W9-BTB-074

Managing with
Microsoft®
Project 2002

Lisa A. Bucki

Gary Chefetz

Managing with
Microsoft®
Project 2002

Premier

Press

© 2002 by Premier Press. All rights reserved. No part of this book may be reproduced or transmitted in any form or by any means, electronic or mechanical, including photocopying, recording, or by any information storage or retrieval system without written permission from Premier Press, except for the inclusion of brief quotations in a review.

Premier
Press

The Premier Press logo, top edge printing, and related trade dress are trademarks of Premier Press, Inc. and may not be used without written permission. All other trademarks are the property of their respective owners.

Microsoft is a registered trademark of the Microsoft Corporation. All other trademarks are the property of their respective owners.

Important: Premier Press cannot provide software support. Please contact the appropriate software manufacturer's technical support line or Web site for assistance.

Premier Press and the author have attempted throughout this book to distinguish proprietary trademarks from descriptive terms by following the capitalization style used by the manufacturer.

Information contained in this book has been obtained by Premier Press from sources believed to be reliable. However, because of the possibility of human or mechanical error by our sources, Premier Press, or others, the Publisher does not guarantee the accuracy, adequacy, or completeness of any information and is not responsible for any errors or omissions or the results obtained from use of such information. Readers should be particularly aware of the fact that the Internet is an ever-changing entity. Some facts may have changed since this book went to press.

ISBN: 1-931841-35-7

Library of Congress Catalog Card Number: 2001099841

Printed in the United States of America

02 03 04 05 BH 10 9 8 7 6 5 4 3 2 1

Publisher:
Stacy L. Hiquet

Marketing Manager:
Heather Buzzingham

Managing Editor:
Sandy Doell

Project Editor:
Estelle Manticas

Editorial Assistant:
Margaret Bauer

Marketing Coordinator:
Kelly Poffenbarger

Technical Reviewer:
Jacqueline Harris

Copy Editor:
Sean Medlock

Interior Layout:
Scribe Tribe

Cover Design:
Mike Tanamachi

Indexer:
Sharon Shock

Proofreader:
Kim Benbow

To my family and friends, whom I appreciate every day.

—LB

Acknowledgments

This fourth edition of *Managing with Microsoft Project* presents coverage to serve a broad array of Microsoft Project users. I appreciate the feedback I receive from Project users and strive in this edition to deliver the information and techniques you need to use Project successfully.

The publisher of Premier Press, Stacy Hiquet, worked long and hard with me to bring this book to you. Thanks for your patience, Stacy. Once again project editor Estelle Manticas brought her expert guidance to bear on this title, ensuring its quality and timeliness. Copy editor Sean Medlock lent spit and polish to the text, and technical reviewer Jacqueline Harris verified the accuracy of everything you'll read here. I'm also grateful to the design and layout team members, who have once again outdone themselves on this beautiful book.

I extend a hearty thanks to co-author Gary Chefetz, who was willing to roll up his sleeves and tackle some of the new chapters in the book. His coverage of the new Enterprise features in Project, Project Server and Web-based features, and other powerful new management tools in Microsoft Project will help you extend your skills even further and investigate whether or not to deploy advanced Project functionality in your work environment. Thanks again, Gary.

Finally, thank you to the folks who manage the Microsoft Project product development and beta testing programs. In particular, I would like to thank Adrian Jenkins, who many times has helped me unravel an issue or problem with the software. It's wonderful to receive such support to ensure that I get the details right.

Lisa A. Bucki, bucki@mindspring.com

About the Authors

Lisa A. Bucki has over twelve years' experience in computer training and computer book publishing. She was Associate Publisher of Alpha Books, an imprint founded to address the needs of beginning users. Bucki has authored or co-authored nearly 50 books and multimedia products, including the previous three editions of Managing with Microsoft Project and Premier's Mac OS X Fast and Easy and Photoshop 6 for Windows Fast and Easy. Bucki leads beginning-to-intermediate Microsoft Project training classes for North Carolina-based SofTrain, Inc. (www.SofTrainInc.com).

Gary Chefetz is an independent project consultant who has spent more than twenty years professionally pursuing his passion for technology. With project management experience in publishing, real estate, and technology, he leverages an extensive and diverse background to assist his clients through their project management improvement initiatives. Chefetz is a 2002 Microsoft MVP (Most Valued Professional) and can be found haunting the Microsoft Project public news groups.

Contents at a Glance

Contents

PART IV   VIEWING, FORMATTING, AND PRINTING PROJECTS 347

Chapter 12   Viewing and Managing Costs and Value 349

Chapter 13   Working with the Different Project Views 379

Introduction

As a team leader or manager, you encounter new challenges every day. In today's resource-scarce business environment, you're probably being asked to accomplish more in a shorter time, with less help. You also may increasingly find yourself working with outside resources (as the trend of increasing outsourcing continues) or resources in multiple facilities. With such complexity on your plate, to-do lists, meetings with lists on white boards, copious e-mail messages, or even clumsy spreadsheets and homegrown databases don't cut it. Project managers need tools that lend efficiency and precision to both the project planning process and each project's execution.

To fill that need, Microsoft has once again raised the bar with the latest release of Microsoft Project 2002. This leading project management program gives you all the tools you need to review and control many facets of a project from start to finish.

With Project, there's a significant payoff for your time investment in learning how to use the software. Not only will you be more organized, but you'll be able to help your team be more effective as well. You'll be able to anticipate problems and your ability to make resource estimates will improve, so that over time you'll become a stronger manager.

This book is designed to help you make the most of your company's financial investment in Project, as well as your professional investment—the time you'll spend learning to work with Project, and the impact Project will have on your performance.

What's New with Project's Editions (and This Book)?

In keeping with its recent strategy for the Office XP suite, Microsoft has differentiated Microsoft Project 2002 into several editions. The editions enable a user to choose the feature set appropriate for his or her business environment. Small business users, for example, may only need core features, while large organizations may want to take advantage of all new enterprise functionality. Following is a review of the various Project 2002 editions and pricing:

◆ **Microsoft Project Standard.** At an estimated retail price of $599 (full version), the Microsoft Project Standard edition provides all the project management tools of prior Project releases, as well as features new to this version. Build projects, manage resources and costs, track progress, and handle reporting with the Standard edition. This is the ideal choice for users who will be using Project in a stand alone or small group setting. In addition, the Standard edition enables users to publish and update Project information to a Project server created with the Microsoft Project Server edition (just as Project 2000 enabled users to publish project information to Project Central).

◆ **Microsoft Project Professional.** When used in conjunction with Microsoft Project Server, the Professional edition ($999) offers additional enterprise features not available in the Standard edition. Using the Professional edition, the project administrator can build the enterprise global template to apply custom fields, calendars, views, and more to all projects in the enterprise. Enterprise resource management enables assignments across all projects to be visible, better helping managers avoid overbooking resources. Query features enable you to find available resources, and the Resource Substitution Wizard matches available resources with a particular project. Choose this edition if you will be publishing projects using Project Server and need the extra enterprise tools not provided by the Standard edition.

◆ **Microsoft Project Server.** This edition replaces Microsoft Project Central 2000, which offered Web-based project management for Microsoft Project 2000. Project Server provides the foundation for sharing project information on the network. With the Project Professional edition, it provides the enterprise functionality not found in prior versions of Microsoft Project. The Server edition also interfaces with SharePoint Team Services for document and issue tracking. If you plan to use Web-based collaboration tools, you must purchase and install Project Server. (The retail cost is approximately $799.) Given the expense for this edition as well as the system requirements,

Project Server is most appropriate in larger organizations with multiple, detailed projects and a heavy emphasis on project management information. As Project Server remains compatible with Project 2000, note that you also can upgrade from Project Central to Project Server without having to replace the client product immediately.

◆ **Microsoft Project Web Access.** Not every project participant will need to build projects. Many will simply need to view assignments and timesheets, as well as providing details about completed work. For such a user, the Microsoft Project Web Access edition provides the appropriate solution. The Web Access edition extends the Internet Explorer browser so that it can connect with project information published to Project Server. At $179 per licensed user, the Web Access client provides a cost-effective way to enable more users to interact with project information on the project server.

We've beefed up this edition of *Managing with Microsoft Project* to include even more information about the Web-based functionality provided via Project Server. If that's your primary area of interest, jump ahead to Chapters 24 through 27. Those chapters provide the information you'll need to deploy Project Server and use it to manage projects. Those chapters will be useful to both network administrators responsible for Project Server installation and project administrators responsible for publishing and updating project information.

The remainder of the book applies to users of both the Standard and Professional Editions of Project 2002, as the core functionality of those two editions is identical. If you want to learn to start using Microsoft Project from the ground up, start with Chapter 1 and work your way through the book. If you have some experience with Project and want to check out new features or learn more about functionality you've never used before, jump ahead to the chapter covering the topic that interests you.

Who Should Read This Book

Whether you or your company have already purchased and installed the Project software or you are trying to decide if Project is right for your organization, this book provides the guidance you need. This book helps anyone who needs to be able to work with Project on short notice, who needs to learn about additional features, or who needs to plan for and implement enterprise-wide use of Project, including:

◆ Managers and assistants whose company has adopted Project

◆ Managers beginning to use Project as a method to standardize the planning process

◆ Project or team leaders who need to use Project to create graphical print-outs of task assignments, or to allocate resources between several projects

◆ Leaders who need to coordinate a diverse set of resources that may include colleagues from many departments, outside consultants, or even cross-company teams

◆ Project or team leaders who want to take advantage of the company network, a company Intranet, or the Internet to communicate about tasks, progress, and completion

◆ IT professionals and decision makers who want to learn more about the ins and outs of deploying Project on the enterprise

◆ Professional, certified project managers who have purchased Project to implement an organized planning system for their companies or clients

 NOTE

While this book teaches you a lot about using Microsoft Project, keep in mind that the book is not intended to teach the principles of the discipline of project management. Chapter 1 notes some additional resources you can consult to learn more about project management.

How This Book Is Organized

Whether you review the chapters from start to finish or browse around to review specific subjects, *Managing with Microsoft Project 2002* is structured for easy use.

Part I, "Easy Introduction to Project," gives you background information on project management and the Microsoft Project software. Here you will learn how to get the most out of Project, and you'll get a jump-start on your Project skills with a look at the new Project Guide that leads you through some of the key Project operations.

Part II, "Project Management Basics," focuses on the minimum you need to know to set up a project. You'll learn how to create a file in Project, set the overall project parameters, define the tasks that must be completed, organize those tasks and establish task relationships, and indicate the resources that will be used to complete each task.

Part III, "Making Adjustments to Projects," teaches you how to work out project kinks. You'll learn how to identify and resolve resource overcommitments, adjust tasks, and track a project's progress.

Part IV, "Viewing, Formatting, and Printing Projects," discusses using the information you so diligently captured in Project. You'll choose different display formats for a project, print, work with forms and reports, review costs, and use outlining features.

Part V, "Handling Multiple Projects," builds on the skills you mastered previously, showing you how to move and copy information between projects, create and use project templates, combine projects and resources, and use master projects and subprojects.

Part VI, "Sharing and Publishing Project Information," covers using information from Project in other Microsoft Office applications, exporting project information, and importing tasks from Microsoft Outlook. It also provides information on online features for sending assignments or updates to team members, deploying Project Server to publish and manage project information on the Web, and more.

Part VII, "Working with Advanced Features," shows you how to customize the way you work with Project and create macros to make your work in Project even more efficient. The book closes with a new chapter introducing you to VBA programming in Microsoft Project.

Conventions Used In This Book

To make it easier for you to use this book, the following conventions are used to present different kinds of information. You should review these conventions before moving on.

- ◆ **Key combinations.** Pressing and holding one key while pressing another key is called a key combination. In this book, key combinations are indicated by a plus sign (+) separating the keys you have to press.

For example, Ctrl+O is a key combination that requires you to press and hold the Ctrl key while pressing the O key.

◆ **Menu commands.** A phrase like "Choose File, Open" means to open the File menu and click on the Open command.

◆ **Text you type.** When you need to type some text to complete a procedure, the text appears in bold, as in the following:

Type the name for the task, such as **Request Price Quotes**.

Special Features of This Book

At times, I'll provide you with information that supplements the discussion at hand. This special information is set off in easy-to-identify sidebars, so you can review or skip these extras as you see fit. You'll find the following features in this book:

 TIP

Tips and more tips. Tips like these provide shortcuts or alternatives for using features, as well as ideas for using a particular feature on the job.

 NOTE

Notes like these provide supplemental information that either clarifies an operation, provides greater technical detail, or gives you background information about the subject at hand.

 CAUTION

Cautions protect you from what can be your worst computing enemy—yourself. When particular operations are risky and might cause you to lose some of your work, I'll forewarn you in these boxes.

 WEB

The publisher of this book, Premier Press, offers a Web page where you can download supplemental files that you can use to practice the skills you learn in this book. That page is **www.premierpressbooks.com/downloads**. A sidebar like this will alert you when supplemental files are available.

PART I

**Easy Introduction
to Project**

Chapter 1

The Project Management Process and Project

In This Chapter

◆ The benefits of project management

◆ Key tools provided in Microsoft Project

◆ Overview of planning a project

◆ What you need to be successful with Microsoft Project

The students I've taught have shared an almost universal feeling about Microsoft Project and project management: Both are difficult and time-consuming. Students who have invested the time to learn more about what Project and project management have to offer, however, know that a disciplined approach offers real advantages over scribbled notes and good intentions. You can get a job done more smoothly, impressing your bosses, clients, vendors, and coworkers in the process. As you read this book and start up Microsoft Project 2002 for the first time, keep in mind that you must build a foundation before you can put up a building.

This chapter provides the foundation for your knowledge of Microsoft Project. Although this chapter (and this book) isn't designed to teach you the overall discipline of project management, I'll try to outline some of the basic project management principles that should guide how you'll use Microsoft Project. This chapter also covers some of the realities and benefits of using Project to plan and manage your endeavors.

Understanding Why You Need to Manage Projects

"Project management" used to be primarily a catchphrase to flesh out a résumé. At best, it involved keeping a long to-do list and dealing with problems after someone else had pointed them out. In its broadest sense, the label "project manager" could describe any individual who could complete most of his or her own work assignments.

In today's business climate, project management has emerged as a serious discipline that is being incorporated into programs at technical schools and universities worldwide. For example, certain MBA programs include project management courses, and you can earn undergraduate and graduate degrees. Some international organizations, such as the Project Management Institute at http://www.pmi.org, train project management professionals, certify them with designations such as Project Management Professional (PMP), and provide accreditation for project management courses. Finally, some consulting firms now specialize in providing project management services, and some businesses have developed formalized project manager positions.

Even if you don't have specific training in project management, you—like millions of others—might discover that project management skills are essential to career success. You need to have a precise understanding of the steps involved in a project, the resources you'll need, the time each portion of the project will take, and the money all of it will cost.

Business trends over the past decade are making people with project management skills increasingly valuable as managers or team leaders. Following are just a few examples of such trends:

◆ The continuing market pressure to run lean, efficient companies compels us all to accomplish more with fewer resources. As resources become scarcer, you must plan further in advance and become more skilled at identifying and eliminating conflicts.

◆ The increasing adoption of technology has led to management reliance on more precise, accurate, and timely information. You need the skills to plan more accurately, respond immediately to information requests, and support your requests for additional resources. You'll have greater credibility and effectiveness when you're more disciplined in your approach.

◆ In today's smaller workgroup or team environment, each team member's role has become less specialized. Thus, you must carefully define each person's role within the context of a particular project.

◆ The efficiency of online communication has led to *virtual teams*—geographically dispersed individuals who need to work together as a cohesive unit. The fact that a team member is halfway across the country doesn't make that person any less important to your overall mission.

With virtual teams, you need to communicate frequently about deadlines and progress, and make sure you're getting feedback about problems so that you can resolve them before they sidetrack your schedule or budget.

◆ To bring products to market more quickly, most companies distribute tasks across several departments so that different project phases can be handled concurrently. In such cross-departmental situations, tracking performance and communicating expectations has become more challenging and necessary.

◆ Companies that are under headcount restrictions, or that are unwilling to invest in specialized technology, increasingly rely on outside contractors for a variety of functions. Project management techniques and tools can help in keeping these outside resources on track.

Management Techniques Offered in Microsoft Project

Even if you're just getting started with Microsoft Project, you'll be surprised at how little time you need to spend with it to look organized and impress your colleagues. Consider this true story. My husband took a job as a project manager with a large international manufacturer of audiocassettes and CDs. A month or so later, his primary client placed an order for several million units of product— one of the largest orders that the plant had ever handled. The pressure was on my husband, both from the head honchos at the plant and from the client.

So, to prepare, he launched Microsoft Project (which few of his colleagues had ever bothered to open, let alone use). He established the project start date, and then he typed in the list of tasks and the approximate length of time each task could take. He added a few summary tasks to make the list a little clearer, and then added the needed list. Finally, he printed only the list of tasks, called the Task Sheet. At the meeting to kick off the project, he handed out the Task Sheet and his other materials, and the clients and his bosses loved it. His company's president even said, "This is exactly what we should be doing for every job."

The order went off like clockwork, and all my husband did to become the hero was type in some information. He didn't even use many of Project's most powerful features!

In the past, you needed several tools to keep track of far-flung details and resources for big projects such as this client order. You would outline the project with a word processor, budget with a spreadsheet, plot progress on paper timelines, and so on. Microsoft Project 2002 handles all the key facets of project planning by blending traditional project management models with more contemporary techniques—such as printing custom calendars, importing information from other programs, and quickly e-mailing assignments. With Project, you can track the completion of various tasks, manage costs, reassign resources, and more.

Overall, the process you follow with Project is to create a schedule by defining the tasks that need to be completed, determining the probable cost for each task, and determining which employees, supplies, contractors, and other resources are needed to complete the task. After you establish the schedule, you can fine-tune it to decrease the total time frame, deal with resource conflicts, and so on. Finally, you can track the team's progress and communicate the schedule to others from start to finish by printing an overall chart, printing charts about individual resources, generating reports for your manager, and e-mailing information to other team members.

Thus, Project offers a variety of techniques for establishing, modifying, and managing the parameters for each project plan you pull together.

Key Benefits of Using Microsoft Project

As with many other new types of software, users often wonder whether it's worth investing the time to learn Microsoft Project and enter all the necessary information about a project. Why not simply stick with a word processor and spreadsheet to get the job done?

Well, because you don't want to use a regular hammer when the job calls for a sledgehammer. Project not only makes the basic job of managing projects easier, but it also offers features and capabilities that give you more control over the scope of the project.

By using Project as a planning and management tool you'll be able to

◆ **Manage more information.** Project can track thousands of tasks and resources per project, as well as many pieces of information about each task and resource. Only your computer's memory and other capabilities limit the amount of information you can store in a Project file.

◆ **Gain accuracy.** Because Project can calculate the task and project schedules based on other information you provide, it helps you create a project plan that's more realistic. Project also performs dozens of calculations that would be difficult or time-consuming for you to perform manually. This increases the number of data points that you can consider when you develop your project plan or need to make schedule and budget decisions.

◆ **Automatically create project diagrams.** Project automatically generates Gantt charts (Figure 1.1), calendars, and other graphs and views to provide a look at how project tasks are related and a method to relay information to others.

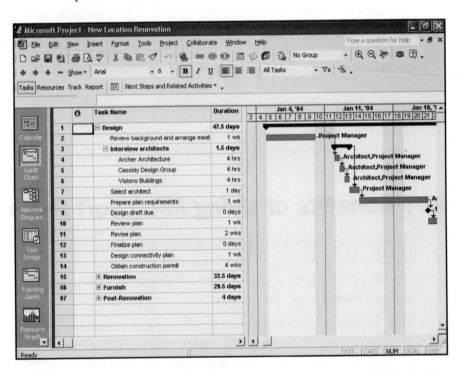

FIGURE 1.1 *A graphical schedule for the project shows you the timing for individual tasks.*

◆ **Track specific aspects of the project and anticipate problems.** You can take a look at the costs, commitments, and available starting date of a particular resource.

◆ **Track overall progress.** As you enter task completion information, you can compare your progress with the original plan. In addition, you can add a status date to help you update the progress more quickly and to clarify when you last updated the project.

◆ **Generate forms and reports to share information.** You can choose from a variety of predefined forms and reports, or create custom forms for particular situations. Figure 1.2 shows an example of such a report.

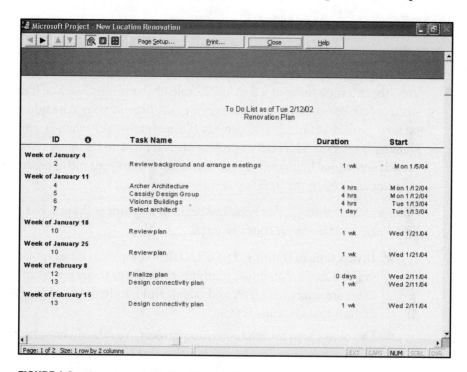

FIGURE 1.2   *Generate reports like this to-do list to communicate more effectively.*

◆ **Communicate via e-mail and the Web.** Project enables you to share project information via existing e-mail tools, such as Microsoft Outlook. You can publish Project information as a Web page or develop a Web site to manage team messages, giving everyone involved in the project a central location to consult for more information.

◆ **Capture historical data.** As you use Project, you gather information to build a history of how tasks and the whole project actually progress. For example, you can see how long a particular type of task takes, whether a particular resource has a tendency to be on-time or run late, and how much the overall plan is costing your company. Then, when you move on to other projects, you can refer to the data you've accumulated in past Project files to refine your latest plan.

Getting the Most Out of Microsoft Project

All the benefits I've laid out so far sound great, and they are. But, as I've found when using Project and through speaking with students and consultants, the "no such thing as a free lunch" rule of thumb applies. You'll need to make a few investments (such as carving out time in your schedule for increased project planning and project file maintenance) when it comes to shifting from a casual model of project management to the more formal approach demanded by Project. If you try to hang onto your old approach, you may not experience the upside you expect.

So, as you work through this book and begin to implement Project, you should be prepared to take some concrete steps.

- ◆ **Invest time in training.** Project is fairly complex as far as applications go. You can use multiple methods to perform many operations, and there are dozens of views and tables, and hundreds of fields of information that you can view.

- ◆ **Develop a plan for implementing Project.** You should not plan to run all your mission-critical projects using this software from day one. Instead, start using Project to track one or two of your smaller assignments. As your proficiency builds, ramp up to using Project across the board.

- ◆ **Make sure the resources are in place to maintain the Project information.** The program delivers a host of calculations to help you drive a project forward, but those calculations depend on the quality and timeliness of the information that you provide. You (or your organization) must decide who will be responsible for maintaining this information in Project, how often that information should be updated, and how updates will be gathered—via regular status meetings or another means. Your company needs to dedicate the person-hours to maintain the Project information, and you (as the project manager) need to ensure you have the discipline to keep an orderly process in place.

TIP

To implement Project on a Web server in your organization, you can purchase and implement the Microsoft Project Server companion product to Microsoft Project. Deploying Project Server helps disperse the responsibility for keeping project information up-to-date. You can request status updates from resources and incorporate the updates you receive into your project plan. The extra expense and setup time required for Project Server can pay for itself many times over in terms of reducing the time you and team members spend communicating about task status.

◆ **Retool your planning style to some degree.** I often alert students that Project forces you to do what you should be doing already. That is, if you aren't accustomed to making a realistic estimate of the time it takes to do every task in a project, typically you don't have a formal schedule for following up with resources about their progress, and so on, you'll find that you won't get what you need from Project unless you change your style.

Don't let any of this dissuade you from using Project, however. You can compare using Project to maintaining a huge customer database. Updating dozens or hundreds of customer records is decidedly tedious, but it's a worthwhile investment because of the value that the database yields to the organization. Similarly, your investment in learning Microsoft Project and building and maintaining project files will be rewarded many times over through the leaps you'll make in effectiveness.

 CAUTION

Microsoft followed the lead of the Project Management Institute in defining a *project* as an endeavor that has a set starting point (start date) and ending point (finish date), with a specific goal to accomplish in that time. The project must have an overall goal or goals, which can be broken down into groups of specific tasks. Each project file you create should pertain to a specific project, not a specific time period or group of resources.

For example, you shouldn't use Project to track all the ongoing assignments for a department or team, especially when those assignments relate to different projects. However, you can create a Project file to track the introduction of a new product, the implementation of a new computer system, the planning and execution of a special event, or a similar specific project.

Deploying Project Server in Your Organization

Chapter 24 of this book will provide the nitty-gritty details on the process of deploying Project Server. Until then, there are a number of factors to deal with if your organization is considering Project Server. Just as employing Project yourself will require changes in your working style, employing Project Server company-wide will require agreement on implementation, changes in policies and procedures, and a change in working style for users throughout the organization.

Implementing Project Server requires additional resources from your organization in terms of server setup, storage, and the installation of other products, such as Internet Information Services and SQL Server. Thus, adding Project Server to the mix calls for cross-departmental planning. Your organization's IT department will need to be involved in the process of preparing for and installing Project Server, as well as supporting it down the line.

Fortunately, Microsoft provides a variety of resources that you and others in your organization can consult as you consider, prepare for, and execute a Project Server installation. Go to the main Project Web page, at http://www.microsoft.com/office/project/, and then consult the section on Project Server to learn more about a successful Project Server implementation.

You'll need to budget time and money to train end users—both those who will be using Project Standard or Project Professional and those who will be using Project Web Access to access information that's published to Project Server.

And finally, you'll need to consider such factors as who will be the manager for particular projects and how frequently status updates should be requested.

The Planning Process in Microsoft Project

As mentioned earlier, all you need to do to get a great deal of benefit from Microsoft Project is enter a list of tasks and schedule them. Then, if you want to start making resource assignments and using other features, you're free to do so.

That said, if you do plan to take advantage of all that Project offers, you should follow this overall process to build and exploit a project file:

1. Establish the initial parameters for the project, including when the project starts and what calendar the work follows—that is, whether work will proceed around the clock, on one shift a day, or on some other basis.

2. Create a list of tasks. This part of the process includes estimating how long each task will take. You'll need to establish relationships (called links) between tasks, identifying whether a particular task must be finished before another task can begin. Via the links, Project calculates the schedule for each task and the overall project schedule. You can use constraints to give Project less flexibility in rescheduling tasks. This process may also involve grouping the tasks in a logical order, if applicable, by using outlining features.

3. Add resources and costs. You will enter a list of people, equipment, and other resources that will complete the tasks in the project, and then you'll enter the costs for using each resource, in terms of hourly rates or cost per unit. (In some cases, you may have to assign a particular cost to a task rather than to a resource.)

4. Make assignments. This part of the process is where you identify which resource or resources will be working on each particular task in your list.

5. Fine-tune your schedule. After you have the basic plan in place, it's time to reexamine it for overbooked resources and opportunities to improve the schedule. Project provides tools for adjusting your schedule. For example, the Resource Graph view, shown in Figure 1.3, tells you when a resource has too much work assigned on a given day.

6. Save a snapshot of your plan. Once you have the plan in place to the best of your ability, you can save that information as the *baseline*. Later, Project can compare the actual project progress to the baseline.

7. Enter actual information. As your project gets under way, you can enter information about the amount of work completed, actual start and finish dates, and actual costs.

8. Communicate with the team. You can use team and Web-based (Project Server) features to make assignments and request updates.

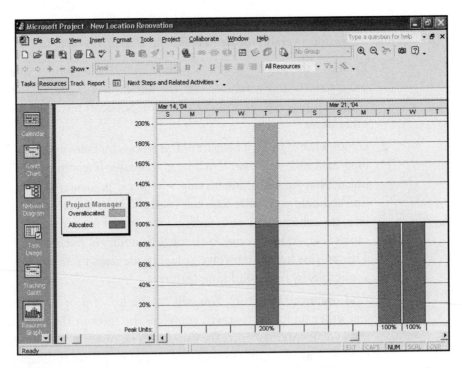

FIGURE 1.3 *Project offers tools like this Resource Graph view to help you ensure your plan is realistic and will proceed smoothly.*

9. Review information and generate reports. Project provides a variety of views so that you can find and print the information that's pertinent. It also offers predefined reports that you can use to communicate about project progress, upcoming tasks, the budget, and more.

This book covers each part of this process, as well as topics such as how to customize Project.

Learning More about Project Management

A book covering every feature of the Microsoft Project program would be well over a thousand pages, so I've had to choose how much Microsoft Project and project management information to include here. If you're interested in learning more about the discipline of project management, or perhaps even pursuing further education in that area, the best site to consult is the Project Management Institute (PMI), at http://www.pmi.org.

PMI offers a variety of publications and educational opportunities, as well as its own certification program. Its site offers valuable links to the following types of information:

◆ **The PMI Bookstore.** This area of the site offers more than 1,000 project management books for sale.

◆ **Links to Registered Education Providers.** These consultants, universities, and educational sites have been approved by PMI to provide project management training and degree or certification programs. Check out http://www.pmirep.org for a listing of Registered Education Providers (REPs). Many REPs also offer a variety of e-Learning opportunities. If you prefer to learn online or via audio tape or interactive CD-ROM, visit http://www.pmi.org/education/e-learning/index.htm and use the links at the bottom of the page to search for appropriate e-Learning materials.

 TIP

The Project Management Institute also has plans to implement online courses. Check the PMI Web site to learn more about upcoming e-Learning opportunities.

◆ **Coverage of upcoming events.** PMI keeps a calendar of seminars, expos, and other events it sponsors, as well as those sponsored by related organizations.

Chapter 2

Getting Started with the Project Guide

In This Chapter

◆ Viewing and using the Project Guide side pane

◆ Specifying basic project information

◆ Viewing information in your project plan

◆ Establishing the overall order for tasks

◆ Adding resources and making assignments

◆ Saving the project starting point

◆ Telling Microsoft Project about completed work

◆ Generating reports

◆ Turning the Project Guide off

If you're a first-timer, this chapter is for you! Microsoft Project 2002 offers a new feature called the Project Guide, which guides users through the process of setting up a Project file and using that file to track and manage a project's progress. In this chapter, you'll work our way through the most important tasks in the Project Guide, using example entries to build and use a Project file.

By working through the examples in this chapter, you'll get a firsthand look at how powerful Project's features are, and how easy it can be to get started with the system. (While this chapter presents a great overview of working in Microsoft Project, I still recommend that you read the rest of this book to learn the theories behind the skills presented here, and to develop a more fully rounded understanding of Project 2002.)

Viewing and Navigating the Project Guide Side Pane

By default, the Project Guide appears in its own *side pane* to the left of the project file window (also called the view area) whenever you create a new project file or open an existing file. (The default view that appears in the view area is called the Gantt Chart view.) The Project Guide offers a variety of links and wizards to guide you through the process of setting up your project file, adding tasks and resources, tracking the project's progress, and reporting project information.

 NOTE

The *side pane* that holds the Project Guide is separate from the *task pane* that appears in Project 2002 and other Office XP applications.

You can use the Project Guide toolbar (also called the Project Guide Bar) to show, hide, and navigate through the Project Guide. Both of them appear in Figure 2.1.

Click these buttons to display different steps in the Project Guide

Click to hide and display the Project Guide side pane

Click to access Project Guide steps when side pane is hidden

Project Guide toolbar

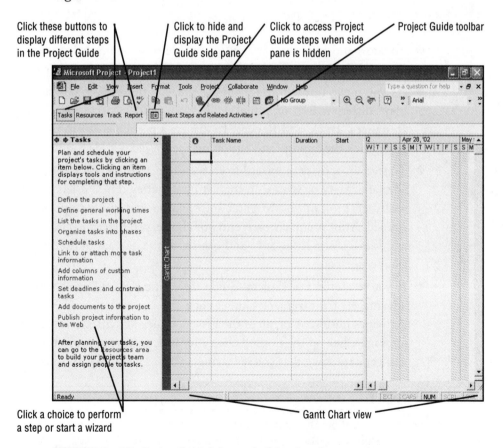

Click a choice to perform a step or start a wizard

Gantt Chart view

FIGURE 2.1   *The Project Guide helps you build and track your project.*

Use the following techniques to work with the Project Guide toolbar and the Project Guide itself:

◆ If the Project Guide toolbar doesn't appear, right-click on any toolbar and then click Project Guide. Alternately, you can open the View menu, point to the Toolbars choice (that is, move the mouse over Toolbars until a submenu appears), and then click Project Guide. Repeat either technique to hide the Project Guide toolbar if you no longer need it onscreen.

 CAUTION

If you do not see the Project Guide toolbar choice on either the toolbar shortcut menu or the View, Toolbar submenu, the Project Guide has been turned off. See the final section in this chapter, "Turning the Project Guide Off (and Back On)."

◆ To show and hide the Project Guide side pane as needed, click the Show/Hide Project Guide button on the Project Guide toolbar.

◆ As you move through the planning process, the Project Guide displays different lists of activities, wizards, and information: Tasks, Resources, Track, and Report. To display a particular list in the side pane, click the appropriate button on the Project Guide toolbar.

◆ To start an activity or wizard from the Project Guide, click the name of that activity or wizard in the list of activities. The Project Guide will then prompt you to enter information and choose options as needed. After you make each entry or choice, you'll need to click Save and Go To Step X (or Save and Finish) at the bottom of the Project Guide side pane.

◆ If you've closed the Project Guide side pane but still want to take advantage of the Project Guide, click the Next Steps and Related Activities button. A menu of the Project Guide activities and wizards appears. Click on the desired choice to work with your project file. If you get a message that you're leaving a wizard, click Yes to continue.

 NOTE

You can use the View Bar to change the view shown in the view area to the right of the side pane. The View Bar is turned off by default. To display or hide the View Bar, choose View, View Bar.

Starting a New Project

Every project plan starts with two vital pieces of information. The project *start date* tells Microsoft Project when work is to begin on the project. By default, Project schedules all tasks from the project start date. The project calendar (or *base calendar*) you choose clarifies how Project should schedule tasks—whether a one-day task takes place over a standard 8-hour workday or over the 24-hour workday that's common in three-shift manufacturing facilities.

 NOTE

This chapter presents only the most essential project planning steps from the Project Guide, as a means to familiarize you with the basic project planning and management process. The Project Guide lists additional activities once you begin to develop more robust project plans.

This first exercise shows you how to specify the project start date and the base calendar for a project file.

 NOTE

Even if you have the Project Guide turned off, by default Project will prompt you (by displaying the Project Information dialog box) to specify the project start date, base calendar, and other information each time you start a new file. If the Project Information dialog box does not appear, choose Tools, Options. Click the General tab, click the Prompt for Project Info for New Projects check box to check it, and then click OK.

Start the exercise now:

 NOTE

At this point, you should have already installed and activated your version of Microsoft Project 2002.

1. Start Project by choosing Start, All Programs, Microsoft Project. (In Windows versions prior to Windows XP, choose Start, Programs, Microsoft Project.)
2. If needed, display the Project Guide toolbar and the Project Guide side pane.

3. Click on Define the Project in the Project guide. This starts the New Project Wizard, and its first step (Enter Project Information) appears in the side pane.

4. Use the drop-down calendar to choose a project start date (choose **3/ 7/05** for this example, as shown in Figure 2.2), or type the desired start date into the text box on the wizard screen.

First step in the New Project Wizard

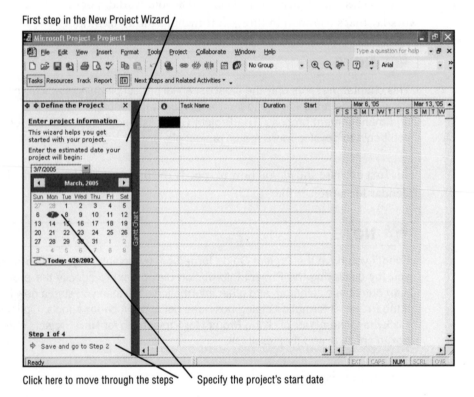

Click here to move through the steps   Specify the project's start date

FIGURE 2.2 *The New Project Wizard appears in the side pane and prompts you to enter basic information, such as the project's start date.*

 TIP

To use a drop-down calendar for any text box holding a date entry in Project, click the drop-down arrow to display the calendar. Double-click the year at the top of the calendar, and then use the spinner buttons that appear to change the year. Next, click the month at the top of the calendar, and then click the desired month. Finally, click the desired date on the calendar.

5. Click Save and Go to Step 2 at the bottom of the side pane. This takes you to the next step of the wizard, Collaborate on Your Project.

6. For this example, leave the No option selected. (If you had plans to publish the project to Project Server, you would choose Yes instead). Click Save and Go to Step 3.

7. Click Save in step 4 of the wizard, or click the Save button on the Standard toolbar. The Save As dialog box appears.

8. Type **Seminar Plan** in the File Name text box to replace the default entry, which should be selected. (At this point, you could also specify a save location other than My Documents, which is the default for most installations.)

9. Click the Save button to finish the save and close the Save As dialog box.

10. Click Save and Go to Step 4 at the bottom of the side pane.

11. Click Save and Finish at the bottom of the side pane to complete the New Project Wizard and redisplay the list of Tasks activities in the Project Guide side pane. At this point, Seminar Plan should appear as the file name in the Project window title bar.

12. Click Define General Working Times in the Project Guide. This starts the Calendar Wizard, shown in Figure 2.3, so you can choose and adjust the base calendar for your project plan.

13. If you need to, click the arrow for the Select a Calendar Template drop-down list, and then click an alternate template. (For more about the default calendars or calendar templates offered by Project, see the section called "Creating and Assigning the Project Base Calendar" in Chapter 4. For this exercise, you can leave the Standard calendar template selected.)

14. Click Save and Go To Step 2. Step 2 of the Calendar Wizard, Define the Work Week, appears in the side pane. Most businesses follow the same hours as the Standard calendar: an eight-hour workday (from 8 a.m. to 5 p.m., minus an hour for lunch), five days a week. For this example, however, the working hours are slightly different: 9 a.m. to 6 p.m., minus an hour for lunch, five days a week.

15. Leave the check boxes for Monday (Mon.) through Friday (Fri.) selected. (If you wanted to specify different working days, you would use these check boxes. Click the bottom option button, I Want to Adjust the Working Hours Shown, and then scroll down the side pane to see additional choices.)

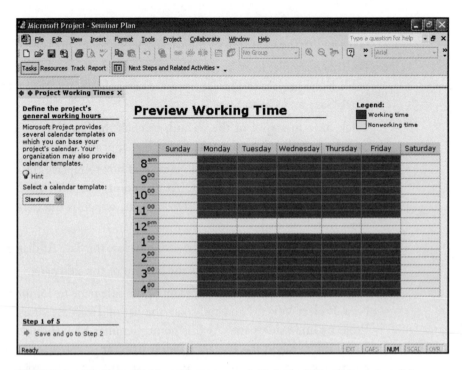

FIGURE 2.3 *The Project Guide enables you to use the Calendar Wizard, shown here. Select a calendar template, and then move through the steps to specify working hours, holidays, and more.*

16. For this exercise, leave Monday selected in the Hours For drop-down list. (Of course, you could select another working day if you needed to change its working hours in your project base calendar.) Using the From and To drop-down lists, specify working hours from 9 a.m. to 1. p.m. and 2 p.m. to 6 p.m., as shown in Figure 2.4. The Preview Working Time display at the right illustrates the adjusted schedule for Monday.

17. Click the Apply to All Days button to apply the new working hours to all working days in the workweek.

18. Click Save and Go To Step 3 at the bottom of the side pane. The next step of the Calendar Wizard, Set Holidays and Days Off, appears in the Project Guide side pane. For this example, let's say the business is closed on 3/24–25/2005 due to Passover and Good Friday. You need to specify those nonworking dates in the project base calendar.

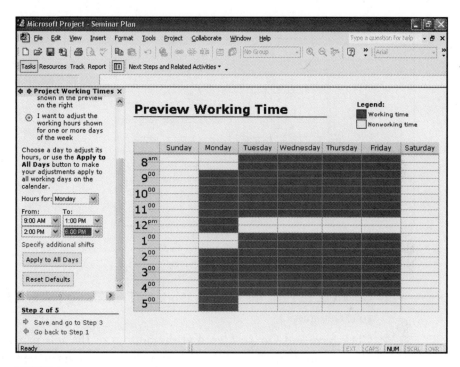

FIGURE 2.4 *Change the daily working hours for one day, and then use the Apply to All Days button so that all working days in the base calendar follow the same schedule.*

 NOTE

Because holidays vary widely from business to business, none of Microsoft Project's default calendars (or calendar templates) have any holidays indicated. You must always make sure that holidays are specified for accurate project scheduling.

19. Click Change Working Time in the side pane. The Change Working Time dialog box will open.

20. Use the scroll bar at the right side of the calendar to scroll to March 2005, if needed.

21. On the calendar, drag over the boxes for March 24 and March 25 to select those dates, as shown in Figure 2.5.

22. Under Set Selected Date(s) To at the right side of the dialog box, click the Nonworking Time option button. This marks the selected dates as holidays. (Of course, you could select and mark additional dates, as needed.)

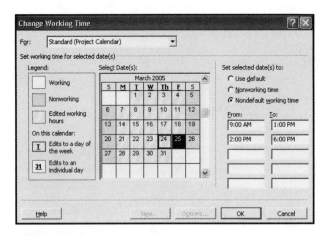

FIGURE 2.5 *You can select the appropriate dates on the calendar to mark them as holidays (nonworking days).*

23. Click OK to close the Change Working Time dialog box and apply your changes.

24. Click Save and Go To Step 4 at the bottom of the side pane. The Define Time Units Step of the Calendar Wizard appears in the Project Guide side pane. If you needed to, you could adjust the Hours Per Day, Hours Per Week, or Days Per Month settings here. These choices should generally reflect the changes to the working calendar that you made earlier, if any. (For example, if you specified only four days per week as working days, the Days Per Month setting would be changed to 16, if needed.)

25. For this exercise, no changes are needed, so click Save and Go to Step 5 at the bottom of the side pane. The final step of the Calendar Wizard advises you that The Project Calendar Is Set.

26. Click Save and Finish to finish the Calendar Wizard and redisplay the list of Tasks activities in the Project Guide side pane.

Adding Tasks

If you've worked with a spreadsheet or table in a database or word processor, you'll have no problem entering new tasks into a project file in Project. Tasks appear in the task sheet at the left side of the Gantt Chart view, the default view that Project uses, to the right of the Project Guide. Each row in the sheet holds a single task. In this case, the Project Guide really just provides you with guidance on how to enter tasks: You click on a cell in the Task Name column, enter the task name, press Tab to move to the Duration column, and then enter the duration.

 NOTE

The *duration* is the amount of time between the start date and finish date for the task. In later chapters, you'll learn how Project calculates *work* (which you can think of as the person-hours required to complete a task) differently than duration.

As indicated in the Project Guide, I recommend that you limit yourself to making only the Task Name and Duration field entries for new tasks. Then you can use the outlining and linking features to have Project calculate actual task schedules for you. (If you manually enter start and finish dates, Project might apply what's called a *constraint*, which gives it less flexibility in recalculating a task's schedule.)

The following exercise illustrates how you can continue with the Project Guide to enter tasks for a project:

1. Click List the Tasks in the Project in the Project Guide. (If needed, display the Project Guide first and then click the Tasks button on the Project Guide toolbar.) The Project Guide will display information to help you enter tasks.

2. Click in the Task Name column of the first blank row in the Gantt chart. This is where you'll start entering new tasks.

3. Enter the new task information exactly as listed in Table 2.1. Press Tab to move to the next column to the right, and use the arrow keys to move around. As you add each task, a row number appears for it at the left. That is the *task number* for the task. Notice that by default, Project schedules each new task from the project start date, 3/7/05. Also notice that when you don't include an abbreviation (such as h for hours or w for weeks) with an entry in the Duration column, Project assumes you're entering the duration in days. So, an entry of **1** becomes **1 day**.

Table 2.1 New Task Entries for Seminar Plan

Task (Row) #	Task Name	Duration
1	Determine budget	1
2	Develop topic and speaker list	1
3	Select date	3h
4	Identify and book site	9
5	Speaker invitations	1w
6	Write brochure	2
7	Design/produce brochure	1w
8	Print brochure	1w
9	Mail brochure	2
10	Write press release	1
11	Mail press release	1
12	Rent audiovisual equipment	1
13	Set menu	4
14	Set room arrangements	1
15	Hire photographer	2
16	Confirm speakers and arrangements	4
17	Finalize schedule and print	1w
18	Create registration packages	1w
19	Mail registration packages	2
20	Verify room/catering arrangements	1h
21	Greet speakers	0.5h
22	Registration	1h
23	Event	12eh
24	Pay bills	1
25	Write thank you letters	2
26	Write event summary	1

TIP

When you include an "e" along with a duration abbreviation, Project schedules that duration in terms of elapsed hours, overriding the project base calendar if needed. Take task 23 in Table 2.1, for example. The Event task duration was entered as **12eh** because you want Project to schedule the full event on a single date, even though the base calendar only allows for eight hours per working date. The elapsed duration prevents Project from scheduling the event to be eight hours on one day and four hours the next, as it normally would be according to the base calendar.

4. Press Ctrl+Home to return to the row for task 1. Your Seminar Plan project entries should look like Figure 2.6.

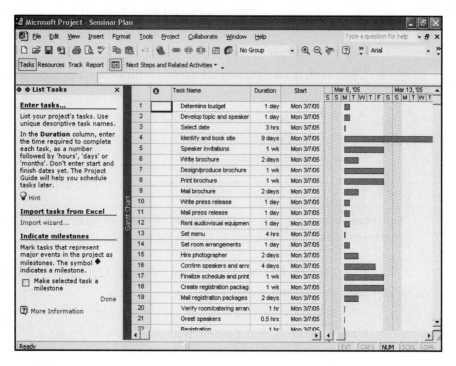

FIGURE 2.6   *The lists of tasks and their durations*

5. Click Done in the bottom-right corner of the Project Guide side pane. The list of Tasks activities reappears in the Project Guide side pane.

Outlining and Linking to Organize and Schedule the Tasks

Outlining helps you group related tasks so that Project can summarize information about that task group for you. Linking establishes relationships between tasks. The default link type, a Finish-to-Start link, tells Project to start the second linked task after the first one finishes.

Continue working with the Seminar Plan file in this exercise to see how the Project Guide can help you use outlining and linking to finish organizing and scheduling your tasks:

1. Click Organize Tasks into Phases in the Project Guide. (If needed, display the Project Guide first and then click the Tasks button on the Project Guide toolbar.) The Project Guide will display information to help you organize tasks.

2. Click a cell in row 1 if needed, and then click the Click Here to Insert a New Row button in the side pane.

   A new, blank task row will be inserted above the old task 1.

3. Click in the Task Name column for the new task 1, type **Planning Phase**, and press Enter.

 TIP

Don't bother entering the duration for any of the new tasks you add here. Project will calculate the durations for you, as you'll see in a moment.

4. Drag over the Task Names for tasks 2 through 12, and then click Click Here to Indent Selected Task(s) in the side pane. (Note that you also can use buttons on the Formatting toolbar to work with outlining.)

5. Click task 13 to clear the selection. As shown in Figure 2.7, Project indented tasks 2 through 12 below task 1.

 NOTE

The indented tasks are *subtasks* or *detail tasks*. In fact, all tasks are detail tasks or subtasks until you start indenting some and *outdenting*, or promoting, others.

The task at the level above the subtasks in the outline is called the *summary task*. You will create multiple summary and subtask levels in this exercise. You'll learn more about task levels in Chapter 5, "Working with Outlining."

Click here to indent tasks you've selected

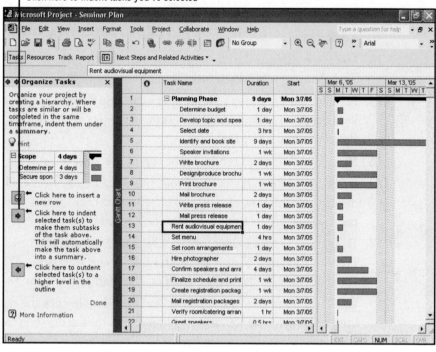

FIGURE 2.7   *Use outlining to group and organize the list of tasks in the Task Sheet.*

6. Use the techniques described in Steps 2 and 3 to add a new task above task 13. Enter **Logistics Phase** as the task name.

7. Click the new task 13, and then click Click Here to Outdent Selected Task(s) in the side pane. This promotes the task so that it is no longer a detail task of task 1, the Planning Phase summary task.

8. Use the technique described in Step 4 to indent tasks 14 through 22. They become subtasks of task 13, the Logistics Phase summary task.

9. Use the techniques described in Steps 2 and 3 to add a new task above task 23. Enter **Event Phase** as the task name.

10. Click the new task 23, and then click Click Here to Outdent Selected Task(s) in the side pane. This promotes the task so that it is no longer a detail task of task 13, the Logistics Phase summary task.

11. Use the technique described in Step 4 to indent tasks 24 through 26. They become subtasks of task 23, the Event Phase summary task.

12. Use the techniques described in Steps 2 and 3 to add a new task above task 27. Enter **Wrap-Up Phase** as the task name.

13. Click the new task 27, and then click Click Here to Outdent Selected Task(s) in the side pane. This promotes the task so that it is no longer a detail task of task 23, the Event Phase summary task.

14. Use the technique described in Step 4 to indent tasks 28 through 30. They become subtasks of task 27, the Wrap-Up Phase summary task.

15. Scroll down the Project Guide side pane, and then click Done in the lower-right corner. The list of Tasks activities will reappear in the Project Guide side pane.

16. Press Ctrl+Home to return to the top of the Task Sheet.

17. Click Schedule Tasks in the Project Guide. The Project Guide will display information to help you schedule tasks. (That is, you'll link tasks so that Project can calculate their schedules.)

18. Drag over the task names for tasks 2 through 12, and then click Click Here to Create a Finish to Start Link in the side pane. (You also could click the Link Tasks button on the Standard toolbar.)

19. Click task 13 to clear the selection, and then double-click the right column heading for the Duration column so that the full duration for task 1 can appear. As you can see in Figure 2.8, Project applies the specified link type to the selected tasks, and it recalculates schedules for the linked tasks so that each one follows the preceding one chronologically. The duration for the Planning Phase summary task also has been recalculated to reflect the overall duration spanned by all the linked tasks it summarizes. (Note that I've adjusted the number of columns displayed in the Task Sheet for some figures so you can better see the changes.)

20. Also use the technique presented in Step 18 to link these groups of tasks: 14–22, 24–26, and 28–30.

21. Now it's necessary to link tasks between the summary (outline) groups, because too many tasks are still scheduled concurrently in the schedule. Scroll up the Task Sheet using the scroll bar along the right side of the file, and then click on the Task Name cell for task 12. Press and hold the Ctrl key, and click on the Task Name for task 14. Release the Ctrl key, and then click Click Here to Create a Finish to Start Link in the side pane or the Link Tasks button. This links tasks between the two summary groups in the outline, and it reschedules the tasks in the lower (later) summary group. Click on another task to remove the selection from tasks 12 and 14.

Click either of these to link selected tasks

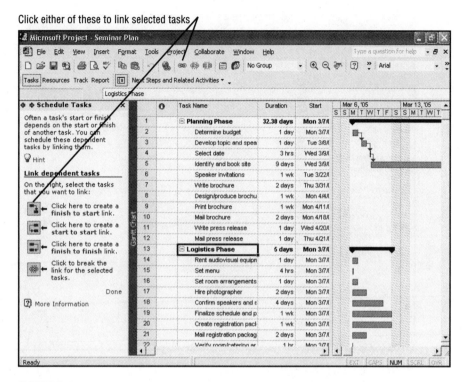

FIGURE 2.8   *Linking establishes the sequence of tasks and enables Project to calculate the task schedule, and the overall schedule for each summary group.*

22. Using the Ctrl+click method, select and link the following pairs of tasks: 22 and 24, and 26 and 28. You can scroll around the chart at the right side of the Gantt Chart view to see the quite extensive links that you've created, as shown in Figure 2.9.

◆ **TIP**

If at any time you need to adjust the Gantt chart portion of the view so that you can see the Gantt bars, click a task in the Task Sheet and then click the Go To Selected Task button on the Standard toolbar. The Gantt bars will immediately scroll back into view.

23. Click Done in the lower-right corner of the Project Guide side pane. The list of Tasks activities will reappear.

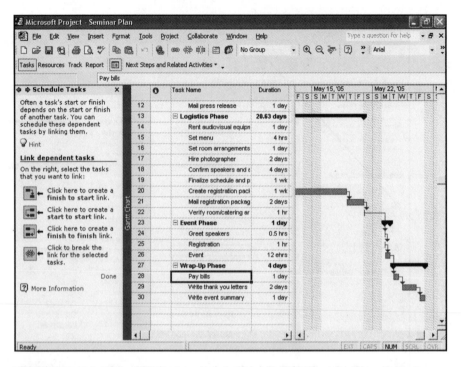

FIGURE 2.9 *Linking enables Project to recalculate task schedules, as well as an overall project schedule.*

Adding Resource Information

Resources comprise the people, equipment, and materials that perform the project tasks. Project 2002 actually offers two different types of resources. *Work resources* are people or equipment that finish a task over time by expending hours of work. You typically pay an hourly fee for using work resources. *Material resources* represent goods consumed by a task. For example, pouring a building foundation might consume 10 cubic yards of concrete. You typically pay by the quantity (cubic yard, dozen, ream) for material resources.

Normally, you add resources into the Resource Sheet for your project to make them available to the project plan, and then you use another view to assign those resources to particular tasks. In this exercise, however, you'll use the list of Resources activities in the Project Guide to practice with adding resources and making task assignments.

One last note before you start. By default, Project uses what's called *effort-driven scheduling,* meaning that adding more resources to a task causes Project to decrease the task's duration. This sort of scheduling makes sense for certain types of tasks and when you are in the early stages of planning. If you think a task will take three weeks' work for one person, two people can probably get it done in a week and a half. On the other hand, in some instances you don't want Project to use effort-driven scheduling; you want the duration to remain fixed. For example, there may be a task that will last a full week no matter how many employees (resources) you assign. If you assigned four employees to the task, you wouldn't want Project to decrease its duration to 1.25 days.

By default, Project 2002 offers the new Feedback feature, similar to smart tags in Office XP. It lets you choose how Project treats the task duration (based on the task type plus whether effort-driven scheduling is left active) when you assign more than one resource to a task. You'll be able to practice with that feature as well in this exercise.

 NOTE

Chapters 7 and 8 include more specific information about task settings and effort-driven scheduling.

Pick up right where you left off in the last exercise, continuing to build the Seminar Plan project:

1. Press F5 (the equivalent of Edit, Go To) to display the Go To dialog box. Type **30** in the ID text box and press Enter. Project jumps to task 30.

2. Double-click on the task name for task 30 to display the Task Information dialog box. Look at the Finish text box on the General tab. Project is currently calculating a finish date of 5/27/05 for the project. Click OK to close the dialog box.

3. Click the Resources button on the Project Guide toolbar. (If needed, display the Project Guide first.)

4. Click Specify People and Equipment for the Project in the Project Guide. The Project Guide will display information to help you specify resources.

5. Although the Project Guide enables you to easily draw in resources from other sources, such as a company Address Book on the network, for this exercise you need to click the Enter Resources Manually op-

tion button. The Project Guide will display further information about manually entering resources.

6. Enter the resource information shown in Table 2.2. You can press Tab to move from cell to cell or skip cells, as well as using the arrow keys and Home key (which moves the cell selector to the first cell in the current row). Note that you're skipping some columns of information to keep this exercise simple.

Table 2.2 New Resource Entries for Seminar Plan

Resource (Row) #	Resource Name	Standard Rate
1	Jan Jones	25
2	Lydia Scott	35
3	Mark Kaiser	25
4	Scott Paul	15

 NOTE

Entering material resources takes a bit of extra work. Chapter 7 covers resource entries in greater depth.

7. Click Done in the lower-right corner of the Project Guide side pane. The list of Resources activities will reappear. It should resemble Figure 2.10.

8. Click Assign People and Equipment to Tasks in the Project Guide. The Project Guide will display information to help you assign resources.

9. Click Assign Resources in the side pane. The Assign Resources dialog box will open.

10. Click on the Task Name cell for task 2. (You can click in the Task Sheet while the Assign Resources dialog box is open, thus moving back and forth between the sheet and the dialog box.) In the Assign Resources dialog box, click on Lydia Scott, and then click on Assign. A check mark will appear beside her name in the dialog box, telling you that she's been assigned to the task.

11. Click task 3 to select it. Click on Jan Jones in the Assign Resources dialog box, and then click Assign. Click on Mark Kaiser, and then

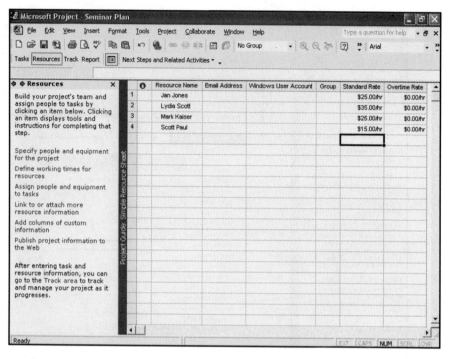

FIGURE 2.10   *Enter the new resource information shown here.*

click Assign. As shown in Figure 2.11, Project will assign both resources to the task. A small button will also appear beside task 3, telling you that the Feedback feature is offering you some choices for rescheduling the task.

12. Click the Feedback button to display a menu of choices for scheduling the task. Click the second menu option, Increase Total Work Because the Task Requires More Person-Hours; Keep Duration Constant. (In essence, this choice turns off effort-driven scheduling for the task but does not change the task type.)

 NOTE

Notice that you've only assigned resources to detail-level tasks, *not* to summary tasks. That's because the summary tasks truly should be used to illustrate summary calculations only. The actual work is occurring for the detail tasks.

13. Make the additional resource assignments outlined in Table 2.3. Note that the table also includes the choice you should click in the Feedback menu if you assign multiple resources to a task.

Feedback button | The assigned resources

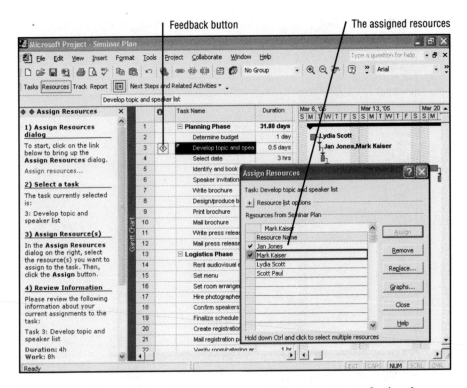

FIGURE 2.11 *You can assign a single resource or multiple resources to a task using the Assign Resources dialog box.*

 NOTE

The Feedback option doesn't work if you select multiple tasks in the Task Sheet before making assignments. Also, wait until you've added all the desired resources to a task before clicking the Feedback button.

14. Click the Close button to close the Assign Resources dialog box.

15. Click Done in the lower-right corner of the Project Guide side pane. The list of Resources activities will reappear.

16. Press Ctrl+Home to go to the first task, drag the divider in the middle of the Gantt Chart view to the left a bit so you can see more of the Gantt bars, and scroll to examine the chart. The assigned resources should appear beside the Gantt bars, as shown in Figure 2.12.

17. Press F5 (the equivalent of Edit, Go To) to display the Go To dialog box. Type 30 in the ID text box and press Enter. Project will jump to task 30.

Table 2.3 New Resource Assignments for Seminar Plan

Task (Row) #	Resource(s) to Assign	Feedback Option*
4	Lydia Scott	
5	Scott Paul	
6	Jan Jones Mark Kaiser	Increase total work
7–10	Scott Paul	
11–12	Jan Jones	
14	Mark Kaiser	
15	Lydia Scott	
16	Scott Paul	
17	Jan Jones Mark Kaiser	Reduce duration
18	Jan Jones Mark Kaiser	Reduce duration
19	Lydia Scott Jan Jones Mark Kaiser	Reduce duration
20	Mark Kaiser Scott Paul	Reduce the hours
21	Mark Kaiser	
22	Scott Paul	
24	Lydia Scott	
25	Scott Paul	
26	Lydia Scott Jan Jones Mark Kaiser Scott Paul	Increase total work
28	Lydia Scott	
29	Jan Jones Mark Kaiser	Reduce the hours
30	Jan Jones	

*The Feedback menu choices have been abbreviated.

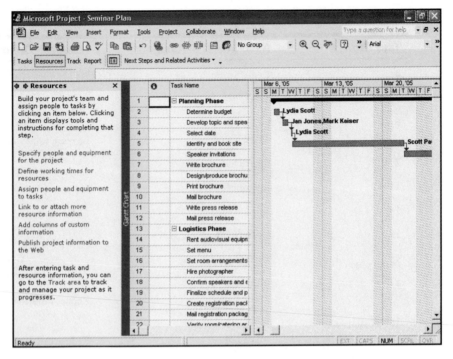

FIGURE 2.12 *At this point, the Seminar Plan file features assigned resources.*

18. Double-click on the Task Name for task 30 to display the Task Information dialog box. Look at the Finish text box on the General tab. Project will now calculate a finish date of 5/20/05 for the project. The improved project finish date has resulted from the changes to the task schedules that you made by using the Feedback button, in some cases allowing effort-driven scheduling to reduce the duration for a task to which you assigned multiple resources. Click OK to close the dialog box.

19. Press Ctrl+Home to return to the top of the project.

Saving the Baseline

Saving a *baseline* stores all the information for your original project plan within the project file: original task start and finish dates, amount of work assigned via various resources, the original cost information Project calculated based on your Standard Rate (and other) entries, and so on. After you save the baseline and start marking work completed or entering actual costs, you can go back and compare your progress versus the original (baseline) plan.

This exercise shows you how to use the Project Guide to store the baseline information, once again continuing to use the example Seminar Plan file that you've been building:

1. Click the Track button on the Project Guide toolbar. (If needed, display the Project Guide first.)

2. Click Save a Baseline Plan to Compare with Later Versions in the Project Guide. The Project Guide will display information to help you specify a baseline.

3. Click the Save Baseline button in the Project Guide side pane. The Project Guide will display the date and time when you saved the baseline, as illustrated in Figure 2.13.

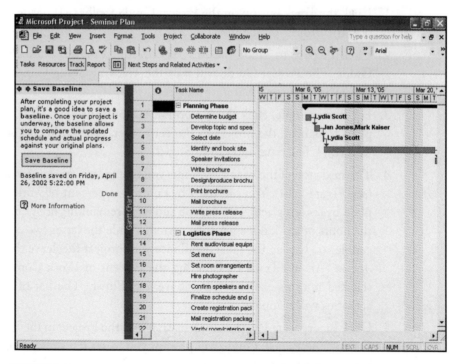

FIGURE 2.13   *Saving a baseline keeps a record of your original project plan in terms of timing, work, and cost.*

4. Click Done in the lower-right corner of the Project Guide side pane. The list of Track activities will reappear.

Tracking Project Progress

As time passes, you'll need to tell Project how much work has been completed on the tasks in the Task Sheet, enter any actual cost information that applies (if it differs from the baseline cost information that Project calculated), and also reschedule tasks as needed. There are many ins and outs to this process, so consult Chapter 11, "Saving the Baseline and Tracking Work Progress," to learn more.

The Project Guide, on the other hand, can simplify the process. Use this exercise to get started, continuing to work with the Seminar Plan file:

1. Click the Track button on the Project Guide toolbar. (If needed, display the Project Guide first.)

2. Click Prepare to Track the Progress of Your Project in the Project Guide. The Project Guide will start the Tracking Setup Wizard and display its first step, Entering Progress.

3. For this example, click the No option button if needed. (If you had plans to publish the project to Project Server, you would choose Yes instead). Click Save and Go to Step 2.

4. The next step of the wizard prompts you to choose a tracking method (see Figure 2.14). You can track by entering a percent of work complete, by entering actual work done and work remaining, or by entering the hours or work done per time period. While the latter two options enable you to plug the most detail into your project file, leave the first option (Always Track by Entering the Percent of Work Complete) selected for this exercise. Click Save and Finish. The list of Track activities will reappear.

5. Click Incorporate Progress Information into the Project in the Project Guide. The Project Guide will prompt you to set the status date and update progress in the side pane.

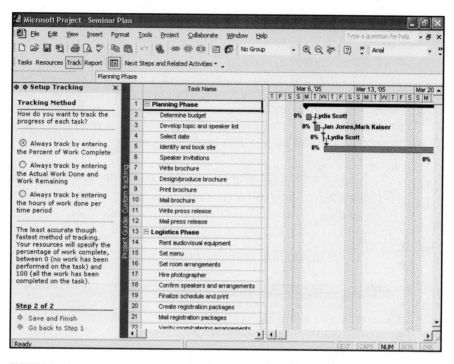

FIGURE 2.14   *The Tracking Setup Wizard prompts you to specify how you prefer to enter information about work completed on tasks.*

6. Change the setting in the Set the Status Date area to **3/31/2005**. While this step doesn't seem necessary for this exercise, you'll see later that Project uses this setting to calculate task and project status as of that date.

7. Click in the % Work Complete column for task 2, type **100**, and press Enter. This marks the task as 100% complete, and 100% appears beside the Gantt bar for the task. Notice that a calculated entry also appears in the % Work Complete cell for task 1, the first summary task. Again, summary tasks have calculated values based on the detail tasks in the summary group, so you never have to mark any work as complete for a summary task. Project does it for you!

8. Click the Work column for task 3, type **24**, and press Enter.

NOTE

If a Feedback button appears, click the Feedback button, and then click the option labeled Increase Task Duration, So the Work Is Done Over a Longer Period of Time. You make this choice when you know that a task takes more person hours to complete, over a longer duration. Project reschedules the scheduled finish for task 3, as well as rescheduling the start and finish dates for successors of task 3 and their successors.

9. Now click in the % Work Complete column for task 3, type **100**, and press Enter. This will mark the task as complete according to its new duration.

10. Mark task 4 as 100% complete and task 5 as 75% complete. Your project should now resemble Figure 2.15.

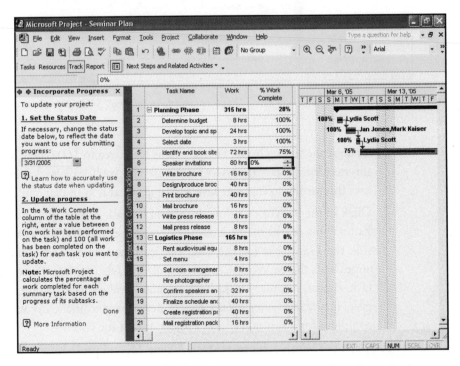

FIGURE 2.15   *You can use the Project Guide to enter a percentage of work completed on a task-by-task basis.*

11. Scroll down the Project Guide side pane and click Done in the lower-right corner. The list of Track activities will reappear.

12. Click Check the Progress of the Project in the Project Guide. The Project Guide will describe each of the status indicators displayed in the Status Indicator column for the tasks. As you can see in Figure 2.16, because you changed the length of task 3 earlier, some tasks now are running late. (The calculation for each task compares it with the baseline plan you saved earlier, the task Work and % Work Complete entries you've made, and the status date you specified.)

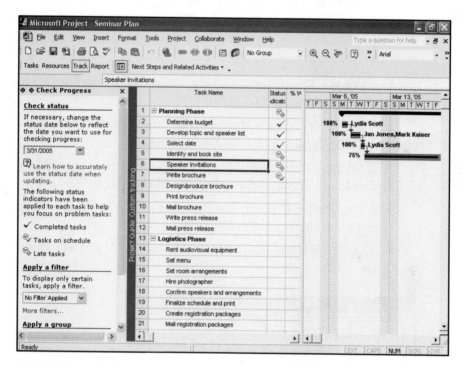

FIGURE 2.16   *The Project Guide uses easy-to-understand indicators to update you about each task's status.*

13. Scroll down the Project Guide side pane and click Done in the lower-right corner. The list of Track activities will reappear.

 NOTE

A special view called the Tracking Gantt view gives you an even clearer picture of how your project's schedule compares with the baseline plan. You'll learn about Tracking Gantt view, as well as other views and tables that you can use to review baseline and progress information, in Chapter 11.

Reporting on Project Results

Project contains a number of built-in report formats to make communicating with your team members and project stakeholders as effortless as possible. You can generate reports about overall project information, assignments, upcoming tasks, and costs, or even create your own specialized reports.

Chapter 16, "Creating and Printing a Report," will cover viewing, printing, and customizing reports in greater detail. For now, follow this exercise to use the Project Guide to display and print a report, working from the example Seminar Plan file that you've built:

1. Click the Report button on the Project Guide toolbar. (If needed, display the Project Guide first.)

2. Click Select a View or Report in the Project Guide. The Project Guide will display choices for views and reports.

3. Click the Print a Project Report option in the side pane. The Project Guide will display Select a Report information.

4. Click Display Reports. The Reports dialog box will appear, displaying the available report categories.

5. Double-click on Costs. The Cost Reports dialog box will appear (Figure 2.17).

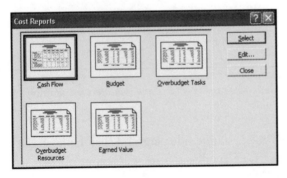

FIGURE 2.17   *Here are Project's cost reports. Project offers other types of reports, and you can create custom reports.*

6. Double-click on Budget. The Budget report will appear onscreen.

7. Click on the Print button at the top of the report preview window.

CAUTION

It's inconvenient, but you can't use Project to keep track of the report data you display and print on any given day. If you need an electronic snapshot of the data from your project, you'll have to export the data to a file. Chapter 21, "Using Project with Other Applications," covers the export process.

8. Change any needed settings in the Print dialog box, and then click on OK to print.

9. Click on the Close button to close the report preview.

10. Click on the Close button in the Reports dialog box to close it.

11. Click the Save button on the Standard (top) toolbar to save the Seminar Plan file, and then choose File, Close to close the file.

 WEB

You can download the finished Seminar Plan file from the Premier Press download page at http://www.premierpressbooks.com/downloads.asp.

Turning the Project Guide off (and Back on)

As you've seen throughout this chapter, the Project Guide can really reduce the learning curve when it comes to creating and working with Project files. Once you're more proficient, however, you may want to turn off the Project Guide and work on your own.

Follow these steps to turn the Project Guide off (and back on) at will:

1. Choose Tools, Options. The Options dialog box will open.

2. Click the Interface tab to display its options.

3. Click the Display Project Guide check box in the Project Guide Settings section of the dialog box (see Figure 2.18).

4. Click OK to close the Options dialog box and apply your change.

Click to turn the Project Guide off and on

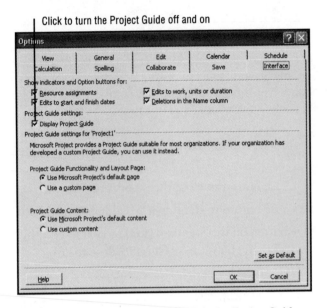

FIGURE 2.18 *Disable (uncheck) the Display Project Guide check box to turn off the Project Guide. Check the check box to turn the Project Guide back on.*

PART II

Project Management Basics

Chapter 3

Working with Files and Help

In This Chapter

◆ How to start Microsoft Project

◆ Help resources in Project

◆ Going online for more help

◆ Managing files

◆ How to exit Project

So you've taken Microsoft Project 2002 out of the box and installed it (or your MIS person has). You're all set up, but where do you go now? With many applications, how to get started is obvious. To begin working in Word, for example, you just start typing. In Excel, you just click on cells and type numbers and formulas.

The starting point with Project is not so obvious, but don't worry. This chapter and the next one will introduce the steps you need to take to begin setting up a project.

Starting Project

As with most other Windows applications, the easiest way to start Project is via the Windows taskbar.

1. Click on the Start menu button.

2. Point to All Programs (Windows XP) or Programs (prior Windows versions).

3. Click on Microsoft Project.

 TIP

In Windows XP, Microsoft Project may appear on the list of recently used applications along the left side of the Start menu. If so, you can skip Step 2 and click directly on Microsoft Project.

Even though Project appears as a choice on the Start menu, you may find it more convenient to add a shortcut icon for starting Project to the Windows desktop.

1. Close all open applications and windows so you can easily see the desktop.

2. Click on the Start menu button.

3. Point to All Programs (Windows XP) or Programs (prior Windows versions).

4. In the submenu, point to the Microsoft Project menu choice, press and hold the right mouse button, and drag the choice over the desktop as shown in Figure 3.1. When you release the mouse button, a shortcut menu will appear. Click on Copy Here.

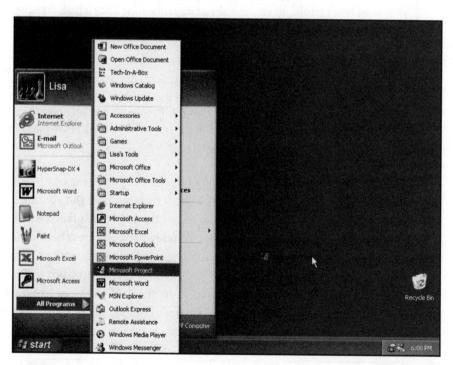

FIGURE 3.1   *After you release the right mouse button, the shortcut icon for Project appears on the desktop.*

5. Drag the shortcut to the location that you prefer on the desktop.

After you add a Project shortcut to the desktop, you can double-click on it at any time to start Project. If the Project Information dialog box appears, you can enter a start date for the new, blank project file and then click OK, or simply click OK to close the dialog box and start using Project.

Understanding the Project Screen

When Project displays a new blank project, the screen looks like Figure 3.2. If the Project Guide is turned off, you'll see the Gantt Chart view for the new project and the New Project task pane at the left. The Gantt Chart view enables you to enter tasks for your project. It features two grid-like panes. In the left pane, you enter the name of the task, its duration, and other columns of task information. (Chapter 4, "Setting Up a Project," covers creating tasks in more detail.) The right pane displays each task you create as a graphical bar in a weekly schedule, so you can see at a glance how long a task lasts, or where tasks overlap in time.

 NOTE

The remainder of this book assumes that the Project Guide has been turned off, unless otherwise specified. To turn the Project Guide on and off, choose Tools, Options, click the Interface tab, check or uncheck the Display Project Guide check box as desired, and then click OK.

Project 2002 looks like the other Microsoft Office applications (Word, Excel, PowerPoint, Access, and Outlook), so it feels familiar and you can quickly find and learn to use its features. The top of the screen displays a title bar and menu bar with commands, as in other Windows applications. Below the menu bar, two toolbars appear by default (on a single row); each toolbar button is a shortcut for executing a particular command. A text entry box appears between the toolbars and the panes that show the data you've entered; you can use this box to enter and edit task entries. The box changes in appearance when you use it, as you'll learn in the next chapter.

 TIP

For more information about Project and other Microsoft products, visit Microsoft's Web site, as described in the "Getting Help on the Web" section later in this chapter.

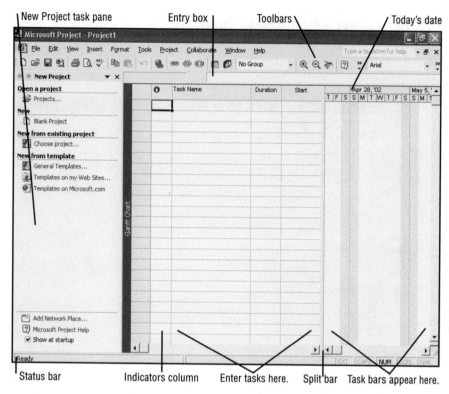

FIGURE 3.2   *The Gantt Chart view is the default view for a new project.*

Opening and Closing the Task Pane

Like the Project Guide side pane, the task pane consumes a lot of screen real estate. If you find that the task pane gets in the way more than it helps your work, you can click the Close button (X) in the upper-right corner of the task pane window. To redisplay the task pane, right-click any toolbar (or choose View, Toolbars), and then click Task Pane. The task pane will also open when it is required, such as when you choose File, New to start a new file. (You must choose the File, New command to see the task pane; clicking the New button on the Standard toolbar simply displays a new, blank file.)

 NOTE

The remainder of this book assumes that the task pane has been closed, unless otherwise specified. This enables the screen shots in this book to better illustrate the example information.

Looking at the View Bar

Project 2002 includes an onscreen feature called the View Bar, shown in Figure 3.3.

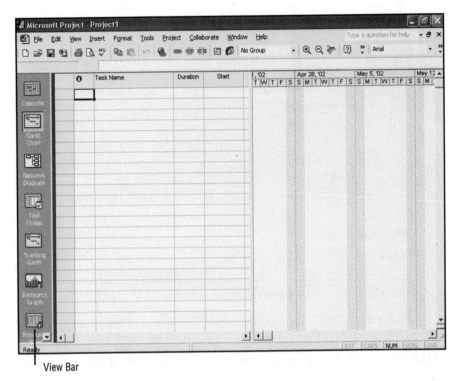

View Bar

FIGURE 3.3   *You can use the buttons on the View Bar to navigate through Project's views.*

As its name suggests, the View Bar enables you to select a different screen layout or view for the various types of information stored in a Project file. For example, a particular view might show a graph you're looking for, and another view might make it easier to enter a certain type of information, such as information about a resource (a person who will be working on a project). Some views are graphical, and some provide information about tasks, and so on. Don't worry about what each view looks like for now. You'll learn more about the various views in the chapters where they apply and in Chapter 13, "Working with the Different Project Views."

Each icon in the View Bar represents a particular view in Project. Click on the icon for the view you want. To scroll the View Bar and see additional view icons, click on the down-arrow button at the bottom-right corner of the View Bar. An up-arrow button appears in the upper-right corner of the View Bar.

When you move the mouse pointer over the icon for a particular view, the icon takes on a 3-D appearance. Then you can click on the icon to change to the view.

NOTE

If you use Outlook to manage your e-mail, to-do list, contact list, and other information, you're familiar with the Outlook Bar, which you use to view various types of information in Outlook. The View Bar in Project looks and works much like the Outlook Bar.

Use the View, View Bar command to hide and display the View Bar. The View Bar is hidden by default. (You also can right-click on the open or hidden View Bar, and then click View Bar in the shortcut menu to hide or open the View Bar.) When you hide the View Bar, the view name appears along the left side of the screen. Each view button on the View Bar corresponds to one of the views listed on the View menu. So, when you've hidden the View Bar, you can use the View menu choices to change the view instead. In fact, many more advanced users prefer to keep the View Bar hidden at all times, opting instead to see more Project information onscreen.

NOTE

In the remainder of this book, you'll probably see a mix of figures both with and without the View Bar. I will generally hide it in a figure, for the sake of clarity.

Looking at the Toolbars

By default, Project displays two toolbars, Standard (left) and Formatting. When you start using Project, it at first displays only one tool for the Formatting toolbar—the Font choice at the far right. To discover what a particular toolbar button does, simply place the mouse pointer on it to display a yellow ScreenTip describing the button (see Figure 3.4).

FIGURE 3.4   *Point to a toolbar button to learn what it does.*

Project enables you to control the toolbar display, select the shortcuts you prefer to work with, and control how much of your screen the toolbars use. As shown in Figure 3.5, you can point to the handle at the left end of a toolbar (the pointer will change to a four-headed arrow), and then drag the toolbar to another location onscreen. The toolbar appears in a floating window that you can resize by dragging any of its borders. To return the toolbar to its original location, double-click on the toolbar window title bar.

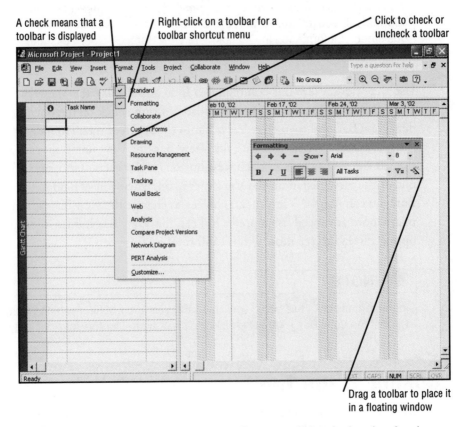

FIGURE 3.5   *In Project, you can make your toolbars more efficient by dragging them into their own floating windows.*

The fastest way to choose which toolbars appear onscreen is to right-click on a toolbar to display the shortcut menu. A check mark beside a toolbar name in the list indicates that the toolbar is presently displayed (toggled on). To select or deselect a toolbar, click on its name on this shortcut menu. To close the shortcut menu without changing a toolbar selection, click outside the menu (or press Esc).

TIP

Chapter 28, "Customizing Microsoft Project," shows you how to customize your toolbars by adding new buttons. It also explains how to create your own toolbar in order to make using Project as easy as possible for you.

Getting Help When You Need It

Project offers several different "flavors" of help, via the Help menu. The fastest way to get help is to use the Ask a Question box at the right end of the menu bar. (It displays Type a Question for Help in grayed-out text until you enter a question of your own.) If you need help with a particular issue or operation, click in the Ask a Question box, type in your question, and then press Enter. As shown in Figure 3.6, a drop-down list of help topics about your problem opens. You can click the See More arrow at the bottom of the list if the initial list doesn't include a topic you think will be helpful. When you do see a topic you want in the list, click it. The Microsoft Project Help window opens at the right side of the screen and displays the requested topic. You can scroll down the instructions, use the buttons at the top of the window to print the topic, or navigate through Help (described later) as needed. When you're finished, click the Close button in the upper-right corner of the Microsoft Project Help window.

Or instead, you may prefer to browse through the list of available Help topics. To do so, choose Help, Contents and Index. The Microsoft Project Help window that appears (see Figure 3.7) offers two panes.

The left pane enables you to choose one of three tabs, each of which offers a different kind of help.

◆ **Contents.** The Contents tab lists several folders or topic areas within the Help system. To view the topics within a folder, double-click on the folder, or click on the plus sign beside it so that its icon changes to an open folder and its contents (additional folders and topics) are displayed. A question page icon indicates specific topics. Click on any topic to view it in the pane at the right or in its own window. To close a folder, double-click on it or click on the minus sign that appears beside it. The Contents tab is ideal for browsing through the available help.

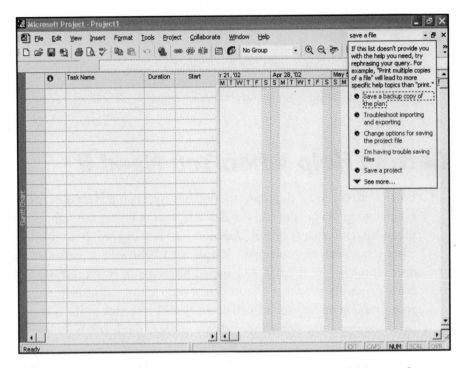

FIGURE 3.6   *The Ask a Question feature on the menu bar helps you with issues and problems you have with Project.*

◆ **Answer Wizard.** The Answer Wizard tab enables you to type in a question and search for matching topics. Type your question or the activity you want to find out about into the What Would You Like To Do? text box on the Answer Wizard tab, and then click on Search. The Select Topic To Display list box will display a list of potentially matching topics. Click on a topic to see help about it in the pane at the right side of the Microsoft Project Help window.

◆ **Index.** If you have a rough idea of the topic you're searching for and how it might be referenced in Help, click on the Index tab. The Type Keywords text box prompts you to type all or part of the topic you want information about. The Or Choose Keywords list scrolls down to display the terms and phrases that most closely match your entry. When you see an entry you want to view in the Or Choose Keywords list, double-click on it. The Choose A Topic list will display help topics relating to the term you've selected. Click on a term in this bottom list to see help about it in the right pane.

FIGURE 3.7 *After you access the Microsoft Project Help window, you can click on a tab in the left pane to select the kind of help you need, or click a link in the right pane to review detailed tutorials and browse for information.*

After you use one of these methods to display a Help topic in the right pane of the Microsoft Project Help window, follow the hyperlinks (which are blue and underlined by default) to browse through all the help about that topic. You can also use the Back and Forward buttons on the Help window toolbar to browse, much as you would in Web browser software like Internet Explorer.

You can click on the Options button on the Help window toolbar to open a menu with options for working with the help topic information. Choosing Print from the menu, for example, enables you to print the Help topic. Drag over text in the right pane of the Help window to select it, and then right-click with the mouse. Choose Copy in the shortcut menu that appears to copy the Help topic contents to the Windows Clipboard. Then you can paste that information into another document—say, an e-mail message to a colleague who needs help with a Project feature. The Hide button on the toolbar hides the right pane of the Help window, at which point the button turns into the Show button. Click on the Help window Close button to close the Microsoft Project Help window altogether.

Looking back at Figure 3.7, the Welcome! pane of the Microsoft Project Help window initially displays a list of specific Help features that you can view or browse to become more comfortable with key concepts.

- ◆ **What's New.** Follow this link if you've upgraded from Project 98 or 2000, and you want to learn about new 2002 features and how they might affect your existing Project files.

- ◆ **Project Map.** Click on this link to view a list or map (see Figure 3.8) that outlines the project management process, both in general and with regard to the use of Microsoft Project. Follow the links to find out about topics of interest. This is a good resource to review if you want to start learning more about project management.

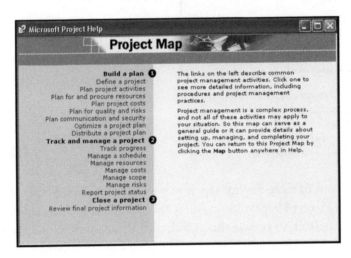

FIGURE 3.8 *The Project Map outlines the project management planning process.*

- ◆ **Tutorial.** Click on this link to use the tutorial, which offers background information about the project planning process and brief lessons that walk you through the creation of a project schedule.

- ◆ **Reference.** Use this link to access Help listings that describe the various Project fields, troubleshooting help, and more.

TIP

After you follow one of the links, click on the Home link near the top of the right pane in subsequent Help windows to return to the Welcome! window. Note that you can access the Project Map, Tutorial, and What's New Help via Getting Started on the Help menu. A command for reviewing the Reference Help appears directly on the Help menu.

When you've finished working with Help, click on the Close button in the upper-right corner of the Microsoft Project Help window. This hides the Help window so you can see more of the Project application window and the new blank project file.

Using What's This?

Another Help menu choice can provide instant help for the task at hand. Open the Help menu by clicking on it, and then click on What's This? to get information about what you're doing. Alternately, you can press Shift+F1. The mouse pointer turns into a question-mark pointer. Click on the onscreen item that you're curious about, and Project will display a pop-up description of it. Click outside the description to close it.

NOTE

If you see a question-mark button next to the Close button at the right end of a dialog box title bar, you can click on it and then click an item in the dialog box for pop-up help about it. If the dialog box doesn't offer a question-mark button, right-click on the dialog box option you want help with, and then click on What's This? in the shortcut menu.

Checking ScreenTips

Like its sister products in the Office XP suite, Project 2002 features ScreenTip help. In addition to displaying ScreenTips about toolbar buttons, you can display ScreenTips about other onscreen features. For example, you can point to part of the timescale to see the precise calendar date or dates that the specified portion of the timescale represents. You also can point to any column header in the Task Sheet portion of the default Gantt Chart view. As shown in Figure 3.9, the ScreenTip includes a link to a help description of the field contents. Click on the link to see that help.

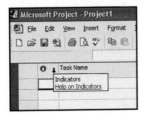

FIGURE 3.9 *Project offers ScreenTips about column headings and the timescale.*

Using the Office Assistant

The Office Assistant enables you to ask for help in plain English, as with the Answer wizard. You type in a question, and the Office Assistant searches the Help system and displays a list of topics that may answer your question. Follow these steps to work with the Office Assistant:

1. You can launch the Office Assistant in a few ways: by choosing Help, Microsoft Project Help; by pressing F1; or by clicking on the Microsoft Project Help button on the Standard toolbar. No matter which method you use, the Office Assistant will open onscreen, and its yellow question bubble will open. The bubble prompts you to type in a question.

2. Type in your question; it will replace the prompt in the bubble. Figure 3.10 shows a question typed into the Assistant: "How do I save a project file?"

3. Click on the Search button, located beneath the area where your question appeared when you typed. The Office Assistant will search all the Help topics and list those that might answer your question. If there are more topics than can appear in the little yellow bubble at one time, See More with a triangle button will appear at the bottom of the topic list. Click on it to review the additional topics. See Previous will appear at the top of the list so that you can redisplay the initial list of topics.

4. When you see the Help topic you want, click on the round button beside it. A Help window will appear, giving you steps, information,

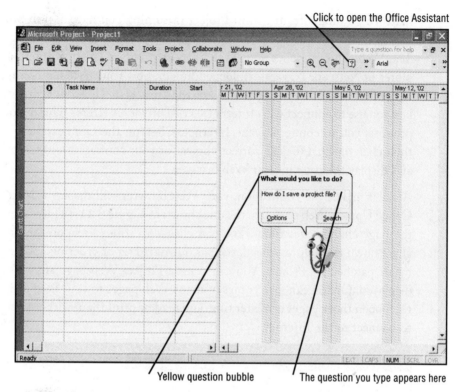

FIGURE 3.10   *Use the Office Assistant to type a help question in your own words.*

or links to more specific topics. Review the Help and follow links as needed, and then click on the Close button to close the window.

5. When you finish working with the Office Assistant, you can right-click on it and choose Hide to remove it from your screen.

Rather than closing the Office Assistant after getting Help about a question, you can leave it onscreen as long as you need to by simply clicking outside the yellow question bubble. To redisplay the yellow question bubble at any time, click on the Office Assistant character (the default character's name is Clippit).

Getting Help on the Web

Although software publishers do provide manuals and online help along with their products, the help that comes with the software itself has become slimmer. To supplement this, Microsoft maintains a Web site providing additional help. To go online from within Project (assuming you have a Web browser installed and your Internet connection is set up), choose Help, Office On The Web. This launches your Web browser program (such as Internet Explorer or Netscape Navigator). Depending on how your system is configured to connect to the Internet, you may see the same Dial-Up Connection dialog box you use to connect with Internet service providers (ISPs). This dialog box prompts you to connect to the Internet. Click on the Connect button and then click on Dial (or the correct choice for your configuration) to connect and display the page in your Web browser.

After it makes the connection, your Web browser will display a Microsoft Office Update Web page like the one shown in Figure 3.11. (The contents of the page change over time.) You can click on various links on the page to chase down the help you need, such as downloading or ordering updates and repair patches for Project. You can print a Project Web page after it's fully displayed. Or you can save copies of many Web pages to your hard disk, and then open those pages at a later time and read or print them without needing to connect to the Internet.

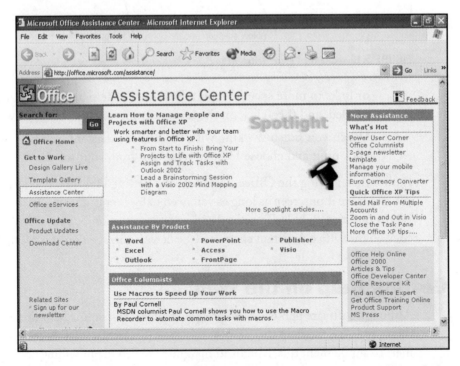

FIGURE 3.11 *Microsoft's Project Web coverage can help you answer your questions or find support products and consultants for Project.*

Use the Browser's File, Save As command to save Web help for later reference. When you finish checking out the Project Web information, you can close your browser and disconnect or surf on to another Web site.

 TIP

If you don't find the help you need on the Project Web site or would have to pay for technical support, you can try visiting the various Project newsgroups, including microsoft.public.project2002. On Internet newsgroups like this, users of all levels post questions or offer help to other users. Questions posted to these very active newsgroups often garner a response in a matter of hours. In my opinion, these are among the best places to get help about specific Project questions, free of charge!

Working with Files

As in all other applications, in Project you must store your work by saving it to a file on your computer's hard disk. You won't be able to track your project's progress if you can't use your file repeatedly, so it's essential to be careful when saving your files and to choose file names that are specific and descriptive. This makes it easy to find the file you need.

This section examines preserving and organizing your work.

Starting a New File

As you learned earlier in this chapter, you can open a new blank file when you launch the Project 2002 application. There might be occasions, however, when you finish working with one file and then want to create a new file without exiting Project. You can start a new file in one of two ways:

◆ Click on the New button on the Standard toolbar (it's at the far left and looks like a piece of paper). This method only allows you to create a new, blank project file.

◆ Choose File, New. The New Project task pane will open (as in Figure 3.12), if it isn't already open. Click on Blank Project. (You also can use a template to create a new project file from the New Project task pane. Chapter 19 explains how to use a template to create a new Project file.)

Click here to open an existing project file   Click here to create a new blank file

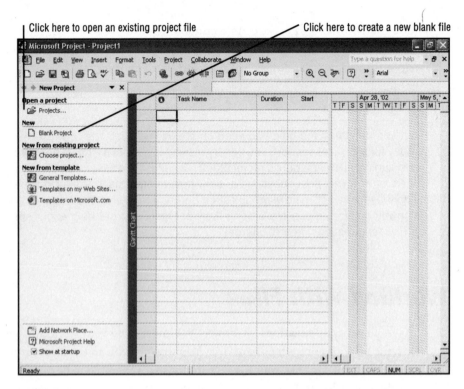

FIGURE 3.11   _The New Project task pane enables you to open and create files._

By default, Project gives the file the temporary name ProjectX, where _X_ is a number sequentially assigned to each new file you open in a Project work session.

Project displays the empty file onscreen. It puts the file's temporary name in the title bar until you save the file and assign a unique name to it. (See the section titled "Saving a File" later in this chapter.)

Opening an Existing File

If you've ever opened files that were created and saved in other Windows applications, you'll be relatively comfortable with Project's Open dialog box. It enables you to open Project files you previously saved, so that you can enter new information, change the view, print the file, and more.

To open a file, follow these steps:

1. Choose File, Open. Alternately, you can press Ctrl+O or click on the Open button on the Standard toolbar. Finally, if the New Project task

pane is open, you can click Projects in the Open a Projects section. No matter which method you use, the Open dialog box will appear (see Figure 3.13).

 NOTE

On Windows 95 (or later) systems, the folder that appears by default in the Look In list is usually My Documents, which is located on the C drive. However, if you're running Project with Windows NT or NT Workstation, the default folder is usually Personal, which is a subfolder of the folder that holds your Windows NT Workstation files.

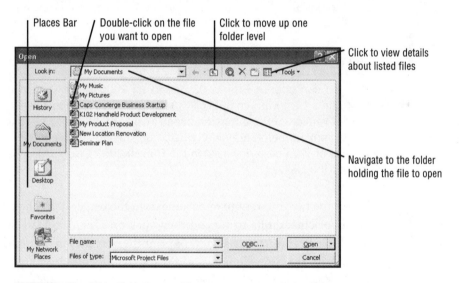

FIGURE 3.13   *This dialog box enables you to open an existing file so that you can work with it again.*

2. Click on the drop-down arrow beside the Look In list and click on the disk drive where your Project file is stored to select it and display its list of folders in the dialog box.

 TIP

The Places Bar appears on the left side of the Project Open and Save dialog boxes. Click on the History button there to see files and folders you've used recently and find a particular file more quickly. The My Documents button takes you back to your default My Documents folder. Desktop lists folders and files stored on the Windows desktop.

NOTE

If you're using a Windows 98 machine that's set up for multiple user logon, you *must* use the My Documents folder icon to return to your My Documents folder, because the actual path to your My Documents folder will be a subfolder holding your Windows profile in the Windows folder. In that case, you'd have to know the full path, based on your user name, to use the Look In list to navigate all the way to your My Documents folder.

3. Double-click on a folder in the list of folders that appears. Doing so displays the contents of that folder in the dialog box list. You might need to double-click on one or more subfolder icons to reach the file you want to open.

 NOTE

Generally, you can open a Project 98 or Project 2000 file in Project 2002 because it offers backward-compatibility. However, if you try to open a file from an older version of Project and it doesn't work, that file may need to be saved in the .mpx format in the older version of Project. Then, choose MPX from the Files of Type drop-down list in the Project 2002 Open dialog box to find and open the file.

4. When the file you want to open appears in the list, double-click on its name (or click on its name and then click on Open) to load the file into Project. If you want to view or print the file but don't want to edit it, click on the drop-down list arrow for the Open button and select Open Read-Only. This option prevents you from making unwanted changes to the file.

After you select the file to open, Project displays it onscreen, ready for you to alter it, print it, or whatever.

 TIP

Project adds a button to the Windows taskbar for every file that you open. So if you open multiple Project files, you can use either the Windows menu in Project or the taskbar buttons to move between open files.

Finding a File with the Open Dialog Box

As the sizes of hard disks on individual computer systems—and the sizes of networked drives—increase to several gigabytes each, it becomes harder for users to keep track of files. It can be tough to keep everything in order on hard disks with dozens of folders and thousands of files, even if you're diligent in organizing everything. Or you might have many files that are similar and need to use a Find feature to distinguish between them. To facilitate this, most Microsoft applications have built-in file-finding help in the Open dialog box.

When you perform a find, you can use wild-card characters if you remember part of a file name. Project will list files with names similar to the name you specified using wild cards. The asterisk (*) wild card stands in for any group of characters within a file name. For example, entering—**a*** in the File name text box results in a list of all file names that begin with the letter a, such as Annual Report and Accidents. The question mark (?) wild card stands in for any single character. For example, entering **anders?n** in the File name text box finds files named Anderson and Andersen.

If you're working in the Open dialog box and can't remember the exact location of the file you want to open, follow these steps to perform a basic find:

1. Click on the Tools button in the Open dialog box, and then choose Search in the menu that appears. The Search dialog will box open.

 TIP

To search for a Project file based on a single word or phrase found in the file, click on the Basic tab. Enter the word or phrase in the Search Text field, and then click Search.

2. Click the Advanced tab in the Search dialog box.
3. For the criterion you're creating, use the Property drop-down list to select the file property that will be used in the find operation, and use the Condition list to indicate how the Property and Value entries should correspond.
4. Finally, enter the value that the Find operation should look for in that criterion. For example, if you have selected Keywords from the Property list, you might enter **development** in the Value text box. If the Value entry contains more than one word, surround the entry with quotation marks, as in **"product development."**

5. Click on the Add button to finish defining the criterion. Figure 3.14 shows an example.

 TIP

If you want to remove one of the criteria you defined from the current search or a prior search, click on it in the list of criteria, and then click on Delete. To remove all the criteria, click on New Search.

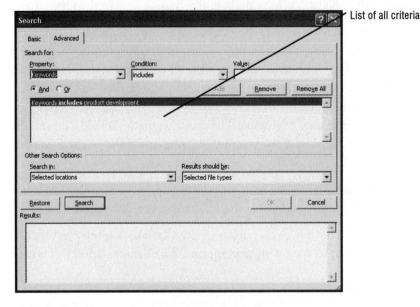

List of all criteria

FIGURE 3.14   *You can create a list of criteria to increase the power of a search operation.*

6. To add a new criterion to the list of criteria, start by selecting either the And or Or option button. Selecting And means that Find must match the original criteria (if any) and the new criterion you're specifying. In contrast, selecting Or means that the file can match any one or more of the criteria you've specified. Then, repeat Steps 3 through 5 to finish each new criterion.

7. Use the Search In drop-down list to specify a disk or folder to be searched. Use the plus or minus sign beside each location to display or hide its contents. Check and uncheck locations as needed to determine whether to search them.

8. Use the Results Should Be drop-down list to limit the search to certain file types, if needed. Again, use the plus or minus sign beside each group of file types to display or hide its contents. Check and uncheck file types as needed to determine whether to include them.

9. Click on the Search button to execute the search. When the search is finished, Project will display a message or list at the bottom of the Search dialog box telling you how many files match the search criteria you specified.

10. Double-click on the name of the file you want to open. Doing so returns you to the Open dialog box, where the file is selected.

11. Click Open to finish opening the file.

Saving a File

Saving a file on disk preserves it (as permanently as possible, given the imperfections of electronic storage media) so that you can work with it again. The first time you save a file, you can give it a unique name. Project 2002 enables you to take advantage of the long file names in Windows. You can enter up to 255 characters, including spaces. This enables you to create useful and descriptive file names. (However, keep in mind that the 255 characters must include the path, slashes, and so on. Therefore, the real limitation for the file name is closer to 230 characters.)

To save a file for the first time and give it the name of your choice, perform the following steps:

1. Choose File, Save. Alternately, you can press Ctrl+S or click on the Save button on the Standard toolbar. The Save As dialog box will appear (see Figure 3.15).

2. Navigate to the drive and folder where you want to save the file using the Save In drop-down list and the folders that appear below it. (Double-clicking on a folder icon opens that folder so you can store the file there.)

3. Type a name for the file in the File Name text box. Try to use something descriptive, even if it's lengthy, such as **Rider Bike Product Introduction**.

4. Click on the Save button to save the file.

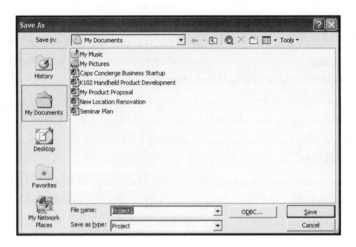

FIGURE 3.15 *Use this dialog box to save and name a file.*

After you save a file for the first time, you can save any subsequent changes you make to it by pressing Ctrl+S (or clicking on the Save button on the Standard toolbar).

However, sometimes you may want to save a file with a new name. For example, if you have a lengthy project, you might want to save a version of the main project file at the end of each month. That way, you can keep a record of your progress and create a series of progressive backup copies of your file. In such a case, you must first save your file to ensure that the existing version reflects your most current changes. Next, reopen the Save As dialog box by choosing File, Save As. In the Save As dialog box, you can (but don't have to) change the selected folder to specify a new location for the renamed file. Then type the new name, such as **March 05 Rider Bike Product Introduction**, and click on Save to finish creating the new version of the file.

 TIP

Each time you use Save As, you create a new copy of your file and leave the older version intact on disk. You might use Save As daily to copy a file, use it monthly to ensure you have a relatively up-to-date spare copy of the file, or even make copies to test the impact of changes you make to your schedule. I recommend you include the date in the file name (as in My Project 5-1-06, My Project 5-8-06, and so on). To create extra copies of your Project files, you also can use My Computer or Windows Explorer to copy and rename the file. Microsoft Project files with larger amounts of task and resource information might tend to become corrupted when you use Save As, so use My Computer or Windows Explorer to copy those files instead.

File Protection and Backup Options

Part of the beauty of Project is that its files can be used easily in a networked environment. At any time, other team members can open the master plan for a project and review where things stand, or update information about tasks as they are completed. The downside to this, of course, is that it is difficult to control who can view the file and how changes are made.

The Save As dialog box provides a method for applying some protection to files. You can protect files the first time you save them, or after the fact. Open the Save As dialog box by choosing File, Save the first time you save the file, or by choosing File, Save As for existing files. If necessary, specify the folder where the file should be saved, and then enter the file name. Next, click on the Tools button, and then choose General Options in the menu that appears to open the Save Options dialog box (see Figure 3.16).

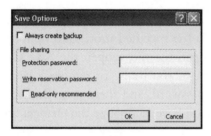

FIGURE 3.16   *Protect your files, especially when they are on a network, by specifying a password protection and backup option.*

If you want Project to automatically create a backup copy of the file each time you save it, select the Always Create Backup check box.

Passwords for Project files can be up to 15 characters and can include letters, numbers, and symbols. Create a Protection Password if you want users to enter a password to be able to open the file. Enter a Write Reservation Password if you want to allow users to view a read-only version of the file without a password, but you want to require a password for a user to be able to edit the file and save the edited version.

CAUTION

Passwords in Project are case-sensitive. Therefore, if happY is the password you create, it will not match user entries such as Happy, happy, or HAPPY. Be careful to record the correct password and its capitalization in a secure location. Also, steer clear of using passwords that others might be able to guess or discover, such as your birth date, your Social Security Number, names (of your spouse, pet, or child), and so on.

Click on the Read-Only Recommended check box if you want Project to display a dialog box allowing the user to open a read-only version of the file each time it is opened.

After you specify any desired save options, click on OK. If you specify a new password (or change a password), Project asks you to enter the password again to verify it. Do so, and then click on OK. Click on Save to close the Save As dialog box and put your protection options in place.

If you ever want to make changes to the specified protection options—for example, change a password—just open the file, reopen the Save Options dialog box, and make whatever changes you want. To remove a password, double-click it to select the whole password, and then press Backspace or Delete. Click on OK and then click on Save to finalize the changes and return to your project file.

Saving and Opening a Workspace

Sometimes you might need to work with several Project files at once. For example, if you frequently copy information between two project files (such as one for all tasks in your group and one for a specific project), it might be more convenient to have them open up automatically and appear side-by-side onscreen. You might even want to have each file appear in a particular view.

Project allows you to create such an onscreen configuration of multiple files and settings as a *workspace*. Then, to reopen multiple files, position them precisely onscreen, and specify the appropriate views and settings, all you have to do is open a single workspace file.

NOTE

Workspace files have a different file name extension to help the Open dialog box distinguish them from regular Project files.

To create a workspace file:

1. Open all the project files that you want to include in the workspace.

2. Arrange the files onscreen (as covered in the next section) and specify the appropriate view for each file. (Views are covered where they apply throughout the book. They are also covered in detail in Chapter 13, "Working with the Different Project Views.")

3. Choose File, Save Workspace. The Save Workspace As dialog box appears, with Workspace automatically selected as Save As Type (see Figure 3.17).

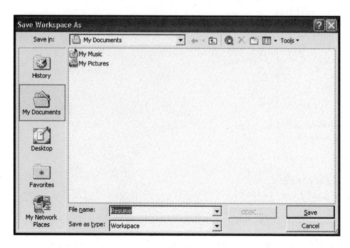

FIGURE 3.17   *Create a workspace so you can easily open multiple files.*

4. Select the folder where you want to save the workspace file by using the Save In list and double-clicking on folders as needed below the list.

5. Type a name for the workspace in the File Name text box. (By default, Project suggests the name Resume, but you can enter any name you want.)

6. Click on Save to finish saving the workspace.

Opening a workspace is virtually identical to opening a file. Use any of three methods: choose File, Open; press Ctrl+O; or click on the Open button on the Standard toolbar. In the Open dialog box, navigate to the folder where the workspace file is saved. Click on the drop-down list arrow to open the Files Of Type drop-down list, and select Workspaces from the list. When you see the name of the workspace file you want to open, double-click on the name.

Selecting, Arranging, and Closing Files

Each time you open a file in Project it remains open until you specifically close it after you finish working with it (and presumably after you save it). If you're viewing each open file at full-screen size (maximized), the easiest way to switch between open files is to use the Window menu. To choose which file to display, open the Window menu and click on the name of the file you want to select (see Figure 3.18). You can also click on the button for the file on the Windows taskbar.

FIGURE 3.18 *Select the file you want to work with from the Window menu.*

Notice that the Window menu offers some other useful options.

◆ New Window opens a new window of an open file. This option enables you to show two different views of the same file onscreen, for example.

◆ Arrange All arranges all the open files and windows so that they fill the screen, with each file at least partially visible.

◆ Hide hides the currently selected file or window. This is handy if you want a file to be out of view during your lunch break, for example.

◆ Unhide displays a list of hidden windows so that you can redisplay one.

◆ Split breaks the current file into two panes so that you can display different areas of a file simultaneously. This command changes to the Remove Split command so that you can unsplit the window and return to a single view when needed.

After you finish working with a particular file and save it, you should close the file so that it is no longer consuming system memory. To close the current file, choose File, Close.

Turning on Auto Save

When you turn on Auto Save, Project will save your file at an interval you designate, whether it's every 5 minutes or every 20 minutes. This protects your files against data losses that might be caused by power fluctuations or system crashes. While I recommend Auto Save for most clients and students (because most of us don't save as often as we should), be aware that Auto Save can cause Project to pause while the save occurs. If those pauses interfere with your work, try specifying a longer time interval between Auto Saves.

To turn on Auto Save, choose Tools, Options. Click on the Save tab in the Options dialog box that appears. Click on the Save Every check box to check it, and then enter an interval in the Minutes text box. Choose either the Save Active Project Only or Save All Open Project Files option button. I also recommend that you click on the Prompt Before Saving check box to uncheck it. Otherwise, you'll have to confirm every Auto Save operation. Click on OK to close the Options dialog box and apply your Auto Save settings.

Exiting Project

When you finish with your work in Project, you can close the program in one of the following ways:

◆ Press Alt+F4.

◆ Click on the Close box in the upper-right corner of the Project application window.

◆ Choose File, Exit.

If you haven't saved your work before you try to close Project, it will ask whether or not you want to save your changes. Click on Yes to do so, or on No to exit without saving.

Chapter 4

Setting Up a Project

In This Chapter

◆ Establishing an overall schedule for your project

◆ Controlling the base calendar schedule for the project

◆ Defining each task in the schedule

◆ Working with the order of the tasks

◆ Setting up milestones

◆ Understanding file properties

Traditionally, when you were assigned a new activity on the job, one of the first things you did was sit down with a yellow notepad and compile a to-do list. You made notes about steps you needed to take to complete the whole project, and perhaps you sketched out schedules for individual assignments. As you completed each step, you simply scratched the item off your list and adjusted subsequent deadlines as needed.

The first step of the planning process in Project 2002 resembles the yellow pad method. You begin by mapping out your time frame and the tasks to be completed.

Managing Project Start and End Dates

As discussed in Chapter 3, "Working with Files and Help," each time you start a new project file by choosing File, New, the Project Guide appears by default. However, if you've turned off the Project Guide (as described in the last section of the chapter), choosing File, New starts a new project file and opens the New Project task pane at the left side of the screen. In contrast, clicking the New button on the Standard toolbar opens a new, blank project file without displaying the New Project task pane.

You need to deal with some important parameters when you create each new project file. One of the most critical is the project's start date. When you open a new project file, it uses by default the current date (per the Windows system settings) as the starting date for the project. Ideally, however, you'll be planning your schedules in advance in Microsoft Project. So, you need to tell Project when you want the work on the project to begin. To accomplish this, you use the Project Information dialog box. (The settings you need do not appear in the New Project task pane.)

To open the Project Information dialog box (see Figure 4.1) after you create a new file, choose Project, Project information. The resulting dialog box will enable you to work with the overall time schedule for your project.

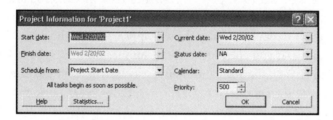

FIGURE 4.1   *Use the Project Information dialog box to establish overall timing for your project.*

The first two text boxes in the dialog box are Start Date and Finish Date. Initially, the Start Date entry displays the system date for your computer, and the Finish Date entry is grayed out (disabled). That's because you enter only one of these dates; Project calculates the other one for you based on the tasks you enter for the project and how long the sequence of the tasks lasts. So to determine how the duration of your schedule is calculated, you can use one of the following two methods:

◆ **Have Project calculate the Finish Date.** Leave Project Start Date as the Schedule From selection, and change the Start Date entry if needed.

◆ **Have Project calculate the Start Date.** Click on the arrow beside the Schedule From drop-down list, and select Project Finish Date. Then, edit the Finish Date entry. However, you should note that with this method, Project schedules all tasks to occur as late as possible, which may not be the scheduling method you prefer.

When you enter or edit either Start Date or Finish Date, you can type the date in m/dd/yy or mm/dd/yy format in the appropriate text box. You don't need to enter the abbreviation for the day of the week; Project specifies it after you finish making changes to the Project Info settings.

If you type the date, however, you need to have a calendar at hand to ensure you type the correct date—for a Monday rather than a Sunday, for example. Project provides a method for entering dates more easily, though. When you see a drop-down arrow on the right side of any text box that holds a date (in the Project Information dialog box and others throughout Project), click on the drop-down arrow to display a calendar you can use to select a date.

For example, Figure 4.2 shows the calendar that opens when you click on the drop-down arrow beside the Start Date text box. Click on one of the arrows near the top of the calendar to display an earlier or later month. You also can click on the month or year at the top of the calendar to change it. If you click on the month, a drop-down list of months will appear, in which you can click on the desired month. If you click on the year, spinner buttons appear. Click on one of them to change the year, and then click elsewhere on the calendar. After you display the correct calendar for the month and year, click on a date to choose it and close the calendar.

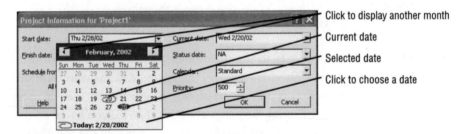

Click to display another month
Current date
Selected date
Click to choose a date

FIGURE 4.2   *Project offers drop-down calendars for quick, accurate date entries.*

The Current Date text box enables you to calibrate your project schedule with the actual calendar. Each time you open the Project Information dialog box, Project uses the system date from your computer as the current date. By default, however, the dates used to schedule all new tasks you add to the project will be the start date or finish date you specified (depending on which of those entries Project is calculating for you).

For example, if you chose Project Finish Date for the Schedule From entry and entered 6/9/04 as the finish date, the tasks you entered will be scheduled with a finish date of 6/9/04, regardless of the Current Date entry. Conversely, if you're scheduling the project from the start date and enter 6/7/04 as the Start Date entry, Project schedules all new tasks you enter with a start date of 6/7/04. You can instead use the Current Date entry to schedule the start date for new tasks you enter into the project plan. See the "Scheduling Tasks from the Current Date" section later in the chapter to learn how this works.

The last two settings that you really need to adjust when you set up your new project are the Calendar and Priority settings. (For information on setting and working with a Status Date, see Chapter 11, "Saving the Baseline and Tracking Work Progress.") The Calendar setting determines the base calendar, or the working hours and days for the project. This calendar determines the number of hours per week available in the project schedule. (You also need to specify the working schedule for each resource, as explained in Chapter 7, "Adding Resources into Your Project Plan.") You can select one of the following choices from the Calendar drop-down list:

◆ **Standard**. This choice, the default, assigns corporate America's standard work week to the project. The project schedule is based on a Monday-Friday work week, with daily working hours of 8 A.M. to noon and 1 P.M. to 5 P.M. Thus, each workday is eight hours and each work week is 40 hours.

◆ **24 Hours**. If you make this selection, the schedule is continuous. Each work day is 24 hours long, and work is scheduled seven days a week.

 CAUTION

Note that if you choose the 24 Hours calendar, it's best to adjust the default Hours Per Day and Hours Per Week settings to sync them up with the calendar. This ensures, for example, that when you enter 1w as the Duration, the Gantt chart will show a Gantt bar spanning a full week and will assume the correct number of hours of work for the task. To change these settings, choose Tools, Options. Click on the Calendar tab, then increase the Hours Per Day value to 24 and the Hours Per Week value to 168, and then click on OK.

◆ **Night Shift**. This option provides a schedule based on a 40-hour night shift week, as scheduled in many companies, from Monday evening through Saturday morning:

Days	Scheduled working hours
Mondays	11 P.M. to 12 A.M.
Tuesday through Friday	12 A.M. to 3 A.M.
	4 A.M. to 8 A.M.
	11 P.M. to 12 A.M.
Saturdays	12 A.M. to 3 A.M.
	4 A.M. to 8 A.M.

CAUTION

The number of working hours per day is important because it affects how Project calculates the schedule for a task. For example, if you estimate that a certain task will take 24 hours under the Standard calendar, Project divides that task into three eight-hour work days. Under a 24-hour calendar, the task gets a single day. Unless your resources truly will be working 24 hours a day, selecting 24 Hours as the Calendar setting can cause Project to underestimate the schedule drastically. The "Creating and Assigning the Project Base Calendar" section later in this chapter explains how you can customize a calendar in Project.

You use the Priority setting in the Project Information dialog box when you share resources between project files, and use Project's automated features for adjusting assignments so particular resources aren't overbooked. (I'll get into those features more in later chapters, because they're intermediate-to-advanced in nature.) Type the Priority setting you want, between 1 and 1000, into the dialog box. Or, you can click on the spinner buttons beside the text box to change the setting. A higher Priority setting means that the project file will have more importance when it shares resources with other project files. If you tell Project to find and fix overbooked resources in the files sharing those resources, Project will tend not to change task scheduling in the files with the highest Priority settings.

After you make your final choices, click on OK to close the Project Information dialog box.

Changing Project Information

After you create project information, it's by no means set in stone. You can reopen the Project Information dialog box at any time to make changes to the options there. In addition, you might want to check the calculated Start Date or Finish Date for the schedule after you specify actual start and finish dates for particular tasks. To view or change schedule information, choose Project, Project Information. When the Project Information dialog box appears, make any changes that you want, and then click on OK to close the dialog box.

Be careful when making changes to the settings in the Project Information dialog box after you add tasks to the schedule. For example, selecting a different calendar can have a drastic effect on your project's timeline. Also, let's say you make a change to the project start date or finish date, and have tasks that you marked as finished or that you set up to start or end on a specific date that falls outside the new overall schedule (see Chapters 11 and 6, respectively). Project will warn you after you click on OK in the Project Information dialog box (see Figure 4.3). You can click on OK and then reschedule individual tasks to fit within the new schedule. If you see a Planning Wizard dialog box instead, you can click the Continue or Cancel option as needed, and then click on OK.

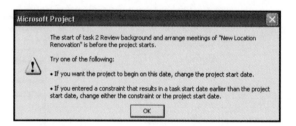

FIGURE 4.3   *Project warns you if you try to schedule tasks outside the new dates you entered for the project file.*

Viewing Project Statistics

Project provides numerous ways to review the information you entered for a project. In fact, it automatically tracks particular project statistics for you, so that you can review the overall status at a glance in the Project Statistics dialog box (see Figure 4.4).

You can open the Project Statistics dialog box using either of two methods:

◆ Display the Tracking toolbar by right-clicking on any onscreen toolbar and then clicking on Tracking. Click on the Project Statistics button at the far left on the Tracking toolbar.

◆ Choose Project, Project Information. Click on the Statistics button in the Project Information dialog box.

Project does not allow you to edit or print the information in the Project Statistics dialog box. When you finish viewing the information, click on the Close button to exit the dialog box.

 TIP

Although Project won't print the Project Statistics dialog box information directly, you can print a report that does include the information—the Project Summary report in the Overview category of reports. After you've built your project file, see Chapter 16, "Creating and Printing a Report," to learn how to print reports.

Compares planned versus actual starting and ending dates   Calculates how much the schedule has varied from the plan

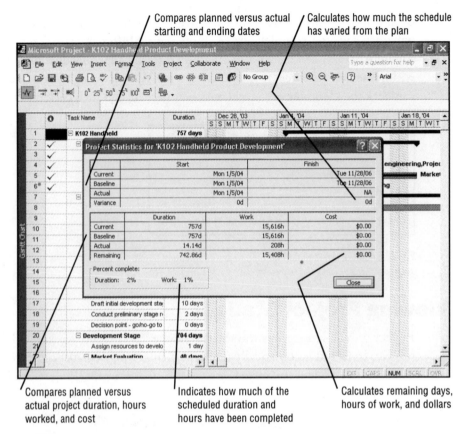

Compares planned versus actual project duration, hours worked, and cost

Indicates how much of the scheduled duration and hours have been completed

Calculates remaining days, hours of work, and dollars

FIGURE 4.4   *Project calculates key statistics about your schedule.*

Creating and Assigning the Project Base Calendar

As you just learned, when you create a new project file you assign a base calendar for the schedule using the Calendar drop-down list in the Project Information dialog box. Thus, unless you select the 24 Hours base calendar, each work day in the schedule is eight hours long and it takes three working days to complete a 24-hour task.

There might be instances, however, when you want to change the working calendar slightly. For example, if the project you are tracking is a plan for some kind of special event that takes place on a Saturday, you need to make that Saturday a working day. If you want certain work days to be 10 hours long, you can make that change. Or you can mark company holidays as non-working days if you need to do so. This section explains how to create and assign the base calendar that's appropriate for your project schedule.

 CAUTION

Make sure that you specify base calendar changes before you begin building your project schedule to ensure that a calendar change doesn't cause unpredictable results. In addition, under the default method of resource-driven scheduling, if you assigned a special calendar to a resource, that calendar overrides your base calendar. Be sure that you base custom resource calendars on the project base calendar you've created. This keeps the resource calendar in sync with the base calendar in terms of working hours, company holidays, and so on.

 NOTE

You can use Project's options to change the default work day and work week schedule, no matter what base calendar you assign to each file. For example, you can specify a different day as the start of the work week, or specify that the default start time for each working day is 7 A.M. Of course, you should edit the project base calendar, or the custom calendar you're using for the project, to match. Otherwise, the default Options settings will override the calendar.

To access these settings (described in Chapter 28, "Customizing Microsoft Project"), click on the Options button in the Change Working Time dialog box (or choose Tools, Options), and then click on the Calendar tab. Just make sure that you change the Calendar options and the base calendar *before* you enter task information. Changing either one after the fact can unexpectedly change task durations and ruin your careful scheduling.

Creating a Custom Calendar

While it's certainly possible, it's not a good idea to make your changes to the base calendars provided by Microsoft Project 2002. Instead, you should keep each of those calendars as a neutral starting form, so you can use it again. Save your changes in a custom calendar, and then select that calendar for the project. (The resources you assign to the project can also use the custom calendar.) To create a custom calendar, follow these steps:

1. In Gantt Chart view, choose Tools, Change Working Time. The Change Working Time dialog box will appear.

2. Click on the New button. The Create New Base Calendar dialog box will appear, as shown in Figure 4.5.

FIGURE 4.5 *Copy an existing calendar or create a custom calendar so that you leave Project's original calendars intact.*

3. Because the Name text is highlighted, you can simply type a new name for the custom calendar.

4. Below the Name text box, click an option button to select whether you want to create a new base calendar or make a copy of an existing base calendar. If you opt to copy a calendar, which is the default setting, select the desired base calendar from the Calendar drop-down list.

5. Click on OK. Project will return to the Change Working Time dialog box, where the custom calendar you created will appear as the For drop-down list selection.

6. Make any schedule changes you want for your custom calendar, as described in the next set of steps.

7. Click on OK to close the Change Working Time dialog box.

 NOTE

When you create a custom calendar as described here, it initially exists only in the current project file. However, you can make it available to all of the project files you create in Microsoft Project by using a tool called the Organizer. To learn more, see the section titled "Using the Organizer to Create Global Calendars, Views, Tables, Macros, and More" in Chapter 13.

Changing Working Hours or Adding a Day Off

Project gives you the flexibility to change the working hours for any day in any base calendar or to specify any day as a nonworking day. To do so, follow these steps:

1. If the Change Working Time dialog box isn't open, choose Tools, Change Working Time. The Change Working Time dialog box appears.

2. Open the For drop-down list to select the calendar you'd like to edit. (As discussed previously, you can edit one of the default calendars that came with Project as well, but that's not the best practice.) The name of the custom calendar will appear as the For selection, as shown in Figure 4.6.

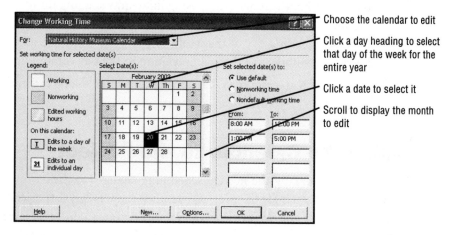

FIGURE 4.6   *Use this dialog box to make changes to a calendar, such as a custom calendar that you've created.*

3. To select a date on the calendar, use the scroll bar beside the calendar to display the month containing the date you want to adjust, and then click on the date. Or, if you want to select a particular day of the week for the entire year, click on the day column heading. For example, click on F to choose every Friday for the entire year. You also can drag across the day headings to select more than one day, or Monday through Friday, for example.

4. To specify the selected date or dates as nonworking, click on Nonworking Time in the Set Selected Date(s) To area of the dialog box. Dates you specify as nonworking should include holidays, vacation days, and other times when no work can be scheduled on the project.

 TIP

The Use Default choice returns selected dates to the default working hours or nonworking time specified in the base calendar.

5. To change the working time (daily working hours) for the selected date or dates, edit or delete the desired From and To entries under Set Selected Date(s) To. (The Nondefault Working Time option button will be selected when you click the next date to edit.)

6. Continue editing the calendar as needed, repeating Steps 3 through 5 to change the schedule for additional dates. As you change the schedule for each date, Project marks the edited date in the calendar with bold and underlined lettering, using light-gray shading for nonworking days and hatched shading for days with edited working hours. (When you edit a day of the week for the whole calendar, an underline appears under the day's abbreviation in the day column head.)

7. Click on OK to close the Change Working Time dialog box and save the changes to your custom calendar.

Assigning the Calendar to the Project

After you finish making the needed scheduling changes to the custom base calendar you've created for the project, you must then assign that calendar to the project file. Use the Project Information dialog box to do so, as reviewed in these steps:

1. Choose Project, Project Information to display the Project Information dialog box.

2. Open the Calendar drop-down list, and choose the newly created calendar (see Figure 4.7).

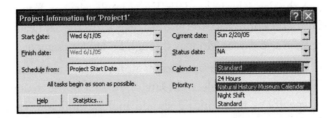

FIGURE 4.7 *Assign the custom base calendar to the project to ensure proper scheduling.*

3. Click OK to close the dialog box and apply the new calendar.

Adding and Deleting Tasks

After you set up the overall parameters for the schedule, you're ready to begin entering the individual jobs that need to be done. This phase of building the project blueprint is most analogous to jotting down a to-do list, with each task roughly equating to a to-do item.

 NOTE

Technically, Project considers your list of tasks the *Work Breakdown Structure*. As you become more comfortable with Project, you can use its outlining features to outline the list of tasks, grouping those tasks into more logical stages of work. See Chapter 5, "Working with Outlining," to learn more about organizing the WBS.

Generally, you add tasks to the schedule in the default Gantt Chart view. In this view, enter basic information about each task in the Task Sheet, located in the left pane.

As shown in Figure 4.8, the Task Sheet resembles a spreadsheet grid. You enter information about each task in a single row in the Task Sheet. You can use the scroll bar at the bottom of the Task Sheet to display more columns. Each column, also called a *field,* holds a particular type of information.

By default, the Task Sheet displays the Entry table. Each table is a particular set of the available fields in Project. The section called "Choosing a Table" in Chapter 13, "Working with the Different Project Views," gives you more information about the available tables and how to display one in the Task Sheet. But the default Task Sheet (with the Entry table displayed) includes the following fields:

◆ **Indicators (i).** This column holds small icons called *indicators* that provide information about the current task. For example, if you add a note to a task, as described later in this section, a note indicator appears in the Indicators field for the task. (You'll learn more about the various indicators later in this section and in later chapters where they apply.) You can't enter information in this column; Project automatically displays and removes applicable indicators as needed.

◆ **Task Name.** This column holds the descriptive label you assign to each task. Use names that are recognizable enough to differentiate

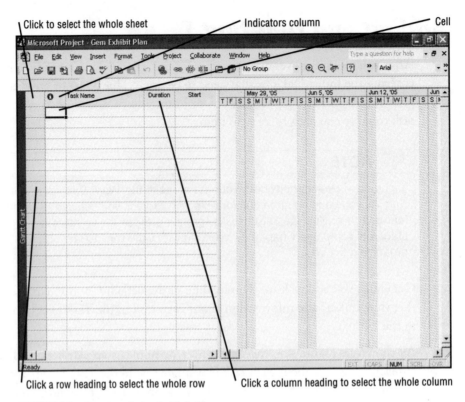

FIGURE 4.8   *Enter tasks in the Task Sheet.*

between individual tasks. The name can include spaces, as well as upper- and lowercase characters. And although the name can include more than 100 characters, as a rule you should stick with names that are as brief and descriptive as possible.

◆ **Duration.** This column holds the time you're allowing between the start date and finish date of each task. If you enter no duration, Project assumes a default duration of one day (*1 day?*, where the question mark indicates that the duration is estimated). Project assumes other durations to be in days unless you specify otherwise (see "Using Differing Durations" later in this chapter).

◆ **Start.** This column holds the date that work is scheduled to begin for a particular task. By default, Project assumes this date is the project start date specified in the Project Information dialog box (or it's calculated from the finish date if you opted to schedule the project from its finish date). To build your project schedule, you use linking to establish task relationships, as described in "Linking and Unlinking Tasks" in Chapter 6, "Building the Schedule and Fine-Tuning Tasks." Based on the links you add, Project will calculate the start date and finish date for each task.

 CAUTION

In general, you don't want to make entries in the Start or Finish column for any task. Let Project calculate these entries for you as you link tasks and otherwise build the schedule. If you instead type in a start date or finish date, Project will add a *constraint* to the task. Constraints limit Project's ability to recalculate the schedule as needed, so they should be used judiciously. See the section called "Setting Task Constraints" in Chapter 6 to learn more about constraints and how to use them.

◆ **Finish.** This column holds the date when work on each task is to be completed. If you specified that Project should schedule tasks from the starting date in the Project Information dialog box, the date in this column is automatically calculated based on the entries in the Duration and Start columns. In other words, you don't have to make an entry in this field when you're building the schedule. Project will calculate it for you. (On the other hand, if Project is scheduling tasks from the ending date, the date in the Start column is calculated.)

◆ **Predecessors.** This column indicates when a task is linked to one or more preceding tasks. Project can fill in this column for you, or you can use this column to establish links.

◆ **Resource Names.** This column enables you to enter one or more resources (team member, outside contractor, and so on) responsible for completing a task. Chapter 7, "Adding Resources into Your Project Plan," explains how to create resources for use in your schedule.

Entering tasks in the Task Sheet works much like making spreadsheet entries. Although later chapters cover some of the entries for a task in more detail, here's an overview of the steps for creating a task:

1. Click on the cell in the Task Name column of the first available row in the Task Sheet. This selects the cell and prepares it for your entry. Alternately, you can press Tab to move from the Indicators column to the Task Name column.

2. Type the name of the task, such as **Determine Exhibit Budget**. As you type, the text will appear in the entry box above the Task Sheet, as shown in Figure 4.9. To complete the entry, press Tab, or click on the Enter button with the green check mark (beside the Entry box above the Task Sheet). Then click on the next cell to the right in the Duration column. Clicking on the Cancel button instead of the Enter button will stop the entry altogether.

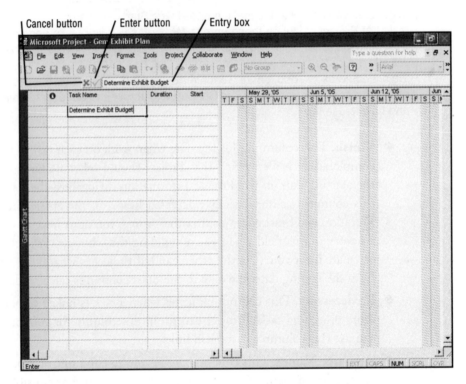

FIGURE 4.9 *You can accept or cancel the entry you make in any cell.*

 TIP

To quickly enter a list of tasks, press Enter after each task name you create. Project will assign each task a one-day duration and the default start date. However, the Duration column displays *1 day?*, with the question mark reminding you to adjust the default duration, if needed, at a later time. You also can adjust the other entries.

3. Type a number, such as **4,** for the new duration entry. Alternately, click one of the spinner buttons that appear at the right side of the Duration cell to increase or decrease the value. The new entry appears in the Entry box as you type. Unless you include more duration information, as described later in the section "Using Differing Durations," Project assumes the duration to be in days. To finish the entry, press Enter. Alternately, you can click on the Enter button. This finishes the basic task creation and creates a bar for the task in the Gantt Chart pane on the right side of the screen (see Figure 4.10).

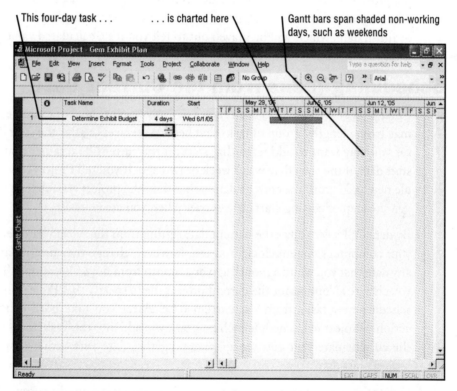

FIGURE 4.10   *Project creates a Gantt Chart bar to represent your task graphically on the schedule.*

 NOTE

When you type in a task's specific start date, Project assigns the *Start No Earlier Than* constraint to the task. This means that Project cannot reschedule the task to an earlier time, even if it's called for by links you create. This is why you should opt not to enter a start date for each task; instead, use linking to schedule tasks (see "Linking and Unlinking Tasks" in Chapter 6).

4. To create the next task, you need to move to the Task Name cell in the next row. Press the Left Arrow key (or the Home key and then the Tab key) to select that cell.

5. Repeat Steps 2 through 4 as many times as needed to enter all the tasks for your project.

As you enter tasks, Project numbers them in the row heading area, starting with task 1. Based on all the tasks you create, the durations you enter for them, and the links you'll add later, Project calculates the total schedule for the project. To check the total schedule, choose Project, Project Information. The Project Information dialog box will then include the calculated start date or finish date, which will be grayed out to tell you it's a calculated value.

Scheduling Tasks from the Current Date

Most project schedules occur in stages or evolve over time. For example, you may have a lengthy group of tasks that begin a few weeks after the start date. Or you may want to add tasks that start on the current date rather than the start date, if the start date was a week or two ago. If you tell Project to schedule new tasks from the current date rather than the project start date, it saves you the step of editing start date entries when you create tasks.

By default, Project takes the current date setting from the system date kept by your computer's system clock. You can, however, change the current date to any date that you want: a month ago or a month from now, for example. Then you change an option for the current project file to specify that Project should schedule new tasks from the current date. After you take both of those actions, Project will schedule each new task you add into the Task Sheet from the current date that you set up, assuming that date isn't earlier than the project start date.

Follow these steps to set up Project to schedule new tasks from the current date:

1. Choose Project, Project Information.

2. Change the Current Date entry to the desired date.

3. Click on OK to close the dialog box.

4. Choose Tools, Options.

5. Click on the Schedule tab.

6. Open the New Tasks drop-down list in the Scheduling Options For area of the dialog box, and choose Start on Current Date. (You would choose Start on Project Start Date to return to the default scheduling method.)

7. Click on OK. At this point, Project will schedule all new tasks you add in the Task Sheets with a start date that's the current date you specified in Steps 1 through 3.

Displaying a Project Summary Task

As you'll learn in Chapter 5, "Working with Outlining," you can organize the tasks in the Task Sheet using outlining tools like those found in Microsoft Word. Ideally, you would think about outlining as you build the task list and outline before you link tasks, but I can't cram every task entry feature into this one chapter; the outlining discussion will have to wait a bit.

But you may want to turn on one special outline feature right from the beginning of the project—the *project summary task*. This appears as task 0 in the list of tasks, so you won't confuse it with other tasks in the list. The project summary task summarizes the overall length of the project; its start date is the start date for the earliest task, and its finish date is the finish date for the latest task. So it provides you with another means of viewing the overall project schedule.

To display the project summary task, choose Tools, Options. The Options dialog box will appear. Click on the View tab, if needed. In the Outline Options For area near the bottom of the dialog box, click on the Show Project Summary Task choice to check it. Click on OK to close the Options dialog box. As Figure 4.11 illustrates, the project summary task appears as task 0 and displays information about the overall project duration, start date, and so on. Also notice that the project summary task uses a special type of bar on the Gantt chart at the right side of the view. You'll learn more about summary Gantt bars like this in Chapter 5.

 TIP

The project summary task initially uses the project file name or the Title entry from the Summary tab of the Properties dialog box (choose File, Properties) as its task name. You can edit the project summary task name to make it more descriptive, if you wish. The next subsection shows you how to edit tasks.

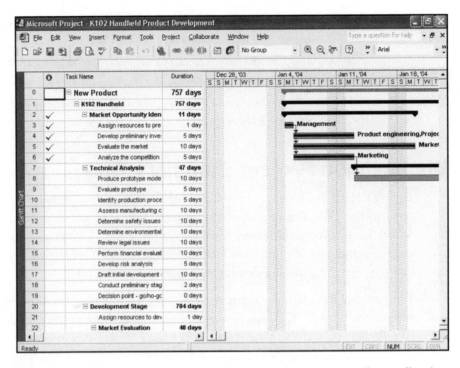

FIGURE 4.11 *The project summary task appears as task 0 and shows you the overall project schedule at a glance.*

Editing a Task

No matter how well formulated a business plan is, you can count on it to change. For example, you might start out using somewhat generic names for your tasks—or even code names. Later, after the project is announced, you might want to replace the temporary names with the real project names. Or, after consulting a particular resource, you might discover that you overestimated the time required to complete a particular task, so you might want to change the duration you specified for that task.

To edit any of the cell entries for a task, click the cell you want to edit to select it. Use one of the following methods to make your changes:

◆ To replace the cell entry completely, start typing. Whatever you type completely replaces the previous entry. Press Enter when you finish making the replacement entry.

- ◆ If spinner buttons or a drop-down arrow appear, use them to change the entry as needed.

- ◆ To make changes to only part of an entry, click to position the insertion point in the entry box, or drag to highlight the text you want to replace. Type your changes. After you place the insertion point in the entry box, you can edit text as you would in most word processors, using the arrow keys, Backspace key, and more. When you finish making your changes, click on the Enter button.

- ◆ To edit the entry directly in the cell, press the F2 key to enter Edit mode (as with other Microsoft products) so you can type in your changes. Press Enter when you finish making the changes.

 NOTE

Project 2002 offers a new feature called Feedback, which is a cousin to the Smart Tags in the other Office XP applications. If you edit certain cells, such as cells in the Start date field, a small Feedback button may appear when you finish the entry. Click on that button to see a menu of options regarding your entry, such as undoing the entry or removing a constraint. Click on the option you want, and then review any additional Help information that appears or change any additional settings as prompted.

Using Differing Durations

As you've seen, when you assign a duration for a particular task, by default Project interprets that duration in terms of days. Each day consists of a full day's worth of working hours, depending on the base calendar you set for the schedule using the Calendar drop-down list in the Project Information dialog box. So, if your project is based on a customized copy of the 24 Hours calendar, each day of duration consists of 24 working hours. On the Standard calendar, each day of duration consists of 8 working hours.

For the Night Shift base calendar, each "day" of duration is eight hours—but each working day spans two calendar days. For example, a task that begins on a Friday and is scheduled to last 1 day starts Friday at 11—P.M., when the working day starts, and spans to 3 A.M. on Saturday. After a one-hour lunch break, the work day and task continue from 4 A.M. to 8 A.M., which is the end of the shift.

NOTE

Keep in mind that when you enter a start date for a task under the Night Shift calendar, Project schedules the task for the work day that begins at 11 P.M. of that start date and runs over to the next day. Thus, if you want work to be completed on a task during the early morning hours of a given day (12 A.M. to 3 A.M. and 4 A.M. to 8 A.M.), specify the preceding date as the start date for the task.

Obviously, not every task requires 8 to 24 hours. Likewise, not every task is completed within the bounds of the work day hours (as much as we wish they would be). For example, if you want to include a key meeting on your schedule, it's likely you only need to block out a few hours for it, not an entire day. On the other hand, if you expect a supplier to work during the weekend to deliver a product, or you know something will be shipped to you on a weekend, you need to schedule the task outside normal working hours.

Project enables you to control the exact amount of time a task will take to finish, based on the abbreviation, or *duration label,* you include with the numeric entry in the Duration column of the Task Sheet. Some duration abbreviations are for *elapsed durations,* where you specify work according to a 24-hour, seven-day-per-week calendar, even though that isn't the base calendar for the project. To specify the new duration, enter the correct abbreviation along with your numeric entry. Table 4.1 lists the basic abbreviations or duration labels.

Project also offers smart duration labels, making it even easier for you to enter durations. Basically, this feature means you can make slight mistakes when you enter duration labels and they'll still work. For example, if you inadvertently include a space and enter **5 h** instead of **5h**, Project can still correctly interpret your entry as five hours.

 TIP

Project 2002 also enables you to indicate when you've estimated a Duration entry. If you include a question mark at the end of your entry, as in **2w?**, Project displays the Duration as **2 wks?**, reminding you that the actual duration might vary dramatically and affect your schedule. You can *filter* the task list so that it shows all tasks with estimated durations, giving you a way to focus on potential trouble spots in the schedule. Chapter 13, "Working with the Different Project Views," explains how to filter the Task and Resource Sheets.

Table 4.1 Duration Labels (Abbreviations)

Time Unit	Abbreviations	Example
Minutes	M Min Mins	30m means 30 working minutes
Hours	H Hr Hrs Hour	30h means 30 working hours
Days	D Dy Day	30d means 30 working days
Weeks	W Wk Week	30w means 30 working weeks
Months	Mo Mons Months	2mo means 2 working months
Elapsed minutes	Em Emin Emins	30em means 30 consecutive elapsed minutes
Elapsed hours	Eh Ehr Ehrs Ehour	30eh means 30 consecutive elapsed hours
Elapsed days	Ed Edy Eday	30ed means 30 consecutive elapsed days
Elapsed weeks	Ew Ewk Eweek	30ew means 30 consecutive elapsed weeks
Elapsed months	Emo Emons Emonths	2emo means 40 consecutive elapsed days*

*Assumes that you've specified each month to be 20 working days using the Calendar tab of the Options dialog box in Project.

When you enter an elapsed time, the Gantt Chart bars at the right reflect how the task falls in terms of real time. For example, Figure 4.12 compares the actual scheduled time for a task entered as three working days (3d) and a task entered as 24 elapsed hours (24eh). When scheduled as standard work days, a 24-hour period covers three days. As elapsed hours, however, a 24-hour period occupies a single day on the Gantt chart.

Scheduled normally (standard 8-hour work days)   Scheduled as elapsed hours

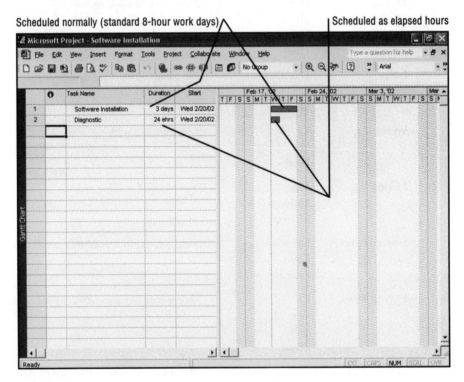

FIGURE 4.12 *Elapsed times are scheduled consecutively.*

Selecting, Inserting, and Deleting Tasks

When you're creating any kind of business plan, you start with the overall framework and refine it as you go along, adding details as you flesh out some ideas and discard others. You might need to adjust the framework for your project by adding new tasks to the Task Sheet as you discover that they're necessary, or by dropping them as you determine that they're extraneous or already included within the scope of other items. Project gives you total flexibility in determining which tasks appear on the Task Sheet.

Use the following steps to add a task to your Task Sheet:

1. Select any cell in the row above where you want to insert a new task. To select the cell, use the scroll bars at the far right and bottom of the screen to display the cell, and then click in it. Alternately, you can use the arrow keys to reach a cell in the appropriate row.

2. Press the Insert key (or choose Insert, New Task) to insert a new blank row.

3. Enter information for the new task, as discussed earlier in this section.

Use the following steps to delete a particular task:

1. Select a cell in the row in the Task Sheet that holds the task. To select additional consecutive tasks after you select a cell in the first one, drag with the mouse (or press Shift and an arrow key) to extend the selection through all the tasks you want to delete. To select additional tasks that are noncontiguous, press and hold down Ctrl while you click in cells in additional rows.

TIP

You can click on the Select All button in the upper-left corner of the Task Sheet to select the entire Task Sheet. To select an entire task row, click on the task number in the row heading at the left side of the Task Sheet.

2. Use one of the following methods to remove selected tasks:

◆ Press the Delete key. A Feedback button will appear to the left of the Task Name cell for the task you're deleting. Click on that button to display a menu of choices for handling the deletion (see Figure 4.13), and then click the desired option in the menu to finish deleting either the task name or the entire task.

◆ Choose Edit, Delete Task.

◆ If you've selected the entire task row by clicking the task number at the left, right-click on the selected task to display a shortcut menu. Then click on Delete Task.

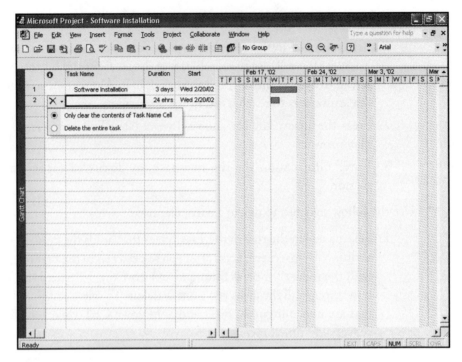

FIGURE 4.13 *When you press the Delete key to delete a task and then click on the resulting Feedback button, Project enables you to specify exactly what to delete.*

CAUTION

If you use the latter two methods, Project doesn't warn you about lost information when you delete a task, even if other tasks are linked to the task you're deleting. If you mistakenly delete a task, *immediately* choose Edit, Undo, press Ctrl+Z, or click on the Undo button on the Standard toolbar—unlike most of the other Office XP applications, Project only enables you to undo your most recent action. Be aware that deleting a task that's linked to other tasks can dramatically affect your schedule, such as causing Project to move tasks that followed the deleted task to a much earlier date.

TIP

Another way to insert a new task row above the currently selected task row is to right-click on a task row number and then click on the Insert Task command in the shortcut menu that appears.

Filling Table Entries

Project 2002 offers a great feature that works just like a popular feature in Excel: the *fill* feature. You can use this feature to copy a cell entry in the Task Sheet (or Resource Sheet) to cells below or to the right. For example, if you have a number of tasks that you expect to last two days apiece, you can fill that duration rather than typing it multiple times. You can fill either contiguous cells or cells scattered throughout the sheet, as described here:

◆ **Contiguous cells.** Make the entry to fill in the desired cell. With the cell selected, point to the black fill handle at the lower-right corner of the cell border until the mouse pointer changes to a pair of crosshairs. Drag the mouse in the direction in which you want to fill (see Figure 4.14), and release the mouse button when you've filled all the cells as needed.

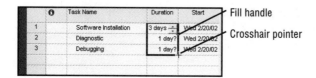

Fill handle

Crosshair pointer

FIGURE 4.14   *Drag the fill handle to copy cell entries on the Task Sheet (or Resource Sheet).*

◆ **Noncontiguous cells.** Again, make the entry to fill in the desired cell and be sure to leave the cell selected. Press and hold the Ctrl key, and click on the other cells that will contain the first entry. Then open the Edit menu, point to the Fill command, and click Down (or press Ctrl+D).

 TIP

You can create a series of entries and drag to fill (repeat) it. For example, you can enter **1d**, **2d**, and **3d** in three consecutive cells in the Duration column. Select all three cells by dragging over them, and *then* drag the fill handle to repeat all three entries.

Moving and Copying Tasks

One of the many features that make Project more efficient than a yellow legal pad for process planning is that you can easily change the order of the tasks on your list. There's no more endless renumbering or trying to figure out which arrow points where to indicate the final order of tasks.

The easiest way to move a task on the Task Sheet is by dragging the task information (see Figure 4.15). Click on the row number for the task you want to move; doing so selects the whole task. Point to one of the selection borders until the mouse pointer turns into an arrow, and then drag the row into its new position. As you drag, a gray insertion bar indicates exactly where the task row will be inserted if you release the mouse button.

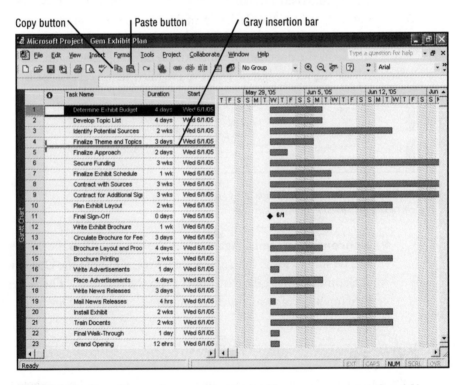

FIGURE 4.15 *Dragging a task to a new location enables you to rearrange tasks quickly.*

 TIP

You can also drag and drop cells to move their contents. Point to the cell border until you see the white arrow mouse pointer, drag, and then release the mouse button to drop the cell into place. However, be sure you're doing what you want to do—if you drop the cell onto a cell that already holds an entry, the dropped cell contents overwrite the old cell contents.

Dragging is convenient when the task you want to move is relatively close to the new location you want for it. It's a bit more difficult to drag a task into place, however, if you have to scroll other tasks to do so. Likewise, when you want to copy a task from one location to another, you need a different process to do the job. For example, if you have two tasks that will run on the same schedule and will be completed by the same resource, it's much easier to copy the original task and then edit the task name on the copy. In such cases, use the following steps to move or copy the task:

1. To select a whole row for the task you want to move or copy, click on the row number.

2. If you want to move the task, choose Edit, Cut Task. Alternately, you can press Ctrl+X, click on the Cut button on the Standard toolbar (if you haven't used this button previously, you may need to click on the Toolbar Options button at the right end of the Standard toolbar to find it), or right-click on the selection to display a shortcut menu. Then select Cut Task.

   If you want to copy the task, choose Edit, Copy Task. Alternately, you can press Ctrl+C, click on the Copy button on the Standard toolbar, or right-click on the selection to display a shortcut menu and then select Copy Task.

3. Click in any cell in the row above where you want to insert the task you cut or copied.

4. Choose Edit, Paste. Alternately, you can press Ctrl+V and click on the Paste button on the Standard toolbar, or right-click to display a shortcut menu and then select Paste. Project will paste the task as a new row.

Cut-and-paste (or copy-and-paste) operations can also be used to move or copy information in individual cells. When you select a cell, the Edit and shortcut menu commands change to Cut Cell and Copy Cell. After copying or cutting the selected cell, as just described for rows, select a destination cell and then paste the cut or copied information. When you paste a cut or copied cell, the pasted information replaces any existing information in the selected destination cell. (It's not inserted above the cell you selected.)

 TIP

You can select more than one row or cell to cut or copy by clicking and dragging over multiple row numbers or multiple cells.

Clearing Task Information

Cutting or deleting a task removes the task from the Task Sheet altogether. The remaining rows close the space vacated by the cut task. However, sometimes you may want to remove the information from a task while keeping the row that was occupied by that task in place. For example, you might want to replace the old task with information about a new task. If you simply change the entries for the old task, however, you might neglect to edit one, resulting in a schedule error.

An alternative to cutting information in a task or cell is to *clear* the information. Clearing removes cell contents but leaves all cells in place. Unlike cut information, cleared information can't be pasted, so you should clear material only when you're sure it's no longer needed.

Use these steps to clear information from your Task Sheet:

1. Select the task row or cell you want to clear.
2. Choose Edit, Clear. A submenu will appear, offering you a choice of the kind of information to clear.
3. Choose the kind of information to clear by clicking on the appropriate submenu item, as follows:

   ◆ **All.** This removes the task contents, formatting, and any notes you added for the task. (The next section explains how to add a note.)

   ◆ **Formats.** This returns the selected task or cell contents to the default formatting, removing any formatting you added (such as a new font or color).

   ◆ **Contents.** This is equivalent to pressing Ctrl+Delete. It removes the contents of the selected task or cell.

   ◆ **Notes.** This clears any notes you added for the task (as described in the next section).

   ◆ **Hyperlinks.** This removes any hyperlinks you created in a task to enable the user to jump to a Web page on the Internet or a company intranet. Chapter 23, "Using Project with the Web," explains how to create hyperlinks.

   ◆ **Entire Task.** This clears the contents of the entire task when you haven't selected the entire task row.

Adding a Task Note

A *task note* enables you to capture information that doesn't need to appear within the Task Sheet, but does need to be recorded with the schedule (and printed, in some instances). For example, you might create notes in situations like these:

◆ If you have a task that is a reminder for a meeting, you can create a note listing materials you need to bring to the meeting.

◆ If a task relates to research-gathering that will be completed by a resource other than yourself, you can include a note mentioning information sources that the designated researcher should check.

◆ If a task deals with proofreading or fact-checking, you can use a note to list the details that need to be reviewed.

Adding a note to a task is a straightforward process. Select the task row—or a cell in the task—for which you want to create a note. Right-click on the selected area, or open the Project menu. Choose Task Notes. Alternately, click on the Task Notes button on the Standard toolbar. (If you haven't used this button previously, you may have to click the Toolbar Options button at the right end of the Standard toolbar to find it.) The Task Information dialog box appears, with the Notes tab selected. Click on the Notes text entry area, if necessary, and then type your note (see Figure 4.16).

Press Enter to start each new line in the note. You can add special formatting to notes by using the buttons at the top of the Notes text area. The first button enables you to change the font for any text you select by dragging over it in the note. It opens the Font dialog box, which is covered in Chapter 17, "Other Formatting." The next three buttons align the current note line (which holds the blinking insertion point) left, center, and right, respectively. The fourth button adds or removes a bullet at the beginning of the current line of the note. The last button enables you to insert an embedded object into the note, such as information from Excel or a bitmap image. Chapter 21, "Using Project with Other Applications," provides more information on working with embedded objects.

When you finish typing the note, click on OK to close the Task Information dialog box. Project will insert an icon in the Indicators column for the task to remind you that you added a note for that task.

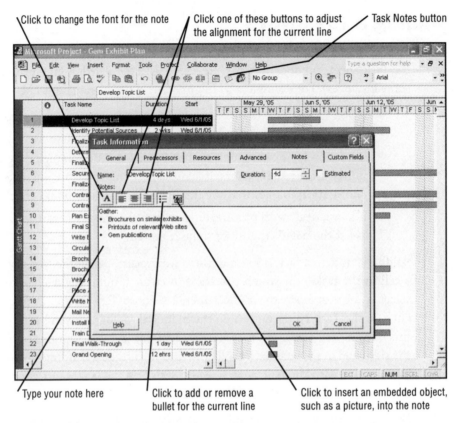

Click to change the font for the note | Click one of these buttons to adjust the alignment for the current line | Task Notes button

Type your note here | Click to add or remove a bullet for the current line | Click to insert an embedded object, such as a picture, into the note

FIGURE 4.16   *Notes enable you to capture more detailed information about a task.*

Understanding Indicators

As you saw earlier in this chapter, an Indicators column appears at the far-left side of the Task Sheet in the default Gantt Chart view. The Indicators column remains blank until you begin entering information in other columns and changing the options for tasks. Then, depending on the settings you choose, indicator icons may appear in the Indicator column. Each indicator icon reminds you of a particular piece of information about a task. For example, the indicator icon in Figure 4.17 shows that a note has been added to task 1 in the Task Sheet.

Other indicator icons tell you whether a task has been completed, whether it has been completed by a date you specified, whether you need to e-mail task information to the resource who will be completing the work, and so on.

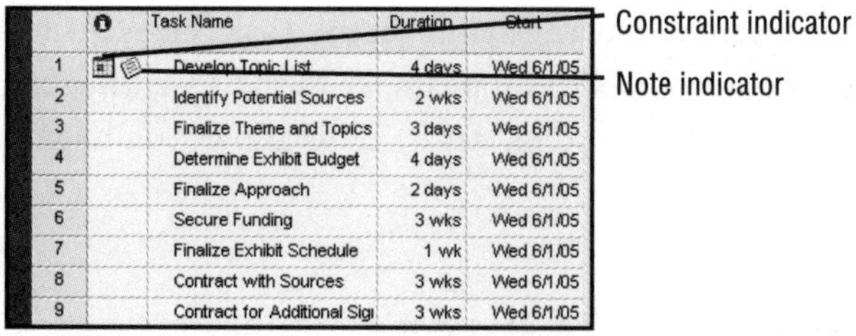

FIGURE 4.17 *Indicator icons appear in the Indicators column to tell you that you specified particular task options or added information, such as a note, to a task.*

When you begin entering resource information, as described in Chapter 7, you'll see that indicators can also give you more information about a particular resource's status. I'll identify particular indicators throughout the book as I describe settings that cause an indicator to appear. If you can't recall what a particular indicator beside a task means, move the mouse pointer over the indicator cell to display pop-up messages like the ones shown in Figure 4.18.

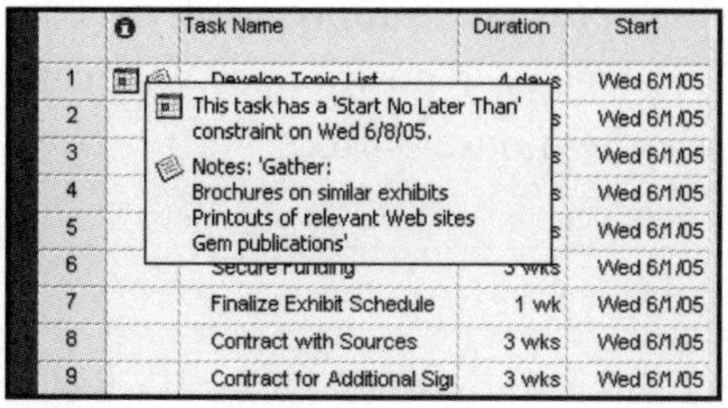

FIGURE 4.18 *Point to the indicators for a task or resource to see a pop-up description of what each indicator represents.*

Adjusting the Task Sheet

By default, the Task Sheet occupies roughly the left third of the screen in Gantt Chart view, and it offers six columns with preset names and sizes. The narrow screen area allocated for the Task Sheet means that you might spend more time than you'd prefer scrolling or tabbing back and forth to display particular cells or columns (fields). Or, if you have a column in which the entries become rather lengthy, the column might be too narrow to display the column contents. Finally, the columns provided by default might not capture all the information you want to have available on the Task Sheet. As you'll see next, Project enables you to control the appearance of the Task Sheet (and the Resource Sheet, which you'll see in Chapter 7). This allows you to customize it for your project creation needs.

Sizing the Sheet and Columns

One of the first changes you might want to make is to display more of the Task Sheet to make editing easier. This change isn't permanent. While you're entering information about various tasks in your schedule, for example, you can fill most of the Project application window with the Task Sheet. After you enter the task information, you can return the Task Sheet to its previous size so that the Gantt Chart pane of the window becomes visible again.

You can resize the screen area occupied by the Task Sheet by dragging. A split bar separates the Task Sheet pane from the Gantt Chart pane on the right. Move the mouse pointer onto that split bar, and the pointer changes to a split pointer with a double-vertical line and left and right arrows. Press and hold the mouse button, and then drag the split bar to move it. A dark line (see Figure 4.19) indicates where the bar will be repositioned. When this line reaches the location you want, release the mouse button.

 TIP

Project prints any view—including the Gantt Chart view—as it appears onscreen. So, if you want the printout to include more columns, display them onscreen. Or, if you want to show the full length of the entries in a column, resize the column.

Just as you can drag to resize the whole Task Sheet area, you can drag to resize the width of any column or the height of any row. To change a column width, point to the right border of the column heading, beside the column name. To change a row height, point to the bottom border of the row, below the row number. The mouse pointer changes to a resizing pointer with a line and a double-headed arrow. Press and hold the mouse button, and then drag the border to change the size of the column or row. A dotted line indicates what the new size of the column or row will be. When the column or row reaches the new width or height you want, release the mouse button.

Dark line indicates the new pane size

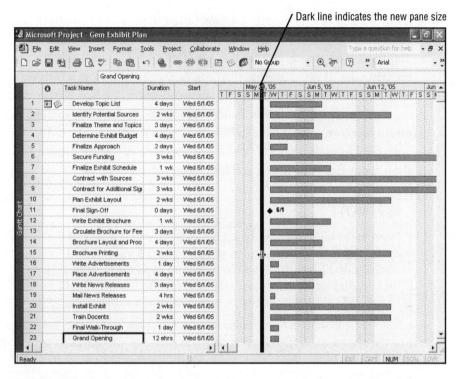

FIGURE 4.19 *With a simple dragging operation, you can view more of the Task Sheet for easier task entry.*

 TIP

To resize a column to the optimum width for all its entries, double-click on the right border of the column heading.

Adding Columns (Fields)

When there are many pieces of data to capture about a particular process, six or seven measly columns cannot do the job effectively. Furthermore, you might want to display some information that Project normally calculates behind the scenes for you. For example, if a given task is being completed by a particular resource at a certain hourly rate, and you've entered the actual hours the resource spent to complete the task, you might want to see the resulting cost onscreen. You might even want the Task Sheet to display certain information that you can print and distribute to others.

Table 4.2 lists several predefined *fields* (also called *columns*), many of which are self-calculating, that you can add to the Task Sheet. Project offers more than 100 fields that you can use for tasks, so Table 4.2 describes only the most significant ones. If you choose to display a *table* other than the default entry table in the Task Sheet, you'll see a whole new collection of fields. Rather than adding a column into the default Entry table on the Task Sheet, you may want to create your own custom table to leave the original intact. Chapter 13, "Working with the Different Project Views," explains how to display different tables in the Task or Resource Sheet, and how to create custom tables.

 NOTE

Project's online help system contains a listing of all the Task Sheet field types, including a detailed description of each one. To view the list, choose Help, Contents and Index. Click on the Index tab, type **field** in the Type Keywords text box, and then click on the Search button. Scroll down the Choose a Topic list box until you see Task Fields, and then click it in the list.

For more information on a particular field, click on it in the list in the right pane of the Microsoft Project Help window. Notice that Project considers certain fields to be *assignment* fields. (Chapter 8, "Assigning Resources to Specific Tasks," explains what assignments are.) You can display assignment fields in the Task Sheet as well.

 NOTE

To make table changes available to all your project files you must create and display a custom table, add and delete fields as needed, and then use the Organizer to make the custom table global. Unless you've displayed a custom table, the following changes will apply to the currently displayed table in the current project file only.

The process for adding a new column resembles adding a new task to the schedule. Here are the steps:

1. Click in any cell in the column next to the location where you want to insert the new column. The inserted column will appear to the left of the column where you selected a cell.

2. Choose Insert, Column. (As an alternative to Steps 1 and 2, you can click on the column heading to select the entire column, right-click

on it, and then click on Insert Column.) The Column Definition dialog box appears (see Figure 4.20).

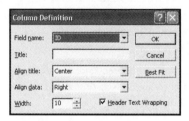

FIGURE 4.20   *This dialog box enables you to create or edit the columns in the Task Sheet.*

3. Click on the down arrow to display the Field Name drop-down list. Use the scroll bar to display the name of the field you want to add, and then click on the name to select it.

4. (Optional) If you want the inserted column to be identified with a name other than the built-in field name (such as "Actual $" rather than "Actual Cost"), click to place the insertion point in the Title text box, and then type the name you want.

5. (Optional) If you want the title for the new column to be left- or right-aligned, rather than centered, click to open the Align Title drop-down list, and then select an alignment choice from the list that appears.

6. (Optional) If you want the entries that Project displays or that you make in the new column to be left-aligned or centered automatically, rather than right-aligned, click on the down arrow to display the Align Data drop-down list, and then select the alignment you want.

7. (Optional) If you know that the contents in the new column will require many characters (for example, a long hyperlink address) or very few characters (for example, a one- or two-character ID number), double-click on the value shown in the Width text box, and then type the new number of characters you want the column to display. Alternately, you can click on the spinner buttons at the right side of the Width text box and use the mouse to increase or decrease the value.

8. Click on OK to finish creating the column. The column you specified appears in the Task Sheet, as shown in the example in Figure 4.21.

Table 4.2 Other Fields You Can Display in the Task Sheet

Field Name	Description
Actual Cost	Calculates the actual cost for the hours or material units required to complete a task, or lets you enter an actual cost if the task was completed for a fee.
Actual Duration	Calculates the actual time that has elapsed since the scheduled start of the task, based on your entry in the Remaining Duration or Percent Complete field (if displayed).
Actual Finish	Lets you enter the actual task completion date, if it differs from the scheduled date.
Actual Overtime Cost and Actual Overtime Work	Calculates the actual overtime expenses or actual overtime work incurred to date for all resources assigned to the task.
Actual Start	Lets you enter the actual task starting date, if it differs from the scheduled date.
Actual Work	Calculates or lets you enter the work completed for the task.
Baseline (various fields)	Displays the total planned cost, duration, finish, start, and work for the task.
BCWP	Baseline Cost of Work Performed: Displays the projected actual cost, calculated from the budgeted baseline cost and the percentage of work actually completed.
BCWS	Budgeted Cost of Work Scheduled: Lets you compare the cost of what has actually been accomplished (BCWP) versus the cost of what you plan to accomplish by a particular date.
Contact	Enables you to enter a contact name for the resource assigned to complete the task, if that contact person's name is different from the resource's name. For example, you may list a consulting company as the overall resource but your contact person in the contact column.
Cost Variance	Calculates the difference between the baseline cost and scheduled work cost for tasks in progress, and between the baseline and actual cost for finished tasks. Negative values indicate that a cost came in under budget.
Critical	Indicates whether a task is critical or noncritical, via calculations based on the Total Slack field entry and some other dialog box entries for the task.
Duration Variance	Displays the difference between the baseline duration for the task and the currently calculated duration.

Table 4.2 (continued)

Field Name	Description
Finish Variance	Calculates the difference between the planned (baseline) finishing date for the task and the currently calculated finishing date. Negative values indicate that the task is now scheduled to finish earlier than initially planned.
Hyperlink	Contains a hyperlink you can click to open a document on your hard disk, a network, or the World Wide Web. For example, you can edit the entry in this column so that it gives only the file name rather than the full path to the file.
Hyperlink Address	Contains the actual address for a hyperlink, no matter what name you assign in the hyperlink column. Clicking the address in this column opens the hyperlinked document.
ID	Identifies a task's current position in the list of tasks, even if two tasks have the same name. (The ID is also referred to as the task number.)
Overtime Cost and Overtime Work	Adds the already incurred and remaining overtime costs or work for all resources assigned to the task.
Percent (%) Complete	Calculates or lets you enter the percentage of a task's duration that has passed.
Percent (%) Work Complete	Calculates or lets you enter the percentage of a task's work that has been completed.
Remaining (various fields)	Calculates or lets you enter the cost, duration, or work still available to complete a task.
Resource (various fields)	Displays the group, initials, or names for the resources assigned to the task.
Start Variance	Calculates the difference between the original (baseline) starting date and the actual starting date for the task.
Successors	Lists later tasks that depend on (are linked to) the current task.
Total Slack	Indicates, when the value is positive, that there is time in the schedule to delay the task.
Update Needed	Specifies when schedule changes need to be communicated to a resource via the Collaborate, Publish, New and Changed Assignments command.
Work	Calculates the total work that all resources are scheduled to dedicate to the task.
Work Variance	Calculates the difference between the baseline amount of work scheduled for the task and the work currently scheduled.

	❶	Task Name	% Complete	Duration	Start
1		Develop Topic List	0%	4 days	Wed 6/1/05
2		Identify Potential Sources	0%	2 wks	Wed 6/1/05
3		Finalize Theme and Topics	0%	3 days	Wed 6/1/05
4		Determine Exhibit Budget	0%	4 days	Wed 6/1/05
5		Finalize Approach	0%	2 days	Wed 6/1/05
6		Secure Funding	0%	3 wks	Wed 6/1/05
7		Finalize Exhibit Schedule	0%	1 wk	Wed 6/1/05
8		Contract with Sources	0%	3 wks	Wed 6/1/05
9		Contract for Additional Sig	0%	3 wks	Wed 6/1/05

FIGURE 4.21 *I've inserted a new column, % Complete, before the Duration column.*

> ● **CAUTION**
>
> You need to be somewhat careful about which fields you add and how to use them. If you add a *calculated* field (one for which Project calculates the entry) into the Task Sheet, such as BCWP, you don't want to make your own entries into that new field—or Project won't let you, depending on the field. You also don't want to add the Baseline fields and enter your own information into them, because Project copies information into those fields when you save your baseline plan.
>
> The safest fields to add and use for your own purposes are the Text fields (Text1 through Text30), which Project offers for custom uses. Chapter 13, "Working with the Different Project Views," also explains how to create a variety of custom fields.

Hiding, Deleting, and Editing Columns

In some instances, you might realize that you don't want to see a Task Sheet column, no longer need it, or need to make changes to it so that it's more useful and relevant to everyone who's using the project schedule you created.

Hiding a column removes it from the currently displayed table but leaves its information intact. Therefore, you may want to hide a column after you have entered all the information for it, or when you'd prefer to focus on other columns. For example, you may decide that you really don't need to see the Indicators column when you're entering basic task information, so you can hide that column.

To hide a column, first you click on the column heading to select the entire column. Right-click on the selected column or choose Edit, Hide Column. Alternately, you can press the Delete key. To redisplay the column and its contents, use the Insert, Column command (as just described) to add the column to the Task Sheet.

NOTE

If you hid the Task Name column, you can redisplay it by inserting the Name column into the Task Sheet. When you do so, enter **Task Name** in the Title text box of the Column Definition dialog box, and choose Left as the Align Data choice. However, I suggest that you make a copy of the default Entry table for the Task Sheet and then make changes to it, so you can always redisplay the default Entry table. Refer to Chapter 13, "Working with the Different Project Views," for more on displaying and customizing tables.

To edit an existing column, you need to display the Column Definition dialog box containing information about that particular column. Double-click on the column name in the column heading. Make the changes you want in the Column Definition dialog box, and then click on OK to accept them. When you edit a column (as opposed to when you create it), you might find it useful to click on the Best Fit button in the Column Definition dialog box. Clicking this button resizes the column so that it's wide enough to fully display every entry already made in that column.

Dealing with the Planning Wizard

As you start entering information about tasks, you might discover that a Planning Wizard dialog box appears from time to time. This wizard points out situations where you might need to make a decision about the information you're entering. It prompts you with specific, easy choices (see Figure 4.22). For example, the

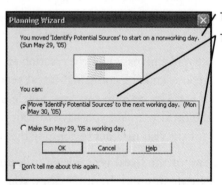

This is what you just did

These are the choices you can make

FIGURE 4.22 *The Planning Wizard helps you make decisions about the task information you are entering.*

Planning Wizard might ask whether you want to establish a link between tasks, or it might point out that you're about to create an error in your schedule.

To continue working after the Planning Wizard dialog box appears, select the appropriate option button to respond to the Planning Wizard's question. If the Planning Wizard has asked you this particular question previously and you no longer want to be reminded of the issue, select the Don't Tell Me About This Again check box. Click on OK to finish working in the Planning Wizard dialog box.

 TIP

Clicking Cancel closes the Planning Wizard dialog box and also cancels the task entry or edit you were making.

You can turn off all the Planning wizard suggestions. Chapter 28, "Customizing Microsoft Project," explains how to use the Options dialog box to control certain Project features, including the Project wizard.

Creating Milestones

Milestones were once stone markers used to identify one's relative position along a road—the particular distance to a certain city. Today, milestones enable you to gauge your progress through life, through a particular phase of your career, or through a particular process. In your Project files, milestones enable you to mark a particular point of progress or a particular event during the course of a project. They indicate events that must occur on time in order for the project to finish on time. However, those events have no work associated with them.

For example, suppose that the project you're managing is the creation and production of your company's annual report, and the company's fiscal year ends June 30. Producing the annual report is tricky, because you want to release it as soon as possible after the close of the fiscal year. Yet you have to wait for the final, audited financial information for the year in order to compile the report.

In this case, you might mark the end of the fiscal year with a milestone to help you keep that key, approaching date in mind. In other cases, you might want to mark particular dates, such as the date when you're 25 percent or 50 percent through your total allotted schedule. You also can use milestones to mark significant events that must occur but require no work, such as the receipt of a signed contract.

Creating a milestone isn't very different from creating a task. You insert a task into the Task Sheet, if needed, and then enter information about the task. To specify the task as a milestone, give it a duration of 0 days by entering **0** in the Duration column. Project then identifies the new task as a milestone and displays a milestone marker for it in your schedule's Gantt chart (see Figure 4.23).

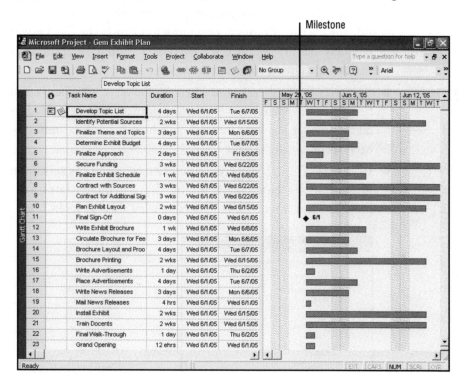

FIGURE 4.23 *This Gantt Chart view shows a sample milestone.*

Looking at Project Properties

As with the files you create in other Microsoft applications, Project tracks certain properties, or details, to search for files more efficiently, to enable you to identify the key people involved with a project, and to help you understand who is working with a particular file and how often. Some of the properties tracked for your Project files include statistics about the task scheduling and tracking information you enter in the file.

You can review the properties for a particular file by opening the Properties dialog box. Choose File, Properties. This dialog box offers five tabs, some that calculate and display information and others that enable you to add details about the file:

◆ **General.** This tab displays the file type, creation date, date the file was last modified, DOS file name, and more.

◆ **Summary.** This tab is selected by default. It enables you to enter or edit information about your name, your company, your manager, a title for the file or project, a category to identify the file, keywords to uniquely identify the file if you're trying to find it using the Windows search capabilities, and more.

◆ **Statistics.** This tab indicates when the file was created and last modified, and also when the file was last printed, who last saved it, how many times it has been revised, and how many total minutes have been spent editing the file.

◆ **Contents.** This tab displays some key facts about the scheduling information you entered, including the scheduled dates and total projected cost. Figure 4.24 illustrates what this tab looks like.

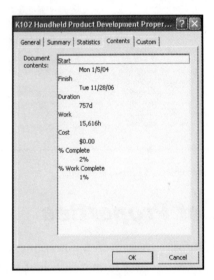

FIGURE 4.24 *You can view schedule information via the Properties dialog box.*

◆ **Custom.** This tab enables you to create a custom property to facilitate finding the file in Windows. For example, you can create a custom property to assign a unique number—such as the job number for the project of the file. If you create a custom job number field for all your Project files, you can search for any project file by its job number. To create a custom property, specify values for the Name, Type, and Value text boxes, and then click on the Add button.

Chapter 5

Working with Outlining

In This Chapter

◆ Promoting and demoting tasks

◆ Controlling the outline display

◆ Using summary tasks

◆ Using WBS Codes

At one time, many artists and writers employed a method called *stream of consciousness*. Basically, this meant that the creator would sit down and just let the brushstrokes or words come out, leading where they would. The artist or writer made no effort to impose any type of structure on the output.

However, most people tend to prefer a more orderly approach to work—especially in the business world, where the most effective professionals excel at spelling out expectations and providing clear directions for what others need to do. To help you become more orderly as you build a structure for your work, Project provides outlining capabilities. This chapter helps you learn how to create a work breakdown structure in online format.

What Outlining Does for You

Different project leaders have different styles. Some fancy themselves "big-picture-thinkers" and like to sketch out overall plans first; such a leader might even hand a project off to someone else charged with "figuring out the details." Other leaders treat project tasks as a puzzle, first laying out all the pieces, and then grouping together pieces for the edges, the sky, the grass, and so on before proceeding to put the puzzle together.

No matter which approach you prefer, you'll find that Project's outlining features can accommodate you as you build the *work breakdown structure*. This is the list of tasks, organized into groups related by activity, and numbered with traditional outline numbering—1, 1.1, 1.2, 2, 2.1, 2.2, 2.3, and so on.

If you like to build a schedule using a *top-down approach*, where you identify and arrange major, general tasks before filling in the details, you can enter those major categories and then break them down into more specific action items. Conversely, if you like to simply do a brain-dump and list every possible task (the *bottom-up approach*), later you can group your list into logical areas.

When you use outlining in Project, the major tasks within your Task Sheet are called *summary tasks* because they summarize a series of actions in a given time frame. The tasks required to complete a summary task are called *subtasks* (or *detail tasks*). Project allows for thousands of outline levels (up to 65,000 if your system has enough resources to handle it), so keep in mind that you can have summary tasks within summary tasks.

Project uses special formatting to help you identify summary tasks and subtasks onscreen, as shown in Figure 5.1. Summary tasks usually appear in bold text in the Task Sheet and use a special summary Gantt bar. By default, an outlining symbol appears beside each summary task. (You can turn these symbols off as described later in this chapter, under "Hiding and Showing Outlining

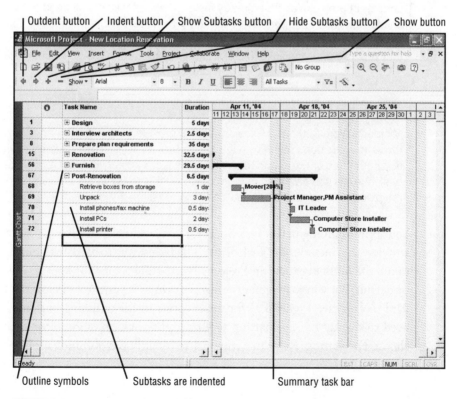

FIGURE 5.1   *The Formatting toolbar offers several buttons that make outlining more convenient.*

Symbols.") Subtasks are indented in the Task Name column of the Task Sheet. If a task is a summary task of a summary task, it's indented twice.

Summarizing work in this way not only gives you an idea of where major completion points in your project will occur, but it can also help you make resource assignment decisions. For example, you may examine a particular summary task and its subtasks, and then decide to farm the whole mess out to a contractor who can provide several people to complete and add continuity to the summary task. Or you may see that the start and finish dates for two summary tasks are about the same and realize that those tasks are creating a "crunch period" in your schedule during which you'll need extra resources—either additions to your team or authorized overtime hours for the existing team.

 NOTE

Keep in mind that if you use the outlining techniques you'll learn about in this chapter in project files that already include linked tasks, you'll need to double-check task links after you insert summary tasks and subtasks. Ideally, you will apply outlining before you link tasks as you build your project plan. This ensures that you'll be applying links to tasks at the appropriate level—the subtask level.

 CAUTION

Microsoft Word 2002 and Excel 2002 also provide outlining features. However, those features don't mesh with the one in Project. If you copy outlined information from Word or Excel and paste it into Project, Project does not recognize the outline levels you assigned in Word or Excel. You still save the time and effort of retyping the information, but you'll have to reassign the outline levels.

You apply outlining in the Task Sheet for your schedule, and you can start from any view that includes the Task Sheet. The fastest way to work with outlining is to use the outlining tools on Project's Formatting toolbar. It appears onscreen by default, but you may prefer to drag it down to its own row, below the Standard toolbar (see Figure 5.1) for easier access to the outlining buttons. If you need to display the Formatting toolbar, right-click on any toolbar and then choose Formatting. Refer to Figure 5.1 to identify the outlining tools.

Promoting and Demoting Tasks in the Outline

Whether you're outlining a list of existing tasks or organizing a list of tasks that you're building, the process is generally the same. You select the Task Name cell (or the entire row) of the task for which you want to define an outline level, and then you *outdent* (promote) it to a higher level or *indent* (demote) it to a lower level.

Since all tasks start on the top outline level by default, it's easiest to begin outlining by demoting subtasks. Demoting a task automatically converts the task above it to a summary task. To demote a selected task by one level (to the next lower level), you can use one of the following techniques:

◆ Click on the Indent button on the Formatting toolbar.

◆ Choose Project, Outline, Indent.

◆ Select the entire task by clicking on its row heading (row number). Then right-click on the row and choose Indent from the shortcut menu that appears.

◆ Point to the first letter of the task name until you see the double-arrow pointer, press and hold the mouse button and drag to the right to move the task down a level. A vertical gray line appears to indicate the outline level to which the task is being demoted.

The demoted task is automatically formatted as a subtask, and the task above it is formatted as a summary task. Project prevents you from demoting a task if doing so would skip a level in the outline, and would result in some task ending up two outline levels below the task above it.

 TIP

You can select multiple tasks that are on the same outline level and demote them simultaneously. To do so, drag across the row numbers to select the group of tasks, and then click on the Indent button on the Formatting toolbar. Figure 5.2 shows an example of multiple tasks that have been selected and demoted.

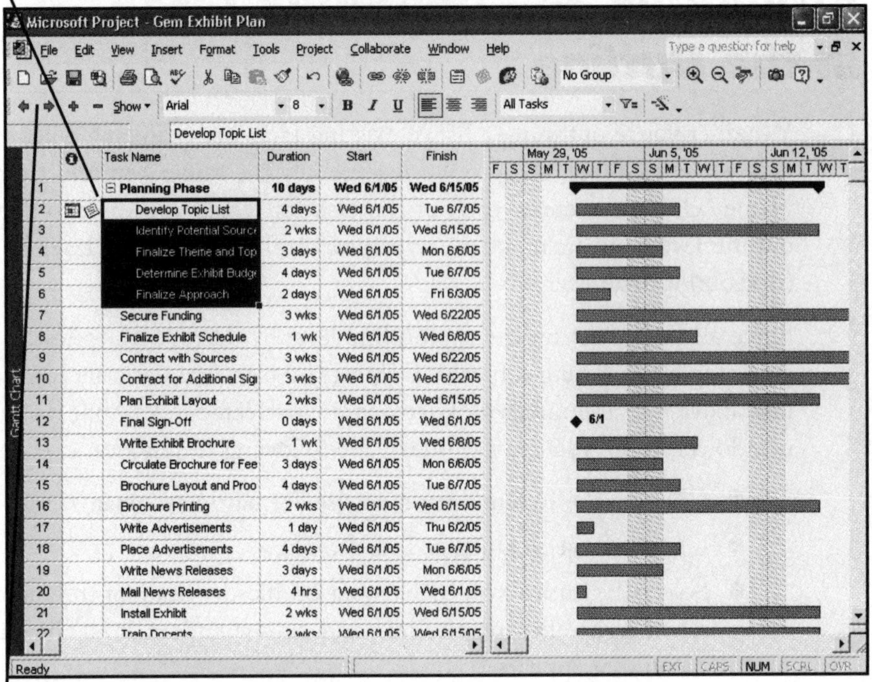

Drag over tasks to select them...

...and then click on the Indent button to make them subtasks.

FIGURE 5.2 *Usually, selecting multiple tasks and indenting them is the speediest way of creating the project outline.*

To promote a selected task, use one of the following methods:

◆ Click on the Outdent button on the Formatting toolbar.

◆ Choose Project, Outline, Outdent.

◆ If the task is a subtask and is not on the top level of the outline, select the entire task by clicking on its row heading (row number). Then right-click on the row and choose Outdent from the shortcut menu that appears.

◆ If the task is not on the top outline level, point to the first letter of the task name until you see the double-arrow pointer. Press and hold the mouse button, and drag to the left to move the task up a level. A vertical gray line appears to indicate the outline level to which the task is being promoted.

If a task is already at the top level of the outline, meaning that it does not appear indented in the Task Name column (keep in mind that there is some space to the left of task names by default), Project will not let you promote it. If the Planning wizard is active when you attempt to promote such a task, the Planning Wizard dialog box appears to inform you that the task can't be promoted (see Figure 5.3). Simply click on OK to close the dialog box. Project returns you to your Task Sheet without making any changes. When you promote a task, the tasks listed below it that were previously on the same level become subtasks of the promoted task, and the promoted task is reformatted accordingly.

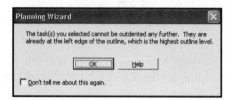

FIGURE 5.3 *If you try to promote a task that is already at the top level, the Planning Wizard tells you that Project can't make the change.*

 NOTE

If you promote or demote a summary task, Project promotes or demotes its subtasks as well.

Inserting a Summary Task

If you're using a bottom-up approach to building your schedule, you may have a list of tasks into which you want to insert summary tasks. It would be nice if Project simply allowed you to simultaneously demote all the tasks you typed in and then insert higher-level tasks, but it doesn't work that way. Instead, follow this process:

1. Insert a blank row above the tasks you want to summarize. To do so, click on the top task in the group you want to summarize, and then press the Insert key.

2. Enter the task name for the new task. You don't have to specify any other task details, even duration. Project makes those entries for you when you define the subtasks for the summary task.

3. If the task above the newly inserted task is a summary task, Project typically treats the new task as a subtask too, and indents the task automatically. To move it back up an outline level, select the new task, and then use the technique of your choice to promote it, such as clicking on the Outdent button on the Formatting toolbar.

4. Drag over the row headings for the tasks you want to convert to summary tasks (to select those rows). Then click on the Indent button on the Formatting toolbar. Alternately, you can choose Project, Outline, Indent, or right-click on the selected tasks and then click on Indent on the shortcut menu (see Figure 5.4). Figure 5.5 shows how the tasks in Figure 5.4 look when the indent operation is completed. A summary task bar has been added in the Gantt chart for the newly designated summary task in row 7.

Drag over the row headings to select tasks to demote or promote simultaneously

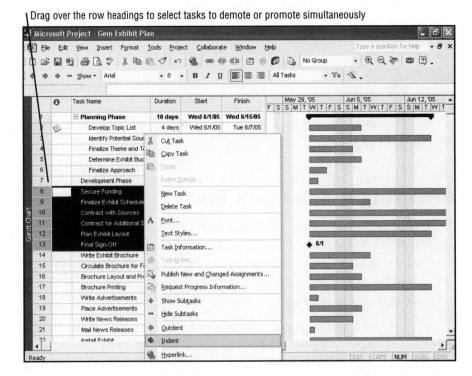

FIGURE 5.4 *You can use the shortcut menu to demote (or promote) selected task rows.*

New summary task bar

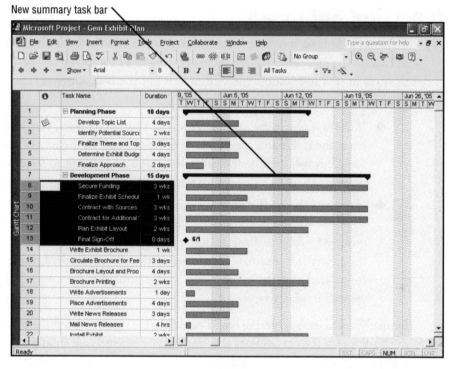

FIGURE 5.5   *The newly inserted row is designated as a summary task.*

 NOTE

If you promote a task that's linked to predecessor and successor tasks and then demote tasks below the newly promoted summary task, Project breaks the link between the summary task and its newly demoted subtasks. This might cause unwanted rescheduling in your project. To ensure proper scheduling the first time around, apply outlining to your list of tasks before you establish links. Then, when you do link tasks, the best approach is to link only subtasks, not summary tasks. That's because summary tasks only summarize work; they don't represent the details in your schedule. The best way to capture how a schedule change in one task might affect other tasks is to create your links at that level of detail—the subtask level.

 WEB

If you want to practice inserting some summary tasks and applying outlining, you can download the Gem Exhibit Plan Chapter 5 file from the Premier Press download page at www.premierpressbooks.com/downloads.asp.

Inserting Subtasks

To insert a subtask, you must insert a new row for it in the Task Sheet. As you learned in the preceding section, when you insert a new row into a Task Sheet the task in that row adopts the outline level of the task above it. Therefore, one of two situations might develop:

◆ If the task above the inserted row is at a summary level, you'll need to enter the task name, and then demote the task in the newly inserted row. This will demote the subtasks as well, so you'll need to select and promote them by one level to get them back where they belong.

◆ If the task above the inserted row is at the correct subtask level, just enter the task name. Notice that if you insert a new task row within a group of subtasks, Project does not demote the tasks in rows below the newly inserted row to a lower outline level. Instead, Project assumes that all tasks in the group should remain at the same level until you tell it otherwise.

Similarly, when you're entering brand new tasks into blank rows at the bottom of the Task Sheet, Project assumes that each newly entered task should adopt the outline level of the task above it. For example, if I type a new Task Name into row 28 of the Task Sheet shown in Figure 5.6, Project assumes it to be a subtask of the row 23 summary task, just like the subtasks in rows 24 through 27.

Adjusting Subtask Scheduling and Moving Subtasks

If you experiment at all with outlining, you might notice that the summary task duration and summary task bar on the Gantt chart adjust to encompass both the earliest task start date for any subtask of the summary task and the latest task finish date for any subtask. For that reason, it's preferable to create your entire list of tasks, apply the outlining you prefer, and then add links and adjust the scheduling information as needed for all subtasks. If you enter dates for a task, convert it to a summary task, and then later demote it to a subtask, you lose the original duration information you entered for the task anyway.

You can change the schedule for a subtask by using any of the methods for rescheduling tasks that are described in Chapter 6, "Building the Schedule and Fine-Tuning Tasks." The duration, start and finish dates, and Gantt chart

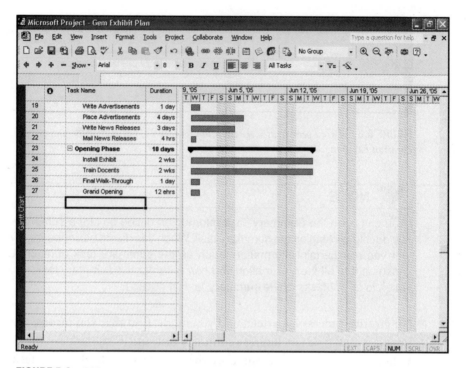

FIGURE 5.6   *If I create another task by typing a Task Name in row 28, it becomes a subtask like the four tasks above it.*

summary bar for the summary task all adjust automatically to reflect the change. Figures 5.7 and 5.8 show how increasing a subtask's duration changes the summary task.

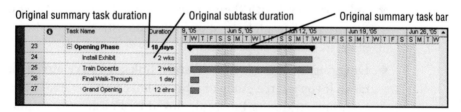

FIGURE 5.7   *The task 23 summary task shows the total duration spanned by all its subtasks: 24 through 27. If the subtasks were linked, making their schedules consecutive rather than concurrent, the duration for summary task 23 would be even longer.*

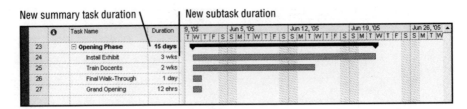

New summary task duration | New subtask duration

FIGURE 5.8 *After I've increased the duration for task 24, notice that the summary task duration has changed.*

 NOTE

You can open the Summary Task Information dialog box for a summary task by double-clicking on the summary task. When this dialog box appears, it won't let you edit certain information, such as the summary task duration. Don't assume that all the information you can enter for the summary task also applies to all subtasks of the summary task; it doesn't.

No creative process is perfect, and you might find that you incorrectly positioned several tasks, including a summary task and its subtasks, in the outline. When this is the case, you can move the tasks as usual, by dragging task rows.

To move a row, click on its row heading (row number). Point to a row border, and then press and hold the mouse button while you drag the row to its new location, dropping the row into place whenever the gray insertion bar reaches the location you want. However, there are a couple of points to remember when dragging outlined tasks:

◆ **Subtasks travel with their summary task.** Therefore, if you drag a summary task to a new location in the task list, when you drop it into place, its subtasks appear below it.

◆ **Dragging tasks around can disturb links, if you've already linked tasks.** If you insert a group of subtasks linked by a series of Finish-to-Start links within tasks already linked by Finish-to-Start links, the typical result is that the moved group will be linked into the sequence— whether or not you want it to be. This is yet another argument for nailing down your outline as much as possible before progressing too far with information about linking, scheduling, or resources.

◆ **A moved task adopts the outline level of the task above it.** When you move a task, Project assumes that you want the task to be on the same outline level as the task above it in its new location. If you move a summary task (and thus its subtasks) to a location that demotes the summary task, click on the Outdent button on the Formatting toolbar to return the group of tasks to the proper outline level before proceeding. Project even demotes or promotes a moved task more than one level, if needed. For example, if you move a task to a Task Sheet row directly below a task that's two outline levels lower, Project demotes the moved task (and any subtasks that travel with it) two levels.

Controlling the Outline Display

As when you're outlining in a word processing application or spreadsheet program, outlining in Project gives you visual cues about how you structured your outline. This can help you make intelligent decisions about scheduling changes and resource assignments. This section explains how you can work with the outlining display features.

Hiding and Showing Outlining Symbols

Outlining symbols help you differentiate summary tasks from subtasks. Any task that has subtasks below it is considered a summary task, and it's indicated with an outlining symbol to the left of the task name. When the summary task has a plus (+) outlining symbol beside it, its subtasks are hidden. When the subtasks for a summary task are displayed, the summary task has a minus (−) outlining symbol beside it. If a task is at a summary task level (most often the top level of the outline) but has no subtasks, no outlining symbol appears beside it. By default, outlining symbols appear for summary tasks in the Task Sheet, at the left of the task names.

To hide outlining symbols, choose Project, Outline, Hide Outline Symbols. To redisplay the outlining symbols, choose Project, Outline, Show Outline Symbols.

For your convenience, you can add a Show/Hide Outline Symbols button to any toolbar. Chapter 28 explains how to customize toolbars. The Show/Hide Outline Symbols button is found on the Commands tab of the Customize dialog box. Click on Outline in the Categories list to display that button in the Commands list.

Specifying Which Outline Levels Appear

Summary tasks wouldn't provide much of a summary if you could never view them without their subtasks. Consequently, Project enables you to hide subtasks from view, for your convenience.

There are a couple of reasons why you might want to hide some or all subtasks in your schedule. First, you might want to print the schedule and have the printout only include summary tasks, not the details shown in subtasks. Second, if you have a lengthy list of tasks in your project, you might find it easier to move up and down through the Task Sheet if you hide subtasks until you need to view or work with the information for a particular subtask.

The fastest way to hide and display subtasks for a summary task is to use its outlining symbol. Click on the minus (–) outlining symbol beside a summary task to hide its subtasks, or the plus (+) outlining symbol to redisplay its subtasks.

When you hide and redisplay subtasks using other commands, you do so for a single summary task by selecting it first. Then, to hide subtasks, click on the Hide Subtasks button on the Formatting toolbar. Alternately, choose Project, Outline, Hide Subtasks. Figure 5.9 shows a Task Sheet with the subtasks for one summary task hidden. Notice that not only the subtask rows but also the corresponding Gantt bars are hidden, leaving only the summary task bar on the Gantt chart.

To redisplay subtasks for selected summary tasks, click on the Show Subtasks button on the Formatting toolbar. Alternatively, choose Project, Outline, Show Subtasks.

If you want to redisplay all subtasks without taking the time to select particular summary tasks, click on the Show button on the Formatting Toolbar and then click on All Subtasks, or choose Project, Outline, Show, All Subtasks. Alternately, first select the whole Task Sheet by clicking the Select All button in the upper-left corner, or select the whole Task Name column by clicking that column heading. Then use the Show Subtasks or Hide Subtasks button on the Formatting toolbar as needed.

 TIP

You can right-click on a summary task's row heading, and then choose Show Subtasks or Hide Subtasks from the shortcut menu as needed.

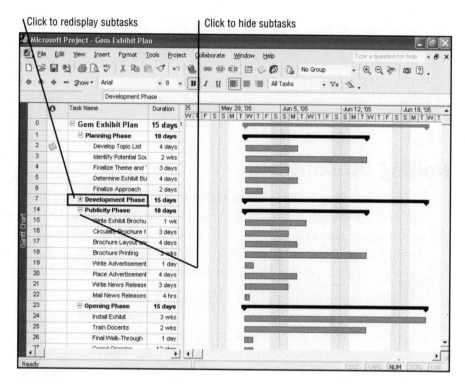

FIGURE 5.9 *The task in row 7 is a summary task; its bold formatting and the plus sign beside it tell you that it contains subtasks.*

The Show button on the Formatting toolbar also offers a handy capability: displaying or hiding tasks down to a particular outline level. For example, you can show only the tasks on the first four outline levels. Tasks at all lower levels will be hidden. To take advantage of this feature, click on the Show button on the Formatting toolbar, and then choose the desired outline level from the menu that appears.

Finally, if you're working in the Task Usage or Resource Usage view, you can hide and redisplay the assignments for one or more selected tasks. To hide assignments, select the desired task and then choose Project, Outline, Hide Assignments. You can also click on the minus (–) button beside the task to hide its assignments. To show assignments, select the desired task and choose Project, Outline, Show Assignments. Or click on the plus (+) button beside the task name.

If you select the Task Name column by clicking on its column heading, the Project, Outline, Hide Assignments command hides all the assignments. You can then later select the entire column and choose Project, Outline, Show Assignments. However, you cannot select the Task Name column and then redisplay all assignments if you hid those assignments on a task-by-task basis. You can only redisplay all the tasks at once if you hid them all at once, a fact that becomes obvious if the Show Assignments choice isn't available on the Project, Outline submenu.

Rolling Up Subtasks

If you have a long list of subtasks within a summary task, you might lose track of how a particular task compares to the summary schedule. Or you might have a particular task near the middle of the summary task range that you want to highlight by having it appear on the summary bar as well as its usual location. To achieve this effect, you *roll up* the subtask to its summary task.

Double-click on the Task Name cell for the subtask to roll up. The Task Information dialog box opens, displaying information about the subtask. On the General tab of this dialog box, click to place a check beside the Roll Up Gantt Bar To Summary choice, and then click on OK. The subtask bar will then appear on the summary bar, as shown in Figure 5.10. To remove the effects of a rollup, reopen the Task Information dialog box for the subtask, clear the Roll Up Gantt Bar To Summary check box on the General tab, and click OK.

Do not select the Hide Task Bar check box in the General tab of the Task Information dialog box when you're rolling up tasks. If you do so, you won't be able to see the rolled-up task.

If you want to roll up several of the subtasks for a summary task simultaneously, drag over the Task Name cells to select the tasks. Click the Task Information button on the Standard toolbar to open the Task Information dialog box, select the Roll Up Gantt Bar To Summary check box on the General tab (you will have to click the check box twice to select it), and click on OK.

 TIP

You can reformat the bars for summary tasks so that they display dates or have a different appearance that makes them stand out more when rolled up. For example, you can make the Gantt bar for a particular subtask red so that it stands out. To learn how to reformat a Gantt bar, see Chapter 17, "Other Formatting."

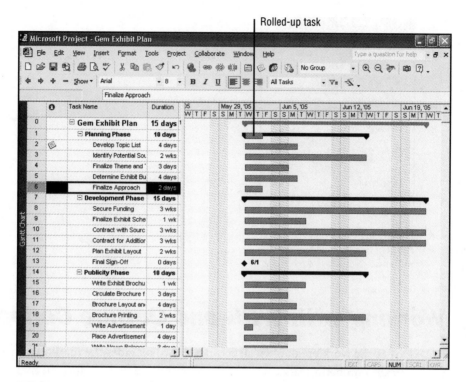

FIGURE 5.10   *The subtask from row 6 has been rolled up onto the summary bar for the summary task in row 1.*

Project enables you to display and remove the rollup bars for all the subtasks at once, which makes the job much easier if you have a lengthy project plan. Choose Format, Layout. The Layout dialog box appears, as shown in Figure 5.11. Click Always Roll Up Gantt bars to roll up the subtask bars for all the tasks in the project file, or clear the check box if you're turning this feature off. With Always Roll Up Gantt Bars checked, the Hide Rollup Bars When Summary Expanded check box becomes active. If you check this check box, Project displays the rollup bars on the summary task bar only when you've hidden (collapsed) the subtasks for the summary tasks. After you finish choosing your layout options, click on OK to close the dialog box.

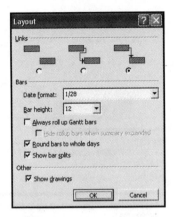

FIGURE 5.11 *Check the Always Roll Up Gantt Bars check box to roll up all the subtask bars in the project file.*

Working with WBS and Outline Codes

Part of the work breakdown structure (WBS) includes the method of hierarchically numbering tasks in a traditional outline numbering format. By default, the WBS numbers (or WBS codes) are the same as the *outline numbers*.

In addition to enabling you to display and use WBS numbers in the Task Sheet, Project lets you create custom WBS numbers (a numbering scheme different from the default outline numbers) to match the needs of your organization. This last section of the chapter explores WBS codes.

Work Breakdown Structure Basics

When you use outlining, Project assigns the WBS numbers automatically, behind the scenes. As you move, promote, and demote tasks, Project updates the outline numbers and WBS numbers accordingly. Tasks at the top outline level are numbered sequentially. For example, the first 10 top-level outline tasks receive WBS numbers 1 through 10. Subtasks on the first level use the top-level number for their summary task plus a decimal value. For example, the first three subtasks of summary task 2 are numbered 2.1, 2.2, and 2.3. For the next outline level down, Project adds another decimal. For example, the first two subtasks under task 2.1 are numbered 2.1.1 and 2.1.2.

The WBS codes or outline numbers aren't the same as the task number. For example, let's say rows 1 through 5 hold a summary task and four subtasks—tasks 1 through 5. The WBS codes for those five tasks would be 1, 1.1, 1.2, 1.3, and 1.4, respectively.

Basically, WBS codes (and outline numbers) do a better job of identifying how your tasks fit into the overall project scheme than the simple task numbers do. And, as your project becomes lengthier, it's easier to refer to the tasks by WBS number rather than task name. For example, if your project has a few hundred tasks, Task Sheet and report printouts will be many pages long. If a question regarding "Task 5.10.7" comes up, it'll be easier to flip through the printout and find that task than to look for its name, such as "Install fourth floor plumbing."

Displaying WBS Codes and Outline Numbers

You can add a field (column) to a Task Sheet table to display WBS numbers and outline numbers. Once you display the desired field, you can even sort by the WBS numbers. The following steps explain how to create a custom table that includes both WBS and Outline number fields:

1. From the default Gantt Chart view, choose View, Table, More Tables. The More Tables dialog box will appear.

2. Make sure Entry is selected in the list of tables, and then click on the Copy button. The Table Definition dialog box will open.

3. Type a name for the new table in the Name text box. For example, type **WBS and Outline**.

4. In the Field Names column, click on the Indicators choice, and then click on the Delete Row button. Also delete the Start, Finish, Predecessors, and Resource Names fields.

5. Click on the Name choice in the Field Names column, and then click on the Insert Row button twice to insert two blank rows. A drop-down list arrow will appear in the Field Name column for the first blank row.

6. Click on the drop-down list arrow to open the list, press the W key on your scroll bar to scroll down the list, and then click on the WBS choice.

7. Press Enter to accept the entry and display the drop-down list arrow for the second new row.

8. Click on the drop-down list arrow to open the list, press the O key on your scroll bar to scroll down the list, scroll down further to display the Outline Number choice, and then click on it.

9. Press Enter. At this point, your table definition settings should appear as shown in Figure 5.12.

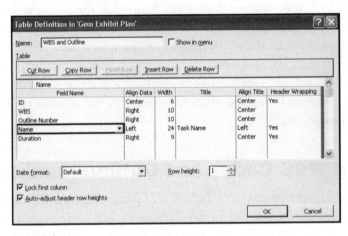

FIGURE 5.12 *As you can see in the Field Name column, I've added the WBS and Outline Number fields into the custom table.*

10. Click on OK to finish creating the custom table.

11. Make sure the new table, *WBS and Outline,* is selected in the list of tables, and then click on Apply. Figure 5.13 illustrates how this custom table appears in the Gantt Chart view. As you can see, both fields display the same numbers by default, because the WBS codes are the same as the outline numbers unless you enter custom WBS codes.

If you prefer a more concise display, you could show outline numbers (which are the same as the default WBS numbers) along with the task name in the Task Sheet rather than creating a custom table. To do so, choose Tools, Options. On the View tab of the Options dialog box, click to place a check beside the Show Outline Number option and then click on OK. The assigned outline number appears to the left of each task name, as shown in Figure 5.14.

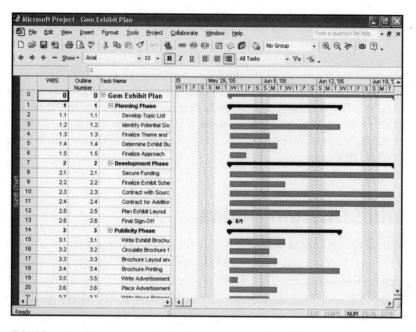

FIGURE 5.13 *The custom table displayed at the left side of the Gantt Chart view includes the WBS and Outline Number fields.*

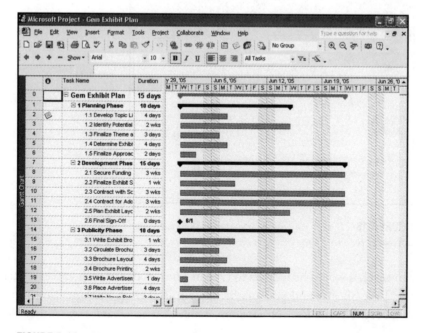

FIGURE 5.14 *If you prefer, you can display each task's outline (WBS) number with the task name.*

NOTE

If you copy the Task Name column into Word 2002 as unformatted text (see Chapter 21, "Using Project with Other Applications"), the WBS numbers are not copied with the Task Name entries, even if the WBS numbers were displayed in Project. If you need to include accurate WBS numbers in documents that are in other applications, create a custom table that includes the WBS column. Then make sure you also copy or export the WBS column information to Word or Excel.

Creating Custom Codes

Your company might mandate a specific set of WBS numbers that you need to follow. You can assign custom WBS codes a task at a time. To do so, double-click on the task in the Task Sheet. In the Task Information dialog box, click on the Advanced tab. Double-click on the entry in the WBS Code text box and type the new entry you want, as shown in Figure 5.15. Click on OK when you finish editing the entry.

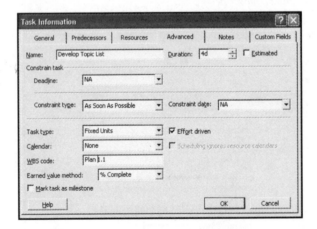

FIGURE 5.15 *If your company requires specific WBS codes, you can change the ones Project creates in the WBS Code text box.*

However, it would be tedious to type in a new code for each and every task in the Task Sheet—and you might make mistakes in incrementing the code numbers. Recent Project versions enable you to create a *mask* that assigns custom WBS codes for all the tasks in the Task Sheet. Follow these steps to create a custom WBS code mask in the current project file:

1. Choose Project, WBS, Define Code. The WBS Code Definition dialog box appears.

2. If you want your WBS codes to include a prefix that's specific to the project name or job number, type that code into the Project Code Prefix text box. You could also use your name, initials, or department number as a prefix.

 TIP

Include a space or underscore character at the end of your Project Code Prefix entry if you need to set it off from the rest of the code.

3. Click in the first blank row in the Sequence column under Code Mask (Excluding Prefix). A drop-down list arrow appears beside the selected cell. Click on the drop-down list arrow, and then click on the type of sequence to use for the top WBS code level. Here are your choices:

   ◆ **Numbers (ordered).** Inserts the specified number of Arabic numerals at that WBS code level.

   ◆ **Uppercase Letters (ordered).** Inserts the specified number of uppercase characters at that WBS code level.

   ◆ **Lowercase Letters (ordered).** Inserts the specified number of lowercase letters at that WBS code level.

   ◆ **Characters (unordered).** Inserts the specified number of asterisk characters at that WBS code level. Or, if you choose Any from the Length column, this choice inserts three numerals, inserting sequential numbers at that WBS code level.

4. In the Length column for the first row, enter the number of characters Project should display for that WBS code level. For example, if you select Numbers (ordered) as the Sequence and then enter 2 as the Length, Project displays 11, 22, 33, and so on in the WBS code for that code level. You can also open the drop-down list for the Length cell and choose Any. This choice tells Project to use the required number of characters at that code level so it can display the proper letter or number (1, 112, 232, and so on).

5. Click on the Separator column for the first row. Open its drop-down list to click on the separator to use between the first level of the WBS code and the next level. Or you can type your own separator, such as the ampersand (&).

6. Using subsequent blank rows, repeat Steps 3 through 5 to add as many levels as are required for your WBS code. If you've outlined your project tasks to six levels deep, you need to create six WBS code outline levels. As you build your code levels, the Code Preview area shows how the WBS codes will look. Figure 5.16 shows the preview of my code, which has a prefix plus two code levels.

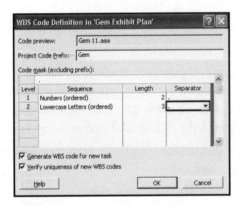

FIGURE 5.16 *Use the blank rows in the Code Mask (Excluding Prefix) area to build the various levels of your WBS code.*

 TIP

To delete a code level row, click on its Sequence column entry, and then press the Delete key.

7. Leave the Generate WBS Code For New Task check box checked to ensure that Project will add the custom WBS codes for any new tasks you add into the project file.

8. Leave the Verify Uniqueness Of New WBS Codes check box checked to ensure that if you try to enter a WBS code in the Task Information dialog box, Project will prevent you from duplicating an existing code. (WBS codes you enter must match the pattern of the mask, however.)

9. Click on OK to finish defining the mask and display the new codes in the WBS column, as illustrated in Figure 5.17.

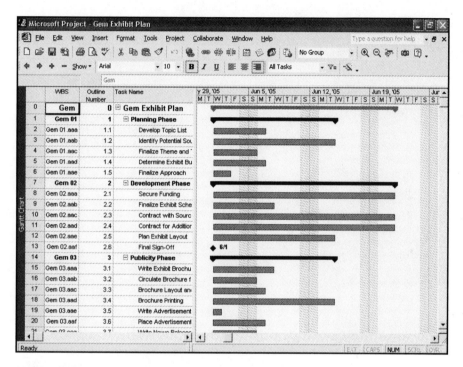

FIGURE 5.17 *The WBS column now displays my custom codes.*

If you move tasks around or make other changes, and Project fails to update the WBS codes, choose Project, WBS, Renumber to make sure your WBS codes are applied according to your custom mask. Leave Entire Project selected in the WBS Renumber dialog box, and then click on OK to finish the renumbering.

Chapter 6

Building the Schedule and Fine-Tuning Tasks

In This Chapter

◆ Working with links that show relationships between tasks

◆ Understanding how lead times and lag times affect your schedule

◆ Identifying and creating tasks that you know will repeat

◆ Applying constraints that further specify when the task should be performed

◆ Reviewing and changing other information that's been stored about a task

Most designers and artists who create masterpieces don't start by drawing subtle shading and fine lines, just as architects don't start a building design by selecting a brick color. In putting the whole picture together, most people—professionals and amateurs alike—start by sketching out a rough idea of what they want. Then they go back and draw in the details.

In Chapter 4, "Setting Up a Project," you learned how to sketch out the schedule for your project in the default Gantt Chart view. Then in Chapter 5, "Working with Outlining," you learned how to organize the list of tasks into functional summary groups. This chapter helps you to continue working in the Gantt Chart view to begin the refinement process, drawing in some details to make your schedule clearer, making changes here and there to fine-tune individual tasks.

Linking and Unlinking Tasks

One major drawback to the "yellow pad" method of project planning is that it forces you into a simplistic way of thinking. Because each task is on a separate line, it is separate and distinct from all other tasks on the list.

That's perception, though, not reality. Most projects don't progress in so neat a fashion. Many tasks are completely independent of one another, but sometimes tasks need to occur simultaneously. Other times, one task cannot start until another one finishes. Some tasks need to start or finish simultaneously. Such a connection between the "destinies" of two tasks is called a *task relationship*. In Project, you define task relationships by creating *links*.

Links in your schedule define how tasks should proceed, which is why linking is sometimes referred to as *sequencing tasks*. The links you add enable Project to calculate adjusted start and finish dates for the linked tasks. Based on the links between subtasks, Project also can calculate the overall schedule for each summary group, as well as the schedule for the project as a whole. As you'll see in this chapter, building your project schedule through linking proceeds much faster than typing numerous entries in the Start and Finish columns of the Task Sheet.

The first task in a linked pair, which usually must be completed before the other linked task can start, is called the *predecessor*. The task or tasks that follow and depend on each predecessor are called *successors*. A predecessor can have more than one successor, and successors can serve as predecessors for other tasks, creating a chain of linked events. A successor task can even have multiple predecessors, such as when three tasks must finish before one successor task can start.

One detail that might be difficult to get your head around is that a predecessor task is identified by its ID number in the Predecessors field on the row for the successor task in the Task Sheet. The predecessor's task ID is based on the task's current position (which row it's in) on the Task Sheet, not its individual schedule. It's perfectly okay to specify the task in row 20 as the predecessor to the task in row 12 in a Finish-to-Start link (described next), as long as the finish date for the row 20 task precedes the start date for the row 12 task.

 CAUTION

You should only create links between subtasks (detail tasks). That's because you want to link at the outlining level that represents the work that will occur. Because the summary tasks represent calculated subtotals, linking the summary tasks won't reflect the true flow of work in the project.

Link Types

Project offers four types of links. Links are visually represented by lines and arrows between tasks in Gantt charts, calendars, and Network Diagram charts that are based on your schedule. Each link is identified with a particular abbreviation:

◆ The most common kind of link is a *Finish-to-Start (FS) relationship*, where you tell Project to adjust the successor task's schedule so that the successor task starts after the predecessor has finished (see Figure 6.1). For example, a product prototype might need to be approved before prototype testing can begin. An FS relationship is the simplest type of link to create. It's the default link type, and Project creates an FS relationship if you don't specify a different link type.

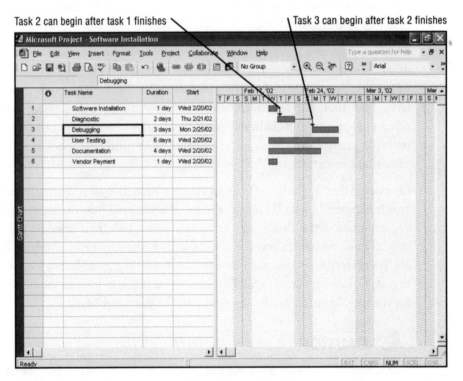

Task 2 can begin after task 1 finishes — Task 3 can begin after task 2 finishes

FIGURE 6.1 *A Finish-to-Start (FS) link means that the predecessor task must finish so the successor task can start.*

◆ A *Start-to-Start (SS) relationship* specifies that the predecessor task must start so that the successor task can start (see Figure 6.2). You'd use this type of relationship in situations where you want resources to work closely together during the same timeframe, such as when an internal engineering department is working on tasks that occur along with tasks handled by freelance resources. With a Start-to-Start link, you're specifying that Project can schedule the successor task so it can start simultaneously with (or after) the predecessor. For example, if your engineering department started work on its task, the freelancers can start work on theirs.

Once task 3 starts, task 4 can start

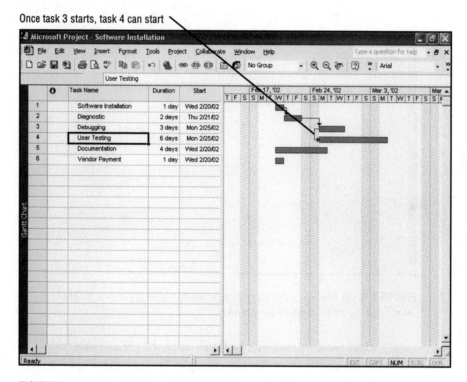

FIGURE 6.2   *A Start-to-Start (SS) link indicates when the predecessor task must be underway so that its successor can start.*

◆ A *Finish-to-Finish (FF) relationship* means that the predecessor task must finish before the successor can finish (see Figure 6.3). Such a situation might arise when multiple tasks must be completed simultaneously, but the predecessor task is more lengthy or resource-intensive than any successor task. For example, say that you're creating the first issue of a new magazine. When the page layout task (the predecessor) ends, the proofreading task (the successor) can end because pages must be completed before they can be proofread. If you added a Finish-to-Finish link between those tasks, Project would schedule them accordingly.

◆ A *Start-to-Finish (SF) relationship* is a bit more complex than the other relationships, and therefore it's used less often. In such a relationship,

Task 4 must end before task 5 can finish

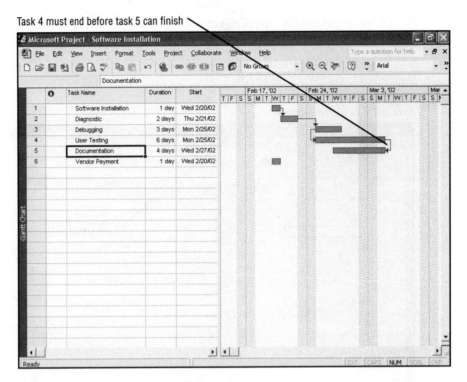

FIGURE 6.3 *A Finish-to-Finish (FF) relationship identifies when the predecessor task must finish before the successor can finish.*

the successor task cannot finish until the predecessor task begins (see Figure 6.4). Consider the example illustrated in Figure 6.4. The link between tasks 5 and 6 indicates that the software documentation process cannot begin until the software vendor has been paid (and the user testing has finished, according to the link between tasks 4 and 5).

 CAUTION

When you create a particular relationship that requires it, and when the successor task has no constraints applied to its schedule, Project will change (recalculate) the schedule for a successor task to be consistent with the link type.

For example, if you create an FF relationship and the successor task's finish date was originally an earlier date than the predecessor's finish date, based on the relative lengths of the tasks, Project shifts the successor task's schedule so that it has the correct finish date but retains its original duration. Project might also shift successor tasks that are attached to any predecessor task you move, so don't be too surprised.

Task 6 must finish before task 5 can start

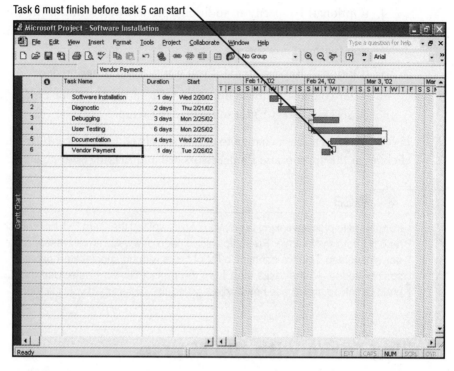

FIGURE 6.4 *A Start-to-Finish (SF) relationship identifies when the successor task must finish before the predecessor can start.*

Linking Tasks on the Task Sheet

Recall from the description of the Task Sheet in Chapter 4, "Setting Up a Project," that one of the columns in the default Task Sheet is the Predecessors column. To use this column to create links, do the following:

1. In the task row for the task that will be the successor, click in the Predecessors cell. For example, if you want the task in row 12 to start when the task in row 10 finishes, click on the Predecessors cell in row 12.

2. Type the row number for the predecessor task.

3. If you want to designate a Start-to-Start, Finish-to-Finish, or Start-to-Finish link rather than the default Finish-to-Start link type, type its abbreviation using upper- or lowercase characters (for example, **10ff**). You don't need a space between the predecessor's row number and the abbreviation.

4. (Optional) To specify an additional predecessor, continue the entry by typing a comma followed by the task number and link type abbreviation (without any spaces).

5. (Optional) Repeat Step 4 if you want to add other predecessors.

6. After you create all the links you want in the successor task's Predecessors cell, press Enter to finalize the setup.

If you decide to make a change to a link, simply edit the link information by clicking in the appropriate Predecessors cell and making your changes.

 WEB

If you want to practice linking tasks, you can download the Gem Exhibit Plan Chapter 6 file from the Premier Press download page at www.premierpressbooks.com/downloads.asp. This file contains a list of tasks with no special start dates or constraints added. All the tasks start from the project file start date. Use that file to practice linking and to see how Project schedules tasks when you link them.

Linking Tasks with the Mouse

To create a default Finish-to-Start (FS) link, you can drag between task bars on the Gantt chart to create the link. Point to either of the task bars until you see the four-headed arrow pointer. Press and hold the mouse button, and drag to the other task bar. As you drag, a Finish-to-Start Link pop-up box appears, as in Figure 6.5. Release the mouse button to finish creating the link.

 CAUTION

Be careful when using this method to link tasks because you can accidentally change a task to a different schedule by dragging its Gantt bar.

Linking Tasks with the Toolbar

Using a toolbar button along with the Task Sheet can make even faster work of creating links between tasks—but only if you want to create the default type of link, an FS relationship. Using this method, you can select multiple tasks and

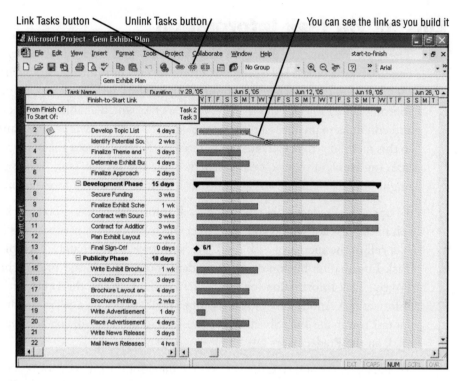

FIGURE 6.5 *Drag between task bars to create a link.*

link them simultaneously. This enables you to forecast your schedule very rapidly because Project recalculates the overall schedule based on the series of links.

The following steps make it easy to link several tasks in a single operation:

1. Drag to select the Task Name cells for two or more adjacent tasks. If you want to select noncontiguous tasks, click a cell in the predecessor task row, press and hold down the Ctrl key, and click a cell in the successor task row—both cells will be selected. (In fact, use the Ctrl+click technique to skip over summary tasks, because you don't want to link those.) If you want to select additional noncontiguous tasks, continue to hold down Ctrl and click the Task Name cells in additional rows.

2. Click on the Link Tasks button on the Standard toolbar. Alternately, press Ctrl+F2, or choose Edit, Link Tasks. Project creates the links between the tasks in the rows you selected.

Linking via Task Information

The Task Information dialog box lets you view and alter numerous crucial details about a task. This dialog box offers six tabs of information, including the Notes tab that you learned about when creating task notes in Chapter 4, "Setting Up a Project," and the Predecessors tab, which enables you to create and edit links to predecessors for the selected task. The obvious disadvantage to this method is that you must be familiar with details about the predecessor task you want to choose or the schedule for the predecessor, because you might not be able to view that information while the dialog box is open.

To open the Predecessors tab in the Task Information dialog box, click in a cell in the task for which you want to create or work with predecessors (that is, a cell in the successor task row). Press Shift+F2. Alternately, click on the Task Information button on the Standard toolbar. Or if you prefer, choose Project, Task Information (or right-click on the task and then click on Task Information). Another method is to simply double-click on a cell in the successor task row in the Task Sheet. When the Task Information dialog box appears, click on the Predecessors tab.

To add a predecessor, type the ID (row) number for the predecessor task in the first cell of the ID column below the Predecessors choice. Press Enter or Tab, or click on the Enter button (it looks like a check mark) beside the Predecessors text box above the column heads. (The text entry area here operates just like the one above the Task Sheet.) Project enters the predecessor's task name.

Project offers a second, easier method of specifying a predecessor task in the Task Information dialog box. Click on the Task Name cell in the first empty row of the Task Name column of the Predecessors tab in the Task Information dialog box. A drop-down list arrow appears at the right side of the cell. Click on the arrow to open a drop-down list giving the task name for each task in the schedule. Click on the name of the predecessor task, as shown in Figure 6.6. Click on the Enter button to finish choosing the predecessor.

Whether you specify the predecessor by ID or task name, by default Project enters Finish-to-Start (FS) in the Type column as the link type. To specify a different type, click on the Type cell for a predecessor and do one of the following:

◆ Select the type that currently appears in the text entry box, type the abbreviation for the preferred type of link, and click on the Enter button (which looks like a check mark).

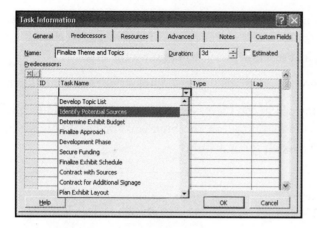

FIGURE 6.6 *Open the drop-down list for the selected Task Name cell, and then click on the name of the predecessor task.*

◆ Click on the down arrow at the right end of the text entry box to display a drop-down list of link types, and then click on the preferred type of link.

You can add additional predecessor tasks in lower rows of the tab. To edit any link, click on the appropriate cell in the predecessor row, and then edit it in the text entry box or use a drop-down list for the cell, if available, to make another choice.

To remove a predecessor, click on the ID cell for it. Then drag over the ID number that appears in the text entry box, press Backspace to remove it, and click on the Enter button. When you finish using the tab to add or edit predecessors, click on OK to close the Task Information dialog box.

 NOTE

For information about the Lag column for predecessor tasks, see the "Working with Lead Times and Lag Times" section later in this chapter.

Unlinking Tasks or Changing the Link Type

To remove a link between tasks or change the type of link, you typically work from the successor task, not the predecessor task. Removing a link does not change the schedule for the successor task, unless that schedule was changed by Project when the link was created. If Project did automatically adjust the successor task schedule based on a link you added, Project returns the successor task to its original schedule when you remove the link.

Use any of the following methods to break a link or change the link type:

◆ Click on any cell in the successor task row to select it. Then click on the Unlink Tasks button on the Standard toolbar. (This technique applies to breaking the link only.)

 TIP

You can select multiple tasks and then click on the Unlink Tasks button to unlink them.

◆ Click the Predecessors cell in the successor task row of the Task Sheet. To remove the link, right-click on the cell and choose Clear Contents. Otherwise, click in the Entry box above the Task Sheet, edit the link type abbreviation, and click on Enter to finish changing the link.

◆ Click on the Task Information button on the Standard toolbar (or use the method of your choice) to open the Task Information dialog box, and then click on the Predecessors tab. Delete the ID number for the predecessor to remove the link. Change the Type column entry for a predecessor to change the link type.

◆ Double-click on the appropriate link line between two tasks in the Gantt chart. To remove the link, choose Delete in the Task Dependency dialog box that appears. Or open the Type drop-down list, click on a different link type, and then click on OK. Note that the (None) choice in the Type drop-down list removes the link, too.

Working with Lead Times and Lag Times

Reality dictates the way your schedule must progress, and the way Project enables you to define task relationships. Time is *analog*, or continuous. Although it can be expressed in discrete units, such as minutes and seconds, it flows continuously. Moreover, events blend together in time. Even though tasks might seem to follow one after another, they probably flow together more loosely, overlapping or occurring after a delay.

Project accounts for the flexibility of time by enabling you to schedule *lead time* and *lag time* for linked tasks. With the default Finish-to-Start link type, adding lead time causes the successor task to overlap with the predecessor task. This means that the successor task can start after the predecessor task has started, but before it has finished.

Adding lag time on a Finish-to-Start relationship enables you to insert a delay between the finish of the predecessor task and the start of the successor task. For example, if a predecessor task is scheduled to end on a Wednesday, you can schedule the successor task to begin the following Wednesday without breaking the link between the two tasks.

With other link types, lead and lag time work a bit differently. In particular, with a Start-to-Start link, lead time schedules the successor to start at the specified interval before the predecessor, and lag time schedules the successor to start at the specified interval after the predecessor starts. With a Finish-to-Finish link, lead time schedules the successor to finish at the specified interval before the predecessor finishes, and lag time schedules the successor to finish at the specified interval after the predecessor finishes.

You can schedule lead or lag time by entering the proper code for it in the Predecessor column entry (by appending it to the predecessor task number and task type specification). Or you can schedule it by entering the code in the Lag column of the Predecessors tab of the Task Information dialog box, or in the Lag text box of the Task Dependency dialog box. You specify lead time using a minus sign (−) and lag time using a plus sign (+). You can specify the timing in terms of duration intervals (2h for two hours, 2d for two days, and so on), or as a percentage of the predecessor task's duration.

For example, if you want to create a Finish-to-Start link to task 7 with a two-day lead time, enter **7FS−2d** on the Task Sheet in the Predecessors cell for the successor task. If you're entering the lead time in the Lag column (Task Information dialog box) or Lag text box (Task Dependency dialog box), you only have to enter **−2d**. A Lag entry using percentages might be **7FS−50%** (on the Task Sheet), which would insert lead time equivalent to 50 percent of the predecessor task's duration before the start date of the successor task, or **−25%** (in either of the dialog boxes), which would do the same thing at 25 percent. To specify lag time (a pause) rather than lead time, you simply use a plus sign (or no operator) rather than a minus sign in your entries.

Figure 6.7 shows lead time and lag time added to tasks in an example schedule.

 CAUTION

By default, the abbreviation for a Finish-to-Start (FS) relationship doesn't appear in the Predecessors column of the Task Sheet. However, you must type that abbreviation when specifying lead time or lag time.

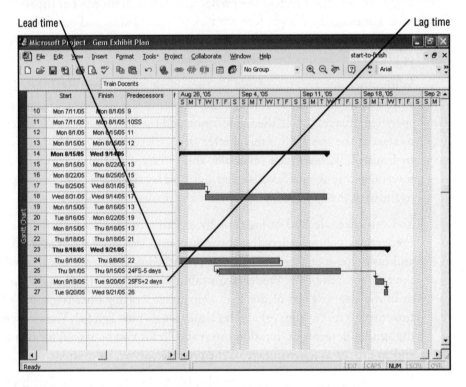

FIGURE 6.7 *Achieve more realistic scheduling with lag time and lead time.*

NOTE

In real life, problems arise, resources are detained, and other delays gum up the works. You should always include a bit of "cushion time" in your schedule to allow for such problems.

Project offers you two ways to build this cushion time into your project schedule. The first is to schedule extra time for some tasks, especially those for which you're less confident about estimating a duration. The second is to assign the anticipated duration for a task, but to build in some lag time after the task.

I prefer the latter method, especially when I need to track costs accurately or when I'm dealing with a resource outside my company. I give the outside resource a task deadline (the finish date for the task as calculated by Project) that is at least a couple of days before the real internal date when I require the task to be completed (as reflected by the lag time period). I recommend this technique because it not only provides cushion time but also gives you, as manager of the project, some time to review the work from the outside resource. This is especially prudent if you haven't previously dealt with that resource. Plus, you can always remove the lag time later if the schedule is running behind and you find that the lag time is no longer needed.

Splitting a Task

Chapter 4 discussed how Project works with durations you enter. If you enter a duration of one week (1 wk) for a task, and the project calendar uses a 40-hour work week, Project assumes the task will take 40 hours of work to complete. However, sometimes you might know that a task won't take 40 hours, even when the start and finish dates need to be a week apart.

For example, if a resource spends all day Monday on the task, waits a few days for information to arrive from a supplier, and then spends Friday afternoon finishing the task, the resource worked only 1.5 days (12 hours) on the task. If the resource is from an outside supplier or another department in your company that charges your department for time, it is in your best interest to zero in on the actual time spent on the task. That way you can accurately account for project costs, while keeping the true schedule dates intact.

Project offers a feature called *task splitting* to help you create an accurate picture of when tasks start and finish (the duration), while also tracking any nonworking periods that occur within the task. When Project tracks working time accurately, it can then calculate costs accurately rather than overstating them.

Returning to the example, let's say you know a task will take about 1.5 days of work hours, and you want it to start on the morning of Monday, 4/3/06. Because of the delay while the resource is waiting to receive information, the finish date will be a week later, on Monday, 4/10/06. Therefore, you should enter the task with a 1.5-day duration. Assume it has a start date of 4/2/06 (based on the project start date or links to other tasks). Then, you should split the task and drag the last half-day of the task to the true finish date, 4/10/06. Then the Gantt bar for the task spans one full week, while Project displays 1.5 days of duration for the task and uses that latter figure to calculate the resource commitments and costs for the work.

Follow these steps to use your mouse to split a task:

1. Scroll the Gantt Chart pane to the task bar for the task that you want to split. Double-check to ensure the task start date is the date when all work will begin. This ensures that when you create the split between tasks, you have a more accurate picture of how long it can be. That way, you don't need to repeatedly move the split task around or adjust the split.

2. Click on the Split Task button on the Standard toolbar. Alternately, choose Edit, Split Task. The Split Task pop-up box will appear, and the mouse pointer changes to a split pointer, with two vertical lines to the left and a right-pointing arrow.

3. Point to the Gantt bar for the task you want to split. Move the pointer left or right until the date listed as the starting date in the Split Task pop-up box is the date when you want the split (the nonworking period between the split portions of the task) to begin. Figure 6.8 shows the Split Task pop-up box.

4. When you see the correct starting date for the split in the Split Task pop-up box, press and hold the left mouse button, and then drag the split portion of the task to the right. When you start dragging, the Split Task pop-up box will change to the Task pop-up box. This box also appears when you drag to create a new task, and it includes start and finish dates for the portion of the task you're moving.

A dotted line indicates the task is split   Split Task button   Shows the Start date for the period between the split portions of the task   Split pointer

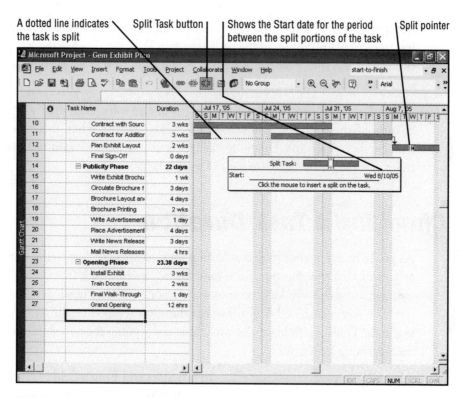

FIGURE 6.8 *You can click on the Split Task button and then drag with the split pointer to move a portion of a task to a later time.*

5. When the Task pop-up box displays the correct starting date—the date you want work to resume on the task—release the mouse button to drop the split portion of the task into place.

 TIP

If you click on the Split Task button and then decide that you don't want to split a task, click on the Split Task button again or press Esc.

You can split as many tasks as you want in a schedule, or even place multiple splits in the same task bar. In fact, if you double-click on the Split Task button on the Standard toolbar, it remains turned on so that you can make as many splits as you want in the project. Click on the Split Task button again to turn it off.

As you fine-tune your schedule, you may find a split task that no longer needs to be split. To remove the split in the task, point to the right-hand portion of the split task bar (that is, the Gantt bar for the split task). Press and hold the left mouse button, and drag the bar to the left. When it touches the left-hand portion of the split task bar, release the mouse button. The portions of the split task will merge back into a single task.

Similarly, if you want to adjust the length of the split, drag the right-hand portion of the split task and release the mouse button when it reaches the starting date you want. Dragging the leftmost portion of a split task bar reschedules the entire task, leaving the split intact.

Changing a Task Duration

As you're building your project schedule, you may realize that you've improperly estimated the duration for a task. Based on feedback from other team members, outside vendors, or your supervisor, you may need to adjust the duration you've assigned. You adjust the duration at any time simply by clicking in the Duration field for the applicable task, typing the new duration, and then pressing Enter.

Although you also could edit dates in the Start and Finish fields as well, the same caution that I gave in Chapter 4 applies here. If you start typing in dates yourself, rather than allowing Project to calculate task dates via linking and other task settings (such as constraints, which are covered later in this chapter), you may be assigning unwanted constraints to your tasks.

On the other hand, if a task has no predecessors to drive its schedule but has to adhere to a particular start or finish date, you can type in the applicable date. This will constrain the task, yes, but you would've had to add a constraint anyway in order to move it.

Furthermore, you can change the duration of a task by dragging the right end of its Gantt bar on the Gantt chart. (You can even create or move tasks around by dragging.) As with typing in dates to edit task parameters, I strongly recommend against using the mouse to edit task schedules, for a few reasons. Project may once again apply unwanted constraints when you drag to work with tasks. Plus, dragging is much less precise, especially when you're dealing with tasks that are already short in duration.

Creating Recurring Tasks

Splitting tasks is a great solution for breaking up work over a span of time. However, there's an even better technique for brief tasks that occur regularly over a particular period of time, such as weekly team meetings, monthly reports to a client, and so on. Rather than entering a separate task for each one-hour meeting or each half-day of report preparation, you can automatically schedule tasks that will occur at set intervals. These are called *recurring tasks*.

You can schedule monthly team meetings, a weekly conference call, or a daily status report. You can even set tasks to occur more than once each week—for example, every Monday and Wednesday.

 TIP

Although you can create recurring tasks from a few different views in Project, adding these tasks from the Gantt Chart view often works best because you get a clear picture of where the recurring task fits in.

To add a recurring task to your schedule, perform the following steps:

1. In the Task Sheet, select the row (or a cell in the row) that the first instance of the recurring task should precede. You do this because the recurring task will be inserted as a summary task on a single row of the Task Sheet, with the subtasks representing each recurrence hidden from view. (See Chapter 5, "Working with Outlining," to learn more about viewing subtasks.) Because the recurring tasks aren't dispersed throughout the task list by default, it's a good idea to place the summary recurring task early in the schedule. Users of the file will notice it there, and it won't disrupt the appearance of other linked tasks on the Gantt chart.

 TIP

Try inserting recurring tasks right after the project summary task, if you've displayed it, or near the top of a summary section.

2. Choose Insert, Recurring Task. The Recurring Task Information dialog box appears, as shown in Figure 6.9.

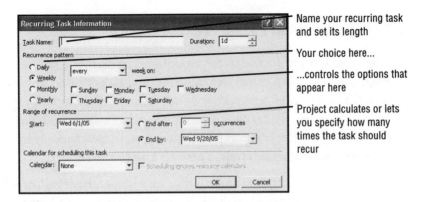

Name your recurring task and set its length

Your choice here...

...controls the options that appear here

Project calculates or lets you specify how many times the task should recur

FIGURE 6.9 *You can specify that a task recurs several times.*

3. Enter the desired values in the Task Name and Duration text boxes. Remember that you can use abbreviations to specify the exact timing you want to assign, such as **2h** for a two-hour task.

4. In the area of the dialog box called This Occurs, select one of these choices: Daily, Weekly, Monthly, or Yearly.

5. Specify the interval between recurrences in the area to the right of This Occurs. The available choices vary depending on the option you've selected. Basically, you can choose from the following:

   ◆ **Daily.** Use the drop-down list to specify whether the task appears every day, every second day, every third day, and so on, up to every twelfth day. The Day choice includes all days in the schedule, and the Workday choice only schedules the recurring task on days included in the calendar for the project.

   ◆ **Weekly.** Use the Week On drop-down list to specify whether the task appears every week, every second week, and so on, up to every twelfth week. Next, select each day of the week on which you want the task to recur. Change the entry in the From text box (in the Length area of the dialog box) only if you want to schedule recurrences starting before—or at a specified interval after—the project start date. Use the To option to specify an ending date for the recurrence. Otherwise, click on the For Occurrences option and specify the number of times that the task should be scheduled after the start date. Note that if you click on the drop-down list arrow beside either the From or the To choices, a pop-up calendar appears so you can make sure you're selecting a working day (rather than a weekend or some other nonworking date).

◆ **Monthly.** Use the Day option button to specify the day of the month (by date number, such as the 25th of every month). Then use the corresponding drop-down list to specify whether to schedule the task in every month of the project time frame. If you want to schedule the recurring task by a day of the week rather than a date within each month, click on the option button labeled The. Then use its drop-down lists to specify particular weekdays when the task should be scheduled, and whether to schedule the task every month. The Length options work exactly like the ones described under Weekly.

TIP

Whenever possible, schedule tasks by selecting a day of the week rather than entering a date. This helps you avoid scheduling any instances of the recurring task on a nonworking date.

◆ **Yearly.** Click on the option button beside the upper text box and enter a single schedule date for the recurring task. Or click on the button labeled The, and then use the drop-down lists to choose a month, week day, and particular week day in that month (first, second, and so on) for the task. Again, the Length options work as described under Weekly.

6. If you want the recurring task to use a particular calendar, choose the proper calendar from the Calendar drop-down list. This will help ensure that Project doesn't schedule a recurrence of the task on dates designated as holidays, for example. Also, if you want Project to ignore calendars you set up for your resources (more on that in the next chapter), click on the Scheduling Ignores Resource Calendars check box to check it.

7. Click on OK to accept your choices. If, by chance, one or more of the recurrences you scheduled appears on a day that's not a working day according to the project calendar, Project asks if you want to reschedule the task (see Figure 6.10). To reschedule the task and continue, click on Yes.

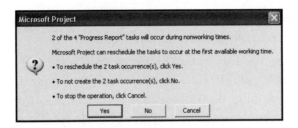

FIGURE 6.10 *If a recurring task doesn't fit into the working schedule, Project offers to reschedule it.*

The recurring task appears in the Task Sheet in boldface, with a minus (−) outlining symbol to indicate that it's a summary task (see Figure 6.11). The subtask rows under the recurring task each contain an individual recurrence. The duration, start date, and finish date for this summary task will span all the recurrences of the task, although you might not be able to see the Duration field entry at first if the Duration column is too narrow. If you see a series

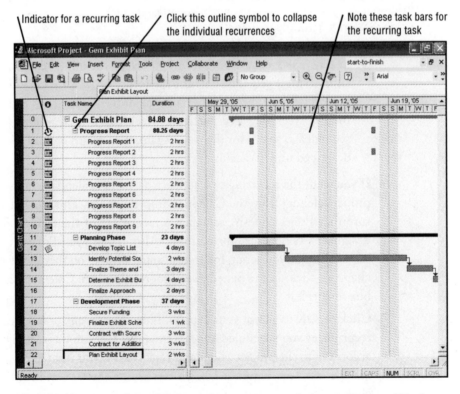

FIGURE 6.11 *A recurring task is inserted as a summary task; you can display or hide the individual instances as needed.*

of pound (#) signs filling the Duration column, double-click on the right border of its heading to increase the column's size.

To adjust the schedule for the recurring task, click in any cell in the summary task row. Press Shift+F2, or choose Project, Recurring Task Information. (You also could double-click or right-click in a cell in the task and then click Recurring Task Information). Make the changes you want, and then click on OK to complete your changes.

To delete the recurring task, select the summary task by clicking on its row number and then press Delete (or open the Edit menu and click on Delete Task). Alternately, right-click on the heading for the summary task row and click on Delete Task. If the Planning Wizard dialog box appears, click on OK to confirm the deletion. This deletes the summary line and all the hidden rows that represent recurrences of the task.

Setting Task Constraints

As you learned elsewhere in this book, Project calculates a project finish date or start date for you depending on the duration, links, and other settings for the tasks you create. This book has focused quite a bit already on the flexibility you have in adjusting links or rescheduling parts of tasks.

That flexibility is great if you're the only person who's able to edit the schedule. If you want to make the schedule a bit more solid, however, in most cases you can establish constraints for tasks. A *constraint* limits Project's ability to move and reschedule a task based on changes to that task's predecessors or successors. Table 6.1 reviews the constraints you can assign.

To create constraints for a task, perform the following steps:

1. Click on a cell in the Task Sheet row of the task for which you want to create constraints.
2. Right-click on the task or choose Project, Task Information. Alternately, press Shift+F2, or click on the Task Information button on the Standard toolbar, or double-click on the Task. The Task Information dialog box appears.
3. Click on the Advanced tab to see the advanced options.

Table 6.1 Constraints for Controlling Individual Task Scheduling

Constraint	Abbrev.	Description	Flexible/Inflexible
As Soon As Possible	ASAP	Ensures that the task starts as soon as possible, based on the completion of any predecessors. This is the default constraint if you enter only the duration for the task for projects scheduled from the project start date.	Flexible
As Late As Possible	ALAP	Ensures that the task starts as late as possible when the project is being scheduled from its finish date and is the default constraint if you enter only the duration for the task in this type of schedule.	Flexible
Finish No Earlier Than	FNET	Prevents a task from finishing when premature. This is the default if you edit or enter the task's finish date.	Inflexible when tasks are scheduled from the project finish date. Flexible when tasks are scheduled from the project start date.
Start No Earlier Than	SNET	Prevents a task from starting before the specified date. This is the default if you edit or enter the task's start date.	Inflexible when tasks are scheduled from the project finish date. Flexible when tasks are scheduled from the project start date.
Finish No Later Than	FNLT	Sets the drop-dead deadline for the task, but enables the task to start earlier if needed.	Inflexible when tasks are scheduled from the project start date. Flexible when tasks are scheduled from the project finish date.

Table 6.1 (continued)

Constraint	Abbrev.	Description	Flexible/Inflexible
Start No Later Than	SNLT	Sets the absolute latest date when the task can commence, but enables the task to start earlier if needed.	Inflexible when tasks are scheduled from the project start date. Flexible when tasks are scheduled from the project finish date.
Must Finish On	MFO	Specifies that a task must finish no sooner or later than a specified date.	Inflexible
Must Start On	MSO	Specifies that a task must start no sooner or later than a specified date.	Inflexible

4. Click on the Constraint Type drop-down list arrow to see a list of constraint types. Select the type of constraint you want for the selected task.

5. Click on the Constraint Date text box drop-down list arrow, and use the pop-up calendar to specify the new date to define the constraint. See Figure 6.12 for example constraint settings.

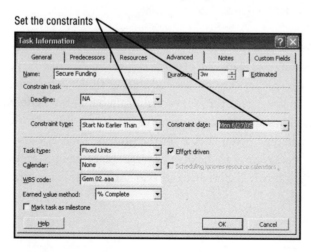

FIGURE 6.12 *Use this tab of the Task Information dialog box to create constraints.*

6. Click on OK to close the dialog box and finalize the constraint.

After you add a constraint, a small, square, grid-like icon appears in the Indicators column. This icon represents a particular type of constraint. If required by the constraint, Project also will move the task so that it honors the constraint. For example, let's say Project is currently calculating a Start date of 4/4/05 for a task (based on its links and other settings). If you then add a Start No Earlier Than constraint to the task, along with a constraint date of 4/11/05, Project will reschedule the task to start on 4/11/05, inserting lag time before the task to account for the gap between it and its predecessor.

 NOTE

Okay, so I've advised you not to move tasks by dragging and not to type in start or finish dates, but you may do it anyway. By default, if you move a task to an earlier or later date (that is, moving the start date for the task), Project gives the task a Start No Earlier Than (SNET) constraint. If you edit the finish date for a task, Project assigns the Finish No Earlier Than (FNET) constraint to the task.

If you do edit the start or finish date for a task, a small green triangle appears in the upper-left corner of the cell holding the edited date. This is another of the new Feedback indicators. If you move the mouse pointer over a cell with the Feedback indicator for the edited date, a button appears to the left of the cell. Click that button to see a menu of choices for adjusting the task schedule with or without the constraint that's been added.

Flexible constraints aren't anchored or restricted to a particular date. They can move within a range of dates as needed as you create links or add resources (until the task reaches the constrained start or finish date, that is). In contrast, an inflexible constraint prevents a task from being rescheduled unless you change the constraint. Some constraints can be flexible or inflexible, depending on the Schedule From choice for the project. Table 6.1 also clarifies when particular constraints are flexible or inflexible. The indicator for an inflexible restraint is slightly different from that for a flexible constraint, as shown in Figure 6.13.

FIGURE 6.13 *The top indicator represents a flexible constraint, and the bottom one represents an inflexible constraint.*

Adding a Task Deadline

Project 2000 and 2002 offer a deadline setting on the Advanced tab of the Task Information dialog box. After you assign a deadline to a task, a marker for that deadline appears on the Gantt bar for the task. If you move your mouse pointer over the deadline marker, a pop-up tip shows you the deadline date. When you're developing and tracking the project and a task is scheduled to finish (or actually finishes) later than the deadline you specified, an indicator appears in the indicators column to alert you, as shown in Figure 6.14. This feature might be useful, for example, if a contract with an outside resource calls for financial penalties for missed deadlines.

Indicator that the task Finish date is after the deadline   Deadline marker on the Gantt bar

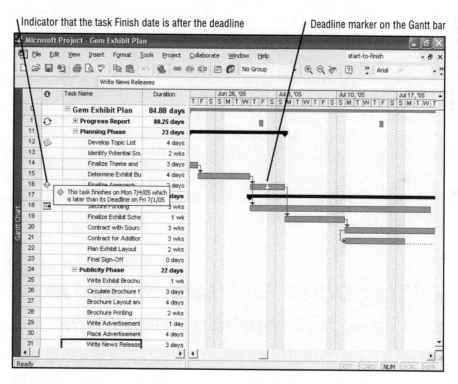

FIGURE 6.14 *You can use the Deadline setting as another way of ensuring that your project will stay on track.*

To specify a deadline, double-click on the desired task to display the Task Information dialog box. Click on the Advanced tab. Enter the deadline date in the Deadline text box or use its drop-down calendar to choose the deadline date, and then click OK to apply the deadline.

Using Go To to Find a Task

Scroll bars enable you to scroll through the various parts of each view. For example, you can scroll up and down to see different rows of the Task Sheet, and you can scroll left and right to see other columns. Pressing Page Down and Page Up moves the display by one screenful of information. Likewise, you can scroll up, down, left, and right to display different areas of the Gantt chart.

Moving around the Task Sheet and clicking a task certainly changes the part of the Task Sheet that you see, but selecting a task in the Task Sheet doesn't automatically scroll the Gantt chart to the task bar for that selected task. Additionally, scrolling to the correct task bar on the Gantt chart could be slow. Instead, you can use the Go To feature to jump directly to the Task Sheet task and task bar you want, or just the task bar.

To use Go To, choose Edit, Go To (Ctrl+G). The Go To dialog box appears (Figure 6.15). Enter the ID number (row number) of the task you want to jump to in the Task Sheet, and scroll the Gantt chart to display the task bar for the selected task. To simply scroll the Gantt chart to a particular date, click on the Date text box drop-down list arrow and select the date you want to see in the Gantt chart. Click on OK to finish your Go To selection and adjust the display.

If you already clicked on a cell in a task in the Task Sheet, and you want to quickly display the task bar for that task on the Gantt chart pane at the right side of the Gantt Chart view, click on the Go To Selected Task button on the Standard toolbar.

Editing Other Task Information in the Task Information Dialog Box

So far, you've worked in the Predecessors, Advanced, and Notes tabs of the Task Information dialog box. The fastest way to display this dialog box is to double-click a cell in the task that you want to learn more about. Or click a cell in the task, and then click on the Task Information button on the Standard toolbar. You can click on any tab in the Task Information dialog box to display its options, edit them as needed, and then click on OK to close the dialog box. This section takes a brief look at the options not examined thus far.

Go to Selected Task button

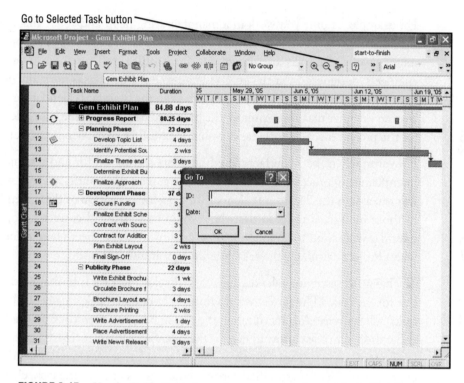

FIGURE 6.15 *Use the Go To dialog box to jump to a particular task in the Task Sheet and Gantt chart, or just the Gantt chart.*

 TIP

You can select multiple tasks by dragging across cells or holding down the Ctrl key while you click on noncontiguous tasks. Then, click on the Task Information button. This displays the Multiple Task Information dialog box so that you can change certain task settings for all the selected tasks. For example, you could apply a constraint for all the tasks or change the duration for all the tasks.

Changing the Task Calendar

In Chapter 4, you learned how to create a custom calendar that takes into account holidays, nonstandard working hours, and so on, as well as how to select that custom calendar as the base calendar for your project file. In Project 2002, you can also specify a calendar for a task, if it varies from the base calendar you've established for the project.

For example, assume you work in a manufacturing plant and you're managing the design and first-run production of a new product. Tasks early in the project might involve primarily the design and front-office staff for the company—engineers, designers, financial analysts, and so on. These tasks normally occur during a standard work day, so you would assign the Standard calendar (or your custom calendar that approximates the Standard calendar) as the base calendar for the project file. The early tasks would then follow that calendar by default.

However, when the manufacturing lines start setting up for and testing the manufacturing process, those lines typically run on three shifts, so you might want to assign the 24 Hours calendar (or a custom variation of that calendar) to those individual tasks so that they would be scheduled correctly. So, any calendar you assign to an individual task overrides the project's base calendar when Project calculates the schedule for that individual task.

To change the assigned calendar for a task, display the Task Information dialog box for the task. (The fastest way to do so is to double-click on any cell in the task.) Click on the Advanced tab in the dialog box, and then click on the Calendar drop-down list arrow to display the calendars (Figure 6.16). Click on the calendar to use in the drop-down list. If you want the specified task calendar to override any calendars specified for the resources assigned to the task, click on the Scheduling Ignores Resource Calendars check box to check it. (If you don't check that check box and the assigned resources also have calendars other than the project base calendar, Project schedules that task only within the time where

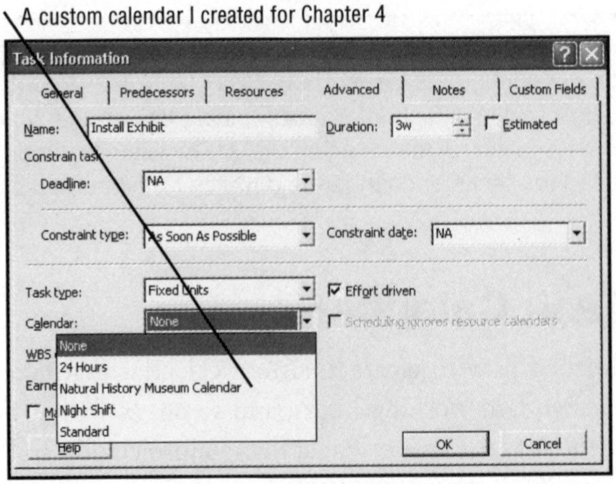

FIGURE 6.16 _To ensure proper scheduling for a task, apply a calendar to the task._

the task calendar and resource calendar coincide.) Click on OK to close the dialog box. An indicator in the Indicators column will specify that you've assigned a calendar other than the project base calendar to the task.

Changing Other Task Information

The first tab in the Task Information dialog box is the General tab (see Figure 6.17). It lets you work with general parameters for the task, like its start and finish date, if needed.

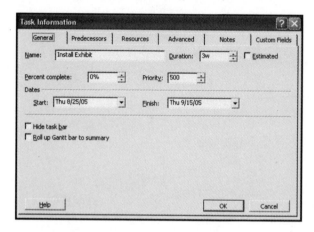

FIGURE 6.17   *Here's another opportunity to revise task basics.*

The Predecessors tab was described earlier in this chapter. It enables you to alter the task name and duration, as well as specify predecessors for the selected task to create links. The Resources tab is covered in Chapter 7, "Adding Resources into Your Project Plan." This tab enables you to assign one or more resources (coworkers, vendors, and so on) to complete the specified task.

In addition to the Constrain Task options you learned about in the preceding section, the Advanced tab (refer to Figure 6.12) offers a few more options of interest. The Mark Task As Milestone check box converts the task bar to a milestone marker without changing the duration.

If you want to use a specialized coding system, enter the code to use for the task in the WBS Code text box, as described in Chapter 5. If you want the number of resources you add to a task to influence task durations, make sure the Effort Driven text box remains checked. The next tab, Notes, is where you enter and edit notes about the selected task, as described in Chapter 4.

NOTE

As an example, you might want to use WBS codes with a special prefix or numbering scheme. See Chapter 5, "Working with Outlining," for more about creating and using WBS codes.

The final tab, Custom Fields, displays any fields you've customized or set up in the current project file so that you can view or edit the custom field information for the current task. Chapter 13, "Working with the Different Project Views," shows you how to create custom fields, such as fields that perform calculations.

Chapter 7

**Adding
Resources
into Your
Project Plan**

In This Chapter

◆ Defining resources in Project

◆ How the resources you select affect the schedule

◆ Adding work and material resources for your project

◆ Determining how much each resource will cost

◆ Controlling how a resource's time is scheduled

The first several chapters of this book have introduced you to the key concepts you need to be familiar with when using Project. In those chapters, you learned the steps for building and scheduling the tasks associated with your plan. All the information you've compiled so far, however, doesn't answer the most critical question of all: How in the world is everything on your to-do list going to get done?

What Is Effort-Driven (Resource-Driven) Scheduling?

Resources complete the tasks you've specified in a plan or schedule. When you think about resources, coworkers or team members may come to mind first, but *resources* can refer to the whole range of essentials. For example, a resource can be an outside freelancer or consulting firm, a vendor that provides printing or manufacturing, or raw materials or supplies needed for a project, such as paper that needs to be purchased for a printing job. It can even be a piece of equipment you might need to use during a project, whether that equipment exists in your company and is shared by others or is leased from an outside firm. In a nutshell, *resources* include all the people, supplies, and equipment used to complete tasks in a project.

You face several challenges when you try to assign resources to a project:

◆ Generally, you have a limited number of resources available to you. That is, you can't ask just anyone in your company to handle a task for you. You have to work with the resources made available to you and figure out how to maximize the contribution each one makes.

◆ You're usually competing with other project managers for each resource's time. For example, a resource from your company's marketing department might be handling items for you and five other colleagues in a given week.

◆ Even if money is no object, you can't just hand an entire project off to outside resources. It takes an insider—you or someone else—to coordinate and manage contracted outside resources and ensure that your tasks don't suffer because of an external resource's commitments to other clients.

◆ Even in the most extreme circumstances, certain tasks require at least a minimal amount of a resource's time. For example, if a task requires a resource to fly from a faraway city to your city with an approval mockup of a new product, and you know the flight plus the commute from the airport requires at least eight hours, you simply can't ask the resource to do it in six hours. People like to deliver excellent, timely work, but most people haven't perfected the ability to warp time.

If you've had any education in economics, you'll recognize that the preceding points sound a lot like the concept of *scarcity*. When resources in a marketplace are scarce, competition for the resources increases so that people pay more for them and have to use them more wisely.

With scarcity of resources (or anything else), what you can accomplish is limited by your access to the resources to do it. You can't make steel, for example, if scarcity makes coal so expensive that you can't afford to buy it for the furnace.

Project takes resource scarcity into account by using *effort-driven scheduling* (also called *resource-driven scheduling*) by default. Under effort-driven scheduling, Project may adjust a task's duration to take into account both the amount of work the task requires and the number of resources assigned to it.

For example, suppose that you have a task with a duration of four days, and the default calendar for the project calls for 8-hour work days. This means that the task's work in hours is 32. Suppose, however, that you assign two full-time resources to the task, each of whom works the full eight hours per day. Under effort-driven scheduling, Project correctly adjusts the task's duration to two days. Each resource will apply 16 hours of work to the task over two days, completing the full 32 hours. So Project adjusts the finish date for the task accordingly. In contrast, if you assigned only one resource and then adjusted its assignment so that it worked less than full time, Project would extend the task's schedule.

 NOTE

You can override the effort-driven duration for any task. See the "Overriding an Effort-Driven Duration" section in Chapter 8.

With effort-driven scheduling, the resources you select have a critical impact on your plan. As you create resources and make the related choices that are described in this chapter, keep in mind how those choices might affect the overall schedule. If you encounter difficulties or conflicts as you create and work with resources, read Chapter 9, "Resolving Overallocations and Overbooked Resources," and Chapter 10, "Optimizing the Schedule."

Viewing and Using the Project Resource Sheet

The Task Sheet, which you learned to work with in earlier chapters, specifies *what* needs to happen in a project and *when* it needs to happen. (I'll assume that someone in your company also knows *why* it needs to happen.) The Resource Sheet for your schedule enables you to specify who will make it happen, and how it will be done.

Use the Resource Sheet to build the list of resources you'll need to complete all the tasks you listed on the Task Sheet for the schedule. To view the Resource Sheet, shown in Figure 7.1, choose View, Resource Sheet. Or, if you have the View Bar displayed, scroll down the View Bar and click on the Resource Sheet icon. Just as each row in the Task Sheet holds information about a single task, each row in the Resource Sheet holds details about a single resource. Each column represents a particular field or type of information. You can add columns that show information Project calculates, or custom columns to hold special resource information.

To select a cell in the Resource Sheet, click on it or drag to select (highlight) groups of cells. Alternately, use the arrow keys to move the cell selector around.

Click on a cell to select it | Click on a row heading to select a whole row | Click on a column heading to select a whole column | Each row holds information about a single resource

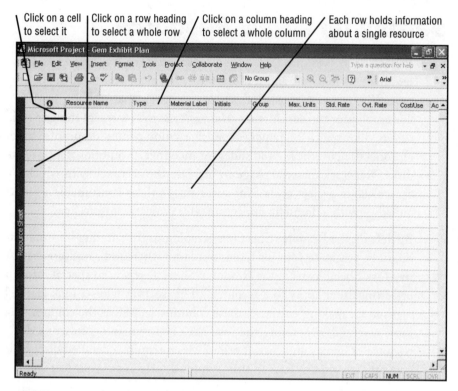

FIGURE 7.1 *You can use the Resource Sheet to add resources to your project file.*

To select an entire column or row, click on the column name or row number. Right-clicking on any selection opens a shortcut menu with commands that you can perform on the selection. To insert a new blank resource at the selected location in the Resource Sheet, for example, you can select a row, right-click, and then click on New Resource on the shortcut menu.

 NOTE

You can make adjustments to the size and position of columns or add columns in the Resource Sheet, just as you did in the Task Sheet. The steps are virtually the same. To learn more, see the section "Adjusting the Task Sheet" in Chapter 4, "Setting Up a Project." One important column you might want to add is for resources' e-mail addresses.

Setting Up a New Resource

Project offers two different types of resources: work resources and material resources. When you add resources to your plan, you need to specify their type. *Work resources* consist of people or entities that perform work for you, like employees and consultants. *Material resources* represent things a task consumes, like reams of paper, expensive color copies or proofs, blueprint reproduction, overheads and slides for meetings, promotional kits, or storage disks. You track material usage to increase the accuracy with which Project can calculate project costs. Not surprisingly, these consumables can add up quickly—with a dramatic impact on your project's bottom line.

By default, the Resource Sheet has 12 columns for entering information that might be crucial to your plan, plus a column where indicators appear. (As for the Task Sheet, icons in the Resource Sheet alert you to special information or settings that apply to a resource.) This section takes a look at the basic method for making entries in these columns, as well as the columns that are most essential in defining the resource. The remaining columns deal with resource calendars and costs, both of which require a detailed discussion. I'll cover those columns later in this chapter, after you get your feet wet here.

 WEB

If you want to practice adding and working with resources in this chapter and the next, you can download the Gem Exhibit Plan Chapter 7 file from the Premier Press download page at www.premierpressbooks.com/downloads.asp. This file contains a list of tasks but no resources.

Work Resources

To start a new work resource, click on the Resource Name cell of a new blank row in the Resource Sheet and type in the resource name. As you type, the Enter button and Cancel button appear beside the text entry box above the column headings (see Figure 7.2). To finish entering the name, click on Enter. Project fills in some default information about the resource, such as *Work* as the resource type and *100%* in the Max. Units column. After you enter the resource name, you can press the Tab key to move to any column to the right, or press Enter to move down to the next row and list all resources by name only.

Cancel button   Enter button   Entry box

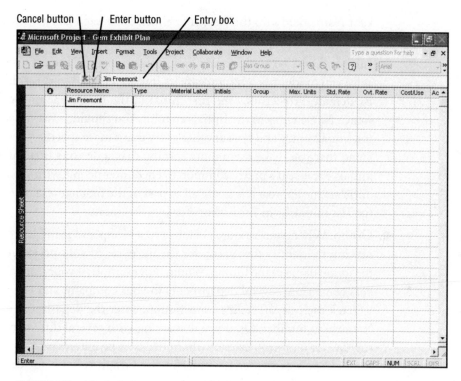

FIGURE 7.2   *Navigate in the Resource Sheet as you do in the Task Sheet.*

 CAUTION

To remove the contents of a cell in the Resource Sheet, right-click on the cell, and then click on Clear Contents to empty the cell while keeping the resource in place. Chapter 8 covers deleting resources from tasks and the project plan.

The style you use to create resources is up to you. You can use the Tab key after each entry to move across the row and complete each field entry for that resource. Or you can simply enter all the resource names, and then come back to each row and fill in the details. As noted at the start of this section, several of the columns or fields are basic, yet essential in identifying each resource as you assign it to tasks in your plan:

◆ **Resource Name.** Enter the full name for the resource, such as the name of a team member, supply vendor, or independent contractor. (If you want to sort the list of resources by last name at any time, enter the resources in this fashion: **last name, first name**. Or, add a custom

Last Name field into the Resource Sheet, enter each last name there, and sort by that column.)

♦ **Initials.** Don't be afraid to use long resource names. Project also enables you to identify a resource by its initials, entered in this column. By default, Project uses the first initial of the first name of the Resource Name entry in the Initials column. You should, however, select the Initials entry and type another entry that's more specific. I recommend that you make them more specific than a person's first and last initials because it's pretty common to encounter people with the same initials. One approach is to use all or part of the first name, along with the last initial, as in JimF, short for Jim Freemont.

♦ **Group.** When your resource belongs to a group and it might be significant to identify that group for the purposes of your project, enter the group name in the Group column. For example, if your team members come from several departments in your company, and you want to track each department's contribution, enter the department name or tracking number. Or, if you're working with several different contractors for a project, each of whom needs to be entered as a separate resource, you can enter Contract in the Group column for each of them to be able to track their collective performance.

 TIP

You can fill entries down a column in the Resource Sheet, just as you can fill entries in the Task Sheet. Select the cell holding the entry to fill (copy), and then drag the fill handle in the lower-right corner of the cell.

♦ **Max. Units.** The default entry for this column, 100%, means that for each scheduled work day, the resource offers one person (or machine, and so on) for the full duration of the resource's work day according to the calendar assigned for the resource. This is known as a single *assignment unit*. Entries of less than 100% indicate part-time work (more on that in Chapter 9), but entries of more than 100% don't assign overtime (more on overtime in Chapter 10). Entries of more than 100% mean that the resource might be offering additional people (or machines) for assignments. So, for example, if a resource offers four people to handle each task, you would change the Max. Units entry for the resource to 400%.

When you select the Max. Units field in a row, spinner buttons appear at the right side of the cell, so you can use the mouse to increase or decrease the entry rather than typing it in. (Alternately, you can specify assignment units in the Max. Units column in decimal values, with 1 in decimal terms being equivalent to 100% in percentage terms. To change this setting, use the Show Assignment Units As A drop-down list on the Schedule tab of the Options dialog box, described in Chapter 28, "Customizing Microsoft Project.")

◆ **Code.** This column at the far right side of the Resource Sheet enables you to enter an alphanumeric code to identify the resource. This code might be a department number that corresponds to your entry in the Group column, or a unique number, such as a Purchase Order number that you obtained for payment of the resource.

After you enter this basic information about several resources, your Resource Sheet might resemble the one shown in Figure 7.3.

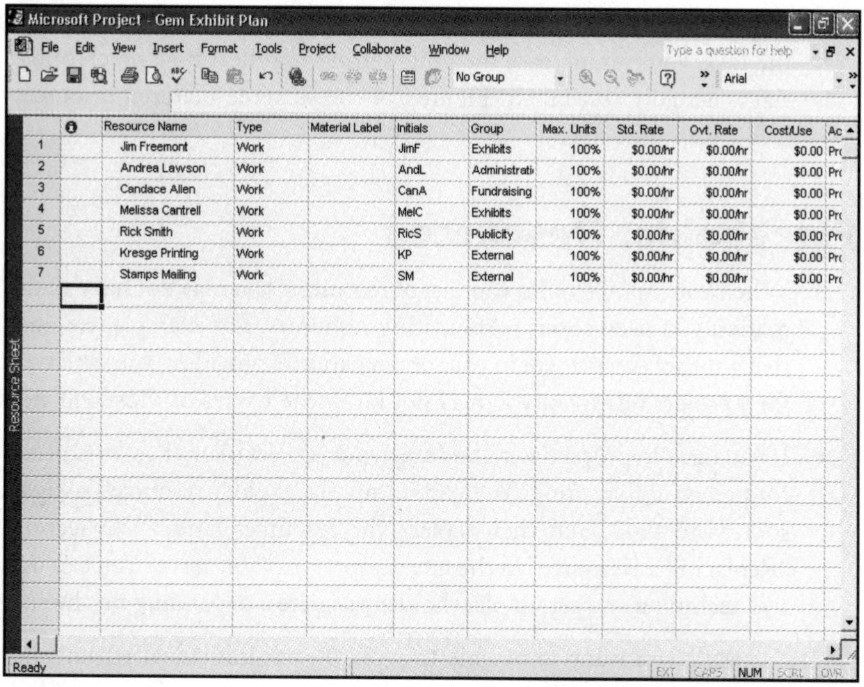

FIGURE 7.3   *Here's what the Resource Sheet looks like after you sketch out resources.*

Material Resources

You use the same process to enter material resources—make the field entries and then press Tab to move between fields—but you need to be sure to choose Material from the Type drop-down list and fill in the Material Label column. The *material label* represents the quantities or units you're using to measure the amount of material purchased and consumed.

For example, if you're buying sets of color proofs, you could enter **set**. If you'll be paying for slides by the page, enter **page**. If your project will consume other materials by the gross, dozen, or thousand, enter the appropriate material label. (The amount you enter in the Std. Rate field should correspond with the material label you've entered, as you'll learn shortly.)

Optionally, you can include an entry in the Initials, Group columns, and Code columns, but note that you cannot make an entry in the Max. Units column. Project assumes a 1 for this column, which can stand for a single item, a ream, a gross, or any other measure you need to use. (Just add a note to the resource entry to clarify which measure you're using.) When you assign the resource to the task, you can increase the units setting to reflect how much of the material is actually consumed. Figure 7.4 shows some material resources added into a Resource Sheet.

Placeholder Resources

When you initially build your list of resources, you may not have all the information you need about participating resources. For example, you may know that another department in your organization is providing you with two people for a project team, but you may not know the names of those individuals.

If you need to proceed with building your project plan, there's no need to wait for precise information. You can set up placeholder resources, assign the resources to tasks, and then replace the resources later. (The section called "Replacing a Resource" in the next chapter explains how.) You can use one of two techniques to set up placeholder resources, depending on the situation.

◆ If you want to be able to replace each individual resource by name later in the project, you can enter placeholder names by job description, such as Engineer1, Engineer2, and so on.

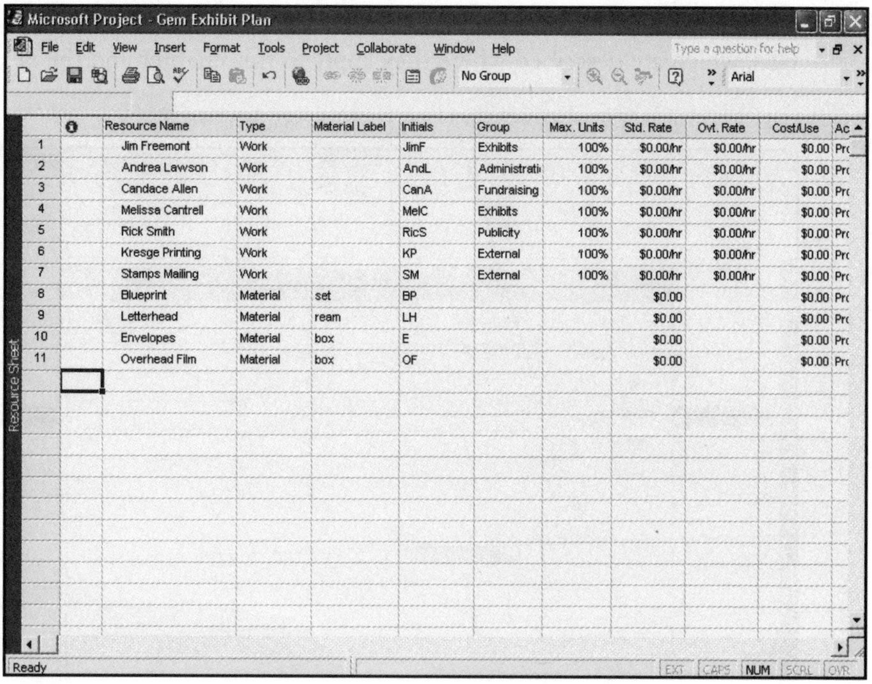

FIGURE 7.4 *Material resources require the Material option in the Type column.*

◆ If you don't think you need to name each individual resource at a later time, you can use a more generic resource name describing the resources' function, such as Programmer. Then, depending on how many programmers the other department or outside resource will provide, increase the Max. Units setting on the Resource Sheet accordingly. For example, if you will be getting help from three programmers for each task, set the Max. Units setting to 300%. You can then adjust the units setting as needed for individual task assignments.

Displaying Resource Information

If you're not comfortable working in the spreadsheet-like cells of the Resource Sheet and would prefer a more convenient format for entering and editing the information about a resource, you can use the Resource Information dialog box shown in Figure 7.5. The General tab of the Resource Information dialog box enables you to enter basic task information, as well as other schedule-related information. The dialog box also offers three other tabs, which are described where they apply in this chapter and the next.

Enter the resource's e-mail address here / | Resource Information button

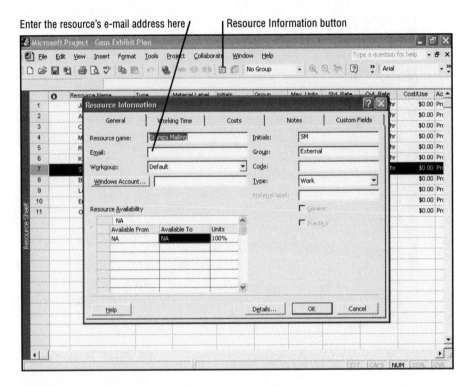

FIGURE 7.5 *After you open this dialog box from the Resource Sheet, you can use it to enter and edit resource information and options.*

To open the Resource Information dialog box for a resource in any view in Project that shows all or part of the Resource Sheet, start by clicking in a cell in the row for the desired resource. Then choose Project, Resource Information (or right-click and then click on Resource Information). Alternately, press Shift+F2 or click on the Resource Information button on the Standard toolbar. Enter or edit information about the resource in the dialog box, and then click on OK to close the dialog box and accept the entries you made. Your changes appear in the appropriate columns for the selected task in the Resource Sheet.

When you open the Resource Information dialog box for a material resource, the dialog box Working Time tab is grayed out, or disabled, as are some of the choices on the General tab. Logically, the tab and fields in question don't really apply to material resources, so Project makes them unavailable.

TIP

You also can display information about a resource by double-clicking in any cell in that resource's row in the Resource Sheet.

TIP

You can create a new resource by clicking on a blank row of the Resource Sheet, opening the Resource Information dialog box, entering information about the new resource, and clicking on OK.

Assigning Costs

There's a cost associated with using every resource, even when the resource is seemingly free because it comes from within your company. (Some costs are associated with tasks rather than resources. I cover task costs later in this section, as well.) In fact, tracking your use of internal resources throughout the year can be useful during year-end budgeting, when your company determines how costs from administrative or service departments are allocated to (charged to) departments that are profit centers. For example, you don't want your department to be charged for a third of the marketing department's time if you only used about 10 percent of that time (based on the hours tracked in your project), while two other profit centers each used 45 percent.

Similarly, you want to be smart about using resources with the correct responsibility level for projects, and resource costs can help you make such decisions. For example, say that one task in a project involves calling various companies for examples of annual reports to use as idea-starters for the project. A designer in your company is paid about $20 per hour, and an administrative assistant is paid $15 per hour, and both resources have the ability and the time to make the calls. In this case, it's much more efficient to have the less expensive resource, the administrative assistant, handle the calls. Such a strategy frees up more of the designer's time for true creative work, yielding better financial and design results on your project and more time for other projects.

NOTE

If your company doesn't require you to track internal resource costs, you can still enter a standard rate (Std. Rate) of some type (even a dummy rate) for the resource. Project needs a standard rate for some of its calculations, such as task cost calculations.

Three columns on the Resource Sheet enable you to assign default costs to the work performed by a resource. For most of these you can simply select the cell and make your entry.

◆ **Std. Rate.** Enter the cost for work performed by a work resource during normal hours. To indicate an hourly rate, simply enter the hourly cost, such as **20** for $20 per hour. However, if the resource is charging or will be paid by the minute (m), day (d), or week (w), enter the appropriate abbreviation along with your cost, such as 2000/w for $2,000 per week. You also can enter yearly salary amounts using the y abbreviation, and Project calculates the appropriate compensation for the actual length of the task. For material resources, enter the cost per unit—material label—for the resource. Make sure you choose a cost that's consistent with the unit of measure you entered in the Material Label column. For example, if one unit of the resource equals one set of color proofs, enter the cost for the entire set of color proofs (such as **500** for $500) as the standard rate, not the cost per proof page. If each resource unit equals a single ream of paper, enter the cost per ream as the standard rate, not the cost per 10-ream box. If you specified thousand as the material label, enter the cost per thousand.

◆ **Ovt. Rate.** Let's say the resource might be working overtime on your project and your company is willing to pay a premium for the overtime (or is required to by law, as for hourly nonexempt workers). Enter the overtime rate for the resource in this column, using the same method and abbreviations described for the Std. Rate column. This helps Project calculate the additional cost of overtime work assigned in the project during estimating and tracking. (You have to authorize overtime manually in order for Project to use the overtime rate in its calculations. The section called "Authorizing Overtime Work for a Task" in Chapter 10 discusses this technique.)

You cannot enter an overtime rate for material resources. However, if the material resource cost will vary, you can set up different cost rate tables for it, as described in the "Creating Variable Pay Rates with Cost Rate Tables" section later in this chapter.

◆ **Cost/Use.** A work or material resource might have a set cost every time you use it. This cost might be the total cost for using the resource, or it might supplement the hourly rate. For example, a courier service might charge you a set fee per delivery rather than an hourly rate. Or a resource might charge you a set travel fee for visits to your office in addition to an hourly rate. Or you might incur a delivery cost for each shipment of a material resource. Enter an amount in the Cost/Use column (such as **15** for $15) to charge that fee to your project each time you assign the resource to a task and the task is completed.

 TIP

If you're a consultant and need to provide both schedules and cost estimates for clients, assigning costs to every resource can help you build a reasonably accurate cost estimate. Unless the client is willing to pay for budget overruns, you should build some cushioning into the cost estimate you provide (especially if the client's requirements are ill-defined).

Setting How Resource Costs Are Calculated

As you just learned, the costs for a resource can be based on units of work completed, a per-use fee, or both. Most people aren't foolish enough to pay for work before it's completed, however—and it isn't a standard accounting practice. On the other hand, it's not reasonable to expect all task costs for any given task to meet your project's bottom line after the work on the task is completed, especially if the task lasts more than a week or so.

To get a realistic picture of the costs incurred for your project at any given date, you need to specify the correct option for the resource's costs using the Accrue At column in the Resource Sheet, or the Cost Accrual drop-down list on the Costs tab of the Resource Information dialog box. After you click on a cell in the Accrue At column, a drop-down list arrow appears at the right end of the cell. Click on this arrow to display the Accrue At options (see Figure 7.6), which are identical to the Cost Accrual drop-down list options on the Costs tab of the Resource Information dialog box.

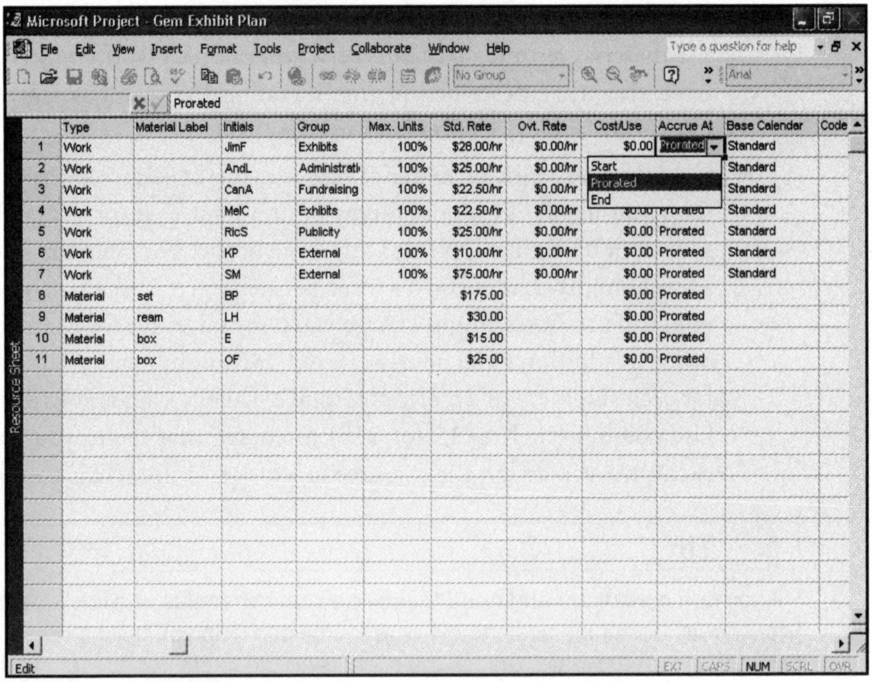

FIGURE 7.6 *Use the drop-down list to select an Accrue At method.*

Then click on the method you want to select for the current resource:

- ◆ **Start.** Specifies that a resource's total cost for a task is expended as soon as work on the task starts. Use this method if you need to pay for contract work when the work begins. This choice also applies when a resource has only a per-use cost that's due in advance, such as having to pay for a supply item when you order it rather than when it's consumed.

- ◆ **Prorated.** Under this method (the default), costs hit your project's bottom line as the work progresses. For example, if a resource charges $10 per hour and you've told Project that the resource has completed 10 hours of work on a task, under this Accrue At method, the project shows $100 in expenses to date for the task. Use this method when tracking expenses for resources within your company or for resources that you need to pay on a monthly basis.

CAUTION

If you use the Prorated Accrue At method for resources that you work with only on a per-use fee structure, it can lead to inaccurate reporting. You might owe the full fee even if you need the resource for less time. For example, if you rent certain equipment, there might be a per-use minimum fee that's due in advance. Make sure that you change the Accrue At method to Start or End for such resources.

◆ **End.** This method specifies that the expense will officially be charged to the project when the task is completed. Use this when you need to approve work before payment, or when payment isn't due until work on a task is completed.

Creating Variable Pay Rates with Cost Rate Tables

To accommodate businesses' ongoing efforts to trim and accurately predict costs, Project offers precise, flexible tracking methods. You can set up cost rate tables to help you account for moving targets such as the following:

◆ **Scheduled pay rate or material cost increases, or volume purchase decreases.** If an internal resource's pay will increase on a particular date during the schedule, Project can automatically increase the standard rate and overtime rate for the resource on the date you specify in the resource's default cost rate table. If the cost for a material resource will increase starting on a particular date, you can indicate when the standard rate will change. Similarly, if an external resource's rates will increase or decrease (due to surpassing a minimum volume breakpoint) on a particular date (typically the start of a new calendar year or the effective date for a new contract), you can have Project automatically apply the rate increase when it kicks in by specifying the rate change on the resource's default cost rate table.

◆ **One resource, many rates.** For some resources, you might pay different rates depending on the nature of the work needed to complete different tasks. You'll typically encounter such a cost structure when you're working with an outside resource, such as a consulting company. Such companies usually charge one rate for work by a partner or account manager, and another rate for work performed by assistants.

Or, for example, the firm might charge one rate for research, another for designing a campaign or publication, and another for account administration. You need to create a separate cost rate table for each rate, and then assign the appropriate cost table for each task you assign to the resource. This is described in Chapter 8 in the section "Changing the Cost Table for an Assignment."

 TIP

If a consulting firm doesn't provide a rate reduction for work handled by assistant-level folks, ask for such a reduction to reduce your costs.

◆ **Mixing hourly fees with per-use costs.** A resource might charge a per-use fee or other type of fee for some types of tasks, but not others. For example, if an outside consulting firm charges a fixed fee for preparing your monthly company newsletter but charges you an hourly fee for all other work, you'll need separate cost rate tables for the resource. One cost rate table would hold the per-use fee, and the other would hold the hourly rate. Then you could assign the rate table that applies to each task assignment.

◆ **Periods with special rates.** If you have to convince a resource to work at a time when that resource wouldn't typically be working, that resource might charge a premium rate. For example, a resource might charge double the hourly rate for work during the week between Christmas and New Year's Day. In such a case, you would enter the increase's starting date and rate on a row of the resource's default cost rate table. Then, on the next row, enter the date when the rate would return to normal, along with the normal rate.

You use the Resource Information dialog box to create cost rate tables for a resource. Follow these steps to edit or adjust a cost rate table:

1. In the Resource Sheet, click in a cell in the row for the resource for which you want to create a cost rate table. Then click on the Resource Information button on the Standard toolbar. Or, double-click in a cell in the resource row. The Resource Information dialog box will appear.

2. Click on the Costs tab to display its options. The Cost Rate Tables area of the dialog box offers five tabs, each of which represents a separate cost rate table. The A (Default) tab's rates will be used for the

resource unless you create entries on another cost rate table tab (B through E) and specify that tab for an assignment, as described later in the chapter.

3. To specify a rate change for the resource, enter an Effective Date on the next empty row of the tab—in this case, the A (Default) tab. Then, enter the new standard rate or overtime rate in the appropriate cell on that row, or a new per-use cost on that row. You have to change each rate. Project does not calculate a new overtime rate if you change the standard rate. You can enter positive or negative percentages to have Project calculate each rate increase or decrease, respectively. For example, if you know an internal resource will receive a 4 percent pay increase on a particular date, you can enter that increase percentage as shown in Figure 7.7 rather than calculate dollars and cents.

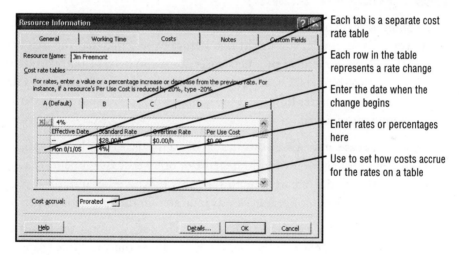

FIGURE 7.7   *You can enter a new rate on each row of a cost rate table. Each table holds up to 25 rates.*

4. Repeat Step 3 as many times as needed to build the A (Default) cost rate table. Each cost rate table can hold up to 25 rate changes.

5. To create a new cost rate table, click on another tab under Cost Rate Tables.

6. If you're working with the first row on another Cost Rate Table tab, don't edit its Effective Date entry. This will designate the rate entries

on that row as the "base" or "default" rates for the new cost table. Otherwise, create the rates on the table as described in Steps 3 and 4.

7. Repeat Steps 5 and 6 to specify additional cost rate tables. You can create up to five for each project file.

8. When you finish making cost rate table changes for the resource, click on OK to close the Resource Information dialog box.

Once you've established an effective date and rate change, Project automatically applies the new rate to work completed and materials consumed starting on that effective date.

Working with Fixed Costs (Assigned to Tasks)

Some tasks have a particular cost no matter which resource handles the work. For example, you might know from experience that the freight for a particular shipment of products costs approximately $1,000 if you use either of two shippers. Or, an external contractor might have quoted a flat fee for a task, no matter how great the quantity of work resources, materials, or equipment required.

In such a case, if the cost won't vary, assign a fixed cost for the task rather than creating a resource entry with a per-use or other cost assignment. You have to go back to Gantt Chart view to start this process—because fixed costs are assigned to tasks, not resources—as indicated in the following steps:

1. Choose View, Gantt Chart, if you're not already at the Gantt Chart view. Or click on the Gantt Chart icon in the View Bar. (Alternately, you could go to the Task Sheet view. Chapter 13 gives you more information on the various views and how to display them.)

2. Open the View menu, point to Table, and click on Cost. (You also could right-click on the Select All button where the sheet row and column headings intersect, and then choose Cost from the shortcut menu that appears.) The Task Sheet pane at the left side of the view will change to display columns specific to tracking costs for the tasks, as shown in Figure 7.8.

3. Select the Fixed Cost cell for the task for which you want to assign a fixed cost.

Enter fixed costs in this column

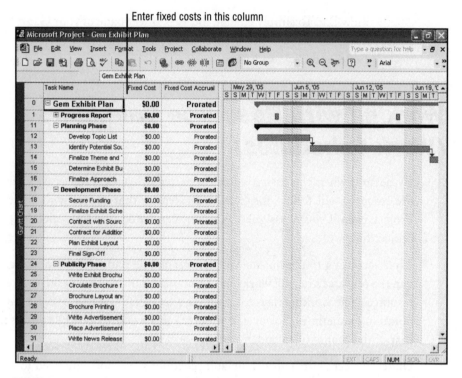

FIGURE 7.8   *You enter a fixed cost in the Cost table of the Task Sheet rather than on the Resource Sheet.*

 CAUTION

Just as you don't enter durations for summary tasks, you don't make Fixed Cost field entries for summary tasks. That's because the summary task rows in the Cost table present calculated cost values for the subtasks in the summary group. So, if you enter a fixed cost for one task in a summary group, the Fixed Cost field in the summary task for that group is recalculated automatically to include the newly added subtask fixed cost.

4. Type the amount (in dollars) of the fixed cost. For example, type **500** for $500. Press Enter or click on the Enter button next to the text entry box to finish entering the fixed cost.

5. (Optional) Return to the view in which you were working by using a choice on the View menu. For example, open the View menu and click on Resource Sheet or click on the Resource Sheet icon in the

View Bar. To simply change the Task Sheet pane of your Gantt Chart view back to its normal entry mode, open the View menu, point to Table, and click on Entry.

Working with Resource Calendars (Work Schedules)

By default, when you assign a work resource to a task, Project assumes that the resource will follow the Standard calendar that comes with Microsoft Project, even if you've assigned another calendar or a custom calendar to the project file.

Thus according to the normal work day schedule under the Standard calendar, the resource's typical work day is 8 hours. Under this scenario, it takes the resource three working days to complete a task that's 24 hours (three days) in duration. Sometimes, however, a resource's real working schedule differs from that of the Standard calendar or the project file.

Under Project's effort-driven default scheduling method, you need to ensure that you specify the real working schedule for each resource to develop an accurate schedule. For example, if the base calendar for the project is set to 24 hours, but the resource works only 8 hours per day, the durations for the tasks you assign to that resource need to be three times longer than the base calendar would cause Project to assign.

Assume you create a calendar for a resource that includes the resource's nonworking days (such as vacation days). Project will change the schedule for any task to which you assign the resource so that the task no longer falls on a nonworking day for the resource. For example, let's say a task is scheduled to start on Monday, 12/8/03. You assign a resource using a calendar that indicates the resource has a vacation day (nonworking day) on 12/8/03. Project will then reschedule the task to begin on 12/9/03, the next available working day for the assigned resource. So generally speaking, the resource calendar overrides the project base calendar.

NOTE

You learned in Chapters 4 and 6 that you assign a base calendar to the project as a whole, and you can assign another calendar to individual tasks as well. Now you're learning to assign calendars to individual resources. This may lead you to wonder how Project handles conflicts between the calendars when a particular task has two or three calendars in the mix.

By default, a task with only an alternate task calendar, or a resource with an alternate calendar assigned, will follow the task or resource calendar rather than the project calendar. Thus, Project overrides the project base calendar and schedules the task according to the task calendar or resource calendar. If a task has both an added task calendar and a resource using an alternate calendar, Project will first disregard the project base calendar. Then it will compare the task's calendar and the resource's calendar, and will schedule the task only within the time when those two calendars coincide.

You don't have to specify a certain calendar for a material resource—and in fact, you can't. Material resources don't have working time or a calendar associated with them.

Choosing a Calendar

Use the Base Calendar column of the Resource Sheet to select the appropriate working calendar for a resource. The base calendars available for resources are the same as those available for projects. The 24 Hours calendar runs round the clock, seven days a week. The Standard calendar provides 40 hours per week, scheduled 8 A.M. to noon and 1 P.M. to 5 P.M., Monday through Friday. The Night Shift schedule also offers 40 hours per week, scheduled from Monday evening through early Saturday morning. If you created a custom calendar for your project, as described in Chapter 4, it appears on the list as well.

To change the base calendar entry for a resource, click on its Base Calendar cell in the Resource Sheet view. (Choose View, Resource Sheet to change back to that view, if necessary.) A drop-down list arrow appears at the right end of the text entry box. Click this arrow to display the calendar choices (see Figure 7.9), click on the calendar you want, and then press Enter or click on the Enter button next to the text entry box.

Specify the calendar the resource will follow

	Type	Material Label	Initials	Group	Max. Units	Std. Rate	Ovt. Rate	Cost/Use	Accrue At	Base Calendar	Code
1	Work		JimF	Exhibits	100%	$28.00/hr	$0.00/hr	$0.00	Prorated	Standard	
2	Work		AndL	Administrati	100%	$25.00/hr	$0.00/hr	$0.00	Pror	24 Hours	
3	Work		CanA	Fundraising	100%	$22.50/hr	$0.00/hr	$0.00	Pror	Natural History Museum	
4	Work		MelC	Exhibits	100%	$22.50/hr	$0.00/hr	$0.00	Pror	Night Shift	
5	Work		RicS	Publicity	100%	$25.00/hr	$0.00/hr	$0.00	Pror	Standard	
6	Work		KP	External	100%	$10.00/hr	$0.00/hr	$0.00	Prorated	Standard	
7	Work		SM	External	100%	$75.00/hr	$0.00/hr	$0.00	Prorated	Standard	
8	Material	set	BP			$175.00		$0.00	Prorated		
9	Material	ream	LH			$30.00		$0.00	Prorated		
10	Material	box	E			$15.00		$0.00	Prorated		
11	Material	box	OF			$25.00		$0.00	Prorated		

FIGURE 7.9 *You choose a calendar for the resource on the Resource Sheet.*

TIP

To account for vacation schedules, you may find it best to create a custom calendar for each resource. If you base the custom calendar for the resource on the custom calendar you created for your organization or project, you won't have to mark company holidays again for the resource's calendar.

TIP

If most of your resources will be using the same calendar, you can fill the calendar selection. Just specify the appropriate Base Calendar choice for the first resource, make sure the Base Calendar cell for that resource is selected, and then drag the fill handle (in the lower-right corner of the cell selector) down the column.

Setting Work Resource Availability

You may find yourself competing for a highly desirable work resource. For example, a resource may be tied up with other projects until three weeks after your project starts. Or, you may only have the opportunity to use a resource during a specific one-week period. In such cases, rather than tediously marking nonworking days in the resource's base calendar (see the next and final part of this section), you should instead specify availability dates for the resource.

Similarly, if you're sharing a resource with another department and the resource is only available to you during certain work periods, Project offers a fast availability setting to account for that—which is faster than adjusting the resource's working calendar. Project uses availability settings and the resource's base calendar together to determine whether a resource can take on a task and to calculate how long it will take the resource to complete the task.

Be aware that Project treats the interaction between the availability setting and the task schedule differently than the interaction between the resource's calendar and the task schedule. As you learned at the beginning of this section, when the resource's calendar has nonworking time or reduced working hours marked, Project will reschedule the task to follow the nonworking time or otherwise conform to the resource's work availability. On the other hand, if you assign a resource to a task and that task occurs during a period for which the resource is not available, Project leaves the task schedule as-is and marks the resource as overallocated. If you change back to the Resource Sheet view (with View, Resource Sheet), you'll see that the resource's name appears in red to indicate that the resource is overallocated.

So, the method that you use—changing the resource's base calendar or adjusting the resource's availability—depends on whether or not you want Project to reschedule tasks based on the resource assigned. Furthermore, when you use availability settings, you have to schedule all periods during which the resource is available for your project. For any periods not specifically included within the availability periods, the resource will be considered completely unavailable (which could result in more overallocations in your schedule).

Follow these steps to change a resource's availability:

1. In the Resource Sheet, click on a cell in the row for the resource for which you want to set availability. Then click on the Resource Information button on the Standard toolbar. Or double-click on a cell in

the resource row. The Resource Information dialog box appears, with the General tab selected.

2. To specify the first date on which the resource becomes available, click on the first line in the Available From column under Resource Availability, and then enter a date or choose it from the drop-down calendar.

3. If the resource will become unavailable again after a certain date, specify that date in the Available To column on the same row. However, leave the Available To cell set to "NA" if the resource will remain available.

 TIP

If you're removing availability dates you entered for a resource, click on the Available For Entire Project option button, which removes the From and To settings.

4. Use the Units text box or spinner buttons to specify how many work units the resource will provide during the period of availability. Figure 7.10 shows an availability period designated for a resource.

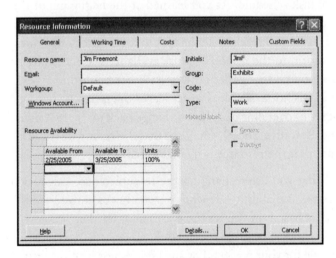

FIGURE 7.10 *If the work resource will only be available between certain dates, you can specify them on the General tab of the Resource Information dialog box.*

5. If the resource will be unavailable for additional periods during the span of your project schedule, indicate the dates and units of availability on subsequent rows under Resource Availability.

6. Click on OK to finish changing the resource's availability settings.

As your project progresses and you view the Resource Sheet, a resource's Max. Units column entry will vary according to the current system date and the periods of availability you've indicated. In other words, if you view the Resource Sheet on a date during which you've indicated the resource would not be available, the Max. Units entry for that resource will be 0%. Don't change the entry in the Resource Sheet at this point, because it will create an unwanted availability entry and could throw off Project's calculations.

Customizing a Resource Calendar

Sometimes you need to adjust the base calendar for a resource. For example, a resource might work one long shift per day, four days per week. Or a resource might be unavailable on Wednesdays, or only available to work half-time for a few days during the schedule. To ensure that the effort-driven scheduling properly adjusts the durations of tasks to which you assign this resource, and to prevent you from scheduling the resource for times when it is unavailable, make sure that you adjust the selected base calendar for any resource that has special scheduling requirements (this method is an alternative to creating a separate base calendar for the resource).

To do so, follow these steps:

1. In the Resource Sheet, use the Base Calendar column to select the working schedule that most closely approximates the actual availability of the resource.

2. In the Resource Sheet, click in a cell in the row for the resource for which you want to set availability. Then click on the Resource Information button on the Standard toolbar. Or double-click in a cell in the resource row. When the Resource Information dialog box appears, click on the Working Time tab to display it, as shown in Figure 7.11. Alternately, after you click in a cell in the resource's row, choose Tools, Change Working Time.

3. To specify whether the resource works on a particular day, click on the date you want to change on the calendar. (Click on a day column head to change that day for the whole year.) Then, in the Set Working Time For Selected Date(s) area of the dialog box, click on Working Time or Nonworking Time as needed. Dates to specify as nonworking include holidays and vacation days.

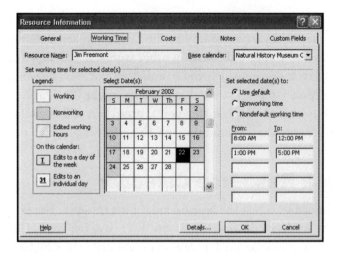

FIGURE 7.11 *You can customize the working hours and days for a resource.*

 TIP

The Use Default selection returns a date to its default scheduling according to the selected base calendar. This includes both rescheduling the task as a working or nonworking day and returning the Working Time entries to the defaults for the selected date.

Unlike a project schedule, a resource doesn't need its own custom calendar. Project already tracks individual base calendar changes you make by resource name.

4. To change the Working Time (daily working hours) for a date, select the date, and then make sure either the Working Time or Use Default option button is selected for it under For Selected Dates. In the Working Time area, edit or delete the desired From and To entries.

5. Continue scrolling the Calendar view as needed, repeating Steps 4 and 5 to change the schedule for additional dates. As you change the schedule for each date, Project indicates the edited date in the calendar by marking the date with bold and underlining and filling the date box with light-gray shading.

6. Click on OK to close the dialog box and implement the scheduling changes you've specified.

Adding a Resource Note

Just as you can add more detailed notes about a particular task you created, you can use a note to capture information about a specific resource. This feature can be particularly important when you're working with outside resources, or when a resource is handling especially complex tasks. For example, you can use a note to record detailed contact information for the person you're working with at an external vendor. Or you can add a note to a resource explaining why the resource has a per-use fee in addition to an hourly rate. You can remind yourself of the names of key clients the resource has served in the past, in case someone working with your project file is interested in knowing more about the project resources.

To enter or edit note information about a resource in the Resource Sheet, do the following:

1. Click in a cell in the row holding the resource for which you want to create a note.

2. Open the Project menu or right-click to open the resource shortcut menu. Click on Resource Notes. Alternately, click on the Resource Notes button on the Standard toolbar. The Resource Information dialog box appears, with the Notes tab selected. (If you double-click on the resource entry instead, you can then click on the Notes tab in the Resource Information dialog box.)

3. Click in the Notes text box, and then type or edit the text of your note (see Figure 7.12). Press Enter to start each new line in the note. You can add special formatting to notes using the buttons at the top of the Notes text area. The first button enables you to change the font for any text you select by dragging over it in the note. It opens the Font dialog box, covered in Chapter 17, "Other Formatting." The next three buttons align the current note line (which holds the blinking insertion point) to the left, center, and right, respectively. The fourth button adds or removes a bullet at the beginning of the current line of the note. The last button enables you to insert an embedded object into the note, such as information from Excel or a bitmap image. Chapter 20 provides more information on working with embedded objects. If you highlight and delete all of this text, Project removes the note from the resource altogether.

Resource Notes button

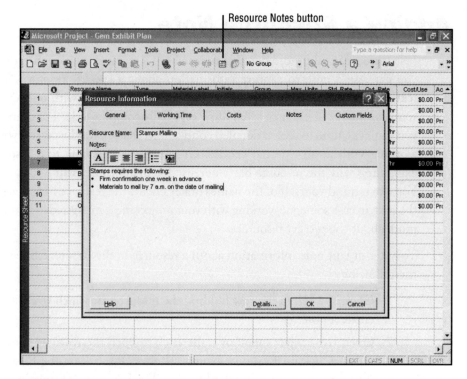

FIGURE 7.12 *Use the Notes tab in the Resource Information dialog box to enter and format your notes about a resource.*

4. Click on OK to close the Resource Information dialog box.

After you add a note to a resource, you can point to the note indicator on the Resource Sheet to display the note in a pop-up box.

Chapter 8

Assigning Resources to Specific Tasks

In This Chapter

◆ Assigning a resource

◆ Verifying resource availability

◆ Fine-tuning schedules for tasks

◆ Removing a resource

◆ Viewing and editing assignments

◆ Sharing resources between files

Assigning a Resource to a Task

Until now, this book has described tasks and resources as somewhat separate, discrete entities. You enter information about tasks in one part of Project and information about resources in another. In this section, you'll learn to mesh these two forms of information in your schedule.

When you specify that a particular resource will work on a particular task, you create what's called an *assignment* in Microsoft Project. If you've specified that two resources will be working on a task, you've created two assignments. If you specify that a particular resource will be working on 10 tasks, you've created 10 assignments for that resource.

Keep in mind that the resources you assign to a particular task might cause Project to adjust the task's start or finish date depending on the availability of the resource. If a resource assignment causes a schedule change you don't want, use one of the methods described later in this section to choose a different resource for the task.

To assign resources to a particular task, you need to return to the location where you list the tasks for your schedule, the Task Sheet in the Gantt Chart view, or (in most cases) another task-oriented view, like the Task Sheet view. To speed up your work with resources, you might also want to display the

Resource Management toolbar by right-clicking on any toolbar onscreen and choosing Resource Management.

 NOTE

You can also work with task and resource information in other views. Chapter 13, "Working with the Different Project Views," introduces more of the available views and helps you work with task and resource information. Most of the options in other views, however, work like the ones described here.

If you're most comfortable working in the Task Sheet, you might prefer to assign resources there by using the Resource Names column, which provides a drop-down list of available resources. Switch to the Gantt Chart view, if necessary, by choosing View, Gantt Chart, or by clicking on the Gantt Chart icon in the View Bar. (If you also need to redisplay the default Entry table in the Task Sheet, choose View, Table, Entry, or right-click the Select All button in the upper-left corner of the sheet and then click on Entry in the shortcut menu.) Scroll down the Task Sheet pane so that it shows the Resource Names column. Click in the cell for the task to which you want to assign a resource. If you remember the full resource name, type it into the selected cell and press Enter. Otherwise, click on the drop-down list arrow that appears at the right end of the cell. Click on the name of the resource you want (see Figure 8.1), and then press Enter or click on the Enter button.

 TIP

If you type the name of a brand-new resource in the Resource Names column of the Task Sheet in Gantt Chart view, Project adds a new row for that resource in the Resource Sheet. You then can choose View, Resource Sheet or click on the Resource Sheet icon in the View Bar to switch to the Resource Sheet. There you can enter the remaining information about the resource.

If you're not comfortable with a lot of typing, or you plan to enter multiple resources and want a faster method, you can use the Assign Resources dialog box.

To open the Assign Resources dialog box, click in a cell in the task for which you want to add resources. Open the Tools menu, point to Resources, and click on Assign Resources. Alternately, click on the Assign Resources button on the Standard or Resource Management toolbar, or press Alt+F10. The Assign Resources dialog box will appear, as shown in Figure 8.2.

Assign Resources button   Resource Management toolbar   Assigning a resource

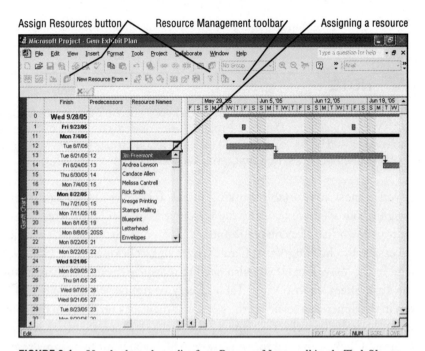

FIGURE 8.1 *Use the drop-down list for a Resource Names cell in the Task Sheet to assign a resource to the task.*

The resource assignment you make applies to the task that holds the selected cell

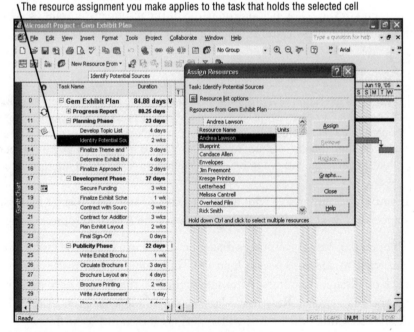

FIGURE 8.2 *When you need to work with many resource assignments, the Assign Resources dialog box might be the fastest way.*

To assign a resource to the task holding the cell you've selected, click on the desired resource name in the Resources From list. Adjust the Units entry as needed. For example, you can change a work resource to 50% units for the task, or assign more than one unit of a material resource (such as 5, if the resource is reams of paper). Click the Assign button to finish assigning the resource. Or, point to the gray box at the left end of the row holding the desired resource in the Assign Resources dialog box, drag the resource, and drop it into place on a task.

You can continue using the Assign Resources dialog box to assign resources to other tasks. Simply select the Resource Names cell for another task, and then use the Resource Assignment dialog box to select and assign the resource. When you finish assigning resources, click on Close to close the Resource Assignment dialog box.

 NOTE

You can double-click on a resource in the Assign Resources dialog box to open its Resource Information dialog box. You can then change resource information in the dialog box rather than returning to the Resource Sheet.

 TIP

If you have information about a resource entered in your Windows Address Book or a Windows Active Directory, click the plus sign (+) beside Resource List Options at the top of the Assign Resources dialog box, click the Add Resources button, and then click the appropriate choice in the menu that appears. You get a dialog box that enables you to add resources into the Project file. This saves you some typing and ensures that the correct e-mail address information for the resource is entered into Project.

A final way to assign a resource to a single task from the Task Sheet is to right-click on the task, and then click on the Task Information command (or click on the Task Information button on the Standard toolbar). In the Task Information dialog box, click on the Resources tab. Click on the first blank Resource Name row, click on the drop-down list arrow that appears beside the cell, click on a resource name, and then click on the Enter button. Click on OK to close the Task Information dialog box.

The biggest drawback to a couple of the resource assignment techniques just described is that unless your screen is big enough to display the whole Task

Sheet, you might not be able to see the name of the task to which you're assigning a resource. You can use another view, Task Entry view, to clarify which task you're entering a resource for. This view is sometimes referred to as the Task Form. To use the Task Entry view to assign resources to tasks, do the following:

1. Click on the Task Entry View button on the Resource Management toolbar. Alternately, choose View, More Views or click on the More Views icon in the View Bar. Then, in the Views list, scroll down to Task Entry, click on it, and click on Apply. The Task Entry view will appear, as shown in Figure 8.3.

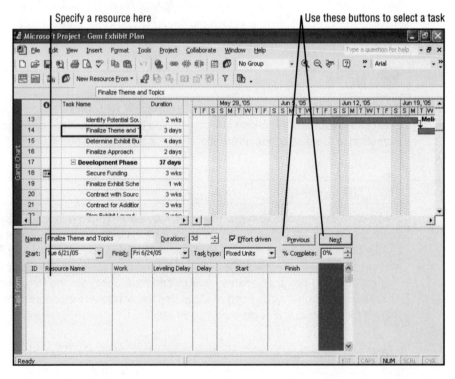

FIGURE 8.3 *You can use the Task Entry view to enter and edit resource assignments.*

2. Select a task by choosing it from the Task Name column of the visible portion of the Task Sheet, or by using the Previous and Next buttons in the Task Form pane.

3. Click on the first blank row of the Resource Name column of the lower portion of the view. The name of the selected task will be highlighted in the Task Sheet.

4. Click on the drop-down list arrow that appears at the right end of the selected cell under Resource Name, and then click on the name of the resource you want to select. Click on OK (which appears in place of the Previous button) to complete your entry. After you do so, information about the selected resource will appear in the lower pane of the display, as shown in Figure 8.4.

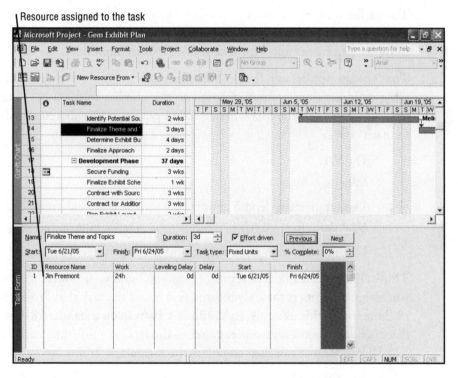

FIGURE 8.4 *Here's how a resource assigned to a task appears when displayed in the Task Form pane of Task Entry view.*

5. Repeat Steps 2 through 5 to assign resources to other tasks.

When you finish working in Task Entry view, open the View menu and click on the appropriate menu command to return to another view, such as Gantt Chart. If the window remains divided into upper and lower panes, remove the split by choosing Window, Remove Split.

CAUTION

It's not a good practice to assign resources to summary tasks because (again) they calculate the assignment totals for the tasks in the summary group. You should only assign resources at the level where the work occurs—for the subtasks.

Understanding the Driving Resource and Effort-Driven Scheduling

The earlier examples showed you what a task looks like if you've assigned a single resource. If you assign additional resources to a task, you'll see something happen by default—the task gets shorter in duration!

That's because by default, Project uses effort-driven or resource-driven scheduling to adjust a task's duration based on the number of resources assigned. Behind the scenes, the following equation powers effort-driven scheduling for each task:

D=W/U

Where

D=Duration (the length of time between the Start and Finish of a task)

W=Work (the number of person-hours required to complete the task)

U=Units (the resource's assignment units for work on the task)

Think about this formula in terms of how you build your project plan. Until you assign a resource, the only information about the task that Project has is its duration. In this example, let's assume a 1w task on a standard 8-hour per day calendar. If you assign one resource to the task on a full-time basis (100% or 1 Units), Project can then complete the formula:

1w=40h/100%

or

1w=40h/1, yielding 40h of work spread over the 1w duration

Project then plugs in the 8h of work per day over five days (the default work-week) for the resource.

You might assume, then, that if you add the first resource at less than full time, Project would increase the task duration. However, that's not the case!

Instead, Project completes the right side of the formula for the first time using the reduced values indicated by the initial resource assignment. Let's consider the 1w task again, but this time assign the first resource at 50%:

1w=40h/50%

or (stay with me here, algebra fans!)

1w=40h*.5, yielding 20h of work spread over the 1w duration

The result here, based on the 50% units setting, is 20h of work spread over the original duration. In this scenario, the resource will be scheduled to work 4h per day (50% of an 8-hour work day) over each of the five days of the task's duration.

These examples illustrate the concept of the *driving resource* in Microsoft Project. The first resource you assign to a task, the driving resource, completes the D=W/U formula. Until that formula is completed by the first assignment, Project cannot adjust the duration of the task because it does not have enough information to do so.

When you add a second resource to a task, however, Project can then adjust the duration accordingly. Let's go back to the beginning of this example, where you assigned one full-time resource to a 1w task:

1w=40h/100%

or

1w=40h/1

Let's say you add another full-time resource, which by default means adding another 100% to the Units figure in the right side of the formula:

40h/200%

or

40h/2, yielding 20h of work per resource

Project then uses the result of the right side of the calculation to adjust the duration accordingly, because it assumes that each resource will begin working from the start date of the task:

.5w=40h/2

So, each resource is assigned 8h, 8h, and 4h of work over the 2.5 days (half a default work week).

Figure 8.5 illustrates how these example tasks look in the Gantt Chart view.

	ⓘ	Task Name	Duration	Feb 24, '02 S M T W T F S	Mar 3, '02 S M T W T F S
1		Task with one full-time resource	1 wk		Joe Simpson
2		Task with one part-time resource	1 wk		Kim Taylor[50%]
3		Task with two full-time resources	0.5 wks		Joe Simpson,Kim Taylor

FIGURE 8.5 *When you assign the first resource (the driving resource) to a task, Project does not adjust the duration, even if you add that resource at less than 100% units (part time). When you add a second resource, Project can decrease the task duration accordingly by default.*

If you're math-averse, you don't have to remember all the formulas I've just presented. Here's everything you need to know when you assign resources in your schedule:

♦ Project does not adjust the task duration when you assign the first resource, no matter what the assignment units are.

TIP

So, what do you do if you *want* Project to extend the duration of a task when you've assigned a single resource at less than 100% units? You trick it! You first assign the resource at 100% units. Then you go back and edit the assignment, reducing the units. Project then recalculates the duration according to the new units setting. The Task Name cell for the affected task will include a green Feedback triangle in the upper-right corner. If needed, click the Task Name cell, click the Feedback button that appears, and then use one of the options on the menu that appears to further adjust the task's schedule.

♦ When you add additional resources (assignment units), Project decreases the task duration accordingly by default.

♦ If needed, you can fix the task duration so that it does not change no matter how many resources you add. The "Overriding an Effort-Driven Duration" section later in this chapter explains how to accomplish this.

Filtering the List in the Assign Resources Dialog Box

By default, the Assign Resources dialog box presents only one bit of information about each resource—its name. When you're dealing with a lengthy list of resources, you may need a bit more information to make appropriate assignments. For example, you may want to know that a resource is part of a particular group (and thus has the needed skill set), or you may want to verify whether the resource has enough available hours of work during the task's duration to handle the task.

Project 2002 offers added functionality to the Assign Resources dialog box, enabling you to identify key facts about particular resources before you assign them. To display these new features, click the plus (+) icon to the left of Resource List Options at the top of the Assign Resources dialog box. Two Filter By choices appear at the top.

The first check box enables you to filter the list of resources so that the Assign Resources dialog box displays only resources matching the specified filter criterion. (See Chapter 13, "Working with the Different Project Views," to learn more about filtering.) Basically, you turn on the filtering option, specify which filter to apply, and specify any filter criteria if prompted. For example, if you want the Assign Resources dialog box to list only resources with a particular entry (such as Administrative) in the Group field of the Resource Sheet, you would apply the group filter.

The following steps illustrate how to filter the list of resources in the Assign Resources dialog box:

1. If needed, click on the plus (+) button beside Resource List Options at the top of the Assign Resources dialog box to expand the filtering options.

2. Place a check in the top check box under Filter By. This will activate the list of available filters.

3. Open the drop-down list of filter choices and click the filter you want to apply, as in Figure 8.6.

 NOTE

Choose All Resources from the drop-down list of filters to remove any previously applied filter.

4. If the filter prompts you to specify a criterion, such as entering the Group field entry to filter by using the Group filter, do so and then click on OK. The list of resources will immediately adjust to show only matching resources, as shown in Figure 8.7. You can then assign any displayed resource as you normally would.

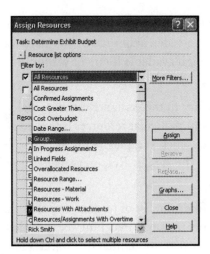

FIGURE 8.6 *Filtering the list of resources in the Assign Resources dialog box enables you to zero in on the resources that best meet the skill requirements for a task.*

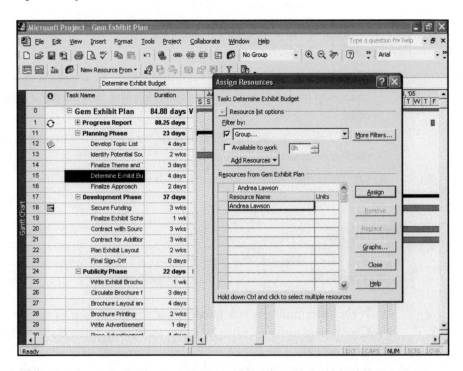

FIGURE 8.7 *I can now evaluate whether the listed resource—from the Administration group in my project plan—is the appropriate resource for the selected task (Determine Exhibit Budget).*

You also can use the Available To Work option near the top of the Assign Resources dialog box (either alone or in conjunction with a filter) to see if a resource has enough unassigned hours available within the duration of a task to handle that task. Here's that process:

1. With the Assign Resources dialog box open, click the task for which you want to check a resource's availability in the Task Sheet.

2. If needed, click on the plus (+) button beside Resource List Options at the top of the Assign Resources dialog box to expand the filtering options.

3. Apply a filter as described in the preceding set of steps, if needed.

4. Place a check in the Available To Work check box under Filter By. This will activate the accompanying text box.

5. Use the spinner buttons (or drag over the text box entry and type a new entry) to indicate the minimum number of hours the resource should be available to work on the task. The Assign Resources dialog box will list only resources meeting that availability requirement. Figure 8.8 shows a resource from the Exhibits group in my project plan whom is available to work 120h on the specified task (according to the resource's calendar and other assignments during the timeframe specified by the task's schedule).

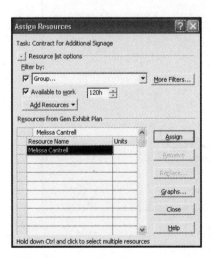

FIGURE 8.8   *You can both filter the list of resources and check for availability, as shown here.*

Checking Resource Availability Graphs

If you want to look at a resource's overall work assignments or remaining availability within a particular timeframe, you can do this as well from the Assign Resources dialog box. The graphs can be a handy tool if you want to check a resource's upcoming availability before you assign it to a task, thus avoiding overbooking the resource.

To check a resource's upcoming work and availability, follow these steps:

1. In the Assign Resources dialog box, click the resource for whom you want to view work and assignment information.

2. Click on the Graphs button to open the Graphs dialog box.

3. Open the Select Graph drop-down list and then click on the graph to view:

   ◆ **Remaining Availability.** Shows a day-by-day graph of the hours that a resource is available to work on additional assignments, based on the resource's calendar. Figure 8.9 shows an availability graph for a resource.

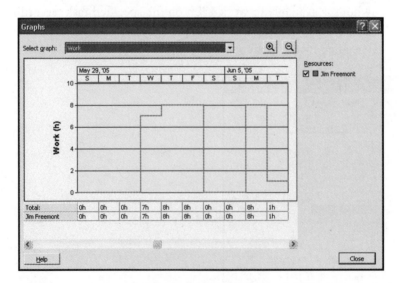

FIGURE 8.9 *You can see the availability for a specific resource (or that resource's scheduled work) in the Graphs dialog box.*

♦ **Work.** Shows a graph of hours of work scheduled for the resource on a day-by-day basis.

♦ **Assignment Work.** Shows the hours of work assigned to the resource for the task that's currently selected in the Task Sheet, as well as other assignments for the resource.

4. If needed, use the scroll bar at the bottom of the dialog box to view the graph information for additional dates.

5. Click on the Close button to close the dialog box when you've finished viewing graphs.

Replacing a Resource

Microsoft Project offers you a great advantage as a project manager, because you can use it to evaluate the impact of particular changes to a project plan. For example, you can change resource assignments at any time to meet changing project needs. This section discusses the techniques you can use to replace resources as the project plan evolves.

For a Single Task

Sometimes you'll learn that a resource has become unavailable or overbooked during the timeframe of a particular task. Or, you may have identified a resource who's more suited for a particular task. In cases like these, you need to replace one resource with another on an individual task. Here's the best technique for such a scenario:

1. With the Assign Resources dialog box open, click the task for which you want to replace the resource in the Task Sheet.

2. In the Assign Resources dialog box, click on the name of the assigned resource that you want to replace.

3. Click on the Replace button in the Assign Resources dialog box. The Replace Resource dialog box will open.

4. In the With list, click on the name of the replacement resource, as shown in Figure 8.10.

5. Click on OK to apply the change and return to the Assign Resources dialog box.

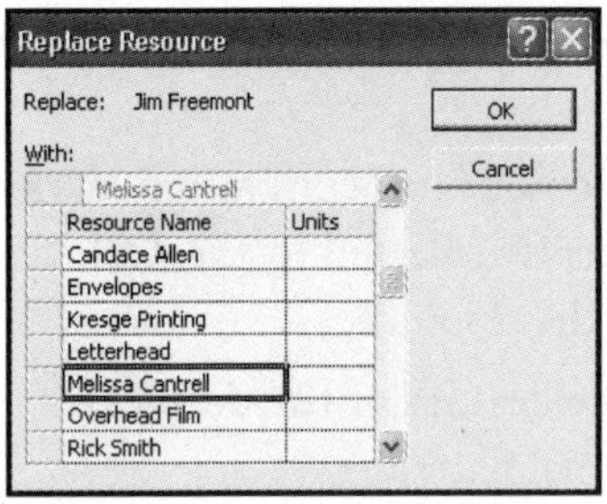

FIGURE 8.10 *Replace a resource on a task with just a few quick steps.*

Throughout the Project

If you need to replace all or part of a resource's assignments in your project plan, you can do so quickly without having to use the Assign Resources dialog box to replace each and every assignment for the resource. Project offers two different techniques for replacing a resource on multiple assignments. The technique you should choose depends on whether you want to replace all or part of a resource's assignments.

Let's start with the first choice. Say you've created a placeholder resource (such as Engineer1) in the Resource Sheet, as described in the previous chapter. You've just learned that the engineer assigned to the project is named Janet Griggs. You want to update all of Engineer1's assignments to reflect the engineer's name, Janet Griggs:

1. Go to the Resource Sheet (View, Resource Sheet).
2. Click on the Resource Name field for the resource to replace (*Engineer1*, for example).
3. Type the new resource name (**Janet Griggs**) and press Enter. Project immediately substitutes the new resource name for all assignments for the old resource.
4. Update any other information about the resource as needed.

> **TIP**
>
> You also can use this technique if you find a more cost-effective resource and want to substitute it throughout the project plan.

If you only want to substitute one resource for another for part of the original resource's assignments, it's best to use Project's Replace feature. (Replacing in Project is very similar to replacing in other Office applications.) You might use this technique if you're working to reduce overallocations for a particular resource in the project plan. Follow these steps to explore the Replace technique:

1. Go to the Gantt Chart view (View, Gantt Chart).

2. Press Ctrl+Home to go to the beginning of the project file.

3. Choose Edit, Replace. The Replace dialog box will open.

4. Open the Look In Field drop-down list, and then click on Resource Names.

5. If needed, open the Test drop-down list, and then click on Contains. (Use this to match and replace a text string.)

6. Enter the name of the resource to find in the Find What text box. Be sure to enter the full resource name, not just the first name.

7. Enter the name of the resource to use as the replacement in the Replace With dialog box. Again, type the full resource name.

8. Click on Find Next. As shown in Figure 8.11, Project will find the first task to which you've assigned the resource it's finding, and it will then highlight the Resource Names cell for that task.

9. Click the Replace button to replace the found resource with the new resource, or click Find Next to skip the selected task. Project will then find and highlight the next match.

10. Continue replacing and finding assignments until Project displays a message box telling you that Project has reached the end of the field. Click on OK to close that dialog box.

11. Click on Close to close the Replace dialog box and conclude the Replace operation.

TIP

You also can use this technique if you find a more cost-effective resource and want to substitute it throughout the project plan.

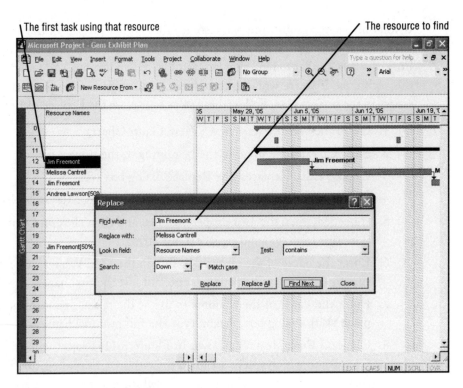

FIGURE 8.11 *The Replace feature in Project automates the process of updating some assignments to use another resource.*

Start Dates and Delays

As you saw in the Task Form pane of the Task Entry view in Figure 8.4, the view shows the task and resource names, task duration, number of work hours the resource will require to finish the project, and start and finish dates. Next to the Start column, you'll find the Delay column. You can use this column to specify that you don't want a resource to begin exactly when the start of the working day begins. It's also useful when more than one resource is assigned to the task (see the next two chapters for more details) and you want one of them to start a certain length of time after the others, perhaps to check their work.

To enter a delay for a resource, switch to Task Entry view by choosing View, More Views, scrolling down the list of views, and double-clicking on Task Entry. Then display the task information by clicking in the Task Name column in the upper pane (or by using the Previous and Next buttons). Click in the Delay column and enter the delay time period, along with a time unit specification such as **h** for hours or **d** for days. Figure 8.12 shows an example.

Enter the delay here...   ...and click here to accept it

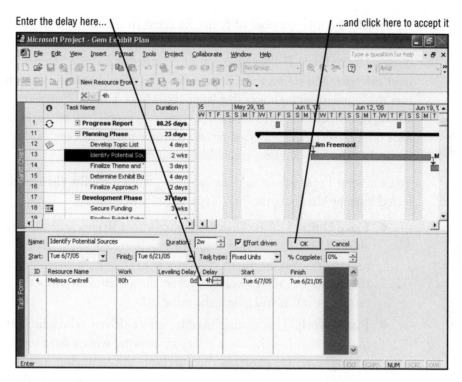

FIGURE 8.12 *You can create a delay to adjust the start of a resource's work.*

Click on OK in the lower pane of the view to finish specifying the delay. If necessary—such as if you're creating a delay for the sole resource assigned to the task—Project adjusts the start and finish dates for the task. Keep in mind that such changes can introduce scheduling conflicts, particularly if other linked tasks depend on the scheduled completion of the task you're working with.

Overriding an Effort-Driven Duration

This chapter has noted repeatedly that under Project's default effort-driven method of scheduling tasks, assigning multiple work resources to a task causes Project to adjust the schedule for the task. The degree of adjustment depends on the added resource's availability—Max. Units on the Resource Sheet, or the Units specified for a particular period of availability on the General tab of the Resource Information dialog box. (Remember, each unit of availability represents one person working full time on the task, as determined by the resource's base calendar, compared with the calendar for the task).

By default, the total number of hours allocated to the task (called the *work*) remains constant as you add more resources (units), with Project adjusting the duration accordingly. For example, say a four-day task has the Standard eight-hour calendar. You assign the first resource (the driving resource) which also uses the Standard eight-hour calendar at 100% Max. Units. Then, you assign a second full-time resource to the task (so now two people will be working full-time on the task). Applying that second resource to the task causes Project to recalculate the task duration and reduce it duration to two days.

You can stop Project from making duration, work, or units changes for selected tasks by changing the Task Type setting:

- ◆ **Fixed Units.** This is the default when effort-driven scheduling is enabled. Once the driving resource has been assigned, adding more resources makes the duration shorter and removing resources increases the duration. Project will not adjust the assignment units for added resources, but it will adjust the duration.

- ◆ **Fixed Work.** This setting disables effort-driven scheduling, and in most cases it has the same effect as working with a fixed units task: adding resources shortens the duration, and removing resources increases the duration. Adding the first (driving) resource sets the hours of work for the task. So, if you have a 1w task (on a Standard calendar) but assign the driving resource at 200%, the task will have 80h of work rather than 40h. From there, adding more resources decreases the duration (by dividing the hours of work between the resources), but not the total hours of work or the units settings for the resource assignments.

- ◆ **Fixed Duration.** This setting keeps the duration constant when you apply resources to the task. For example, if your project requires filing accounting information by a particular federal filing deadline, you'll want the duration and schedule for the task to remain fixed. Adding resources to this task decreases the amount of work each resource contributes on each day. For example, if you apply two full-time resources to a four-day task, Project doesn't cut the duration in half; it cuts the number of hours (work) each resource supplies each day in half.

  Note that the impact of the Fixed Duration task type varies depending on whether or not you leave effort-driven scheduling turned on with that task type. If you leave it turned on, Project fixes both the duration and the total hours of work for the task when you assign the driving resource. Therefore, adding additional resources reduces the units setting for each resource to keep the hours of work per day constant over the duration of the task. If you turn off effort-driven scheduling for a Fixed Duration task, Project sets the duration for the task when you assign the driving resource, doesn't change the units setting for any resource assignments, and changes the total hours of work for the task.

Figure 8.13 illustrates the impact of various task types on how Project adjusts duration, work, and units when you've assigned multiple resources.

	❶	Task Name	Work	Duration	Details	2					
						M	T	W	T	F	S
1		⊟ Fixed Units with Two Resources at 100%	40 hrs	0.5 wks	Work	16h	16h	8h			
		Jim Freemont	20 hrs		Work	8h	8h	4h			
		Andrea Lawson	20 hrs		Work	8h	8h	4h			
2		⊟ Fixed Work with Two Resources at 100%	40 hrs	0.5 wks	Work	16h	16h	8h			
		Jim Freemont	20 hrs		Work	8h	8h	4h			
		Andrea Lawson	20 hrs		Work	8h	8h	4h			
3		⊟ Fixed Duration, Effort-Driven On	40 hrs	1 wk	Work	8h	8h	8h	8h	8h	
		Andrea Lawson	20 hrs		Work	4h	4h	4h	4h	4h	
		Jim Freemont	20 hrs		Work	4h	4h	4h	4h	4h	
4		⊟ Fixed Duration, Effort-Driven Off	80 hrs	1 wk	Work	16h	16h	16h	16h	16h	
		Andrea Lawson	40 hrs		Work	8h	8h	8h	8h	8h	
		Jim Freemont	40 hrs		Work	8h	8h	8h	8h	8h	

FIGURE 8.13   *Adjusting the task type and working with the effort-driven scheduling option affects how Project schedules a task when you assign a second resource after assigning the driving resource.*

You can change the task type in the Task Entry view by selecting the task in the top pane of the view. Then click on the Task Type drop-down list in the bottom pane of the view, and click on the desired type. You also can specify a task's type in any view that shows the Task Sheet. Right-click on the task you want to fix, and then click on Task Information. Alternately, click on the task, and then click on the Task Information button on the Standard toolbar. The Task Information dialog box appears. Click on the Advanced tab. Open the Task Type drop-down list (see Figure 8.14), and then click on the desired type. Click on OK to close the dialog box.

 NOTE

If you want all new tasks to be scheduled with the task type you select, use the Default Task Type drop-down list on the Schedule tab of the Options dialog box. Chapter 28, "Customizing Microsoft Project," explains how to change this and other default settings.

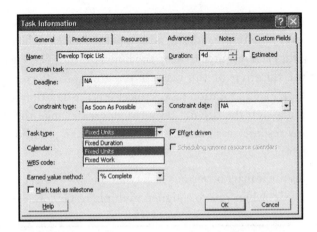

FIGURE 8.14 *Use the Task Type drop–down list to control whether Project adjusts the task's schedule.*

Turning Off Effort-Driven Scheduling

You also can turn off the effort-driven scheduling feature for a task to disable the Duration = Work/Units equation. That way, adding more resources doesn't automatically decrease the duration, but instead adds more units and work. On the Advanced tab of the Task Information dialog box, clear the check mark beside Effort Driven. Then, to fix the task duration, choose Fixed Duration as the task type using the Task Type drop-down list.

Deleting Resources

There are instances when a resource is no longer needed, either within a task assignment or within the Resource Sheet. At that point, you'll want to delete it.

Deleting a Resource from a Task

To delete a resource from a task, you can use any of a number of methods, depending on the current view. From the Task Sheet view, click in any cell in the task for which you want to remove the resource. Open the Assign Resources dialog box by clicking on the Assign Resources button on the Standard or Resource Management toolbar (or by pressing Alt+F10). In the Assign Resources dialog box, click on the resource to delete, which has a check mark beside it to indicate that it's assigned to the current task.

Click Remove to remove the resource. From here, you can use the dialog box to add and remove resources for other tasks, or you can simply click on Close to close the dialog box.

You can use Task Entry view to make removing a resource from a task even easier. Simply click on the name of the resource you want to delete in the Resource Name column of the bottom pane, press Delete, and then click on OK.

Selecting a cell in the Resource Names column and pressing Delete deletes the whole task entry, not just the resource. To delete the Resource Names entry only, right-click on the appropriate cell and click on Clear Contents.

Deleting a Resource from the Project

Just as you can use the Resource Sheet to add new resources to a project, you can use it to remove entries for resources you no longer use. For example, say that you've added the name of a person from another department to the resource list, but that person has been transferred to another city and is no longer available to work on the project. After you open the View menu and click Resource Sheet or click on the Resource Sheet icon in the View Bar, use either of the following methods to remove the resource:

◆ Select any cell in the resource you want deleted, and then press Delete.

◆ Click on the row number for the resource you want deleted; this selects the whole row. Choose Edit, Delete Resource (or right-click on the selected row to access the shortcut menu, and then click on Delete Resource).

Working with Assignments

Project provides a way of looking at the interplay between tasks and the resources assigned to complete them. A view that shows assignments lists each task in the Task Sheet as a summary task, with each resource assigned to the task listed in a subtask row below it. Each resource listing under the task is an assignment—a specific task assigned to a specific resource. So if you have a task to which you assigned three resources, it has three assignments—one for each resource.

Assignments not only enable you to reexamine which resources will be handling which tasks, they also provide an additional level of detail for adjusting your schedule. For example, you can adjust start and finish dates for one assignment (one resource working on a particular task) without adjusting the start and finish dates for the task as a whole or the other resources assigned to the same task.

Viewing Assignments

The Task Usage view offers a Task Sheet that includes both tasks and assignments. To switch to Task Usage view, choose View, Task Usage. Or, click on the Task Usage icon on the View Bar. The view—complete with tasks and assignments—appears onscreen, as shown in Figure 8.15. Click the Go To Selected Task button, if needed, to scroll the actual task schedule for the selected task into view in the right pane.

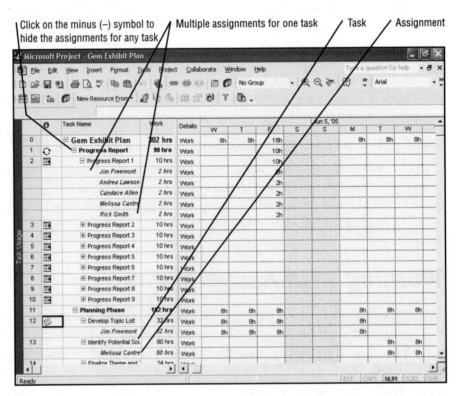

FIGURE 8.15 *Assignments provide more detail about each resource involved with each task.*

NOTE

You can also view assignments in the Resource Usage view, covered in the next chapter. It lists each resource as a summary task, with individual assignments for that resource listed as subtasks.

In the Task Usage view, each task has a symbol that you can use to display or hide the assignments for that task. Click on the minus (–) symbol to hide the assignments and the plus (+) symbol to redisplay them. Or you can use the outlining buttons on the Formatting toolbar (see Chapter 5, "Working with Outlining") to hide and display assignments for a task.

Displaying Assignment Information

The Assignment Information dialog box offers the settings for fine-tuning a selected assignment. To display the Assignment Information dialog box, click in a cell in the assignment row, and then click to open the Project menu or right-click in the selected cell. In the menu or shortcut menu that appears, choose Assignment Information. After you click in a cell in an assignment row, you also can click on the Assignment Information button on the Standard toolbar. Finally, you can simply double-click on a cell in the assignment row. No matter which method you choose, the Assignment Information dialog box appears (see Figure 8.16).

I'll discuss specific settings in this dialog box where they apply later in the book, but I'll touch on its three tabs here. After you make your changes in the Assignment Information dialog box, click on OK to close it and make your changes take effect.

- ◆ **General.** This tab enables you to adjust how much time the resource can spend on the assignment, such as when the resource can start work, how many units the resource can allocate to the assignment, and more.

- ◆ **Tracking.** Use this tab to enter actual work the resource has completed on the assignment and the actual timing of that work.

- ◆ **Notes.** Use this tab to add a note for the assignment, using the same process described in Ch. 7. You can display this tab for an assignment directly by clicking on the Assignment Notes button on the Standard toolbar.

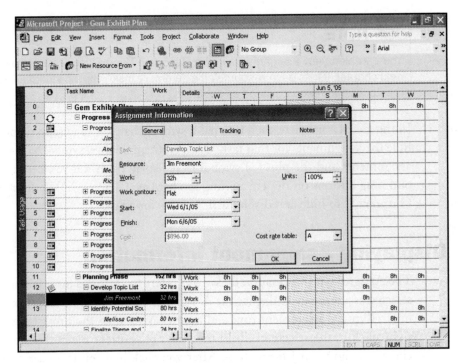

FIGURE 8.16 *The Assignment Information dialog box offers settings not found elsewhere.*

Changing the Cost Table for an Assignment

Earlier in this chapter you learned how to create different cost rate tables for a resource, which you can use when a resource charges a different rate or fee for different types of work. Although rate changes within the A (Default) rate table apply automatically to all tasks on the dates that you specify, you must manually apply a different rate table to any assignment to which it applies.

You do so by using the Assignment Information dialog box in the Task Usage view. Click in a cell in assignment's row to specify the assignment. Then click on the Assignment Information button on the Standard toolbar, or use one of the other methods described earlier for displaying the Assignment Information dialog box. On the General tab, click to open the Cost Rate Table drop-down list, and then click on the cost rate table to use it. Click on OK to close the dialog box and accept your change.

Working with Resource Pools

If you plan to build multiple project files that use the same resources, you could copy the list of resources from the Resource Sheet in one file to the Resource Sheet in another file. (Select the resources in the original file by dragging over their row headings, and then choose Edit, Copy. Change to the Resource Sheet in the destination file and choose Edit, Paste.)

However, Project gives you a more efficient method of using the same resources in multiple files: resource sharing. Using this technique, you build the resource list in a single file, referred to as a *resource pool*. This file should hold only resources and resource information—no tasks. You can name the resource pool file anything you like.

Once you've created and saved the resource pool file, you then open other project files that have task information but no resources on the Resource Sheet, and distribute the resources among the individual project files, as illustrated in Figure 8.17. The beauty of this process is that once you've set up all the detailed information in the resource pool file—including cost information, cost rate tables, resource calendars, resource availability settings, and so on—you don't have to repeat that work in your other project files. Even better, you'll know when you've overallocated a resource between projects because you'll be able to see that overallocation in the resource pool file.

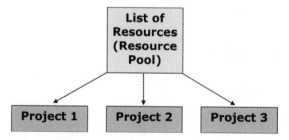

FIGURE 8.17 *You can share the resources from a centralized file, called a resource pool, into individual project files with task information.*

 NOTE

Chapter 20, "Consolidating Projects," will explain more of the benefits of using a resource pool, especially when you're reviewing multiple project files.

Sharing Resources

Even though resource sharing provides immense benefits, it surprisingly requires only a few straightforward steps:

1. Open a blank file and create the list of resources in the Resource Sheet. Specify all needed resource settings, including cost, calendar, and availability information.

2. Save the file and leave it open. (The resource pool file must be open, or you won't be able to share its resources.)

3. Open or create the file that will share the existing resource information. Initially, this file will hold information about tasks only. The Resource Sheet will be blank.

4. Choose Tools, Resource Sharing, Share Resources. The Share Resources dialog box will appear.

5. Click on the Use Resources option button, and then use the From drop-down list to select the file containing the resources you want to share (see Figure 8.18).

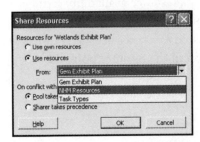

FIGURE 8.18 *Select the file containing the information about all your resources.*

6. In the On Conflict With Calendar Or Resource Information area, select Pool Takes Precedence (Project will make changes to the resource list in individual files based on changes to the pool file), or Sharer Takes Precedence (Project will make changes to the file holding the resource pool based on changes to the individual file sharing the pool).

7. Click on OK to finish sharing the resources. The resource pool from the file you specified is now used for the current file. Save the current file to save the resource sharing information.

NOTE

Hundreds of files can share the same resource pool in Project. Be aware, though, that this strategy may lead to a huge resource pool file if everyone in your organization is using the same pool file stored on a shared network drive. Even on a fast network, a huge resource pool file can slow down the performance of the individual files sharing the resources from the pool.

Opening and Refreshing the Pool and Sharer Files

By default, the resource pool file remains linked to the individual project files sharing its resources. When you save and close a file that uses the resource information from a resource pool file, Project keeps track of the fact that the two files are linked. When you reopen the file containing the link to resource information, Project must open the resource pool file. It displays the Open Resource Pool Information dialog box asking if you want to open the resource pool or not. Make your choice and click on OK. If you've made changes to the resource information in the shared resource pool file, those changes appear in the file that shares the information.

Conversely, if you reopen the file where you originally entered the resources, the Open Resource Pool dialog box presents a few options (Figure 8.19). You can open the resource pool as read-only, open the resource file normally so that you can make changes to it (although if your files reside on a network, other users won't be able to change the resource pool), or open the file with the resource pool and any other files using the resource pool in a new master project file.

You can make changes, such as updating rates for the resource information in the file that holds the resource pool, and then simply open the other files that also use that resource pool to update the resource information for those files too. However, if the resource pool file is stored on a network and others can make changes to the pool, and you have left a file using that resource pool open for several hours, your resource information won't be up to date.

You can refresh the resource information (to get the latest information) without closing and reopening the sharer file. Instead, choose Tools, Resources, Refresh Resource Pool. This pulls the latest changes from the resource pool

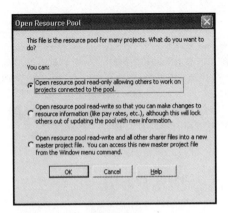

FIGURE 8.19 *When you open the project file that holds your resource pool, you have to specify whether or not you want to be able to make changes to it.*

file (in the event that another user is editing it on the network) into the individual sharer file.

Conversely, if you make changes in any file that uses the resource pool on the network, and you want the pool to be updated with those changes, choose Tools, Resources, Update Resource Pool. This ensures that any new assignment information will be visible to all users of the pool, helping prevent problems with overallocating resources between projects.

If you open a file that uses resource information from another file, you can edit the resource link information. To do so, reopen the Share Resources dialog box by choosing Tools, Resources, Share Resources. In the Share Resources dialog box, make the changes you want (such as selecting another file to use resources from, or opting not to use resources from another file at all), and then click on OK. Project will close the dialog box, and your resource sharing changes will take effect. Make sure that you save the current file to save these changes.

PART III

Making Adjustments to Projects

Chapter 9

Resolving Overallocations and Overbooked Resources

In This Chapter

◆ What it means to overallocate a resource

◆ Finding overallocation problems in your plan

◆ Using leveling to eliminate overbooked schedules

◆ Addressing overallocations on your own

I'm sure you've heard colleagues moan, "I wish there were more than 24 hours in a day, because I can't seem to get enough done." It might be a cliché, but only because it reflects our common tendency to cram too many activities into each and every day. As a leader under pressure, you'll need to fight this natural tendency when creating your project plans.

Project 2002 provides features designed to help you make your schedule realistic and attainable. Some of the best of these features quietly point out when you may have created an unrealistic schedule, such as giving a resource 16 hours' worth of work on an 8-hour workday.

Discovering Overallocation

Early in the book, you learned to sketch out your schedule by simply listing the tasks to accomplish. You then learned to organize the list of tasks via outlining, establish the project schedule via linking, add resources for the project, and assign those resources to tasks. Before the work begins on your project, you need to go back and look at whether the resources you assigned to your project make sense. In this chapter and the next, you'll look for problems with your plan so that you can deal with them before they negatively affect the project's completion.

Because Project uses effort-driven scheduling by default, you don't generally have to worry about having too few or too many resources assigned to a particular task. If the resource's working hours enable the resource to handle the task more quickly, Project shortens the task duration. Conversely, Project automatically lengthens the task if you reduce the number of resource units assigned. For example, suppose that your schedule is based on a 24 Hours base calendar and you've adjusted the default Hours Per Day to 24 and the default Hours Per Week to 168. However, the resource you want to use follows the Standard calendar with 8-hour days. A task scheduled for one 24-hour day will be rescheduled to take three days if you assign the 8-hours-per-day resource to it, even if Project doesn't display an adjusted duration value. (That is, the Gantt Chart bar will reflect the calculated Start and Finished dates based on the resource's work being spread over three days.)

Instead, what you need to be concerned about is assigning a resource to separate tasks that occur simultaneously. If your list includes 25 different tasks, in theory, any number of them could partially occur during the same week. Say that the task in row 5 (task 5) begins on the Monday of the third week of your project. The task in row 7 (task 7) begins the same week, but on Thursday. You assigned the same resource to both tasks. Each of the tasks needs to be handled as quickly as possible, so the assigned resource must give it full-time attention during the eight-hour workday defined for the project schedule. The problem is obvious. During Thursday and Friday, the resource needs to handle two full-time tasks. Thus, for Thursday and Friday, you've overallocated (overbooked) the selected resource.

You might be able to quickly spot overallocations in Gantt Chart view when tasks are close together in your list. Generally, though, you'll only be able to see 25 or so task rows onscreen at any time (depending on your screen resolution), so you can't visually compare the tasks in, let's say, rows 1 and 55 without scrolling back and forth. For that reason, Project provides a couple of other methods for quickly finding overallocations, described next.

 NOTE

Even if a resource is overbooked by only a few minutes on a given date, Project will still identify an overallocation on that date. As a manager, you should review all the overallocations in your project plan and decide whether each one is substantial enough to warrant changes in your plan. In many cases, especially if your resources are salaried employees, you may leave small overallocations in the schedule, assuming the resource will work the extra minutes to cover a particular task. On the other hand, if you've consistently booked a resource for 10 or 12 hours of work per day, your project plan is probably unrealistic and you will need to rethink some of that resource's assignments.

Finding Overallocations with the Resource Management Toolbar

If you need to identify an overallocation in the default Gantt Chart view, display the Resource Management toolbar by right-clicking on any toolbar onscreen and selecting Resource Management. To go to a task in the Task Sheet that's assigned to an overallocated resource, click on the Go To Next Overallocation button on the Resource Management toolbar. Project selects the indicator cell of the task with the overallocated resource, as shown in Figure 9.1. Clicking on the Go To Next Overallocation button again takes you to the next task in the list with an overallocation. If you click on the Go To Next Overallocation button when there are no more overallocated tasks in

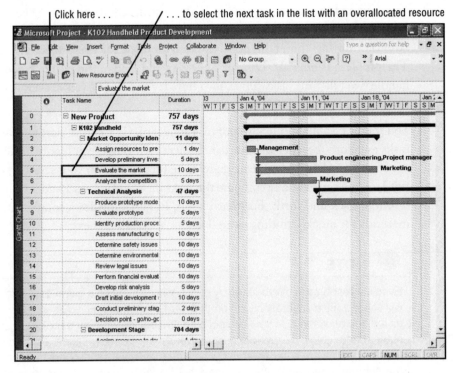

FIGURE 9.1 *The Resource Management toolbar offers a fast way to find a task with an overallocated resource.*

the list, you'll see a message saying that there are no further overallocations. Click on OK to close the message box and continue.

Looking at Resource Usage in Other Views

To make a good decision about how to fix an overallocation, you have to know when the overallocation occurs and how extensive the overallocation is. Have you assigned 24 hours' worth of work for an 8-hour day, or have you assigned only an extra hour or two? For more extensive schedules, you might have multiple overallocations, and you might even have overallocated more than one resource on the same date.

Project offers a couple of options for getting a clearer overall picture of the overallocations in your schedule. (These are views, which you'll learn more about in Chapter 13, "Working with the Different Project Views.")

First, you can display the resource usage in a tabular format. Choose View, Resource Usage, or click on the Resource Usage icon on the View Bar. The Resource Usage view appears, as shown in Figure 9.2. The Resource Name column in this view lists each resource you added to the schedule, as well as each of the resource's assignments. The Work column shows you the total amount of work (in hours) that you scheduled for the resource, as well as the amount of work scheduled for each assignment. The scrolling pane on the right side of the screen shows you the amount of work you assigned to each resource on each date. You can see which resources are overallocated at a glance, because Project displays the Resource Name and Work entries in bold red text and an indicator tells you the resource needs leveling. Figure 9.2 shows overallocations for both the Jim Freemont and Andrea Lawson resources.

If you look to the right along the row of an overallocated resource, you'll see that Project also highlights the particular dates on which you overbooked the resource according to the resource's work calendar. For example, on Friday during the week of May 29, Jim Freemont is scheduled for 10 hours of work, 2 hours more than his calendar (and Max Units setting) allows him to handle.

Project looks at three factors when determining whether a resource is overallocated on a given day: the hours of work available according to the resource's calendar, the total hours of work assigned to the resource, and the total units assigned to

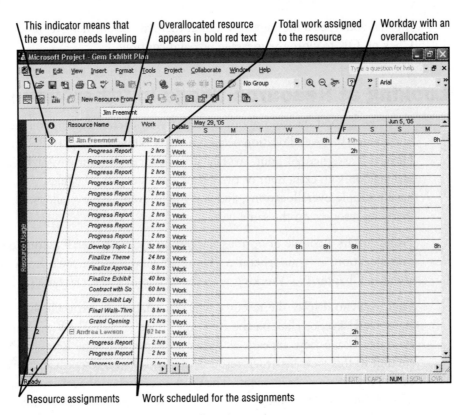

FIGURE 9.2 *The Resource Usage view summarizes how much work you've assigned.*

the resource. Sometimes one of these factors causes a resource to be flagged as overallocated on a given date when that's really not the case.

For example, by default, any resource you assign to a recurring task will be assigned at 100% units. Let's say you assign John Smith (who follows the Standard calendar and has a 100% Max. Units setting) to a recurring meeting task, and it's a 2h task. On that same day, you assign John Smith at 50% units to another task. On that day, Project correctly calculates 6h of total work for John, but shows him as overallocated even though his calendar allows 8h of work per day! Based on the two assignments for the day, his units of work add up to 150%, or 50% more than allowed by his Max. Units setting.

This is another instance where you need to examine the nature of the overallocation and decide how to handle it. In the preceding example, no action is required because the resource isn't really overallocated. Or, if you really want to get technical and make the overallocation disappear, you could reduce the Units for John's meeting assignment to 25%, reflecting the actual amount of his calendar that he will expend on that assignment.

The Resource Allocation view combines the tabular layout for the Resource Usage view with a lower pane where you can see the assignments for the selected resource as a Gantt chart. Click on the Resource Allocation View button on the Resource Management toolbar. If you haven't displayed that toolbar, choose View, More Views and then double-click on Resource Allocation in the Views list of the More Views dialog box.

Project displays your schedule in the Resource Allocation view. When you select a resource from the Resource Usage view in the upper pane, a Gantt chart in the lower pane shows you the tasks for the resource, so that you can see which ones overlap. Figure 9.3 shows that Jim Freemont has overlapping tasks. This view is ideal for changing the schedule for overallocated resources, as you'll see in the "Manually Cutting Back the Resource's Commitments" section later in the chapter. If you switch back to the Resource Sheet (by choosing View, Resource Sheet), overallocated resources are also indicated in bold red text. You won't get any information about where in the schedule the overallocation occurs, however.

 CAUTION

When you display another view from the Resource Allocation view, the screen may remain split into upper and lower panes. Choose Window, Remove Split to restore the view to normal.

Creating and Printing an Overallocated Resources Report

Project can automatically create and print a report that lists each overallocated resource and the tasks assigned to that resource. This report can be a good tool

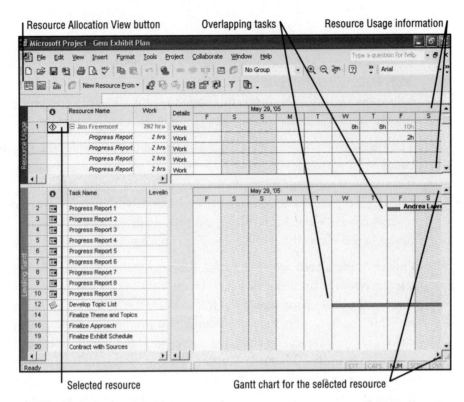

FIGURE 9.3 *The Resource Allocation view shows the work summary and a Gantt chart for the selected resource.*

if you're seeking additional funding or resources to complete your project plan.

Reports don't let you edit the information entered into your schedule, but, when you're making a decision, they're convenient tools for looking at particular types of information. Chapter 16, "Creating and Printing a Report," provides more details about generating and printing the various types of reports in Project. Until then, here's how to make Project compile an Overallocated Resources report:

1. Choose View, Reports to access the Reports dialog box.

2. Double-click on Assignments, or click on it once and then click on Select. The Assignment Reports dialog box will appear (see Figure 9.4).

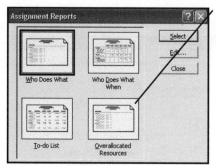

Double-click here to compile your Overallocations Report

FIGURE 9.4 *Project offers reporting about resource assignments.*

3. Double-click on Overallocated Resources, or click on it once and then click on Select. Project will display a list of overallocated resources for you.

4. To take a closer look at the information, click on the report with the zoom pointer, which looks like a magnifying glass (see Figure 9.5).

5. To print the report, click on the Print button on the toolbar. Or you can click on the Close button, and then click on Close again in the Reports dialog box.

Using Leveling to Fix Overallocations

When you've overbooked a resource, something has to give. You want to eliminate huge peaks in a resource's workload to achieve an even, realistic flow of work. The process of smoothing out the workloads for resources is called *resource leveling*. Project can level resource schedules automatically, when you specify it, for any schedule where Project calculates the finish date automatically.

To level resources, Project delays a conflicting task, or splits the task and moves part of it to a later time when the resource has available working hours. (You'll learn how to manually specify delay time later in this chapter, in the "Creating a Delay" section.) Project decides which tasks to delay by

Click here to print the Overallocated
Resources report as is

Click here to leave the
report without printing

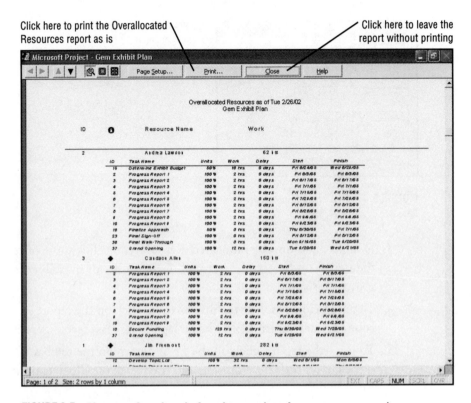

FIGURE 9.5 *You can take a closer look at the reporting about your resource assignments.*

examining the information you entered about tasks. In particular, it's looking for *slack*, which occurs when a task can be moved to a later date without
delaying another task or the end date of the project.

When tasks are linked, Project takes tasks' links and constraints into consideration before delaying a particular task. This is important because
linked tasks may be handled by different resources, and you don't want to
create a problem for another resource as a result of the leveling. For example, if two tasks are linked using the default Finish-to-Start (FS) link
type, and there's no lag time between the two tasks, the first task can't be
moved without moving the second task as well unless you change the nature of the link.

NOTE

The next chapter provides more details about working with slack, but here's a quick example. Suppose that a resource is scheduled to handle a task that begins on Monday, 12/1/03, and has a duration of four days. The next task assigned to the resource begins on Monday, 12/8/03, and has the Start No Later Than (SNLT) constraint with a 12/8/03 constraint date, meaning that it cannot move beyond its scheduled start date. Thus, there's one day of slack between the two tasks. The 12/1/03–12/4/03 task can only be delayed one day to a 12/2/03–12/5/03 schedule, because the resource must start working on the second task on the following Monday.

Here are a few more important issues to keep in mind before you level:

◆ Schedules built backwards from the finish date have no slack, so there's nowhere to move any tasks. You have to work manually to level resources for this type of schedule.

◆ By default, it's conceivable that Project may move a task that's listed earlier in the schedule, such as in row 2, rather than a conflicting one in row 5. Project moves whichever task is easier to move based on links and other factors, regardless of its ID number or order in the Task Sheet.

For example, compare the tasks for Steve Poland before and after leveling in Figure 9.6. Task 5 has a Must Start On constraint, so Project moved Task 4. This created a problem, because Steve needs to conduct research for the presentation before he can write it. In some cases, such moves do not make sense. Be sure to double-check leveling results carefully.

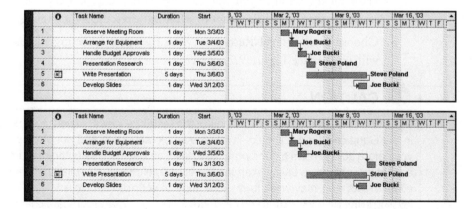

FIGURE 9.6 *Leveling decisions aren't based on a task's order in the Task Sheet, as shown in this example of the same set of tasks before and after leveling.*

◆ Project can't change history. If a task has already started, Project can't move it altogether when leveling a resource schedule.

◆ Automatic leveling can have a massive impact on the flow of your schedule. If your schedule is very complex, or you want to limit the scope of the changes made but still take advantage of leveling, use leveling for one resource at a time. (See the following steps that explain how to use leveling.) Check the results after leveling each resource.

Setting Options and Leveling

Project enables you to level resources with the Resource Leveling command on the Tools menu. As you proceed through the leveling process, Project allows you to set numerous leveling options:

1. Open the file with the resources you want to level and make any desired adjustments to tasks, such as changing link types and priorities.

 TIP

If you want to level a schedule but also want to be able to see the original dates, create a copy of the schedule file by choosing File, Save As, and then giving the file a new name. Then apply leveling to the copied file. Reopen the original file if you want to compare the dates.

2. (Optional) If you want to level a single resource, change to Resource Sheet, Resource Usage, or Resource Allocation view. Then click on the resource name for the resource you want to level. (Press Ctrl and click on other resource names if you also want to select those resources for leveling.)

3. Choose Tools, Level Resources. The Resource Leveling dialog box will appear (see Figure 9.7).

 CAUTION

If you don't select a resource from one of the resource views, or you're working in the Gantt chart view, Project levels the whole schedule and does not warn you before doing so. It's a good practice to level one or more selected resources so that you can more easily examine the schedule changes applied by the leveling. In fact, you may want to make a copy of your project file and apply the leveling in the file copy so that you can more easily identify and compare changes.

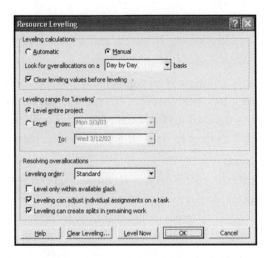

FIGURE 9.7   *Select leveling options in the Resource Leveling dialog box.*

4. If you want Project to automatically level the schedule each time you make a change in a task or resource assignment, select the Automatic option button in the Leveling Calculations area of the dialog box. Otherwise, you have to reopen the Resource Leveling dialog box to level the schedule again after you make any changes. If you want to retain control of when and how leveling occurs, however, leave the Manual option button selected.

 CAUTION

I don't recommend automatic leveling, because it forces you to give up some control over scheduling decisions. Plus, it increases the difficulty of communicating schedule changes as the schedule evolves.

5. The Look For Overallocations On A ... Basis option specifies how precise the leveling is. The default option, Day By Day, compares the hours of work assigned to a resource on each day, with the working hours available in the resource's calendar for that day. For the Standard calendar, then, any day with more than eight hours of work is marked as overallocated and will be leveled. But what if you don't need to be that precise? If you assign a resource 12 hours of work that happens to fall on the same day, but that work really can be completed any time within the week, you can choose Week by Week so the work won't be leveled. The Look For Overallocations On A ... Basis offers

these options, in order from most to least precise: Minute By Minute, Hour By Hour, Day By Day, Week By Week, and Month By Month.

6. If you previously leveled the schedule and want Project to remove the old leveling as it applies the new leveling, leave the Clear Leveling Values Before Leveling check box checked. If you turn this option off and Project has already delayed a task when you previously applied leveling, it's possible for Project to delay the task even further if you level again.

7. If you don't want to level the entire project schedule, you can specify a range of dates to level in the Leveling Range For area of the dialog box. To specify the schedule date when you want the leveling to start, click on the Level From option button. Then click on the drop-down list arrow on the accompanying text box and select a date from the pop-up calendar that appears. Click on the drop-down list arrow beside the To text box, and use the pop-up calendar to select a date beyond which you don't want to level resources. If you want to level the remainder of the project, select a To date that is later than the project's finish date.

8. Use the Leveling Order drop-down list in the Resolving Overallocations area of the dialog box to tell Project how to choose which tasks to delay or split. This drop-down list offers three options. The default is Standard, in which Project considers links, slack, dates, and priorities to determine which task to delay. If you select ID Only, Project delays the overlapping task that appears latest in the Task Sheet and thus has the highest ID number. If you select the final option, Priority, the priority you assigned to tasks takes precedence over other factors in determining which tasks to delay.

9. By default, the Level Only Within Available Slack option is not selected, meaning that Project can adjust the finish date of your schedule as needed when it moves tasks. However, this could lead to a delay of weeks or even months in your schedule, depending on the scope of your project. If you don't want the leveling operation to change the finish date, check this option so that Project moves tasks only within available slack time.

10. You may have several resources assigned to a task, and if only one of those resources is overallocated, Project can level only the overallocated resource. To have leveling work on individual resources in this way,

leave the check mark beside Leveling Can Adjust Individual Assignments On A Task. Clear the check box if you would prefer Project to reschedule the entire task, even when only one of the resources handling the task is overbooked.

11. If you want Project to delay tasks and not split them, remove the check beside Leveling Can Create Splits In Remaining Work.

12. Click on the Level Now button. If you selected a particular resource to level, as described in Step 2, or you're displaying your schedule in one of the resource views, Project will open the Level Now dialog box (see Figure 9.8).

FIGURE 9.8 *Specify whether to level all resources in your project.*

13. Leave the Entire Pool option selected to level all resources, or click on Selected Resources to tell Project to level only the resources you selected in Step 2.

14. Click on OK to complete the leveling operation. When a resource has been leveled, it no longer appears in bold red type.

TIP

You may have to apply leveling more than once to the selected resource in order to remove all of the resource's overallocations.

15. (Optional) If you're not happy with the leveling changes, immediately click on the Undo button on the Standard toolbar, press Ctrl+Z, or choose Edit, Undo Level.

If you have leveled the resource and view information about that resource in the Resource Allocation view, the Gantt chart pane at the bottom of the view clearly shows the effects of leveling. As shown in Figure 9.9, each Gantt bar becomes a double bar, with the top portion showing the original schedule for the task and the bottom portion showing the leveled schedule.

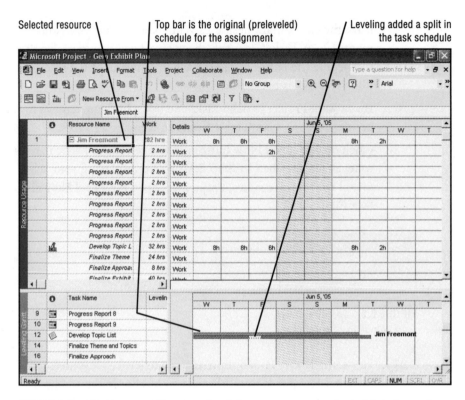

FIGURE 9.9 *The Resource Allocation view helps you compare a task schedule before and after leveling.*

Clearing Leveling

As illustrated, you work with resources to add leveling—but when you need to *remove* leveling, you work with tasks. Thus, you need to be in a view where you can select tasks, such as Gantt Chart view. The Task Sheet appears in the left pane, or Resource Allocation view, and you can select task assignments for a particular resource in the lower pane of the view.

 CAUTION

You can't just select a resource name from any Resource Sheet and clear leveling. You have to be working from a task-oriented view or pane. You'll know you're in an incorrect place if the Clear Leveling button isn't available in the Resource Leveling dialog box.

Removing leveling removes any delay or split that Project inserted for a task or tasks during leveling. To remove leveling, perform the following steps:

1. Select a task-oriented view.

2. (Optional) If you only want to remove leveling from a particular task, click on that task name. (If you select the Resource Allocation view, you'll also have to select a resource that has been leveled in the upper pane, and then click on the task assignment to level in the lower pane.) To select more than one task, press and hold down the Ctrl key and click on additional task names.

3. Choose Tools, Resource Leveling. The Resource Leveling dialog box will appear.

4. Click on the Clear Leveling button. Project will open the Clear Leveling dialog box (see Figure 9.10).

FIGURE 9.10   *Choose whether to remove the delay from all or selected tasks.*

5. If you chose to have leveling removed from one or more particular tasks in Step 2, make sure the Selected Tasks option button is selected. Otherwise, click on Entire Project to remove all of the leveling.

6. Click on OK to remove the leveling. Note that even after you clear leveling from a resource or task, the bottom pane of the Resource Allocation view will continue to show split bars for the tasks that were previously leveled.

Reprioritizing Tasks Before Leveling

The last section of Chapter 6 provided an overview of the settings in the Task Information dialog box. To open it, double-click on any task in the Task Sheet of the Gantt Chart view. The first tab in that dialog box, the General tab, enables you to enter and edit the basic information that defines the task, such as its name and duration. One of the settings in that dialog box is the Priority option, as shown in Figure 9.11.

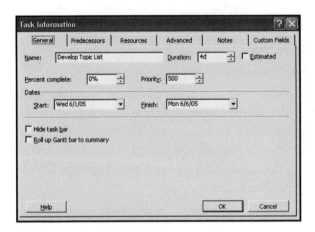

FIGURE 9.11 *The Priority option enables you to define the relative importance of tasks.*

By default, all regular tasks are assigned a priority setting of 500, meaning that each task is equally important in the schedule. You can specify which tasks are more important by changing the Priority setting to a value between 1 and 1000, with a higher value symbolizing a greater priority. (You can prevent Project from delaying a task at all during leveling by entering 1000.)

Project uses the priority settings as a factor in automatic leveling, and the priority is given even more precedence if you select the Priority, Standard option in the Resource Leveling dialog box. Project delays tasks with lower priority settings before moving those with higher priority settings.

 TIP

You can sort your list of tasks by priority. See Chapter 13, "Working with the Different Project Views," for details.

You should change task priorities before leveling, when necessary. Assuming that you'll be doing much of your leveling work in the Resource Allocation view, here's how to change a task's priority from that view:

1. In the upper pane of the Resource Allocation view, click on the resource that's scheduled to handle the task for which you want to set the priority (usually an overallocated resource).

2. In the lower pane, right-click on the task for which you want to set the priority. This opens the shortcut menu shown in Figure 9.12. Then click on Task Information.

Click on this button for task information . . .   . . . or right-click on the task and
                                                       then click on Task Information

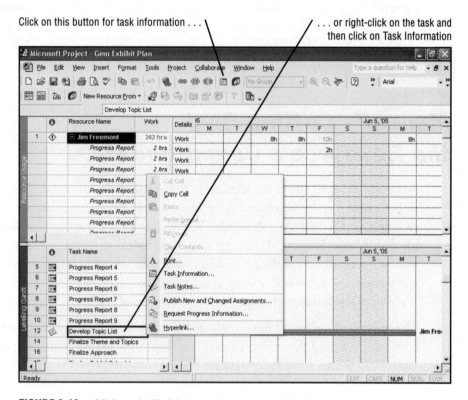

FIGURE 9.12 *Click on the Task Information option in this shortcut menu on your way to changing the selected task's priority.*

3. On the General tab of the Task Information dialog box, drag over the entry in the Priority text box, and then type the new Priority value you want.

4. Click on OK to close the Task Information dialog box.

Use a similar approach to make such changes from other views that show a list of tasks.

CAUTION

Recurring tasks are automatically set with a priority of 1000. Changing this setting for a recurring task could have unwanted results, such as Project delaying a recurring task when leveling. Obviously, in the real world, the meeting or other repeating event that the recurring task represents would likely occur as scheduled, so the unwanted delay could create issues with resource schedules.

Manually Cutting Back the Resource's Commitments

Although Project's automatic leveling is a no-brainer way to ensure that your resources can handle the work you've assigned, some resource adjustment chores require more thought. As noted earlier in this chapter, if you set up your schedule file to have Project calculate its start date based on a finish date you've entered, you can't use automatic leveling to deal with overallocations. Nor would you want to use automatic leveling if the tasks involved are high in priority, or if you need a solution that is more creative than simply delaying some tasks.

The methods described in this section will enable you to resolve overallocations with precision and flexibility. To perform most of these adjustments, you'll work in Resource Allocation view. In the next chapter, you'll learn to adjust the schedule and make some resource adjustments from the Task Entry view.

Creating a Delay

Automatic leveling creates a delay for a task, so that tasks for a resource no longer overlap in the schedule. Without considering task linking, lead time, or lag time, generally this delay means that the second task starts after the first task ends, so the work flows in a continuous stream. If you enter a delay manually, you can create a delay of any length. For example, you might want to do the following:

◆ Build in extra delay time of a day or two (or more) between the tasks, in case the resource's first task takes longer than planned.

◆ Enter a smaller delay that still lets the two tasks overlap by one day, for example. Then you can use another method, such as adding another resource or specifying overtime, to take care of the smaller overallocation.

To enter a delay of the length you prefer, do the following:

1. In Resource Allocation view, click on the resource name for the overallocated resource in the upper pane.

2. In the lower pane, click on the task name for the task you want to delay. Remember that entering the delay will move the task's start date. This technique doesn't work for schedules calculated backward from the project's finish date.

3. Press the right arrow or Tab key to scroll one column to the right, to the Leveling Delay column. You can also use the horizontal scroll bar below the Task Sheet in the lower pane to scroll over. Then click on the desired cell in the Leveling Delay column.

4. Enter the amount of delay you desire (see Figure 9.13) and press Enter.

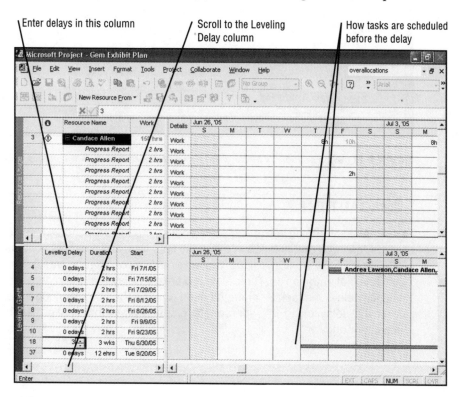

FIGURE 9.13 *It's possible to manually enter a delay.*

When you press Enter, Project pushes out the task. It adjusts the task's Start column entry and moves the task to the right on the Gantt chart. For example, compare Figure 9.14 with Figure 9.13.

The moved task

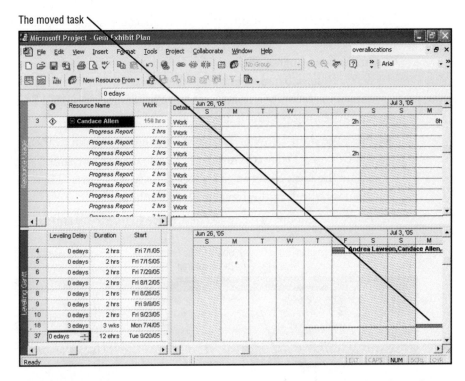

FIGURE 9.14   *After you specify a delay value, Project moves the task based on that value.*

 CAUTION

Delays are scheduled in elapsed days (edays), meaning that nonworking days for the resource are included in the delay time frame. You cannot schedule a delay in terms of workdays (d). If you enter a delay of 1w (one week), Project converts that entry to 7ed. Thus, after you enter a delay, make sure that Project actually delays the task far enough based on the schedule's working days. Or enter the delay using the appropriate elapsed time abbreviation, such as eweeks or ehours.

Removing or Replacing an Overbooked Resource

There will be times when delaying a task is not an option. For example, you might be required to finish a product by a particular date or else lose a customer's order. Additionally, certain tasks might need to be completed before the end of a financial period. Or a task might be so pivotal in your schedule—and linked to so many successor tasks down the line—that delaying it will ruin your entire schedule.

In situations like this, you need to look closely at the resource you've assigned, rather than at the schedule. You might be forced to remove a resource from a task (especially if you've assigned more than one task to the resource), or you may need to replace the resource with another one that's available to complete the task. Here's how:

1. In Resource Allocation view, click on the resource name for the overallocated resource in the upper pane.

2. In the lower pane, click on the task name for which you want to remove or replace the resource.

3. Choose Tools, Resources, Assign Resources (or press Alt+F10). The Assign Resources dialog box will appear.

4. Select the assigned resource, which should have a check mark beside it.

5. To take the resource off the task, click on the Replace button. Project immediately removes the resource from the task and opens the Replace Resource dialog box.

6. Click on a new resource for the task in the With list, and then click on OK. Project reassigns the task, removing it from the task list for the original resource and adding it to the task list for the newly selected resource. (You can then click Close to close the Assign Resources dialog box, if you prefer.)

Changing resource assignments in this way can fix one overallocation but create another. If the new Resource Name entry changes to bold red text, then you've got a new overallocation to deal with. Pay careful attention to the results of your resource reassignment.

Part-Time Work

Sometimes you may not be in a position to delay one task or another altogether. Perhaps a third successor task is unable to start until its predecessor starts, as in an SS relationship. Or you might not want to remove a resource from a task altogether, but you do want to scale back its commitment to the task and add another resource to help finish the task in a timely fashion.

In such cases, you have the option of cutting back a resource to a part-time commitment to a task:

1. In Resource Allocation view, click on the resource name for the overallocated resource in the upper pane.

2. In the lower pane, click on the name of the task for which you want to reduce the resource assignment.

3. Choose Tools, Resources, Assign Resources (or press Alt+F10). The Assign Resources dialog box appears.

4. Click on the Units cell for the assigned resource, which should have a check mark beside it. Type in your replacement for the existing Units entry, as shown in Figure 9.15. If the original number was 100%, type a number that's less than 100% to indicate how much of

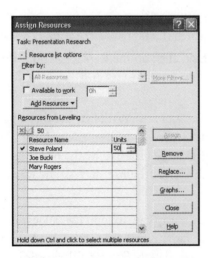

FIGURE 9.15 *You might want to change the resource's time commitment during the duration of the task.*

each workday you want the resource to spend on the selected task. For example, if you want the resource to work on the task for half the day, type 50. If the original number was 1.00, type a decimal value, such as .5 for half-time work.

5. Press Enter to finish your entry, and then close the Assign Resources dialog box. On the Gantt chart for the task, an indicator beside the Resource label tells you what portion of the workday the resource will spend on the assignment (see Figure 9.16). If the task uses a resource-driven duration type, Project adjusts the task's duration (lengthening the Gantt chart bar) so that the resource works the same total number of hours on the task. For example, if a task originally has a one-week duration and you reduce the resource's commitment to half-time, the duration is extended to two weeks.

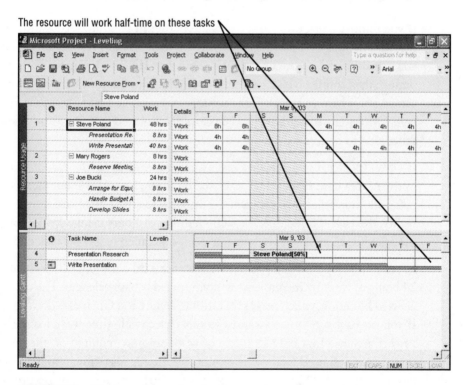

FIGURE 9.16   *Check any Gantt chart bar for part-time resources.*

CAUTION

If you enter a number that's greater than 100%, Project does not assume that you want the resource to work overtime. It assumes that the resource has the proportion of extra time available within the bounds of the workday. For example, if the resource is a consulting firm you're working with, and you change the Units entry to 200%, Project assumes that two members of the firm will work on your task each day. Or if the resource has a defined 8-hour-a-day calendar, Project assumes you have just assigned that resource 16 hours that day. To learn how to specify overtime for a task, see "Authorizing Overtime Work for a Task" in Chapter 10.

Avoiding Underallocations

If you remove a resource from a task altogether in Resource Allocation view, that task no longer appears on the assignment list for any resource. Therefore, you should make a note of the task name and ID (row) number before you remove its resource. Make sure that you go back to Gantt Chart view (or any other view where you can assign resources to tasks) and add a resource for the task. Otherwise, the task is completely underallocated and there's no resource scheduled to handle it.

It's even trickier if you change a resource from a full-time to a part-time commitment to a task. If the task has a fixed duration, Project will not increase the task's duration when you cut back the resource to a part-time commitment. In reality, the task still requires the same number of hours it initially did, but on the schedule there are fewer hours of work scheduled to get the task done.

For example, suppose that you have a task with a 3d duration, which equates to 24 hours of work by the project's 8-hours-per-day base calendar. The task type is Fixed Duration, which means that the task's start and finish date don't change. If you cut back a resource assigned to this task to half-time work for the task, Project assumes that only 12 hours of work are now required on the task. In such a case, you need to add one or more additional part-time resources to the task to replace the 12 hours of work that the first resource no longer provides. (The "Adding More Resources" section in Chapter 10 covers how to do this.)

If you cut back a resource assignment to part-time but the task duration doesn't change, you should check the task type. If it's Fixed Duration, make sure that you add more resources for the task as needed.

 TIP

Remember that you can quickly check a task's duration type by clicking on the task name in any task list and then clicking on the Task Information button on the Standard toolbar. Click on the Advanced tab, and then check the Task Type drop-down list. Click on OK to close the dialog box.

Changing the Resource's Work Schedule

The "Working with Resource Calendars (Work Schedules)" section in Chapter 7 explains how to assign a calendar for a resource to determine how many hours per week the resource works, and to set the days that the resource has off. Rather than cutting back a resource's commitment to a project, you can change a resource's schedule, adding more hours or days to remove the overallocations. Although you might not have much leeway to do this for resources within your company (you can't make certain people work extra hours without paying them overtime, for example), sometimes adjusting a resource's calendar, or selecting a new calendar, can resolve an overallocation.

Consider the following examples:

◆ If a salaried employee is willing to give up a holiday or weekend day to complete a task, you can make that day a working day in the calendar. For example, if an employee has to attend a trade show on a weekend, you can specify those weekend days as working days.

◆ On a day that requires an evening or morning meeting, you can adjust the working hours for the resource.

◆ If you're working with a vendor that normally has a standard eight-hour workday but can work around the clock when you request it, make the request and change that resource's schedule.

Although you can refer to Chapter 7 to review how to make changes to a resource's working days and hours, here's a quick way to select a different calendar for a resource:

1. Double-click on the resource's name in any view or resource list, or in the Resources From list in the Assign Resources dialog box. The Resource Information dialog box will appear.

2. Use the Base Calendar drop-down list on the Working Time tab to select another calendar, as shown in Figure 9.17.

3. Click on OK to complete the change.

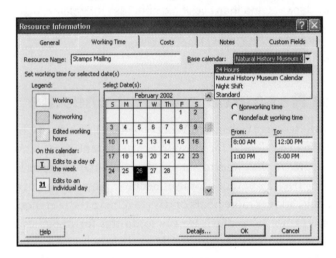

FIGURE 9.17   *You can quickly change the base calendar for a resource.*

Using Contouring to Vary Workload

Microsoft Project offers another feature intended to help you plan workloads realistically—*workload contouring*. Although contouring doesn't necessarily resolve all overallocations, it can help. Also, it does enable you to adjust how many hours per day a resource is scheduled to work on a task. This gives you more flexibility to work in smaller tasks around other tasks, or to overlap tasks without creating an overallocation.

Simply put, contouring an assignment adjusts the hours per day that a resource is scheduled to work on the assignment. You can choose one of several contouring patterns to automatically distribute the hours for an assignment.

For example, say you have a two-week task, and you assign a single full-time resource to handle it. If you apply a bell curve contour to that assignment, Project extends the task schedule to four working weeks so it can redistribute the hours per day that the resource works on the task in a bell-shaped pattern. The first two days, the resource is scheduled to work .8h on the task, the next two days, 1.6 hours, and so on. The resource's work will peak at a full day during the middle of the task schedule, and then it gradually drops back to .8h for the last two days.

You can set these kinds of contouring for an assignment in the Resource Allocation view, Resource Usage view, Task Usage view, or any other view where you can open the Assignment Information dialog box for an Assignment.

- ◆ **Front- or back-loaded.** This contour increases the hours per day from the start to the finish of the task, or decreases the hours per day from the start to the finish.

- ◆ **Early, late, or double-peak.** The work peaks to a full eight-hour day near the start or finish of the project (but not on the first or last day, as under a front- or back-loaded schedule), or both.

- ◆ **Bell.** As described, this contour smoothly allocates the hours per day to peak during the middle of the task. Generally, this contour doubles the task's duration.

- ◆ **Turtle.** Similar to a bell curve, this schedule peaks in the middle. However, it allocates more full-time workdays, so the duration isn't extended as far as it would be under a bell contour.

- ◆ **Edited.** When you edit the hours for one or more days of the assignment in the Resource Usage or Task Usage view, you've created an edited or custom contour (described later in this section). This is the only type of contour that's not automatic or predefined.

- ◆ **Flat.** Choose this contour to return to the default, scheduling the same number of work hours per day through the completion of the task.

To use the Assignment Information dialog box to assign an automatic or predefined contour to an assignment, follow these steps:

1. In the Resource Usage or Task Usage view, double-click on the assignment to which you want to apply an automatic contour. Or click on the assignment and then click on the Assignment Information button on the Standard toolbar, which is the equivalent of choosing Project, Assignment Information. The Assignment Information dialog box will appear.

2. Open the Work Contour drop-down list on the General tab, as shown in Figure 9.18. Then click on the type of work contour you want to use.

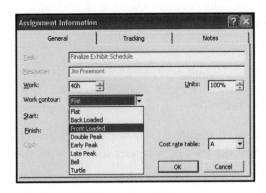

FIGURE 9.18 *Set a work contour in the Assignment Information dialog box.*

3. Click on OK to finish setting the contour.

4. If the Planning wizard warns you that the change may cause a scheduling conflict due to constraints, click on the Continue option button and then click on OK. Figure 9.19 shows a contoured work assignment. Applying the contour didn't completely remove the overallocation, but it reduced the scheduled work on the overallocated days to a level that's only slightly above the resource's full workday.

If you experiment with various contours and none of them resolves an overallocation, you can edit assignments on a day-by-day basis in the Task Usage or Resource Usage views. This is called *editing the assignment* or *creating an edited contour*.

To edit a work assignment, click on the cell for the day that you need to adjust. As shown in Figure 9.20, I clicked on the cell for F (Friday), 8/12/05 for the Plan Exhibit Layout assignment. Type the new value for the cell, including the hours (h) abbreviation (although you don't need to because Project assumes the value you enter will be in hours), and then press Enter. Project reduces the work scheduled for that date of the assignment and adds a This Assignment Work Has Been Edited contour indicator for the assignment.

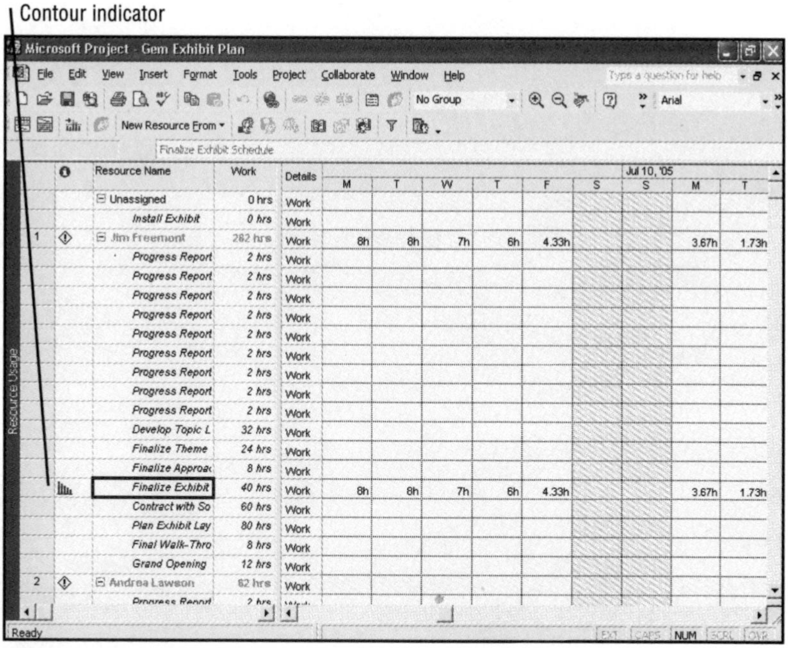

Contour indicator

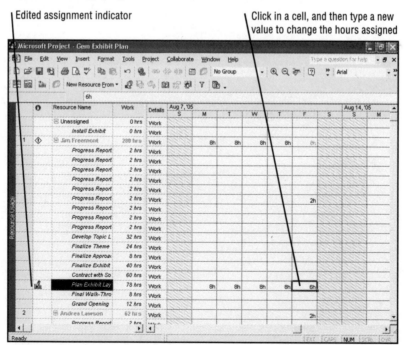

FIGURE 9.19 *Applying the contour has rescheduled some work.*

Edited assignment indicator

Click in a cell, and then type a new value to change the hours assigned

FIGURE 9.20 *Editing the assigned hours for a particular date within a particular assignment creates an edited assignment.*

Chapter 10

Optimizing the Schedule

In This Chapter

◆ Understanding which tasks are critical and how they affect your schedule

◆ Looking for ways to finish critical tasks more quickly

◆ Finding "dead" time in the schedule and taking it out

◆ Giving yourself more room by adjusting the project base calendar

When you lead a project, you have to use a lot of creativity to bring everything together on time and within budget. You need to look at different ways to apply the resources you have, check for every place where you can trim time, and do everything you can to ensure that as many tasks are moving along simultaneously as possible.

In Chapter 9, you looked at how to make your schedule attainable by ensuring that you didn't assign too much work to any particular resource. Now you can apply your managerial creativity to tightening up your schedule and ensuring that it gets the job done as quickly as possible.

Identifying and Tightening the Critical Path

In the Midwest and the northern regions of the United States, the building industry is seasonal because certain building tasks can't be completed under certain weather conditions. For example, if the weather isn't right, the foundation can't be constructed; if the foundation isn't constructed, the framing for the walls and roof can't be erected; and without the framework, other key systems can't be installed. After the most important features of the building are in place, however, the schedules for many tasks are a bit more flexible. For example, work on the exterior can proceed at the same time as work on the interior. The tasks that can't be delayed without drastically affecting the overall schedule—the foundation and framing work, for example—are called *critical tasks*.

Your schedule will have critical tasks as well. If any of these tasks slip (either begin late or take more time than you allowed), the finish date for your project will move further out. Together, the critical tasks form the *critical path* for your schedule—the sequence of tasks that must happen on time for the project to finish on time. Although moving tasks that aren't on the critical path might even out your resource assignments or help you improve milestones, such changes typically won't improve the full schedule for your project. (If you've set up the Project file so that Project calculates the schedule from a specified Finish Date, the schedule does not have a critical path.)

Thus, if you want to reduce the overall timeframe for your project, you need to reduce the length of time it takes to complete the critical path. You need to be able to identify which tasks form the critical path and focus on compressing the schedules for those tasks without needlessly inflating costs. You'll have the greatest impact on reducing a project's overall schedule if you add more resources to critical tasks. Or, you may want to rethink the order flow of tasks—see if more of them can run simultaneously, for example.

 CAUTION

The techniques covered in this chapter can introduce resource overallocations. After you make any of these changes, check for resource overallocations as described in Chapter 9, "Resolving Overallocations and Overbooked Resources."

You can use a formatting technique to identify critical tasks in the Task Sheet in Gantt Chart or Task Entry view (you'll learn about the latter shortly); this is the easiest way to highlight critical tasks. You can also format critical tasks in the lower pane of Resource Allocation view, but that formatting won't appear if you switch back to Gantt Chart or Task Entry view. Furthermore, you can format the color of the Gantt bars for critical tasks in the Gantt Chart view. You can also run the Gantt Chart wizard to format the Gantt bars for critical tasks. The section called "Quick and Dirty Gantt Chart Formatting" in Chapter 13, "Working with Different Project Views" describes the Gantt Chart wizard.

 WEB

If you want to practice formatting and working with a critical path, you can download the Seminar Plan Chapter 10 file from the Premier Press download page at www.premierpressbooks.com/downloads.asp.

To highlight the critical tasks in your schedule, follow these steps:

1. Click in the visible portion of the Task Sheet in whichever view you're presently using. For example, in Gantt Chart view, click in the left pane of the screen. Or in Task Entry View, click in the upper pane.

2. Choose Format, Text Styles. The Text Styles dialog box will appear.

3. Click on the drop-down list arrow to display the Item To Change options, and then click on Critical Tasks (see Figure 10.1). This means that the formatting choices you make next will apply to any task that's part of the critical path.

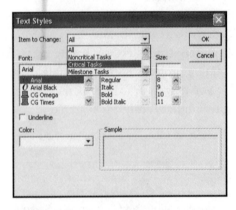

FIGURE 10.1 *Use this dialog box to specify how you'd like to identify critical tasks in the Task Sheet.*

4. In the scrolling Font list, display and click on the name of a font to use for the critical task text.

5. Use the Font Style list to apply attributes such as bold or italic to the text. Depending on the font, italic is often a better choice than bold because it more clearly differentiates the text when it's printed.

6. Use the Size list to select a size for the critical task names in the list. Enlarging the type emphasizes the critical task names and makes them easier to read.

7. Select the Underline check box if you want to apply underlining to the critical path tasks.

8. Finally, open the Color drop-down list (see Figure 10.2) and click on the color you want to apply to the critical task text in the Task Sheet.

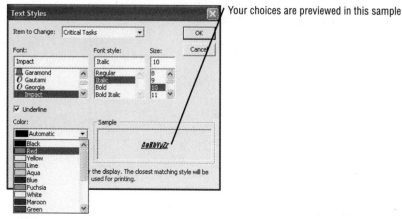

Your choices are previewed in this sample

FIGURE 10.2 *Finish up these formatting selections to tell Project how to identify critical tasks.*

9. Click on OK to apply your changes and close the Text Styles dialog box. The text formatting changes that you've specified now apply to all the tasks that are critical to your schedule in the Task Sheet.

10. Choose Format, Bar Styles. The Bar Styles dialog box appears.

11. In the list of bar types near the top of the dialog box, click on the cell that holds *Split* in the Name column.

12. Click on the Insert Row button.

13. Type **Critical** as the Name column entry for the new row.

14. Open the Show For ... Tasks drop-down list for the new row and click on Critical, as shown in Figure 10.3.

15. On the Bars tab at the bottom of the dialog box, choose another color, such as red, from the Color drop-down list under Middle.

16. Click on OK to finish formatting the Gantt bars for critical tasks.

Figure 10.4 shows how your project might look in Gantt Chart view, with special formatting applied to the critical tasks in both the Task Sheet and the Gantt chart.

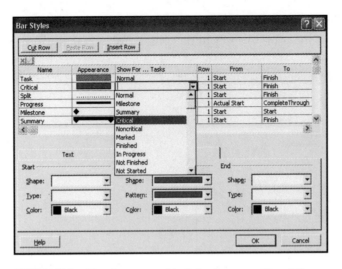

FIGURE 10.3 *You also can use this dialog box to specify a different look for the Gantt bars for critical tasks.*

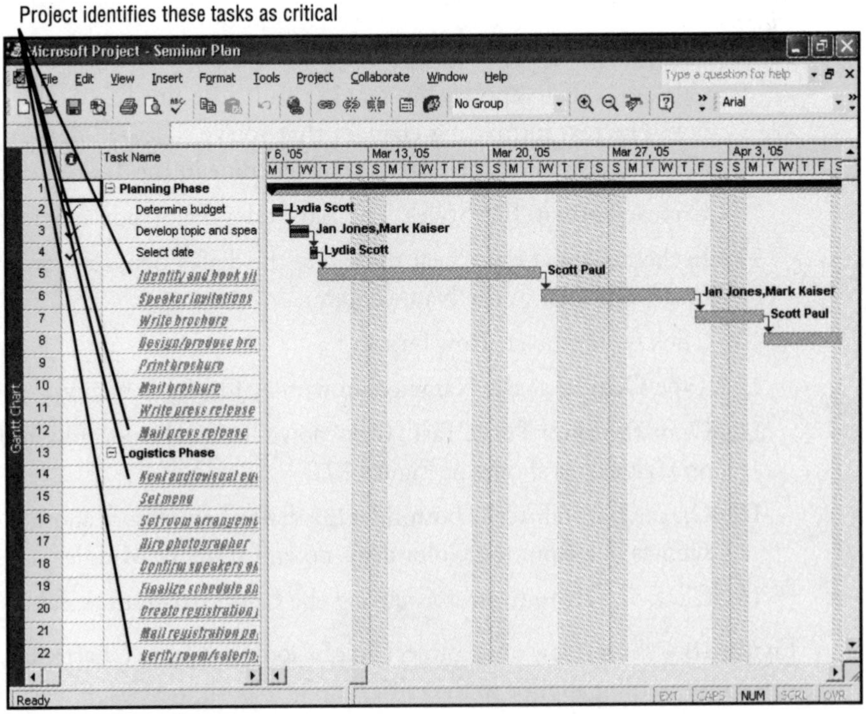

Project identifies these tasks as critical

FIGURE 10.4 *Critical path tasks now appear as you've specified in the Task Sheet.*

CAUTION

Your changes might cause a column in the Task Sheet to be filled with pound signs so that you can't see the data the column contains. If this happens, try repeating the preceding steps with different settings (especially the font size) until you find settings that work. Or you can autofit the column width by double-clicking on the right border for the header of the column to be widened.

 TIP

You can use filtering to limit the displayed lists of tasks to critical tasks only. To learn how to filter the Task Sheet, see "Filtering the Task Sheet or Resource Sheet" in Chapter 13.

If you use the preceding steps and only one task changes (typically the last one), Project isn't making an error. It simply means that your schedule doesn't include a true critical path. Perhaps you don't have many tasks linked, you've included a lot of lag time, or you haven't assigned many constraints.

However, using the Advanced tab of the Task Information dialog box, you can go back and define task relationships (links) and add constraints to tasks (such as defining that a task should start no later than a particular date). When you make alterations to task information that identifies some tasks as critical, Project applies the critical path formatting.

 NOTE

To tighten up the schedule for critical tasks if you're assigning more resources to them, Project needs tasks that have the effort-driven task type. Double-click on the task in a Task Sheet, click on the Advanced tab, check the Effort Driven check box, and make sure the task is using the default Fixed Units task type.

Using Task Entry View

After you identify which tasks are critical in your schedule, you can begin examining them, one by one, for possible adjustments to decrease the duration of each critical task. You could simply double-click on each task in the Task Sheet and use the Task Information dialog box to make your changes, but that would be time-consuming—and you wouldn't immediately see the effects of your changes on other tasks that were linked. It's better to use another view you haven't yet seen, Task Entry view, which displays Gantt Chart view in the upper pane and an area for entering and changing task and resource information in the lower pane. Switch to Task Entry view in one of the following ways:

◆ Click on the Task Entry View button on the Resource Management toolbar, if that toolbar is displayed.

◆ Choose View, More Views (or click on the More Views icon in the View Bar). In the Views list of the More Views dialog box, double-click on Task Entry.

No matter which method you use to reach it, Task Entry view appears onscreen as shown in Figure 10.5.

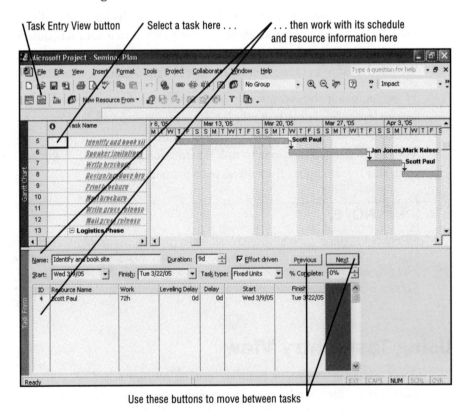

FIGURE 10.5 *Task Entry view combines the Gantt chart with a lower pane for working with different types of information.*

You can vary the details that appear in the lower pane of Task Entry view. In fact, some of the details you can modify here aren't available in other areas, such as the Task Information dialog box. To change the information in the lower pane of Task Entry view, right-click on the pane to open its shortcut menu (see Figure 10.6). Then click on one of the options to change the pane. The top option on the shortcut menu, Hide Form View, closes the bottom pane of Task Entry view, essentially returning to Gantt Chart view.

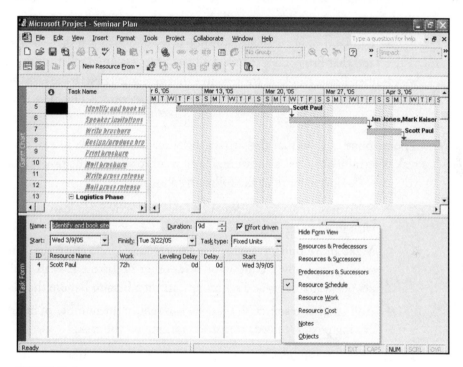

FIGURE 10.6 *It's possible to adjust the lower pane of the Task Entry view.*

When you're working in Task Entry view, you can jump back and forth between panes. You can select a task in the upper pane, make changes in the lower pane, select a different task in the upper pane, change its settings in the bottom pane, and so on.

 NOTE

When you make an entry or change a setting in any form, such as the bottom pane of the Task Entry view, you must click on the form's OK button to complete the entry. Simply pressing the Enter key does not work.

Revisiting Driving Resources

So far, for simplicity's sake, you've been looking primarily at tasks with a single resource assigned to them. Imagine how restricted your options would be, though, if each task your team handled could only be assigned to one resource! By definition, a *team* means people working together to accomplish a goal. You can think of a goal in terms of the overall project, or in terms of any individual task. This means that you can use more than one resource (a mini-team, if you will) to accomplish each task in your schedule.

Before I explain how to assign additional resources to a task, you need to understand that Project doesn't treat all resources assigned to a task the same way. Rather, Project looks at the resource that's assigned first to the task (which is typically also the resource that handles the most work). This first resource is called the *driving resource*.

The amount of time that the driving resource has available to work on the task determines the task's duration. If you want to shorten the task's duration you must do one or more of the following things:

◆ Add more hours to the resource calendar, which you learned to work with in Chapter 7.

◆ Make more units available for the resource, indicating that the resource (typically a contractor or another department with multiple people available) is adding more staff members to handle the task.

◆ Add another resource so that you can reduce the number of hours the driving resource needs to spend working on the task.

The latter two techniques are described in the next subsection.

Adding Resources for a Task

If a critical task is being handled by a resource outside your company or department, you can start optimizing your schedule by asking that resource to assign more workers or equipment to the task to finish it more quickly. For example, the resource might be willing to assign three people or three pieces of equipment to your task to get it done in a third of the time originally planned.

Keep in mind, though, that adding more resource units to a critical task can be tricky. Project always decreases the task duration directly in proportion to the number of additional resource units. Thus, if you increase the units from

100% or 1 (one full-time person) to 200% or 2 (two full-time people), Project automatically cuts the task duration in half. However, the two resource units might not get the task done in half the time. It might take a little longer, because the resources need to communicate among themselves.

To allow for this possibility, consider building a lag time between the critical task and any successor tasks that depend on its completion. Then, when you track the actual finish date, Project will accurately capture the amount of work applied.

To increase the number of units for a resource assigned to a critical task, follow these steps from Task Entry view:

1. Click on the task name of the critical task in the top pane, or use the Previous and Next buttons in the bottom pane to display the information for the critical task.

2. Right-click in the bottom pane of the Task Entry view, and then click on Resource Work.

3. Click in the Units column of the bottom pane and type in a new value, as shown in Figure 10.7.

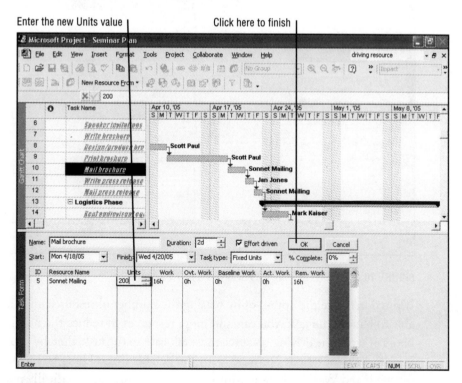

FIGURE 10.7 *You can add more resource units to shorten the task duration.*

4. Click on the OK button in the bottom pane of the Task Entry view to finish the entry. Project adjusts the duration of the task to reflect that the added resource units will finish the task more quickly.

You can also change the Units setting via the Assign Resources dialog box. Click on the critical task in the Task Sheet of Gantt Chart view or in the upper pane of Task Entry view. Click on the Assign Resources button on the Standard toolbar or the Resource Management toolbar. Or choose Tools, Resources, Assign Resources. Click in the Units column for the resource assigned to the task, type a new value (see Figure 10.8), and press Enter or click on the Enter button to finish changing the entry. Then close the Assign Resources dialog box.

Click here or press Enter to finish   Enter the new Units value

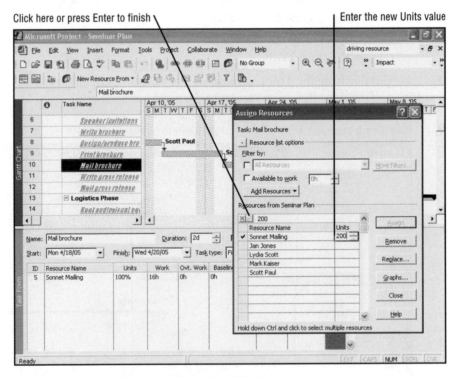

FIGURE 10.8   *This is another way to adjust resource units.*

If you don't have the option of increasing the number of resource units available to handle the task, you can add more resources to reduce the number of hours of work the driving resource must allocate to the task, thereby shortening the task's duration. For tasks with the default Fixed Units task type and for the Fixed Work task type, adding another resource automatically reduces the task duration. (Remember, Project uses the equation Duration = Work/Units to adjust the duration.) If you add one more resource, Project automatically gives each resource half of the work. Project assumes the resources will work concurrently, so the task can be completed in half the time.

Follow these steps to add more resources to a critical task and decrease the task's duration:

1. Change to Task Entry view. (If needed, also right-click in the bottom pane and then click on Resource Work.)

2. In the upper pane, click on a cell to select the critical task for which you want to add more resources.

3. In the lower pane, click in the first blank row of the Resource Name column. A drop-down list arrow will appear at the far-right end of the text entry box.

4. Display the drop-down list, and then click on a resource in the list to select it (see Figure 10.9).

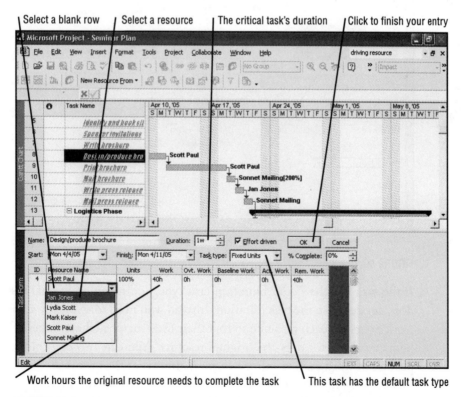

Select a blank row | Select a resource | The critical task's duration | Click to finish your entry

Work hours the original resource needs to complete the task | This task has the default task type

FIGURE 10.9 *Here's one way to add another resource to a task.*

5. Click on the OK button in the lower pane or the Enter button beside the text entry box to finish your entry. The new resource appears in the lower pane (see Figure 10.10). In Figure 10.9, notice that the Work column for the original resource holds 40h, for the 40 hours of work required to complete the task in the assigned duration. In Figure 10.10, these working hours have been adjusted in light of the new resource. The new resource offers 20h in the Work column, for a total of 40h between the two resources. The Duration entry drops from 1w in Figure 10.9 to .5w in Figure 10.10.

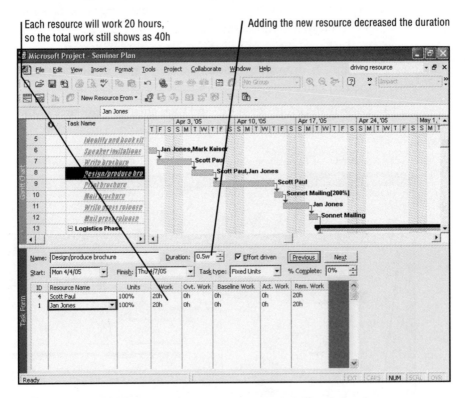

FIGURE 10.10 *By default, adding a new resource decreases the task duration.*

If the task has the Fixed Duration task type, adding an additional resource does not decrease the task duration. Instead, you need to manually adjust the work hours for each resource so that their total matches the number of work hours available for only the original resource. You can also control the proportion of work each resource has, no matter what the task type, by splitting the work evenly between the two resources or letting the driving resource retain the bulk of the work. Using the examples in Figures 10.9 and 10.10, you can specify 30 hours of work for the original resource, Scott Paul, and 10 hours of work for the new resource, Jan Jones. The total work given for the two resources then equals the 40 hours originally scheduled for Scott Paul (see Figure 10.11). To change each resource's Work entry, click in the Work column for the resource, type a new value (Project assumes you're specifying hours), and click on the OK button in the lower pane.

This resource works more and was assigned first, so it's the driving resource

The duration reflects the work hours scheduled for the driving resource

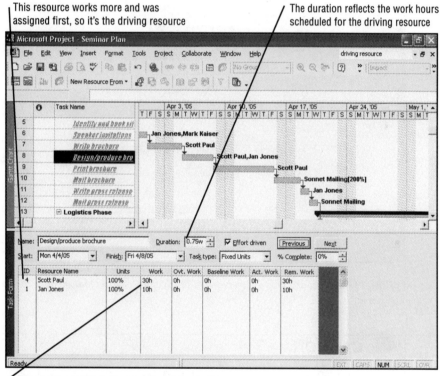

The work hours for both resources add up to the work originally scheduled for the first resource

FIGURE 10.11 *Here are the same two resources with the working hours adjusted.*

As an alternative to using the bottom pane of the Task Entry view to add resources, you can open the Assign Resources dialog box. (Click on the Assign Resources button on the Standard toolbar after clicking on the top pane of Task Entry view.) Then you can drag new resources from the assignment box to the critical task. Click on the resource you want to drag, and then point to the gray box at the left of the resource name until you see the resource pointer (see

Figure 10.12). Press and hold down the mouse button, drag the resource to the correct task name in the top pane, and release the button.

Resource pointer

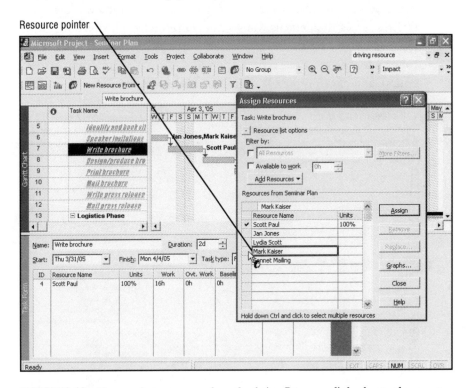

FIGURE 10.12 *You can drag a resource from the Assign Resources dialog box to the correct task name.*

 CAUTION

There are a couple of other ways to add resources, but those methods don't let you adjust the hours each resource will spend on the task to tighten up the task duration. You can add resources by typing them into the Resource Names columns of the Gantt Chart view and separating the entries with a comma. Or you can use the Resources tab of the Task Information dialog box. But your best bet is to add more resources by using the techniques described in the preceding section.

Authorizing Overtime Work for a Task

Companies, particularly large ones, are obligated to compensate most hourly employees for overtime work.

In some cases, you might also need to pay overtime charges for outside resources you bring in for your project. Overtime costs are required, especially for any resources who are union workers. To protect the bottom line, generally Project doesn't let you add extra shifts (overtime hours) for a resource by changing the Units entry to a value greater than 100% (or 1.00, if you're using decimal values). As you learned earlier, changing the Units entry generally assumes that more than one worker from the resource will work on the task simultaneously, or that a salaried employee will devote time outside the normal workday to get the task done.

You also can't specify overtime by changing the working calendar so that a resource has more hours in the day. (You can use that technique to resolve overallocations for salaried resources, however.) Project forces you to enter overtime hours in another way to ensure that overtime costs are calculated correctly, according to the overtime rate you entered when you added the resource to the file (see Chapter 7, "Adding Resources into Your Project Plan"), and to ensure that you've approved the overtime work.

The Task Entry view allows you to allocate overtime work for a task. After you add overtime, Project changes the task's duration to reflect the extra working hours per day provided by the overtime. Here's how to authorize overtime hours for a resource assigned to a critical task:

1. Change to Task Entry view.

2. In the upper pane of Task Entry view, click on a cell in the critical task to which you want to assign overtime work. Information about the resources assigned to the task appears in the lower pane.

3. Right-click on the lower pane and click on Resource Work. The pane changes to display more information about the resource's work schedule (see Figure 10.13).

4. Click in the Ovt. Work cell belonging to the resource for which you want to specify overtime hours. Type the number of overtime hours you want to authorize, and then click on the OK button in the lower pane. Project enters the overtime hours and tightens the task's Duration entry accordingly (see Figure 10.14).

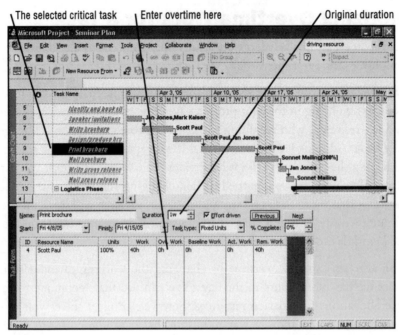

FIGURE 10.13 *You can enter overtime when you view Resource Work information in the lower pane of Task Entry view.*

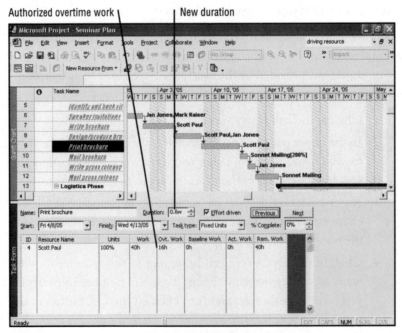

FIGURE 10.14 *Here's the revised Resource Work information.*

In these examples, adding resources and authorizing overtime reduces the overall critical path for the project. The individual tasks, however, remain critical. Adding overtime introduces slack into the schedule, which in turn might remove the critical designation for the task to which you add overtime or (depending on task links and other task information) for one or more predecessor tasks.

Creating a Hammock Task

Sometimes you may have a task with start dates that are based on the start or finish dates of two other tasks, without being really dependent on those tasks. In such a case, you can create a special type of task called a *hammock task*. The start and finish dates for the hammock task come from the start or finish dates for other tasks in the schedule. As those other tasks move around in the schedule, the start date, finish date, and duration for the hammock task will change accordingly.

 CAUTION

A hammock task may not have predecessors. If a hammock task is linked to a predecessor task, its schedule will not be recalculated correctly.

Use these steps to add a hammock task into a schedule:

1. Use the Insert key to insert the task that will be the hammock task in your project plan, and enter its Task Name. Or, select the existing task that you want to set up as a hammock task.

2. Because new tasks are linked into any existing sequence of tasks by default, remove any links added to the new hammock task. (You may need to relink other tasks as a result.)

3. If needed, drag the divider bar in the Gantt Chart view to the right so that you can see the Start and Finish columns for each task.

4. Click on the Start or Finish date cell (for another task) that holds the date that will determine the Start date for the hammock task.

5. Choose Edit, Copy Cell.

6. Click on the Start date cell for the hammock task.

7. Choose Edit, Paste Special. The Paste Special dialog box opens.

8. Click on the Paste Link option button (see Figure 10.15), and click on OK.

The pasted date will become the Start date for the hammock task

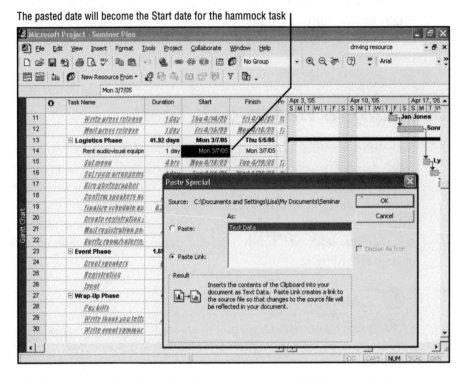

FIGURE 10.15 *Use Edit, Paste Special to link the start and finish dates and create a hammock task.*

9. Repeat Steps 4 through 8 to create the linked finish date for the hammock task.

 TIP

Once you've created the hammock task, its Start, Finish, and Duration field entries should be recalculated if either of the linked dates change. If the values aren't recalculated as you'd expect, press the F9 key twice to recalculate the schedule manually.

Using Multiple Critical Paths

In most instances, a task needs to have links to successor tasks (other tasks that cannot start or finish until the predecessor task starts or finishes, depending on the nature of the link). Or particular constraints must be marked as critical and be part of the critical path. But that doesn't mean that tasks without successors or constraints can be finished late without affecting the overall schedule. For example, if you set a project finish date of 6/30/05, all tasks must be finished by that date for the project to be finished on time.

Project enables you to display *multiple critical paths* to mark more tasks as critical and help you identify potential trouble spots that could bog down your project. This feature becomes particularly important if you're working in a consolidated project file, where you might have multiple series of concurrent tasks. (See Chapter 20, "Consolidating Projects," to learn how to set up consolidated project files.) When you display multiple critical paths, Project resets certain information for tasks that have no constraints or successors to make those tasks (and often any predecessors) critical.

Chapter 4 explained that even though a Task Sheet or Resource Sheet typically shows only a half-dozen or so fields (columns) in any given view, there are dozens of other fields you can display if needed. Many of these fields contain information that Project calculates to help it make decisions, such as determining which tasks are critical. Project uses two of these calculated fields to determine whether a task has slack and therefore isn't critical: the *late finish date* and the *early finish date*.

A task cannot miss its late finish date without delaying the finish of the whole project. When a task has no constraints or successors, Project sets the task's late finish date as the project's finish date. This makes sense, because a task without constraints or links can move around in the schedule without affecting other tasks, but it still must finish by the project completion date. A task cannot be finished before its early finish date, which Project calculates based on the task's duration, start date, resources, links, and so on.

In other words, Project assumes that a task with a 2w duration requires a minimum of two weeks. Therefore, if a task without successors or constraints falls in the middle of a lengthy project schedule, there could be weeks between the early start date and the late finish date. Project considers this time *total slack*, but you might consider it crucial lead time that you don't want to waste.

When you turn on multiple critical paths, Project changes the late finish date for such tasks to the same date as the early finish date, eliminating that slack to make the tasks (and some predecessors) critical. Therefore, turning on multiple critical paths can highlight other groups of related tasks in the schedule to which you might want to add more resources or overtime, to ensure those tasks finish on time. To display multiple critical paths in Project, choose Tools, Options. Click on the Calculation tab, and then place a check beside Calculate Multiple Critical Paths, as shown in Figure 10.16.

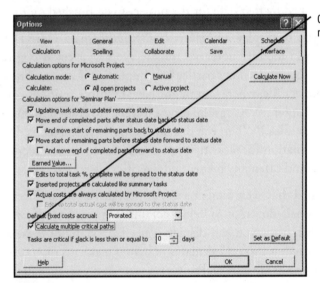

Checking this option displays multiple critical paths

FIGURE 10.16 *Turn on multiple critical paths using the Options dialog box.*

Working with Slack

Part of what defines a critical task is its impact on other tasks, depending on the relationships you've established between tasks. Sometimes there's room between related tasks, so the task scheduled first can slip without delaying the start or completion of the successor task. That room between tasks is called *float time* or *slack*. (As noted in the preceding section, if a task doesn't have a successor task, the task's slack is any time between the task's early start date and late finish date.) Slack between tasks is called *free slack*. Slack between a particular task and the project's finish date is called *total slack,* and basically it tells you how long the task can slip without affecting the project finish date.

Total slack measurements can be negative. That happens when you have two linked tasks, both of which are constrained to start on particular dates. If you change the duration of the predecessor task to make it longer, and you don't add any lead time for the successor task (so it can start before the finish of the predecessor), you'll create negative slack. In optimizing your schedule, make sure that you look for negative slack measurements and make changes to eliminate them, ensuring that the critical path is realistic.

If the total slack for a task is less than a minimum amount you've specified (which you'll learn to change shortly), Project identifies the task as a critical task.

You can display the free slack and total slack for the tasks in a schedule in the Task Sheet portion of Gantt Chart view or Task Entry view. Follow these steps to check the slack measurements for tasks:

1. Display Gantt Chart or Task Entry view.
2. Click anywhere in the Task Sheet portion of the view.
3. Choose View, Table for a submenu of options (see Figure 10.17), and click on Schedule.

FIGURE 10.17 *Select a way to see how much free slack and total slack your tasks have.*

4. Scroll to the right in that portion of the window until you see the Free Slack and Total Slack columns (see Figure 10.18).

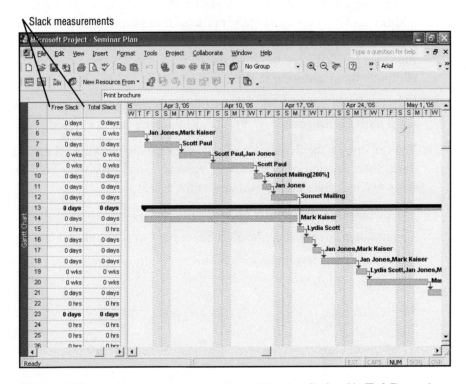

FIGURE 10.18 *Here's what the slack columns look like when displayed in Task Entry view.*

Changing How Much Slack Makes a Task Critical

Although Chapter 28, "Customizing Microsoft Project," covers how to adjust many important Project features, one feature relating directly to slack and critical tasks bears mentioning here. You can change the minimum amount of slack that tasks must have to avoid being designated as critical tasks. By default, any task with 0 or fewer days of total slack is designated as a critical task.

Increasing this setting designates more tasks as critical, allowing you to scrutinize them and look for ways to tighten the schedule:

1. Choose Tools, Options. The Options dialog box will appear.

2. Click on the Calculation tab to display its settings (see Figure 10.19).

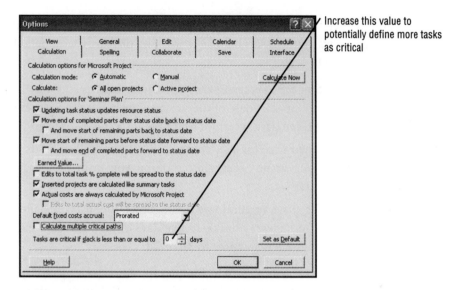

Increase this value to potentially define more tasks as critical

FIGURE 10.19 *Use the Calculations tab in the Options dialog box to control which tasks are critical.*

3. Double-click on the entry in the Tasks Are Critical If Slack Is Less Than Or Equal To ... Days text box, and type in a new entry. For example, type in **3** to have Project designate any task with less than or equal to three days of total slack as a critical task.

4. Click on OK to close the dialog box. Project updates critical task designations in light of the new setting.

Adjusting Lead and Lag Times

Lead times and lag times can have a great impact on the slack available for a task, as well as the critical path. (The "Working with Lead Times and Lag Times" section in Chapter 6 explains the basics of lead and lag times.)

Constraints allowing, you can add slack time by removing lead time or adding lag time. For example, you might change the Lag entry for a successor task from -2d to 0d to remove lead time. Adding slack time generally lengthens the schedule to some degree. Depending on how much slack you add, Project might remove a task from the critical path. This can be beneficial in your planning if you're really unsure how well you estimated the schedule for a task.

In contrast, here are a few things you can do to use lead and lag times to tighten the critical path (assuming you're working primarily with default finish-to-start links):

◆ Add lead time for a successor task where none exists, assuming that you can move up the start date of the successor task. For example, entering **-3d** creates three days' worth of lead time for a successor task.

◆ Add more lead time for a successor task with an FS link to its predecessor, as long as no constraints prohibit you from moving up the successor task.

◆ Cut back lag time, or eliminate it altogether, if constraints allow. For example, a 5d lag entry builds in five days of lag time. You might be able to change such an entry to **3d** or **2d**.

You can choose any of a number of techniques to adjust the lead and lag times for a task. For example, you can double-click on a task name, click on the Predecessors tab in the Task Information dialog box, and then edit the Lag column in the Predecessors list. Or you can use the lower pane of Task Entry view to work with lead and lag time, as follows:

1. In the upper pane, click on the name of the critical task for which you want to work with lead and lag times.

2. Right-click on the lower pane. Then choose Predecessors & Successors on the shortcut menu that appears. The lower pane changes to show other tasks linked to the selected task, either as predecessors or successors (see Figure 10.20).

3. Click on the cell in the Lag column for the link you want to edit. Type a new lag setting, and then click on OK in the lower pane. Project adjusts any task schedule as needed, according to your change. For example, Figure 10.21 shows the result of adding lead time to task 7's link with its predecessor task, task 6. Because both the selected task and its predecessor are critical, adding the lead time (so that the tasks overlap in the schedule) reduces the overall schedule for the project.

4. To adjust lead and lag times for another task, select the task in the upper pane and make changes as needed in the lower pane.

The selected critical task — Its predecessor

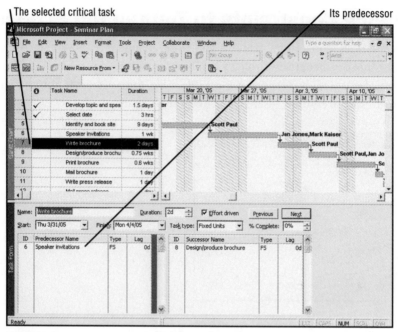

FIGURE 10.20 *The bottom pane has been adjusted to let you work with linked tasks.*

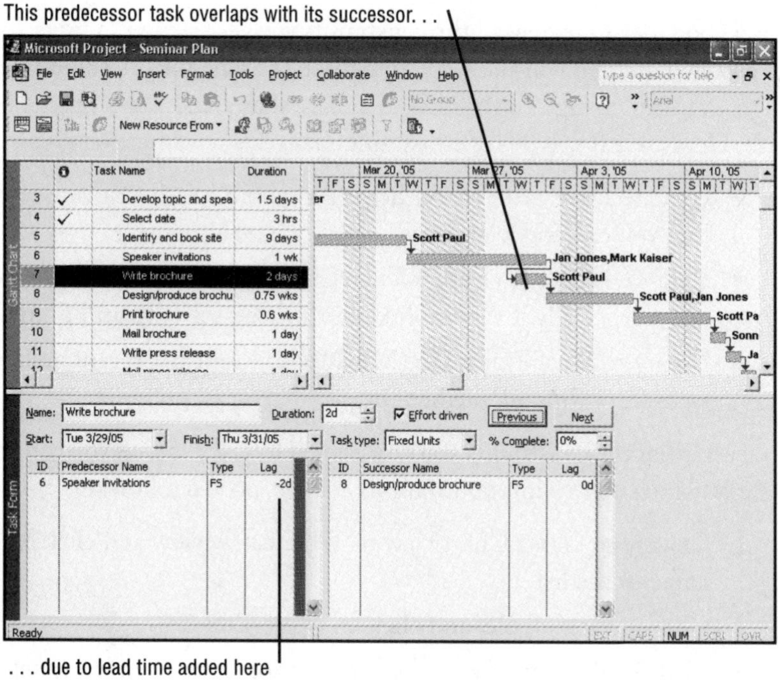

This predecessor task overlaps with its successor. . .

. . . due to lead time added here

FIGURE 10.21 Here's an example of working with linked tasks.

Changing Constraints to Tighten the Schedule

Sometimes, constraints prohibit you from changing lead and lag time, or a schedule conflict arises if you try to add a constraint. If you have the Planning wizard enabled, it warns you if a lead or lag time or constraint change will create such a conflict, as shown in Figure 10.22.

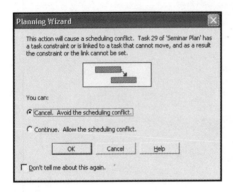

FIGURE 10.22 *Constraints can keep you from making the schedule adjustments you want.*

It is a good idea to review all the constraints you've assigned to tasks, looking for any changes that will allow you to tighten the schedule. In some cases, you might want to change constraints to ensure that a task stays on the critical path. Here are a few types of constraint changes you can make:

- Change more tasks to As Soon As Possible (ASAP) constraints so that you can add lead times.

- Remove Finish No Earlier Than (FNET) constraints for predecessor tasks, especially if they're linked to a successor with an FS link.

- Use more Must Finish On (MFO) constraints to prevent predecessor tasks from slipping further out.

To see a list of the constraints you've assigned to tasks so that you can quickly identify which constraints you want to change, do the following:

1. Change to Gantt Chart view or Table Entry view and click on a task name in the list.

2. Choose View, Table, and click on More Tables.

3. In the Tables list (with the Task option button above it selected), double-click on Constraint Dates, or click on it once and then click

on Apply. The Task Sheet changes to include Constraint Type and Constraint Date columns. You can drag the split bar from the upper pane and use the scroll bar for the task list to display those columns (see Figure 10.23).

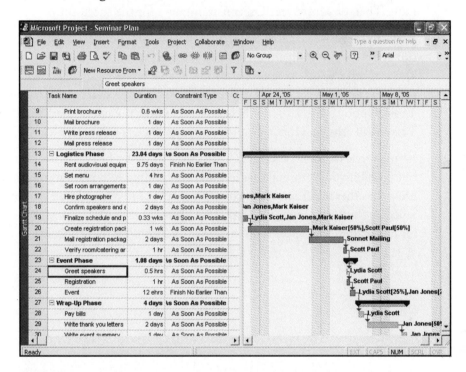

FIGURE 10.23 *Project lists constraints. Scroll through the list to check for constraints you might want to change.*

Chapter 6 covers the different types of task constraints in more detail. To quickly change constraints while the list of task constraints is onscreen, double-click on the desired task name to display the Task Information dialog box. Click on the Advanced tab. In the Constraint Task area, use the Type drop-down list and Date text box to specify a change to the constraint.

Ignoring Constraints to Remove Negative Slack

If your project has hundreds of tasks, manually reviewing and changing constraint types could take quite some time. Although you may want to use the manual route to really fine-tune your schedule, Project offers an alternative for situations where you only want to eliminate negative slack from the schedule. (For example, negative slack occurs when a successor task can't start until its predecessor finishes, but the predecessor's finish date is after a Start No Later Than or Must Start On constraint date for the successor.)

Basically, negative slack means that accomplishing both tasks within all the constraints is physically impossible, so you need to remove that negative slack. You can tell Project to ignore constraints and move tasks where needed in order to remove every instance of negative slack in the schedule. First, choose Tools, Options. Click on the Schedule tab. Clear the check mark beside the Tasks Will Always Honor Their Constraint Dates option. Click on OK.

It's okay to leave some tasks marked as critical in your schedule. After all, reality can prohibit you from building in lead time, adding resources or overtime, or using the other techniques covered in this chapter. Just remember, if your project schedule starts running behind, you should always look to the critical tasks first for opportunities to apply more resources and improve the schedule.

Chapter 11

**Comparing
Progress
Versus Your
Baseline Plan**

In This Chapter

- ◆ Capturing the original project information and schedule
- ◆ Reporting work that has been completed
- ◆ Preserving updated information, adding another baseline, and saving an interim plan
- ◆ Checking if your project is on time, ahead of schedule, or running behind
- ◆ Deleting a baseline
- ◆ Comparing project plans

Because a project often calls on a varied combination of resources, tasks, and other factors, you need to act as a "deejay." You need to make sure that the right tune plays at the right time (tasks stay on schedule), that the volume is right (everything's done correctly), and that the floor stays full of dancers (your resources remain available and able to work when you need them).

This chapter shows you how to compare actual progress on a project with the schedule you had planned. That way, you can make adjustments, if needed, to meet your project goals.

Final Considerations Before Saving the Baseline

By this point, you should have everything in your project plan in place. You should have entered all the tasks, created links between them, and used constraints and other features to control their schedules. You should have entered all your resources in the Resource Sheet, including costs for using each resource. After assigning resources to tasks, you should have adjusted the assignments, costs, and schedules as needed to perfect the plan.

In other words, you should strive to make your plan as accurate as possible before you proceed with the subject of this chapter—saving and using baseline information. In the real world, you should verify the following items to confirm that your plan is realistic before you save the baseline:

◆ If the plan requires resources outside your department or company (or resources otherwise not under your control), verify each outside resource's availability and willingness to take on the required tasks.

◆ Make sure you have accurate cost quotes when required, particularly for very expensive tasks or those that require highly specialized or custom work. Being disciplined in this regard may take a bit longer, but it reflects more positively on you in the long run—and ensures that you'll have an adequate budget in place to complete the project.

◆ If you have to verify the project budget, goals, or time frame with your company's leadership or with the client, be sure to do so. This gives you the opportunity to make any needed adjustments before you save the baseline.

Creating the Baseline

When you're relatively young and your doctor puts you through your first thorough physical, he's not being paranoid and looking for imaginary illnesses. He's gathering your vital statistics while you're in good health, so that there will be a basis for comparison if you ever begin feeling ill. If your blood pressure is very low when you're healthy, a slight climb in the pressure can signal to your doctor that something serious is going on. But a doctor who doesn't have your normal blood pressure reading might not catch the fact that your new reading is higher than normal. Those original health measurements your doctor takes become the baseline, the starting point for future comparison.

Project enables you to take a baseline reading of your schedule, too. Thus, you'll have a record of where you started, and you can use it to diagnose any problems that crop up in the schedule and budget. When you save a baseline for your schedule, Project records all timing, work, and cost details about your plan. Then you can look at the information you've entered about the actual work performed, actual task duration, start and finish dates, and actual costs, and compare it with your original plans. (You'll learn how to do this later in this chapter.)

Prior versions of Microsoft Project automatically queried you about whether or not to save a baseline the first time you saved any project file after adding information to it. That feature is not available in Project 2002. Instead, you must save the baseline manually.

CAUTION

Every time you save the baseline, it overwrites any baseline information you saved previously. If you want to take a snapshot of your task's start and finish dates at any given time and leave the original baseline intact, you can save another baseline or save an interim plan. See the "Saving Additional Baselines" and "Saving and Viewing an Interim Plan" sections later in this chapter.

You shouldn't save a baseline until you enter all your task and resource information, as described in the first section of this chapter. You can also save a baseline for only part of the project by selecting certain tasks to track in detail.

 WEB

If you want to practice saving and working with a baseline, you can download the Gem Exhibit Plan Chapter 11 file from the Premier Press download page at www.premierpressbooks.com/downloads.asp.

Here are the steps for creating your schedule baseline:

1. Enter all the task and resource information you want to save as part of the baseline. It doesn't hurt to double-check that everything's in place, including links and fixed task costs you might have overlooked.

2. (Optional) If you want to save baseline data only for certain tasks, select the rows you want in the Task Sheet in Gantt Chart view. (Make sure you're in Gantt Chart view by choosing View, Gantt Chart, or by clicking on the Gantt Chart icon on the View Bar.) Select the tasks you want by pointing to the row number for the top row and dragging down to highlight (select) the rows. To select noncontiguous rows, press and hold down Ctrl and then click on each additional row.

3. Choose Tools, Tracking. A submenu of commands appears.

4. Choose Save Baseline. The Save Baseline dialog box will appear (see Figure 11.1).

5. To save baseline information for all the tasks, leave the Entire Project option button selected. If you selected specific tasks for the baseline, click on the Selected Tasks option button, and then select either or both of the following options under Roll Up Baselines if needed:

FIGURE 11.1   *Using this dialog box, you can save baseline information easily at any time.*

- ◆ **To All Summary Tasks.** Saves the summary task baseline data to reflect the baseline data for the selected subtasks.

- ◆ **From Subtasks Into Selected Summary Task(s).** For a selected summary task, ensures that the summary task data reflects subtasks that have been inserted or deleted within its summary group.

6. Click on OK. Project stores the baseline information.

Viewing Baseline Information

After you save the baseline information, you might want to look at the baseline values for reference or print them out for others on the team. To view the baseline information, use a variation of the Task Sheet called the Baseline Table. The "Choosing a Table" section in Chapter 13, "Working with the Different Project Views," provides more details, but here are the basic steps for viewing this table of baseline information:

1. Make sure that you're in Gantt Chart view by choosing View, Gantt Chart, or by clicking on the Gantt Chart icon in the View Bar. Gantt Chart view appears with a cell selected in the Task Sheet.

2. Choose View, Table: (table name) and click on More Tables. The More Tables dialog box will appear (see Figure 11.2).

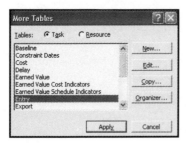

FIGURE 11.2 *Selecting a table here changes the columns that appear in the Task Sheet.*

3. Make sure that you leave the Task option button selected at the top of the dialog box. In the Tables list, select Baseline by double-clicking on it, or by clicking on it once and then clicking on Apply. Project displays the baseline columns in the Task Sheet.

4. Scroll the Task Sheet to the right a bit and drag the vertical split bar to the right. This will display more of the Task Sheet so that you can see the baseline columns (see Figure 11.3).

If you want to return to the regular Task Sheet view at any time, choose View, Table: (table name), Entry. You can also display the Variance Task Sheet table, which includes the Baseline Start and Baseline Finish fields, plus variance fields that show the difference between the baseline fields and the information currently in the Start and Finish fields.

Entering Completed Work

Project would be an even better product if you could attach a "work meter" to each and every resource that would automatically capture what the resource does and report that information to Project. Because the world isn't that high-tech yet, you'll have to tell Project which work has been completed on scheduled tasks.

Although Project gives you several ways to enter information about actual work completed, one of the most convenient methods is the Tracking toolbar.

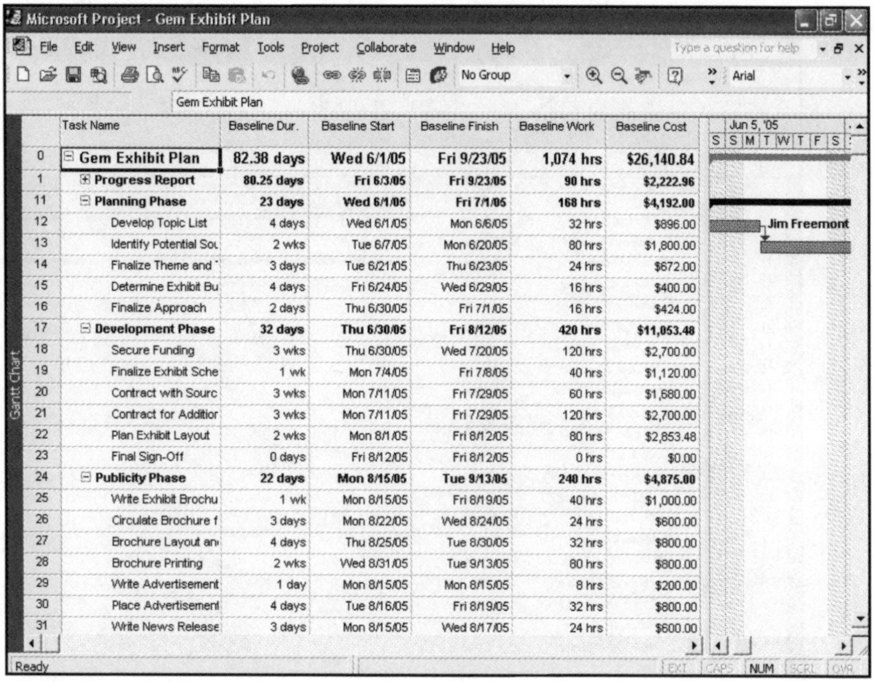

	Task Name	Baseline Dur.	Baseline Start	Baseline Finish	Baseline Work	Baseline Cost
0	Gem Exhibit Plan	82.38 days	Wed 6/1/05	Fri 9/23/05	1,074 hrs	$26,140.84
1	Progress Report	80.25 days	Fri 6/3/05	Fri 9/23/05	90 hrs	$2,222.96
11	Planning Phase	23 days	Wed 6/1/05	Fri 7/1/05	168 hrs	$4,192.00
12	Develop Topic List	4 days	Wed 6/1/05	Mon 6/6/05	32 hrs	$896.00
13	Identify Potential Sou	2 wks	Tue 6/7/05	Mon 6/20/05	80 hrs	$1,800.00
14	Finalize Theme and	3 days	Tue 6/21/05	Thu 6/23/05	24 hrs	$672.00
15	Determine Exhibit Bu	4 days	Fri 6/24/05	Wed 6/29/05	16 hrs	$400.00
16	Finalize Approach	2 days	Thu 6/30/05	Fri 7/1/05	16 hrs	$424.00
17	Development Phase	32 days	Thu 6/30/05	Fri 8/12/05	420 hrs	$11,053.48
18	Secure Funding	3 wks	Thu 6/30/05	Wed 7/20/05	120 hrs	$2,700.00
19	Finalize Exhibit Sche	1 wk	Mon 7/4/05	Fri 7/8/05	40 hrs	$1,120.00
20	Contract with Sourc	3 wks	Mon 7/11/05	Fri 7/29/05	60 hrs	$1,680.00
21	Contract for Additior	3 wks	Mon 7/11/05	Fri 7/29/05	120 hrs	$2,700.00
22	Plan Exhibit Layout	2 wks	Mon 8/1/05	Fri 8/12/05	80 hrs	$2,853.48
23	Final Sign-Off	0 days	Fri 8/12/05	Fri 8/12/05	0 hrs	$0.00
24	Publicity Phase	22 days	Mon 8/15/05	Tue 9/13/05	240 hrs	$4,875.00
25	Write Exhibit Brochu	1 wk	Mon 8/15/05	Fri 8/19/05	40 hrs	$1,000.00
26	Circulate Brochure f	3 days	Mon 8/22/05	Wed 8/24/05	24 hrs	$600.00
27	Brochure Layout an	4 days	Thu 8/25/05	Tue 8/30/05	32 hrs	$800.00
28	Brochure Printing	2 wks	Wed 8/31/05	Tue 9/13/05	80 hrs	$800.00
29	Write Advertisement	1 day	Mon 8/15/05	Mon 8/15/05	8 hrs	$200.00
30	Place Advertisement	4 days	Tue 8/16/05	Fri 8/19/05	32 hrs	$800.00
31	Write News Release	3 days	Mon 8/15/05	Wed 8/17/05	24 hrs	$600.00

FIGURE 11.3 *You can now view the baseline information you saved.*

To display it, right-click on any onscreen toolbar and then choose Tracking. It's shown in Figure 11.4. You'll use several of its buttons as you update and view information about completed work in the Gantt Chart view. I'll describe each button when you need it.

Choosing a Status Date

In this chapter and the next one, you'll learn that Project automates some features for updating completed work. In addition, Project calculates how much work has been completed, which costs have accumulated, and whether the project is ahead or behind schedule and budget.

Normally, when you're updating the work completed in a schedule, Project assumes that you're marking all the work completed as of the current date (which is determined by your computer's system clock, by default). However, sometimes you may want Project to use a different date when it's updating work and performing calculations regarding completed work and accumulated costs.

Tracking toolbar

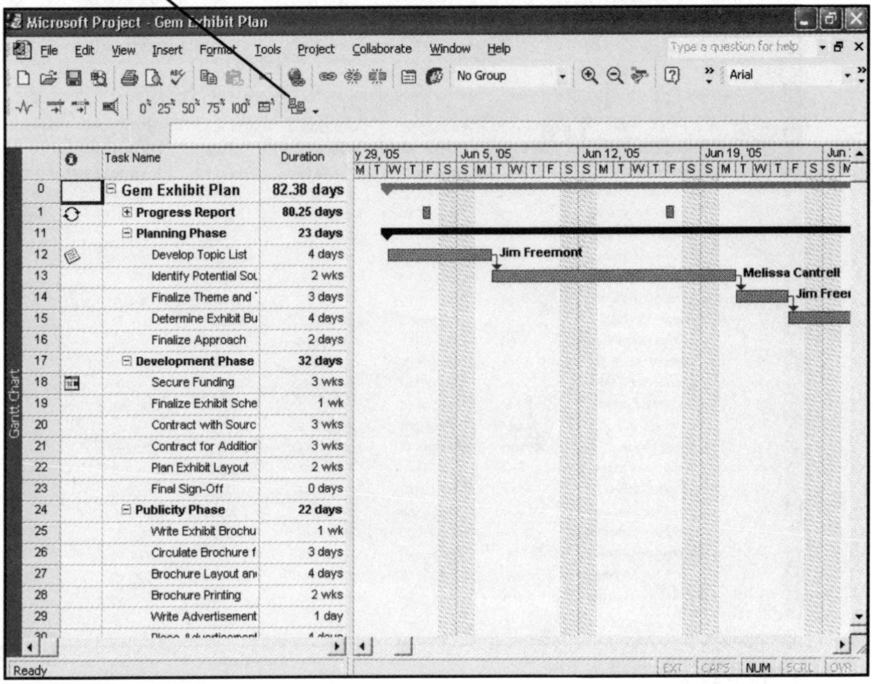

FIGURE 11.4 *The Tracking toolbar speeds up the process of entering specific information about tasks.*

For example, say that every Friday at 4 P.M., your group has a status meeting to discuss progress on individual tasks. You check with your resources on Wednesday so you can update information about work completed as of the day of the meeting (Friday). The date that your status information really applies to is the following Friday. So, to make it easier to use some methods to enter your updates, and to ensure that Project's status calculations are accurate, you should enter that Friday's date as the status date. However, it is important to remember that the Update Project dialog box and the Update as Scheduled button on the tracking toolbar use the current date for project updates, unless the status date is a later date. In the latter case, work will be marked completed as of the status date.

Project also uses the status date setting to reschedule all or parts of tasks, based on the amount of work marked as completed. Project can reschedule portions of future tasks that are completed early back to the status date, when you mark those tasks as complete. Or, it can reschedule uncompleted work on a task that was scheduled prior to the status date to resume, beginning on the status date. The options controlling how Project works with the status date appear on the Calculation tab of the Options dialog box. Chapter 28, "Customizing Microsoft Project," describes these options so you can decide whether or not to enable them as you work.

To change the project status date before you enter completed work information, follow these steps:

1. Choose Project, Project Information. The Project Information dialog box will appear.

2. Open the Status Date calendar and use it to specify an alternate date. Or, if you want to use the Current Date setting as the status date and remove a Status Date entry you made previously, drag over the entry in the Status Date text box and then type **NA**.

3. Click on OK to close the Project Information dialog box and finish setting the status date.

If you haven't yet saved your baseline, you can change the Current Date setting in the Project Information dialog box to a much earlier date. Then go back and adjust the original task schedules, as long as you haven't marked any work completed on them. You might need to do this, for example, if you're trying to backtrack and enter tasks that you left out of the project plan but now need to include. Changing the Current Date as needed just makes the job a little faster, so you don't have to respond to a number of Planning wizard warnings.

Updating Task by Task

There are at least three ways to tell Project about work that has been completed on a task or a selected set of tasks.

The first method is updating completed work information with the mouse. This is probably the most time-consuming, but it allows you to get an indication of the completed work immediately. With this method, you can update work using the calendar to indicate that, for example, someone has completed three out of five days of work scheduled for a task. Project calculates the percentage of work completed.

To update task completion information using your mouse, work with the Gantt bars in Gantt Chart view. Point to the left end of the bar for the task you want to update, so that the mouse pointer changes to a percentage pointer. Press and hold the left mouse button and drag to the right (see Figure 11.5).

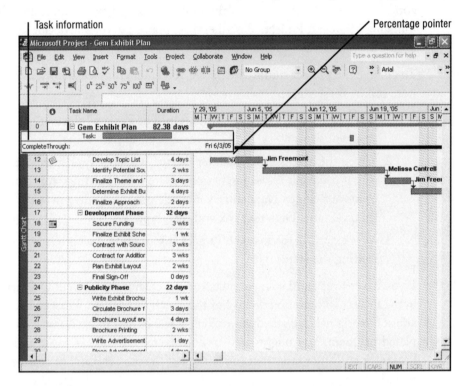

FIGURE 11.5 *The percentage pointer indicates that you can update your task by dragging.*

As you drag, a Task information box appears, telling you how many days will be marked as completed. When you release the mouse button, Project indicates the percentage of the task that has been completed by placing a dark *progress bar* (completion bar) within the Gantt bar for the task you've modified (see Figure 11.6). If a task has not started on time and you need to enter information about the actual starting date, use the method described next to update the task.

The second method also allows you to update tasks one at a time, but it gives you some options about how you specify that the work is completed. This method enables you to specify the actual start and finish dates for the task when those dates differ from the dates you scheduled. To use this method, follow these steps:

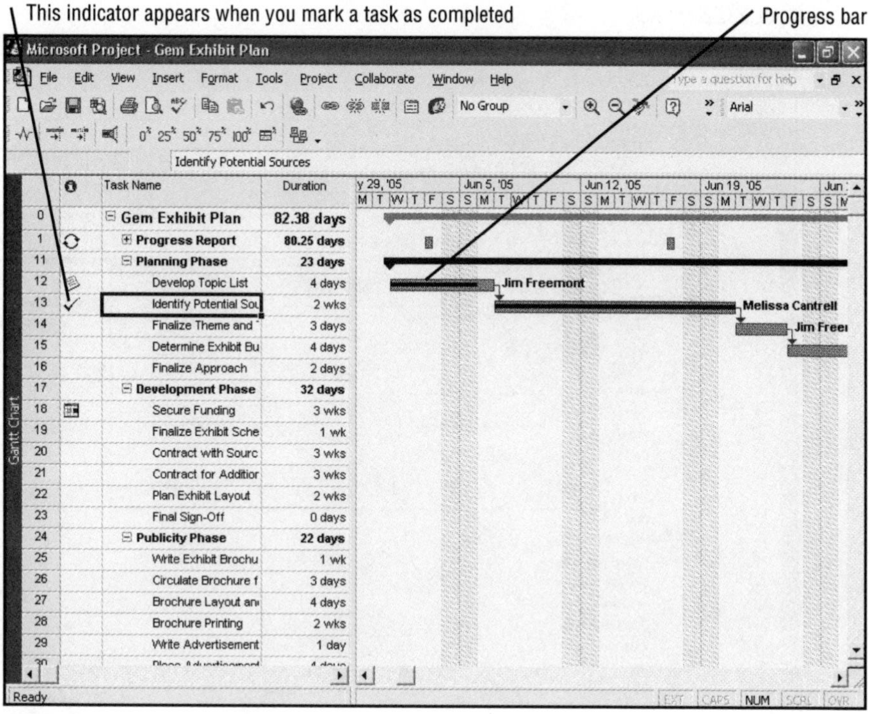

This indicator appears when you mark a task as completed   Progress bar

FIGURE 11.6 *The dark bar within the Gantt bar for the first task shows the portion of work completed on the task so far (in this case, all of it).*

1. Select the task or tasks you want to update in the Task Sheet. Keep in mind, though, that you can't select a summary task (the "master" task for a set of recurring tasks) to update it. You can only select the subtasks within a summary task. For more on working with summary tasks and subtasks, see Chapter 5, "Working with Outlining."

2. Choose Tools, Tracking, Update Tasks. Alternately, click on the Update Tasks button on the Tracking toolbar. The Update Tasks dialog box will appear (see Figure 11.7).

3. Enter information about the work that has been completed using one of the following three methods:

   ◆ Enter a percentage value, such as **10** for 10%, in the % Complete text box, which is highlighted by default when you open the Update Tasks dialog box. Project changes the duration settings for you when you finish updating the task.

Update Tasks button

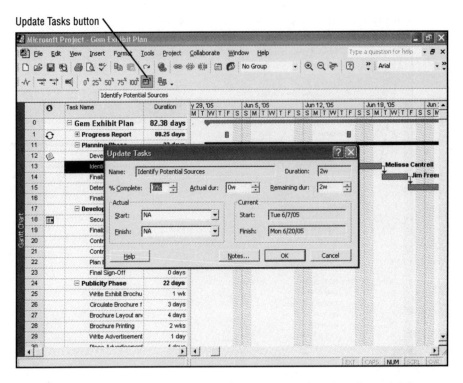

FIGURE 11.7 *Here you enter actual data about a task's schedule and work completed.*

◆ Enter the number of days of work completed in the Actual Dur text box. If you want to use a duration other than the default (days), enter the duration abbreviation with the value you enter, such as **w** for weeks. Project calculates the percentage completed and the remaining duration.

◆ Enter the estimated number of days of work remaining for the task in the Remaining Dur text box. Again, if you want to enter a duration that's not in days, include the appropriate duration abbreviation. When you specify work completed this way, Project calculates the percentage completed and duration.

4. If it looks like the actual starting or finishing date for the task will differ from those dates entered in the Current area of the Update Tasks dialog box, change the Start and Finish text box entries accordingly. Enter the new dates in mm/dd/yy format, or click on the drop-down arrow beside either text box and use the pop-up calendar to specify the date. (By default, these text boxes contain **NA**.) Note

that if you make a date entry in the Finish text box in the Actual area of the Update Tasks dialog box, Project will mark the task as 100% complete. A task can't have an actual finish date if it's not finished.

5. If you want to add notes describing special circumstances about why a task might be ahead of or behind schedule, click on the Notes button, enter the information in the Notes dialog box that appears, and then click on OK.

6. Click on OK in the Update Tasks dialog box. Project updates the tasks, moving and adjusting any tasks as needed to reflect your changes in the Actual Start or Finish dates. It also uses a dark bar to mark the percentage of completed work you indicated for the selected tasks.

The third and final method for updating tasks is more "quick and dirty," and it gives you less flexibility in specifying exact percentages or days of completed work. For this method, select the task or tasks you want to update in the Task Sheet, and then click on one of the five percentage buttons (0%, 25%, 50%, 75%, or 100%) on the Tracking toolbar. Project updates the Gantt chart accordingly. Of course, you use the 0% button to remove any completed work that you previously specified. For example, if you thought an external resource had completed half a task, but you discover that no work has actually been completed (maybe your contact person initially fibbed to you), you can select the task and click on the 0% button to show the true percentage measurement.

 CAUTION

If you select multiple tasks in the Task Sheet before opening the Update Tasks dialog box, you can enter the actual duration or the actual start and finish information. Keep in mind, however, that these changes apply to all of the selected tasks. Such a global change might be useful if the project starting date becomes delayed and a number of tasks are started later than planned. Generally, you should select multiple tasks only when you want to enter the same % Complete value for all of them.

The Update As Scheduled button (second from the left on the Tracking toolbar) specifies work completed for the selected tasks based on the scheduled start dates and the status date (or the current date, if the status date is set before the current date). Project assumes that all work scheduled between those dates has been completed and enters the work update information accordingly, adding dark tracking bars to the Gantt chart.

Updating Tasks by Resource Assignment

Sometimes, you might not have information to enter about the work completed for all the tasks that were under way recently. For example, say that in the last week, you've received a progress report from only one outside contractor. However, other outside contractors and internal resources assigned to some of the same tasks have not reported. When such a situation arises, you need to be able to enter work completed on an assignment-by-assignment basis. You can use either the Task Usage view or Resource Usage view to enter actual work completed by a specific resource.

Using Task Usage View

If you still want to view tasks in a certain order according to their ID or order in the Task Sheet, you can switch to the Task Usage view, which lists the tasks in order and then lists the resource assignments below each task. Then you can find the task you need and enter a value for completed work for the resource assignment. Follow these steps to enter completed work for a resource in Task Usage view:

1. To change to Task Usage view, choose View, Task Usage, or click on the Task Usage icon on the View Bar.

2. Choose View, Table: (table name), Work. This changes the columns that appear in the Task Sheet portion of the view so that the sheet now displays the column where you enter completed work.

3. Drag the vertical split bar to the right so that you can see the Actual column of the Task Sheet portion of the view. You enter completed work values in this column.

4. Scroll to the task for which you want to update resource work. Then click in the Actual column (in the left pane) for the resource's assignment under the task.

5. Enter a completed work value in the cell, as shown in Figure 11.8. Project assumes that you're entering a value in hours.

6. Press Enter or click on the green Enter button on the Entry box to complete the entry.

Task   Assignment   Enter work the resource has completed for the assignment here

	ask Name	Work	Baseline	Variance	Actual	Details	W	T	F	S	Jul 3, '05 S
0	**Gem Exhibit Plan**	**1,074 hrs**	**1,074 hrs**	**0 hrs**	**56 hrs**	Work	4h	16h	26h		
1	⊞ **Progress Report**	**90 hrs**	**90 hrs**	**0 hrs**	**0 hrs**	Work			10h		
11	⊟ **Planning Phase**	**168 hrs**	**168 hrs**	**0 hrs**	**56 hrs**	Work	4h	8h	8h		
12	⊟ Develop Topic List	32 hrs	32 hrs	0 hrs	24 hrs	Work					
	Jim Freemont	*32 hrs*	*32 hrs*	*0 hrs*	*24 hrs*	Work					
13	⊟ Identify Potential Sou	80 hrs	80 hrs	0 hrs	32 hrs	Work					
	Melissa Cantre	*80 hrs*	*80 hrs*	*0 hrs*	*32 hrs*	Work					
14	⊟ Finalize Theme and T	24 hrs	24 hrs	0 hrs	0 hrs	Work					
	Jim Freemont	*24 hrs*	*24 hrs*	*0 hrs*	*0 hrs*	Work					
15	⊟ Determine Exhibit Bu	16 hrs	16 hrs	0 hrs	0 hrs	Work	4h				
	Andrea Lawson	*16 hrs*	*16 hrs*	*0 hrs*	*0 hrs*	Work	4h				
16	⊟ Finalize Approach	16 hrs	16 hrs	0 hrs	0 hrs	Work		8h	8h		
	Jim Freemont	*8 hrs*	*8 hrs*	*0 hrs*	4	Work		4h	4h		
	Andrea Lawson	*8 hrs*	*8 hrs*	*0 hrs*	*0 hrs*	Work		4h	4h		
17	⊟ **Development Phase**	**420 hrs**	**420 hrs**	**0 hrs**	**0 hrs**	Work		8h	8h		
18	⊟ Secure Funding	120 hrs	120 hrs	0 hrs	0 hrs	Work		8h	8h		
	Candace Allen	*120 hrs*	*120 hrs*	*0 hrs*	*0 hrs*	Work		8h	8h		
19	⊟ Finalize Exhibit Sche	40 hrs	40 hrs	0 hrs	0 hrs	Work					
	Jim Freemont	*40 hrs*	*40 hrs*	*0 hrs*	*0 hrs*	Work					
20	⊟ Contract with Sourc	60 hrs	60 hrs	0 hrs	0 hrs	Work					
	Jim Freemont	*60 hrs*	*60 hrs*	*0 hrs*	*0 hrs*	Work					
21	⊟ Contract for Additior	120 hrs	120 hrs	0 hrs	0 hrs	Work					

FIGURE 11.8   *You can enter the work completed on an assignment by a resource in the Task Usage view.*

▶ TIP

If you want to enter the total work completed on a task in Task Entry view, select the Actual cell for the row that holds the task information (rather than an assignment row below the task) and enter the work value.

Using Resource Usage View

If only one or two resources have reported completed work to you, you don't want to have to sift through the Task Sheet in Gantt Chart view or Task Usage view to update each task handled by the resource. Instead, you can use the Resource Usage view, which lists assignments by resource. This method works best if your organization uses timesheets where resources identify how many hours per day they spend on each assigned task. At the end of the week, you'll find that it's easiest and fastest to update the work information from the timesheets and track progress on the job if you're in Resource Usage view.

To update completed work in Resource Usage view, follow these steps:

1. To change to Resource Usage view, choose View, Resource Usage, or click on the Resource Usage icon on the View Bar.

2. Choose View, Table: (table name), Work. This adds several more columns to the Resource Sheet portion of the view, including the column where you enter completed work.

3. If necessary, drag the column header for the Resource Name column to the right so that you can clearly see the assignment names indented beneath each resource. Then drag the vertical split bar to the right so you can see the Actual column for the Task Sheet portion of the view. You enter completed work values in this column.

4. Scroll to the resource for which you want to update completed work. Then click on the Actual column cell for the appropriate assignment under the task.

5. Enter a completed work value in the cell, as shown in Figure 11.9. Project assumes that you're entering a value in hours.

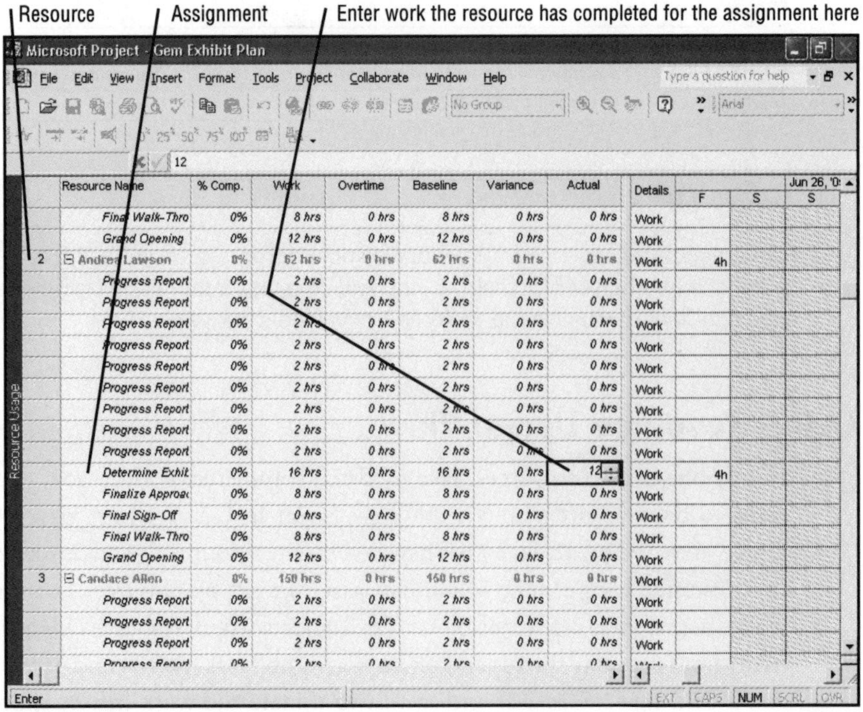

FIGURE 11.9 *You can also enter the work completed on an assignment by a resource using the Work table of the Resource Usage view.*

6. Press Enter or click on the green Enter button on the Entry box to complete the entry.

Using Assignment Information

In either the Task Usage or Resource Usage view, you can double-click on any assignment to open the Assignment Information dialog box. Click on the Tracking tab to display its entries. Then enter the completed work value (in hours) in the Actual Work text box (see Figure 11.10), or adjust the % Work Complete entry to specify the percentage of work completed. If the assignment began early or late, change the Actual Start date, too. Click on OK to finish entering the work.

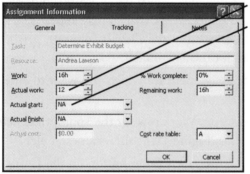

Enter completed work here

If work began early or late, adjust this setting

FIGURE 11.10 *On the Tracking tab of the Assignment Information dialog box, you can enter completed work as well as actual start and finish dates for an assignment.*

Entering Daily Values (Custom Time Period Tracking)

Chapter 9, "Resolving Overallocations and Overbooked Resources," explained how to tell Project to distribute hours worked on a task in the pattern of your choice. By default, when you assign a resource to a task, Project uses the flat contour and divides the work evenly over the duration of the project. That is, for a four-day task, the resource will be scheduled to work eight hours per day for four days. If you apply a contour to the assignment, however, Project extends the task duration and reallocates the daily work in a pattern such as a bell curve, in which the resource works fewer hours at the start and finish of the assignment and full-time during the middle of the assignment. In addition, Chapter 9 explained how to create an edited contour so that you could control how many hours on a given day the resource is scheduled to work.

Similarly, you may need exact control over how you enter completed work for a resource to ensure that your project tracking is accurate. For example, say a resource is assigned to work full time on a task for five days, but actually he or she only completes six hours of work per day for the first three days. Here's how to enter such precise settings for work completed:

1. Change to the Task Usage view or Resource Usage view.

2. Right-click on the right pane of the view (the yellow area that displays work per day). Then click on Actual Work. Alternately, choose Format, Details, Actual Work. In the right pane, the schedule for each assignment is split into two rows. The top row, Work, holds scheduled entries. The bottom row, Act. Work (which may appear as "Act. W" unless you increase the width of the Details column), is where you enter work completed for the assignment.

3. Scroll to the resource assignment for which you want to enter daily work values.

4. Click in the cell in the Act. Work row for the appropriate date, and then type the work value. Figure 11.11 shows an example.

5. Press Enter or click on the green Enter button on the Entry box to complete the entry.

 NOTE

When you enter daily Act. Work values that are less than the scheduled values in the Work row, Project automatically extends the assignment duration (unless a constraint prevents it from doing so), adding an hour to the end of the resource assignment for each hour of shortfall.

Having Project Calculate Work Completed to the Current Date or Status Date

As if the preceding methods weren't enough, Project offers one final path for indicating how much work has been completed for tasks you select, or for all the tasks in the project: the Update Project dialog box. To open and use this

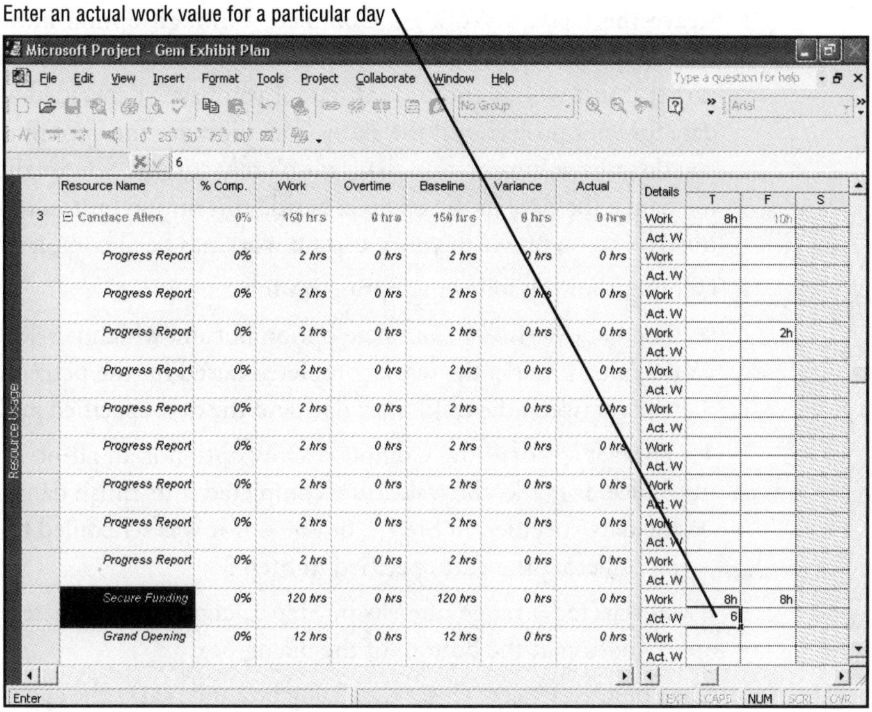

Enter an actual work value for a particular day

FIGURE 11.11 *You can use the right pane of either the Task Usage or Resource Usage view to enter daily values for completed work.*

dialog box to update completed work information for the tasks in your schedule, follow these steps:

1. (Optional) If you want to update only selected tasks, select the tasks in the Task Sheet in Gantt Chart view by dragging over the task row numbers or dragging to select cells in the rows for the tasks you want.

2. Choose Tools, Tracking, Update Project. The Update Project dialog box appears (see Figure 11.12).

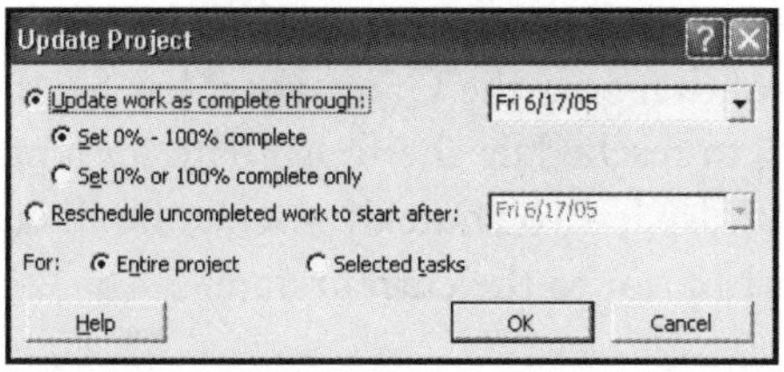

FIGURE 11.12 *This is yet another method for updating information about work completed.*

3. Leave the Update Work As Complete Through option button selected. By default, the date that appears here is the status date (described earlier), or it will be the current date if you haven't specified a status date for your project or if the status date precedes the current date. If you don't have information that's absolutely current, you might want to change the date in the text box beside this option button to reflect the date through which you're certain work has been completed.

4. Choose from the following option buttons:

   ◆ The Set 0%–100% Complete option button, which is selected by default. It marks the work completed based on the percentage of work between the task's start date and the date specified in Step 3.

   ◆ The Set 0% or 100% Complete Only option is an all-or-nothing choice. It marks the task as 0% completed if its finish date is after the date specified in Step 3, or 100% if it was scheduled to finish on or before the date specified in Step 3.

5. If you selected a range of tasks in Step 1, choose the Selected Tasks option button at the bottom of the dialog box.

6. Click on OK. Project closes the dialog box and marks the appropriate tasks with indicators of how much work has been completed.

Rescheduling Work

Things happen, and work doesn't always start as planned. For example, if you schedule painters to handle some outdoor painting and it rains that day, there's no choice but to start the painting on a drier day. Or a resource might begin work on a task, but can't finish it on the scheduled date because of scheduling conflicts or unforeseen absences from work. In such instances, you need to reschedule the task to a time frame that's realistic—which means moving all or some of the work after the current date in the schedule. When a task needs to be rescheduled, it has *slipped*.

Of course, you have the option of dragging the Gantt chart bar for the task into a new position, or dragging to reschedule the finish date for a partially completed task. However, Project also lets you quickly reschedule all tasks for which work was to start (or finish) prior to the current date.

When you reschedule a task and indicate that no work has been completed on it, Project moves the task so that its start date becomes the status date or the current date. If you mark the task as partially complete, Project leaves the original start date in place but extends the task schedule so that the work yet to be done begins on the status date or current date. This is called *splitting* an in-progress task. The Gantt chart bar for the task displays the split. (Review the topic "Splitting a Task" in Chapter 6 to learn more about split tasks.)

Select the tasks that you want to update in the Task Sheet, and then choose one of the following methods to reschedule the task:

◆ Display the Update Project dialog box as just described. Click on the Reschedule Uncompleted Work To Start After option button (refer to Figure 11.12). Then enter the date when the rescheduled work should begin in the accompanying text box. Click on the Selected Tasks option button, and then click on OK to let the work slip.

◆ Click on the Reschedule Work button on the Tracking toolbar (the third button from the left) to move the selected tasks so that uncompleted work begins on the status date or the current date.

 CAUTION

Always keep in mind, however, that rescheduling work can have a dramatic impact on your schedule when you're rescheduling linked tasks, especially those that are critical. The Planning wizard may display warnings when you try to reschedule work, as well. Always make sure that you check the impact of rescheduling work on the overall project plan, and then deploy more resources if warranted.

Using Progress Lines

Progress lines on a Gantt chart mark a particular date and compare how in-progress tasks are advancing with relation to that date. They help you see at a glance how drastically a task may be lagging or exceeding its schedule. The fastest way to add a progress line to the schedule is with the mouse. Click on the Add Progress Line button on the Tracking toolbar, and then click on the date for the progress line on the Gantt chart. The progress line appears, as shown in Figure 11.13.

Click this button . . .   . . . then click on a date to add a progress line

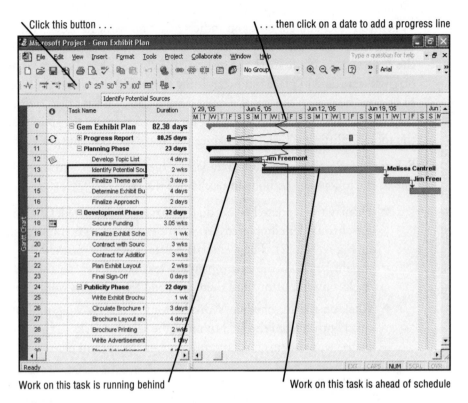

Work on this task is running behind   Work on this task is ahead of schedule

FIGURE 11.13 *Progress lines let you know when tasks are on schedule.*

If you want to add several progress lines that recur at regular intervals, or to control certain progress line settings, follow these steps:

1. Choose Tools, Tracking, Progress Lines. The Progress Lines dialog box will appear.

2. Click on the Dates and Intervals tab, if it isn't selected.

3. To display a *current progress line,* which has special highlighting and is meant to highlight the current date or a status date you set (so you can have a daily look at where you stand), check the Always Display Current Progress Line check box. Then click on an option button to specify whether you want that current progress line to appear At Project Status Date or At Current Date.

4. To add recurring progress lines to the schedule, click on the Display Progress Lines At Recurring Intervals check box. This activates the options below it, as shown in Figure 11.14. Choose whether to add

the lines daily, weekly, or monthly. As with setting a recurring task, the choices that coincide with each option button are slightly different, but they all involve making schedule choices. For example, for the Weekly option, you need to select a day of the week and choose whether the lines should appear every week, every other week, or at intervals up to 12 weeks apart. Finally, next to Begin At, specify whether the progress lines should start appearing from the Project Start or a particular date that you specify.

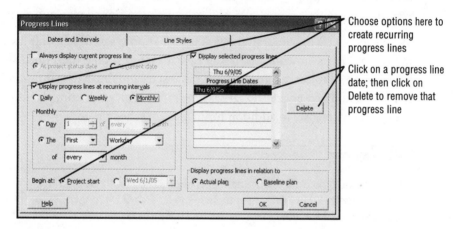

FIGURE 11.14   *Use the Progress Lines dialog box to manually add progress lines, especially recurring ones.*

5. Under Display Progress Lines In Relation To, specify whether the progress lines should compare the project with the actual plan or the baseline plan.

6. If you want to delete a progress line you added with the mouse, click on the date in the Progress Line Dates list and then click on the Delete button.

7. Click on OK to finish creating progress lines.

Saving Additional Baselines

For more lengthy project plans, you may want to save multiple baselines to track the project's evolution as it progresses. In addition to the original baseline (named Baseline), you can store up to 10 additional baselines (named Baseline

1 through Baseline 10) in your project plan file. Ideally, you would save an additional baseline if something has happened to drastically alter the project plan after work has begun.

For example, let's say that about a quarter of the way through the project, your company's CEO changes the parameters of the project and increases the number of deliverable results it must provide. As a result, you need to add tasks, change cost information, secure additional outside vendors, and so on. Saving a second baseline (rather than replacing the old baseline information) enables you to compare the original plan and costs with the revised plan and costs.

When you save a baseline, all the task information is saved: schedule, assignments, and costs. In contrast, if you save an interim plan (described in the next section), Project records only the task's start and finish date information. So, you should save an additional baseline rather than an interim plan if you're concerned with costs in addition to the project schedule.

 NOTE

The new Multiple Baselines Gantt view charts the first three interim plans you save—Baseline, Baseline 1, and Baseline 2. The Gantt chart portion of this view uses a different bar color for each of the three baselines. Of course, if you save additional baselines, you can create a custom version of this view to show alternative baselines instead.

Here are the steps for saving an additional baseline in your project plan file:

1. Update all the task, resource, and cost information as needed.

2. (Optional) If you want to save new baseline data only for certain tasks, select the rows you want in the Task Sheet in Gantt Chart view. (Make sure you're in Gantt Chart view by choosing View, Gantt Chart, or by clicking on the Gantt Chart icon on the View Bar.) Select the tasks you want by pointing to the row number for the top row and dragging down to highlight (select) the rows. To select noncontiguous rows, press and hold down Ctrl and then click on each additional row.

3. Choose Tools, Tracking. A submenu of commands will appear.

4. Choose Save Baseline. The Save Baseline dialog box will appear.

5. Leave the Save Baseline option button selected, open the accompanying drop-down list, and click on the name of the new baseline plan

you want to save (Baseline 1 for the second baseline plan, Baseline 2 for the third baseline plan, and so on). This is shown in Figure 11.15.

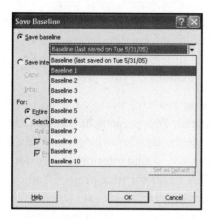

FIGURE 11.15 *Saving an additional baseline enables you to record major adjustments to your project plan.*

6. To save the additional baseline's information for all the tasks, leave the Entire Project option button selected and click on OK to continue. If you've selected specific tasks for the baseline, click on the Selected Tasks option button. Select either or both of the following options under Roll Up Baselines, if needed:

   ◆ **To All Summary Tasks.** Saves new summary task baseline data to reflect the baseline data for the selected subtasks.

   ◆ **From Subtasks Into Selected Summary Task(s).** For a selected summary task, ensures that the summary task data reflects subtasks that have been inserted or deleted within its summary group.

7. Click on OK. Project will store the information for the added baseline.

Saving and Viewing an Interim Plan

Baseline plans let you look at where you started with your schedule and resource plans. In contrast, an interim plan serves as a snapshot of how the schedule has changed down the line, and it shows how far you've come with a project. For example, you can set a milestone for the date when the project is 25 percent completed and get a record of how things stand at that point. You may find that your baseline plan has become meaningless because the schedule and assignments have changed so much. In such a case, your interim plan allows you to compare the current schedule to the baseline schedule. If you save an interim plan, it captures the current start and finish information for each task. (In contrast, saving a baseline stores about 20 different fields of information about each task.) You can save up to 10 interim plans for your project.

Consider a hypothetical situation. Your resource has completed task 1 but took twice as long as you had anticipated. You can look at similar tasks later in your schedule, adjust them to reflect the new knowledge, and save an interim plan. Any changes you make after saving that interim plan are not added to it, but rather to the main scheduling fields for your project. You can save numerous interim plans to keep a record of where significant schedule changes occur. This could be helpful if, for example, your company routinely uses follow-up meetings after the completion of a project to analyze what worked well and troubleshoot things that didn't. You can arm yourself for the discussion by creating interim plans and adding task notes about when and why key tasks slipped.

The initial steps for creating an interim plan resemble the initial steps for saving the baseline. Here are those initial steps and the rest of the steps needed to save your interim plan and view its information:

1. Enter all of the task and resource updates that affect the current schedule. For example, make changes to the Duration field for tasks, or change resource assignments that were in place when you saved your baseline plan.

2. (Optional) If you want to save selected tasks, select the rows you want in the Task Sheet in Gantt Chart view.

3. Choose Tools, Tracking, Save Baseline. The Save Baseline dialog box will appear.

4. Click on the Save Interim Plan option to select it. This will enable the Copy and Into drop-down lists.

5. From the Copy drop-down list, select the two fields of information from the Task Sheet that you want to save in your interim plan. Typically, you should select either Start/Finish (the default) or Baseline Start/Finish.

6. Use the Into drop-down list (see Figure 11.16) to specify the fields into which Project will copy (and save) the interim plan dates. For your first interim plan, use Start1/Finish1, for your second interim plan, use Start2/Finish2, and so on.

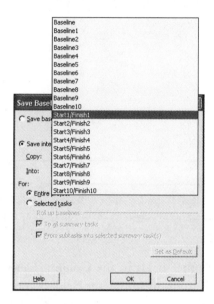

FIGURE 11.16 *The interim plan captures information from two Task Sheet fields that you specify here.*

7. If you want to save interim dates for only the tasks you selected in Step 2, select the Selected Tasks option and specify any Roll Up Baselines choices as needed.

8. Click on OK. Project saves the interim plan dates in the specified fields. You can add them to the Task Sheet to view their contents by completing the rest of these steps.

9. In the Task Sheet, click on the name of the column to the right of where you want to insert an interim plan field.

10. Choose Insert, Column (or right-click and then click on Insert Column on the resulting shortcut menu). The Column Definition dialog box will appear.

11. Click on the drop-down list arrow to display the Field Name list. Then scroll down and click on the name of the interim plan field to

be inserted at that location. For example, you would click on Start1 to display the first field from your first interim plan (see Figure 11.17).

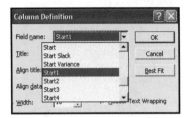

FIGURE 11.17   _You can add an interim plan field to the task sheet._

 TIP

To select a field name more quickly, open the Field Name drop-down list and then type a letter to scroll the list. For example, typing **S** scrolls quickly to the fields that start with S.

12. If needed, make changes to other fields in the Column Definition dialog box. Then click on OK to finish adding the field. It appears in the Task Sheet, as shown in Figure 11.18.

13. Repeat Steps 10–13 to add any other interim plan fields that you want to view to the Task Sheet.

Viewing Baseline versus Actual Information

Because there are so many different kinds of information captured in your Project file, the baseline information you store and the actual information you enter about work completed doesn't appear automatically. I'll show you a few different ways to view this information, depending on how much and what kind of detail you want to see.

The interim plan field

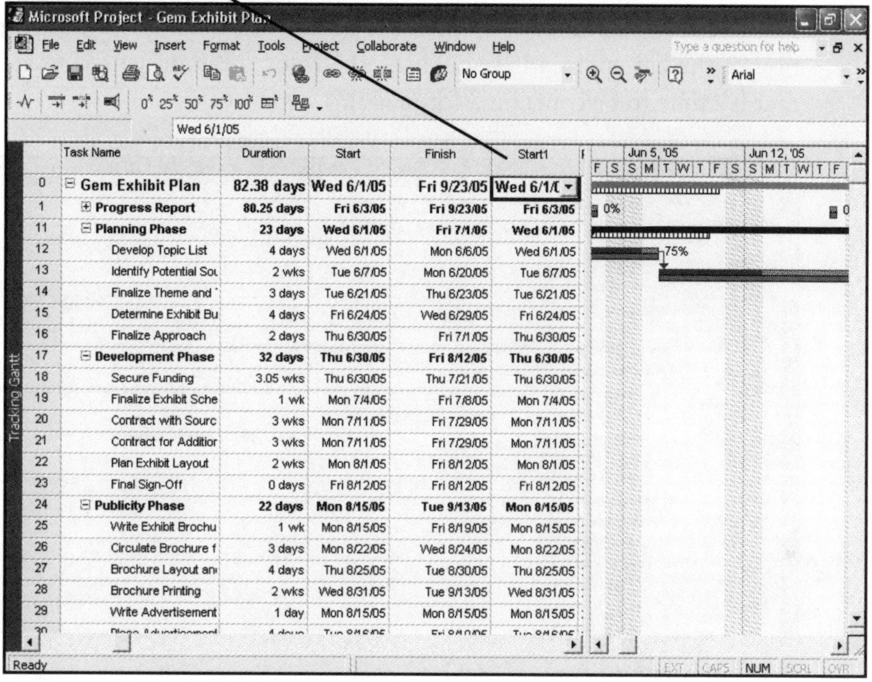

FIGURE 11.18   *This interim plan field has been added to the Task Sheet.*

Using Tracking Gantt View

The Tracking Gantt view in Project lets you do virtually everything you can do in Gantt Chart view, such as dragging and moving tasks, updating links, or entering information about work that has been completed for a project. In addition, though, Tracking Gantt view uses Gantt bars that provide greater detail about work progress on tasks so you can see at a glance which tasks are on schedule or are falling behind. This is much more convenient than scrolling through various columns on the Task Sheet.

In this view, each Gantt bar is really two bars (see Figure 11.19). The bottom portion, usually gray even on a color monitor, shows you the baseline schedule for the task, assuming you saved a baseline plan for the project. The top portion shows the current schedule for the project, in a lightly shaded bar. As you enter actual work information for the task, the portion of the bar representing the work completed becomes solid rather than shaded. By default, the top portion of the bar is blue if the task is on schedule or work has not yet begun on it. If the task is behind schedule (meaning that its finish date has passed but you haven't yet marked the task as 100% complete), the top portion of the bar appears in red. That's the color commonly used to alert you that it's time to be concerned (or panic).

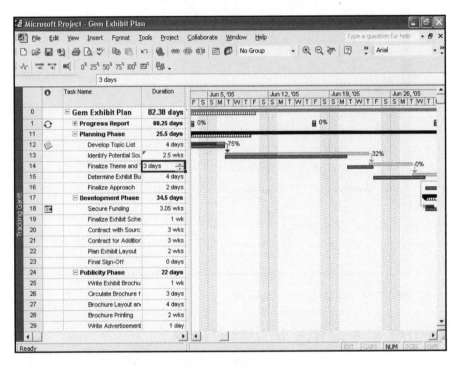

FIGURE 11.19 *Tracking Gantt view works like regular Gantt Chart view, but the bars provide you with more information about your tasks.*

To display Tracking Gantt view, choose View, More Views or click on the More Views icon in the View Bar. In the More Views dialog box, scroll down the Views list to the Tracking Gantt choice. Double-click on this choice (or click on it once and click on Apply).

 CAUTION

At times, Tracking Gantt view can be a bit unpredictable. If you switch to this view and don't see anything in the Gantt chart pane at the right, first make sure that Project hasn't scrolled the displayed dates beyond the schedule for the project. Press Alt+Home to go to the beginning of the project in the Gantt Chart view. If that's not the solution, click on the Go To Selected Task button on the Standard toolbar.

Other Tracking Views

If you want access to the baseline and tracking information in tabular form, you can change the Task Sheet so that it displays the information you want. To do so in any view that contains the Task Sheet, click in a cell in the Task Sheet and then choose View, Table: (table name), Tracking. The Task Sheet now displays tracking information (see Figure 11.20).

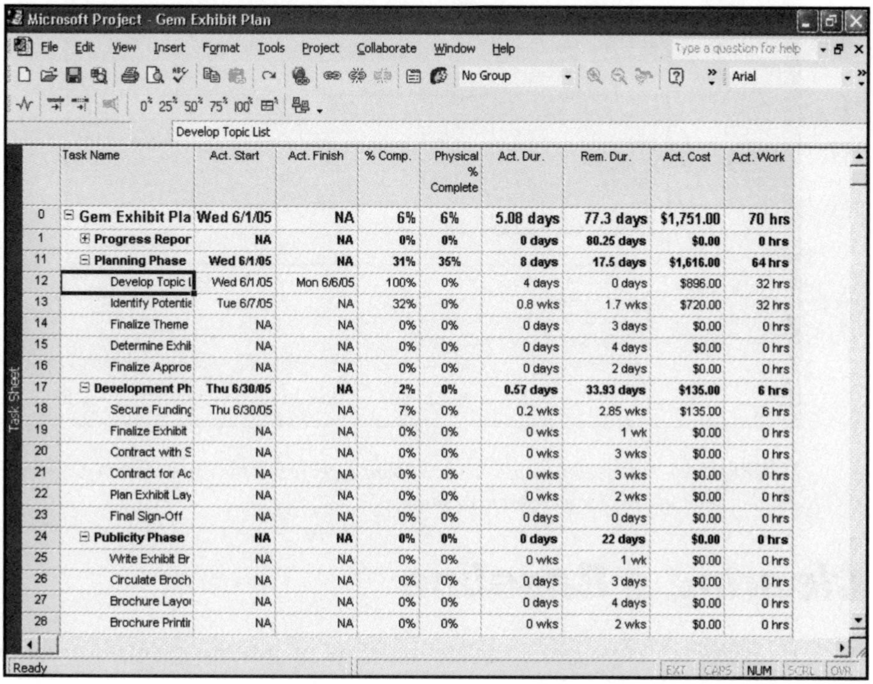

	Task Name	Act. Start	Act. Finish	% Comp.	Physical % Complete	Act. Dur.	Rem. Dur.	Act. Cost	Act. Work
0	Gem Exhibit Pla	Wed 6/1/05	NA	6%	6%	5.08 days	77.3 days	$1,751.00	70 hrs
1	Progress Repor	NA	NA	0%	0%	0 days	80.25 days	$0.00	0 hrs
11	Planning Phase	Wed 6/1/05	NA	31%	35%	8 days	17.5 days	$1,616.00	64 hrs
12	Develop Topic L	Wed 6/1/05	Mon 6/6/05	100%	0%	4 days	0 days	$896.00	32 hrs
13	Identify Potentia	Tue 6/7/05	NA	32%	0%	0.8 wks	1.7 wks	$720.00	32 hrs
14	Finalize Theme	NA	NA	0%	0%	0 days	3 days	$0.00	0 hrs
15	Determine Exhil	NA	NA	0%	0%	0 days	4 days	$0.00	0 hrs
16	Finalize Approa	NA	NA	0%	0%	0 days	2 days	$0.00	0 hrs
17	Development Ph	Thu 6/30/05	NA	2%	0%	0.57 days	33.93 days	$135.00	6 hrs
18	Secure Funding	Thu 6/30/05	NA	7%	0%	0.2 wks	2.85 wks	$135.00	6 hrs
19	Finalize Exhibit	NA	NA	0%	0%	0 wks	1 wk	$0.00	0 hrs
20	Contract with S	NA	NA	0%	0%	0 wks	3 wks	$0.00	0 hrs
21	Contract for Ac	NA	NA	0%	0%	0 wks	3 wks	$0.00	0 hrs
22	Plan Exhibit Lay	NA	NA	0%	0%	0 wks	2 wks	$0.00	0 hrs
23	Final Sign-Off	NA	NA	0%	0%	0 days	0 days	$0.00	0 hrs
24	Publicity Phase	NA	NA	0%	0%	0 days	22 days	$0.00	0 hrs
25	Write Exhibit Br	NA	NA	0%	0%	0 wks	1 wk	$0.00	0 hrs
26	Circulate Broch	NA	NA	0%	0%	0 days	3 days	$0.00	0 hrs
27	Brochure Layou	NA	NA	0%	0%	0 days	4 days	$0.00	0 hrs
28	Brochure Printir	NA	NA	0%	0%	0 wks	2 wks	$0.00	0 hrs

FIGURE 11.20 *The Task Sheet now shows tracking information in tabular form.*

In Chapter 4, "Setting Up a Project," you learned how to display the Project Statistics box via the Project Information dialog box. The Project Statistics dialog box offers information about the baseline schedule for the project, including work and cost information, as well as the actual work completed and dollars spent. You can also open this dialog box by clicking on the Project Statistics button (the first button) on the Tracking toolbar. The dialog box is shown in Figure 11.21. Click on the Close button when you finish reviewing this information.

Project Statistics button

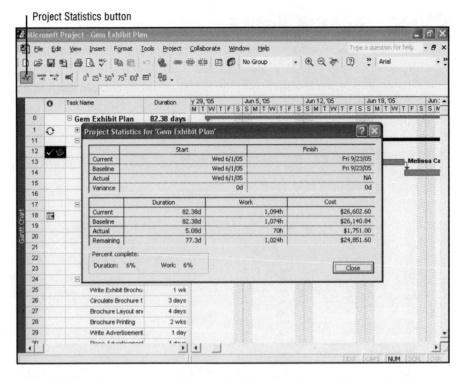

FIGURE 11.21 *As you enter actual data about tasks using the methods covered in this chapter, the statistics for your project change.*

Clearing a Baseline

Project enables you to clear any baseline or interim plan information that you've saved. You might want to use this feature to get back to square one with the information in a project file, or to save a project file as a template (both reasons to discard the baseline information). Follow these steps to clear a baseline or interim plan from your project file:

1. If you want to clear baseline information for selected tasks only, drag over those tasks in the Task Sheet to select them.

2. Choose Tools, Tracking, Clear Baseline. The Clear Baseline dialog box will appear (see Figure 11.22).

3. If you want to clear the baseline plan, leave Clear Baseline Plan selected. To clear an interim plan instead, choose the Clear Interim Plan option button, and then use the drop-down list beside the option button to choose the fields that hold the interim plan information to clear.

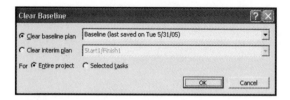

FIGURE 11.22   *If your baseline or interim plan information becomes obsolete, you can remove it from the project file.*

4. If you selected any tasks in Step 1 and want to clear the plan information for those tasks only, click on the Selected Tasks option button.

5. Click on OK. Project clears the baseline information without warning or alerting you.

Comparing Two Project Versions

If you failed to save a baseline (or you're still in the planning process for your project), you can load a special feature called an Add-In that enables Project to compare two different project files. The Compare Project Versions Utility Add-In generates a new project file that reports changes between the two files you select. You can save the report file if needed.

The Compare Project Versions Utility Add-In may not be loaded for you by default. If that's the case, you need to add the command for Add-Ins to the Tools menu and then make sure the Compare Project Versions Utility Add-In is loaded. Follow these steps to load the Add-In:

1. Choose Tools, Customize, Toolbars. The Customize dialog box will appear.

2. Click on the Commands tab.

3. Click on Tools in the Categories list at the left side of the tab. The commands and features available in that category appear in the Commands list at the left side of the tab.

4. Scroll down the Commands list until you see the COM Add-Ins, and then drag it over the Tools menu. When the tools menu opens, drag the COM Add-Ins option to the desired position on the menu (see Figure 11.23), and then release the mouse button to finish adding the command.

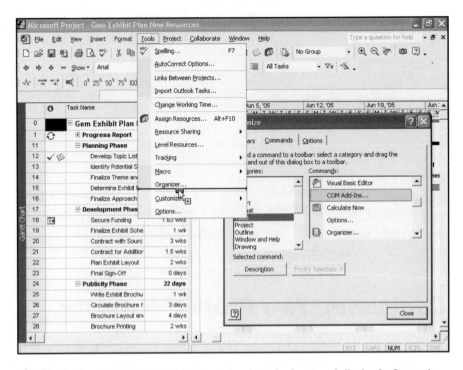

FIGURE 11.23 *Drag the COM Add-Ins option from the Commands list in the Customize dialog box onto the Tools menu.*

5. Click on Close in the Customize dialog box to close the dialog box and finish adding the command to the tools menu.

6. Choose Tools, COM Add-Ins. The COM Add-Ins dialog box will appear (see Figure 11.24).

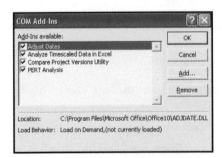

FIGURE 11.24 *Use this dialog box to load, unload, and run COM Add-Ins. Checked Add-Ins are currently loaded.*

7. Click on the Compare Project Versions Utility option in the Add-Ins Available list to check the Add-In if it's not already checked. Then click OK to finish loading the Add-In.

Once you've ensured that the Compare Project Versions Utility Add-In has been loaded, follow these steps to use it to compare two project files:

1. Open the files to compare. (This step isn't absolutely necessary. It just saves you the trouble of browsing to find the files later.)

2. Choose View, Toolbars, Compare Project Versions. Or, right-click on any toolbar and click on Compare Project Versions. The Compare Project Versions toolbar appears.

3. Click on the Compare Project Versions button at the far left end of the Compare Project Versions toolbar. The Compare Project Versions dialog box will appear.

4. Select the names of the files to compare from the Project Version 1 and Project Version 2 drop-down lists (or use the accompanying Browse buttons). Figure 11.25 shows sample files selected for a comparison.

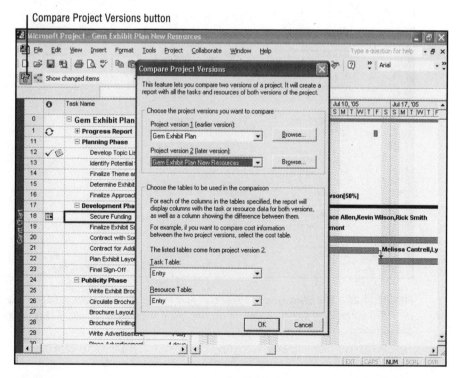

Compare Project Versions button

FIGURE 11.25 *Choose the files to compare in the Compare Project Versions dialog box.*

5. If you want the comparison file to display particular tables in the Task Sheet or Resource Sheet, choose the desired table from the Task Table and Resource Table drop-down lists.

6. Click on OK. Project generates the comparison information in a new project file, and the Compare Project Versions-Done dialog box will appear.

7. Click Yes to view more information, or click No to close the dialog box and view the comparison file directly.

8. You can review the comparison information as needed to see changes. As Figure 11.26 illustrates, the Duration: V1 column holds the task durations from the first project file. The Duration: V2 column holds the task durations from the second project file. The Duration: Diff field calculates the difference between the two.

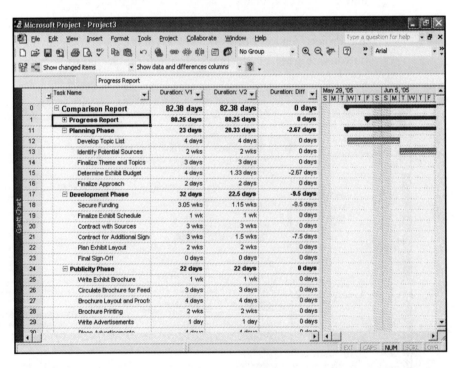

FIGURE 11.26   *The file generated by the Compare Project Versions Utility Add-In calculates the difference between various values in the two files being compared, such as the difference in task durations.*

9. While you're working in the report file generated by the Compare Project Versions Utility Add-In, you can use other tools on the Compare Project Versions toolbar to adjust or limit the results displayed in the report. For example, to show only changed items or unchanged items, you can use the Select Tasks/Resources to Show in the Comparison Report drop-down list. You also can use the Select Columns to Show in the Comparison Report drop-down list to show only the data columns from the original files, only the differences columns, or both.

10. When you've finished working, you can save the comparison file and hide the Compare Project Versions toolbar as needed.

PART IV

Viewing, Formatting, and Printing Projects

Chapter 12

Viewing and Managing Costs and Value

In This Chapter

◆ Viewing and finding task costs

◆ Looking at resource costs

◆ Previewing cost reports

◆ Reporting costs to others

◆ Managing costs and cash flow

When you're an independent contractor, you have to keep your eye on three key aspects of any project you manage for your client. First, you have to ensure that the work you deliver is of the highest quality. Second, you have get the job done on time—or even earlier. Finally, you have to track costs like a maniac to ensure that you not only charge the client a fair price, but also make a fair profit.

Even a project manager within a company needs to think like an independent contractor. The work your team delivers has to be top-quality and on time—and delivered at a cost that helps your company stay profitable.

This chapter shows you how to get crucial mileage from all the resource and task cost information you've entered into Project.

Viewing and Finding Task Costs

Chapter 11, "Comparing Progress versus Your Baseline Plan," explains how to tell Project how much work has been completed on a task. In addition, although you might not be able to see it immediately, Project can use the task completion information you entered to calculate the actual cost for that completed work, based on hourly rates for resources and other cost information you've entered.

You might not be able to see the costs immediately because Gantt Chart view doesn't display any cost information by default. You have to learn techniques for examining cost information in various ways, depending on what type of information you want to view. Project enables you to view accumulated costs (costs based on actual work completed, plus any fixed and per-use costs) by task, by the whole project, or by the resources completing the work. The remainder of this section describes how you can access each type of cost information and make sure that task costs are calculated for you.

 WEB

If you want to practice working with cost information, you can download the New Location Renovation Chapter 12 file from the Premier Press download page at www.premierpressbooks.com/downloads.asp.

Controlling Whether Costs Are Updated Based on Work Completed

By default, Project automatically updates the calculated costs for a task or resource when you update information about how much work has been completed on a task. Project calculates cost values by multiplying the number of hours of work completed for a task by the standard rate for the resource completing the task. Project also adds any applicable cost-per-use or fixed-cost figures.

You can turn calculation off if you need to, however. The primary reason not to have Project calculate these values as you go is to avoid calculation delays while you're updating information about the work completed on various tasks. You will also want to turn off automatic calculation if you need to enter actual cost information before you indicate that work has been completed on the project. (See "Changing How Costs Add Up" later in this chapter to learn more about entering actual costs.)

To ensure that Project correctly calculates information about actual costs based on the work you mark as completed, or to turn off automatic calculation, follow these steps:

1. Choose Tools, Options. The Options dialog box will appear, with many tabs.
2. Click on the Calculation tab to display its options (see Figure 12.1).
3. If you want Project to update all calculated cost information whenever you update task completion information, leave the check mark in the Actual Costs Are Always Calculated By Microsoft Project check

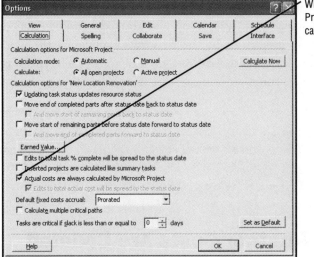

When this option is checked, Project automatically calculates actual expenses

FIGURE 12.1 *The Calculation tab offers options for controlling how Project reacts when you enter scheduling information.*

box. Clear the check box if you prefer to enter actual cost information or calculate actual costs periodically. When this option is turned on, it's enabled for all files you open in Project.

 CAUTION

If you check the Actual Costs Are Always Calculated By Microsoft Project check box after you've already entered actual cost information, the calculated costs will wipe out the actual costs you've entered.

4. Click on OK to close the Options dialog box. If you turned on automatic calculation, a message box warns you that actual cost entries will be overridden. Click on OK to close the message box. Your change takes effect immediately.

Viewing Task Costs

One way to look at the expenses associated with your project is task by task. For example, your plan might include particular tasks for which you really need to watch expenses, such as work handled by an outside contractor with a particularly high hourly rate. Or you might need to provide information about the costs you've estimated for a particular task to a team member who is negotiating to have that task completed, so the team member will know the highest price you're willing to pay to have the task completed.

Project gives you a couple of methods of looking at how costs are adding up for a task based on the work completed for that task. Both methods enable you to enter or edit cost information when you need to, such as when the actual fixed cost turns out to be less than the fixed cost you initially estimated.

The first method involves adjusting the columns shown in the Task Sheet. Do this in any view that displays the Task Sheet, such as Gantt Chart view or Task Entry view. To display actual cost information in the Task Sheet, choose View, Table: (table name), Cost. The Task Sheet changes to include several columns with cost information. Drag the vertical split bar (if there is one) to the right to display additional columns of cost information, as shown in Figure 12.2. To return the Task Sheet to its regular view, choose View, Table: (table name), Entry.

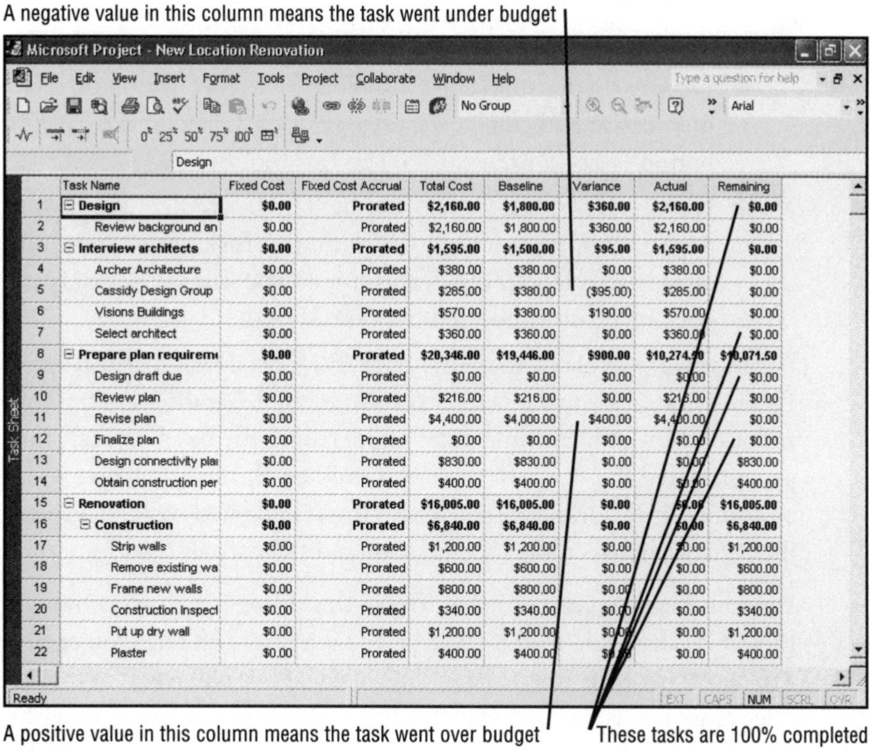

A negative value in this column means the task went under budget

A positive value in this column means the task went over budget   These tasks are 100% completed

FIGURE 12.2 *You can adjust the Task Sheet so that it displays cost information.*

TIP

Before you save a project baseline or enter information about completed work, don't forget to use the Task Sheet shown in Figure 12.2 to enter a fixed cost for any task that includes one in the Fixed Cost column. Even if you have only rough estimates for these costs, you should add them to ensure that you won't see too much of a budget variance after you enter actual costs. Remember, fixed costs apply on a task-by-task basis. Any other hourly or per-use costs you enter for resources assigned to the task will be added to the fixed cost to yield the task cost (total cost).

Displaying cost information in the Task Sheet is useful when you want to view the costs for many tasks. However, sometimes you may not want to change the Task Sheet's appearance, but you may still want to view the cost information for a particular task. You can do so by displaying the Cost Tracking form. (You'll learn more about forms in Chapter 15, "Working with Forms"). Use one of the following methods to access the Cost Tracking form after you select the task in the Task Sheet:

◆ Display the Custom Forms toolbar by right-clicking on any toolbar onscreen and clicking on Custom Forms. Click on the Cost Tracking button (second from the left) on this toolbar.

◆ Choose Tools, Customize, Forms. The Customize Forms dialog box appears (see Figure 12.3). Click on the Task option button if it isn't already selected. In the Forms list, double-click on Cost Tracking (or click on it once and then click on Apply).

When you use either of these methods, the Cost Tracking form appears (see Figure 12.4). As you can see, this form offers several text entry boxes with various bits of task cost information, including the baseline cost (how much you estimated the work on the task would cost), the actual cost of the work performed so far, and any remaining (Rem) budgeted costs. It also calculates the variance between the baseline cost and the current cost.

You can change several of the entries in this dialog box. Note, however, that if Project is calculating the task cost based on hourly cost rates you've entered for a resource, any edits you make in the Total text box will revert to the calculated value as soon as you close the dialog box (unless you turn off automatic calculation). To close the dialog box after making the changes you want, click on OK.

Cost Tracking button on the Custom Forms toolbar

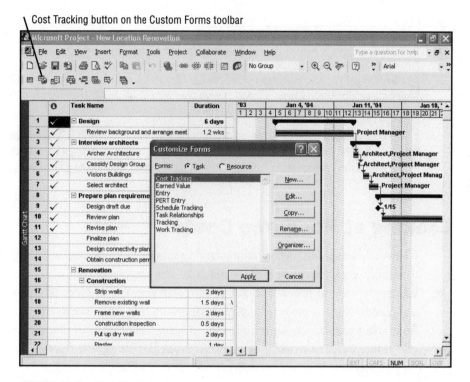

FIGURE 12.3 *Use this dialog box to display a form giving you cost information about a single task.*

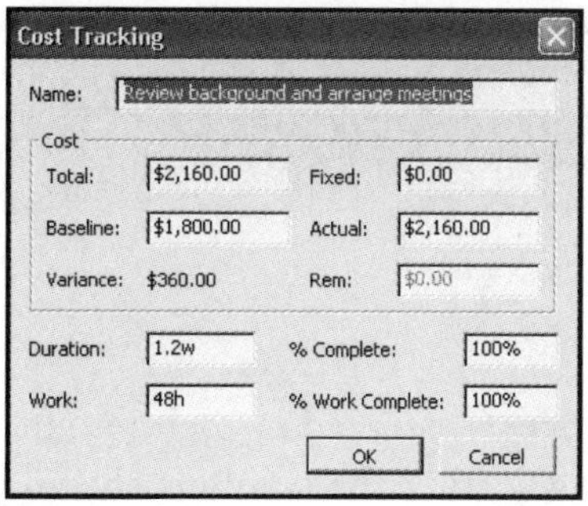

FIGURE 12.4 *This form displays cost information for a single task.*

TIP

For most variance fields, a positive variance means that a task has gone over budget or over duration. A negative variance means that the task costs remain under the baseline budget and the task schedule remains under the baseline duration.

The only exception to this rule of thumb occurs with some of the earned value fields, like SV. For that field, positive values mean a task is ahead of schedule. The Microsoft Project Help system gives detailed descriptions of all these fields.

Looking at Resource Costs

Chapter 9, "Resolving Overallocations and Overbooked Resources," explained how to identify when you've assigned too much work to a resource. Similarly, sometimes you might want to review the cost of each staff member or piece of equipment associated with your project. This information can help you make intelligent decisions about cost-cutting, or refresh your memory about invoices that are coming due as the project schedule progresses. As usual, Project gives you several options for precisely how to view resource costs. These options are covered next.

 NOTE

If you haven't finished adding all the resources to your schedule, you can use the General tab in the Options dialog box to change the default standard hourly rate and overtime rate for new resources so that it's no longer $0 for each. Chapter 28, "Customizing Microsoft Project," explains how to set this type of option.

Individual Resource Costs

Typically, you'll want to view the total costs assigned to each resource. You can view this kind of information by adjusting the columns shown in the Resource Sheet. Chapter 7, "Adding Resources into Your Project Plan," showed you how to use the Resource Sheet to add resources to your schedule. Here are the steps for displaying the Resource Sheet and displaying resource cost information in it:

1. If the Resource Sheet isn't currently onscreen, choose View, Resource Sheet, or click on the Resource Sheet icon on the View Bar. The Resource Sheet will appear.

2. Choose View, Table, Cost. The Resource Sheet will display columns of cost information, as shown in Figure 12.5.

	Resource Name	Cost	Baseline Cost	Variance	Actual Cost	Remaining
1	Architect	$19,950.00	$19,000.00	$950.00	$10,708.50	$9,241.50
2	Project Manager	$5,841.00	$5,436.00	$405.00	$3,321.00	$2,520.00
3	PM Assistant	$500.00	$500.00	$0.00	$0.00	$500.00
4	Mover	$592.00	$592.00	$0.00	$0.00	$592.00
5	Electrician	$1,920.00	$1,920.00	$0.00	$0.00	$1,920.00
6	Plumber	$2,160.00	$2,160.00	$0.00	$0.00	$2,160.00
7	IT Leader	$2,015.00	$2,015.00	$0.00	$0.00	$2,015.00
8	Inspector	$640.00	$640.00	$0.00	$0.00	$640.00
9	Construction Worker	$6,500.00	$6,500.00	$0.00	$0.00	$6,500.00
10	Interior Designer	$910.00	$910.00	$0.00	$0.00	$910.00
11	AC Installer	$2,940.00	$2,940.00	$0.00	$0.00	$2,940.00
12	Computer Store Instal	$700.00	$700.00	$0.00	$0.00	$700.00

FIGURE 12.5 *You can adjust the Resource Sheet to display cost information, as shown here.*

NOTE

To return to regular Resource Sheet view, choose View, Table, Entry.

Each column in the Resource Sheet contains a particular type of cost information, and most are self-explanatory. One that isn't so obvious is the Cost column, which contains the current total cost of the work scheduled for the resource, taking into account any task duration changes, as opposed to the baseline amount you initially planned. The cost information in all columns consists solely of calculated information. You can't edit any of these values. In fact, if you click on a cell in one of the cost columns, you'll see that the entry in the text entry box above the Resource Sheet is grayed out—if you try to edit it, you can't.

TIP

After you change the Task Sheet or Resource Sheet to display cost information, you can print that information. See Chapter 14, "Proofing and Printing a View," for more details.

Resource Group Costs

You might recall that one of the columns in the default version of the Resource Sheet is the Group column. In this column, you enter information to tell Project that a particular resource has something in common with other resources. For example, you might enter Comm in the Group column to identify each resource from the Communications department in your company. Or you might enter Contract to identify each freelance or contract resource on the team. You might enter Equipment to distinguish nonhuman resources with an hourly cost.

After you display resource cost information, you can reduce the list to display only resources that are part of a particular group and associated costs for only those resources. (This is a filtering operation. You'll learn more about filtering in Chapter 13, "Working with the Different Project Views.") To reduce the list, follow these steps:

1. Display cost information in the Resource Sheet as previously described.

2. On the Formatting toolbar (move and resize it, if needed), click on the arrow beside Filter to display a drop-down list (see Figure 12.6).

3. Click on Group in the Filter drop-down list. The Group dialog box will appear.

4. Enter the name of the group for which you want to view costs in the Group Name text box (see Figure 12.7). You don't have to match the capitalization you used when you identified the resource group in the Group column, but you do have to use the exact spelling.

TIP

You can use wildcard characters, however. For example, if you enter **d*** as the group name, any entry in the Group column that starts with a d—such as Design, Delivery, Data, and so on—will be a match.

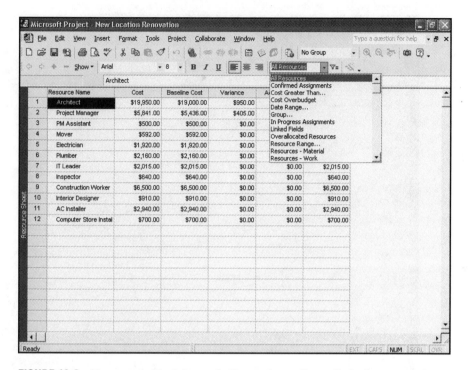

FIGURE 12.6 *You can use this choice on the Formatting toolbar to limit the resources that Project lists.*

FIGURE 12.7 *Specify a resource group for which you'd like to see cost information.*

5. Click on OK to close the dialog box. The Resource Sheet displays cost information for only those resources that you've identified as part of the specified group (see Figure 12.8).

If you want to return to displaying all your resources in the Resource Sheet, choose All Resources from the Filter drop-down list on the Formatting toolbar.

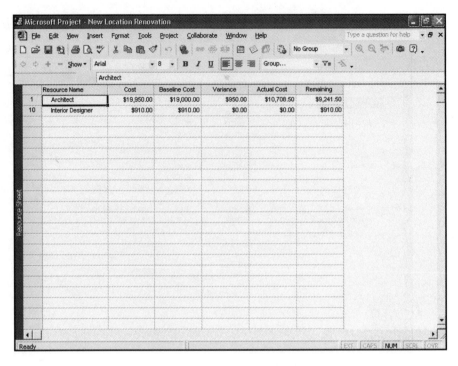

FIGURE 12.8 *Here's the cost information for a group of resources.*

Graphing Individual Resource Work and Costs

In addition to showing task information in graphical form with a Gantt or Network Diagram chart, you can show some resource information in a chart. You'll learn more about adjusting various views in the next chapter, but here's a quick look at how to display graphical information about resource costs:

1. Choose View, Resource Graph, or click on the Resource Graph icon on the View Bar. By default, Project shows a graphical representation of the work scheduled for the resource that you've selected in the Resource Sheet.

2. Right-click on the right pane of the view (where the graphical information appears), or choose Format, Details. On the shortcut menu (see Figure 12.9) or submenu that appears, choose Cost or Cumulative Cost. Project adjusts the graph in the right pane to show the exact cost amounts on the dates when they accrue (see Figure 12.10), or a running total of the costs for the selected resource as they will accumulate (see Figure 12.11).

Use this scroll bar to display the graph information for other resources

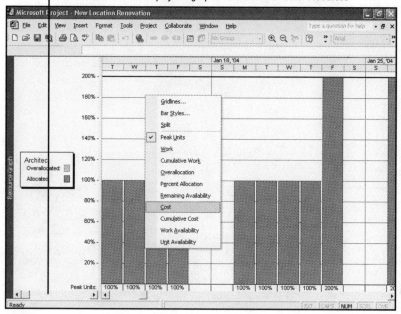

FIGURE 12.9 *You're en route to changing the resource information to a cost graph.*

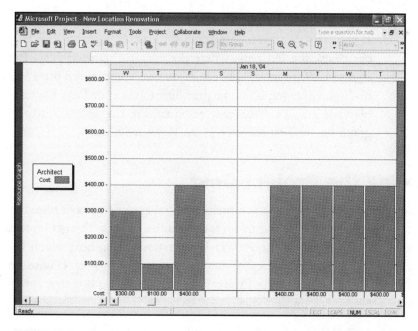

FIGURE 12.10 *Here you're graphing costs for a particular resource on particular dates.*

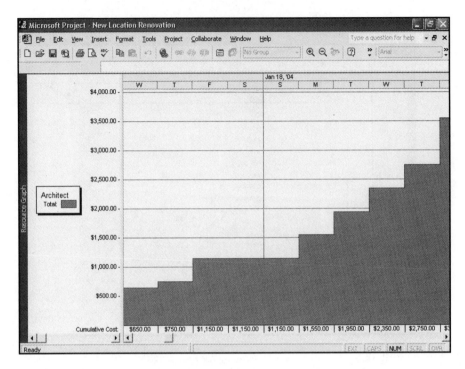

FIGURE 12.11 *Here you're graphing how resource costs accumulate over time.*

3. If you want to view a cost graph for another resource, use the scroll bar below the left pane where the resource name appears (refer to Figure 12.9) to move between resources. You can also press Page Up to display the graph for the previous resource, or Page Down to display the graph for the next resource. Pressing Alt+F5 displays the graph for the first resource in the Resource Sheet.

Viewing the Project Cost

In addition to viewing cost information about specific tasks or resources, you can view how costs are adding up for the entire project. You get information about project costs via the Project Information dialog box, which you saw earlier in this book. To display total costs for your project, choose Project, Project Information. In the Project Information dialog box that appears for your project, click on Statistics.

The Project Statistics dialog box appears (see Figure 12.12). After you review the cost information, click on Close to exit this dialog box.

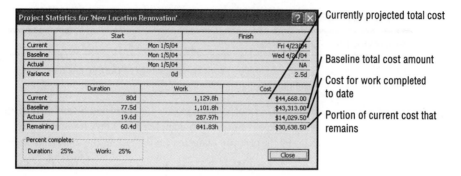

Currently projected total cost

Baseline total cost amount

Cost for work completed to date

Portion of current cost that remains

FIGURE 12.12 *This dialog box contains information about how much all your project work is costing.*

A Word about Earned Values

The term earned value measures whether particular tasks are on budget and on schedule.

In fact, when you view earned value information in either the Task Sheet or the Earned Value dialog box, you actually get to look at several statistics, which are listed in Table 12.1. That's a lot of ways to slice up the information, and it might be more than you ever wanted to know about the costs associated with your tasks.

There are two places to view all this cost information: the Task Sheet or the Earned Value dialog box. To display earned value information in the Task Sheet, follow these steps:

1. Change to the Task Sheet view by choosing View, More Views and then double-clicking on Task Sheet in the Views list of the More Views dialog box.

2. Choose View, Table, More Tables. The More Tables dialog box appears.

3. Make sure that the Task option is selected, and then double-click on Earned Value in the Tables list (or click on it and then click on Apply). The Task Sheet shows all the earned value amounts (see Figure 12.13).

 NOTE

Many of the earned value calculations use the current date. As such, you can calculate the earned value as of a given date by changing the Current Date setting in the Project Information dialog box (Project, Project Information).

Table 12.1 Earned Value Statistics Tracked by Project

Abbreviation	Description
BCWS	Budgeted Cost of Work Scheduled up to the current date in your baseline plan.
BCWP	Budgeted Cost of Work Performed is calculated by multiplying the percentage of work actually completed on a task (as of the current date) by the cost you budgeted for the task in the same time frame.
ACWP	Actual Cost of Work Performed to date on a task, based on the hourly, per-use, and fixed costs you entered.
SV	Schedule Variance is the difference between BCWS and BCWP (BCWS–BCWP). This value compares the money you planned to spend (in your baseline) by the current date to the money you budgeted to spend for work performed by the current date. This figure simply shows how your budgeted costs have changed since you established the baseline. A positive SV value indicates that your current plan calls for spending more than your original plan did.
CV	Cost Variance shows how reality compares with the current budget. It subtracts BCWP from ACWP to tell you whether the work completed is over budget (indicated by a positive value) or under budget (indicated by a negative value).
BAC	Budgeted At Completion is the amount you budgeted for the complete task, including fixed costs and per-use costs. This amount is from your baseline plan.
EAC	Estimate At Completion, also called Forecast At Completion (FAC), projects the total actual cost of the task by comparing measures of budgeted work versus measures of actual work.
Variance	Compares the EAC with the BAC to see whether you'll be spending more (indicated by a positive value) or less (indicated by a negative value) than initially planned to complete the task.

If you want to view the earned value information for a single task in a convenient format, click on its task row in any view that includes the Task Sheet. Next, click on the Task Earned Value button on the Custom Forms toolbar, if you've displayed that toolbar (as described earlier in this chapter). Alternatively, choose Tools, Customize, Forms, or click on the Forms button on the Custom Forms toolbar. In the Customize Forms dialog box, make sure that

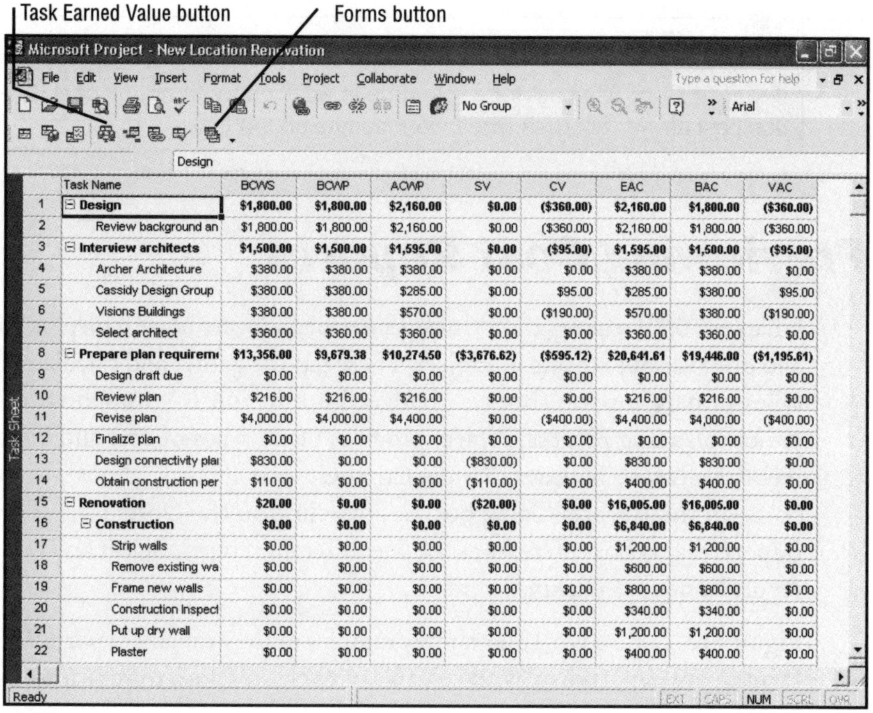

Task Earned Value button · Forms button

FIGURE 12.13 *You now can view a listing of earned value amounts.*

the Task option is selected, and then double-click on Earned Value in the Forms list. Either way, the Earned Value dialog box appears (see Figure 12.14). When you finish viewing the earned value information, click on OK to close the dialog box.

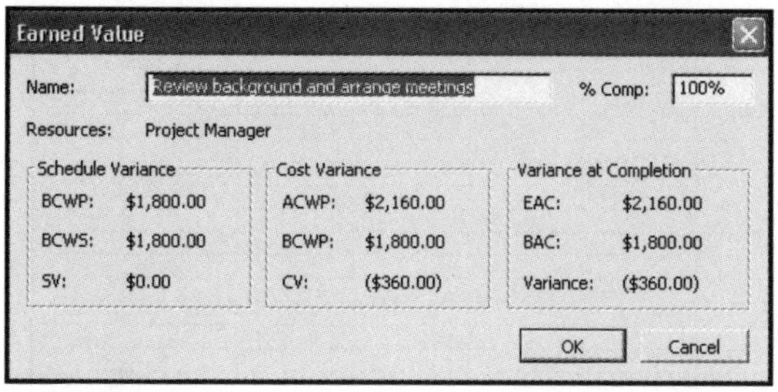

FIGURE 12.14 *Project lets you see earned value information for a single task.*

> **NOTE**
>
> If there's a per-use cost for a resource in addition to an hourly cost, the per-use cost always accrues when work begins on the task.

Previewing Cost Reports

Chapter 16, "Creating and Printing a Report," covers how to display, format, and print various reports in Project. These reports gather and calculate myriad types of data for you. Because budget information is so important to any project planning process, Project provides many types of cost and budgeting reports—five, to be exact. To display these cost reports, choose View, Reports. In the Reports dialog box, double-click on the Costs icon. The Cost Reports dialog box offers icons for five different reports. Select and compile a report by double-clicking on its icon.

Figures 12.15 through 12.19 show examples of the available reports. Click on Print in any report display to print it, or click on Close to return to the Reports dialog box.

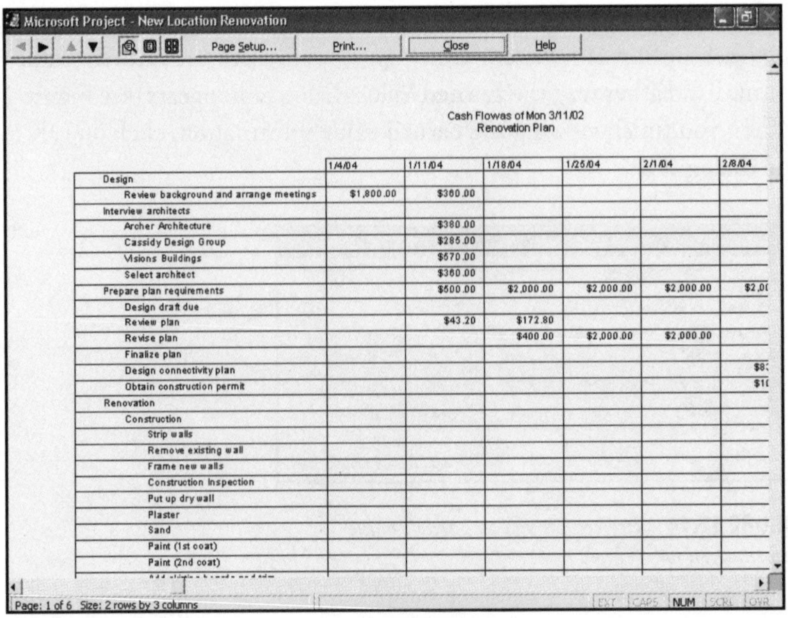

FIGURE 12.15 *The Cash Flow report presents an update of how much you spent per task each week.*

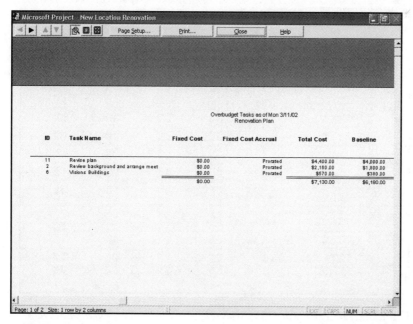

ID	Task Name	Fixed Cost	Fixed Cost Accrual	Total Cost	Baseline
			Budget Report as of Mon 3/11/02		
			Renovation Plan		
11	Revise plan	$0.00	Prorated	$4,400.00	$4,000
2	Review background and arrange meet	$0.00	Prorated	$2,160.00	$1,800
45	Install pipes	$0.00	Prorated	$1,600.00	$1,600
32	Install ducting	$0.00	Prorated	$1,260.00	$1,260
17	Strip walls	$0.00	Prorated	$1,200.00	$1,200
21	Put up dry wall	$0.00	Prorated	$1,200.00	$1,200
38	Upgrade wiring	$0.00	Prorated	$960.00	$960
33	Install vents	$0.00	Prorated	$840.00	$840
13	Design connectivity plan	$0.00	Prorated	$830.00	$830
19	Frame new walls	$0.00	Prorated	$800.00	$800
18	Remove existing wall	$0.00	Prorated	$600.00	$600
6	Visions Buildings	$0.00	Prorated	$570.00	$380
34	Install main unit	$0.00	Prorated	$560.00	$560
50	Install LAN backbone	$0.00	Prorated	$520.00	$520
40	Electrical Inspection	$0.00	Prorated	$500.00	$500
46	Plumbing Inspection	$0.00	Prorated	$500.00	$500
14	Obtain construction permit	$0.00	Prorated	$400.00	$400
22	Plaster	$0.00	Prorated	$400.00	$400
24	Paint (1st coat)	$0.00	Prorated	$400.00	$400
25	Paint (2nd coat)	$0.00	Prorated	$400.00	$400
29	Lay new flooring	$0.00	Prorated	$400.00	$400
30	Install appliances	$0.00	Prorated	$400.00	$400
4	Archer Architecture	$0.00	Prorated	$380.00	$380
7	Select architect	$0.00	Prorated	$360.00	$360
20	Construction Inspection	$0.00	Prorated	$340.00	$340
55	Final Inspection	$0.00	Prorated	$340.00	$340
39	Install new switches and outlets	$0.00	Prorated	$320.00	$320
47	Install sink and faucets	$0.00	Prorated	$320.00	$320
5	Cassidy Design Group	$0.00	Prorated	$285.00	$380
35	Install thermometers and controls	$0.00	Prorated	$280.00	$280
52	Install phone lines and jacks	$0.00	Prorated	$260.00	$260

FIGURE 12.16 *The Budget report presents the total costs you've scheduled for your project, and the cost per task. This report sorts tasks in order, from most expensive to least expensive.*

ID	Task Name	Fixed Cost	Fixed Cost Accrual	Total Cost	Baseline
			Overbudget Tasks as of Mon 3/11/02		
			Renovation Plan		
11	Revise plan	$0.00	Prorated	$4,400.00	$4,000.00
2	Review background and arrange meet	$0.00	Prorated	$2,160.00	$1,800.00
6	Visions Buildings	$0.00	Prorated	$570.00	$380.00
		$0.00		$7,130.00	$6,180.00

FIGURE 12.17 *The Overbudget Tasks report points out where expenses are going to get out of hand.*

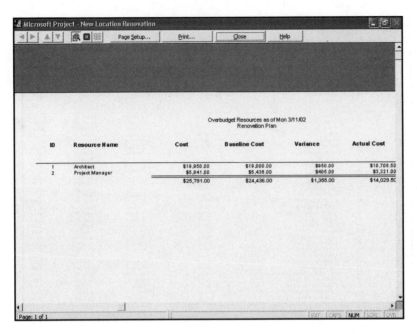

FIGURE 12.18 *The Overbudget Resources report identifies when a resource has had to work more (and therefore costs more) than you had planned in your baseline.*

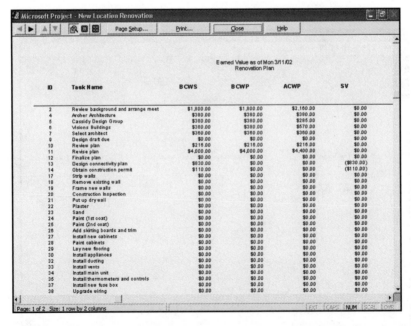

FIGURE 12.19 *The Earned Value report shows earned value calculations for each task, as well as totals for the project.*

Changing How Costs Add Up

When you added resources to the project file using the default view of the Resource Sheet, you used the Accrue At column to note when costs for work performed should be charged to the project as actual costs. Most costs accrue in a prorated fashion. For each percentage point of the task that's marked as completed, a corresponding amount of the budgeted expense is charged as an actual cost. For a task that has the Start setting in the Accrue At column, the total budgeted cost becomes an actual cost as soon as any work is completed on that task. In contrast, for a task where Accrue At is set to End, no actual costs accumulate until you mark the task as 100% completed.

In most cases, cash flow is as important to project management as the ultimate bottom line is. One of the biggest scams on consumers is when certain unscrupulous home repair contractors give the best estimate for a repair job, but ask for all or a large part of the money up front. You hand over a check, and the contractor disappears into thin air without doing anything. Just as you'd certainly want to delay payments to a home repair contractor, it's in the interest of any business to delay project expenses until the work is completed to your satisfaction.

If you review task costs and it seems that too many costs have accrued too early in the schedule, look for tasks for which you can postpone accrued costs. (Negotiate with your resources, of course, to ensure that your changes reflect reality.) You want to be able to change as many tasks as possible to accrue at the end of work on the task. (This isn't the realistic choice for most internal resources, of course—they're getting paid all the time, and your company cheerfully assigns you the cost as soon as you use them.) If you can't have tasks accrue at the end, at least lobby for prorated cost approval and minimize the number of tasks that accrue at the start of work on the task.

To review or change Accrue At information, display the Resource Sheet and review or change your choice in the Accrue At field. Alternately, right-click on a resource in the Resource Sheet, and then click on Resource Information to open the Resource Information dialog box for that resource. On the Costs tab, change the entry in the Cost Accrual drop-down list box as needed.

NOTE

If you changed the Resource Sheet to display earned value or other information instead of the default entry information, you need to change it back to adjust how costs accrue. With the Resource Sheet onscreen, open the View menu, point to Table, and click on Entry.

Changing a Fixed Task Cost

After work has been completed on a task, most external resources present you with a bill. Or, your company's accounting department might inform you how much of an allocated (shared) cost your group or department has to pay for the completion of a task. Even though you usually aren't dinged for a fixed cost until the work on the task is completed, Project automatically prorates fixed costs based on how much of the task work has been completed. If you want Project to add in entire fixed costs at the start or end of the work on the task, follow these steps:

1. Choose Tools, Options. The Options dialog box will appear, with many tabs.

2. Click on the Calculation tab to display its options.

3. Open the Default Fixed Costs Accrual drop-down list and choose Start or End.

4. Click on OK to close the Options dialog box. Your change will take effect immediately.

Whether the actual (fixed) cost for a task is higher or lower than what you budgeted in the Task Sheet, when you receive the bill or charge, you need to compare it with the Fixed Cost entry you made for the task and adjust the entry upward or downward. Follow these steps to enter the actual, final fixed cost for a task:

1. Change to the Task Sheet view by choosing View, More Views and then double-clicking on Task Sheet in the Views list of the More Views dialog box.

2. Choose View, Table, Cost. The Task Sheet adjusts to show columns of cost information.

3. Click on the Fixed Cost cell in the row for the task for which you want to enter actual data.

4. Type the new entry (see Figure 12.20).

You also can change the accrual method for a single task's fixed cost

	Task Name	Fixed Cost	Fixed Cost Accrual	Total Cost	Baseline	Variance	Actual	Remaining
1	⊟ **Design**	**$0.00**	**Prorated**	**$2,160.00**	**$1,800.00**	**$360.00**	**$2,160.00**	**$0.00**
2	Review background an	$0.00	Prorated	$2,160.00	$1,800.00	$360.00	$2,160.00	$0.00
3	⊟ **Interview architects**	**$0.00**	**Prorated**	**$1,595.00**	**$1,500.00**	**$95.00**	**$1,595.00**	**$0.00**
4	Archer Architecture	$0.00	Prorated	$380.00	$380.00	$0.00	$380.00	$0.00
5	Cassidy Design Group	$0.00	Prorated	$285.00	$380.00	($95.00)	$285.00	$0.00
6	Visions Buildings	$0.00	Prorated	$570.00	$380.00	$190.00	$570.00	$0.00
7	Select architect	$0.00	Prorated	$360.00	$360.00	$0.00	$360.00	$0.00
8	⊟ **Prepare plan requireme**	**$0.00**	**Prorated**	**$20,346.00**	**$19,446.00**	**$900.00**	**$10,274.50**	**$10,071.50**
9	Design draft due	$0.00	Prorated	$0.00	$0.00	$0.00	$0.00	$0.00
10	Review plan	$0.00	Prorated	$216.00	$216.00	$0.00	$216.00	$0.00
11	Revise plan	$0.00	Prorated	$4,400.00	$4,000.00	$400.00	$4,400.00	$0.00
12	Finalize plan	$0.00	Prorated	$0.00	$0.00	$0.00	$0.00	$0.00
13	Design connectivity plan	$0.00	Prorated	$830.00	$830.00	$0.00	$0.00	$830.00
14	Obtain construction per	600	Prorated	$400.00	$400.00	$0.00	$0.00	$400.00
15	⊟ **Renovation**	**$0.00**	**Prorated**	**$16,005.00**	**$16,005.00**	**$0.00**	**$0.00**	**$16,005.00**
16	⊟ **Construction**	**$0.00**	**Prorated**	**$6,840.00**	**$6,840.00**	**$0.00**	**$0.00**	**$6,840.00**
17	Strip walls	$0.00	Prorated	$1,200.00	$1,200.00	$0.00	$0.00	$1,200.00
18	Remove existing wa	$0.00	Prorated	$600.00	$600.00	$0.00	$0.00	$600.00
19	Frame new walls	$0.00	Prorated	$800.00	$800.00	$0.00	$0.00	$800.00
20	Construction Inspect	$0.00	Prorated	$340.00	$340.00	$0.00	$0.00	$340.00
21	Put up dry wall	$0.00	Prorated	$1,200.00	$1,200.00	$0.00	$0.00	$1,200.00
22	Plaster	$0.00	Prorated	$400.00	$400.00	$0.00	$0.00	$400.00

FIGURE 12.20   *Adding a fixed cost amount includes flat costs (not based on hourly work) charged for a task.*

5. Click on the Enter button or press Enter to finish your edit.

NOTE

If you want to change the accrual method for a single fixed cost rather than all of them, change the entry in the Fixed Cost Accrual column, as shown in Figure 12.20.

Overriding a Calculated Resource Cost

Just as your original Fixed Cost entry might not reflect the final, actual cost, a calculated expense based on the amount of hourly work completed by a resource might not reflect the final charge to you for that work. This might happen when a resource (particularly a freelance resource) has to work more hours or days than you estimated, but because of a contractual obligation, the resource only bills you the original amount. In such a case, entering all the hours the resource worked would make the calculated cost higher than the final bill. Other times, a resource might have reason to bill you more for a task than had been initially agreed upon, even if the days or hours of work completed remained consistent with your estimate.

In either case, you need to adjust the actual costs for the task without changing the number of hours or days of work on the task. There's only one way to do so before a task is 100% completed:

1. Choose Tools, Options. The Options dialog box will appear, with many tabs.

2. Click on the Calculation tab to display its options.

3. Clear the check mark beside the Actual Costs Are Always Calculated By Microsoft Project option.

 CAUTION

Remember that once you disable automatic calculation, turning it back on will override all the actual costs you've entered while it was turned off. Therefore, it's best to follow these steps only after your project is finished. Project offers another approach for entering actual costs that's the best of both worlds. You can override a calculated resource cost after you mark a task as 100% completed, and remaining costs (Rem. Cost) for the tasks are calculated as $0 without turning off automatic calculation.

4. By default, actual costs you enter are distributed (accrued) along the full duration of the task. If you want to spread the actual cost only through the project status date you entered, check the Edits To Total Actual Cost Will Be Spread To The Status Date check box.

5. Click on OK to close the Options dialog box.

6. Switch to Gantt Chart view and click on the task for which you want to enter an actual cost that's different from the cost calculated by Project.

7. Choose View, More Views, or click on the More Views icon on the View Bar. The More Views dialog box appears.

8. Scroll down the Views list and double-click on Task Entry (or click on it and click on Apply). Project displays the Task Entry form in the lower pane.

9. Right-click on the lower pane and click on Resource Cost. The pane changes to display cost information about the resource.

10. Click on the Act. Cost column and edit the entry as needed (see Figure 12.21).

The real cost you've entered

Click here for your change to take effect

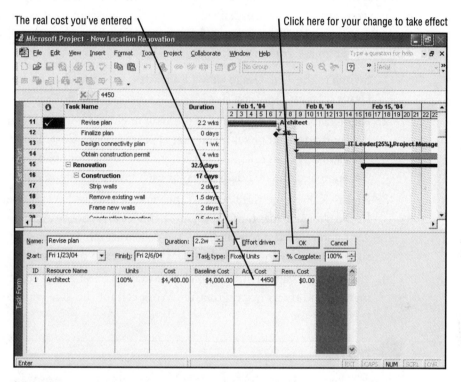

FIGURE 12.21 *You can edit the actual cost for a resource's work when it's different from the calculated amount. Either turn off automatic calculation (be cautious in doing so) or wait until the task is 100% completed.*

11. Click on the OK in the form pane to finish your entry.

12. (Optional) Use the Previous and Next buttons to display information about the resource work for other tasks, and repeat Steps 5 and 6 to edit the Act. Cost entries.

To remove the lower pane and return to regular Gantt Chart view, choose Window, Remove Split.

Entering Exact Daily Costs

You can use the Task Usage view to see and enter actual costs per day for an assignment. To do so, you must first turn off automatic calculation (refer to "Controlling Whether Costs Are Updated Based On Work Completed"), because you can't edit Act. Cost entries for a particular assignment even when work on a task is 100% complete. Then, follow these steps to see and edit daily costs for an assignment:

1. Switch to the Task Usage view. (The fastest way is to click on the Task Usage icon on the View Bar.)

2. Right-click on the right pane of the view, or choose Format, Details. In the shortcut menu or submenu that appears, choose Cost. This choice adds a row of Cost cells for each assignment to the right pane, showing the original calculated daily costs for each resource assignment.

3. Right-click on the right pane of the view, or choose Format, Details. In the shortcut menu or submenu that appears, choose Actual Cost. This choice adds a row of Act. Cost cells for each assignment to the right pane, showing the daily actual cost for each resource.

4. Display the assignment for which you want to enter actual cost information, and then click on the Act. Work cell for the date you want in the right pane.

 NOTE

The cells in the grid in the right pane of Task Usage or Resource Usage views are called *timephased fields* or *timephased cells*. That's because they let you focus in on a particular date and enter precise work and cost measurements for that date.

5. Type the new cost figure (see Figure 12.22), and then press Enter or click on the Enter button on the entry box to finish your entry. Project updates the Act. Cost and the cost information for the assignment for that date.

Cutting Back Costs

When you're developing your overall project schedule, or after work is under way and you're seeing that some of your actual cost amounts are exceeding

Selected assignment | Actual cost entered for the date | Original cost

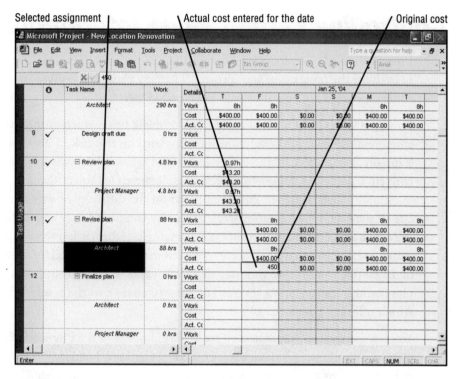

FIGURE 12.22 *For more precise final cost information, you can enter the actual cost for a particular date of an assignment after displaying actual cost information in the right pane of Task Usage view.*

the amounts you budgeted, you might need to look for ways to cut back costs. Here are just a few ways that you can reduce your overall budget:

◆ Look at the schedules for more expensive tasks—the Budget report (refer to Figure 12.16) can help you identify them—and see if you can decrease the scheduled work for them or negotiate a more favorable fee or hourly rate.

◆ Cut back the working time allotted for later tasks.

◆ Return to your cost estimates, and see if you have time to substitute less expensive resources for more expensive ones.

◆ Cut back the amount of work handled by an expensive resource, perhaps by adding resources with lower hourly rates to share the expensive resource's workload.

Controlling Earned Value Information

Project 2002 adds several new earned value fields that you can view and use to evaluate the progress of your project. The new version also gives you more control over exactly how it calculates earned values.

Project 2002 includes a new Physical % Complete field, which enables you to enter your estimate of the actual work completed on the task, if it varies substantially from the % Complete. To calculate the % Complete (when you haven't entered a particular completion percentage yourself), Project divides actual duration by total duration. However, based on the difficulty of work early or late in the task, the amount of work physically completed may vary dramatically from the completion percentage. For example, if the hardest work in a task comes last, the task may be 75% complete but may have a Physical % Complete of 25%. You would have to enter that 25% value in the Physical % Complete field. (Choose View, Table, Tracking to change to the tracking table, which offers this new field.)

You can specify that Project uses either the % Complete or the Physical % Complete to control how earned value is calculated—in terms of duration (% Complete) or in terms of your estimate of work completed (Physical % Complete). In addition, you can choose which baseline Project will use in earned value calculations. To change these settings for the current project file, follow these steps:

1. Choose Tools, Options. The Options dialog box will open.
2. Click on the Calculation tab.
3. Click on the Earned Value button. The Earned Value dialog box will open, as in Figure 12.23.

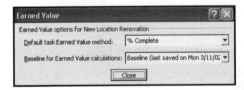

FIGURE 12.23 *Project enables you to control some of the values used in earned value calculations.*

4. Choose either % Complete or Physical % Complete from the Default Task Earned Value Method drop-down list.

5. Choose the baseline to use for calculations from the Baseline for Earned Value Calculations drop-down list.

6. Click on Close to close the Earned Value dialog box.

7. Click on OK to close the Options dialog box and apply the new settings.

 NOTE

To use % Complete or Physical % Complete to calculate the earned value for a single task, double-click the task in Gantt Chart view. This displays the Task Information dialog box. Click on the Advanced tab and choose the desired field from the Earned Value Method drop-down list near the bottom. Then click on OK to apply the change.

In addition to the Physical % Complete field, Project 2002 adds a few more new earned value fields:

◆ **CPI (Cost Performance Index)** divides BCWP by ACWP as of the current date to compare baseline costs to actual costs.

◆ **SPI (Schedule Performance Index)** divides BCWP by BCWS to find out whether work is ahead of schedule or behind schedule, overall. Values greater than 1 indicate the project is ahead of schedule. Values less than 1 mean you need to crack the whip!

◆ **CV% (Cost Variance Percent)** divides CV by BCWP and then multiplies by 100, to yield a percentage that shows the variance between how much a task should have cost for completion to date and how much it actually cost.

◆ **SV% (Schedule Variance Percent)** divides SV by BCWS and then multiplies by 100, to yield a percentage that expresses the ratio between the variance for work actually performed to date and the budget for work scheduled to date.

◆ **TCPI (To Complete Performance Index)** requires a bit more involved calculation: (BAC – BCWP)/(EAC – ACWP). This statistic helps you identify whether the remaining work on a project is in line with the remaining budget available to pay for it, as of a given status date. Values greater than 1 reflect a negative situation, where the remaining amount of work outstrips the remaining budget and resources need to perform at a higher level. Values less than 1 tell you that resources have been getting more done that you estimated, meaning you can focus more on quality or profit as opposed to work flow.

Chapter 13

Working with the Different Project Views

In This Chapter

◆ Reviewing the views

◆ Choosing a view

◆ Working with tables, including how to control table information by sorting and filtering

◆ Grouping sheet information

◆ Using Gantt Chart Wizard

◆ Adjusting whether charted information is displayed on a weekly, monthly, or other timescale

◆ Creating your own views and organizing views

Project enables you to capture a huge amount of information about the tasks and resources associated with your plan. In theory, you could use a spreadsheet program or word processor to store all these details. To a limited degree, those programs let you chart or display information in alternative formats. But they don't provide the same flexibility in viewing and presenting your information that Project does.

Project enables you to be efficient at entering schedule and resource information, and to be proficient at reviewing the schedule and gleaning key facts. The different ways that Project presents information are called *views*, and this chapter reviews them.

Reviewing the Views

Earlier chapters periodically explained how to change the view so that you could work with different kinds of information. The views used in earlier chapters included the Gantt Chart, Resource Graph, Resource Sheet, Task Usage, Resource Usage, and Task Entry views.

Project views can present information in a table or spreadsheet-like grid (as the Task Sheet and Resource Sheet do), in a graphical format (as Gantt bars do), or in a fill-in form format (where you select fields or text boxes and then enter the information you want to view). Some views use a single method to present information, and some present information in various ways by having multiple panes onscreen. When a view uses only one method to organize information, such as a form, it's called a *single-pane view*.

> **NOTE**
>
> Project prints information using the currently selected view. However, Project doesn't print forms or the Relationship Diagram view, so a view that includes only a form won't print at all. When printing is unavailable, the Print button on the Standard toolbar is disabled (grayed out).

In addition to thinking about how views appear onscreen, you need to select a view based on the type of information you want to work with. Some views primarily provide information about tasks, and other views primarily provide information about resources. Here are the predefined views you'll find in Project:

♦ **Bar Rollup, Milestone Date Rollup, and Milestone Rollup.** Use these views after running the Rollup_Formatting macro that comes with Project to roll up the Gantt bars for subtasks onto the summary task Gantt bar. Each view provides slightly different formatting for the rolled-up tasks. See the section "Using the Rollup Views" near the end of this chapter for a look at how to use these views.

♦ **Calendar.** This single-pane view (see Figure 13.1) displays tasks on a monthly calendar, using a bar and label to indicate each task duration.

♦ **Detail Gantt.** In this variation of Gantt Chart view, the Task Sheet includes Delay information, and the Gantt bars indicate slack time and any task slippage (changes in the task schedule since you saved the baseline). Figure 13.2 shows Detail Gantt view.

♦ **Gantt Chart.** This is the default view in Project. It includes the Task Sheet in the left pane and Gantt bars showing task durations and relationships in the right pane.

♦ **Leveling Gantt.** In this variation of Gantt Chart view, the Task Sheet includes a Leveling Delay column to indicate any tasks that Project delayed when you used automatic resource leveling. (Refer to Chapter 9, "Resolving Overallocations and Overbooked Resources," to learn more about resource leveling.) In addition, each Gantt bar is each split into two smaller bars. The upper bar shows the task's original

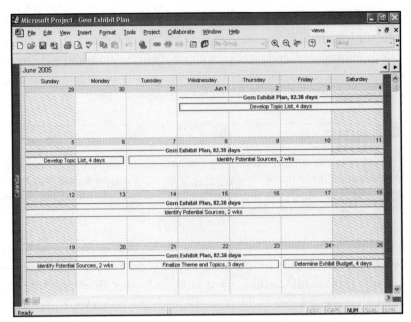

FIGURE 13.1 *Use the Calendar view to show a monthly calendar for a project.*

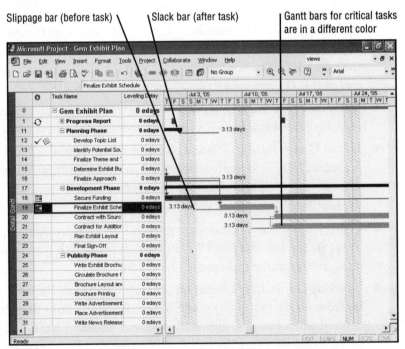

FIGURE 13.2 *Detail Gantt view presents more information than regular Gantt Chart view.*

schedule, and the lower bar shows its current schedule, with darker shading indicating the percentage of work completed on the task.

◆ **Multiple Baselines Gantt.** This view charts the first three baselines using colored bars on the Gantt chart portion of the view. You can use this view to compare how the project plan has evolved, based on the first three baselines you've saved.

◆ **Network Diagram, Descriptive Network Diagram, and Relationship Diagram.** The Network Diagram view (which is similar to the PERT Chart view in the previous version of Project) displays tasks in a format resembling a flow chart (see Figure 13.3). You can drag to link tasks, or right-click on a task and click on Task Information to adjust the task schedule and resource assignments. The Descriptive Network Diagram view resembles the Network Diagram view. The nodes in the Descriptive Network Diagram view offer slightly different information, such as identifying the resource(s) assigned to the task. The Relationship Diagram shows a more simplified diagram of how tasks flow.

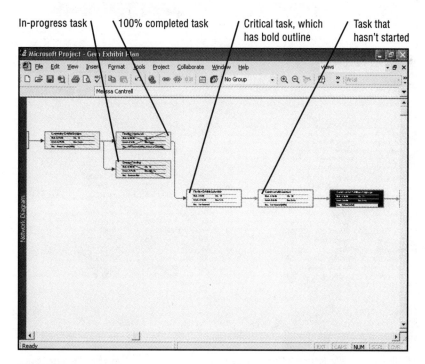

FIGURE 13.3 *If you prefer a flow chart–like format, use the Network Diagram view.*

TIP

On the Network Diagram chart, you can also drag to add new tasks to the schedule. Drag diagonally to create a box with the mouse, right-click on the new task box, and then click on Task Information. Provide the details about the task in the Task Information dialog box, and then click on OK.

To delete a task in Network Diagram view, click on the chart box (node) to select it and press Delete. Or, to select multiple boxes, drag over an area that surrounds the boxes to be deleted. When you release the mouse button, a gray selector appears around the boxes. Press the Delete key to remove the task boxes from the chart.

◆ **Resource Allocation.** This view presents the Resource Usage view in the upper pane and the Task Sheet and Gantt chart in the lower pane.

◆ **Resource Form.** This is a form you use to enter and edit information about a specific resource. It lists all the tasks assigned to that resource, resource cost information, and more (see Figure 13.4).

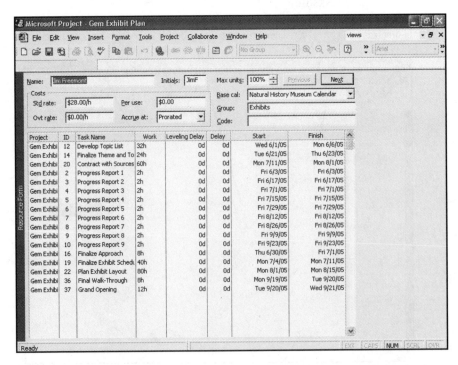

FIGURE 13.4 *The Resource Form view captures all the information about the displayed resource.*

- **Resource Graph.** This view (examples of which are shown in Chapter 12, "Viewing and Managing Costs and Value") can graph information about a resource's daily and cumulative costs, scheduled work and cumulative work, overallocated times, percentage of work allocated, and availability. To change the type of information on the graph, right-click on the chart area of the view and use the resulting shortcut menu to choose which information is charted.

- **Resource Name Form.** This abbreviated version of the Resource Form lists the resource name and its assigned tasks.

- **Resource Sheet.** This view provides a grid of cells you can use to add resources to your project file. Chapter 7, "Adding Resources into Your Project Plan," covers the Resource Sheet in detail.

- **Resource Usage.** This view, covered earlier in the book, has a Resource Sheet that identifies the assignments for each resource on the left, and a timephased grid on the right that you can use to enter daily actual costs, daily scheduled work and completed work, and more. Right-click on the right pane to choose which details you want to view or enter in it.

- **Task Details Form.** Similar to the Resource Form, this full-screen form displays task scheduling information, constraints, assigned resources, and more. You can view or edit information in this form, as you can in other forms.

 TIP

You can right-click on a blank area of any form to adjust what it displays.

- **Task Entry.** This view displays the Gantt chart in the upper pane and the Task Form in the lower pane. It lets you perform detailed editing of task information in the lower pane, so you can see how your changes affect the Gantt chart. You can right-click on the Task Form to select which information it displays.

- **Task Form.** This form (see Figure 13.5) enables you to change the task name, schedule, work completion information, and assigned resources.

- **Task Name Form.** This is the simplest variation of the Task Details Form. It enables you to change the task name and assigned resources.

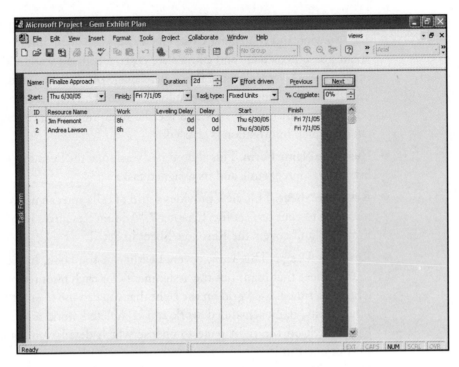

FIGURE 13.5 *Task Form view lets you focus on task assignments.*

◆ **Task Sheet.** This view shows the Task Sheet at full-screen size rather than in combination with other view panes.

◆ **Task Usage.** Various chapters have already covered how to display and work with this view, which groups resource assignments by task. Use the timephased grid at the right to view and enter daily work and cost values. Right-click on the right pane to choose which details you want to view or enter in it.

◆ **Tracking Gantt.** Chapter 11, "Comparing Progress versus Your Baseline Plan," discusses this variation of regular Gantt Chart view. In Tracking Gantt view, the Gantt bars are divided into upper and lower segments. The lower portion of each bar shows the task's original schedule, and the upper portion shows the task's current schedule.

Choosing a View

It's pretty obvious where to begin when you want to select a new view—the View menu. The top eight commands on this menu take you directly to the specified view: Calendar, Gantt Chart, Network Diagram, Task Usage, Tracking Gantt, Resource Graph, Resource Sheet, and Resource Usage. In addition, the View Bar offers an icon for each of those eight views. Choose View, View bar to display the View Bar, if needed, and then click on an icon to display the view it represents.

NOTE

If you're changing from a combination view that includes more than one pane to a view that includes only a single pane, the extra pane often won't close on its own. To close it, choose Window, Remove Split (or double-click on the dividing line between the panes). If the bottom pane is a form, you can also right-click on it and then choose Hide Form View. Finally, if you're changing from a split view to a single-pane view, press and hold the Shift key when you select the new view from the View menu to both remove the split and display the selected view.

If you want to display a view that's not listed on the menu or the View Bar, follow these steps:

1. Choose View, More Views, or click on the More Views icon on the View Bar. The More Views dialog box will appear (see Figure 13.6).

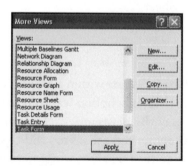

FIGURE 13.6 *The More Views dialog box enables you to choose a view that's not on the View menu or View Bar.*

2. Scroll the Views list, if needed, to the view you want.
3. In the Views list, double-click on the name of the view you want (or click on the name and click on Apply).

In views that include upper and lower panes, click within the pane you want to work in to make that pane the active view, or press F6. The Active View

Bar along the edge of the screen darkens to indicate which pane you've selected to work in.

If you switch to any view that includes a Gantt chart and you don't see anything in the pane, first make sure that Project hasn't scrolled the chart to any dates before or beyond the schedule for the project. Try clicking on the Go To Selected Task button on the Standard toolbar to scroll to the right area. Or, press Alt+Home to go to the project start task/milestone, or press Alt+End to go to the project end task/milestone.

Adjusting a Sheet

The Task Sheet and Resource Sheet present information in various columns (fields). Depending on the operation at hand, you may want to view columns that contain different information. For example, Chapter 12, "Viewing and Managing Costs and Value," explains that you can display columns of actual and projected cost information in the Task Sheet. You can also control which rows appear in the current sheet, and the order in which those rows appear. This section covers how to adjust the appearance or content of information presented in the Task Sheet or Resource Sheet.

Changing Row Heights

In previous versions of Project, you couldn't wrap text within a column when the column entries were too wide to fit. Your only option was to resize the column to make it wide enough to display the new entries. Now you can resize the height of a row that contains a column entry that's too wide. When you do so, Project wraps cell entries to more than one line, where needed, so they fit within the column width. Since Project prints information as it appears onscreen, resizing the rows will ensure that your printouts are easier for recipients to read.

To resize the row height, drag the bottom row border below the row number. As shown in Figure 13.7, Project immediately wraps cell text. To return the row to its original height, drag the bottom row border up until it touches the bottom border for the row above. When you release the mouse button, Project automatically snaps the row back to its original height.

Drag bottom boundary to resize row

FIGURE 13.7 *Project's new row resizing feature enables you to wrap text in cells.*

Choosing a Table

In Project, each particular group of columns shown in a Task Sheet or Resource Sheet is called a *table*. To display one of the predefined sets of columns, therefore, you choose a different table for the currently displayed sheet. Of course, different tables are provided for the Task Sheet and Resource Sheet, because you track different information for tasks than you do for resources. When you select a particular table for a sheet and then print the view that includes the sheet, Project prints only the columns that are part of the presently selected table. Table 13.1 lists the many table types that are available.

> **NOTE**
>
> If you try to use a table that's not available for a Resource Sheet, Project displays a message box telling you that you need to choose or create another table.

When you want to establish which table is used by a Task Sheet or Resource Sheet, first select the sheet. Next, choose View, Table, and click on the name of the table you want. If the desired table is not listed, choose More Tables. The More Tables dialog box appears (see Figure 13.8). If needed, select Task or Resource at the top of the dialog box to list the appropriate kinds of tables. Select a table from the Tables list by double-clicking on it (or by clicking on it and clicking on Apply).

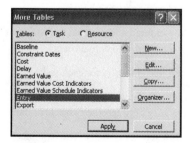

FIGURE 13.8 *Here's where you choose a table that's not on the Table submenu.*

Table 13.1 Tables Available for a Task Sheet or a Resource Sheet

Table	Description
Task Sheet Tables	
Baseline	Displays the baseline schedule dates, work, and cost for tasks.
Constraint Dates	Lists constraint types and dates you entered for tasks.
Cost	Shows fixed cost information you entered for a task, as well as calculated resource costs.
Delay	Tells you when a task has been delayed as a result of resource leveling.
Earned Value	Includes columns that provide earned value analysis for cost and schedule variance.
Earned Value Cost Indicators	Includes fields that provide earned value amounts for costs and cost variances.
Earned Value Schedule Indicators	Includes fields that provide earned value amounts for schedule and schedule variances.
Entry	The default. Provides columns that enable you to set up new tasks.
Export	When you export task data, Project uses this table, which includes more task fields than many of the others.
Hyperlink	Displays links you created to Web pages or files on a network, such as a link to a memo file with more information about a task.
Rollup	When you use the Rollup views, this adds columns so you can control Gantt display features such as whether text appears above the rolled-up bars.
Schedule	Presents task start and finish information, as well as information about slack time.
Summary	Presents scheduled task start and finish dates, percent of work completed, and budgeted cost and work hours.
Tracking	Presents information you entered about actual task start and finish dates, remaining duration, and actual costs.
Usage	Shows start, finish, work, and duration for each task.
Variance	Lists baseline start and finish dates along with the current dates, and shows the variance between the two sets of dates.
Work	Enables you to track work statistics, such as the baseline number of hours scheduled for a task, the actual hours worked, variance between the two, and so on.

Table 13.1 (continued)

Table	Description
Resource Sheet Tables	
Cost	Displays the baseline cost you estimated for resources, the current scheduled cost, the cost actually incurred, and more.
Earned Value	Displays the calculated earned value statistics described in Table 12.1. For example, displays the earned value schedule and cost variance.
Entry	The default. Provides columns that enable you to define new resources.
Entry— Material Resources	Displays only the Resource Sheet columns needed for entering material resources. For example, this table doesn't include the Ovt. Rate column.
Entry— Work Resources	Displays only the Resource Sheet columns needed for entering work resources. For example, this table doesn't include the Material Label column.
Export	When you export resource data, Project uses this table, which includes applicable resource fields.
Hyperlink	Displays links you created to Web pages or files on a network, such as a link to a resource's Web page.
Summary	Includes information about hourly rates and work hours scheduled for a resource on a project, and more.
Usage	Displays the resource name and number of hours of work by that resource scheduled for the project.
Work	Lists scheduled and actual work hours by a resource, overtime work authorized, percentage of work completed, and more.

Filtering and Sorting Sheet Data

When you build the list of tasks or resources in a project plan, the list appears in the order that you entered it and includes all the tasks or resources you entered. However, you can control the display of the list in any Task Sheet or Resource Sheet by sorting the entries (to change the order) or filtering the entries (to hide entries that don't match criteria you specify). Once you sort or filter a list, you can then print it to present the data you want in the order you want. This section discusses how to filter and sort information in Microsoft Project 2002.

Filtering the Task Sheet or Resource Sheet

By default, each Task Sheet or Resource Sheet displays all of the tasks or resources you entered for the project, no matter which table you've selected. Sometimes, though, you might want to see only some of the tasks or resources listed. For example, if you need to provide your client with a list of tasks that have been completed, or a list of all resources from a particular resource group, you can filter the sheet to display only certain rows.

 TIP

Filtering a sheet and then printing it is a quick and dirty method of creating a report about key facts from your schedule.

To filter the current sheet, use the Filter drop-down list on the Formatting toolbar, as shown in Figure 13.9. (Note that you may want to move the Formatting toolbar below the Standard toolbar to make it easier to access the Filter drop-down list and other tools described in this chapter.) The available filter options differ depending on whether a Task Sheet or Resource Sheet is currently displayed. Figure 13.9 shows the Task Sheet options. Some filter options are followed by an ellipsis, which indicates that if you choose that particular filter, Project will ask you to supply more information to help it select the entries to display. For example, if you select Date Range..., Project displays the dialog box shown in Figure 13.10. It asks you to specify the time frame within which the displayed tasks must fall. In this case, you enter a starting date, click on OK, enter an ending date, and click on OK again so that Project can filter the list.

To return to the full listing of tasks or resources after you're done with the filtered version, select All Tasks or All Resources from the Filter drop-down list.

If you prefer not to use the Formatting toolbar but still want to filter tasks and resources, choose Project, Filtered For to display a submenu, and click on the name of the filter you want. If the name doesn't appear, choose More Filters to open the More Filters dialog box (see Figure 13.11). Here you can select the filter you want.

An ellipsis (. . .) means the filter will prompt you for details about which entries to select

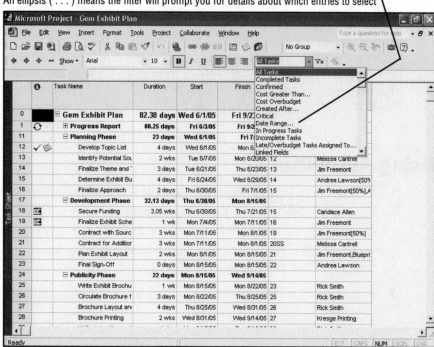

FIGURE 13.9 *Use the Filter drop-down list on the Formatting toolbar to control which rows appear in a sheet.*

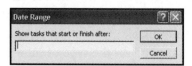

FIGURE 13.10 *A filter might request that you provide more information. In this case, you need to enter the first date for a range.*

Highlights the matching entries

FIGURE 13.11 *Access more filters via this dialog box.*

NOTE

Optionally, you can click on the Highlight button in the More Filters dialog box to apply a highlight color to the filtered tasks or resources, rather than hiding the rows that don't contain the right type of information. If you do this, all rows still appear onscreen, with the filtered tasks in the highlight color. You can also hold down the Shift key and select the filter from the Project, Filtered For submenu.

Using AutoFilter

Project offers yet another type of filtering called AutoFilters, which work just like those in Microsoft Excel. Basically, you turn on the AutoFilters feature, and then you choose an AutoFilter using the drop-down filtering arrow that appears on a Task Sheet or Resource Sheet column header. AutoFilters offer two advantages over the filtering just described:

◆ You can filter by any column, which you can't really do with regular filtering.

◆ You can choose specific criteria for filtering the list.

To apply AutoFiltering to a Task Sheet or Resource Sheet, choose Project, Filtered For, AutoFilter. Alternately, click on the AutoFilter button on the Formatting toolbar. An AutoFilter button appears on the header for every column in the displayed Task Sheet or Resource Sheet. Click on the AutoFilter button for a column head to display the available AutoFilters for that column. The AutoFilters that are available depend on the type of information contained in the column.

For example, because the AutoFilter list shown in Figure 13.12 is for a column that holds dates, you can filter the Task Sheet to list only tasks that have a start date that's this week, this month, and so on. The Duration column's AutoFilters enable you to filter the list to show only tasks with a duration that's more than a week, only tasks with a duration that's less than a week, or other tasks with similar durations. If you want to list only the tasks being handled by a particular resource, choose one of the AutoFilters for the Resource Names column. To remove the AutoFilter from any column, open the AutoFilter drop-down list and click on (All).

You can create a more complex AutoFilter by specifying your own filter criteria. Open the AutoFilter drop-down list for the column that contains the

The AutoFilter button on the Formatting toolbar

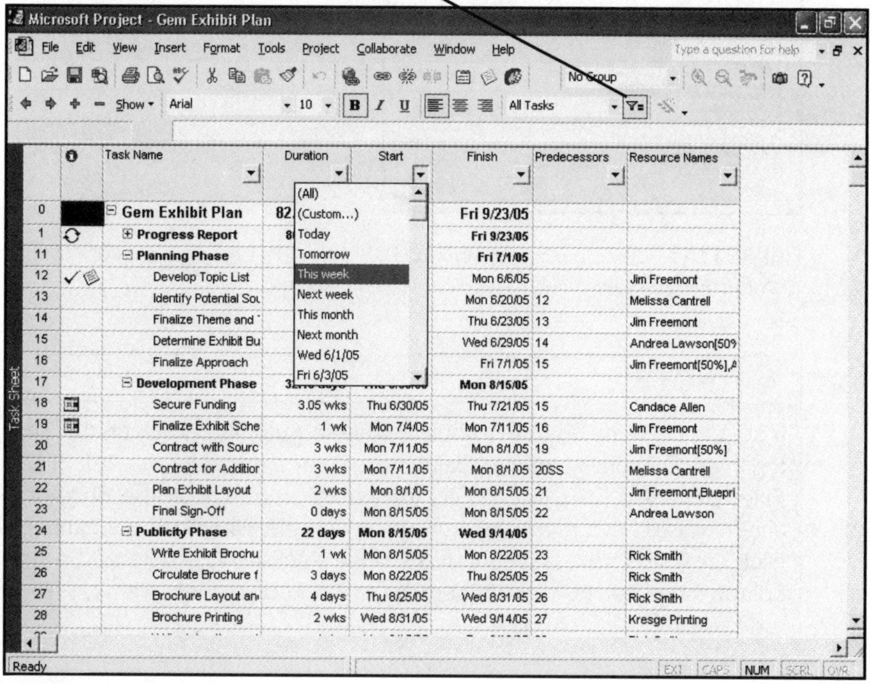

FIGURE 13.12 *After you turn on AutoFiltering, open an AutoFilter list and then click on an AutoFilter.*

information you want to use to filter the list. Choose (Custom...) to display the Custom AutoFilter dialog box. Open the first drop-down list, as shown in Figure 13.13, and then click on an operator (test) option.

For example, to display all dates later than a particular date (in a date-oriented column), choose the Is Greater Than operator. Open the drop-down list to the right on the first row and choose the entry representing the value that the operator should use to evaluate the list, such as the particular date the Is Greater Than operator should use. If you choose Is Greater Than for a date field and then choose Fri 10/3/03, Project filters the list to display only tasks with an entry after Fri 10/3/03 in the filtered column.

If the field entries must match two criteria, leave the And option button selected. If the field entries can match either of two criteria, click on the Or option button. Choose the operator and value from the bottom two drop-down lists in the dialog box to specify the second criterion. Click on OK to apply the custom AutoFilter for the column.

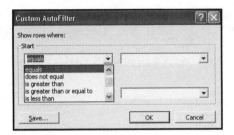

FIGURE 13.13 *Enter criteria for your own AutoFilter in this dialog box.*

NOTE

Instead of clicking on OK to apply a custom AutoFilter, click on the Save button in the Custom AutoFilter dialog box. Enter a name for the AutoFilter in the Filter Definition in '(Current File)' dialog box, and check the Show In Menu check box to have the AutoFilter appear on the Filtered For submenu. Then click on OK to save it. You can also use this dialog box to add even more criteria for a filter, by choosing entries in the And/Or, Field Name, Test (operator), and Value(s) column.

You can AutoFilter as many columns as you want. For example, you can choose the This Month AutoFilter for the Start column. Then choose the AutoFilter for a particular resource in the Resource Name column to display only tasks that the selected resource is scheduled to begin working on during the current month. This will give you a clear picture of current and upcoming near-term assignments for that resource.

When you finish working with all AutoFilters, turn the AutoFiltering feature off (it toggles on and off). Choose Project, Filtered For, AutoFilter, or click on the AutoFilter button on the Formatting toolbar. Project removes the AutoFilter buttons from the sheet column headers.

Sorting Information

By default, the information in your Task Sheet or Resource Sheet (and any accompanying charts in the view you selected) appears in the order in which you added it to the project. Even if you select a different table or filter, the basic order of the rows remains static unless you adjust that order. For example, you might want to sort the Resource Sheet by the name of the resource.

If you're sorting by name, keep in mind that by default Project sorts by the first letter listed, which is generally the first name if the resource is a person. If you want to be able to sort the resource list by last name, I suggest creating a Resource Sheet table (see "Creating a Table or Filter" later in this chapter) that includes a new column for last names. You'll need to reenter the last names there, after which you can sort by that column instead of the one that lists the whole name.

To sort a sheet, choose Project, Sort, and then click on the name of the field (column) to sort by. The fields listed vary depending on whether you're working in a Task Sheet or a Resource Sheet. For a Task Sheet, you can sort by Start Date, Finish Date, Priority, Cost, or ID. For a Resource Sheet, you can sort by Cost, Name, or ID. If the field you want to sort by does not appear on the Sort submenu, click on Sort By. The Sort dialog box will appear (see Figure 13.14).

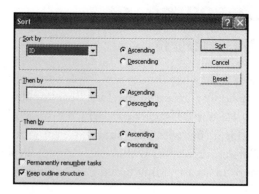

FIGURE 13.14 *Use this dialog box to access more fields to sort by.*

Open the Sort By drop-down list, and then choose the name of the field that contains the information by which you want to sort. Choose Ascending or Descending to specify whether the information should be sorted in lowest-to-highest order (A–Z) or highest-to-lowest order (Z–A). For example, when you sort tasks by the Cost field, by default Project reorders them from most expensive to least expensive. You might prefer to see the least expensive items first, though.

To sort by additional fields as well, use the other drop-down lists provided in this dialog box. Click on OK to complete the sort.

CAUTION

When you select the Permanently Renumber Tasks check box or the Permanently Renumber Resources check box, Project changes the ID numbers for the sorted tasks and resources to reflect their new order. This prevents you from resorting tasks in the Task Sheet by the ID field to return them to their original order, which can destroy your project plan.

Similarly, you wouldn't be able to return your list of resources to its original order. If you've filtered tasks or resources already, or if you've deselected the Keep Outline Structure check box in the Task Sheet, the permanent renumbering option is unavailable. If Keep Outline Structure is deselected, subtasks will not remain with their summary tasks after the sort.

Grouping Task, Resource, or Assignment Information

Project includes a feature that's somewhat akin to a multiple sort—the new *grouping* capability. When you apply a group to the Task Sheet or Resource Sheet (or the Task Usage and Resource Usage views, which display assignment information), Project adds a row with the name for each group and places the appropriate task or resource rows within each group. Typically, Project also arranges the groups in an ascending order, generally from lesser values to higher values.

For example, if you group the Resource Sheet by Complete and Incomplete Resources, Project first lists the group of resources with 0% of their work complete, and then it lists the group of resources with 1–99% of their work complete, and then it places resources with 100% of their work complete in the last listed group. The yellow group rows also display value subtotals, where applicable, in instances where sheet columns display cost information.

You can group tasks using the Complete and Incomplete Tasks, Constraint Type, Critical, Duration, Duration Then Priority, Milestones, Priority, Priority Keeping Outline Structure, and Team Status Pending groups. You can group resources using the Complete and Incomplete Resources, Resource Group, Response Pending, Standard Rate, and Work vs. Material Resources groups. Project displays the proper grouping choices depending on whether you're working in a view that includes the Task Sheet or Resource Sheet.

To apply a group, choose Project, Group By, and then click on the name of the group to apply. Or open the Group By drop-down list near the right end of the Standard toolbar, and then click on the group to apply. In Figure 13.15, I displayed the Entry table of the Resource Sheet in a project plan, and then applied the Resource Group group. So the yellow group rows display the cost subtotals for each group.

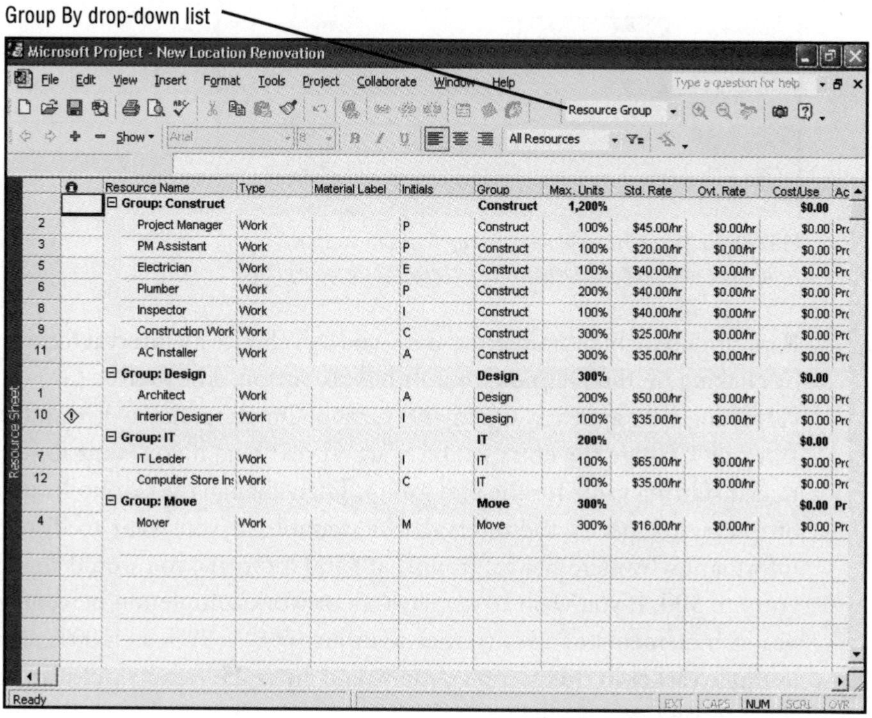

FIGURE 13.15 *Yellow bars define groups in the Task or Resource Sheet.*

You can customize the group display, too. First, apply the group you'd like to use. Then choose Project, Group By, Customize Group By. The Customize Group By dialog box appears. To add another group, choose the first blank cell under Field Name in the Group By The Following Fields area near the top of the dialog box. Click on the drop-down list arrow that appears, and then choose the name of the new field to group by. To choose a sort order for the group, use the drop-down list for the Order cell beside the new group cell. You can use the Font, Cell Background, and Pattern options to change the display settings for the new group or any existing group you choose in the Group By The Following Fields list. Figure 13.16 shows a new group added to the list.

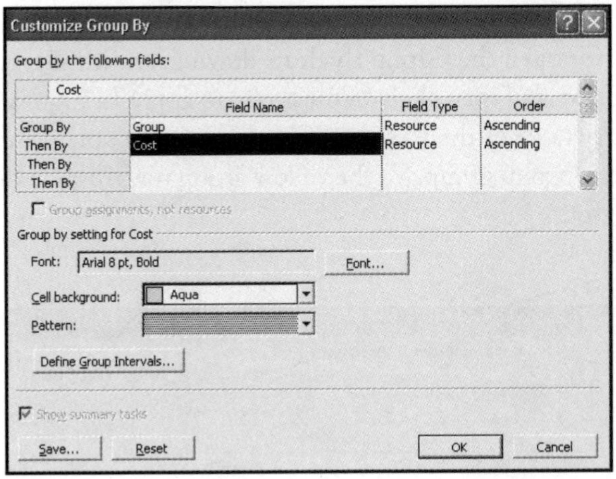

FIGURE 13.16 *Creating a new group is as easy as specifying a field name and choosing formatting settings for the new group.*

If any group includes numerical data, you can choose an interval for the group by clicking on the Define Group Intervals button. The Define Group Interval dialog box appears. Open the Group On drop-down list and choose Interval. Change the entry in the Start At text box, if you want to set a particular starting value for the first group. Then change the Group Interval text box entry to specify the interval. For example, if you want to display cost information by increments (groups) at $500 intervals, you would change this entry to **500**. If you want to display task or work completion percentage values in increments of 25% (rather than just 0%, 1–99%, or 100%, as in the example earlier in this section), you would enter **25**. After you finish making the interval settings, click on OK.

Back in the Customize Group By dialog box, click on the Save button if you want to save the custom group. Enter a name for the group in the Name text box of the Save Group dialog box. Check the Show In Menu check box if you want to be able to access the group via the Project, Group By submenu or the Group By drop-down list on the Standard toolbar. Then click on OK. Click on OK in the Customize Group By dialog box to close the dialog box and apply the new group.

NOTE

You can use the Project, Group By, More Groups command to open the More Groups dialog box to select and work with groups.

To remove a group you've applied, choose Project, Group By, No Group, or choose No Group from the Group By drop-down list on the Standard toolbar.

Quick and Dirty Gantt Chart Formatting

Chapter 17, "Other Formatting," details all the options for formatting bars in a Gantt chart, as well as for formatting information in the Task Sheet and elsewhere. Right now, however, you might want a quick way to adjust the Gantt bars appearing in any view that includes a Gantt chart: To avoid having to master the commands on the Format menu, you can use the Gantt Chart Wizard to walk you through adjusting the appearance of Gantt chart bars.

To start the Gantt Chart Wizard, click on the Gantt Chart Wizard button on the Formatting toolbar, or choose Format, Gantt Chart Wizard. The Gantt Chart Wizard—Step 1 dialog box appears. Click on the Next button to open the next Gantt Chart Wizard dialog box (see Figure 13.17). In this dialog box, select the type of information you want to reformat in your Gantt chart. For example, choosing Critical Path will format all Gantt bars for critical tasks in red (see Figure 13.17).

 NOTE

If you select any custom option (listed last in each Gantt Chart Wizard dialog box), the dialog box enables you to specify details about the option. Obviously, the details you can specify vary depending on that particular option. Additionally, the step number of the subsequent dialog box varies depending on the dialog box from which you selected the custom option.

Make your selection and click on Next to continue. The next Gantt Chart Wizard dialog box appears, enabling you to indicate what kinds of labels you want to appear with the Gantt bars. The default is to label the task bars with both the resources and dates assigned to the task, but you can change this. Specify your choice, and then click on Next. The next Gantt Chart Wizard dialog box appears. Select whether you want Project to include lines indicating links between tasks in the Gantt chart, and then click on Next. The final Gantt Chart Wizard dialog box appears so that you can finish the process. Click on Format It, and Project formats your Gantt chart exactly as you've specified. Then click on Exit Wizard to return to your project.

This sample changes to reflect the option button you select \ | Gantt Chart Wizard button

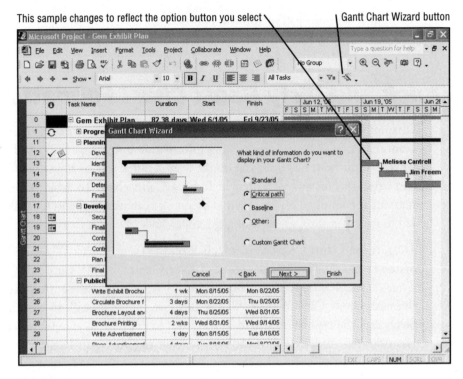

FIGURE 13.17 *Gantt Chart Wizard makes changing the appearance of your Gantt bars idiot-proof.*

Changing and Zooming the Timescale

The graphical portion of any view usually presents information in terms of a schedule. The schedule units used in that portion of the view, usually shown along the top of the view, are called the *timescale*. By default, Project uses a weekly timescale at the top of the graphical display in most views. This is the *middle tier timescale*. Below each week, the *bottom tier timescale* slices the schedule into days. In Project 2002, you can now add a third level, the *top tier*, to any timescale.

Why would you want to change the timescale? Well, you might want to make the schedule more compact for easier printing (select a monthly timescale), or more extended to provide greater detail. To change the timescale, follow these steps:

1. Make sure that the pane that includes the graphical display is the active view.

2. Choose Format, Timescale. The Timescale dialog box appears (see Figure 13.18). You can also right-click on the timescale onscreen and then click on Timescale, or double-click on the timescale onscreen.

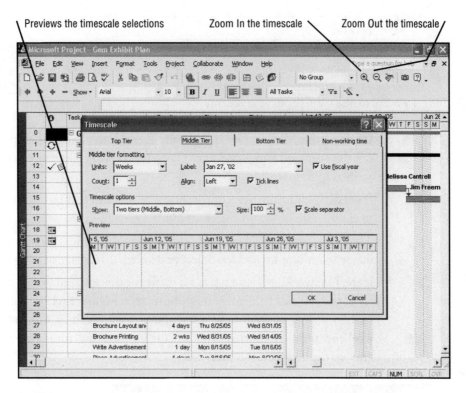

FIGURE 13.18 *Adjust how your chart measures time by changing the timescale.*

3. To add a top tier timescale, click on the Top Tier tab. Open the Show drop-down list in the Timescale options area of the dialog box, and then click on Three Tiers (Top, Middle, Bottom).

4. Then use the Units drop-down list to adjust the measurement (quarters or months, for example). In the Count text box, enter a value to control how many of the timescale units are labeled. (For example, **2** means that Project groups the specified number of units on the timescale tier, such as showing increments of two quarters rather than 1.) Select a date numbering style from the Label drop-down list, and use the Align drop-down list to specify how the labels will be aligned. Select the Tick Lines check box if you want vertical dividing lines to appear between timescale units. And leave the Use Fiscal Year check

box checked if you want the timescale to adjust the major scale labels according to the current fiscal year. This is crucial when you choose Quarters as the major scale Units setting.

 NOTE

To select the month on which your fiscal year starts (which in turn affects the timescale display), choose Tools, Options. Click on the Calendar tab, and then choose the proper month from the Fiscal Year Starts In drop-down list. Click on OK to finish the fiscal year setting.

5. Click on the Middle Tier or Bottom Tier tab to change the options for the specified timescale tier. The settings work like the ones described in Step 4.

6. If needed, adjust the percentage shown in the Size text box on any tab to show more or less of the charted information in the same space.

7. The Scale Separator check box adds a horizontal line to separate the major and minor timescales. Select or deselect this option as you prefer.

8. If the Nonworking Time tab is available for the selected Gantt chart, click on that tab to display its options (see Figure 13.19). This tab enables you to control how nonworking time (such as holiday and weekend time) is charted. By default, nonworking time appears as gray vertical bars on the timescale.

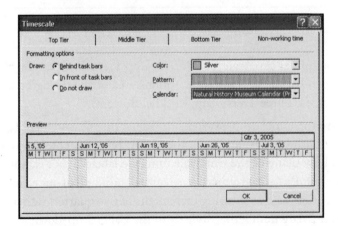

FIGURE 13.19 *You can use these options to specify whether nonworking time is charted.*

9. You might want to change how the working time is charted for a calendar other than the Standard calendar. For example, you could highlight nonworking time for a particular calendar. In such cases, select the calendar to adjust from the Calendar drop-down list. (Figure 13.19 shows the custom calendar created for the project file selected as the calendar for the Gantt Chart portion of the view).

10. Use the Color and Pattern drop-down lists to specify the charted appearance of the nonworking time.

11. In the Draw area, select an option button to control how the charted nonworking time interacts with the charted tasks. Behind Task Bars means that Project always draws the task bars over the nonworking time. In Front of Task Bars means that the nonworking time "bars" appear in front of the charted task bars. Do Not Draw tells Project not to indicate nonworking time at all.

 CAUTION

If you specify nonworking time in days, you must schedule the minor timescale in days or smaller units. Otherwise, Project can't chart the nonworking time.

12. Click on OK to finish making your timescale settings. Your chart adopts a new appearance, as shown in Figure 13.20. This figure illustrates a three-tier timescale.

You can change the timescale in the Calendar view by right-clicking on one of the day names and then clicking Timescale. For the Calendar view, the Timescale dialog box offers three tabs: Week Headings, Date Boxes, and Date Shading. Use the Week Headings tab to specify how the monthly, weekly, and daily headings appear on the calendar. You can specify whether each week displays 7 days or 5 days (the latter means that weekends are hidden). Also, select the Previous/Next Month Calendars check box if you want the calendar to include small thumbnail views of the months before and after the current month. Use the Date Boxes tab to control what appears in the gray shaded area along the top of each date box, or to display another shaded row (and control its contents) at the bottom of each date box. You specify what appears at the left or right side of each shaded area, and you can control the pattern and color of the shading. Finally, use the Date Shading tab to control the shading for working days, nonworking days, and other types of dates in the base calendar for the schedule or in resource calendars.

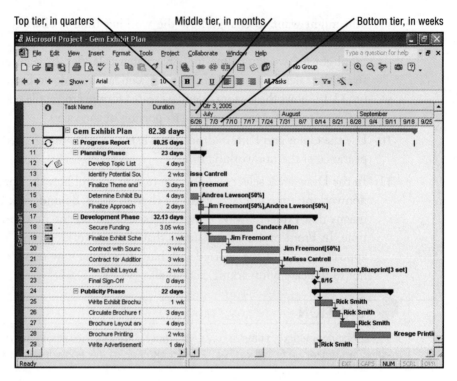

FIGURE 13.20 *The Gantt chart reflects the adjusted timescale.*

Creating a Table or Filter

The More Tables and More Filters dialog boxes each contain New and Copy buttons at the bottom. You can use these buttons to create tables and filters from scratch, or based on an existing table or filter. For example, you might want to be able to quickly display a few added fields (columns) in a particular sheet. You might also want to create a set of fields completely different from the tables that Project provides. (For example, you might want only the task name, resource initials, and remaining work for tasks.)

Creating your own tables or filters is actually a better approach than making a change to one of Project's default offerings. If you create and save your own custom table or filter, you can display it as needed. Then, when you need the default table or filter, it's still available.

NOTE

You can use the Edit button in the More Tables, More Filters, or More Views dialog box to edit the selected table, filter, or view. Make changes using the dialog box that appears, and then click on OK to finish. But remember, it's not a good practice to edit a default table, filter, or view. Rather, copy and rename it first, and then edit the copy.

To create and save a custom table, follow these steps:

1. Display the More Tables dialog box by choosing View, Table, More Tables.

2. (Optional) If there's an existing table similar to the table you want to create, click on its name in the Tables list to select it.

3. Click on the New or Copy button. No matter which button you choose, the Table Definition dialog box appears (see Figure 13.21).

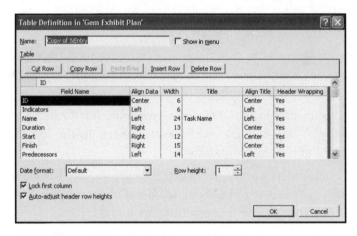

FIGURE 13.21 *You can add and remove fields here to create a custom table.*

4. Edit the name for the table, if needed.

5. If you want the custom table to appear as an option on the Table submenu, leave the Show In Menu check box selected. Otherwise, clear this check box so that the table is listed only in the More Tables dialog box.

6. To remove a row in the list (if you're working on a copy of an existing table), click on the Field Name cell in that row. Then click on the Cut Row button.

7. To add a new field, click on the Field Name cell in the first blank row. Next, click on the field drop-down list arrow to display a scrolling list of all available fields. Click on the field you want. If needed, edit the Align Data, Width, Title, Align Title, and Header Wrapping settings for the new field. If you don't make an entry in the Title column, Project displays the Field Name in the column header for the field.

 NOTE

Table header wrapping is a new feature in Project 2002. When this feature is on, as it is by default for most fields, Project won't hide part of the field name if you resize the field to a smaller width. Instead, it will increase the height of the gray header area and wrap the header text to multiple lines. You can edit any table to turn this feature on and off for given fields, as required.

8. Continue adding and adjusting field rows. You can use the Copy Row, Paste Row, and Insert Row buttons to move selected rows or to insert a new blank row between existing rows.

9. If your table includes date fields and you want to change how they appear (for example, you want to spell out the month's name), use the Date Format drop-down list.

10. If you want increase the height of each table row to make it more attractive or legible, click on the existing entry in the Row Height text box and type in a higher value.

11. The Lock First Column check box "freezes" the far-left column so that you can't edit it and it won't scroll out of view. Clear this check box if you don't want either condition to apply.

12. The Auto-Adjust Header Row Heights check box works along with the Header Wrapping settings. Basically, if you have Header Wrapping set to Yes for one or more fields in the table, you should leave Auto-Adjust Header Row Heights checked. If you clear that check box, Project instead displays only the first row of text in the wrapped header.

13. Click on OK. Project saves your table and adds it to the Tables list in the More Tables dialog box.

14. Click on Close to exit the More Tables dialog box without applying the table, or click on Apply to apply the new table to the current sheet.

Just as you can save a custom table, you can save a custom filter using a process very similar to the one just described. Choose Project, Filtered For, More

Filters. In the More Filters dialog box, select the filter you want to use to create the custom filter, if any. Click on the New or Copy button. The Filter Definition dialog box appears.

 TIP

I strongly recommend creating a custom filter by copying an existing filter. It's easier and faster to edit filtering criteria than to create new ones from scratch.

Edit the filter name and specify whether you want it to appear as an option on the Filtered For submenu. Each row you edit or create in the Filter list area contains a single filter criterion. The Field Name cell for each row contains the name of the field you want to filter by. To specify a field, click on the Field Name cell, and then click on the field's drop-down list arrow to display the list of field names. Click on the one you want. Next, click on the Test cell for this criterion. This holds the operator that Project uses to evaluate the selected field. To change the test, click on the arrow to display the field box drop-down list, and then click on the operator you want.

Next, use the Value(s) column to specify which data the test will compare to the field contents. You can type a value or a date in this column (see Figure 13.22), or use the field drop-down list to select another field to compare the data with. If you enter a value that involves a work amount or schedule amount, be sure to include a time abbreviation with your entry. For example, you might build a criterion with Remaining Work under Field Name, Does Not Equal under Test, and 0h under Value(s). Finally, if you want to filter by more crite-

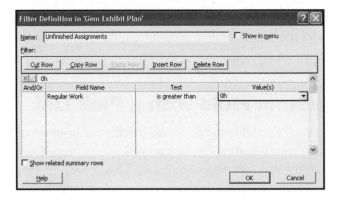

FIGURE 13.22 *You can type an entry in the Value(s) column, or open its drop-down list and specify a field entry to compare with the Field Name entry.*

ria, use the And/Or column to specify whether the filtered rows must match all entered criteria (And) or just one of the entered criteria (Or).

Click on the Show Related Summary Rows check box to select it, if you want the filtered list to display summary tasks that match the filter specifications. Click on OK to finish creating the filter, and then close the More Filters dialog box by clicking on Apply. Project applies your new filter to the current sheet.

You can create a filter that's interactive—meaning it opens a dialog box prompting you to enter the information to filter for—using the Value(s) column in the Filter Definition dialog box. Specify the And/Or, Field Name, and Test options you want. Then enter the message the dialog box should display, surrounded by quotes, with a question mark following the quotes.

For example, you can create an interactive filter that prompts you to specify a percentage of work complete, and that then filters the list by the percentage you enter. Choose % Complete from the Field Name drop-down list in the Filter Definition dialog box, and choose equals from the Test drop-down list. Then, click on the Value(s) cell for that row, type **"Enter percentage:"?**, and press Enter. Click on OK to finish creating the filter. Then, if you choose the filter from the More Filters dialog box, a dialog box appears, using the words you typed in the Value(s) cell to prompt you to enter a percentage.

If you want the interactive filter to prompt you for a range of dates or values, choose *is within* or *is not within* as the Test, and then enter **"From:"?,"To:"?** in the Value(s) cell. Using two sets of quotation marks, two question marks, and the comma tells the filter to prompt for two values. Note that you need to make sure that the prompt you enter in the Value(s) column makes it clear whether the reader should enter a value or a date. For example, if the Field Name that the filter uses contains dates, prompting the user to enter a number or percentage would cause the filter not to work.

Creating a Custom Field with a Pick List

Project 2002 offers you flexibility in customizing fields you insert into a table you create. You can create a custom field with a *pick list*—a drop-down list of entries from which the user can select an option. This speeds up data entry, since the user doesn't have to type a particular entry in that field. Follow these steps to customize a field so it includes a pick list:

1. Create and display the new table. In the table you create, add in a "placeholder" column for the custom field. I suggest inserting one of the text fields (Text1, Text2, and so on), with the title you want to use for the custom field. As an example, I'll enter **Location** as the title for a field I've added to a custom resource sheet table. This Location field will offer a list of three locations: New York, Reno, and Denver. This field will be used to specify the city where each resource is located.

2. Right-click on the field header you want to customize, and then choose Customize Fields in the shortcut menu. The Customize Fields dialog box appears (see Figure 13.23). Under Field, it should have Task or Resource correctly selected, depending on the nature of the custom table you selected. The Type drop-down list should have the proper field type selected (in this case, Text). If not, choose the proper field type. Then select another placeholder field, if needed, in the list of fields.

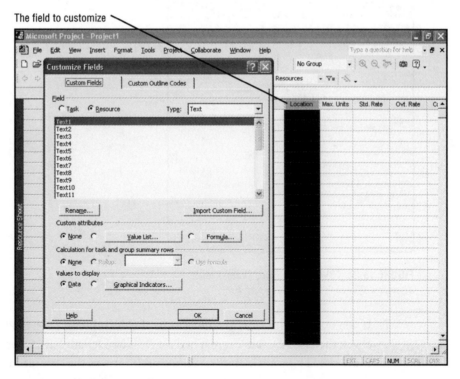

FIGURE 13.23 *After you add a field to a custom table, you can automate or customize the field.*

3. To supply a unique field name (not just a field title) to the field you selected, click on the Rename button. Enter the new field name in the text box of the Rename field dialog box, and then click on OK.

4. Under Custom Attributes, click on the option button beside the Value List button to tell Project that you want to create a pick list of potential values for the entries in the field. Click on OK to close the warning dialog box that appears. You're working with your own new field, which has no data to overwrite, so you don't have to worry about it.

5. Click on the Value List button. The Value List for "Field Name" dialog box will appear.

6. Use each row in the Enter Values To Display In Dropdown List area of the dialog box to enter the value and description for each item in the pick list. Figure 13.24 shows the city entries for my example.

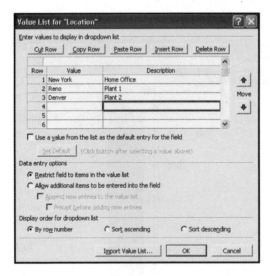

FIGURE 13.24 *Type in the Value (name) and description for each item in your pick list.*

7. If you want one of the list values to be the default entry for the field, check the Use A Value From The List As The Default Entry For The Field check box, click on the Value entry to use as the default in your list of entries, and then click on the Set Default button.

8. If you want users to be able to make unique entries in the field (entries other than those on the pick list), choose the Allow Additional

Items To Be Entered Into The Field option button. To have Project add any new entries into the value list, check the Append New Entries to the Value List check box. To be prompted to verify such additions, check Prompt Before Adding New Entries.

9. Finally, change the setting under Display Order For Dropdown List if you want to use the Sort Ascending or Sort Descending order for the pick list, instead of the default By Row Number order.

10. Click on OK to close the Value List For "Field Name" dialog box, and click on OK again in the warning dialog box. This takes you back to the Customize Fields dialog box.

11. Click on OK to finish customizing the field. A drop-down list arrow should appear immediately beside the first blank cell in the newly customized field. Clicking on this arrow will give you the list you specified, as shown in Figure 13.25.

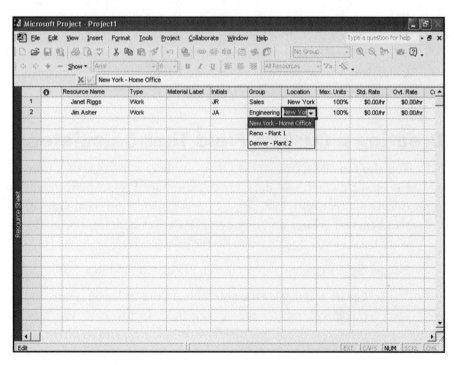

FIGURE 13.25   *Click on an option in your custom pick list to enter it into the field.*

NOTE

If your task list has summary rows or you plan to use grouping, you can click on the Rollup Option button under Calculation for Task and Group Summary Rows in the Customize Fields dialog box, and then choose the calculation type to display in the custom field position from the Rollup Drop-down list. Or, if you want to display graphical indicators for the data in the Task or Resource Sheet rather than actual values, click on the Graphical Indicators button under Values To Display in the Customize Fields dialog box. Use the options at the top of the resulting dialog box to specify whether you want to display graphical indicators for summary or nonsummary (subtask) rows. Then use the first Test For drop-down list to specify a comparison operator, enter the comparison value in the Value(s) column, and choose the graphical indicator to display in the field when the data matches the comparison from the Image drop-down list on the same row. Create any other needed tests (comparisons) on subsequent rows, and then click on OK.

When you customize a field in your custom table, make sure you copy the custom table and custom field into the GLOBAL.MPT file to make it available to all your project plan files. See "Using the Organizer to Create Global Calendars, Views, Macros, Tables, and More" later in this chapter to learn how to copy items into GLOBAL.MPT.

Creating a Custom Field That Calculates

You also can add a custom field that calculates numerical data from existing Project fields that hold data. Or you can have Project perform any custom calculation that you'd like. Using Project's calculation capabilities brings you two benefits: greater accuracy because Project is doing the math, and less work because you don't have to do the calculations.

Follow these steps to create a custom calculated field in a custom table:

1. Create and display the new table. In the table you create, add a placeholder column for the custom field. In this case, you may want to insert one of the cost fields (Cost1, Cost2, and so on) or value fields (Value1, Value2, and so on) with the title you want to use for the custom field. As an example, I'll enter **Cost Plus Markup** as the title for a Cost1 field I've added to a custom resource sheet table. This field will take the resource cost (total cost for work assigned to the re-

source) and mark it up by 15 percent. Let's say I need to know that value, because that 15 percent represents a markup fee that will be passed along to the client.

2. Right-click on the field header you want to customize, and then choose Customize Fields in the shortcut menu. The Customize Fields dialog box appears (refer to Figure 13.23). Under Field, it should have Task or Resource correctly selected, depending on the nature of the custom table you selected. The Type drop-down list should have the proper field type (in this case, Cost) selected. If not, choose the proper field type. Then select another placeholder field, if needed, in the list of fields.

3. To supply a unique field name (not just a field title) to the field you selected, click on the Rename button. Enter the new field name in the text box of the Rename Field dialog box, and then click on OK.

4. Under Custom Attributes, click on the option button beside the Formula button to tell Project that you want to create a calculated field. Click on OK to close the warning dialog box that appears. You're working with your own new field, which has no data to overwrite, so you don't have to worry about it.

5. Click on the Formula button. The Formula For "Field Name" dialog box appears.

6. The insertion point appears in the large Edit Formula text box by default. Build your formula by choosing fields and functions from the Field and Function drop-down lists (buttons), by clicking on the mathematical operator buttons, and by typing in values as needed. For example, Figure 13.26 shows a formula I've created by inserting the

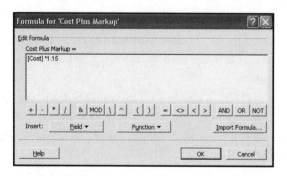

FIGURE 13.26 *You can set up a custom field to calculate information for you.*

Cost field (it's in square brackets), choosing the multiplication operator (*), and entering **1.15**. This formula multiplies the Cost field value
for each resource by 1.15 (115 percent), to arrive at the value of the
cost plus a 15 percent markup.

7. Click on OK when you finish creating the formula, and then click on
OK again to close the Customize Fields dialog box. Project immediately displays the results of the custom calculations if the project file
already holds the needed data, as shown in Figure 13.27.

	Resource Name	Cost	Cost Plus Markup	Baseline Cost	Variance	Actual Cost	Remaining
1	Janet Riggs	$5,400.00	$6,210.00	$0.00	$5,400.00	$0.00	$5,400.00
2	Jim Asher	$22,000.00	$25,300.00	$0.00	$22,000.00	$0.00	$22,000.00

FIGURE 13.27 *The Cost Plus Markup field holds the results of the custom
calculation illustrated in Figure 13.26.*

Creating and Using Custom Outline Codes

If using the default or custom WBS (Work Breakdown Structure) codes doesn't
suit your needs for sorting and filtering tasks, you can create and assign custom outline codes throughout your project. This process involves creating a
new table that holds a field for the custom codes, defining the custom codes,
and then assigning the custom codes:

1. Create and display the new table. Add a placeholder column for the
   custom field. In this case, insert one of the outlines (Outline Code1,
   Outline Code2, and so on) with the title you want to use for the custom field. As an example, I'll enter **My Code** as the title for a Outline
   Code1 field I've added to a custom task sheet table. This field will
   hold the custom codes you'll assign later.

2. Right-click on the field header you want to customize, and then choose
   Customize Fields in the shortcut menu. The Customize Fields dialog
   box will appear.

3. Click on the Custom Outline Codes tab. Under Field, it should have
   Task or Resource correctly selected, depending on the nature of the
   custom table you selected. Select another placeholder field, if needed,
   in the list of fields.

4. To supply a unique field name (not just a field title) to the field you
   selected, click on the Rename button. Enter the new field name in the
   text box of the Rename Field dialog box, and then click on OK.

5. Click on Define Code Mask. The Outline Code Definition for "File Name" dialog box will appear.

6. For each code level you want to create, specify a sequence setting (numbers, uppercase letters, lowercase letters, or characters). Then, specify an accompanying length (the number of characters the mask will allow at that level) and separator (the operator used to separate the code levels). Figure 13.28 shows an example mask.

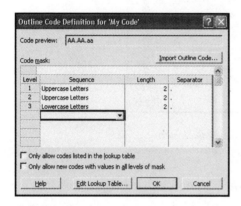

FIGURE 13.28   *The outline code mask defines the number and type of characters allowed for each level in your custom outline code.*

7. If you want to be able to choose entries from a pick list for the field, rather than typing in entries that match the mask, click on Edit Lookup Table. The Edit Lookup Table for "File Name" dialog box opens. You use this dialog box to specify the nesting levels of actual entries available for your custom outline codes. (Yes, you do have to create each level explicitly.)

8. To add each entry, click on the next blank Outline Code cell. If needed, click on the Indent button at the top of the dialog box to indent to the appropriate level. Then type the allowed code characters. Figure 13.29 shows an example code lookup table corresponding to the mask shown in Figure 13.28.

9. Click on Close to finish creating the lookup table and close the dialog box.

10. Click on OK to close the Outline Code Definition for "File Name" dialog box.

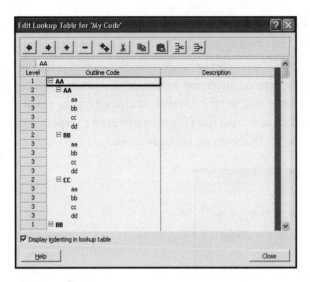

FIGURE 13.29 *Be specific in creating the available outline codes allowable with the mask. Be sure to create all nesting levels.*

11. Click on OK to close the Customize fields dialog box.

12. To edit outline codes for tasks in the custom field, you can type in an entry that matches the outline code mask you created (see Figure 13.28). Or you can open the pick list (drop-down list) for the custom field, if you created a lookup table (see Figure 13.29), and click on the code to use, as shown in Figure 13.30.

Creating a View

Unlike a table or filter, a new view is often easier to create from scratch than by editing one that already exists. Project enables you to create and save a single-pane view that combines a specified table and filter. Thus if you want to create a view that uses a custom table or filter, you need to create that custom table or filter first. To create a new single-pane view, follow these steps:

1. Choose View, More Views, or click on the More Views button on the View Bar. The More Views dialog box appears.

2. Click on the New button. Project uses the Define New View dialog box to ask if you want to create a Single View or Combination View. Leave Single View selected, and then click on OK. The View Definition dialog box appears (see Figure 13.31).

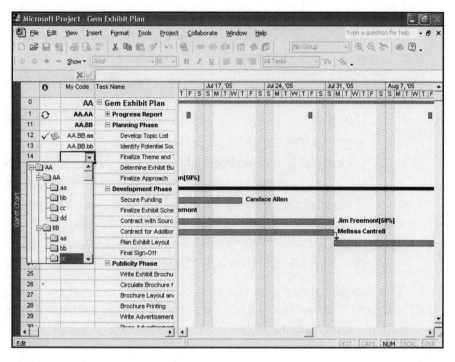

FIGURE 13.30 *If you created a lookup table, you can choose the proper code from a pick list. Otherwise, type an entry that matches the code mask you created.*

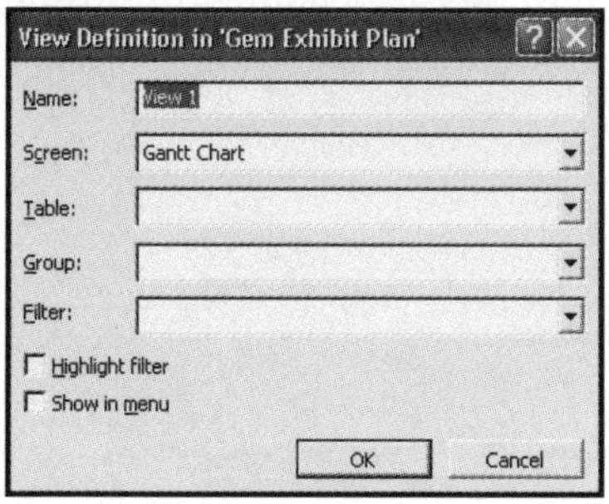

FIGURE 13.31 *Project helps you view your schedule exactly as you want to.*

3. Enter a name for your new view.

4. Use the Screen drop-down list to specify whether you want your view to offer a sheet, form, or chart. For example, select Relationship Diagram to display task information in your view using the abbreviated form of the Network Diagram chart.

5. If you selected a sheet style for your screen, use the Table drop-down list to specify a table that controls which columns of information appear in your view.

6. Use the Group drop-down list to apply a predefined group to the sheet portion of the view.

7. Use the Filter drop-down list to control which rows of information appear in your view.

8. If it's available, click on Highlight Filter to highlight data that matches the filter, rather than hiding the data that doesn't match the filter.

9. If you want the new view to appear as an option on the View menu or an icon on the View Bar, click on the Show In Menu check box.

10. Click on OK to finish creating your view, and then apply the view by clicking on Apply. Or simply close the More Views dialog box.

A combination view displays two single-pane views in upper and lower panes onscreen. If you want a combination view to include a custom single-pane view, you need to create the single-pane view first and then create the combination view.

To create a combination view rather than a single-pane view, select Combination View in the Define New View dialog box (Step 2 in the preceding set of steps). The View Definition dialog box appears again, but this time it resembles Figure 13.32.

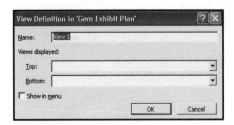

FIGURE 13.32   *This dialog box is where you specify details of the combination view you're creating.*

Type in the name you want for the view. Use the Top drop-down list to select the view that will appear in the upper pane, and use the Bottom drop-down list to select the single-pane view that will appear in the lower pane. Select the Show In Menu check box if you want the new view to appear as an option on the View menu or as an icon on the View Bar. Then click on OK to finish making the view and return to the More Views dialog box. Exit this dialog box as described in the preceding set of steps.

Using the Organizer to Create Global Calendars, Views, Macros, Tables, and More

By default, the custom tables, filters, views, reports, and other items that you create are saved with the open, active project file only. This means that you can select one of these custom items only when that particular project file is open and active. If you want a custom view, filter, or other item to be available to other project files, you need to copy the custom item to the GLOBAL.MPT file. To do this, you use the Organizer, which enables you to specify where custom items are stored.

You might have noticed earlier in this chapter that the More Tables, More Filters, and More Views dialog boxes all contain an Organizer button. Clicking on that button in any dialog box opens the Organizer dialog box. You can also display the Organizer by choosing Tools, Organizer. The tab that appears at the top of this dialog box varies depending on which dialog box you were in when you clicked on the Organizer button. For example, if you were in the More Views dialog box, the Views tab is selected when the Organizer dialog box opens. To deal with a different type of item, click on the appropriate tab. Also choose the Task or Resource option button, if applicable, to display the applicable custom items. For example, Figure 13.33 shows the Tables tab, with the custom tables I created earlier to hold my custom pick list and calculated fields.

Each tab in the Organizer dialog box contains two lists. The list on the left shows the views (or tables, or filters, or whatever) that are saved in GLOBAL.MPT. The list on the right shows the elements that are saved in the current project file. To copy an item from the list on the left to the list on the right (that is, from GLOBAL.MPT to the current project file), click on the item name and then click on Copy>>.

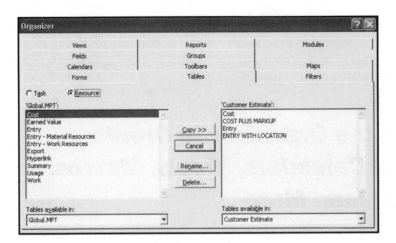

FIGURE 13.33 *The Organizer enables you to move custom items between files.*

To copy an item from the project file to GLOBAL.MPT, click on the item name and then click on <<Copy. (The arrows change direction depending on which side you copy an item from.) If the file to which you're copying includes an item with the same name as the one you're copying, you'll be prompted to confirm that the copied file should overwrite the existing file.

 TIP

The Available In drop-down list appears in the lower-left corner of any tab in the Organizer dialog box. The list name will specify the kind of item available. Use this list to control the file for which you're listing items on the left side of the tab. Similarly, use the Available In drop-down list (in the lower-right corner of the tab) to control the file for which you're listing items on the right side of the tab. If you want to copy a view or other item between two project files, rather than between a project file and GLOBAL.MPT, make sure that you change the Available In selection on the left to display the name of the second project file.

If you select an item from either list and then click on Rename, Project displays the Rename dialog box. Type a new name, and then click on OK. If you select an item from either list and then click on Delete, Project permanently deletes the item from the list for that file only, not from any other files that use the same item. Deleting an item from the GLOBAL.MPT file makes it inaccessible to all files, unless you previously copied the item to an individual schedule file. If you copied a custom item to multiple individual schedule files, remember that you need to remove it from each and every file to permanently delete it.

When you're finished working in the Organizer, click on the Close button, and click on Close again to exit the More dialog box, if applicable.

To save an item such as a view or table that you added to any project file, be sure to save the file. When you exit Project, the application automatically saves changes that have been made to GLOBAL.MPT.

Using the Rollup Views

Three other views—the Rollup views that affect how subtasks look when rolled up to summary tasks—warrant special mention because you need to perform a preliminary step before you use one of these views. The Rollup views are as follows:

- ◆ **Bar Rollup.** Rolls up subtasks to the summary task bar and displays the Task Name for each task.

- ◆ **Milestone Date Rollup.** Rolls up subtasks to the summary task bar, displays each subtask as a milestone, and displays the Task Name and start date.

- ◆ **Milestone Rollup.** Rolls up subtasks to the summary task bar, displays each subtask as a milestone, and displays the Task Name only.

These views can be more helpful than simply rolling up subtasks to a summary task bar, because they enable you to show more information on the rolled-up summary task. Thus they let you summarize your project but still have a clear picture of which tasks it contains.

Before you display one of the Rollup views in the current project file, you have to roll up subtasks and run the Rollup_Formatting macro, as follows:

1. In the Task Sheet of the Gantt Chart view, select the subtasks to roll up.

2. Click on the Task Information button on the Standard toolbar, click twice to check Roll Up Gantt Bar To Summary on the General tab, and then click on OK.

3. Repeat Steps 1 and 2 to roll up other groups of subtasks as needed. If you want to use the Rollup views for all summary tasks in your project, you'll need to use Steps 1 and 2 to roll up all subtasks for each summary task.

4. Choose Tools, Macro, Macros. The Macros dialog box will appear.

5. Double-click on Rollup_Formatting in the Macro Name list. The Rollup Formatting dialog box appears (see Figure 13.34).

FIGURE 13.34 *Specify whether you want your rolled-up tasks to appear as bars or milestones on the Gantt chart, using this dialog box from the Rollup_Formatting macro.*

6. Specify whether to display rolled-up tasks as bars or milestones, and then click on OK. The Task Sheet changes to display summary tasks only, and rolled-up Gantt bars that are specially formatted (depending on your choice in this step) appear in the Gantt chart at the right.

7. Click on the More Views button in the View Bar, and then choose the Bar Rollup, Milestone Date Rollup, or Milestone Rollup view, as needed. Figure 13.35 shows the Milestone Rollup view applied to a rolled-up summary task.

8. You can choose Gantt Chart view to display regular Gantt bars but return to one of the Rollup views as often as needed during the current work session.

Using PERT Analysis

If you aren't confident that the timeline you're building for a project is accurate, and you're not comfortable making an educated guess about the overall schedule, Project offers special PERT analysis views to help. You create your list of tasks and durations and then enter resource information to evaluate

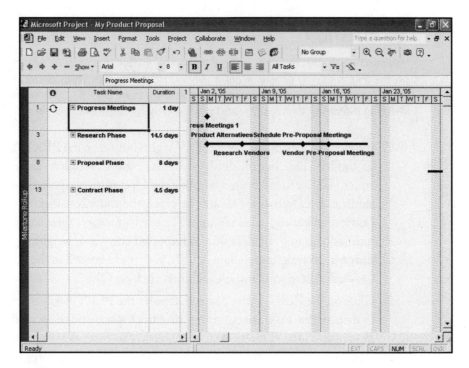

FIGURE 13.35 *The rolled-up summary task at right displays milestones and Task Names in the Milestone Rollup view.*

whether the schedule can be completed in the time frame you estimate. Then you enter Optimistic (best case), Expected (most likely), and Pessimistic (worst case) durations that could occur for each task. Then you click on a toolbar button, and Project creates a weighted average of the Optimistic, Expected, and Pessimistic duration for each task, and changes the task duration to that average. You can then display the estimate in Gantt Chart view. You can display the optimistic, expected, and best case dates you entered in the PA_Optimistic Gantt (Optimistic Gantt), PA_Expected Gantt (Expected Gantt), and PA_Pessimistic Gantt (Pessimistic Gantt) views, respectively.

Here are the basic steps for making PERT analysis calculations:

1. Display the PERT Analysis toolbar, which offers you the best access to all the PERT analysis views and other tools. To display the toolbar, right-click on another toolbar and click on PERT Analysis.

CAUTION

You can't undo a weighted average calculation, so use the Save As command on the File menu to create a copy of your schedule file. Then perform the PERT analysis calculation on the file copy, print the PERT Entry Sheet view showing the calculated results, and compare them to the original file.

2. (Optional) Click on the Set PERT Weights button on the PERT Analysis toolbar. This button displays the Set PERT Weights dialog box, which you use to tell Project whether the Optimistic, Expected, or Pessimistic dates you enter should be given the most consideration (the heaviest weighting) in calculations. The entries for these three weightings must add up to 6. By default, the Expected entry is 4, weighting it the heaviest. To weight each date equally, you would enter **2** in the text box beside it. Make your entries, and then click on OK.

3. Click on the PERT Entry Sheet button on the PERT Analysis toolbar to display the Task Sheet for entering the Optimistic, Expected, and Pessimistic Dur. (Duration) for each task. (To enter these settings for a single task, select the task, click on the PERT Entry Form button on the PERT Analysis toolbar, enter the durations, and click on OK.)

4. Click on the Calculate PERT button on the PERT Analysis toolbar. The Duration column changes to display the calculated weighted averages.

5. To display the estimated (calculated durations), switch to the Gantt Chart view. Or click on either the Optimistic Gantt, Expected Gantt, or Pessimistic Gantt button on the PERT Analysis toolbar to see the Gantt Chart with the dates you entered for the desired scenario. (You can also choose these views from the More Views dialog box. Each one will have "PA_" in front of its name.)

Chapter 14

Proofing and Printing a View

In This Chapter

◆ Making sure you've spelled everything correctly

◆ Replacing entries

◆ Telling Project and Windows which printer you want to use, and what settings it should use

◆ Setting up the appearance of the printed pages

◆ Adjusting what information appears on each printed page

◆ Getting a sneak preview of your printed document

◆ Printing your document

Unless you've developed mental telepathy or you're connected to everyone involved with your project via network or e-mail, you're going to need some method of sharing information. The most traditional way to share information is via printed hard copies. While "virtual" information-sharing has its benefits, certain situations—such as meetings or bound copies of proposals made for clients—call for printouts.

Like other Microsoft applications, Project 2002 gives you a great deal of control over what you print and how it appears in the hard copy. This chapter focuses on the steps you need to take to prepare and print information from your schedule.

Checking your Project's Spelling

To put your best foot forward, you should always—I repeat, *always*—spell-check your files in Project and any other business documents you create. Project's Spelling feature checks all the information in your schedule for correct spelling, starting from the first task in the Task Sheet and progressing through all your task information, whether it's currently displayed or not. It even checks any information you've entered as a Task Note or Resource Note. To spell-check a project file, follow these steps:

1. Make sure that the file you want to check is the open, active file.

2. Choose Tools, Spelling. Alternately, press F7 or click on the Spelling button on the Standard toolbar. The spell-check will start, and when it encounters a word it doesn't recognize, it will display the Spelling dialog box (see Figure 14.1).

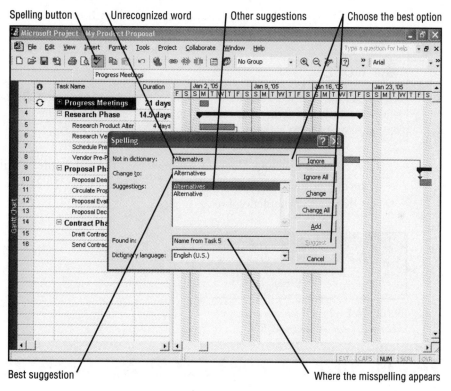

FIGURE 14.1   *The Spelling feature asks you to how it should deal with each word it doesn't recognize.*

3. Look at the Not In Dictionary entry to see which word Project doesn't recognize. Then use one of the following methods to adjust its spelling, if needed:

  ◆ If the word isn't misspelled, click on Ignore to leave it intact, or Ignore All if you know that the word is used several times in the file.

◆ If the word is wrong and the spelling in the Change To text box is correct, click on Change or Change All. Change corrects only the presently highlighted instance of the word, and Change All corrects it everywhere it appears in the Project file.

◆ If the word is wrong and the Change To spelling isn't correct either, you can edit the Change To text box entry, or you can click on another spelling in the Suggestions list to place that spelling in the Change To text box. Then click either on Change or Change All.

4. After you tell Project how to adjust the unrecognized word, it will display the next unrecognized word. Deal with each unrecognized word as explained in Step 3.

 NOTE

If you edit the Change To entry (such as entering the client name "Blalock") and want Project to remember that as the correct spelling for future files, click on the Add button to include the spelling in Project's dictionary.

5. When the Spelling Checker has reviewed the entire file, it will inform you that the spell-check is finished (see Figure 14.2). Click on OK to close the dialog box.

FIGURE 14.2 *Project lets you know you when it has checked the entire file.*

Using AutoCorrect for Entry Accuracy

When you learned to type, you had to learn the pattern of the letters on the keyboard. If you've learned a particular pattern incorrectly, chances are that you'll make the same typographical error (typo) over and over for the rest of your typing career—and you need a way to deal with the necessary repetitive fixes. Or, you might be a fine typist but would like a way to quickly enter certain words that you use often and are tricky to type.

Project's AutoCorrect feature can help in these situations. In essence, you train Project to automatically replace your frequent typos (or abbreviations) with the correct (or full) terms you're trying to type. This ensures that certain terms are entered correctly in the first place, so you don't have to rely on the spell-checker to catch those errors. Use the following steps to create an AutoCorrect entry:

1. Choose Tools, AutoCorrect Options. The AutoCorrect dialog box will appear (see Figure 14.3).

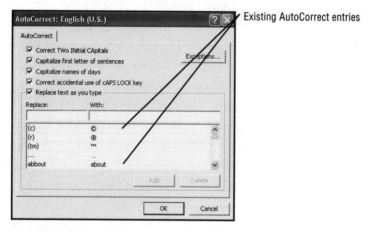

Existing AutoCorrect entries

FIGURE 14.3   *This is your chance to train Project to help you type more effectively.*

2. If you want Project to change the second letter in any word from uppercase to lowercase whenever you mistakenly type two capital letters, leave the Correct TWo INitial CApitals check box selected. Otherwise, clear this check box. You might want to clear it if you'll be typing a lot of state abbreviations, for example.

3. If you want an uppercase first letter in the first word of each entry, leave the Capitalize The First Letter Of Sentence option checked. Alternately, clear the check box to capitalize new sentences only when you specify. This option only works in fields that contain generic text entries, or in Task Names fields that contain task names with punctuation included. It doesn't work in any Notes fields, though.

NOTE

You can create exceptions that won't be corrected when you turn on the options described in Steps 2 and 3. Click on the Exceptions button in the AutoCorrect dialog box. To identify an instance when you don't want to capitalize the first word after a period (normally, this is after any abbreviation), type the abbreviation in the Don't Capitalize After text box on the First Letter tab, and then click on Add. If a specialized term begins with two capital letters, as in "CSi," click on the INitial CAps tab, type the term in the Don't Correct text box, and click on Add. Click on OK to finish creating your exceptions and return to the AutoCorrect dialog box.

4. Leave the Capitalize Names Of Days check box selected if you want Project to automatically capitalize day names when you type them.

5. If you have a habit of accidentally pressing the Caps Lock key when you're aiming for the nearby Shift or Tab key, leave the Correct Accidental Use Of cAPS LOCK Key check box selected. This feature applies in particular to Task Name entries and Resource Sheet entries.

6. For AutoCorrect to work, make sure that a check mark appears beside the Replace Text As You Type check box. If this option is not checked, Project will not make automatic replacements.

7. To create a new AutoCorrect entry, go to the Replace text box and type in the typo or abbreviation you want Project to catch and replace. You can't include any spaces or punctuation in the Replace entry, but it can be up to 254 characters long.

8. In the With text box, enter the correction you want AutoCorrect to make.

9. Click on Add to finish creating the AutoCorrect entry. Project will add this entry to the list of AutoCorrect entries, as shown in Figure 14.4.

10. Click on OK to close the AutoCorrect dialog box. New AutoCorrect entries take effect immediately.

Replacing Entries

Other business changes might require that you make a correction to a term or entry that appears frequently in your project file. For example, a resource company may have changed names, or your company may have changed the accounting code used to track work by a particular department. In some cases

FIGURE 14.4 *Project adds your AutoCorrect entry to its list.*

you could run a spell-check to make the global correction, but that would also mean you'd have to review and work with other unrecognized words, making the process slower than needed. If you've already added the term to replace to the Spelling feature's dictionary, however, running a spell-check won't work because the Spelling dialog box will never stop on that term.

Instead, you can use the Replace feature in Project to find one or more occurrences of a particular entry in a field and replace those occurrences with a new entry that you specify. Follow these steps to replace information in a field:

1. Display either the Task Sheet or the Resource Sheet, depending on which one contains the information to find and replace. If you want the search to begin with a particular row, click on a cell in that row.

2. Choose Edit, Replace, or press Ctrl+H. The Replace dialog box will appear.

3. Type the entry to search for in the Find What text box.

4. Type the new entry that you want to use as the replacement for each found entry in the Replace With text box.

5. Choose the field that holds the entries to find and replace from the Look In Field drop-down list. (Choose Name to search the Task Name field in the Task Sheet or Resource Name in the Resource Sheet, depending on which one you displayed before opening the Replace dialog box.)

6. If you want to use an operator in the Find What entry—for example, if you're searching for all numeric entries greater than a particular number—choose the operator from the Test drop-down list.

TIP

If you're working with a template that contains basic resource assignments, you can replace them and adjust the template schedule using Find and Replace. This is a particularly good trick if you want to extend the duration for a task based on an assignment of less than 100% units.

First, assign the desired resources at 100%. Then, open the Replace dialog box. Choose Resource Names as the Look In Field and leave the Test set to Contains. Enter the name of the resource to replace in the Find What text box. Then, enter the name of the replacement resource (it can be the same resource) followed by the new assignment units in brackets, as in **John Smith[50%]**. When you perform the replace operation, task durations will be extended based on the assignment percentage.

CAUTION

I recommend using the Contains Exactly option in the Test drop-down list as often as you can. For example, if you only use the Contains option and are searching for an entry like "004," Project would stop on entries like "1004," "A004," or "10040," too. This could give you too many entries to sort through. Plus, you could inadvertently make a replacement you don't want.

7. Make a choice from the Search drop-down list to change the direction of the search. Project can search either down or up from the current row.

8. If you want each replacement to match the case (capitalization) of the entry in the Replace With text box, and you only want to replace entries matching the capitalization in the Find What text box, check the Match Case check box.

9. After you enter all the information to tell Project which entries to find and where to find them (see Figure 14.5 for an example), click on the Find Next button. Project highlights the first instance of the entry you told it to search for.

10. You can handle the highlighted entry in one of three ways:

   ◆ Click on Find Next, which skips the highlighted instance without changing it and highlights the next matching instance of the Find What entry.

◆ Click on Replace to change the matching instance to the Replace With entry, and then highlight the next instance.

◆ Click on Replace All to change all matching instances without it pausing to ask you about them.

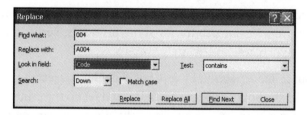

FIGURE 14.5 *These options find a particular Code field entry in the Resource Sheet, replacing each occurrence with a new code entry.*

11. When Project finishes searching the field and making replacements, a message box will tell you the search is complete. Click on OK to close the message box.

12. Click on Close to close the Replace dialog box.

If you want to find an entry instead of replacing it, display the Find dialog box by choosing Edit, Find (Ctrl+F). The Find dialog box is nearly identical to the Replace dialog box, but without the Replace With text box (because you're not replacing anything) or the Replace All button. It does have a Replace button, which you can click to change the Find dialog box to the Replace dialog box. Otherwise, the Find dialog box offers the same options as the Replace dialog box, and you can use it just as described in the preceding steps for a replacement operation.

Changing Printer Settings

If you're using Project in a small business or home office, you'll probably have only one printer attached to your computer system. If you work in a larger company, however, you might have access to multiple printers. For example, you might have one in your office and one attached to your company network. In any environment, your computer also might have a built-in FAX/modem that you can "print" to, thereby faxing documents without making a hard copy. This is the same as having multiple printers.

If you have multiple printers attached to your system, you need a way to select the printer you want to send your Project file to. In addition, each printer offers more than one set of capabilities. For example, your laser printer might be capable of printing at 600 dots per inch (dpi), but you might want to print at 300 dpi for faster everyday printing. Similarly, many dot matrix and inkjet printers offer a choice between letter-quality and draft modes. Or, you might need to use a slower inkjet color printer for some printouts, versus a faster laser printer for everyday black-and-white printouts.

Before you set up your printout pages in Project, you should first select the printer you want to use and set the options you prefer. Select and set up the printer first, if needed, because different printer capabilities might affect the page setup options available in Project. Note that you don't have to set up a document or open any project file to print before setting up the printer. After you adjust printer settings, they remain in effect until you change them or exit Project.

If you're using an older dot matrix or inkjet printer, any Project printouts that include graphical information might not be as crisp and clean as you desire, and printing might be slow. In addition, depending on your printer's limitations, Project might present fewer options for altering the page setup. If you need to print many Gantt or Network Diagram charts, you should buy a laser printer, or even a color inkjet printer. (Or a plotter, if your organization has other purposes for it, such as printing CAD files.)

 NOTE

Remember, Project prints the view or report that currently appears onscreen, so make sure you adjust your settings accordingly. Make sure also you filter, sort, or group the Task or Resource Sheet before printing, if needed.

To select and set up a printer, follow the steps below. There's quite a bit of variation between printers, and it's impossible to cover every option for every printer, so these steps cover only the most important options:

1. Choose File, Print. Alternately, press Ctrl+P. (*Don't* click on the Print button on the Standard toolbar, though. That sends the current view to the specified printer, bypassing the Print dialog box.) The Print dialog box will appear (see Figure 14.6).

2. Click on the drop-down list arrow to display the Name selections in the Printer area. The printers listed here have already been installed

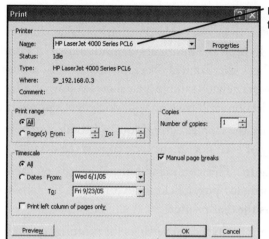

Use this drop-down list to select a printer that's set up on your system

FIGURE 14.6 *Part of the purpose of the Print dialog box is to enable you to choose and set up a printer.*

to work with Windows on your system, or with a Windows NT or Windows 2000 network you're connected with. (To learn how to set up a printer using the Windows Control Panel, see the Windows documentation or online help.) In this list, click on the name of the printer you want to print your Project files to.

3. After you select the correct printer, click on the Properties button beside it. If this is the first time you've worked with printer properties during the current Project work session, Project will open a dialog box alerting you that your printer settings will apply to all views you subsequently print—not just the currently displayed view.

4. Click on OK to continue. The Properties dialog box for the selected printer will appear, as shown in Figure 14.7.

 NOTE

In Windows, properties include information about a file, program, or piece of hardware, as well as the settings or options available for that item.

5. Most printers enable you to control the following options, arranged on various tabs within the dialog box:

◆ **Paper size.** Use the list to display the sizes of paper your printer can handle. Click on the appropriate size to select it.

◆ **Orientation.** Select whether you want to print in a format where the paper's taller than it is wide (Portrait) or wider than it is tall (Landscape). To print the information upside-down in a landscape orientation, check the Rotated check box. Generally, a thumbnail picture in the preview or sample area shows you what effect your orientation selections will have on your document's printed layout.

◆ **Copies.** Change the Copies entry if you want Project to print more than one copy of each document (one copy is the default).

◆ **Restore Defaults.** This command button appears on each tab of the Properties dialog box. Clicking on it restores the tab's settings to the defaults for that printer.

◆ **Other.** Your printer may offer settings for printing multiple pages per sheet, choosing a resolution or toner-saving print quality, reducing, enlarging, or fitting a printout to a page, and more.

FIGURE 14.7 *The Properties dialog box offers different options, depending on the capabilities of the selected printer.*

 TIP

If you need information about one of the Properties settings for your printer, click on the question mark button near the right side of the Properties dialog box title bar. Then use the question mark pointer to click on the item you want information about.

6. After you specify all the property settings for your selected printer, click on OK to close the Properties dialog box and return to the Print dialog box.

7. At this point, you can click on the Close button to return to Project and alter the Page Setup for your project file, as described in the next section. Or you can use the Print dialog box to print your document, as described in the last section of this chapter, "Finishing the Print Job."

Controlling the Page Setup

In Project, the first step in determining what appears on your printout is to select a view. Project creates a printout of that view. So if you've displayed Gantt Chart view, the printout contains the columns at the left and the Gantt bars on a schedule at the right. If you display only the Resource Sheet, Project prints the contents of the Resource Sheet. In a Task Sheet or Resource Sheet, you need to be sure that you display the correct table and filter the information, if needed, before printing. (See Chapter 13, "Working with the Different Project Views," to learn more about selecting and filtering a table.)

There are only a couple of limitations on what you can print. Project doesn't print any information or any view pane that's a form.

In the selected view, you also need to specify formatting—such as adjusting the appearance of Gantt bars, changing the timescale, and changing column breaks (see the next section in this chapter)—to control how information appears in the final printout. The formatting changes you make appear both onscreen and in the printed document.

In contrast, the Page Setup options control only how the printed information appears. For example, you can adjust the header or footer that appears on each page of a printout, or specify how many pages you want the printout to occupy. To adjust the Page Setup options before printing, choose File, Page Setup to open the Page Setup dialog box for the selected view (see Figure 14.8).

The available options vary slightly, depending on the selected view. The default options that Project suggests also differ depending on the selected view. (In Figure 14.8, for example, Project suggests printing the Gantt chart in the Landscape orientation.)

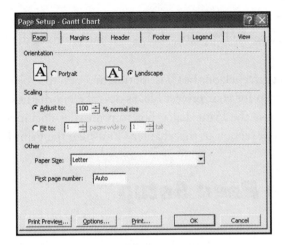

FIGURE 14.8   *The Page Setup dialog box offers options specific to the selected view, which in this case is the Gantt Chart view.*

Finally, some of the settings you see in the Page Setup dialog box resemble the ones provided in the Properties dialog box for the printer. Remember that the printer properties settings become the default for all Project files that are printed. Any Page Setup options you select for the current view take precedence over the Properties settings.

The remainder of this section describes the settings on each tab of the Page Setup dialog box. (Keep in mind that some of them might not be available in your selected view, in which case they'll be grayed out.) After you choose the settings you want from all tabs, click on the OK button to close the dialog box and make your changes take effect.

Page Tab Settings

Figure 14.8 shows the first tab in the Page Setup dialog box, the Page tab. In the Orientation area of the dialog box, specify whether you want the printout to appear in Portrait (tall) or Landscape (wide) format. The Scaling options enable you to scale the printed view or report to a particular size or page count. When the Adjust To option button is selected, you can enter a percentage that makes the printed image smaller (down to 10%) or larger (up to 500%) than its original size.

I prefer to use the Fit To option, which enables you to tell Project how many pages wide and tall to make the printout. This is my preference because it's more error-proof. Otherwise, you might have to print at a few different percentages to get a printed document that fits your needs. In most professional situations, I prefer to have a printout that's one page tall but as many pages wide as needed. That format is easier for an audience to understand in a bound report. For a Task Sheet or Resource Sheet printout, on the other hand, you might prefer a result that's one page wide and multiple pages tall.

Under Other, you can use the Paper Size drop-down list to select a size, such as Legal, to use for the printout. The selected printer and its available paper sizes dictate the Paper Size options in the Page Setup dialog box. Finally, you can enter a number in the First Page Number text box to specify the page number where Project starts printing (if you specify page numbering in the header or footer). For example, if you enter **4** and the printout requires four pages, Project numbers the pages 4, 5, 6, and 7. This is useful if you need to include the Project printout in a bound report that includes pages from other programs, such as a Word document. Adjusting the numbering for your Project printout enables you to seamlessly integrate its pages with the rest of the report.

Margins Tab Settings

The second tab in the Page Setup dialog box is the Margins tab. Click it to display its options (see Figure 14.9). When you change the margin settings, you're changing the amount of white space that Project leaves around the information printed on a page. The Margins tab offers four text boxes—Top, Bottom, Left, and Right—where you can type the margin setting you want to use for your printout, in inches by default. To change one of the settings, double-click on its text box and type the new value or use the spinner buttons (the arrows at the right side of the box).

By default, Project also prints a thin border around the information on every page of the printout. If you wish, you can change that setting in the Borders Around area of the Margins tab. If the selected view is the Network Diagram chart, you can select the Outer Pages option button, which prints a border around only the first and last pages of the printout. For other views, you can click on the None option button to completely eliminate borders from the printout.

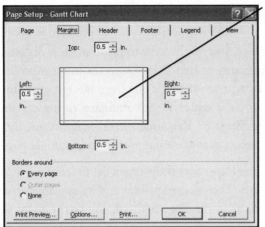

This preview shows how wide the specified margins will look

FIGURE 14.9 *Use this tab to control the margins around the information in your printout.*

 NOTE

Headers, footers, and legends are printed within any border included on the printout.

Header Tab Settings

Moving on, you can click on the Header tab in the Page Setup dialog box. A *header* appears at the top of a printout and provides information about the printout. It can consist of any text you want to type in. For example, you might want to designate the printout as "In Progress" or something similar. Alternately, you can build the header components using the tabs and buttons in the Alignment area of the Margins tab.

Start by clicking on a tab in the Alignment area to select whether the header information will align to the left, center, or right. (Note that you can designate header information to appear simultaneously in two—or even all three—of these tabs.) To enter information simply by typing, click in the blank area below the tab and type the information you want.

As indicated in Figure 14.10, you can use several of the buttons in the Alignment area to enter calculated fields of header information. For example, suppose that you want your header to include the printout date. Click within any information already entered for the header to specify where the date should be inserted, and then click on the button that inserts the printout date. A code that identifies where the printout date will be positioned appears in the header (see Figure 14.10).

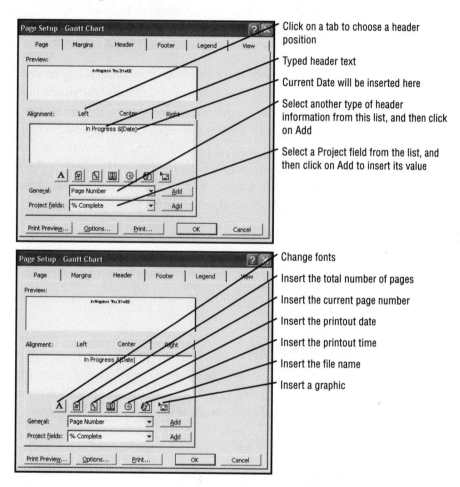

FIGURE 14.10   *Build a header using a variety of techniques.*

Project enables you to automatically insert other kinds of information in the header—such as the Project Author or Project Start Date from the file's Properties or Project Information dialog box settings—by using the General drop-down list at the bottom of the Alignment area. First, click to position the insertion point where you want the information to be inserted in the header. Open the General drop-down list to see the kinds of information you can insert, click on the name for the type of information you want to insert, and then click on the Add button beside the drop-down list. Project inserts a code for that kind of information in the header. The Project Fields drop-down list works in the same way and lists a number of calculated fields. Select the field you want from the drop-down list, and then click on the Add button beside it to insert the actual calculated value contained in that field into the header.

You can format the appearance of the text or inserted codes in any header area by dragging over the information to format until it's all highlighted, and then clicking on the Formatting button in the Alignment area. (This button is on the far left and has the letter "A" on it.) Project then opens the Font dialog box, in which you can choose a new font, size, and so on for the selected text. Chapter 17, "Other Formatting," covers how to use the Font dialog box, which also appears when you format text in a Task Sheet or Resource Sheet. Make the changes you want, and then click on OK to return to the Page Setup dialog box.

TIP

If you want your company's logo to appear on every page of a printout, insert the logo in the header or footer.

Footer Tab Settings

Click on the next tab to move to the Footer options (see Figure 14.11). A footer resembles a header, except it's at the bottom of each printed page. Refer to the preceding information about creating a header to learn how to work with the Footer tab options.

Legend Tab Settings

You can insert a legend explaining what the graphical chart symbols mean on your printouts. To specify whether or not a legend appears on your printout, click on the Legend tab in the Page Setup dialog box. The Legend tab options appear as shown in Figure 14.12.

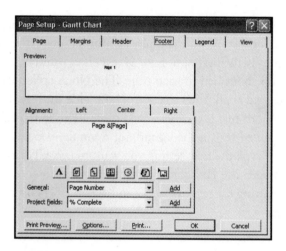

FIGURE 14.11 *The Footer options work just like the Header options.*

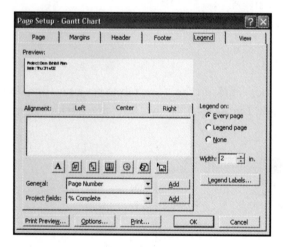

FIGURE 14.12 *For graphical printouts, you can include a legend—and set it up—on this tab.*

Because a legend can include text, Project offers the kind of text formatting options available for creating headers and footers. Those settings work just like the ones on the Header and Footer tabs, so I won't explain them again here.

The Legend On area at the right side of the tab enables you to control whether the legend appears on a given page. By default, Every Page is selected, meaning that the legend appears on every page of the printed hard copy. If you select the

Legend Page option button, Project prints the legend on its own separate page so that there is more room for the schedule's graphical information on the other printed pages. This is typically the best option for Gantt chart printouts. Otherwise, the legend takes up about half of each page. The None option causes the printout to have no legend at all. You can control how wide the legend area is with the entry in the Width text box. If you need more room in the legend area—to include more detailed text in the legend, for example—double-click on the Width text box and type the new setting you want to use. Click on the Legend Labels button to open the Font dialog box, where you can choose the settings you want for formatting the text in the Legend. Chapter 17 covers how to use the Font dialog box.

 NOTE

If you define any custom bar styles for the Gantt Chart view, the legend will include those custom bar styles.

View Tab Settings

In the Page Setup dialog box, click on the View tab to set a few final options specific to the selected view. Figure 14.13 shows how this tab looks for Gantt Chart view.

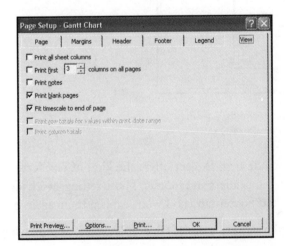

FIGURE 14.13 *Fine-tune how your view is printed by using the options on this tab.*

Here's how to work with each of the listed options, when they're available:

- **Print All Sheet Columns.** When a view contains a chart with a timescale, Project prints only the columns in the accompanying Task Sheet or Resource Sheet that appear onscreen. If you drag the split bar so that only one sheet column is visible, only that column is printed. Select the Print All Sheet Columns check box if you want to print all the sheet columns, not just the presently displayed columns.

- **Print First ... Columns On All Pages.** If you want to choose exactly how many columns in a Task Sheet or Resource Sheet are printed, select this check box and enter the number of columns to print in the accompanying text box. You can only use this option if you're printing a view that includes information charted on a timescale. printout is more than a page deep and a page wide, all the far-left pages include the visible columns, not the number of columns you specify here. Thus, you ideally want to use this option only when you're sure that the printout will be one page deep but many pages wide.

- **Print Notes.** When you select this option for the views where it's available, Project prints the notes you entered for a task or resource, depending on the view you are printing, on a separate page at the end of the printout.

- **Print Blank Pages.** For some of the views that contain charted information, you might end up with pages that don't actually contain any data. An example is the lower-left page of any Gantt chart printout that's more than one page deep and one page wide. If you want to save paper by not printing these blank pages, clear the check mark beside this option. However, if you plan to assemble the multiple pages of your printout into a large, single chart—perhaps by taping them together and hanging them on the wall of your office—leave this option selected.

- **Fit Timescale To End Of Page.** You saw earlier in this chapter that if your printer allows it, you can scale your printout by a certain percentage to control how small or large it's printed. That's somewhat of an eyeball approach, and it doesn't ensure that your schedule fits neatly on the printed pages. You might end up, for example, with half a blank page at the end of your printout. If you want to ensure that the graphical portion of your printout (the timescale) takes advantage of all the available space on your pages, make sure that this check box is selected. Project then stretches the timescale (for example, by making each day take up slightly more space) to ensure that the graphical information fills the last printout page.

◆ **Print Row Totals for Values within Print Date Range.** Available when you print the Task Usage and Resource Usage views, this option (when checked) includes a new column in the printout that totals values across the row for the specified range of dates.

◆ **Print Column Totals.** Available when you print the Task Usage and Resource Usage views, this option (when checked) includes a new row in the printout that totals values in the field above.

Controlling Page Breaks

You just learned that in any view that combines a Task Sheet or Resource Sheet with graphical or timescale information at the right side of the page, you must drag the vertical split bar to control how many columns of the sheet appear in the printout.

In addition, you might want to control which rows of task or resource information appear on each page of a printout. For example, you might know that Task 17 holds a summary task, so you want to end the prior page at Task 16. You can control where the pages break in printouts of Gantt Chart view, Resource Usage view, and Task Sheets or Resource Sheets by inserting a manual page break. A manual page break tells Project to stop printing on the current page with a particular row and to begin the next page down with the information in the next row.

 TIP

Manual page breaks don't affect how many pages wide your printout is. They only affect how many pages tall it is.

To add a manual page break, follow these steps:

1. Switch to the view you want to print.

2. In the Task Sheet or Resource Sheet, select a cell in the row that should be at the top of a new page. (You also can select the whole row by clicking its row number.) Project will insert the manual break above the selected row.

3. Choose Insert, Page Break. Project inserts a dotted line in the sheet to show you where the page break will occur (see Figure 14.14).

Inserted page break

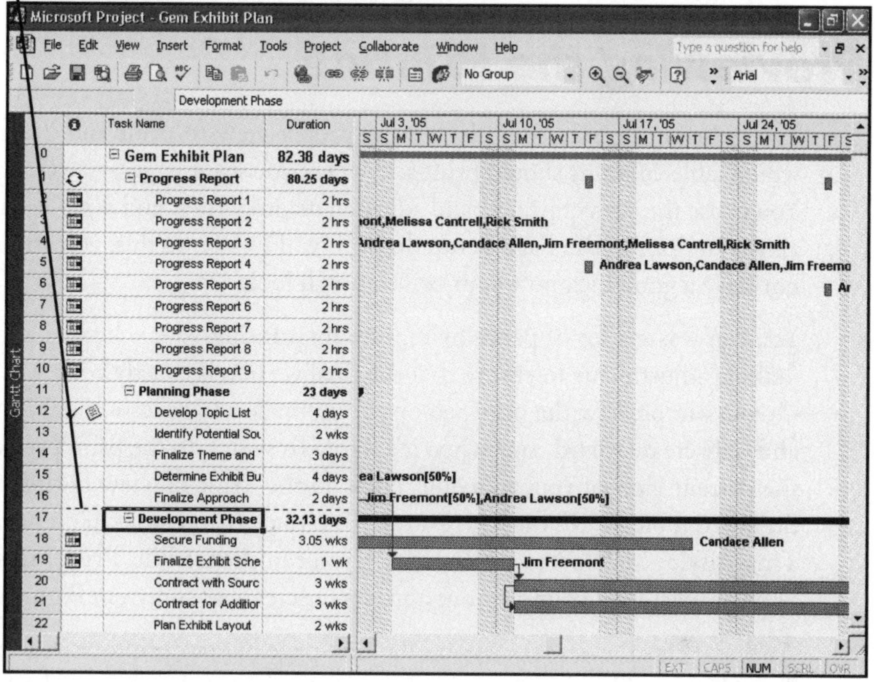

FIGURE 14.14 *A manual page break appears as a dotted line above the row you selected.*

Your inserted page breaks do not work immediately, so if you go directly to the Print Preview (described in the next section), you won't see your inserted page breaks. You have to turn on a print option for the manual page breaks to take effect. To do so, choose File, Print to display the Print dialog box. Check the Manual Page Breaks check box. Then you can either click on the Preview button in the Print dialog box to display the Print Preview and see your manual page breaks or click on OK to send the print job to the printer.

CAUTION

Inserted page breaks can cause unexpected results in printed reports (see Chapter 16, "Creating and Printing a Report," for an in-depth look at reports). I recommend that you remove manual page breaks after you use them, unless you're sure that you won't be working with any reports.

To remove manual page breaks, either select the row just below the break by clicking on its row number, or click on the Select All button in the upper-left corner of the sheet. Choose Insert, Remove All Page Breaks.

Previewing the Printing

You've been diligent. You selected the proper view to print and designated which table columns should print and where you want page breaks to appear. You chose the correct printer and adjusted its properties, and double-checked all the options in the Page Setup dialog box. Despite all this, you still might not have a good idea how your printout will look.

You can waste a lot of paper by repeatedly printing your schedule and then making adjustments to ensure that the final version is exactly what you want. Or you can preview the print job onscreen, make any necessary adjustments, and only create a hard copy when it's right. To switch to the print preview for the current view of your schedule, click on the Print Preview button on the Standard toolbar. (It's the fifth button from the left and looks like a page with a magnifying glass over it.) Alternately, you can choose File, Print Preview. A preview version of your printout appears onscreen, as shown in Figure 14.15.

At first, Print Preview shows you the first page of your printout in a reduced view that provides a look at the overall page layout. You'll see whether the printout includes a legend, how the margin spacing looks around the data, where the headers and footers appear, and more.

If the printout includes more than one page, you can use the left and right arrow keys to move forward and backward through the pages. The up and down arrows only activate if there are too many rows to fit on a single page. You can use the up and down arrows to view the extra rows, which will be on separate pages when you print the hard copy.

You might, however, want to zoom in to read particular details in the printout before printing. For example, you might want to check to see if a heading you added looks the way you want it to. You can either click on the Zoom button at the top of the preview to zoom in on the upper-left corner of the page, or click the zoom pointer (which appears by default in Print Preview) to zoom in on a specific area. After you've zoomed in, you can click on the button for displaying one full page (this button has a page on it) to return to the default view.

Arrows   Zoom in   Show one full page   Show multiple pages

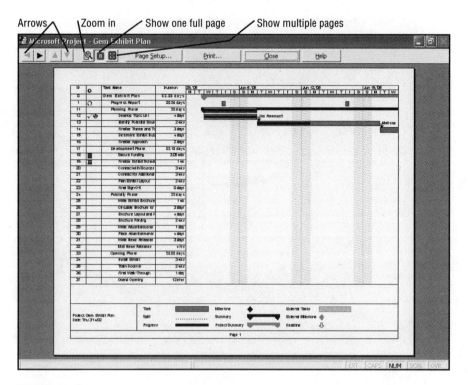

FIGURE 14.15 *Preview a printout to see what setup changes you need to make without wasting paper.*

If the printout has more than one page and you want to view multiple pages, perhaps to see how the information is divided between pages, click on the button that looks like a stack of papers. Project displays multiple pages of the printout onscreen, as shown in Figure 14.16. Again, to return to the default view, click on the button for displaying one full page.

If the printout doesn't look the way you want it to, you need to make changes. Making most changes requires you to return to the normal schedule view, so click on the Close button to exit the print preview. In other cases, you can make your changes directly from the preview. For example, you may think that you've squeezed the printout into too few pages, making the information small and difficult to read. If you need to change a page setup option in such a case, click on the Page Setup button at the top of the preview to open the Page Setup dialog box. Make the needed changes, and then click on OK to close the Page Setup dialog box. If the preview then meets with your approval, click on the Print button at the top of the Print Preview to go directly to the Print dialog box and complete the printout, as explained in the next section.

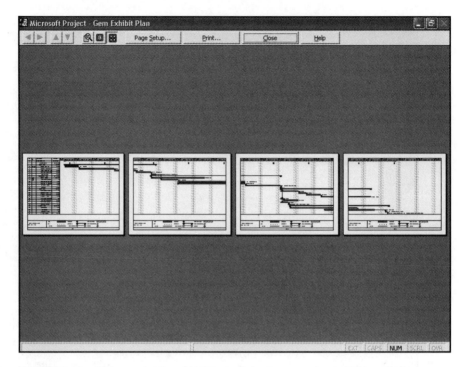

FIGURE 14.16 *If the printout has multiple pages, you can preview more than one page at a time.*

 TIP

To limit the printout to fewer pages, you can limit the tasks in the printout by decreasing the date range for the printout. To do so from the Print Preview, click on the Print button. In the Timescale area of the Print dialog box, click on the Dates option button, and then specify From and To dates as needed. Then click on the Preview button in the Print dialog box to return to the Print Preview and double-check your changes.

Finishing the Print Job

Figure 14.17 shows the Print dialog box, which you saw earlier in this chapter when you learned how to select and set up a printer. To open the Print dialog box from any view but the Print Preview, choose File, Print (or press Ctrl+P). (Click on the Print button in the Print Preview view to display the Print dialog box.)

Print button \ | Print Preview button

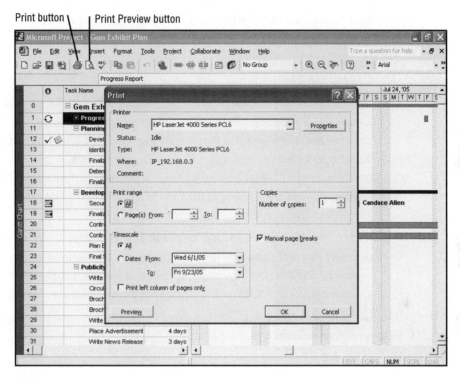

FIGURE 14.17 *Make your final settings before sending a job to the selected printer.*

 TIP

If you want to print your schedule without going through the Print dialog box to specify final options, click on the Print button on the Standard toolbar. When you print using this method, Project automatically prints with the current printer settings and current Page Setup options.

The settings in the Print dialog box override any settings you have made elsewhere, such as when you initially set up your printer. Here's a review of the final choices you can make from this dialog box before sending your schedule to the printer:

◆ In the Print Range area, leave the All option button selected to print all the pages in your schedule. Or, if your printout includes more than one page and you don't want to print the entire document, click on the Page(s) From radio button, and then enter the page number of the first page you want to print. In the To text box, enter the page number of the last page you want to print.

◆ To print more than one copy, change the entry in the Number Of Copies text box.

◆ You can use the Timescale options to control which tasks are printed. Leave the All option button selected to print all the tasks. To print only tasks starting within a particular range of dates, click on the Dates From option button and enter the starting date for the range in that text box. In the To text box, enter the ending date for the range. If you want only one page's worth of Timescale tasks to print, select the Print Left Column Of Pages Only check box.

◆ When the Manual Page Breaks check box is selected, the printout uses any manual page breaks you've inserted. If you don't want to remove the page breaks you've set up, but you don't want Project to use them for this particular printout, clear the check box for this option.

After you finish changing the Print dialog box settings as needed, click on OK to send your schedule to the printer.

Chapter 15

Working with Forms

In This Chapter

◆ Understanding forms

◆ Creating a custom form

In Chapter 13, "Working with the Different Project Views," you learned how to change the view that Project uses to display and organize your schedule information onscreen. You learned that some views include forms (either alone or with other types of information) that are intended to make it easier to enter and edit information.

This chapter shows you how to work with forms on their own, rather than working with them as part of a view.

Understanding Forms

Over time, many easier ways of communicating with programs have evolved. Interface designers study how users interact with programs to find the best method to prompt users for information. Not surprisingly, a good ol' "fill in the blanks" approach tends to work best, both in programs and on Web pages.

So far, you've seen that in Project you can enter information via spreadsheet-like tables or sheets, by dragging on a Gantt chart or Network Diagram chart, via dialog boxes, and more. Forms, which resemble dialog boxes, are yet another method for entering data.

Forms include text boxes to let you enter and edit information—fill in the blanks, so to speak. Forms also enable you to look at other information that you cannot edit, such as calculated costs. Although some views consist solely of a large form—or include a form in a lower pane—you can also display a form in its own floating dialog box (see Figure 15.1).

Project offers some forms for resource information (see Figure 15.2) and others for task information. Table 15.1 lists the predefined forms available in Project.

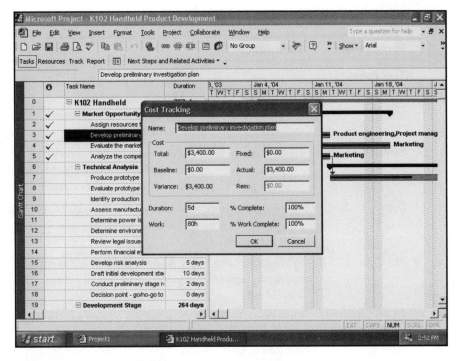

FIGURE 15.1 *When you display one of the many forms offered in Project, it appears in its own dialog box.*

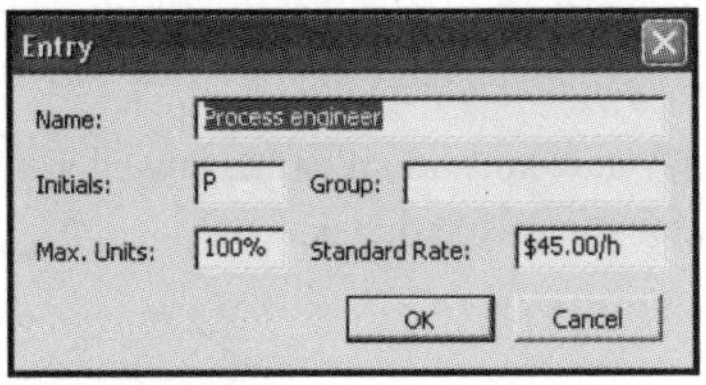

FIGURE 15.2 *Here's an example of a form displaying resource information.*

Table 15.1 Task Forms and Resource Forms in Project

Form Name	Description
Task Forms	
Cost Tracking	Displays cost information for the selected task, including baseline budget, current budget, and actual costs to the current date or status date based on work performed.
Earned Value	Displays earned value and cost variance information, such as the budgeted cost of work performed based on schedule and cost. Only lets you edit the task name and completion percentage.
Entry	Enables you to enter or edit basic information about the selected task (except for summary tasks), including its name, duration, start date, and finish date.
PERT Entry	When you're using PERT Analysis use this form to enter optimistic, expected, and pessimistic durations for the selected task.
Schedule Tracking	Shows the selected task's baseline and currently scheduled start and finish dates, and calculates the variance between the baseline and current dates.
Task Relationships	Displays and lets you edit the predecessors and successors linked to the selected task.
Tracking	Enables you to enter actual start and finish dates, as well as completion information, for the selected task.
Work Tracking	Enables you to enter actual start and finish dates, as well as completion information, for the selected task.
Resource Forms	
Cost Tracking	Displays cost information for the resource selected in the Resource Sheet, including baseline cost, total cost (currently budgeted), and actual cost for work performed to date (or to the status date). None of these values can be edited.
Entry	Enables you to edit the basic information defining the resource, such as the resource's name, initials, and standard rate.
Summary	Summarizes the amount of work and budget for costs scheduled for the resource, including the amount of work assigned, Max Units, and cost and work variances.
Work Tracking	Displays the amount of work scheduled for a resource, the percentage completed, and variance in work completed to date or to the status date. These calculations can't be edited.

Selecting a Form

The process for selecting a form differs a bit from selecting some of the other types of view information, because there's no way to directly display a form via a menu or submenu choice. You have to use the Custom Forms dialog box, as described in the following steps:

1. From the Task Sheet or Resource Sheet, select the task or resource for which you want to display form information by clicking the Task Name or Resource Name cell in the appropriate row.

NOTE

If you're working in a task view, you can't display resource forms, and vice versa. Thus, it's critical to select a task or resource view to ensure that the correct form choices are available.

2. Choose Tools, Customize, Forms. The Customize Forms dialog box will appear (see Figure 15.3).

TIP

It can be faster to use the Custom Forms toolbar. Right-click a toolbar, and then click Custom Forms. On the Custom Forms toolbar that appears, click the Forms button near the right end of the toolbar to display the Customize Forms dialog box.

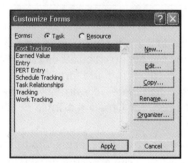

FIGURE 15.3 *Use this dialog box to select and manage forms.*

3. In the Forms list, select the form you want by double-clicking on its name (or by clicking on the name once and then clicking on Apply). Project closes the Customize Forms dialog box and displays the form you selected onscreen.

4. If you need to edit any information in the form (assuming the form offers editable text boxes), click in each text box and then edit its contents.

5. Click on OK when you finish with the form.

Creating a Custom Form

You might find that none of the forms in Project capture the information you want to show. For example, you might need a quick way to check actual task costs along with the resource name and group, to keep an eye on how much work by another department in your company you'll need to pay for. That is, you may want to track the costs for work performed by resources from another group that are coming from your project budget.

Project enables you to create your own custom forms, and you don't need any programming experience. You can add text to your form, or you can add information from any field in the Task Sheet or Resource Sheet. If a field contains a calculated value that you shouldn't edit, Project automatically formats the field so that it can't be edited on your form.

 TIP

If you've created a custom field, you can add it to your form. For a calculated field, you won't be able to use the form to change the calculated result. For a pick list field, you won't be able to select a value from the form. You have to add the field to a table and make your selection there. To learn how to create custom fields, see the section in Chapter 13 titled "Creating a Table or Filter."

While you can create a nearly infinite number of custom forms, the following steps should give you a good start. Afterward, you can experiment on your own to discover the combinations of form information you'll find most useful.

1. Choose Tools, Customize, Forms. The Customize Forms dialog box will appear.

2. To indicate whether your form will display information from the Task Sheet or Resource Sheet, click on either the Task or Resource option button at the top of the dialog box. This is a critical step, because your choice here affects which fields you can add to your form.

3. Click on the New button. The Define Custom Form dialog box will appear (see Figure 15.4).

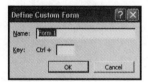

FIGURE 15.4 *This dialog box enables you to begin defining your custom form.*

4. Enter the form name in the Name text box. For example, if you're creating a form showing actual task cost, resource name, and resource group information, you might enter **Cost and Group**.

5. If you want to be able to use a shortcut key combination to display the custom form, enter the second key for the combination in the Key text box. Project allows only letters here. You can't enter numbers, function keys, or special characters such as punctuation marks.

6. Click on OK to continue defining the form. Project displays the Custom Form Editor, with a new blank form background, as shown in Figure 15.5. Notice that the toolbar tools have been hidden, and that the available menus have changed to reflect that you're working with the Form Editor functions.

7. By default, a dotted outline appears around the border of the blank form dialog box to indicate that this box is selected. If needed, you can change the size of the form by dragging the dotted line on any side of the dialog box, as shown in Figure 15.6.

8. Now it's time to begin adding elements to the form. To add a text label, choose Item, Text. Project will add placeholder text to the form, surrounded by dotted boundary lines. Point to this text so that a four-headed arrow appears with the mouse pointer (see Figure 15.7). Then drag the text box placeholder to a different location. You can adjust the size of the text by dragging one of its boundary lines.

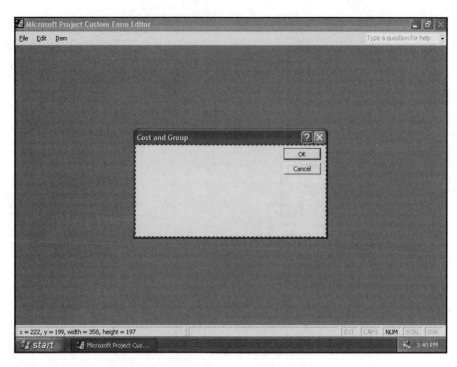

FIGURE 15.5 *Create custom forms with the Custom Form Editor shown here.*

FIGURE 15.6 *It's easy to resize the form by dragging its boundary lines.*

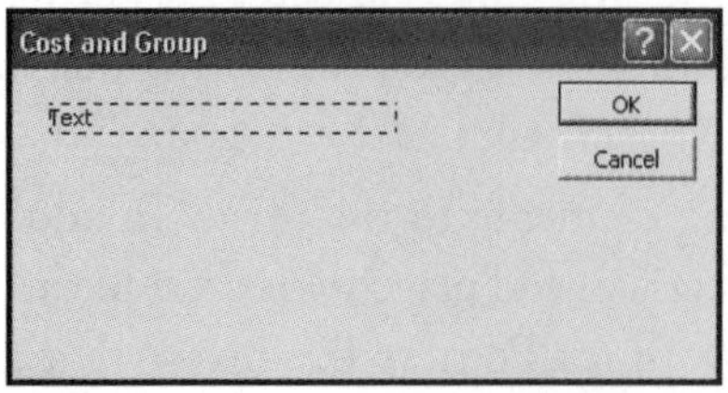

FIGURE 15.7 *You can drag the text box placeholder into the position you prefer on the form.*

9. After you position and size the text placeholder, double-click on it on the form (or choose Edit, Information). The Item Information dialog box will appear, as shown in Figure 15.8.

FIGURE 15.8   *After you place an item on the form, you need to edit the information it displays.*

10. You shouldn't need to edit any of the top four text boxes, because you already defined the placeholder's size and position in Step 8. Simply double-click in the Text text box, and then type the text you want to appear in that area of the form, such as **Task Name**. Click on OK to close the Item Information dialog box.

11. To add a field to the form, choose Item, Fields. Project opens the Item Information dialog box immediately, because you have to specify which field to display.

12. Open the Field drop-down list and click on the name of the field you want to appear on the form. For example, select Name to display the task name, as shown in Figure 15.9.

FIGURE 15.9   *Tell Project which field information you want to display on the form.*

CAUTION

If you clicked the Task option button in Step 2, select the Name field to include the task name on your form and the Resource Names field to show the resources assigned to the selected task. If you clicked the Resource option button in Step 2, the reverse is true. In that case, adding the Name field to your form displays the resource name, and you can choose the Task Outline Number field to identify the task on the form.

13. If you know that a field typically appears in an editable format on forms—as the Name field usually does—and you don't want Project to enable editing of that field information in your form, check the Show As Static Text check box.

14. Click on OK. The field appears on the form, ready for you to resize and drag into place (see Figure 15.10).

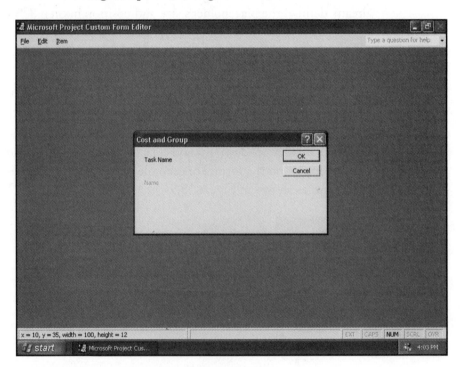

FIGURE 15.10 *A field has just been added to the form.*

TIP

To delete any item you added to a form, click on the item once so that a dotted selection line appears around it, and then press the Delete key.

15. Continue adding items to the form, following the same general process of making a choice from the Item menu, using the Item Information dialog box (if needed) to define what the item displays, resizing the item, and dragging it into position. For example, Figure 15.11 shows my completed form. I've used the Group Box selection on the Item menu to create the Stats box.

Fields display as static text that you can't edit

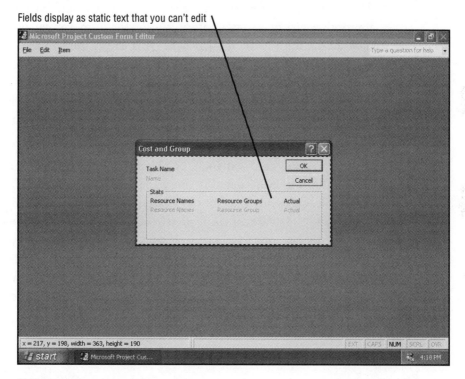

FIGURE 15.11 *Here's how the final form looks.*

16. Choose File, Save to save your form with the name you provided in Step 4.

17. Choose File, Exit. Project closes the Form Editor and returns to the Custom Forms dialog box. Your new form appears in the list there, as shown in Figure 15.12.

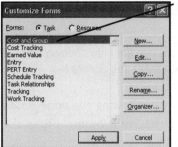 My custom form

FIGURE 15.12 *You select the forms you created via the Custom Forms dialog box.*

18. At this point, if you displayed the appropriate sheet and selected the appropriate task or resource before creating the form, you can double-click on the form name to display it. (If you're at the wrong view or haven't selected the appropriate task or resource, you have to close the Customize Forms dialog box, switch to the appropriate sheet, click the desired task or resource, redisplay the Customize Forms dialog box, and then select your form.) Figure 15.13 shows how my custom form appears when displayed.

It takes a little practice, but soon you'll be able to create a variety of useful forms. Pay attention to every detail if you want to achieve professional results. For example, make sure that your text boxes and field boxes are aligned at both the left and right sides of the form whenever possible, and make sure that information looks centered when you intend it to. Also, make sure you're creating the right type of form. You can only display custom task forms in a task-oriented view like the Gantt Chart or Task Usage views. You can only display custom resource forms from a resource-oriented view like the Resource Sheet or Resource Usage view.

 TIP

If you're not satisfied with a form you've created, open the Customize Forms dialog box, click Task or Resource, click the form in the list, and then click the Edit button so you can make changes to the form.

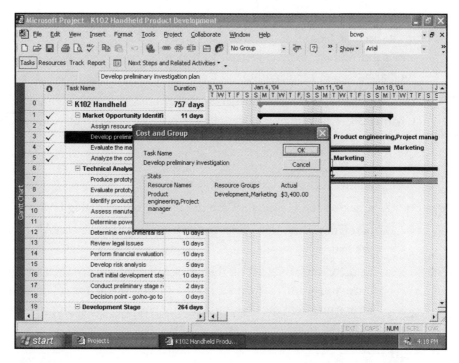

FIGURE 15.13 *A custom form that you create can look just as good as the forms that come with Project.*

 NOTE

Custom forms that you create are saved only with the current project file, until you either copy them to Project's GLOBAL.MPT master file or delete them. To make a form available to all files or to delete a form, click on the Organizer button in the Custom Forms dialog box and use the Forms tab of the Organizer to make your changes.

Creating a Toolbar Button or Menu Command to Display a Form

Note that each form only lets you display information about one task or resource at a time. Unlike forms used as part of a view, forms that you display on their own don't offer Previous and Next buttons to enable you to display information about other resources or tasks without closing the form. Because it can become tedious to use the Tools menu to display a form over and over, and a shortcut key can be difficult to remember, you might want to create a toolbar button or menu command that displays this form.

Here are the steps for adding such a toolbar button or menu command (see Chapter 28, "Customizing Microsoft Project," for an in-depth look at creating menu commands and toolbar buttons):

1. Choose Tools, Customize, Toolbars. Or, right-click on any toolbar and then choose Customize.
2. Click on the Commands tab in the Customize dialog box.
3. Scroll down the Categories list on the tab. Then click on All Forms in the list.
4. In the Commands list on the tab, scroll until you see the name of the form you want to create a button or command for. Then drag the form name from the Customize dialog box onto the appropriate toolbar or menu.

 CAUTION

Although you can change an existing toolbar button so that it displays a form rather than executing its currently assigned command, I don't recommend it. You might not be able to recall what the button's original command was if you ever want to reinstate it.

5. Right-click on the form name you just dragged onto the toolbar to display a shortcut menu with options for customizing the button or menu command (see Figure 15.14). Chapter 28 explains how to use the commands on this shortcut menu to control such features as the picture that appears on a button, the menu command name, and more. Refer to that chapter for details about using the shortcut menu.
6. After you finish using the shortcut menu to make changes to the new button or command, click on Close to finish creating the button and close the Customize dialog box. Figure 15.15 shows an example form button.

I dragged this form onto the toolbar

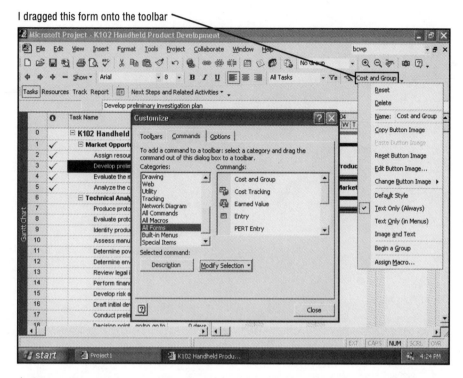

FIGURE 15.14 *You can customize a toolbar button or menu command with this shortcut menu.*

FIGURE 15.15 *I've added a custom form toolbar button near the right end of the Formatting toolbar. Its ScreenTip is displayed.*

Chapter 16

Creating and Printing a Report

In This Chapter

◆ Learning which predesigned reports Project offers

◆ Selecting the correct report

◆ Fine-tuning and printing a report

◆ Designing a unique report

Software developers have placed a good deal of emphasis on offering more ways to manipulate and present the information you gather in a particular program. That's because the typical businessperson needs to share information with a variety of audiences, and each audience needs only a particular subset of the information.

For a Project file, for example, you might need to prepare a weekly report of the current expenses for a project to give to your boss, a listing of upcoming tasks to give to the participants in a planning meeting, or a weekly to-do list to refresh your memory about issues you need to follow up on.

Project can generate these kinds of reports (and more) automatically. This chapter introduces you to reporting in Project.

Understanding the Report Types

Project's predefined reports contain the most common types of summary information that you might need to provide to others, both within and outside of your organization. In Chapter 14, "Proofing and Printing a View," you learned how to select and filter different views for printing and how to control the information appearing in your printout. Although that method of selecting and printing information works fine in many cases, it has a few drawbacks:

◆ It frequently requires several steps to display just the information you want to see.

◆ You often can't capture totals for data in the format you prefer.

◆ There are some kinds of lists you just can't print from a view, such as a list of working days for the schedule.

Project's reports address these issues for you, providing a streamlined approach for selecting and printing information. In addition, using a report rather than printing a view yields a printout with an attractive layout that's suitable for distribution to readers you need to impress. Finally, the reports capture information in key columns; there's no need for the reader to wade through extraneous data in a report printout.

To create reports in Project, you work with the Reports dialog box. Start from any view and choose View, Reports. The Reports dialog box will appear (see Figure 16.1). It offers five icons for different categories of reports: Overview, Current Activities, Costs, Assignments, and Workload. The sixth icon, Custom, enables you to create your own reports, as described later in this chapter.

FIGURE 16.1   *Use this dialog box to select from the report categories offered in Project.*

To select a report category, click on its icon and then click on Select (or simply double-click on the icon). Project displays a dialog box showing the different kinds of reports available in that category, including an icon for each report with a thumbnail view of what it looks like. There's not enough room in this book to show you a printout of every report type, but the rest of this section introduces you to the reports in each category via its dialog box.

The reports that work best for you will depend on what information you're required to report to others, as well as how concerned you are about having frequent updates on specific information, such as upcoming tasks or tasks that are under way. After you review the dialog boxes shown here for the various report categories, do some experimenting on your own to discover which reports you prefer to work with.

TIP

Click on Cancel in any dialog box that lists specific reports to close that dialog box and go to the Reports dialog box.

Overview Reports

When you select the Overview Reports icon in the Reports dialog box, the Overview Reports dialog box will appear (see Figure 16.2).

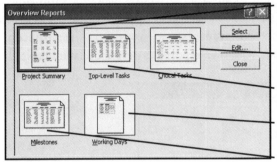

Reviews the numbers of tasks and resources, schedule by project and task, costs, and start and finish dates

Displays critical tasks, summary and successor tasks, and notes

Shows the tasks in the top outline level, including summary tasks and notes

Lists information about the Standard calendar

Lists milestones, summary tasks, and notes

FIGURE 16.2 *Reports provide project summaries at a glance.*

Current Activities Reports

The next category of reports, Current Activities, appears in the Current Activity Reports dialog box (see Figure 16.3), which appears when you select Current Activities in the Reports dialog box.

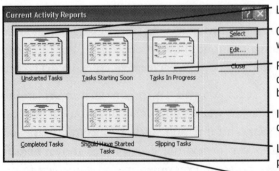

Lists tasks for which work hasn't started

Creates a list of upcoming tasks, along with needed resources and notes

Provides a month-by-month overview of tasks for which work has begun but has not been completed

Indicates tasks that might not be completed when scheduled

Lists tasks scheduled to start by a particular date

Compiles a month-by-month list of completed tasks

FIGURE 16.3 *Reports that enable you to zero in on upcoming priorities.*

> **NOTE**
>
> Two of the report types in the Current Activities category, Tasks Starting Soon and Should Have Started Tasks, require you to enter dates. Whenever Project prompts you to enter a date, type it using the mm/dd/yy format and then click on OK to continue.

Costs Reports

To take a look at the dollars and cents you're spending on your project, select the Costs category in the Reports dialog box to display the report types shown in Figure 16.4. It's likely that you'll get a lot of mileage from these report formats. One of the key aspects of project management is monitoring the bottom line and adjusting planned expenditures as required. These reports not only compile the expenses you specify, but also total various expenses by column (category).

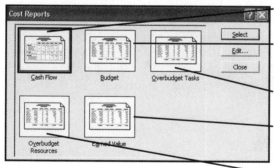

Compiles a week-by-week summary of costs for each task

Summarizes the total project budget, from the most expensive task to the least expensive

Lets you know which tasks might cost more than you've planned

For each task, compares the budgeted expenses with the value of the work actually completed

Lets you know which resources might cost more than you've planned

FIGURE 16.4 *These reports track and sum up costs.*

Assignments Reports

The Assignments selection in the Reports dialog box displays four report types (see Figure 16.5). Although you can print much of the same information by printing a Gantt chart, these reports summarize the information in a more accessible format that's suitable for presentation. For example, you can print them out and bind them as part of a project plan to be distributed at a meeting.

Two of these reports provide particularly valuable management tools. The To-Do report List lets you prepare a list of all the scheduled tasks for a selected resource you select (when prompted) from the Using Resource dialog

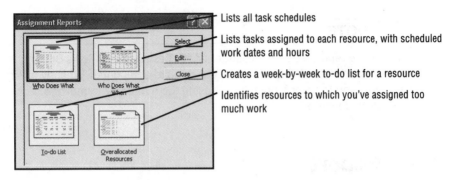

Lists all task schedules

Lists tasks assigned to each resource, with scheduled work dates and hours

Creates a week-by-week to-do list for a resource

Identifies resources to which you've assigned too much work

FIGURE 16.5 *Some reports allow you to provide information about task assignments.*

box. The Overallocated Resources report provides you with ammunition you might need to request more resources for a project—or for particular tasks— during a given time frame. It does this by showing when currently available resources have too many assignments.

 CAUTION

Surprisingly, when you generate a To-Do List report, it doesn't display the name of the resource for whom that list applies! My suggestion for handling this is to use the Page Setup button from the Print Preview of the report to add the resource's name into the report header or footer.

Workload Reports

While the Assignments reports focus on enabling you to view work schedules by resource, the two reports you get when you select Workload in the Reports dialog box enable you to examine the total workload scheduled during each week of the project. The schedule can be grouped by either task usage or resource usage (see Figure 16.6).

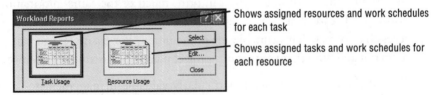

Shows assigned resources and work schedules for each task

Shows assigned tasks and work schedules for each resource

FIGURE 16.6 *These report options generate crosstab reports that summarize assignments.*

The Workload reports and some of the other reports you've seen are referred to as *crosstab reports* because they present information in rows and columns over intervals of time. At the intersection of each row and column is a cell with specific information about the resource or task listed in that row, on the date indicated by the selected column.

Selecting, Setting Up, and Printing a Report

As noted at the beginning of this chapter, the report creation process begins with the Reports dialog box. After you select the report you want, Project compiles the report information and displays the report onscreen in Print Preview mode. There you can make modifications to its layout before printing it out. This section describes how you can tackle these tasks.

 NOTE

Reports appear as a print preview only. The report information for a particular date cannot be stored in the project file. If you need to keep accurate records of how your project data appeared on particular dates, you can either save a copy of the project file on each date as needed or export the needed data on a particular date and capture it in another application.

To select the report you want to work with and print out, open the project file for which you want to create the report and then follow these steps:

1. Choose View, Reports. The Reports dialog box will appear. (Be sure that you expand all subtasks in the Gantt Chart view before printing the report. If you don't expand the subtasks, the report won't include detail information.)

2. In the Reports dialog box, select the category of report you want by double-clicking on a category icon. Project displays the dialog box for the report category you've selected.

3. Double-click the thumbnail icon for the type of report you want to use.

4. Some report types require you to specify a date or resource name (see Figure 16.7). If a date is requested, enter it in mm/dd/yy format. If the dialog box prompts you to select a resource, do so by using the drop-down list that's presented. After you specify either a date or a resource,

click on OK to finish. (Some report formats prompt you for another date. If this happens, enter the date and click on OK again to finish.)

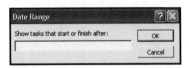

FIGURE 16.7 *Project may prompt you to specify a date or select a resource to report about.*

After you complete the preceding steps, Project compiles the report and presents it onscreen for viewing, fine-tuning, or printing.

But what if you've selected a report type that Project cannot compile, or you've entered a date for which there's no data to report? For example, if you try to print a report about Slipping Tasks from the Current Activities category, and there are no tasks that are behind schedule on the date for which you try to print the report, Project displays the dialog box shown in Figure 16.8. Click on OK to close the message dialog box, and Project returns you to the Reports dialog box so that you can try again. Select a different report type, or try specifying a different date for the report you want.

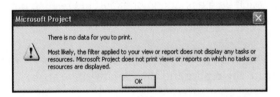

FIGURE 16.8 *This message tells you there's no information to print for the report or date you've specified.*

Whenever you want to close the preview area where the report appears, click on the Close button near the top of the screen. Project returns to the Reports dialog box. Click on the Cancel button to close that dialog box and return to the active view for the project file.

Navigating in the Report

The report you've selected appears onscreen in a Print Preview view, similar to the one you learned about in Chapter 14. This view offers a few special tools and icons that enable you to view different parts of the report, or to take a closer look at particular items in the report (see Figure 16.9).

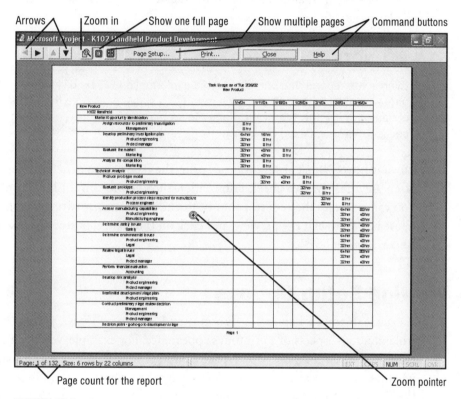

FIGURE 16.9 *Project offers special tools that enable you to work with a report preview.*

Use the left and right arrow keys to move forward and backward through the pages in the report. The up and down arrows are enabled only if there are too many rows to fit in a single report page. The extra rows appear on separate pages when the report is printed.

By default, you'll see one page of the report, shown at a size that keeps the whole page visible in the preview. However, you might want to zoom in to read particular details in the report before printing. You can click on the Zoom button at the top of the preview to zoom in on the upper-left corner of the report, or use the zoom pointer to zoom in on a specific cell. After you zoom in, click on the button for displaying one full page (the button has a page icon on it) to return to the default view.

If the report has more than one page and you want to view multiple pages, perhaps to see how the information is divided between pages, click on the button that looks like a stack of papers. Project displays multiple pages of the report onscreen. Again, to return to the default view, click on the button for displaying one full page.

 NOTE

Even some reports that contain very little information will be divided into two pages by default. To reduce such a report to a single page, use the Adjust To option on the Page tab of the Page Setup dialog box (covered in the next section, "Viewing Setup Options").

Obviously, you won't always want to print the reports you generate. Reports often are a fast way to check information such as the current budget total. You can generate the report, zoom in to check a detail or two, click on the Close button to exit the preview, and click on the Cancel button to close the Reports dialog box.

Viewing Setup Options

As you learned in Chapter 14, "Proofing and Printing a View," you can control numerous aspects of a printout's appearance. For example, you can adjust margins to allow for more or less space around printed data, or you can specify whether a page number appears on every page. You adjust these options using the Page Setup dialog box, which you open from the Print Preview by clicking on the Page Setup button at the top of the screen. The Page Setup dialog box for the report appears (see Figure 16.10).

Although the dialog box offers six tabs, two of them aren't available for many reports. These are the Legend and View tabs, which offer options that apply when you're printing certain charts and views. Additionally, other tabs may become disabled (grayed out) when you select a report type for which they don't apply. For example, you cannot adjust the header or footer for a Project Summary report.

As you learned in Chapter 14, when you want to change a Page Setup option in the Page Setup dialog box, first select the tab that offers the option, and

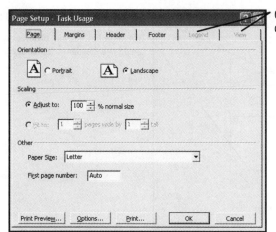

Grayed out tabs aren't available for the current printout

FIGURE 16.10 *This dialog box allows you to adjust how the final printout will look.*

then make your changes. Finally, click on OK to close the Page Setup dialog box (or click on Print to send the report to the printer). The four tabs of available Page Setup options for reports are as follows:

◆ **Page.** Enables you to specify whether the printout is wide (Landscape) or tall (Portrait). You can also scale the printed information by entering a size percentage, choose another paper size, or specify the page number to use for the first page of the report printout.

◆ **Margins.** Allows you to enter a separate margin measurement for each of the four edges of the page, or to specify a printed border for report pages.

◆ **Header.** Enables you to edit the header that appears at the top of the report pages (see Figure 16.11). You can specify what it contains (page number, company names, and so on) and whether it's centered or aligned left or right. (See Chapter 12 for more information about creating printout headers and footers.)

◆ **Footer.** Its options are similar to those found on the Header tab, but it places the specified text at the *bottom* of each printed report page.

Printing

After you check the Page Setup dialog box to ensure that you've chosen the report you need, and you've made any changes you want, you're ready to print your report. To initiate the print process, click on the Print button in either

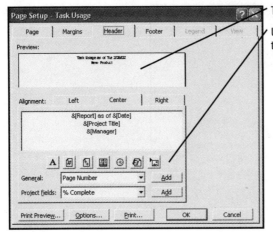

The header or footer is previewed here

Use these buttons and drop-down lists to add new header or footer contents

FIGURE 16.11   *You can specify the header for the report pages on the Header tab. The Footer tab is nearly identical.*

the Page Setup dialog box or the Print Preview screen. The Print dialog box will appear.

This dialog box is covered as part of Chapter 14's in-depth look at printing. However, a few of its options might be particularly attractive to you when you're printing reports:

◆ **Print Range.** By default, Project prints all pages in a report if it's more than one page. You might only want to print part of a report, however. To do so, click on the Page(s) From option button in the Print Range area, and then enter the starting page in the From text box and the final page in the To text box. For example, enter **4** and **5** to print only pages 4 and 5 of the report.

◆ **Copies.** To print more than one copy at a time (such as 10 copies to distribute at a meeting), change the Number Of Copies text box by double-clicking on the current entry and typing a new entry (such as **10**).

◆ **Timescale.** Normally, unless a report asks you for a particular timeframe by default, the report covers the full duration of the project schedule. If you want to print only the report pages that pertain to particular dates in the schedule, select the Dates From option button in the Timescale area. Then enter the starting date in the From box and the last date of the range you want to print in the To box. This helps you zero in on only the data that's relevant to you at a given time.

After you specify the options you want in the Print dialog box, click on OK. Project sends the report to the printer and closes the print preview for the report. To close the Reports dialog box, which reappears onscreen after printing, click on Cancel.

Creating a Custom Report

The sixth category icon in the Reports dialog box, the Custom button, allows you to control various features of any available report, create a new report based on an existing report, or build an entirely unique report to suit your needs. The features you can change vary depending on the report you start working with. For some reports, such as the Project Summary report, you can only change the font and text formatting to adjust the report's appearance. For other reports, Project displays a dialog box enabling you to edit the report's name, the time period it covers, the table it's based upon, filtering, and more.

To change, copy, or create a custom report, double-click on the Custom option in the Reports dialog box to open the Custom Reports dialog box (see Figure 16.12). The scrolling Reports list in this dialog box enables you to select a report to customize, if needed.

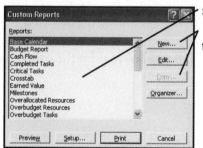

Select the report to work with . . .

. . . and then click on a button to specify how you'd like to work with it

FIGURE 16.12 *The Custom Reports dialog box enables you to show and format specific report information.*

After you select a report in the Reports list, click the Preview button to display the selected report in Print Preview mode, click the Setup button to go to the Page Setup dialog box for the report, or click the Print button to go to the Print dialog box for the report. After selecting one of these buttons, you can work with the preview, setup, or printing options for the report just as described previously in this chapter. Click on Cancel to close the Custom Reports dialog box, and then click on Cancel again to close the Reports dialog box.

Making Changes to an Existing Report

If you want to customize a report and get both the contents and formatting you need, the fastest way is to choose the report that most closely resembles what you want and then make changes to it. To start this process, click on the name of the report to edit in the Reports list of the Custom Reports dialog box. Then click on the Edit button. Alternately, you can click on the icon for a report in the dialog box for that report category, and then click on the Edit button (refer to Figures 16.2 through 16.6).

What happens next depends on the report you've selected for editing. If it's the Base Calendar or Project Summary report, Project only allows you to change the fonts specified for the report, and therefore gives you the Report Text dialog box shown in Figure 16.13. Use the Item To Change drop-down list if you want the change to apply only to the Calendar Name or Detail information in the report. Then use the Font, Font Style, and Size lists to select the text attributes you want. The sample area shows a preview of what your selections will look like when applied to text in the report. To underline the text, for example, select the Underline check box. To specify a color for text, use the Color drop-down list. After you've made the desired font selections, click on OK to implement your changes and return to the Custom Reports dialog box. From there, you can preview or print the edited report.

Choose which report text to change

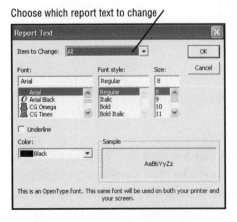

FIGURE 16.13 *For some reports, you can change only the appearance of the text.*

> ● **CAUTION**
>
> After you make changes to a report offered in your project file, those changes remain in effect until you specifically return the report to its original format. There's always a chance, however, that you might forget what the original format was. If you're planning to make major changes to a report, you're always safer working from a copy of the original report (as described next), rather than working from the original.

For other reports you select from the Reports list, a different dialog box appears when you click on the Edit button. Depending on the selected report type, the dialog box that appears is named Task Report, Resource Report, or Crosstab Report. Each of these dialog boxes has three tabs, but the tab contents vary slightly, depending on the report category (as described next). After you specify the options you want in one of these dialog boxes, click on OK to implement your changes. From the Custom Reports dialog box, you then can preview, set up, or print the report.

Task Reports

A *task report* generally has the word "task" or "what" in its name in the Reports list of the Custom Reports dialog box. When you select one of these reports and then click on the Edit button, the Task Report dialog box appears (see Figure 16.14). The first tab of this dialog box, the Definition tab, enables you to work with the most basic information about the report, such as the report name. You might want to change the report name to reflect your changes, perhaps calling it "Weekly Budget Report" instead of simply "Budget Report." This tab also allows you to control the time frame for which information is reported, and to specify whether or not to apply a filter to display only some tasks in the project. (Chapter 13, "Working with the Different Project Views," covers filtering in detail.)

After you set the project definition options, click on the Details tab. The options on this tab (see Figure 16.15) control which details appear for the tasks you've chosen to display using the Definition tab.

Finally, click on the Sort tab to determine how to sort the tasks that appear in your report. Display the Sort By drop-down list (see Figure 16.16). Then choose the name of the field that contains the information you want to sort by. Select Ascending or Descending to specify whether the information is

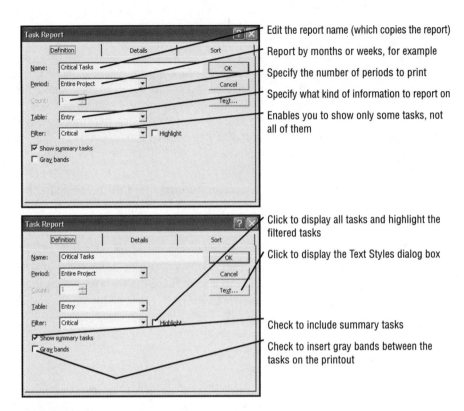

Edit the report name (which copies the report)

Report by months or weeks, for example

Specify the number of periods to print

Specify what kind of information to report on

Enables you to show only some tasks, not all of them

Click to display all tasks and highlight the filtered tasks

Click to display the Text Styles dialog box

Check to include summary tasks

Check to insert gray bands between the tasks on the printout

FIGURE 16.14 *Use the Task Report dialog box to specify key information for a task report.*

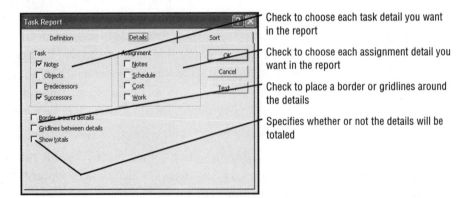

Check to choose each task detail you want in the report

Check to choose each assignment detail you want in the report

Check to place a border or gridlines around the details

Specifies whether or not the details will be totaled

FIGURE 16.15 *Here's where you specify which details appear in the report.*

sorted in A–Z order (lowest-to-highest) or Z–A order (highest-to-lowest). For example, by default the Budget Report lists the most costly tasks first, but you might want to see the least expensive items first.

To sort by other fields as well, use the additional drop-down lists provided on this tab. To specify that there's no field to sort by for one of the Then By drop-down lists in the Sort tab, select the blank line at the top of the drop-down list.

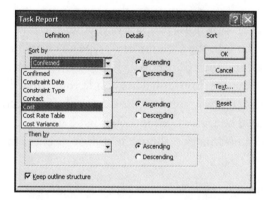

FIGURE 16.16 *The final touch in organizing your report is to sort it.*

Resource Reports

A *resource report* provides information about resources, and generally it includes the word "resource" or "who" in its name. For example, the Overallocated Resources and Who Does What reports are both resource reports.

When you select a resource report from the Reports list in the Custom Reports dialog box and then click on the Edit button, the Resource Report dialog box appears. This dialog box offers three tabs that look and work exactly like the tabs for the Task Report dialog box (refer to Figures 16.14 through 16.16).

 NOTE

You can edit a resource report so that it shows resource cost rate tables, and then print that report. To do so, click on the Resource report in the Reports list of the Custom Reports dialog box, and then click on Edit. Click on the Details tab to select it, and then click on the Cost check box to select it. Click on OK, and then click on the Preview button in the Custom Reports dialog box to display the edited report onscreen.

Crosstab Reports

A *crosstab report* is the last type of custom report you might want to customize. These reports summarize information in a grid of rows and columns and include reports such as Cash Flow. When you select a crosstab report from the Reports list in the Custom Reports dialog box and then click on the Edit button, the Crosstab Report dialog box appears (see Figure 16.17).

You'll notice that the first tab here differs from that for the two previous report types. Use the Row drop-down list to specify whether the rows contain task or resource information. In the Column area, type an entry for how many units of time to display, and then (if needed) change the time unit type to something like **Months** using the drop-down list beside your entry. These choices determine how many columns appear in the crosstab (for example, eight weeks or two months). Then, in the drop-down list below your time selections, select what kind of information about the task or resource to display in each column below the date.

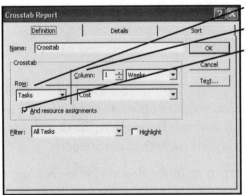

Specify what appears in each row

Specify what appears in each column

Specify whether to include assignments with the row information

FIGURE 16.17 *The Definition options for a crosstab report differ from those of other report types.*

The Details tab also offers a couple of unique choices for crosstab reports. On this tab, select the Show Zero Values check box if you want to have zeros displayed rather than blank cells. Make sure that the Repeat First Column On Every Page option is selected if you want to repeat the names of the listed tasks or resources on every report page for easier reference. Finally, use the Date Format drop-down list to control the appearance of any dates listed for your crosstab report.

The Sort tab for crosstab reports works just like the Sort tab for the Task Report dialog box (refer to Figure 16.16).

Creating a Report Based on an Existing Report

If you want to leave an existing report intact but create a new report based on it, follow these steps:

1. Open the Custom Reports dialog box.

2. In the Reports list, select the name of the report that you want to use as the basis for your custom report.

3. Click on the Copy button. Depending on the type of report you've selected, the appropriate Report dialog box (such as the Task Report dialog box) will appear.

4. In the Name text box of the Report dialog box, Project shows "Copy of" plus the name of the report you selected in Step 2. Be sure to edit this name to ensure that your custom report has a name you'll recognize. For example, you might edit it to read **Monthly Budget Report** if that's the kind of report you're creating.

5. Make any changes you desire to the various options in the three tabs of the Report dialog box, and make any font changes using the Text button.

6. Click on OK. Your custom report appears, with the name you gave it, in the Reports list of the Custom Reports dialog box (see Figure 16.18).

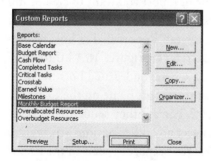

FIGURE 16.18 *The highlighted report name is the custom report I've created based on the Budget report.*

Saving a Unique Report

If you ever want to define a new report completely from scratch to avoid the possibility of making an unwanted change to one of your existing reports, click on the New button in the Custom Reports dialog box. The Define New Report dialog box appears (see Figure 16.19).

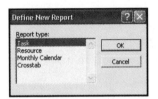

FIGURE 16.19 *This dialog box enables you to build a report from scratch.*

 NOTE

Custom reports that you create are saved with the current project file until you either copy them to Project's GLOBAL.MPT master file, copy them to another project file, or delete them. To make a report available to all files or to delete a report, click on the Organizer button in the Custom Reports dialog box and then use the Reports tab to make your changes. Chapter 13, "Working with the Different Project Views," discusses working with the Organizer.

In the Report Type list, select the type of report you want to create, and then click on OK. If you select Task, Resource, or Crosstab, Project displays the Task Report, Resource Report, or Crosstab Report dialog box, respectively. You work in any of these dialog boxes (refer to Figures 16.14 through 16.16) just as described earlier in this chapter, when you learned how to edit different types of reports. Make sure to edit the report name on the Definition tab (it starts out as "Report 1," "Report 2," or another sequentially numbered name) to make it more descriptive. Select any other options you want on the applicable tabs, and then click on OK. Your report appears in the Reports list of the Custom Reports dialog box.

If you select the Monthly Calendar choice from the Define New Report dialog box, Project displays the Monthly Calendar Report Definition dialog box, as shown in Figure 16.20. Most of the options in this dialog box work just like options you've seen on various tabs of the Report dialog boxes. Some options, however, are unique to calendar formats.

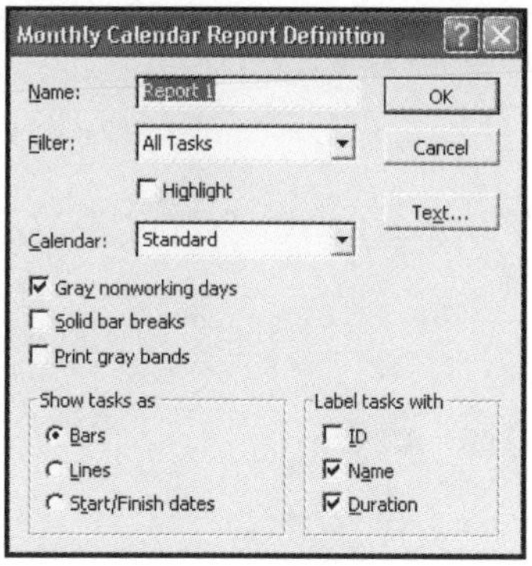

FIGURE 16.20   *This dialog box offers some options that are particular to calendar reports.*

For example, use the Calendar drop-down list to specify whether the calendar is based on one of the default schedule base calendars (Standard, Night Shift, or 24 Hours), a custom base calendar you have created, or the calendar for a particular resource. Use the Solid Bar Breaks and Show Tasks As options to specify whether or not to gray out nonworking days, and to control how the bars representing tasks appear on the report. Finally, use the Label Tasks With check boxes to specify whether each task is identified with its ID number, task name, or task duration (or any combination of these pieces of information).

When you finish setting all these options, click on OK to close the Monthly Calendar Report Definition dialog box and add your new calendar report to the Reports list of the Custom Reports dialog box.

Chapter 17

Other Formatting

In This Chapter

◆ Changing the appearance of selected text in a Task Sheet or Resource Sheet

◆ Working with a single chart bar or box

◆ Controlling progress lines and gridlines that appear on a chart

◆ Adjusting the appearance of a particular style of sheet text or a particular style of chart bar or box

◆ Controlling the display of details and choosing a layout for links

◆ Working with Project's drawing tools

When you're learning how to use Project, the way that text and other elements look may be the furthest thing from your mind. At first, you worry about setting the schedules for your tasks, figuring out how different kinds of links work, determining how to allocate resources most effectively, and working out any kinks that unnecessarily extend your overall schedule.

After you get all that settled, however, you may begin to look at your schedule in a new light. You may become more interested in ensuring that your schedule is not only accurate but attractive, and that it also highlights key facts clearly. This chapter examines the tools that enable you to control the appearance of information in Project.

 TIP

Consider leaving Project's original views intact and using the techniques described in this chapter to make changes to custom views that you create. That way, you'll be able to revert to the desired default view at any time.

Formatting Selected Sheet Text

Fonts are different types of lettering used for text. Within Project, you can select a different font—along with a particular font size, color, and so on—for any cell, row, or column that you select in a Task Sheet or Resource Sheet.

The fonts you can choose depend on the fonts that you installed to work with Windows on your system. When you reformat selected text, the formatting changes appear both onscreen and in printouts, including the formatted text.

 NOTE

Font sizes are measured in *points*. Each point is 1/72 inch; 12 points equal 1/6 inch. Unfortunately, you can't make an exact prediction about how much space a font will take up based on its point size. The number refers to the height of the letters rather than their width, and some fonts are much denser than others. If the text isn't fitting the way you prefer, try a different font.

An easy way to apply formatting to selected text is to use the tools in the Formatting toolbar, shown in Figure 17.1. To display the Formatting toolbar if you've removed it from the screen, right-click on any toolbar and then click on Formatting. If you plan to do a lot of formatting, you can drag the Formatting toolbar into its own toolbar window or onto its own row below the Standard toolbar, as illustrated in Figure 17.1.

Note that the three alignment buttons—Align Left, Center, and Align Right—realign all cells in the sheet column, even if you have selected a single cell in the column. If you select a single row and then click on an alignment button, all columns in the sheet are realigned.

In addition to using the Formatting toolbar, you can format text by using the Font dialog box:

1. Select the cell that contains the text you want to format. Alternately, click on a column header to select the entire column, or click on a row header to select the entire row.

2. Choose Format, Font, or right-click and then click on Font in the shortcut menu. The Font dialog box will appear (see Figure 17.2).

3. Scroll the Font list and select the font you want to use.

4. If you want to format the text with an effect such as bold or italic, select the effect from the Font Style list.

5. Scroll the Size list and select the font size you want to use, or double-click on the Size text box and type the appropriate size.

6. If you want to apply an underline to the selected text, click on the Underline check box to check it.

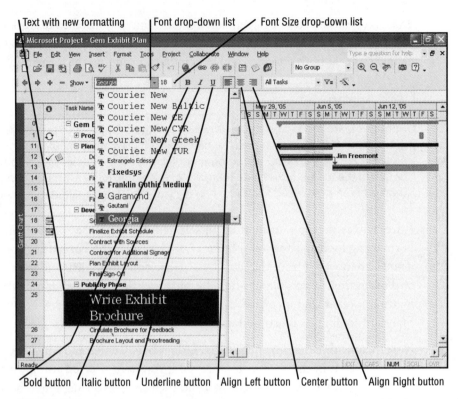

Text with new formatting   Font drop-down list   Font Size drop-down list

Bold button   Italic button   Underline button   Align Left button   Center button   Align Right button

FIGURE 17.1   *Select text in a Task Sheet or Resource Sheet, and then use a tool in the Formatting toolbar to change its appearance.*

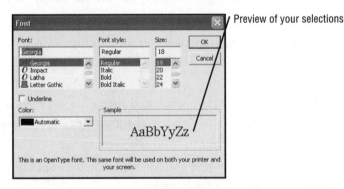

Preview of your selections

FIGURE 17.2   *The Font dialog box enables you to specify formatting for selected text.*

7. If you want to format the selected text with a particular color (perhaps to call more attention to it onscreen or in color printouts), select the color from the Color drop-down list.

8. Click on OK to close the Font dialog box and apply your selections.

If you've added several formatting selections to some text, and you'd like to use those same settings for other cells in the sheet, you can quickly copy all the formatting selections to other cells with the Format Painter button on the Standard toolbar. Select the cell that holds the formatting to copy, click on the Format Painter button, and then click on the cell to which you want to apply the formatting settings.

Formatting the Bar for a Selected Task

Just as you can use formatting selections to call attention to specific text in a Task Sheet or Resource Sheet, you can reformat the Gantt bars for selected tasks in your schedule. Suppose that you want to call attention to the Gantt bars for all the tasks that begin next week. You could make each of those bars yellow so that they're brighter onscreen or in a printout. Alternately, you could include the text of a particular field of task information (such as the Actual Start date) in the Gantt Chart bar.

To adjust formatting options for one or more Gantt bars, follow these steps:

1. Click on the Task Name cell to select the task you want to reformat, or select row headers (or adjoining cells) to select multiple rows.

 TIP

If you want to skip Step 1 and use the Format Bar dialog box to reformat a single Gantt bar, double-click on the Gantt bar itself. If you've marked the task as partially completed, be sure to double-click on the edge of the larger Gantt bar, not the smaller bar marking the completed work.

2. Choose Format, Bar. The Format Bar dialog box will appear (see Figure 17.3).

3. Click on the Bar Shape tab, if needed, to display the Bar Shape options. This tab enables you to specify the appearance of the selected Gantt bars, including overall thickness, color, and ending shapes or symbols.

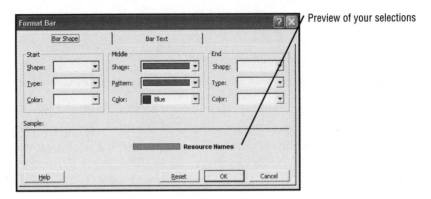

Preview of your selections

FIGURE 17.3 *The Format Bar dialog box contains numerous options for formatting selected Gantt bars.*

4. To add a symbol to the left end of the selected bar(s), select the desired symbol from the Shape drop-down list in the Start Shape area. (If you leave this option blank, the Start Shape will be invisible.) Then use the Type drop-down list to specify the ending fill pattern, such as Solid. Finally, to apply a color to the selected Start Shape, select that color from the Color drop-down list. Figure 17.4 shows some possible Start Shape selections.

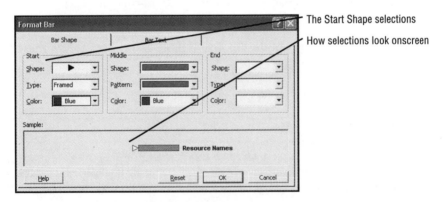

The Start Shape selections

How selections look onscreen

FIGURE 17.4 *I've added a start shape for the selected Gantt bar.*

5. In the End Shape area of the dialog box, use the Shape, Type, and Color drop-down lists to specify and format a shape for the right end of the selected Gantt bars. These options work the same as the corresponding options in the Start Shape area.

NOTE

The Start Shape and End Shape settings do not have to match.

6. In the Middle Bar area, specify how the center of the selected bars will look. The Shape drop-down list enables you to specify how thick you want a bar to be and how you want to position it in relation to the start and end shapes—slightly up or down, or centered.

7. If the bar shape that you specified is more than a thin line, use the Pattern drop-down list to adjust the relative density and hatching of the color used for the bar.

8. Select a color for the bar. Figure 17.5 shows some selected bar shapes.

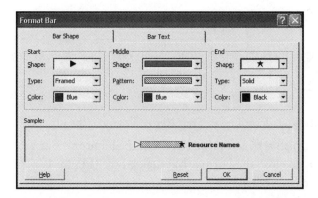

FIGURE 17.5 *The final result of my bar color and shape adjustments.*

9. Click on the Bar Text tab to display the Bar Text options. You use this tab to specify how you want to display text in relation to the selected Gantt bars: Left, Right, Top, Bottom, or Inside. The tab offers a separate line for each of these options. You can enter text in any of them or a combination of them. (By default, resource names are displayed to the right of each bar.)

10. To add text that will appear with a particular part of the bar, click on the cell beside the area name. Then select the field of information to display with the Gantt bar from the drop-down list of fields (see Figure 17.6).

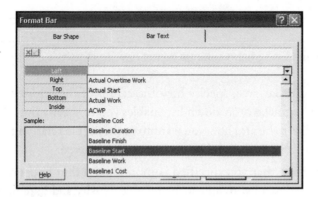

FIGURE 17.6   *You can specify a field of text to appear at the left end of the Gantt bar.*

TIP

If you want to remove text from a particular display area, highlight the existing field name, delete it, and then click on the Enter button that appears in the upper-left corner of the tab.

11. Use the technique described in Step 10 to edit any of the other text areas.

12. When you finish setting options in the Bar Shape and Bar Text tabs, click on OK to close the Format Bar dialog box. (Figure 17.7 shows a sample formatted bar.)

To return a Gantt bar to its default formatting, select the bar, open the Format Bar dialog box, and click on the Reset button on either tab.

Formatting a Progress Line

Chapter 11, "Comparing Progress versus Your Baseline Plan," introduced the Project feature called *progress lines*. You add a progress line to a particular date on the Gantt chart to highlight in-progress tasks and to provide a graphical representation of which tasks have not been completed by that date, or which are ahead of schedule. By default, the progress line for the current date or project status date (if you've displayed it) is red and has circular shapes at each point on the line. Progress lines for other dates are black and have no graphics. Because progress lines contribute to the appearance of your project screens,

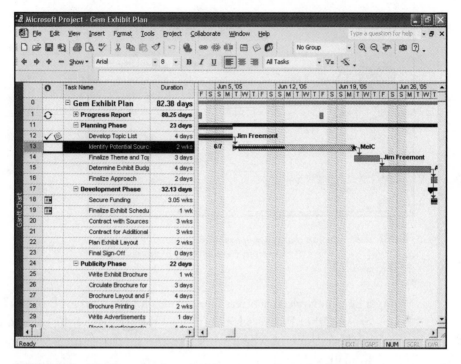

FIGURE 17.7   *The Gantt bar for task 13 has new starting and ending markers, a patterned bar, and new labels.*

you'll want to be able to enhance them as needed for clarity and eye appeal. For example, you can change the pattern or color of a progress line.

Follow these steps to change the appearance of progress lines on your Gantt chart:

1. Right-click on the Gantt chart and click on Progress Lines. The Progress Lines dialog box appears.

2. Click on the Line Styles tab to display its options, as shown in Figure 17.8.

3. Click on one of the designs shown in the Progress Line Type area to change the overall shape of the progress lines. The choices here enable you to specify whether the progress line points are sharp angles or blunted shapes. Also, choose whether the progress line itself moves straight from point to point or returns to travel along the progress line date.

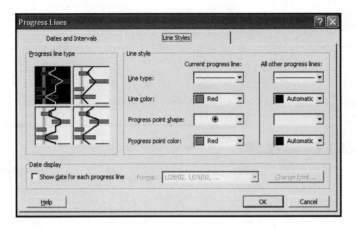

FIGURE 17.8 *You can change the appearance of progress lines with the settings shown here. For example, you can choose a different color for progress lines.*

4. The Line Style area offers four settings for the Current Progress Line or All Other Progress Lines (change the settings in the column that applies), some of which work like the similar settings you saw for formatting Gantt bars:

◆ **Line Type.** Choose a dashed line style (or no line at all) for the actual line that travels between progress line points.

◆ **Line Color.** Choose a color for the progress line.

◆ **Progress Point Shape.** Choose a shape (or no shape) to appear at each progress line point.

◆ **Progress Point Color.** Choose a color for the progress point shape you selected, to make that shape stand out from its progress line or the Gantt bar to which it points.

5. If you want a date to appear at the top of each progress line to identify the progress date being charted, check the Show Date for Each Progress Line check box. Then you can open the Format drop-down list to select another date format for the displayed date, such as **Jan 28, '02.** Click on the Change Font button to open the Font dialog box, and choose a different font for the displayed dates on the progress lines. This Font dialog box works as described earlier in this chapter.

6. Click on OK to apply your changes and change the display of the progress lines. Figure 17.9 shows some example progress lines that I've reformatted.

Other progress lines now have shapes

Dates added

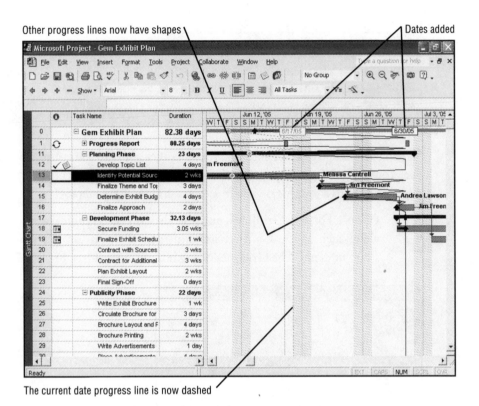

The current date progress line is now dashed

FIGURE 17.9 *Reformatting progress lines makes them more distinct and attractive.*

Working with Gridlines

Gridlines in Project, like gridlines in other applications that display graphical information, help your eye determine whether objects line up or where particular measurements occur. If you add gridlines to separate Gantt bars, you can easily tell which Gantt bars align with which Task Sheet rows. By default, the timescale in Gantt Chart view shows vertical gridlines that identify the major columns, which generally represent workweeks.

Some gridlines are horizontal, such as those that identify Gantt bar rows. Other gridlines are vertical. Generally, if the items for which you want to add gridlines appear in rows, the gridlines will be horizontal. If the items for which you want to add gridlines are organized in columns, the gridlines will be vertical.

NOTE

The lines that separate the rows and columns in Task Sheets and Resource Sheets are also considered to be gridlines and can be removed or reformatted. These gridlines are identified as the Sheet Rows and Sheet Columns options in the Line To Change list of the Gridlines dialog box.

When you change gridline settings, your changes apply to the entire schedule file. You can't change only the gridlines that correspond to selected tasks. To add gridlines to a graphical view in Project, follow these steps:

1. Choose Format, Gridlines, or right-click on the graphical area of the view (such as the Gantt chart) and then click on Gridlines on the shortcut menu. The Gridlines dialog box will appear (see Figure 17.10).

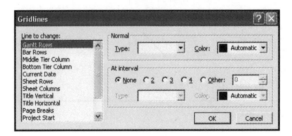

FIGURE 17.10 *The Gridlines dialog box enables you to add gridlines to the Gantt chart area of your view.*

2. In the Line To Change list, select the item for which you want to add or edit a gridline. If the selected item already has some type of gridline applied, the specified formatting options for that gridline appear on the right side of the dialog box.

3. In the Normal area (the upper-right portion of the dialog box), specify the gridlines that you want for your Line To Change choices. Use the Type drop-down list to select the overall gridline appearance, such as dotted or dashed. Use the Color drop-down list to apply a color to the gridlines.

 NOTE

If you want to remove displayed gridlines for the selected Line To change item, select the blank option at the top of the Type list. If you want gridlines to appear at intervals and not for every column or row, make sure that no line Type is selected.

4. In the At Interval area, you can specify the appearance of gridlines at a specified interval. If the normal gridlines are black, for example, you may want every fourth gridline to be red. Click on the 2, 3, 4, or Other option button (and edit the default Other value, if necessary) to specify which gridlines should use the alternative formatting. Then select the alternative gridline Type and Color.

5. Click on OK to close the dialog box and display your gridlines.

Figure 17.11 shows dotted gridlines used to separate Gantt rows. Every fifth gridline is a solid red line.

Dotted Normal gridlines   Every fifth gridline is a solid red line

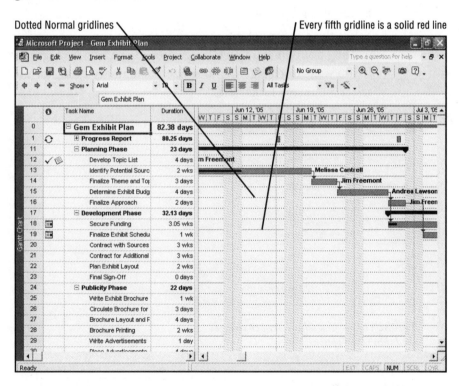

FIGURE 17.11   *This Gantt chart shows gridlines separating the Gantt bar lines.*

Formatting Text Styles

Based on the information you add to your schedule, Project classifies certain tasks based on their impact. The program marks all tasks on the critical path as being critical tasks, for example, and treats summary tasks differently from subtasks. Even though Project can track task categories easily, tracking might be a bit more difficult for you. To make the job easier, Project enables you to apply special text formatting to any category of task or resource information in the Task Sheet or Resource Sheet. In Project, when you apply formatting to a particular category of information, you're defining a special text style. To work with a text style, follow these steps:

1. Display the view that includes the Task Sheet or Resource Sheet to which you want to apply the style.

2. Choose Format, Text Styles. Alternately, select a column, right-click on it, and then click on Text Styles on the shortcut menu. The Text Styles dialog box appears.

3. Select the category of information for which you want to adjust formatting from the Item To Change drop-down list (see Figure 17.12). If you want to change the font size of summary tasks, for example, select Summary Tasks here.

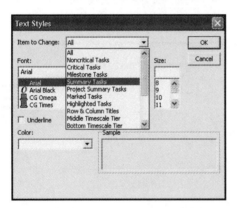

FIGURE 17.12 *You select a style to change and then set its options.*

 NOTE

The Item To Change list contains such items as column and row heads. The list is rather long, so check out everything that you can change.

4. Specify the text-formatting options for this category of information, just as you did for selected sheet text in the "Formatting Selected Sheet Text" section earlier in this chapter. The text-formatting options here work just like those you saw in Figure 17.2.

5. (Optional) If you want to set the formatting for other categories of information, repeat Steps 3 and 4.

6. Click on OK to close the Text Styles dialog box and apply the styles. All text in that category displays your formatting changes. (Figure 17.13 shows an increased font size for summary tasks.)

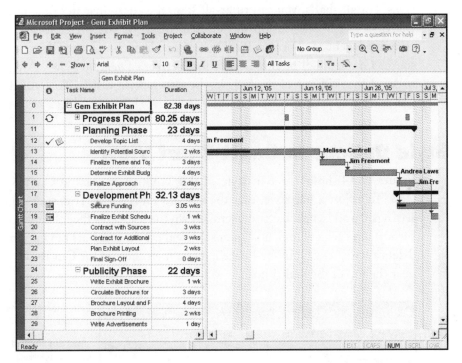

FIGURE 17.13 *The summary tasks in rows 1, 11, 17, and 24 now appear in a larger font size.*

Adjusting the Bar or Box Styles for Charts

Just as Project applies a particular style of text to different categories of tasks or resources, it applies a particular style of formatting to the corresponding charted information. The adjustments that you can make in charted information depend on the selected view in Project. The formatting options are different for Calendar view bars, Gantt Chart view bars, Network Diagram view boxes, and Resource Graph bars. The following sections provide an overview of the most important options for each type of display.

The formatting options that are available for bars and boxes vary, depending on whether the graphical information appears in a combination view or in a single pane. The options also might change based on the type of information displayed.

For all views but Calendar view, you can by double-click on the chart area to open a dialog box that contains the appropriate bar or box-formatting options. For all charts, you can right-click on the chart area and then click on Bar Styles or Box Styles on the shortcut menu. If you prefer to use menu commands, choose Format, Bar Styles (for Calendar, Gantt Chart, or Resource Graph view) or Box Styles (for Network Diagram view). After you make changes in one of these dialog boxes, click on OK to close the dialog box and apply your selections to the appropriate bars and boxes.

Style Options in Gantt Chart View

Figure 17.14 shows the Bar Styles dialog box that appears in Gantt Chart view. To adjust a bar style, edit the column entries and Text and Bars tab settings. To add a new bar style, scroll down the list, enter the information for the style in each column, and then specify the Text and Bars tab options. To delete a style, select it in the Name list and then click on the Cut Row button near the top of the dialog box.

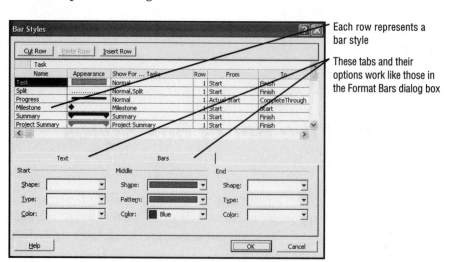

Each row represents a bar style

These tabs and their options work like those in the Format Bars dialog box

FIGURE 17.14   *These options enable you to adjust Gantt bar styles.*

Figure 17.15 shows an example of the formatting possibilities for the summary task bars.

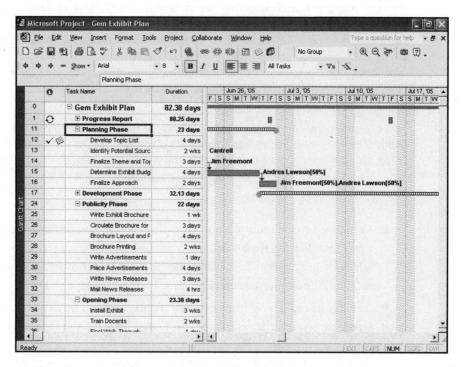

FIGURE 17.15 *This example shows reformatted Gantt bars for summary tasks.*

Not all the style columns are self-explanatory, so the following list reviews them:

- ◆ The **Name** column displays the name you enter for the style.
- ◆ The **Appearance** column displays the style's settings, which you specify by using the Text and Bars tabs at the bottom of the dialog box.
- ◆ The **Show For... Tasks** column specifies which fields or types of tasks the bars represent. Use the drop-down list to select a field. (You could create a bar style that applies to tasks Not Started Yet, for example.) If you want to add multiple fields, type a comma in the text box after the last listed field and then select an additional field from the drop-down list.

NOTE

You can use the placeholder Flag fields (Flag1, Flag2, and so on)—which offer Yes/No pick lists—to create a unique bar style. Let's say you want the Gantt bars to use a particular color based on the department handling the tasks. You would set up a Flag field for each department, add the fields to a new table, and then select Yes in the appropriate department field for each task. Then, to create each bar style, add a new row in the Bar Styles dialog box. You can name the bar and adjust its color as you like.

The choices in the Show For... Tasks column tell Project when to use the bar style for the selected department. Open the drop-down list in the Show For... Tasks column and select Normal. Then type a comma, open the drop-down list again, and select the flag field representing the department for which you're adding the bar style.

◆ When you create multiple bars for each task, you also can enter a value other than 1 in the **Row** column to position one of the bar styles. Generally, a value greater than 1 places the new bar below other bars for the task, and it may insert space depending on the bar shape you've selected.

◆ The **From** and **To** columns can also display fields. The fields that you select determine the length of the Gantt bars for the style. For the Not Started Yet bars, for example, you might want to specify Baseline Start in the From column, and Start (for the currently scheduled starting date) in the To column. Those options draw a bar that leads up to the default bar for the task. Use the drop-down list at the far right of the text box to make your entries for these columns. However, for milestones, the From and To columns should show the same time period. For example, it might be From *Start* To *Start*.

Style Options in Calendar View

If you displayed the Bar Styles dialog box in Calendar view, select a Task type from the list in the upper-left corner. Then choose the various Bar shape options (which work just like those for Gantt charts). This dialog box offers a few options that are unique to Calendar view (see Figure 17.16):

◆ Use the **Split Pattern** drop-down list to specify whether you want a dashed, dotted, or solid line, or no line, between the bar segments for split tasks.

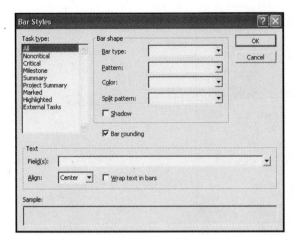

FIGURE 17.16   *Change the bar styles for Calendar view by using these options.*

◆ If you choose the **Shadow** option, Project displays a drop shadow below the bars of that style to give them a 3-D appearance.

◆ The **Bar Rounding** option makes bars of that style appear in full-day increments, even when an actual task's duration is less than a full day.

◆ The **Field(s)** box enables you to specify which field information is used to label bars of the selected style. You can select fields from the drop-down list at the far-right side of the box. Again, you can separate multiple fields in the text box with commas.

◆ The **Align** options enable you to specify where in the bars the specified text should appear.

◆ The **Wrap Text In Bars** option allows the specified text to occupy more than one line, if necessary.

Style Options in Resource Graph View

Figure 17.17 shows the Bar Styles dialog box for Resource Graph view.

The options available in this dialog box vary radically, depending on whether this graph appears by itself or in the lower pane of a combination view. The Filtered Resources options apply only to filtered resources when the Resource Graph appears by itself onscreen or is in the top pane of a split window. Otherwise, the settings apply to all resources. The Resource options apply to the displayed resource.

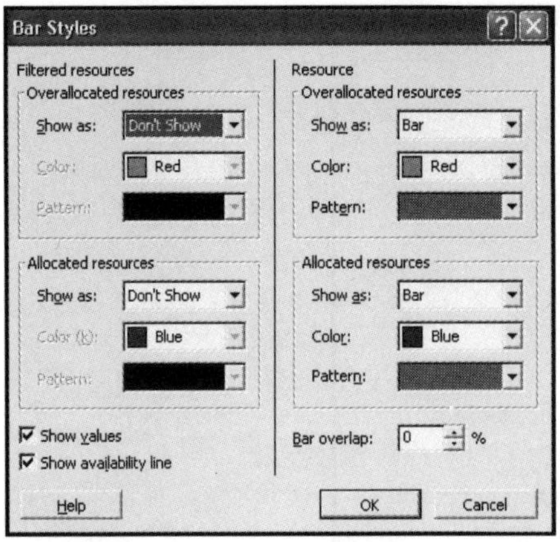

FIGURE 17.17 *Resource Graph view offers these bar-style options.*

Another factor that affects the options in this dialog box is which details you have chosen to display (see the "Working with Details" section later in this chapter). If you have chosen to display cost information in the graph, for example, the Bar Styles dialog box looks like Figure 17.18.

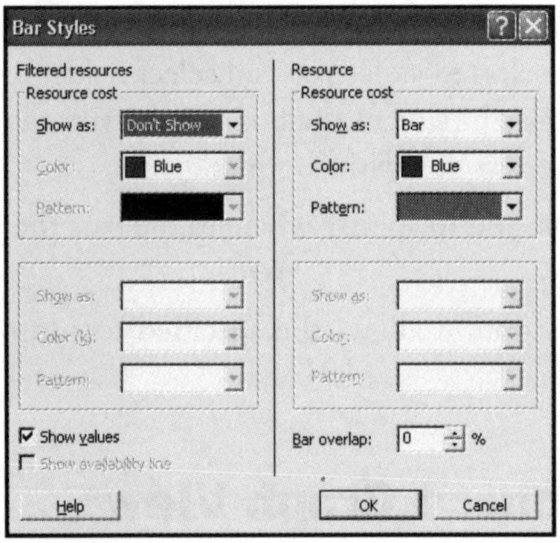

FIGURE 17.18 *The Resource Graph bar-style options have changed because cost information now appears in the graph.*

No matter which kinds of information you can format, the options are similar:

◆ Use any **Show As** drop-down list to specify whether the information appears as a bar, line, area, or other type of chart indicator.

◆ Select a color for the graphed information from the corresponding **Color** drop-down list.

◆ Select a pattern from the corresponding **Pattern** drop-down list.

◆ The **Show Values** option displays the values for the charted information at the bottom of the graph.

◆ The **Show Availability Line** option displays an indicator that shows whether the resource has any available working time. (This option is available when you're charting work information, as opposed to cost information.)

◆ If you want to display more than one type of bar for each time period in the graph, you can specify a **Bar Overlap %** option to allow the charted bars to overlap slightly. That way, more information fits into less horizontal space. Figure 17.19 shows bars with a 25 percent overlap. The legend at the left side of the display shows what each style of charted information means.

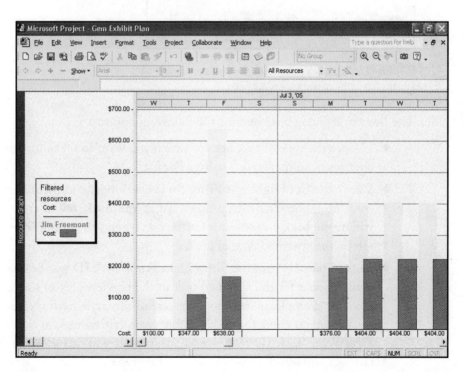

FIGURE 17.19 *Creating overlapping bars is only one of your options in Resource Graph view.*

Style Options in Network Diagram View

In Network Diagram view, you adjust box styles (instead of bar styles) by using the Box Styles dialog box shown in Figure 17.20.

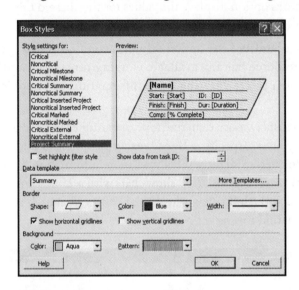

FIGURE 17.20   *Full Network Diagram view enables you to control the appearance of the boxes.*

The Box Style dialog box contains the following options:

◆ Choose the type of task box for which you want to make formatting changes from the **Style Settings For** list.

◆ Check the **Set Highlight Filter Style** check box, and then choose a color from the Color drop-down list in the Background area. This will be the background color for the box when you apply a filter that affects the specified type of task.

◆ Enter a task ID into the **Show Data From Task ID** text box to display the data for the specified task in the preview area of the dialog box. For example, if you chose Critical in the Style Settings For list, you'd want to enter the task number for a critical task in the Show Data From Task ID text box to ensure that you can see how your changes will affect a task of the specified type.

◆ By default, each Network Diagram node box is divided into seven cells. If you want to show other information, click on the **More Templates** button. Click on the New button in the Data Templates dialog box. Type a name for the new template in the Template Name text box. If you want to show more than three rows and columns of cells in each node, click on the Cell Layout button and use the settings in the Cell Layout dialog box to choose the number of cells, cell widths, and merging for blank cells. Then click on OK.

Back in the Data Template Definition dialog box, use the cells in the Choose Cell(s) area to define what field data to display. Click on each cell, and then choose the desired field from its drop-down list. At the bottom of the dialog box, use the Font button to choose font formatting for the cells. Change the Horizontal Alignment and Vertical Alignment settings using those drop-down lists, if needed. Use the Limit Cell Text To drop-down list to specify whether each cell can hold multiple lines of text. Check Show Label In Cell if you want the field name to appear.

Finally, if you've added fields that hold date information, choose a date format from the Date Format drop-down list. Click on OK to finish creating the new data template, and then click on Close to close the Data Templates dialog box. Back in the Box Styles dialog box, open the **Data Template** drop-down list and choose the name of your new template.

◆ Use the **Border** options to set up the box outline. Select the style of box (for a particular type of task) from the Shape drop-down list. Then select a color and width for the box outline using the drop-down lists. Clear the Show Horizontal Gridlines and Show Vertical Gridlines check boxes to remove the gridlines that separate the cells in the node box, if desired.

◆ Under **Background**, use the Color and Pattern drop-down lists to specify the fill for the box.

After you specify all the Box Styles settings for one type of Network Diagram node, you can choose another type of box from the Style Settings For list, and then choose its settings. After you finish making all the box formatting adjustments you want, click on OK to close the Box Styles dialog box and apply your changes.

Working with Details

In the "Graphing Individual Resource Work and Costs" section in Chapter 12, you learned that you can right-click on the graph area on the right side of Resource Graph view to open a shortcut menu, from which you select the information you want to view. You can select Percent Allocation, for example, to display a daily percentage of how much of the workday a resource will spend on a given task.

Similarly, you learned in Chapter 13 that you can right-click on any form in a combination view to open a shortcut menu that enables you to specify which information the form displays. In the lower pane of Task Entry view, for example, you can right-click on the form and then click on Predecessors & Successors on the shortcut menu. The form then displays information about all predecessor and successor tasks for the selected task.

The equivalent of these shortcut menus is the Details submenu of the Format menu (see Figure 17.21). This submenu becomes available only when you select a pane that can morph to display different information. The submenu

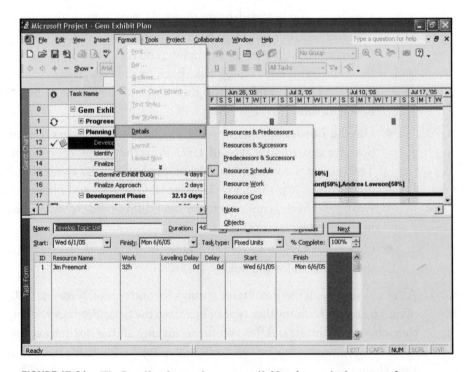

FIGURE 17.21 *The Details submenu becomes available when you're in a pane that can display various types of information.*

options vary depending on the nature of the selected pane. Simply select the type of information you want to display in the selected pane. The submenu closes, and the display changes accordingly.

Choosing a Layout

The layout features control how graphed bars appear in relation to one another in Calendar, Gantt Chart, and Network Diagram views. The layout options for bar and box styles vary, depending on the selected view. To display the layout options for one of these views, choose Format, Layout, or right-click on a blank space of the chart area and then click on Layout on the shortcut menu.

Layout Options in Calendar View

The layout options for Calendar view are simple, as Figure 17.22 shows. If you want each week to show more task information, select the Attempt To Fit As Many Tasks As Possible option. To ensure that bars for split tasks are divided into segments, make sure the Show Bar Splits check box is checked. Select the Automatic Layout option to tell Project to adjust the calendar to accommodate inserted and moved tasks.

 NOTE

As you might surmise from the presence of the Automatic Layout option in the Layout dialog box, Calendar view doesn't update automatically when you move or reschedule tasks in Gantt Chart view. Neither does Network Diagram view. If you need to update Calendar view or Network Diagram view to reflect the current schedule and task relationships, choose Format, Layout Now, or turn on the Automatic Layout option in the Layout dialog box.

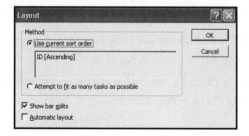

FIGURE 17.22 *The layout options are limited in Calendar view.*

Layout Options in Gantt Chart View

Figure 17.23 shows the Layout dialog box for Gantt Chart view.

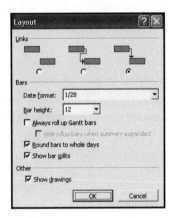

FIGURE 17.23   *The Gantt Chart view layout options enable you to control the appearance of links and more.*

This dialog box contains the following options:

◆ Select the **Links** option to specify how (and whether) you want task-link lines to appear.

◆ The options in the **Date Format** for Bars drop-down list enable you to control the display of any date information that accompanies Gantt bars.

◆ The **Bar Height** option enables you to make all bars (and their rows) larger or smaller.

◆ You can check the **Always Roll Up Gantt Bars** option to display rollup bars for individual subtasks on the corresponding summary task bar. Also check Hide Rollup Bars When Summary Expanded if you want to hide the rollup bars when the subtasks for the summary task are expanded (displayed) rather than collapsed.

◆ The **Round Bars To Whole Days** option tells Project to format each bar as a full day—even for, say, a three-hour task.

◆ To ensure that bars for split tasks are divided into segments, make sure the **Show Bar Splits** check box is checked.

◆ If you added a drawing to the Gantt chart area, make sure that the **Show Drawings** check box is selected so that the drawing appears. To hide the drawing temporarily (such as for printing), clear this check box.

Layout Options in Network Diagram View

Figure 17.24 shows the Layout dialog box for Network Diagram view.

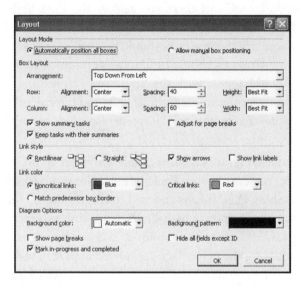

FIGURE 17.24   *These layout options are available for Network Diagram view.*

This dialog box contains the following options:

◆ Under **Layout Mode**, leave Automatically Position All Boxes selected to tell Project that boxes cannot be dragged on the chart. Check Allow Manual Box Positioning if you want to be able to drag boxes into the position you desire on the chart.

◆ Under **Box Layout**, use the Arrangement drop-down list to specify how Project arranges the node boxes. For example, you can choose Centered From Top rather than Top Down From Left, the default. Then, use the Row and Column Alignment, Spacing, and Height/ Width choices to adjust how the boxes align within the specified arrangement. Clear the Show Summary Tasks check box if you want to hide the node boxes for summary tasks. If you leave summary tasks enabled, however, you may want to check the Keep Tasks With Their Summaries check box to keep summary tasks and subtasks together on the diagram. Make sure that the Adjust For Page Breaks option is selected. Later, when you choose Format, Layout Now, Project moves task boxes that appear on a page break to one page or the next so that the box doesn't split in the printout.

◆ Just as you can do for a Gantt chart, you can use the **Link Style** and **Link Color** choices to specify how links appear on a Network Diagram chart. Choose whether the links should be rectilinear or straight. Check the Show Arrows and Show Link Labels options to indicate if those features should appear with the links. You can use the drop-down lists to specify a color for noncritical links and critical links. Or, to have each link use the formatting of its predecessor link, leave Match Predecessor Box Order selected instead.

◆ The settings under **Diagram Options** enable you to set up the overall chart appearance. You can choose a Background Color and Background Pattern. Leave Show Page Breaks checked to display dotted lines in the view so that you'll know which boxes will print together on a page. The Mark In-Progress And Completed check box determines whether lines marking the percentage completed appear in task node boxes. If you want to simplify the layout, you can check Hide All Fields Except ID, which changes all the node boxes so they display only the task ID number (task number).

Creating a Drawing in Project

In Chapter 21, "Using Project with Other Applications," you will learn how to insert a drawing from another application into your Gantt chart as an object. Although Project is by no means a drawing application, it includes some basic drawing tools that you can use to add simple graphics to your Gantt chart. You might want to display a box with some text to call attention to a particular task, for example. If you have a great deal of time, you can be creative and layer numerous drawn objects for a nice effect. By default, the drawn objects that you add will appear onscreen and in any printout of a view that contains your Gantt chart.

The drawing tools in Project work like those in Word, Excel, and many other Microsoft applications. An exhaustive discussion of drawing is beyond the scope of this book, but this section shows you how to draw objects, select and format them, and position them in relation to the correct date or task in the Gantt chart. Follow these steps:

1. In Gantt Chart view, scroll the chart to the blank area where you want to create the drawing.

2. Display the Drawing toolbar by choosing Insert, Drawing, or by right-clicking on any toolbar onscreen and then clicking on Drawing.

3. The seven buttons at the center of the Drawing toolbar—Line, Arrow, Rectangle, Oval, Arc, Polygon, and Text Box—enable you to create those objects. To use each of these buttons, just select the tool and then drag. (There are two exceptions. To use the Polygon button, you have to click for each point and double-click to finish. To use the Text Box button, you have to type in text.) When you finish drawing the object, release the mouse button (black selection handles appear around the object). Figure 17.25 shows an example of using the Oval tool.

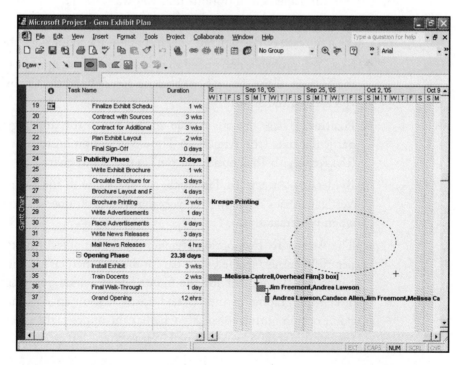

FIGURE 17.25 *Click on a drawing button, and then drag to create a shape.*

4. Double-click on the object you just drew. The Format Drawing dialog box appears (see Figure 17.26). Alternately, click on the object to select it (if it's not already selected), and then choose Format, Drawing, Properties.

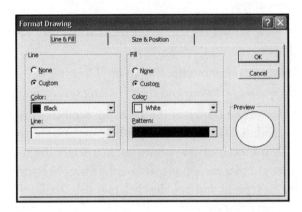

FIGURE 17.26 *Format an object with this dialog box.*

5. Choose the Line & Fill options that you want to use. The Preview area shows the result of your choices.

6. Click on the Size & Position tab, which contains the following options:

   ◆ **Size.** You probably don't need to worry about these options (near the bottom of the dialog box) because you defined the size when you created the object.

   ◆ **Position.** These options enable you to attach the drawing to a particular date (the Attach To Timescale option button) or task (the Attach To Task option button) in the Gantt chart.

   By default, Attach To Timescale is selected, with the Date and Vertical entries reflecting the way that you positioned the object when you created it.

   The Attach To Task option attaches the drawn object (by its upper-right corner) to the Gantt bar for the specified task in the list. Enter the ID number for the Gantt bar to which you want to attach the graphic in the ID text box. Click on an Attachment Point option button to specify whether the upper-right corner of the graphic should be positioned relative to the left or right end of the Gantt bar. Adjust the Horizontal and Vertical entries to control how close the upper-right corner of the graphic is to the specified end of the Gantt bar.

NOTE

I find using the Horizontal and Vertical entries counterintuitive. Entering higher values moves the graphic down and to the right of the Gantt bar. To move the graphic above or to the left of the Gantt bar, you need to enter negative values. For example, if you attach a graphic to the right end of the Gantt bar, you might need to enter –1.00 as the Vertical setting to place the graphic above the selected Gantt bar.

7. When you finish selecting options, click on OK to close the Format Drawing dialog box.

8. Create another object, if you want. Figure 17.27 shows a newly created text box.

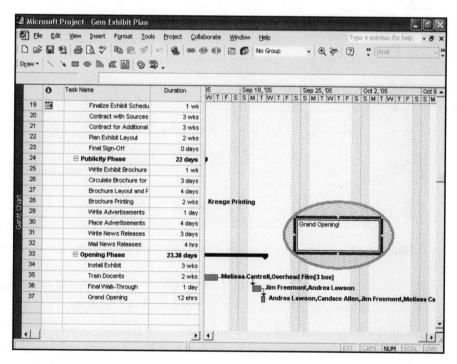

FIGURE 17.27 *This is a second new object.*

9. Double-click on the new object to set its formatting options. If you're adding a text box over an oval and you want the text to look like part of the oval, choose None for both the Line and Fill Color options (on the Line & Fill tab) in the Format Drawing dialog box. Close the dialog box.

10. You have to use a special method to format the text in a drawn text box. Click on the box to select it (you select any drawn object), and then drag over the text within the box to select (highlight) it. Next, choose Format, Font. Finally, use the Font dialog box to specify the formatting you want. Close the dialog box. Figure 17.28 shows the resulting text box.

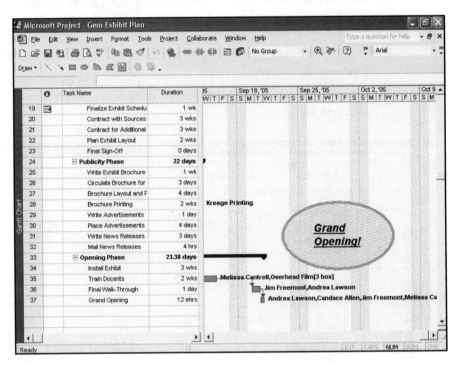

FIGURE 17.28 *A text box superimposed over another object can be an attention-getting reminder.*

11. Save the file to save your drawing on the Gantt chart. If you close the Project file without saving it, you lose your drawing.

The objects you draw appear in invisible layers, with the object drawn most recently appearing on the top layer. You can use the Bring To Front or Send To Back choices in the Draw menu on the Drawing toolbar to send the selected object to the top or bottom layer, respectively. If you want to move the selected drawing object up or back by a single layer, use the Move Forward or Move Backward commands.

PART V

Handling Multiple Projects

Chapter 18

Copying and Moving Project Information

In This Chapter

◆ Copying data between projects

◆ Moving data between projects

◆ Understanding how copying and moving affects task links

There's no shame in using shortcuts. In fact, smart businesspeople seek them out and use them as tools for repeating successes. If you wrote a new-sales-call follow-up letter that enabled you to close a sale, you'd be silly to write a new follow-up letter after the next call. Instead, you'd reuse as much of the letter that had already worked for you as you could.

When you have invested a good deal of time entering information about resources and certain kinds of tasks in Project, and you find that information to be valuable, you may want to reuse it. If different projects that you manage have similar tasks or use some of the same resources, you can save time by copying or moving information between those projects.

Copying Information between Projects

When you copy or move information in Windows applications, Windows places the information on the Clipboard—a holding area in your computer's memory. (When you copy something, it leaves the original information intact. When you move something, it deletes the original.) When you put data on the Clipboard, you can paste it into a new location or several locations. The file or location from which you copy or move information is called the *source,* and the place where you paste the information is called the *destination.*

The following sections show you how to copy information between two Project files. The steps that you take vary a bit, depending on whether you're copying all or only part of the information about a particular task or resource.

NOTE

You can copy and move information within a Project file as well. Simply select the information, cut or copy it, select another location for it in the Task Sheet or Resource Sheet, and then paste it into place.

Project 2002 does not use the Office Clipboard in Office XP. Each time you cut or copy a selection, Windows discards the prior contents of the Clipboard.

Copying Task and Resource Information between Projects

When you select and copy an entire task row (or multiple rows), the entire set of information related to that task from the current table is copied—such as the task name, resources assigned to that task, duration, start time, and so on for the Entry table of the Task Sheet. If you select two or more linked tasks and paste them into another project, the link information that connects the tasks is copied, too.

You can also copy resource information to other projects. Copying resource rows picks up all the fields defined in the current table of your Resource Sheet. If you frequently copy the same resource information to new projects, you can choose Tools, Resources, Share Resources to create a common set of resources that are available to multiple projects. To learn more about shared resources, see Chapter 20, "Consolidating Projects."

To copy tasks or resources between projects, follow these steps:

1. Open the files for the two projects in question, select the same view in each project window (Gantt Chart view, for example), select the same Task Sheet or Resource Sheet table in each view, and arrange the project windows so a portion of each window is visible. You can choose Window, Arrange All to tile the project windows automatically. Alternately, you can press Ctrl+F6 to toggle between the active files.

2. Select the entire task or resource row to copy by clicking on the row number. To select multiple consecutive rows, hold down the Shift key and click on each row heading. To select multiple nonconsecutive rows, hold down the Ctrl key and click on each row heading.

3. Open the Edit menu and click on Copy (Task) or Copy (Resource). Alternately, do one of the following: right-click on the selection and then click on Copy (Task) or Copy (Resource) in the shortcut menu, press Ctrl+C, or click on the Copy button on the Standard toolbar. (The command name reflects the type of information that you selected—task or resource.)

4. If you're copying the information to another Project file, click on a portion of the destination window (such as the title bar) to tell Project that you want to copy information to that file. Then select the first cell of the row in which you want to place the copied information. No need to create a new row—Project does not paste the information over the contents of the current row. It will instead insert a new row for each copied task.

5. Choose Edit, Paste. Alternately, do one of the following: right-click on the row to paste to and then click on Paste in the shortcut menu, press Ctrl+V, or click on the Paste button on the Standard toolbar. The task or resource information will be pasted into the selected row, and the existing information will be pushed down as needed.

You can also use Project's drag-and-drop feature to copy task or resource rows between project windows.

1. Open the project files and arrange the windows so that the source and destination rows are visible.

2. Select the rows to copy by clicking on the appropriate task or resource row numbers.

3. Position the mouse pointer on the border of the selected area. The pointer will change to an arrow.

4. Drag the selected information to the first cell of the destination row. As you drag, the pointer will change to an arrow and a plus sign, indicating that the copy operation is in progress.

5. Release the mouse button to drop the copied information in the new location.

Figure 18.1 shows the drag-and-drop operation in progress.

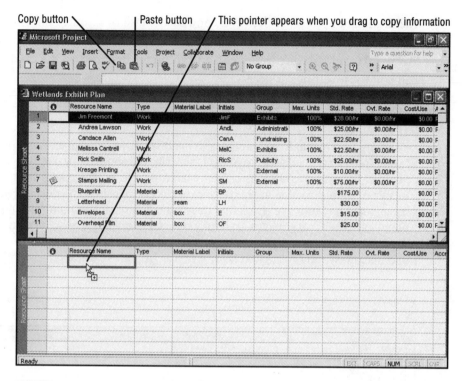

Copy button — | Paste button — / This pointer appears when you drag to copy information

FIGURE 18.1   *You can use the drag-and-drop feature to copy Task Sheet or Resource Sheet rows to other project files.*

> **NOTE**
>
> When you drag and drop to copy information, Project also inserts a new row for the pasted information.

Copying Cell and Column Information between Projects

In some cases, you want to copy selected information about tasks or resources from one Task Sheet or Resource Sheet to another. You can copy a list of task names only, for example, or you can copy the hourly and overtime rates for one resource to the corresponding cells for another resource.

When you copy information from cells, all the other original information for the task or resource is left behind. Only a copy of the cell contents is placed in the destination project. When you copy partial task or resource information to another project, the default values for Duration and Start Date (tasks), Accrue At and Baseline (resource), and so on are assigned to the task. You can edit those settings as necessary.

CAUTION

Keep the field (column) format types in mind when you copy information between Task Sheets or Resource Sheets. Typically, you should copy only between fields of the same type—from a Task Name field to a Task Name field, for example. Otherwise, you might get unexpected results. In some cases, if you try to paste an entry into a cell that needs a different kind of data (pasting a name into a cell that contains an hourly rate, for example), Project displays a warning, as shown in Figure 18.2. Also, Project does not allow you to paste information into any calculated field.

I tried to copy this name . . .   . . . to this rate cell

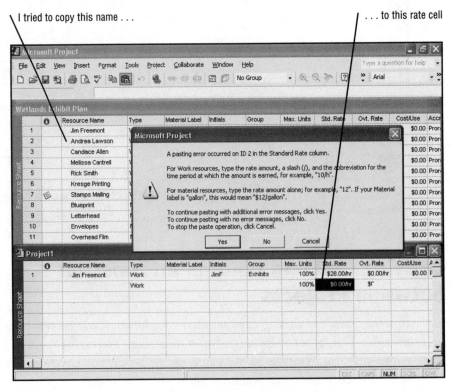

FIGURE 18.2 *You'll see a message if a copy operation could create unwanted results.*

To copy cell information between projects, follow these steps:

1. Open the two projects between which you want to copy information, select the same view in each project window, and arrange the project windows so that a portion of each is visible.

2. Select one or more cells to be copied. To select multiple consecutive cells (a range or block of cells), select the upper-left cell of the range, and then hold down the Shift key and click on the lower-right corner of the range (see Figure 18.3). To select multiple nonconsecutive cells, hold down the Ctrl key and click on each cell that you want to copy.

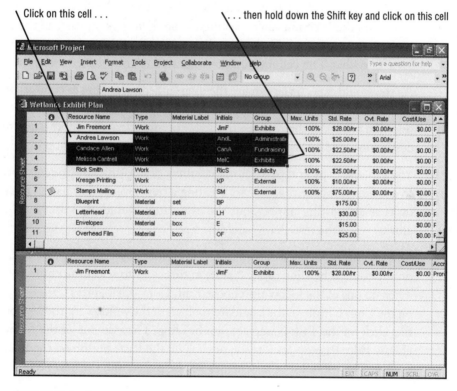

FIGURE 18.3 *You can select a range of cells.*

3. Choose Edit, Copy (Cell). Alternately, right-click on your selection and click on Copy (Cell) in the shortcut menu, press Ctrl+C, or click on the Copy button on the Standard toolbar. (The command name reflects the type of information that you selected—in this case, a cell.)

4. If you're copying the information to another Project file, click on a portion of the destination window (such as the title bar) to tell Project that you want to copy information to that file. Then select the first cell of the row in which you want to place the copied information.

 CAUTION

When you paste a copied cell range (selection), the information you paste replaces any information in the destination location. Make sure you select blank cells to avoid overwriting project information that you need.

5. Choose Edit, Paste. Alternately, do one of the following: right-click on the selection you're pasting to and then click on Paste in the short-cut menu, press Ctrl+V, or click on the Paste button on the Standard toolbar. The cell information is pasted in the selected area.

As you would expect, you can use the drag-and-drop feature to copy cell infor-mation between projects. Select the cells that you want to copy, point to the selection border so that you see the arrow pointer, drag the information to the destination, and release the mouse button to drop the information in place.

You can also copy and paste entire columns of information from one project to another. Suppose that you are creating a new project that has all the same tasks as an existing project, but the associated Duration, Start, and Finish entries—and the resources—are different.

To copy the Task Name entries from the existing project to the new one, click on the column heading (Task Name, in this case) to select the entire column. Then do one of the following: choose Edit, Copy (Cell), press Ctrl+C, or click on the Copy button on the Standard toolbar. In the window for the new project file, click on the Task Name column heading. Then do one of the following: choose Edit, Paste, press Ctrl+V, or click on the Paste button on the Standard toolbar. The entire list of task names will be pasted into the new project.

 TIP

If you often work with multiple projects at the same time, you can save the open projects and window positions as one unit. Save each of the open projects indi-vidually, and then choose File, Save Workspace. Give the workspace a meaningful name and click on OK to save it. The next time you open the workspace file, the project windows will open in the positions where you last left them. Chapter 3, "Working with Files and Help," covers saving a workspace in more detail.

Finally, you can make entering information in a single column easier by *filling*—an operation that's similar to copying. Start by selecting the cell that contains the information you want to copy to other cells that are lower in the list. Next, hold down the Shift key and click on the bottom cell of the group of cells that you want to fill, or hold down the Ctrl key and click on other noncontiguous cells lower in the column. Then choose Edit, Fill Down (or press Ctrl+D). Project fills all the selected cells with the information that appears in the first cell that you selected.

Moving Information between Projects

In addition to copying, you can move information between Task Sheets or Resource Sheets in open Project files. Moving information is almost identical to copying. The difference is that rather than leaving the information in place, you cut it from the source file, leaving the selected row, column, or cells empty. Then you paste the information where you want it.

As in copying, the moved information replaces existing information, unless you're moving an entire row. In that case, the moved information is inserted between existing rows. Finally, moving an entire row of information carries all the task or resource information for that row, except for linking information.

 TIP

To ensure that the information you're moving doesn't overwrite existing entries in your destination Task Sheet or Resource Sheet, press the Insert key one or more times before you perform the move. Project inserts a new row in the location of the currently selected cell and moves existing rows down in the sheet.

The possibilities for moving information are almost endless. You may want to move information if you have more than one project under way and decide to move a resource from one project to another. In such a case, you need to move the contents of the row that contains that resource from the Resource Sheet of the first project file to the Resource Sheet of the second project file.

To move information between two Task Sheets or Resource Sheets, follow these steps:

1. Open the files for the two projects in question, select the same view in each project window (Gantt Chart view, for example), choose the same

table for the Task Sheet or Resource Sheet in each file, and arrange the project windows so that a portion of each is visible. You can choose Window, Arrange All to tile the project windows automatically.

2. Select the task or resource row, column, or cells that you want to move.

3. Open the Edit menu and click on Cut (Task) or Cut (Resource). Alternatively, do one of the following: right-click on the selection and then click on Cut (Task) or Cut (Resource) in the shortcut menu, press Ctrl+X, or click on the Cut button on the Standard toolbar. (The command name reflects the type of information that you selected—task or resource.) Cutting removes the information from its original location and places the information on the Windows Clipboard.

   If the Cut button doesn't initially appear on the Standard toolbar, click on the Toolbar Options button at the far-right end of the Standard toolbar, and then click on the Cut button in the palette that appears.

 CAUTION

Information stays on the Clipboard only while your computer is on. If you shut off the computer, or if it loses power for some reason, the Clipboard is emptied. Also, if you cut or copy anything else to the Clipboard, the new information wipes out the existing contents. Therefore, make sure that you paste information as quickly as possible after cutting it.

4. If you're moving the information to another Project file, click on a portion of the destination window (such as its title bar) to tell Project that you want to move information to that file. Then select the first cell of the row in which you want to place the moved information.

5. Choose Edit, Paste. Alternately, do one of the following: right-click on the selection you're pasting to and then click on Paste in the shortcut menu, press Ctrl+V, or click on the Paste button on the Standard toolbar. The task or resource information is pasted into the area.

To use the drag-and-drop feature to move information between projects, you use a process that's similar to copying. First, select the information that you want to move. Next, point to the selection border so that you see the arrow pointer, hold down the Ctrl key, and drag the information to the destination. Release the mouse button to drop the information in place, and then release the Ctrl key.

Affecting Links When You Copy and Move Information

Many of the tasks in the Project files that you create are part of a series of tasks linked via Finish-to-Start (FS) links. The tasks are strung together like beads on a string. If one of the beads cracks and falls off, the remaining beads slide together to fill the gap.

When you copy or move a group of linked tasks from one project file to another, the links stay intact within the group. If you move or copy a single task, link information doesn't travel with the task.

By default, when you move a task that's linked via FS links to a series of other tasks within a Project file, Project adjusts the linking information so that the linked tasks still flow continuously. If you move the linked task to a location that's higher or lower in the Task Sheet list, the links are updated to reflect all new task predecessors and successors.

In Figure 18.4, for example, the tasks in rows 1 and 4 are linked via an FS link, as are the tasks in rows 2 and 3. If you drag the task from row 1 to a location between tasks 2 and 3, the links are rearranged, as shown in Figure 18.5. If the linking change will create a scheduling problem, the Planning wizard warns you by default.

Pasting a copied task within a series of linked tasks can also disturb the linking relationships. If you want to be able to move tasks that are linked by FS relationships without changing the links, choose Tools, Options to open the Options dialog box. Click on the Schedule tab, clear the Autolink Inserted Or Moved Tasks check box, and click on OK. Otherwise, you can avoid screwing up links simply by not moving or pasting tasks within a series of linked tasks, or by moving only tasks that aren't connected to a predecessor or successor via an FS relationship.

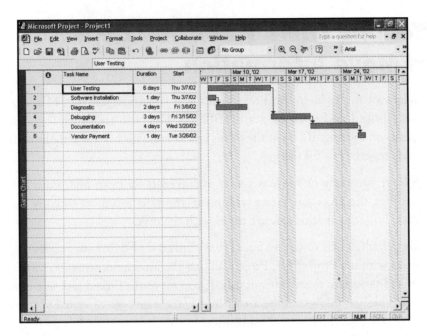

FIGURE 18.4   *These two pair of tasks are linked via Finish-to-Start (FS) links.*

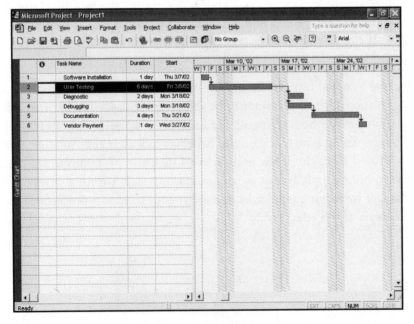

FIGURE 18.5   *Moving the task that was originally in row 1 changed the links.*

Chapter 19

Working with Templates

In This Chapter

◆ Understanding the benefits that templates provide

◆ Reviewing templates that come with Project

◆ Creating a new file from a template

◆ Creating a new template from a file

◆ Finding other template files

A century or two ago, clothing-makers had to have strong powers of visualization. Unless someone had an old garment to take apart and copy the pieces from, he or she had to envision how each piece of fabric should be shaped to create a garment.

Then some genius determined that you could make a prototype for a garment out of cheap muslin, and the muslin pieces could be copied as a paper pattern to use when cutting fabric for duplicates of the garment.

The pattern did the grunt work, freeing the user to focus on improvements and fine-tuning, and that's exactly what a template file does for you in Microsoft Project 2002. In this chapter, you'll learn how to put a template to use.

Why Templates Can Save Time

When you save a file in Project 2002, by default it's saved as a regular project file (with the MPP file name extension) and includes all the task and resource information you entered. When you open the file, it opens the one and only copy of that file, and when you save the file, it saves changes to that file.

In this scenario, it's not necessarily convenient to reuse all the information stored in your Project file. If you have a similar project and want to save the trouble of reentering all the information, you'll have to do some careful saving (and saving *as*) to reuse the information you want without overwriting the original file.

A better way to make your basic task and resource information available for reuse is to save it as a *template file*. This is like a pattern of project tasks and resources that you can use as many times as you want. Using a template saves you the trouble of entering similar task and resource information over and over.

The template file sets up your basic task and resource information for you. Then you can edit it to fine-tune it for the unique requirements of your current project.

Before I launch into describing the templates that Project provides and how to work with them, here are a few situations where you might want to create a template:

◆ You have a project that recurs on a regular basis, such as an equipment diagnostic or equipment maintenance procedure.

◆ You have a schedule file into which you've entered a tremendous amount of task or resource information, and you think you might have other, similar projects.

◆ You want to create an example file of how numerous links work so you don't have to create the links again.

◆ Members of your company's sales force need a basic tool for plotting out schedules for customers, and you want to provide a schedule blueprint with typical task durations.

◆ You're training others to manage a particular type of project in your company, and you want to provide a framework to help them with planning and to ensure that they don't miss any steps.

Using a Template

When you install the typical Project features, the setup process copies a number of predesigned templates to your system. Although you can create your own templates (as you'll learn later in this chapter), and the process for using one of your own templates is the same as the process for using a template provided with Project, it's worth reviewing the templates that come with Project. Some of them may be useful to you.

Table 19.1 lists the templates that ship with the Standard edition of Project 2002.

Table 19.1 Templates Installed with Project Standard 2002

Template	Description
Commercial Construction	Offers a detailed plan for designing and building a commercial space such as an office building, including all phases of preparation and construction
Engineering	Holds a plan for the engineering design phase of a new product
Home Move	Provides a detailed list of tasks for moving your household, including budgeting for movers, arranging for child care, transferring bank accounts, and more
Infrastructure Deployment	Outlines plans for implementation of a major infrastructure (technology or plan change) for a facility
Microsoft Active Directory Deployment	Details the steps for designing, implementing, and testing an Active Directory deployment consistent with business goals and structure
Microsoft Exchange 2000 Deployment	Details the steps for designing and implementing Exchange 2000, taking into consideration such special issues as security
Microsoft Office XP Corporate Deployment	Details the steps for implementing Office XP company-wide, covering such situations as desktop versus laptop installation, existing operating systems and hardware, custom user settings, legacy software interoperability, and file server issues
Microsoft SharePoint Portal Server Deployment	Provides a plan for implementing SharePoint Services on the enterprise
Microsoft Windows XP Deployment	Provides a plan for migrating to the Windows XP operating system, including interoperability issues, networking issues, security considerations, and user training
MSF Application Development	Details a Microsoft standard plan for software product development
New Business	Helps you organize and move through the tasks for launching a brand new business
New Product	Provides a blueprint for launching and marketing a new product offered by your company
Office Move	Provides a comprehensive plan for relocating a business or branch office, including such tasks as designing new office space, ordering furniture, arranging for services at the new location, and updating all business information to reflect the new location

Table 19.1 (continued)

Template	Description
Project Office	Gives a plan for setting up a project management office
Residential Construction	Maps out the steps for building a single-family residence
Software Development	Maps out the process of developing and launching new software, including feature set planning, programming, testing, manufacturing, market planning, advertising and public relations, developing relationships with vendors and customers, and the product release announcement; this plan could be adapted for other products.
Software Localization	Presents a detailed plan for localizing (customizing) and testing a particular application

 NOTE

Not all of the templates listed in Table 19.1 install by default. If you select a template that's not installed, you'll be prompted to install it and to insert the Project Setup CD-ROM to do so.

 TIP

You can use one of Project's templates to create a practice file to help you learn to work with Project features. That way, you only risk messing up sample information, not vital schedule information that you had to spend your own time entering.

Project and Windows identify template files with an MPT file name extension (which normally is hidden) instead of the MPP extension used for normal Project schedule files. Because the template files are identified differently behind the scenes, opening a template file is slightly different from opening a regular Project file.

To open a template file that came with Project, follow these steps:

1. Choose File, New. The New Project options will appear in the task pane at the left side of the Project application window.

2. Click the General Templates option in the New from Template section of the task pane. The Templates dialog box will open.

3. Click on the Project Templates tab. Icons for the templates appear on the tab, as shown in Figure 19.1. On systems using most Windows versions, these templates are stored in the C:\Program Files\Microsoft Office\Templates\1033 folder by default. (The templates appear in a different folder on Windows NT or multi-user systems.) As you'll learn later, you'll store user templates you create in another location. This cuts down on the possibility of accidentally deleting one of Project's templates.

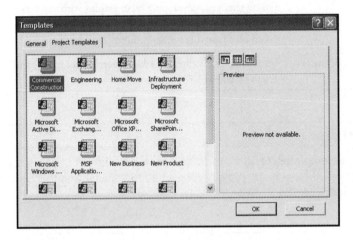

FIGURE 19.1   *You can use the Project Templates tab in the Templates dialog box to open templates offered in Project.*

4. Click on the icon for the template you want to use. If available, a preview of the template will appear in the Preview area at the right side of the dialog box.

5. Click on OK to open the template. At this point, Project might open the Project Information dialog box to prompt you to enter a start date. Fill in the Project Information dialog box as needed, and then click on OK.

6. Before you make any changes, save the template as a Project file. By default, when you try to save a template file, Project assumes you want to save a copy of the template file as a regular Project file. To start the save, choose File, Save (or press Ctrl+S). Alternately, click on the Save button on the Standard toolbar. The Save As dialog box will appear.

7. In the Save As dialog box, navigate to the disk and folder to which you want to save the file using the Save In list. (To avoid confusion, you shouldn't save the file in the default templates folder.)

8. In the File Name text box (see Figure 19.2), edit the suggested file name to save the file with a name that's different from the template name—one that's more descriptive of your project. For example, you might include the name of the product you're marketing in the file name for your copy of the New Product template, as in **Caps Concierge Business Startup**.

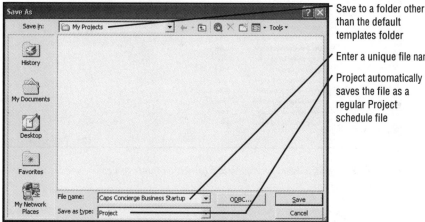

Save to a folder other than the default templates folder

Enter a unique file name

Project automatically saves the file as a regular Project schedule file

FIGURE 19.2 *When you save a template, you're really saving a copy of it as a new schedule file, so the original template remains intact. This enables you to use the basic template repeatedly.*

8. Click Save to finish saving your file. The file's contents will appear onscreen.

 NOTE

If a dialog box prompts you to specify whether or not to save certain data like baselines or actual values, click to check the check boxes for the types of data to exclude from the save, and then click Save.

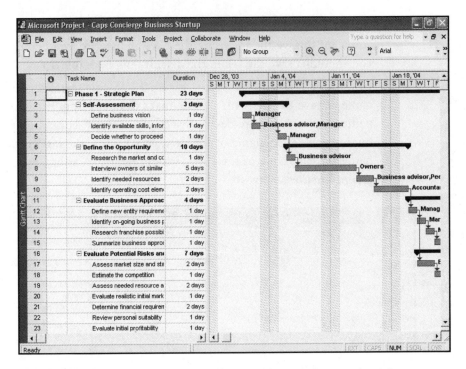

FIGURE 19.3 *A file based on the New Business template can give you a leg up in your business planning.*

 NOTE

You may see a prompt asking if you want to save the baseline. I recommend saving the plan *without* a baseline because you haven't yet entered your real schedule information. Select the Save '(Current File)' Without A Baseline option button, if needed. Then click on OK.

After you open the template you want and save a copy of it as a regular file, you can begin editing it to include your actual schedule information. The types of edits you need to make and the available bells and whistles vary, depending on the contents of the template. For example, the Microsoft Office XP Corporate Deployment template (Figure 19.4) provides a suggested list of tasks and a suggested duration for each task, but no suggested resources. Therefore, you need to build a list of resources in the Resource Sheet and assign resources. In some templates, like the New Business template, a suggested list of resources and suggested resource assignments are already plugged in.

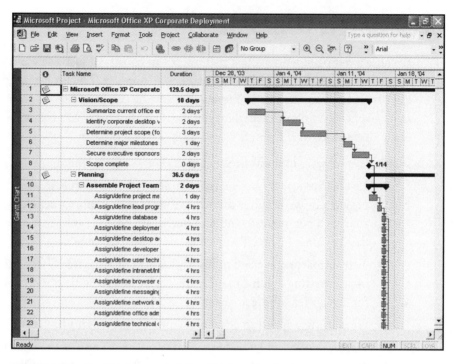

FIGURE 19.4 *Project's Microsoft Office XP Corporate Deployment template offers a road map for implementing Office XP in your organization. The template does not supply any suggested resources or assignments.*

 TIP

You can replace a resource throughout the project by displaying the Resource Sheet, typing over the name of the existing resource, and then editing other information pertaining to the resource. Project will replace the old resource name with the new resource name (as well as replacing other resource information) throughout the project plan.

In other templates you may find and use, the text and Gantt bars may be attractively formatted and color-coded to make them easy to tell apart. Still other templates might include special tables and views you can apply or other kinds of formatting. Simply make the edits and formatting changes you want, saving and printing when needed. After you save your copy of the template, it behaves as other Project files do.

Creating a Template

Because a template works like a pattern, it can consist of just a few pieces or as many pieces as are needed to create the final product. Thus, a Project planning template can include numerous pattern pieces (types of information) that anyone opening the template can use. Any template you create can include these kinds of information and tools, among others:

- ◆ Lists of tasks in the Task Sheet, including suggested durations and links.
- ◆ Lists of resources in the Resource Sheet. For example, if a particular project always requires a resource, such as a shipping company that charges a per-use rate and an hourly rate, include information about that resource (especially its costs) with the template.
- ◆ Text formatting applied in the Task Sheet or Resource Sheet, including formatting applied to individual cells, as well as Text Style changes for categories of information.
- ◆ Formatting applied to chart elements, such as Gantt bars.
- ◆ Custom views, tables, reports, and filters that you created and stored with the file using the Organizer. (See "Dealing with the Organizer To Work with Views, Macros, Tables, and More" in Chapter 13 to learn how to use the Organizer to save special elements with a file rather than in the default Project template, GLOBAL.MPT.)
- ◆ Macros and custom toolbars or toolbar buttons (see Chapters 29 and 30 for more information about macros) that you saved with the file or added to the file using the Organizer.

To build your own template, start by opening a new file and creating all the elements you want the template to include, such as the types of elements just listed. If you want to use a project file you previously created as a template, open that file. For example, if you created a My Product Proposal schedule that worked well for you, such as the one shown in Figure 19.5, you can save it as a template.

 WEB

I've included the *My Product Proposal* file on the Premier Press download page at http://www.premierpressbooks.com/downloads.asp. You can use it to try saving a template.

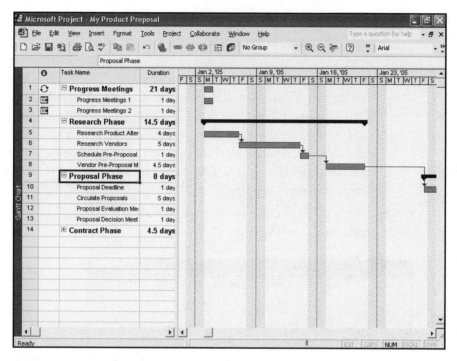

FIGURE 19.5 *This project schedule file worked well, so I'll save it as a template to reuse it.*

Make sure that you include as much file Properties information and as many Task Notes and Resource Notes with your template file as possible. This information will remind you and other users how to use the template, and will help you recall what particular entries mean.

Next, follow these steps to save your creation as a template:

1. Use the Organizer to ensure that you save all custom elements, such as views, reports, macros, and toolbars, to the file that you want to save as a template (see "Dealing with the Organizer to Work with Views, Macros, Tables, and More" in Chapter 13). If you don't, those elements won't be available in your template.

2. Choose File, Properties. The project file's Properties dialog box will appear.

3. Click on the Summary tab, if needed. Then check the Save Preview Picture check box. This option saves a thumbnail picture of the file so that you'll be able to see that preview of the template before you select and use it. Click on OK.

4. Choose File, Save As. The Save As dialog box will appear.

5. Open the Save As Type drop-down list, and then click on Template. Project will automatically change to the C:\Documents and Settings\Your User Name\Application Data\Microsoft\Templates folder (in Windows XP; it's the C:\Windows\Application Data\Microsoft\Templates folder in older Windows releases for single-user setups) in the Save In drop-down list. When you save your templates in that default folder, they will appear on the General tab of the Templates dialog box. This makes it easier for you to access and use your custom templates.

6. Edit the File Name entry to make it easy to see that the file is a template, as shown in Figure 19.6.

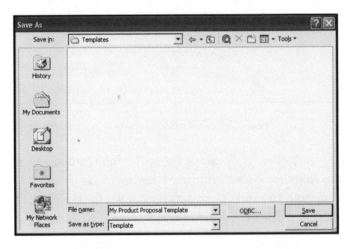

FIGURE 19.6 *Edit the File Name entry to clarify that the file's a template.*

7. Click the Save button. The Save As Template dialog box (Figure 19.7) appears, asking whether you want to exclude certain information from the template file.

8. I recommend that you save the template without a baseline so as not to interfere with baseline calculations for schedule files based on the template. I also recommend that you exclude actual values you may have entered in the file that you're saving as a template. So check both the Baseline Values and Actual Values check boxes, as shown in Figure 19.7. If you also want to exclude resource rate information from

the Resource Sheet and Fixed Costs information you've entered, click the appropriate check boxes. Finally, to facilitate reusing the template information with Project Server, check the Whether Tasks Have Been Published to Microsoft Project Server check box.

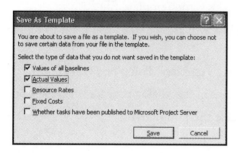

FIGURE 19.7 *Project prompts you to specify if there's any project plan information that you don't want to save in the template.*

9. Click on Save. The title bar for the file changes to indicate that the currently opened file is a template file.

10. Choose File, Close. This removes the template file from the screen. At any time, you can reopen the template file and save a copy of it (as described in the next section) to begin working with the copy.

Sometimes you might want to make changes to one of your custom template files, or one that came with Project. Say, for example, that you have a template file in which you've included resource information, and you discover that the standard hourly rates and overtime rates for several of the resources have increased. You can open the template file, edit the template, and resave it as a template file. Here are the steps:

1. Choose File, Open.

2. Open the Files Of Type drop-down list in the Open dialog box, and then choose Templates.

3. Use the Look In list to navigate to the folder that holds the template. If you saved it in the default folder, that will be C:\Documents and Settings\Your User Name\Application Data\Microsoft\Templates folder in Windows XP, or C:\Windows\Application Data\Microsoft\Templates in other Windows installations.

4. Double-click on the name of the template file to open it.

5. Make any changes you want to make in the template.

6. Choose File, Save As.

7. In the Save As dialog box, select Template from the Save As Type drop-down list. Leave all other settings intact to ensure that your changes are saved within the same template file.

8. Click on Save. A dialog box will ask whether you want to replace the existing file.

9. Click on OK. The Save As Template dialog box will appear.

10. Choose the settings you want in that dialog box, and then click on Save.

11. Choose File, Close to close the template file.

Opening a Template You Created

If you saved a template that you created in the default folder, you'll have no trouble finding and using it. Project displays user-created templates stored in the default folder on the General tab of the Templates dialog box. Use the following steps to access and use a custom template:

1. Choose File, New. Project options will appear in the task pane at the left side of the Project application window.

2. Click the General Templates option in the task pane. The Templates dialog box will open.

3. Click the General tab, if needed. Your custom templates appear on the General tab of the New dialog box, along with the Blank Project icon, which you could select to open a blank project file.

4. Click on the icon for the custom template you want to open. If you saved a preview of the template, it will appear at the right side of the dialog box in the Preview area, as shown in Figure 19.8.

5. Click on the icon for the template to use. If available, a preview of the template will appear in the Preview area at the right side of the dialog box.

6. Click on OK to open the template. At this point, Project might display the Project Information dialog box to prompt you to enter a start date. Fill in the Project Information dialog box as needed, and then click on OK.

7. Immediately save the project file, giving it a new name if needed. You're ready to go with your template!

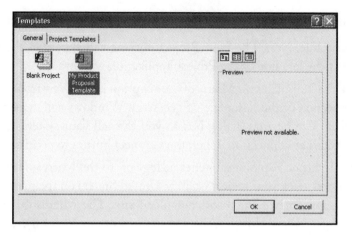

FIGURE 19.8 *The General tab in the Templates dialog box lists templates you've created and saved in the default templates folder.*

If you saved your template to a folder other than the default folder for templates, you have to use the File, Open command to find and use it instead. In the Open dialog box, you would choose Templates from the Files Of Type drop-down list, use the Look In list to navigate to the appropriate folder, and then double-click on the desired template file.

Finding More Templates Online

You may have noticed that when the task pane lists the New Project options, the General Templates section includes a link called Templates on Microsoft.com. You can use that option to go to the Microsoft Web site and download any new templates available for Microsoft Project. Because Microsoft increasingly strives to keep its products fresh by supplying a wealth of supplementary material online, you may be well rewarded if you use the Templates on Microsoft.com option every month or two.

 NOTE

If you want to look for templates on other Web sites where you have read/write privileges, such as the site of a vendor who may be developing custom templates for your organization, use the Templates on My Web Sites option in the New from Template section of the New Project task pane.

Review these steps to see the overall process for finding templates online:

1. Choose File, New. The New Project options will appear in the task pane at the left side of the Project application window.

2. Click the Templates on Microsoft.com option in the New from Template section of the task pane. If necessary, Windows will display the Dial-Up Connection dialog box so you can tell your system to dial your Internet connection. Click the Connect button to continue.

3. After Internet Explorer launches, it logs on to the Microsoft site. If prompted, click your region (such as United States) on the map to go to the appropriate Microsoft download site. The Microsoft Office Template Gallery Home Web page appears, as shown in Figure 19.9.

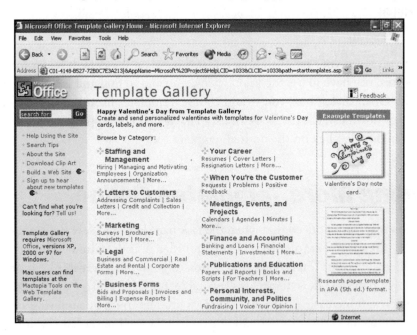

FIGURE 19.9 *Microsoft now offers a wealth of supplementary downloads on its Template Gallery page.*

4. Enter **"Project 2002"** (including the quotation marks) in the search text box near the upper-left corner of the page, and then click the Go button beside it. A Search Results page appears, with a list of potentially matching templates.

5. Browse the available templates, clicking the template name to either initiate the template's download or view its contents.

Chapter 20

Consolidating Projects

In This Chapter

♦ Consolidating projects

♦ Using and adjusting the consolidated information

♦ Linking individual tasks between projects

♦ Sharing resources between projects that aren't consolidated

After you become a Microsoft Project guru (and I know you will, with this book in hand), you'll use the program to manage more forms of work than you could have imagined.

You can have two, three, or more project plans running simultaneously. As the project leader, the challenge for you in such a situation is to understand and prioritize work between projects, as well as work between tasks in a project.

This chapter shows you how to better manage all of the work on your plate by consolidating information from multiple project files.

When to Combine Projects

If you need a single printout of the tasks from two projects, you can print them out separately, trim the excess, tape the two together, and make a photocopy so that you have a single, solid document. This solution, however, is clearly inelegant and forces you to do the dirty work rather than having your computer do it.

Project offers a workaround for situations like this, called *consolidating* projects. When you consolidate two or more schedule files, Project places all the information from each of the selected files (sometimes called *subprojects* or *source projects*) into a single consolidated file (sometimes called the *master project*). Then you can change the view, print, and otherwise work with the combined information. You can consolidate up to a thousand different project schedules (assuming your system has the horsepower to do so) in a single consolidated file, but that's really not practical. Once you consolidate a few dozen files or so, you can see a real degradation in system performance and file corruption is likely.

Here are just a few situations in which you might want to consolidate projects into a single file:

◆ You're managing multiple projects, and you want a list of in-progress tasks to jog your memory about things that you need to follow up on. You consolidate the tasks and then filter the Task Sheet so that it lists only the in-progress tasks.

◆ You want to display a list of all the tasks in your projects that will start in the near future. You can print them before a meeting with your boss, so the two of you can discuss shifting priorities and identify some tasks to reschedule.

◆ You have two projects that use the same resources, and you want to see if there are any resource overallocations. You can consolidate the files and switch to Resource Usage view to find overallocations.

Combining Projects

Consolidating schedule files places all the information from the specified individual files into a new file, the consolidated file. The "live" information it contains helps you see multiple projects in perspective. When you save it, you can assign it a unique name of your choosing. Alternately, you can insert other schedule files into the current file to consolidate them. The current file then becomes the consolidated file. The rest of this section explains the details of creating and working with a consolidated file.

Consolidation Methods

A consolidated file can work in two different ways. It can exist independently of the files from which its information came, or it can remain linked to the original source files. The first situation is fine if you want to work with the consolidated file on a one-time basis only. However, if you want to reuse the consolidated file over a period of days, weeks, or longer, the schedules for the individual original project files might change, making the consolidated file obsolete—unless you link it to the original files when you create it.

Using the first method, described next, you can create consolidated files with or without links. The second method is faster and can be used only when you want to consolidate project files with links.

Inserting a Project to Consolidate Files

The primary method for consolidating files in Project 2002 is to insert a schedule file into a row in an existing project file, which then becomes a consolidated or master project file. Each inserted source project or subproject file is linked to a single Task Sheet line in the master project. At first, you don't see all the tasks for the inserted subproject. Instead, you see a single summary task and Gantt bar summarizing the inserted project. By default, the start date entered in the inserted subproject file is the same date it uses in the master project file. When the files are linked, you can change the start date in either file to update it for both. The duration of the full schedule for the inserted subproject file becomes the duration for the subproject summary task entry in the master project Task Sheet. So, if all the tasks listed in the subproject will take 95 days to complete, the master project shows 95d as the duration entry for the subproject task, and you can't edit that entry.

 NOTE

There will be times when you need to readjust the start date for a subproject. See the "Controlling Dates in Consolidated Projects" section later in this chapter for more details.

You have to create the source or subproject files before adding them to the consolidated project file. You can't insert a file that doesn't exist, after all. However, you don't have to create the tasks within the subproject file initially. You can simply open and save the file with the name you want, and then close it and add it to the consolidated master project. You can reopen the subproject file at any time to enter its tasks. This approach works best in many cases, because it ensures that you don't have to go back and manually update a subproject start date. If needed, you also should share the resources from the resource pool into the individual subproject file before you insert the subproject file into the master project.

To insert a project (source project or subproject) within an existing project file (which becomes the consolidated or master project), follow these steps:

1. Create and save the subproject files.

2. Create the file where you want to insert other files. This file will become the consolidated or master project file.

3. Click on the Task Name cell for a blank Task Sheet row in which you want to insert the subproject.

 NOTE

You can insert a project at any outline level and later demote or promote it by demoting or promoting the summary task that represents it. However, when you insert a subproject into a master project file that already contains other subprojects, be sure that all the subprojects are collapsed so that only the subproject file task appears. Otherwise, you may inadvertently insert a new subproject file at the wrong outline level.

4. Choose Insert, Project. The Insert Project dialog box will appear, as shown in Figure 20.1.

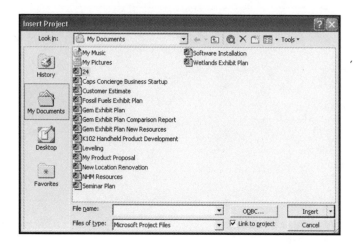

FIGURE 20.1 *Use this dialog box to choose which files to consolidate.*

5. If needed, use the Look In drop-down list to navigate to the disk and folder that contains the file to insert.

6. Click on the file you want to insert. If you want to insert more than one file stored in the same drive and folder, you can click on the first file. Then press and hold Ctrl and click on additional files to select them.

7. By default, the inserted subproject file is linked to the consolidated (master project) file, so the Link To Project check box will be checked. If you do not want the files to be linked (meaning that changes you make in one of the files will not appear in the other), clear the Link To Project check box.

8. Click on Insert. The inserted (subproject) task will appear in the file, as shown in Figure 20.2.

Indicator for an inserted project | Summary Gantt bar for inserted project

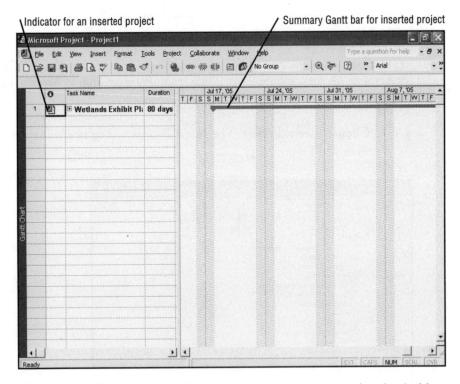

FIGURE 20.2 *This is how a consolidated file appears. One source project (or subproject) has been inserted into this project.*

 TIP

To insert a project file as read-only (preventing you from making any changes to the original subproject file from the consolidated file), click on the drop-down list arrow beside the Insert button, and then click on the Insert Read-Only option in the submenu that appears.

9. Save the master project file to save the links to subprojects.

You can use the preceding steps to link other subprojects to the master project file.

When you're working with the information in a consolidated file, the name for each of the subproject or source project files you've inserted appears as a numbered summary task row in the Task Sheet of any view that includes the Task Sheet (such as Gantt Chart view). When you consolidate multiple files into a new window, these rows are treated by Project as summary tasks at the highest level of the outline. (See Chapter 5, "Working with Outlining," to learn more.)

Combining Multiple Projects in a New Window

There is a somewhat faster way to create a consolidated file, but as usual with such matters, you have to give up a little flexibility to save time.

To use this method, begin by opening each of the files you want to consolidate. Make any changes you want to the files and save them. Choose Window, New Window. The New Window dialog box appears. In the Projects list, click on the name of the first file to consolidate. Press and hold down the Ctrl key. Then click on additional files to select them (see Figure 20.3).

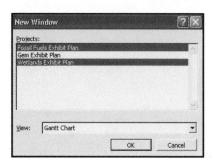

FIGURE 20.3 *This is a quicker but less flexible method to select files for consolidation.*

Click on OK, and Project compiles the consolidated file onscreen into a brand new file. (By default, the consolidated file is linked to the original subproject or source files. In addition, the resource pools for the individual files are not consolidated.) You can then save and work with the consolidated file. The source files remain separate and intact on disk. So, with this method, you're creating a brand new file rather than altering an existing one.

Working with Resources in Consolidated Projects

As you learned in Chapter 8, you can create a resource pool file that holds all the resources you want to use. Then you can share those resources from the resource pool into individual project files. If you then consolidate projects and display the Resource Sheet, Project indicates when a resource is overbooked between multiple projects (see Figure 20.4).

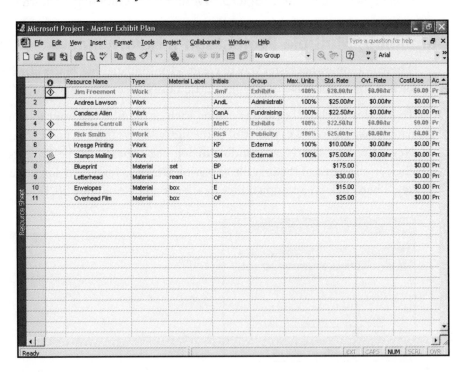

FIGURE 20.4   *The Resource Sheet in the master project file shows when resources have been booked between subproject files.*

If inserted subprojects include their own lists of resources, the Resource Sheet lists all the resources. However, you have to first expand each project file in the Gantt chart view by clicking on the plus sign beside the subproject name. Then, when you switch to the Resource Sheet, all the resources will appear. The row numbers start over where the resource list for each inserted subproject starts.

Similarly, when you first open a master project file whose subprojects share resource information from a resource pool file, the pool file doesn't open automatically. You have to click on the plus sign beside the name of the inserted subproject, and then click on OK in the Open Resource Pool Information dialog box that appears.

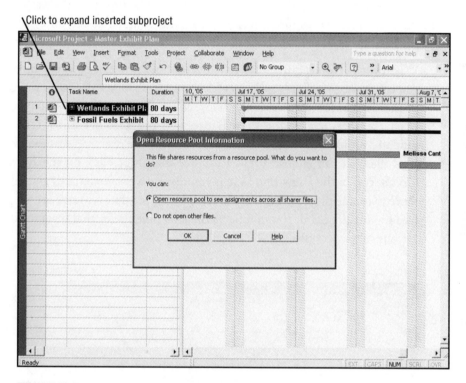

FIGURE 20.5 *When you expand the tasks in an inserted subproject that shares resources, Project prompts you to open the resource pool file.*

 NOTE

If the master project file will include tasks that don't exist in a separate subproject file, and you need to assign resources to those tasks, you need to share the resource pool into the master project file itself. Otherwise, the resources from the resource pool file will not be available to the tasks that exist only in the master project file.

Working with Your Consolidated Information and Viewing Overallocations

To work with the consolidated information, you must expand the subprojects in the Gantt Chart view (by clicking on the plus sign beside each subproject name), in addition to opening the resource pool. Once you've expanded the subprojects, the reports and views in the master project file summarize the information—particularly resource-related information—from all the inserted subprojects.

When you're working with the consolidated file, you can do everything that you can do in an individual Project file. You can change any entries you want, or change the view. For example, choose View, Resource Sheet or click on the Resource Sheet icon in the View Bar to view the Resource Sheet for a consolidated project file. If the inserted subprojects share resources from a resource pool file, you can choose View, Resource Graph or click on the Resource Graph icon in the View Bar. When you display a resource that's assigned to more than one project, the overallocated hours for that resource are graphed (see Figure 20.6). The graph reflects the assignments for that resource in the various subproject files.

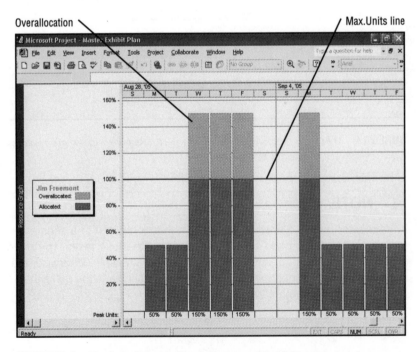

FIGURE 20.6 *Here's the Resource Graph for a consolidated file with shared resources.*

Similarly, the Task Usage and Resource Usage views show a resource's assignments in all subprojects so that you can identify problem assignments or overallocations. Figure 20.7 shows a resource who's overallocated between projects, assigned 4h for one project and 8h for another on the same day.

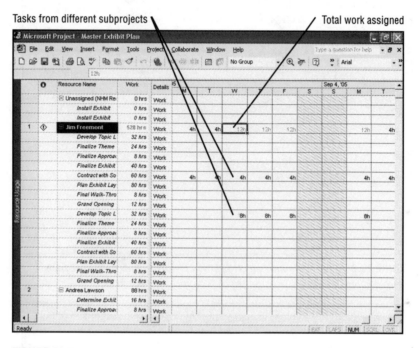

FIGURE 20.7 *You can identify overallocations between subprojects in the Resource Usage view.*

You can work with the outline levels in the master project file just as you would in an individual file. When you've expanded the subprojects, the top-level tasks from the subproject files appear as subtasks. (However, if you consolidated the file by inserting a file, the summary task for the inserted file appears at the same outline level as the task below which it was inserted.) All individual project tasks holding subtasks appear in bold (see Figure 20.8).

If you click on the Task Name column and then click on the Hide Subtasks button on the Formatting toolbar, the Task Sheet displays only the names of the consolidated files (see Figure 20.9).

By now, you get the idea. The consolidated file behaves much like other project files in terms of how you can change its contents.

The next subproject

This bold task is a top-level task in the
source file and includes subtasks

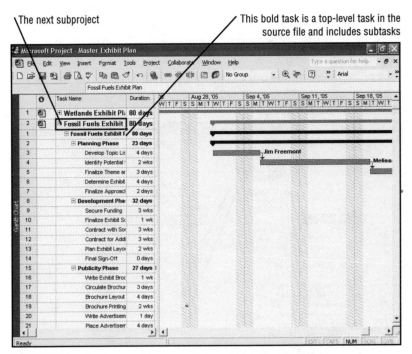

FIGURE 20.8 *Project provides cues to help you identify which tasks came from
which subprojects (source files), and which tasks include subtasks.*

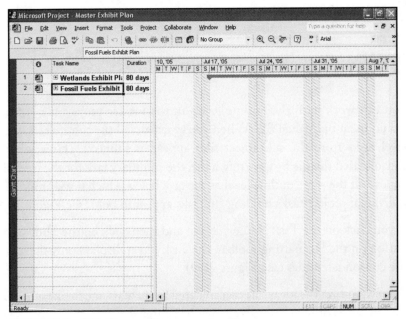

FIGURE 20.9 *This file consolidates two other files.*

NOTE

This may sound odd, but you have to display all subtasks for a report you run to include information from those subtasks. For example, if you have a recurring meeting task set up, you need to expand all its subtasks before you generate the report to ensure that the information gets included in the report.

Opening Subprojects

Even though the subproject files and consolidated (master project) file remain as separate entities on disk, by design they share information so that they always reflect the same dates. For example, if you reschedule several tasks in a subproject to make the total subproject duration longer, you'll want the new duration to be reflected in the master project file. It helps to understand how this automatic updating occurs. It takes place through opening files.

To update subproject and consolidated project information, open each subproject file as usual, update its contents, and save it. Then you open the consolidated (master project) file, which is automatically updated with the latest information you added into each subproject file. Make sure that you then save the consolidated file to save its changes, too. When you save or close a consolidated file, you will be prompted to save changes to the individual subproject files, as well as the resource pool. This ensures that all your files are in sync and have the latest information. Click the Yes to All button in the first dialog box that prompts you to save changes. This greatly speeds up the saving process.

Working with Subprojects

In most cases, working with an inserted subproject is identical to working with other summary tasks and subtasks. You can expand and collapse the inserted task's subtasks, and you can update information such as actual start dates and work completed for any subtask. However, you'll need to use some unique steps when you're working with the inserted subproject's summary task, covered in this section.

Changing Subproject (Inserted Project) Information

When you double-click on the summary task for an inserted subproject, or click on the task and then click on the Task Information button on the Standard toolbar, the Inserted Project Information dialog box appears. In most respects, this dialog box resembles the Task Information dialog box. It offers the same five tabs, which in most cases have identical options:

♦ **General.** This tab appears in Figure 20.10. You can use it to change the inserted project's summary task name and priority, or to control the display of the summary task's Gantt bar and any rolled-up subtask bars.

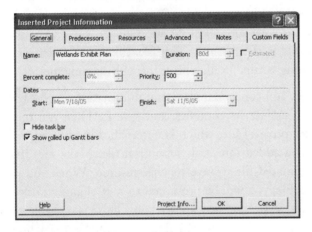

FIGURE 20.10 *Some options on the General tab of the Inserted Project Information dialog box are dimmed, meaning you can't edit them.*

♦ **Predecessors.** Use this tab to link the inserted project's summary task to another task in the consolidated file. For example, if two inserted projects need to finish by the same date, you could create a finish-to-Finish relationship between their summary tasks. The settings on this tab work just like those for a regular task.

♦ **Resources.** Use this tab to assign resources to the summary task for the inserted subtask. You might want to do this if you're making a resource responsible for all aspects of the inserted project (in other words, making the resource a supervisor). Again, the settings on this tab work just like those for a regular task.

◆ **Advanced.** This tab (see Figure 20.11) differs most significantly from the corresponding tab in the Task Information dialog box for a regular task. In the Source Project area of the dialog box, you can specify whether the inserted subproject is linked to the consolidated project (Link To Project), and if so, whether the link is read-only. If you want to verify the name of the inserted file, it appears in the text box in the Source Project area. To insert another subproject file in the same location in the Task Sheet instead, click on the Browse button to reopen the Inserted Project dialog box and then choose a different file to insert.

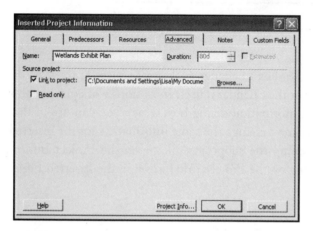

FIGURE 20.11   *Use this tab to control which project file is inserted and how it's inserted.*

 CAUTION

If you break the link between an inserted subproject and the master project file, you can't reinstate it. Instead, you have to reinsert the subproject file. Also, breaking the link affects the task numbering within the master project file, treating the now-unlinked tasks just like the tasks you typed directly into the master project.

◆ **Notes.** Use this tab to insert, format, and edit a note for the inserted task's summary task. Use the same techniques on this tab that you would use on the Notes tab for an individual task.

◆ **Custom Fields.** Use this tab to view the custom fields you've created within the master project file.

At the bottom of the first five tabs in the Inserted Project Information dialog box is a Project Info button. Click on that button to open a Project Information dialog box similar to the one shown in Figure 20.12.

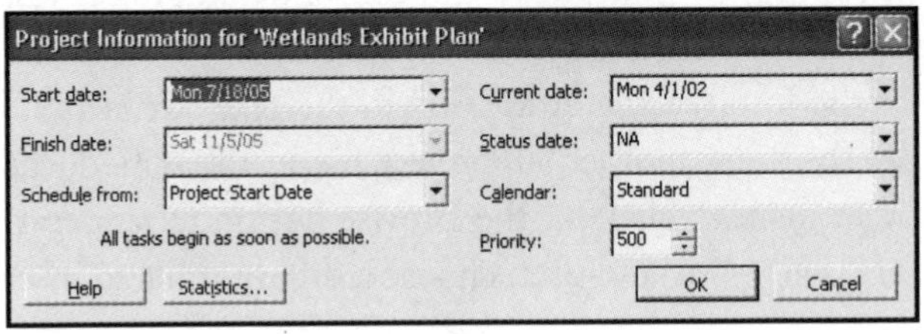

FIGURE 20.12 *Use this dialog box to change overall schedule information for the inserted project.*

You can use this dialog box to change such key features as the start date for the inserted project or the calendar it uses. Its options work just like those for the regular Project Information dialog box, which you can use in the open subproject. If you want to change the same information for the inserted subproject without opening the subproject file, open the Project Information dialog box by clicking on the Project Info button in the Inserted Project Information dialog box.

Deleting a Subproject

If you want to delete the source project or subproject, right-click on its row number and then click on Delete Task. If the Planning Wizard is enabled, a dialog box appears asking you to confirm the deletion (see Figure 20.13).

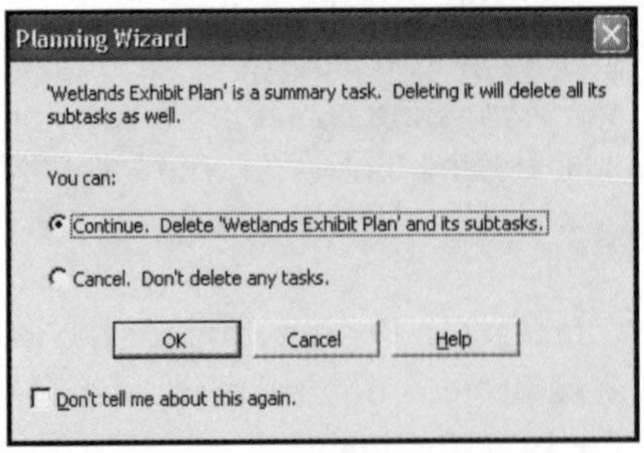

FIGURE 20.13 *The Planning Wizard asks you to verify whether to delete the inserted project's summary task.*

To finish the deletion, leave the first option button selected and click on OK. If you made changes to any of the inserted project's information in the consolidated project file, you'll also be prompted to specify whether or not to save those changes to the subproject file before the subproject is removed from the consolidated project. Click on Yes to do so, or No to remove the inserted subproject without saving changes.

Controlling Dates in Consolidated Projects

Sometimes you'll need to make manual adjustments to ensure that the schedules in your subproject files and master project file are in sync.

For example, an inserted subproject file might include old schedule information, so you might need to adjust its start date to match the master project's start date. This would happen, for example, if you created the subproject file on April 7 (so that its original project start date was April 7), but then waited until April 8 to create the master project file and accepted that date as the master project's start date. You'd then need to change the inserted project's start date to April 8 to make sure its schedule falls within the consolidated master project schedule. If updating the inserted project's start date doesn't fully work, you can update a subproject file so that its start date reflects the start date you entered in the master project, and so the work for all its subtasks is correctly rescheduled. To reschedule the subproject work, follow these steps:

 NOTE

Keep in mind that the following steps also reschedule the start date and scheduled work in the individual subproject (source project) file if the files are linked. Changes you make in the subproject file appear in the consolidated file, and vice versa, for linked files.

1. Open the master project file.
2. In the Task Sheet, display the summary tasks for the inserted subproject. (Click on the plus sign beside the inserted project's summary task, or click on the summary task and click on the Show Subtasks button on the Formatting toolbar.)

3. Drag over the row headers for the inserted project's summary task and all the displayed subtasks to select all the task rows.

4. Choose Tools, Tracking, Update Project. The Update Project dialog box will appear.

5. Select the Reschedule Uncompleted Work To Start After option button (see Figure 20.14). Click on the drop-down arrow for the date text box shown beside that option button. Then use the calendar that appears to select the new start date (which should be the start date for the consolidated master project or a later date).

Select inserted project and subtasks

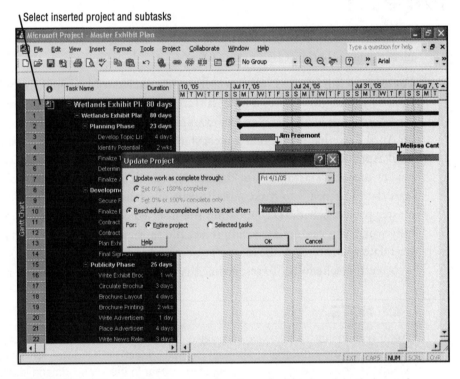

FIGURE 20.14 *Use this dialog box to synchronize uncompleted work in the inserted subproject with the start date for the consolidated master project.*

6. Click on the Selected Tasks option button to ensure you don't inadvertently reschedule tasks that aren't subtasks of the inserted project.

7. Click on OK. If automatic recalculation is on, you've properly established links, and tasks don't use constraints that prevent them from

moving. Project reschedules the inserted subproject to start on the adjusted dates. The subtasks are rescheduled accordingly, with each subtask's duration, link, constraint, and other settings controlling exactly how it's rescheduled. If the inserted subproject and its subtasks don't move automatically, press F9 to recalculate the schedule.

Although links stay intact, you should review the moved tasks to ensure that they still make sense in light of the newly scheduled dates. For example, if a task is rescheduled during a period when a resource is on vacation, the task duration might have been greatly increased. You might want to move the task manually or select another resource for it.

In some cases, task constraints will interfere with your ability to move out one or more tasks. For example, if a task has a Must Start On, Must Finish On, Finish No Later Than, or Start No Later Than constraint entered in the Constrain Task area of the Advanced tab of the Task Information dialog box, and the associated constraint date is earlier than the date you want to reschedule the task to, Project warns you that there's a scheduling conflict when you try to move the task. Click on OK to continue. Then remove the task's constraint or select another constraint type, such as As Soon As Possible, As Late As Possible, Start No Earlier Than, or Finish No Earlier Than. (Remember that you can open the Task Information dialog box simply by double-clicking on the task.)

Another problem occurs if you try to move out a single linked task rather than all the tasks. If you move a task and the link creates a scheduling conflict, you can remove the conflict by clicking on the task name for the successor task, and then clicking on the Unlink Tasks button on the Standard toolbar.

 NOTE

If the subproject contains work that's already marked as completed, and the start date for that work precedes the start date you specified for the master project file, you can remove the conflict by removing the work specified as completed. To do so, choose Tools, Tracking, Update Tasks. Change the % Complete entry to 0, and then click on OK. Or, if the work really has started for the task, move the start date for the subproject entry in the master project to an earlier date, and also change the start date for the master project (choose Project, Project Information to open the proper dialog box) so that it begins earlier.

Linking Tasks between Projects

Another reason to consolidate files is to create a Finish-to-Start link between two tasks in different (separate) project files. Such a link lets you ensure that the tasks happen in the proper order, even if they're in different project files. For example, you may have an external resource scheduled to handle both tasks, and you might want to link them to get a clear picture of the impact on both projects if the resource begins to run behind. Follow these steps to create a link:

1. Open the consolidated file and display subtasks as needed.

2. In the task list, click on the Task Name cell for the earlier task, which will be the predecessor task for the link.

3. Press and hold the Ctrl key, and then click on the Task Name cell for the second task to link, which will be the successor task.

4. Click on the Link Tasks button on the Standard toolbar. Project links the tasks, and it adjusts the schedule for the successor task and any tasks linked to it as needed to honor the new link. Figure 20.15 shows such a link.

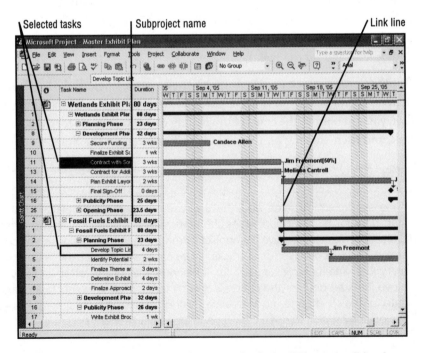

FIGURE 20.15 *You can create links between subtasks for different consolidated or inserted projects.*

If you then open one of the subproject (source) files, you'll see that a special task has been inserted to identify the external *predecessor* or *successor* task. For example, Figure 20.16 shows the external predecessor task for one of the consolidated files linked in Figure 20.15. Note that the external task's name is dimmed, meaning that you can't edit it. Its Gantt bar is gray as well, because you can't move or otherwise reschedule the task.

When you open the subproject file that holds the successor linked task, the task row displays a special Predecessor field entry that points to the full path and file name for the file holding the predecessor task, followed by a backslash and the task ID number. If you want to link tasks between two files without first consolidating them, simply open the file that holds the successor task to link and make an entry in the Predecessor column for that task. That entry should give the full path and file name for the Predecessor entry, followed by a backslash and the ID number, as in **C:\My Documents\Work\Budget.mpp\14**.

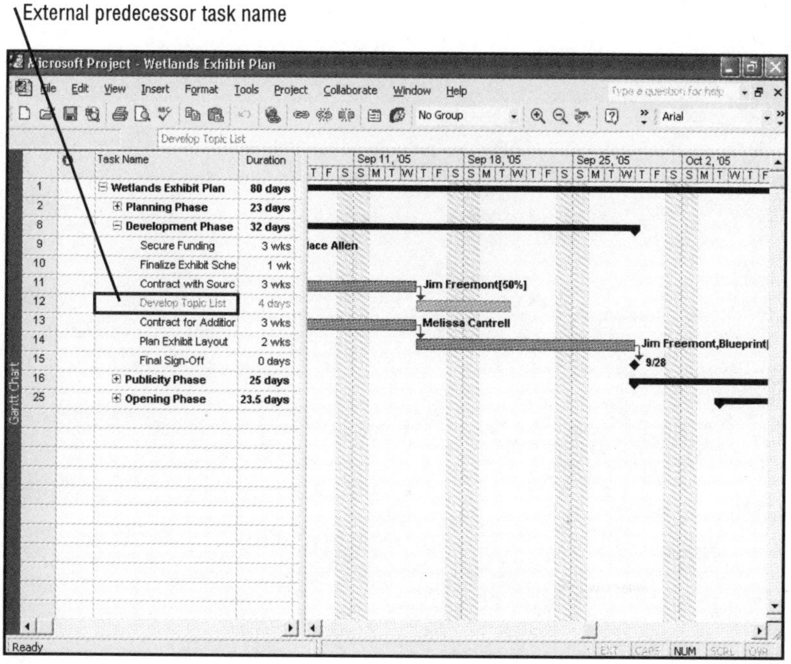

FIGURE 20.16   *Project inserts a special task to let you know when individual tasks are linked between projects.*

If you want to break the link between tasks in different files, you can clear the Predecessor field entry in the file that holds the successor task. Or you can redisplay the consolidated file, if you saved it. Click on a cell in the successor task row, and then click on the Unlink Tasks button on the Standard toolbar.

 NOTE

To view more details about external predecessor or successor tasks in the current project file, choose Tools, Links Between Projects. In the Links Between Projects dialog box that appears, you can view and delete links as needed.

PART VI

Sharing and Publishing Project Information

Chapter 21

Using Project with Other Applications

In This Chapter

◆ Importing tasks you've already listed in Outlook or Excel

◆ Enhancing a project's Gantt Chart views with graphics from other applications

◆ Copying Gantt charts and other Project images into other applications

◆ Using OLE objects to create dynamic links between applications

◆ Understanding data maps

◆ Importing and exporting Project data

No single software program can handle all your business functions, even though different applications can work with similar information. You may need to use features from one application to accent your work in Microsoft Project 2002. Or you may have to share information with a colleague who doesn't use Project. This chapter covers features that let you share tools and data between Project and other applications.

Importing Outlook Tasks

In the past, Project didn't communicate directly with Outlook. To reuse a list of tasks you'd created in Outlook, you had to copy and paste to specific cells in the Task Sheet. Or, you could export the list of tasks from Outlook to a text-based file, and then import the tasks from there into Project. Neither approach was very elegant or saved much time.

Because Outlook has become more sophisticated in terms of a project manager's ability to delegate tasks, Microsoft's programmers have made Project more sophisticated so that it can take advantage of the Outlook Tasks list. Project can now directly import a list of tasks from your Outlook Tasks list.

Project can import three pieces of information about each task from Outlook:

◆ **Subject.** Project places this information in the Task Name field in the project file.

◆ **Notes.** Project places this information in the task Notes field in the project file.

◆ **Total Work.** Make this entry on the Details tab of the new task window when you create the task (see Figure 21.1). Project uses this entry to calculate the duration of the task and plugs that value into the project file.

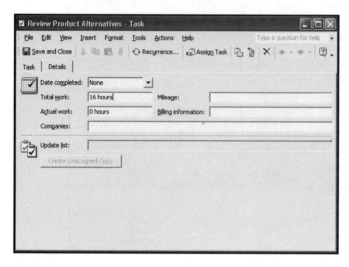

FIGURE 21.1   *Project uses the Total Work entry to specify the duration of the imported task.*

Project also lets you select which tasks to import into the project file, so that you don't have to delete tasks that aren't needed for the import from your Outlook Tasks list.

Once you've received or created your list of tasks in Outlook, follow these steps to import them into a new project file:

1. Open a blank project file in Project.

2. Specify the project start date by choosing Project, Project Information, entering the date in the Start Date text box (or using the drop-down calendar to select the date), and then clicking on OK.

3. Choose Tools, Import Outlook Tasks. (If more than one user profile is set up for Outlook, the Choose Profile dialog box may appear. Choose the appropriate profile from the Profile Name drop-down list, and then click on OK.) The Import Outlook Tasks window opens.

4. Place a check mark in the check box to the left of each task you want to import into Project. (See Figure 21.2.) Clicking the check box to the left of the folder name selects all the tasks in the folder, while clicking the check box beside a category name selects all the tasks in the category.

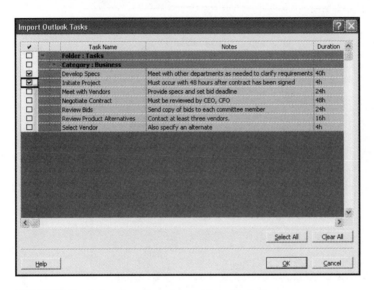

FIGURE 21.2 *Select the tasks to import from Outlook.*

5. Click on OK. Project imports the tasks in alphabetical order, calculates the duration based on the total hours of work, and schedules each task to start from the project start date, as shown in Figure 21.3.

6. From there, you can drag and drop tasks or sort the task list as needed to place the tasks in the appropriate order.

Building a Task List in Excel

When you installed Project, it made two additional templates available in Excel: the Microsoft Project Plan Import/Export template and the Microsoft Project Task List Import template. Both of them make it easier to share information between Project and Excel. The former template can be used to develop Project information for import into Project or to create a file to store information exported from Project. The latter template enables you to build a

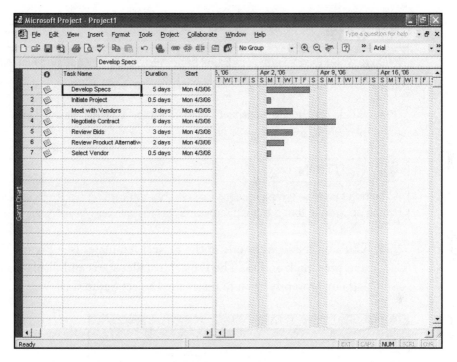

FIGURE 21.3   *Project imported these tasks from Outlook and calculated each one's duration.*

task list in Excel for easier import into Project. So, if you prefer to work in Excel to build your initial task list, review this section to see how to take advantage of these templates.

Installing a Template for Project Information

While the typical Project installation makes icons for the new templates appear on the Spreadsheet Solutions tab of Excel's Templates dialog box, the templates typically aren't installed by default. Follow these steps to install each of the templates when you need it:

1. Start Excel, if needed.

2. Choose File, New to display the New Workbook task pane (if it hasn't appeared).

3. Click on the General Templates option in the task pane. The Templates dialog box will open.

NOTE

If you're working in a version of Excel prior to Excel 2002, choosing File, New immediately opens the Templates dialog box.

4. Click on the Spreadsheet Solutions tab. The list of available templates will appear.

CAUTION

If you don't find the template icons in Excel, try performing a custom install of Project to ensure that the templates for Excel install.

5. Click on the icon for one of the Project templates (see Figure 21.4), and then click on OK. The Project installer starts and displays a dialog box prompting you to insert the Project Setup CD.

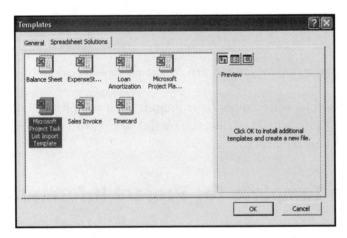

FIGURE 21.4 *Select the icon for one of the templates to be prompted to install the template in Excel.*

6. Insert the CD as prompted, and then click on OK. The installer will install both templates and open a new file based on the template you selected in Step 5.

Using a Template for Project Information

The Microsoft Task List Import Template enables you to build a list of tasks to import into Project. As shown in Figure 21.5, the template creates an Excel file that defines various fields of data—one field per column, with the field names in row 1 (called the header row). After you save and close the file in Excel, you can switch to Project and use the Microsoft Project Import Wizard (described later in the section called "Using Lists from Other Applications") to import the file. The wizard will prompt you to specify the data type. To correctly import the template data, choose the Project Excel Template option and continue the wizard.

You can use the other template, Microsoft Project Plan Import Export Template, either to use Excel to build lists of project information to import into project or to serve as the basis for project information exported from Project to Excel. In either instance, the Microsoft Project Import Wizard or Microsoft Project Export Wizard prompts you to specify Project Excel Template as the data type if you prefer to use the template format and field names.

 TIP

Using these templates for Excel imports and exports saves you the trouble of creating a data map to control field names. Data maps are described later in this chapter.

Using Text and Graphics from Another Application

As a companion to the Microsoft Office suite of applications, Project was designed with information-sharing in mind. All Office applications (and many other Windows applications) enable you to share information between applications easily. You can create information in one application and then use it in another application.

Suppose that your boss types a list of key operations for a project in a word processing program, such as Microsoft Word. The list is about three pages long. If you're not a skilled typist, typing such a list could take you an hour or more. If you have Word installed on your computer, however, and your boss e-mails you a copy of the file that contains the list, you can get the job done in minutes by copying the list from the Word file to a Project file.

 TIP

Every time you retype information, there is the potential to make errors. When information has already been spell-checked or proofed for errors, always copy it rather than retyping it.

The following are just a few other examples of text and graphics from other applications that you can copy and paste into Project:

◆ You can convert a to-do list created in Word to a list of tasks in Project.

◆ You can use a list of committee members assigned to a project as the foundation of a Resource Sheet list.

◆ You can paste the names of people in your department from a spreadsheet to a Resource Sheet.

◆ You can include graphic images, such as company logos, in a Gantt chart to make the printouts more attractive and informative.

◆ You can paste electronic images of product designs or chart images of product information in the Objects box of the Task Form for particular tasks.

◆ If you've scanned in photos of colleagues or of equipment to be used to complete a task, you can add those images to the Objects box for the resources in the Resource form.

The procedures for copying text and graphics are different, so the following sections cover those procedures separately.

 NOTE

When you paste information into blank rows in a Task Sheet or Resource Sheet, Project automatically creates new tasks or resource entries in those rows and adds the default settings for fields (columns) into which you do not paste information. If you paste a to-do list in the Task Name column of a Task Sheet, for example, Project adds a default duration of 1d (one day) for each task and sets the defaults for remaining columns.

Using Lists from Other Applications

You can copy information from any application that supports OLE and enables you to create lists—which includes most Windows-based word processing and spreadsheet programs—and then paste that information into a Project file. (See "Working with OLE Objects," later in this chapter.) You only can paste the information into a Task Sheet or Resource Sheet. Therefore, you can paste information into any view that shows the Task Sheet or Resource Sheet, or into any table that's a variation on those sheets.

Keep in mind that if you're copying cells from a spreadsheet program (such as Excel), Project tries to paste to an area that's similar in shape—say, three columns wide by two rows deep. Also, no matter what kind of application you're pasting from, Project won't allow you to paste a type of information that's inappropriate for the destination. You can't paste text into a cell that calls for an hourly rate, for example. In most cases, you'll simply paste a one-column list into the Task Name or Resource Name column of the Task Sheet or Resource Sheet.

To copy text from an application and paste it into Project, follow these steps:

1. Open the document that contains the text that you want to copy to Project.

 CAUTION

Text that you paste in replaces any information that's in the selected destination cells. If you don't want to wipe out any existing information, be sure to select only a blank area of the Task Sheet or Resource Sheet.

2. Select the text and then choose Edit, Copy (or click on the Copy button, if available). Figure 21.5 shows an example.

3. Open or switch to the Project application. You can press Alt+Tab or click on the Project button on the Taskbar to switch to Project. If Project isn't open, use the Windows Start menu to start Project.

4. Select or open the Project file where you want to paste the copied information.

5. You need to specify the project start date. Choose Project, Project Information, enter the desired date in the Start Date text box (or use the drop-down calendar to select the date), and then click on OK.

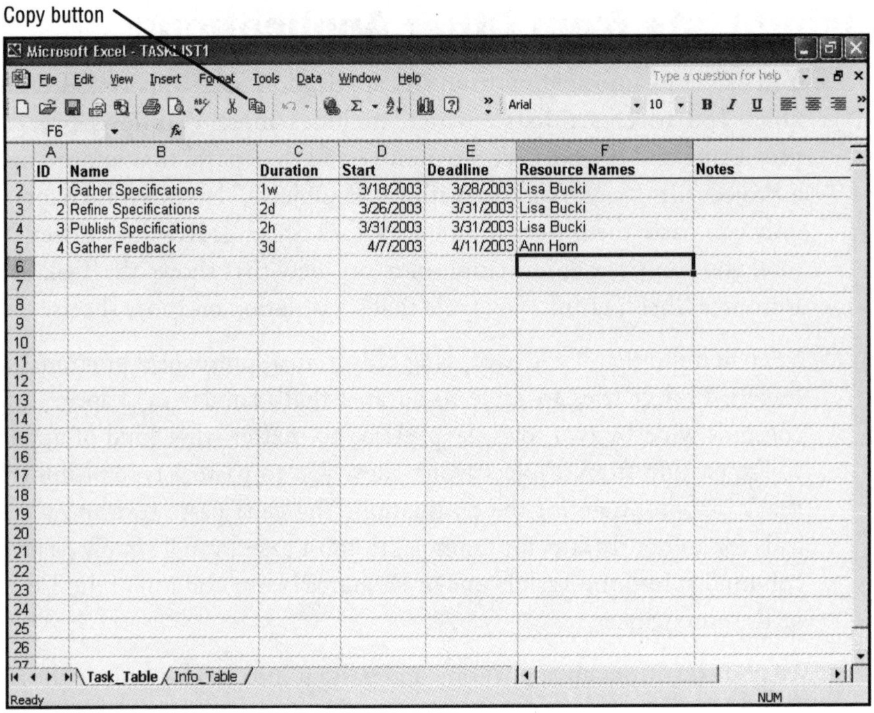

Copy button

	A	B	C	D	E	F	
	ID	Name	Duration	Start	Deadline	Resource Names	Notes
1							
2	1	Gather Specifications	1w	3/18/2003	3/28/2003	Lisa Bucki	
3	2	Refine Specifications	2d	3/26/2003	3/31/2003	Lisa Bucki	
4	3	Publish Specifications	2h	3/31/2003	3/31/2003	Lisa Bucki	
5	4	Gather Feedback	3d	4/7/2003	4/11/2003	Ann Horn	

FIGURE 21.5   *You can copy information from a word processing program.*

6. Select the view that you want to use, such as Gantt Chart or Re-source Sheet.

7. Select the upper-left corner of the range of cells into which you want to paste the information. To paste a list of tasks, for example, you could click on the top cell of the Task Name column.

8. Choose Edit, Paste. Alternately, right-click on the selection to paste to and do any of the following: click on Paste on the shortcut menu, press Ctrl+V, or click on the Paste button on the Standard toolbar. The text is pasted into the selected cells.

 CAUTION

When you copy and paste specially formatted text from another application into Project, you will lose the special formatting. For example, if you copy an outline from Word and paste it into Project, you end up with simple text that lacks the outline formatting.

Figure 21.6 shows the text copied from Figure 21.5 pasted into the Task Sheet.

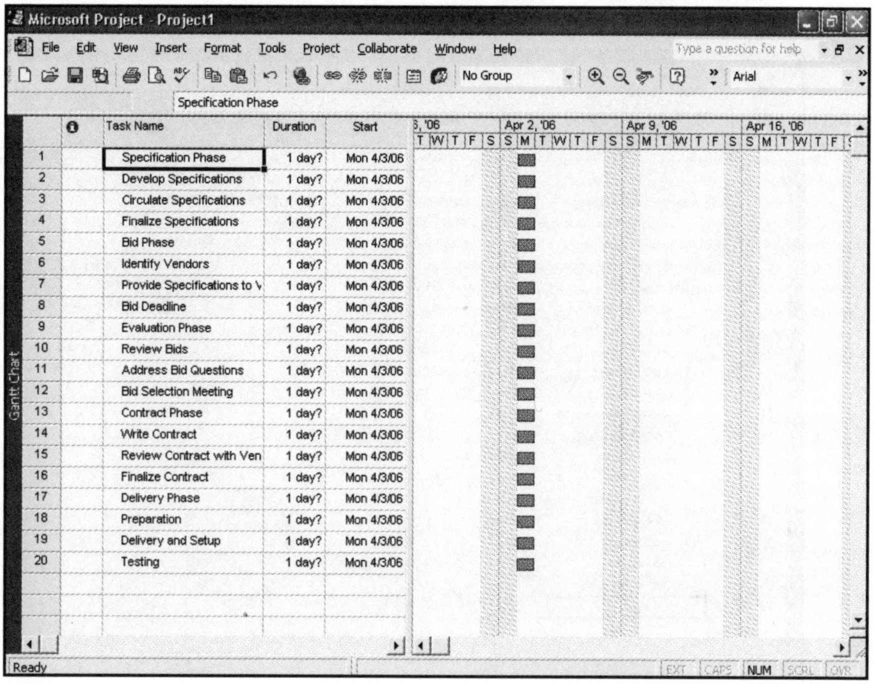

FIGURE 21.6 *The word processing list is now a list of tasks. Each one has been assigned the default duration and has been scheduled to start from the project start date.*

Using Graphics to Enhance Your Project

You can copy graphics created in other applications—such as electronic images of company logos, products, and charts—into Microsoft Project graphic areas. These graphics can range from purely decorative (an image that you use to jazz up a Gantt chart) to purely informational (a graphic of a resource that enables widely separated team members to recognize one another). Although Project offers drawing capabilities, you may want to use a graphic that already exists in another application, or that may need to be created with tools that Project doesn't offer (as with scanned images). For these reasons, Project enables you to use graphics copied from other applications.

You can copy a graphic to any view that shows a Gantt chart, such as Gantt Chart view (see Figure 21.7). When you paste a graphic into a Gantt chart, Project enables you to format the graphic just as you would format a drawing that you created in Project. (For more information on formatting, refer to Chapter 17, "Other Formatting.")

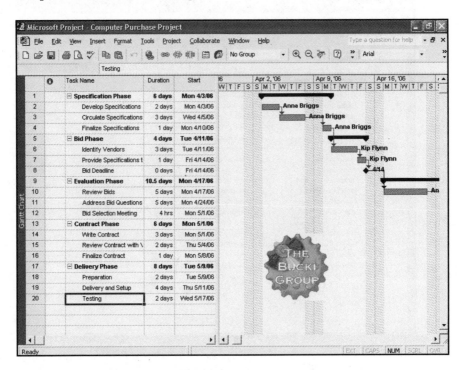

FIGURE 21.7 *Here's an example of a graphic pasted into a Gantt chart.*

You can also paste a copied graphic into the Objects box of the Task Form or Resource Form, or into any view that offers one of these forms. The Task Form, for example, appears as the bottom pane of the Task Entry view.

To display the Task Form or Resource Form, choose View, More Views to open the More Views dialog box. Then double-click on Task Form or Resource Form in the Views list. To display the Objects box for the form, right-click on the form and then click on Objects on the shortcut menu. The Objects box is the big blank area at the bottom of the form. Figure 21.8 shows a graphic pasted into the Task Form.

To copy a graphic image from another application, follow these steps:

1. Start the application that contains the graphic object that you want to copy to Project. (Windows comes with a graphics program called Paint for working with graphic images.)

Objects box

FIGURE 21.8   *Here's an example of a graphic pasted into the Task Form.*

2. Open the file for the graphic image, or create the new image.

3. Select the image (or any portion of the image) that you want to use in Project, using the program's selection method. (Many programs offer a Select All command on the Edit menu to enable you to quickly select the full image.) Figure 21.9 shows a graphic selected in Windows Paint.

 NOTE

Graphics files can be rather large. If you'll be sharing your Project files with other people via e-mail or floppy disks, adding numerous graphics to your project files can make the transfer more time-consuming and difficult. Under such circumstances, you should use graphics files sparingly.

4. Choose Edit, Copy to copy the graphic to the Clipboard.

5. If this object is the only one that you need to copy, exit the application.

FIGURE 21.9   *The selection border surrounds the selected information that will be copied.*

6. Open or switch to the Project application. (You can press Alt+Tab or click on the Project button on the Taskbar to switch to Project, if it's open.)

7. Select or open the Project file where you want to paste the copied information.

8. Select the view that you want to use, such as Gantt Chart view, or display either the Task Form or Resource Form to paste the information into the Objects box on the form.

9. In a Gantt chart, scroll to the section of the view where you want the graphic to appear. In a Task Form or Resource Form, click in the Objects box.

10. Choose Edit, Paste. Alternately, right-click on the location to paste to, and then click on Paste on the shortcut menu (or press Ctrl+V). The graphic object will be placed in the upper-left corner of the Gantt chart area or Objects box.

If you don't like the location of the graphic in the Gantt bar chart area, you can drag the object to the exact position you want. Move the mouse pointer over the object. A four-headed arrow appears on the selection pointer, indicating that you can drag the object to a new location. When you finish moving the object, click outside it to deselect it. In an Objects box, however, you can't move an object after it's been placed.

Using Project Information in Other Applications

You can copy almost all the information and views in Project to other applications. Copying information into Project saves time and reduces errors, and copying information from Project and using it elsewhere does the same thing.

The following are a few examples of how you can use Project information in other applications:

- You can copy Gantt chart timelines as *pictures* (graphics that can't be edited) and paste them into a weekly status report in Word.
- You can copy resource cost tables, showing how much time various people have spent on the project, and paste that information into a spreadsheet.
- You can paste a list of tasks from Project into a project update memo for company executives.
- If you added the field for e-mail addresses to your Resource Sheet, you can copy resource names and addresses into a note that will be distributed to all team members.

Project enables you to copy information as straight text, as an object (for more information on objects, see "Working with OLE Objects," later in this chapter), or as a picture. Information that appears in the timescale area on the right side of a view (such as the chart portion of Gantt Chart view or the schedule portion of Resource Usage view) can be copied only as a picture or an object, not as text. In addition, the table information that appears to the left of the charted information is always copied as well. You can't copy a picture of a few Gantt chart bars without copying a picture of the accompanying task information.

Copying Project Information as Text

When you paste to most programs, such as a spreadsheet program like Excel or a word processing program like Word, Project assumes that you're pasting the information as text. The pasted cell entries will appear in spreadsheet cells, or as entries separated by simple tab characters in a word processor.

If you select the task or resource row before copying, the entire set of task or resource fields is copied and pasted at the destination. If you don't want to copy all the fields (columns) from the Task Sheet or Resource Sheet, select the individual cells that you want to copy and paste.

 NOTE

The text in Calendar and Network Diagram views cannot be copied to other applications. These views can be copied only as pictures or Microsoft Project objects.

To copy information from Project as text, follow these steps:

1. Select the Project view that contains the text that you want to copy to another application.

2. In the Task Sheet or Resource Sheet, select the task row resource row, or individual cells that you want to copy. (To select noncontiguous groups of cells, drag over the first group, press and hold the Ctrl key, drag over additional groups of cells, and then release the Ctrl key.)

3. Open the Edit menu and click on Copy (Task), Copy (Resource), or Copy (Cell). Alternately, right-click on the selection, and then click on the appropriate command on the shortcut menu (or simply press Ctrl+C). The command name on the Edit or shortcut menu reflects the type of information you selected: task, resource, or cell. The text is copied to the Windows Clipboard.

4. If this is the only copy operation you need to perform, exit Project. (Otherwise, you can leave Project open for further work.)

5. Open or switch to the destination document.

6. Select the area in which you want the Project text to appear. In a spreadsheet application, select the upper-left cell of the range of cells in which you want to paste the text. In a word processing application, position the insertion point where you want to paste the text.

7. Choose Edit, Paste, or click on the application's Paste button if one is offered. The text will appear in the document as unformatted text.

Figure 21.10 shows some resource information pasted into Excel.

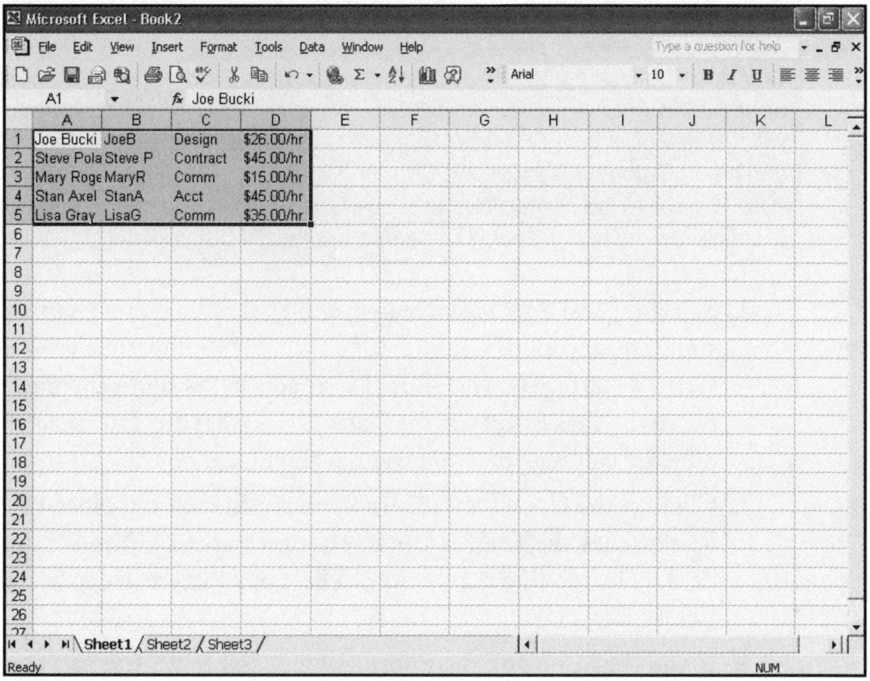

FIGURE 21.10   *Resource information that's pasted into Excel appears where you specify.*

If you use the Paste button on the Standard toolbar and the text is pasted as Microsoft Project Graphic objects, you must use the Paste Special command on the Edit menu. In the Paste Special dialog box that appears, click on the Text or Unicode Text option in the As list, and then click on OK to paste the text.

Pasting a Picture of Project Information

Pasting a picture of Project information enables you to insert that image into the destination application as a graphic. This is the method to use if you won't need to edit the information in the destination application, if you don't want to reformat any text after pasting, and if you want to include Gantt bars, Network Diagram charts, or timescale information in the destination application.

To copy Project information as a picture, rather than text that can be edited, follow these steps:

1. Select the Project view that contains the information you want to copy.

 NOTE

When you copy and paste Project information as a picture-formatted object (a noneditable graphic), only the portion of the current view that corresponds with the selected Task Sheet or Resource Sheet information is copied. Whether you are in Calendar view, Gantt Chart view, or any of the Resource views, be sure to scroll to the appropriate section of the view and select the right rows in the table before using Copy. (The same applies to Cut operations as well.)

2. Select the task row, resource row, or Network Diagram chart area that you want to copy. If you've selected whole task rows in a view like the Gantt Chart view, you should also adjust the vertical split bar between the Task Sheet and the Gantt area so that the Task Sheet displays only the columns that you want in the linked object.

3. Click on the Copy Picture button on the Standard toolbar. (You may need to click the Toolbar Options button on the right end of the Standard toolbar to find that button.) The Copy Picture dialog box appears (see Figure 21.11).

4. If you want to copy the information at the same size as the current screen view, leave For Screen selected. If you want to copy a larger view, select For Printer. If you want create a GIF graphic file of the image (perhaps to include it in a Web document), select the To GIF Image File option. The path and suggested name for the graphic file appear in the accompanying text box. If you want to change either one, use the Browse button.

5. If you've copied from some views, like the Gantt Chart view, the Copy and Timescale options near the bottom of the dialog box are enabled. In the Copy area, you can select Rows On Screen to copy all the information currently displayed. Or, if you selected specific rows of information to copy in Step 2, keep Selected Rows as the choice. Similarly, you can copy the Timescale portion of the view as shown onscreen.

Or, you can choose a specific period of the timescale to include. Click on the From option button, and then use its drop-down calendar and the To drop-down calendar to specify the time period.

Copy Picture button

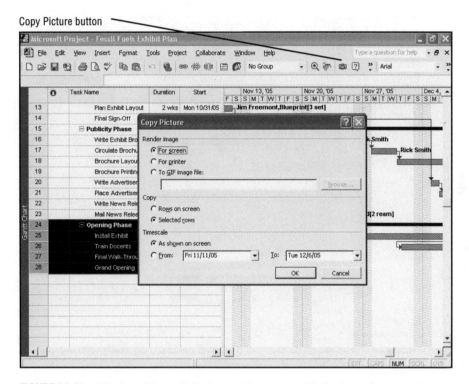

FIGURE 21.11   *The Copy Picture dialog box enables you to specify the picture format, and more.*

6. Click on OK to copy the Project view to the Windows Clipboard (or create the GIF file, in which case you don't have to perform any further steps).

7. Switch to (or open) the document where you want to paste the picture.

8. Place the insertion point where you want the picture to appear. (Or, in PowerPoint, select a graphics image placeholder.)

9. Choose Edit, Paste. Alternately, press Ctrl+V or click on the Paste button on the Standard toolbar. The Project picture appears in the document.

Figure 21.12 shows a Gantt Chart view selection copied to a PowerPoint slide.

Working with OLE Objects

Object linking and embedding (OLE) allows applications to share information dynamically. Basically, the information is created with the source

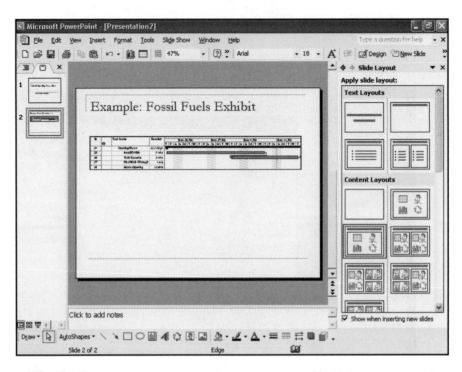

FIGURE 21.12 *Gantt chart information can be copied into another Office document, such as a PowerPoint presentation.*

application or its tools. Then that information is displayed in the container application. If the information in the container application is linked to the original information in the source application, you can make changes in the source document and they'll show up in the linked information in the destination document.

Embedding enables you to take an object that was created in another application and edit it within the current application. You can edit a chart that was created in Excel and has been embedded into a Word document by using the menus, commands, and other features of Excel from within Word. You don't have to exit Word, start Excel, edit the object, cut or copy the object, and paste it back into your Word document.

The following sections cover the basic procedures for creating linked and embedded objects based on Project data. Keep in mind that you can also do the reverse—you can link and embed information from other applications in Project files.

Creating a Linked Object

When you link information from a view, the linked object looks like a picture in the container document. Thus, the linked object can include Gantt bars and timescale information.

To link information from Project to a document in a container application, follow these steps:

1. Select the information that you want to place in another document. The information can be from a Task Sheet, a Resource Sheet, or even a Network Diagram chart. If you've selected whole task rows in a view like the Gantt Chart view, you also should adjust the vertical split bar between the Task Sheet and the Gantt chart area so that the Task Sheet displays only the columns that you want in the linked object.

2. Choose Edit, Copy. Or, right-click on the selection and then click on Copy on the shortcut menu. Project will copy the information to the Windows Clipboard.

3. Open or switch to the document into which you want to paste the linked Project object.

4. Position the insertion point where you want the linked object to appear.

5. Choose Edit, Paste Special. The Paste Special dialog box will appear.

6. Click on the Paste Link option.

7. In the As list box, select Microsoft Project Document Object. (Your choices should now resemble Figure 21.13.) You can also select the Picture object

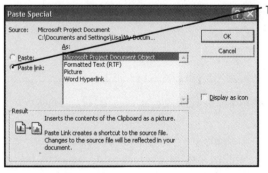

This option creates a linked object

FIGURE 21.13   *The Paste Special dialog box lists the object types that can be applied to the object on the Windows Clipboard.*

type in the As list box if you want to paste the object as a bitmap graphic. The bitmap object will still be linked to the Project document.

 NOTE

Working with the paste options for a particular application may take some experimentation. Excel's options, for example, include weird-looking items called BIFF, BIFF3, and BIFF4. These options represent different kinds of Excel text and will paste the copied information into a group of cells, for example.

8. Click on OK. The Project information will appear in the destination document, as shown in Figure 21.14.

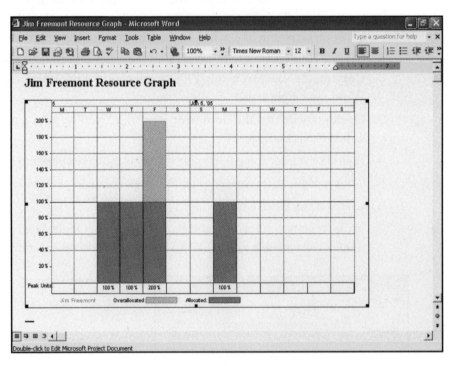

FIGURE 21.14 *Linked Project information looks like this in a Word document.*

A link can be even more beneficial if you have some information—particularly in Excel—that you want to use in Project and that will be updated automatically via the link. For example, let's say you've developed an extensive materials cost list in Excel. You want to continue to use the Excel file, but you'd also like to use that information in a Resource Sheet in a project file or resource pool file. (The information even might be a calculated value.) You'd also like the cost information to be updated automatically in Project anytime you change the source information in Excel.

Here's how to set up this kind of useful link:

1. Select the Excel worksheet cell holding the information that you want to use in a Resource Sheet in Project.

2. Choose Edit, Copy. Or, right-click on the selection and then click on Copy on the shortcut menu. Excel will copy the information to the Windows Clipboard.

3. Open or switch to the project file into which you want to paste the linked Excel information.

4. Select the view and then the location into which you want to paste the linked information. (Typically, this is one of the cost cells in the Resource Sheet.)

5. Choose Edit, Paste Special. The Paste Special dialog box will appear.

6. Click on the Paste Link option.

7. In the As list box, leave Text Data selected.

8. Click on OK. The linked Excel information will appear in the project file, as shown in Figure 21.15.

		Resource Name	Type	Material Label	Initials	Group	Max. Units	Std. Rate	Ovt. Rate	Cost/Use	Ac ▲
1		Kip Flynn	Work		K		100%	$25.00/hr	$0.00/hr	$0.00	Prc
2		Anna Briggs	Work		A		100%	$32.00/hr	$0.00/hr	$0.00	Prc
3		Stan Stevens	Work		S		100%	$44.00/hr	$0.00/hr	$0.00	Prc
4		Network Cabling	Material	Ft.	N			$0.20		$0.00	Prc

FIGURE 21.15 *A small gray marker in the lower-right corner of a cell (such as the cell in the Std. Rate field for resource 4) tells you that the cell holds linked information.*

Whenever you need to view the source data in Excel, simply double-click on the linked cell in the project file. Excel will launch, and the file holding the linked information will open. Whenever you change the source data in Excel, that change will appear in the linked location in the project file as well.

Managing a Link's Update Setting

By design, a linked object is updated each time the object's source document is changed or updated. By using the Links command, you can specify when the changes in the source document are reflected in the linked object. You have two choices of link-update timing: You can update the linked object automatically each time the source document changes, or you can update the object manually by making menu and dialog box choices.

To select a link's update setting, follow these steps:

1. Open the document that contains the linked OLE object.
2. Click on the linked object to select it.
3. Choose Edit, Links. The Links dialog box will appear, displaying a list of linked objects in the document. It shows the link name and the path name of the source document, and indicates whether the link is set to be updated automatically or manually. Also, the name of the object that you selected in Step 2 is highlighted.
4. Select the Manual Update option button.
5. Update the link by clicking on the Update Now button. The object is updated with any changes that have taken place in the object's source document.
6. Click on OK. The Links dialog box will close, and the link is set for manual updating.

With the link set for manual updating, you must open the Links dialog box and click on the Update Now button to update the object with the latest changes in the source document. In some cases, depending on the application and document holding the linked information, you can right-click on the linked object and then click on Update Link on the shortcut menu.

Using Other Linking Options

The Links dialog box contains a few other buttons that enable you to manage the links to objects in your documents:

◆ **Open Source.** This button opens the source document of the currently selected link. With the source document open, you can make changes in the source object, investigate surrounding information, or just refresh your memory as to the name and location of the source file.

TIP

You can open any OLE object's source application without displaying the Links dialog box. Just double-click on the linked object.

♦ **Change Source.** This button opens the Change Source dialog box, which enables you to select a new file as the source document for the linked object.

♦ **Break Link.** This button removes the link to the selected object. If you click on this button, a dialog box asks whether you're sure you want to break the link to the selected object. If you're sure, click on OK. Otherwise, click on Cancel. After you break a link, you must perform a cut-and-paste operation to reestablish the linked object.

Creating Embedded Objects

The process of creating an embedded object is similar to the process of creating a linked object, but the connection between the source document and the destination document is different. The information in the embedded object does not depend on the source document. That is, you can make changes in the embedded object that don't show up in the source document.

NOTE

Unlike linking an object, when you embed an object, Project copies all the tasks or resources in the selected Task Sheet or Resource Sheet. This means that after you choose Edit, Paste Special to place the embedded information in the container document, you can click on the object and then drag the black resizing handles to control how much of the information appears.

To create an embedded object, follow these steps:

1. Select the view that you want to use to create the embedded object. If the view includes a Task Sheet or Resource Sheet, click on any cell in the sheet and drag the vertical split bar to control which columns appear (the same ones will appear in the embedded object).

2. Choose Edit, Copy. Alternately, right-click on the selection and then do any of the following: click on Copy on the shortcut menu, press Ctrl+C, or click on the Copy button on the Standard toolbar.

3. Open or switch to the destination document.

4. Position the insertion point where you want the embedded object to appear.

5. Choose Edit, Paste Special. The Paste Special dialog box will appear (refer back to Figure 21.13), listing the available paste options.

   The default Paste Special options are set up to create an embedded object. That is, the Paste option should be selected, not the Paste Link option.

6. In the As list, click on the object type Microsoft Project Document Object. Notice that the Results area of the dialog box indicates that the selected settings enable you to use Microsoft Project to edit the object.

7. Click on OK to paste the object. The object will appear at the insertion point.

 NOTE

You cannot create an embedded object from an image that you copied by using the Copy Picture button on the Standard toolbar. The Copy Picture button creates a bitmap image of the selected area. It does not maintain the information that is necessary for embedding.

Editing an embedded object is a simple, straightforward process. The primary advantage of embedding comes into play because you don't need to recall the name and location of the source document that created the object. You simply double-click on the object and you get the tools for the source application (in this case, Project), enabling you to edit the object.

When you finish making changes to the object, click outside the object. The source application tools close, and you return to the container document and application. (In some applications, you may have to choose File, Exit to close the source application.)

You can also embed or link an object in the Notes tab of the Summary Task Information or Resource Information dialog box. For example, the following steps show how to embed a resource's picture along with other resource notes:

1. Display the Resource Sheet for the project file.

2. Double-click on the name of the resource in the Resource Name column to open the Resource Information dialog box.

3. Click on the Notes tab.

4. Enter any notes you have in the Notes text box at the bottom of the tab, and then position the insertion point at the location where you'd like the inserted picture to appear.

5. Click on the Insert Object button which is the far-right button at the top of the Notes text box. The Insert Object dialog box will open.

6. Click on the Create From File option button.

7. Click on the Browse button to open the Browse dialog box.

8. Use the Look In list to navigate to the disk and folder that holds the picture file to insert.

9. When the picture file name appears in the list of files at the left, click on it and then click on the OK button to return to the Insert Object dialog box.

10. If you want to link the inserted picture to the original picture file, check the Link check box.

11. Click on OK to finish inserting the picture. It will appear on the Notes tab, as shown in Figure 21.16.

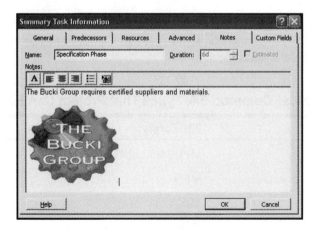

FIGURE 21.16 *Embed or link a picture or other object in the Resource Information or Summary Task Information dialog box.*

12. Click on OK to save your changes and close the Resource Information dialog box.

Importing Other Project-Management Files

Project enables you to work with information stored in a variety of file formats. If you need to bring in information from an application that saves information in tabular format (such as a spreadsheet or database program), you can import that information using the Microsoft Project Import Wizard rather than copying it. Table 21.1 lists some of the file formats that Project can accept.

In order for Project to recognize the data that you import, it needs to be properly formatted. For example, the first row in an Excel workbook file should contain field names that identify the data in the column (field). If you have any questions about how the type of data you want to import needs to be set up in its source application, export some test data from Project into that format (including choosing the corresponding export map, if needed). Then open the exported file in its source application to see how Project set up the file, named fields, and so on. Exporting is covered later in this chapter.

 TIP

If your software (especially other project-planning software) isn't listed in Table 21.1, see whether the program enables you to use its File, Save As command to save files in one of the listed formats.

Table 21.1 The Most Common File Types That Project Can Read

Application	File Format
Microsoft Project	MPP, MPX, MPT
Microsoft Project Database	MPD
Microsoft Excel	XLS
Microsoft Access (as well as FoxPro and dBase III and IV, which share the same format)	DBF
Plain text (ASCII)	TXT
Comma-separated values	CSV
Extensible Markup Language	XML

The procedure for importing a file is similar to the procedure for opening a file that you learned in Chapter 2, "Getting Started with the Project Guide." Follow these steps:

1. Choose File, Open, press Ctrl+O, or click on the Open button on the Standard toolbar. The Open dialog box will appear.

2. In the Look In drop-down list, select the disk where the file that you want to import is stored.

3. Double-click on a folder to display its contents. (You may need to double-click on subfolder icons to find the name of the file that you want to open.)

4. In the Files of Type drop-down list (see Figure 21.17), select the format for the file that you want to import.

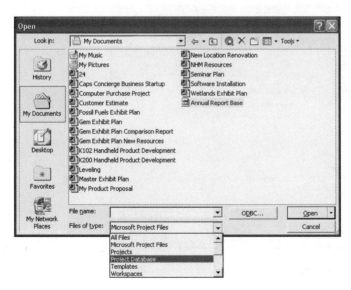

FIGURE 21.17 *Select the type of file to import.*

5. When the file that you want to open appears in the list, double-click on its name, or click on it and then click on Open, to load it into Project. The Microsoft Project Import Wizard will start. (Click the Next button to move past the Welcome screen of the wizard, if it appears.) Figure 21.18 shows two examples of the first screen of this wizard.

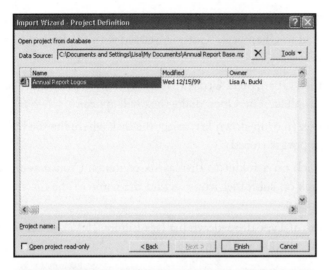

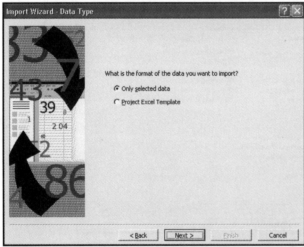

FIGURE 21.16 *The Import Wizard dialog box provides different options depending on the type of file you're trying to import.*

6. The type of file you chose to import in Step 4 determines what steps you take next in the Import Wizard:

◆ For database formats such as Microsoft Project Database, click on the Finish button. Project imports the database file.

◆ For importing an Excel file you've created with one of the Excel Project templates described earlier in the chapter, choose the Project Excel Template option in the Import Wizard - Data Type dialog box and click Next. Choose an Import Mode (creating a new project, appending to it, or merging the data) in the next screen of the wizard, and then click Finish. The data is imported directly. If you instead click Only Selected Data in the Import Wizard - Data Type dialog box and then click Next, the Import Wizard - Map Selection dialog box appears.

◆ The Import Wizard - Map Selection dialog box is used for other types of files, such as Access databases or Excel files created without the use of one of the Project templates. Click either the New Map or Existing Map option button, and then click on Next. If you chose Use Existing Map, the Import Wizard - Map Selection dialog box appears, as shown in Figure 21.19. The Choose A Map For Your Data list displays "maps" that specify which fields of information to import. For example, the Default Task Information option imports the ID, Task_Name, Duration, Start_Date, Finish_Date, Predecessors, and Resource_Names fields. Click on your selections from the list, and then click Finish. If you instead chose New Map Selection in the Import Wizard - Map dialog box, you have to create a data map to import the data. For more on creating maps, see the next section, "Understanding Data Maps."

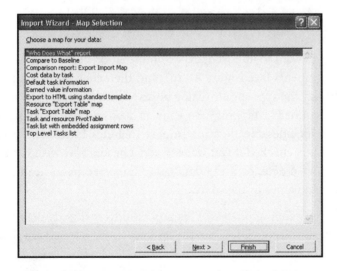

FIGURE 21.19 *A data map tells Project which fields should hold imported (or exported) data.*

If necessary, Project adds default information for columns that are not filled in by the imported information, such as the Duration column. Conversely, it warns you if the data being imported doesn't work for a particular field, and it skips the import for that information.

Understanding Data Maps

When you're importing or exporting data, you may not want to include all the fields of information from the original file. Or, your file may use field names that Project doesn't immediately recognize. In such cases, you can use a data map in Project to tell it which fields to import or export, and to give it the location for the imported or exported fields. In Figure 21.19, you saw that Project comes with multiple data maps.

However, you may need to create your own data map. For example, let's say you want to export information from the Name (Resource Name) field on the Resource Sheet to a column called Full Name in a new Excel workbook. To *map* the data to a new field, you need to create your own data map.

First, click on the New Map button in the Import Wizard - Map Selection (or Export Wizard - Map Selection) dialog box, and then click Next. Specify an import (export) mode in the Import Wizard - Import Mode (or Export Wizard - Export Mode) dialog box, and then click Next. The Import Wizard - Map Options (or Export Wizard - Map Options) dialog box appears.

Specify whether you want to import or export information pertaining to tasks, resources, or assignments (see Figure 21.20), and then click Next. This tells the wizard to display the appropriate dialog boxes—Task Mapping, Resource Mapping, or Assignment Mapping—so you can map the fields. Be sure to leave the Export Includes Headers (or Import Includes Headers, if you're importing) check box checked if you want to add a header row with the field names to the exported data, or if the data being imported has a header row identifying the field names in the source file.

Now you begin the mapping process. This process differs slightly depending on the import or export application, but the options on the selected tab should be fairly straightforward. If you need to name a destination worksheet or apply an import or export filter, or you need to select a sheet or table that holds data to import, do so. Then, using the grid in the middle of the dialog box, identify how the applicable fields from Project should match up with each field of data being exported or imported.

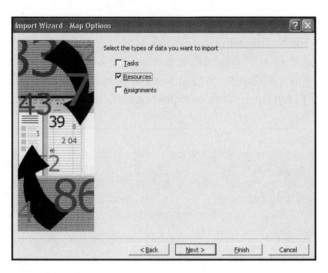

FIGURE 21.20 *Start your map by identifying what type of data to import or export.*

For example, in Figure 21.21, I selected the Name field from the drop-down list of Project field names on the first row. Then, in the To column on the same row, I entered the field name to use in a new Excel worksheet created by the export operation.

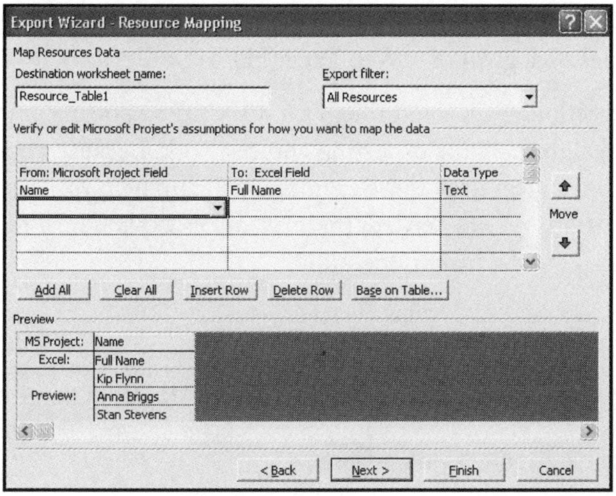

FIGURE 21.21 *Note that a preview shows how the mapped fields will look in the exported data.*

When you finish mapping the fields, click on Next in the dialog box to continue the wizard. In the Import (Export) Wizard - End of Map Definition dialog box, click on the Save Map button. In the Save Map dialog box, type a name for your map in the Map Name text box and then click on Save. Finally, click on Finish to finish the import or export operation using your map.

 TIP

Project stores new maps you save in GLOBAL.MPT, so you need to use the Organizer to move a map into any new file that you intend to send to someone else or move to another computer. Refer to "Using the Organizer to Create Global Calendars, Views, Tables, Macros, and More" in Chapter 13 to learn more about working with the Organizer.

Exporting Project Files

The flipside of importing is exporting, and the Microsoft Project Export Wizard walks you through the process. When you export information from a Project file, you save it in a format that another application can use. The formats to which you can export are generally the same as the import formats listed in Table 21.1, with two exceptions. You can also export project information as an Excel PivotTable (a dynamic table that you can reorganize by dragging categories on a grid) or a Web Page (HTML) file.

The next few subsections walk you through a few specific exporting examples, so you can get a feel for how the exporting choices work. Because importing resembles exporting a great deal, these examples will also help you learn how to import information. Where needed, these examples explain how to create a data map to complete the export operation.

 WEB

I've included the *Computer Purchase Project Chapter 21* file on the Premier Press download page at www.premierpressbooks.com/downloads.asp. You may want to use it to export file information.

Example: Exporting to an Excel Worksheet

You can export task, assignment, or resource information to a worksheet in a new Excel workbook file. Follow the steps to export resource information to a workbook file:

1. Open the file holding the information to export in Project, and then choose File, Save As. The Save As dialog box will appear.

2. Navigate to the disk and folder where you want to save the file, using the Save In drop-down list and the folders that appear below it. (Double-click on a folder icon to store the file there.)

3. In the File Name text box, type the name you want to give the file.

4. Open the Save as Type drop-down list, and then choose Microsoft Excel Workbook from the list.

5. Click on the Save button. The Export Wizard dialog box will appear.

6. Click on Next. The Export Wizard - Data dialog box will appear.

7. Click the Selected Data option button, and then click on Next. The Export Wizard - Map Selection dialog box will appear.

8. Click on the New Map button, and then click Next. The Export Wizard - Map Options dialog box will appear.

9. Check the Resources check box under Select the Types of Data You Want To Export, and leave the Export Includes Headers check box checked as well. (Of course, you would click on Tasks or Assignments to export that type of information instead.) Click on Next.

10. Enter a new name for the exported worksheet tab in the Destination Worksheet Name text box, if desired. For example, you could enter **Name and Rate**.

11. If you want to filter the exported information to export only information that matches the filter, select the filter from the Export Filter drop-down list.

12. Using the rows near the center of the dialog box, choose the fields to export and specify the names to use for the exported fields (columns) in the worksheet. For example, Figure 21.22 shows some export fields I've specified. In the From column, I clicked on each of the first two cells, and then I used the drop-down list arrow that appeared to display the list of fields and select the fields I wanted. Then I edited the suggested field names for the exported data in the To column.

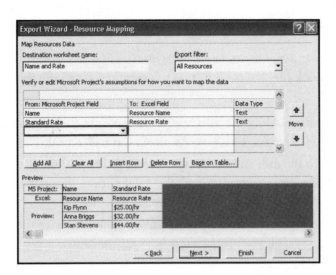

FIGURE 21.22   *This map will export resource information from two different fields.*

13. Click on Next to finish creating the map. The Export Wizard - End of Map Definition dialog box will appear.

14. Click on Save Map. The Save Map dialog box will appear.

15. Type a name for your map in the Map Name text box, and then click on Save.

16. Click on Finish. Project exports the file, saving it with the name you specified in Step 3.

17. Open Excel and open your exported file. Figure 21.23 shows how the map settings from Figure 21.22 result in two columns of exported data.

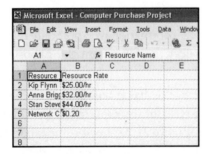

FIGURE 21.23   *In this case, the data map exported two columns of data. From here, I could format the data (changing the Rate entries to currency, for example) or sort it. If I exported fields with numeric information, I could perform calculations on that information.*

You can export *timescaled data* (that is, data from one or more selected fields broken out by day, week, month, or another time unit) from Project to Excel, and you can even graph the data during the export operation. However, you need to load an Add-In to get the job done, and this isn't a well-documented process in Project.

To start, choose Tools, Customize, Toolbars. Click on the Commands tab in the Customize dialog box. Click on the Tools option in the Categories list, and then drag the COM Add-Ins option from the Commands list and drop it onto any toolbar. Click on the Close button to close the Customize dialog box. Then click on the new COM Add-Ins button that you added to a toolbar. In the COM Add-Ins dialog box that appears, click on the Add button. Make sure the Analyze Timescaled Data in Excel Add-In is checked in the Add-Ins Available list, and then click on OK to close the COM Add-Ins dialog box.

Next, right-click on any toolbar and click on the Analysis option to display the Analysis toolbar. Click on the Analyze Timescaled Data in Excel button on that toolbar. This starts a wizard that leads you through the process of choosing the fields, the timescale periods, and whether or not to graph the timescaled data in Excel.

Example: Exporting an Excel PivotTable

Project offers a data map that enables you to export information to an Excel *PivotTable*—a special table you can use to analyze your project information. I'm not going to cover how to use a PivotTable (consult an Excel how-to book to learn more about it), but the following steps demonstrate how to export information into a PivotTable that enables you to view cost information by resource:

1. Open the file with the information to export, and then choose File, Save As. The Save As dialog box will appear.

2. Navigate to the disk and folder where you want to save the file, using the Save In drop-down list and the folders that appear below it. (Double-click on a folder icon to store the file there.)

3. In the File Name text box, type the name you want to give the file.

4. Open the Save as Type drop-down list, and then choose Microsoft Excel PivotTable from the list.

5. Click on the Save button. The Export Wizard dialog box will appear.

6. Click on Next. The Export Wizard - Map dialog box will appear.

7. Click on the Use Existing Map option button, and then click Next. The Export Wizard - Map Selection dialog box will appear.

8. Click on the Task and Resource PivotTable option in the Choose a Map for Your Data list, and then click Next. The Export Wizard - Map Options dialog box will appear.

9. Click check boxes as needed to specify whether the exported file should include information about tasks, resources, assignments, or any combination thereof.

10. Click on Finish. Project exports the file, saving it with the name you specified in Step 3.

11. Open Excel and open your exported PivotTable file. As Figure 21.24 illustrates, the exported file holds several worksheet tabs. Two of them—Task PivotTable and Resource PivotTable—hold predefined

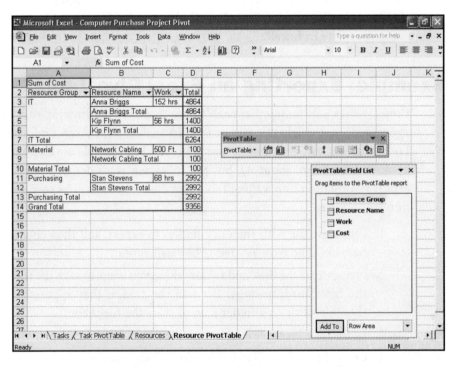

FIGURE 21.24 *Several quick steps in Project can produce a powerful Excel PivotTable.*

PivotTables that you can use to manipulate data and control how you want to view information about work and costs.

Example: Exporting to Access

When you export information from Project to Access, you can either export all the Project data or use a map to select which data elements to export. If you export the entire project file, the export operation breaks the information out into numerous database tables, each of which contains numerous fields of calculated coded information that won't mean anything to you at first glance.

 NOTE

Also note that Access doesn't do a good job of displaying some types of Project data, such as calculated duration information. So you may need to experiment with the data maps you create and the formatting in the Access table to get the export operation to work as you want.

This makes it extremely difficult to find and use the information you need, so I recommend using or creating a map:

1. Open the file with the information you want to export in Project, and then choose File, Save As. The Save As dialog box will appear.

2. Navigate to the disk and folder where you want to save the file, using the Save In drop-down list and the folders that appear below it. (Double-click on a folder icon to store the file there.)

3. In the File Name text box, type in the name you want to give the file.

4. Open the Save as Type drop-down list, and then choose Microsoft Access Database from the list.

5. Click on the Save button. The Export Wizard dialog box will appear.

 TIP

If you're saving to some database formats, you can append additional tables to an existing database file. Navigate to and select the file in the Save dialog box, so that its name appears in the File Name text box. Select the file type from the Save as Type drop-down list. After you click on Save, a dialog box appears to warn you that you've chosen an existing file. Click on the Append button, and then enter a unique name for the project table in the Name to Give the Project in the Database text box.

6. Click on the Only Selected Data button, and then click on Next. The Export Wizard - Map Selection dialog box will appear.

7. Click on the New Map option button, if needed, and then click on Next. The Export Wizard - Map Options dialog box will appear.

 TIP

To create a map based on an existing map, click on Use Existing Map Instead, and then click on Next. In the Export Wizard - Map Selection dialog box, click on the map to use, and then click on Next. Then continue with the following steps, altering the map as needed and making sure to save it under a new name.

8. Check the Tasks check box. (Of course, you would click on Resources or Assignments to export that type of information, instead.) Click Next. The Export Wizard - Task Mapping dialog box will appear.

9. Enter a new name for the exported database table in the Destination Database Table Name text box, if desired. For example, you could enter **NameStartCost**.

10. If you want to filter the exported information, select the filter you want to use from the Export Filter drop-down list.

11. Using the rows near the center of the dialog box, choose the fields to export and specify the names to use for the exported fields (columns) in the worksheet. For example, I chose to export the Name, Start, and Cost fields, so I entered **Task_Name, Start_Date,** and **Cost** (respectively) as the names for the fields in the exported table.

 TIP

In earlier versions of the software, you always had to use an underscore to separate the words in the name of an exported table, worksheet, or field. Project still suggests using the underscore in many instances, but you can use a space instead if you're exporting to Excel. In Access, however, you still need to use the underscore rather than a space.

12. Click on Next. The Export Wizard - End of Map Definition dialog box will appear.

13. Click on Save Map. The Save Map dialog box will appear.

14. Type a name for your map in the Map Name text box, and then click on Save.

15. Click on Finish. Project exports the file, saving it with the name you specified in Step 3.

16. Open Access, open your exported file, and open the table that the export map created for you. As you can see in Figure 21.25, my table data would look more attractive if I adjusted the formatting for the Start_Date and Cost fields.

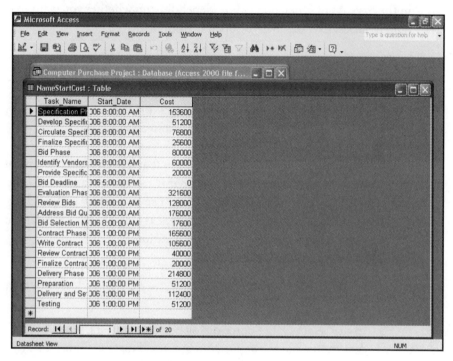

FIGURE 21.25   *I've exported data from Project into an Access table.*

Sharing Project Data with ODBC Databases

Project can also share information with database programs that are ODBC-compliant, meaning that those databases can communicate in a particular way. For this feature to work, ODBC drivers need to be installed on your system using the Data Sources (ODBC) icon in the Windows XP Control Panel. (Describing how to do this is beyond the scope of this book. If your company requires you to work with its central databases, your computer support staff will have set up this capability for you already. The installation process for some versions of the Microsoft Office 2002 suite also set up some of the ODBC drivers by default.) When you install those drivers, you can save Project data in a database from any other ODBC-compliant database application that your system is set up to save to, or you can use information from those databases in Project.

To work with ODBC database information, you click on the ODBC button in the Save As or Open dialog box, depending on whether you want to export data to an ODBC database or open it from one.

 NOTE

Only text or numerical information from the project is stored in the database, such as task names, start and finish dates, resource names, and resource assignments. No formatting or graphical information is stored.

Saving Project data to an ODBC database requires two general operations. First, you have to create the *data source* if it doesn't already exist. The data source tells Project which ODBC driver to use in creating and working with the database. Next, you save the Project data as a database in the data source. Follow these steps to accomplish both operations:

1. Create and save your schedule information in Project.

2. Choose File, Save As. In the Save As dialog box, click on the ODBC button.

3. In the Select Data Source dialog box that appears, type a name for the data source file in the DSN Name text box (see Figure 21.26). Then click on New.

4. In the Create New Data Source dialog box that appears, select the database driver you want from the list of drivers. (The list will vary depending on which drivers have been installed on your system.) Then click on Next.

5. Type a name for the data source in the next Create New Data Source dialog box. (This assigns a name to the data source you're creating to hold the database file. Use the same name you entered in the DSN Name text box.) Then click on Next.

6. Review your choices in the final Create New Data Source dialog box that appears, and then click on Finish.

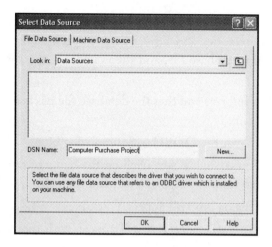

FIGURE 21.26 *The data source you create and select here tells Project which driver to use to connect with the database you're creating.*

 NOTE

Some ODBC drivers don't require some of the following steps. Just follow the instructions in the dialog boxes to set up your ODBC data source.

7. In the ODBC ... Setup dialog box, click on the Create button to open the New Database dialog box, as shown in Figure 21.27.

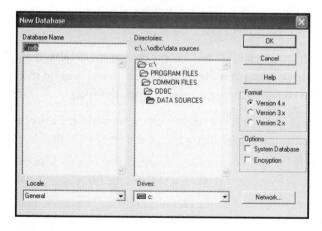

FIGURE 21.27 *At this point, specify a name for the database file itself.*

8. Type a name for the database file in the Database Name text box. If necessary, use the Directories and Drives lists to specify a different location for saving the database file, and then choose a save format. Click on OK.

9. When a message box informs you that the database file has been created, click on OK again.

10. Click on OK again to exit the ODBC ... Setup dialog box.

11. In the Select Data Source dialog box, click on the name of the data source you just created from the Look In list, and then click on OK.

12. The Export Wizard dialog box will appear. Click Next.

13. The Export Wizard - Data dialog box will appear, with the A Full Project option selected. Click Next.

14. The Export Wizard - Project Definition dialog box will appear. Type a name to use for the project information in the Project Name text box. Then click on Finish.

 NOTE

Some ODBC drivers are for spreadsheets such as Excel. If you use one of these drivers, the Selective Data tab will be selected instead. Use it as described in earlier examples to map the imported or exported data.

15. The Planning Wizard dialog box may ask you whether or not to save the information with a baseline. Click on the option you want, and then click on OK. Project saves the database.

After information from a schedule has been saved as an ODBC-compliant database, you need to open it from the database file to use it again in Project. Follow these steps to retrieve the information from the file:

1. Choose File, Open, or click on the Open button on Project's Standard toolbar. In the Open dialog box, click on the ODBC button.

2. In the Look In list of the Select Data Source dialog box, click on the name of the data source you created when you saved the file. Click on OK.

3. In the Import Wizard - Project Definition dialog box, click on the title you assigned to the project data (in Step 14 of the preceding set of steps).

4. Click on Finish. Project opens the information from the database file.

Chapter 22

*Communicating
with the Team*

In This Chapter

◆ Entering resource e-mail addresses

◆ Setting up for workgroup messaging

◆ Sending a collaboration message to assign work

◆ Sending a collaboration message to tell resources about changes in a task schedule or work completion status, or to send a note about a task

◆ Requesting a status update for one or more tasks

◆ Entering task information in Outlook

Like most other business-oriented applications, Project 2002 has evolved to allow you to work with information online. Its new features enable you to connect quickly to information you need, or to make schedule information easily available to your colleagues and contacts.

In addition, Project 2002 offers paperless, automated project management alternatives through its workgroup (collaborative) message-handling capabilities. Workgroup messaging works in conjunction with e-mail in Windows to allow you to automatically send assignment and update information to—and receive status reports from—resources that you communicate with via e-mail.

This chapter walks you through Project's e-mail workgroup messaging features.

Preparing to Communicate with a Workgroup

The workgroup for a project includes all the resources you've entered in the Resource Sheet. You can use Project's collaborative features to send automatic messages to the workgroup via e-mail. (See Chapters 24 through 27 to learn how to use these collaborative features via a Web workgroup.) This capability is called *workgroup messaging* or *team messaging*.

Setting Up for E-Mail Messaging

You first need to select e-mail as the default workgroup communication method for the current project file.

 NOTE

The e-mail system used with workgroup e-mail features must be 32-bit, MAPI-compliant. The e-mail program you use will depend on your operating system and the version of Office you've installed—and on the standards for your company. Project 2002's *Workgroup Message Handler*—the behind-the-scenes software that formats team messages and routes them between Project and the e-mail program—supports Microsoft Exchange, Microsoft Mail (for Windows NT only, not for Windows 95 or 98), Lotus cc:Mail 7.0 for Windows and Windows NT, Lotus Notes 4.5a for Windows and Windows NT, and Outlook. The figures in this book show examples only from Microsoft Outlook 2002.

Follow these steps to set up the current project file for communicating with the workgroup via e-mail:

1. Choose Tools, Options. The Options dialog box will appear. Click on the Collaborate tab.

2. Near the top of the dialog box, open the Collaborate Using drop-down list. Then click on E-mail Only (see Figure 22.1). This tells Project that you'll be communicating with resources via e-mail rather than a Web server.

3. In the message box that reminds you that you've chosen to collaborate by e-mail only, click on OK.

4. If you want this e-mail choice to apply to all of your schedule files, click on the Set As Default button near the bottom-right corner of the dialog box. Otherwise, your changes apply only to the currently opened file.

5. Click on OK.

Specifying Resource E-Mail Addresses

Just as you have to put an address on paper mail or regular e-mail, you need to give Project each resource's e-mail address to ensure that Project properly addresses the messages you send. You also need to verify whether the resource is set up to use e-mail messaging to ensure that Project sends the message correctly.

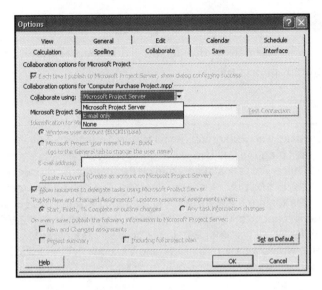

FIGURE 22.1 *Choose E-mail Only to send workgroup messages via e-mail.*

To tell Project a resource's e-mail address and messaging method, follow these steps:

1. Switch to the Resource Sheet view by choosing View, Resource Sheet, or by clicking on the Resource Sheet icon in the View Bar.

2. Double-click on the name of the resource for which you want to specify the e-mail address.

3. Click on the General tab of the Resource Information dialog box, if needed, to display its options.

4. Enter the e-mail address in the Email text box. Figure 22.2 shows an example. Or, if you've entered information about the contact into your Address Book, you can type the resource's name exactly as it appears in the Address Book, rather than the e-mail address. To check the resource's name or e-mail address in your Address Book (for Microsoft Exchange, Windows Messaging, or Outlook), click on the Details button. The Check Names dialog box appears. The Summary tab shows the exact name or e-mail address to use. Click on OK, and then enter the name or e-mail address into the Email text box.

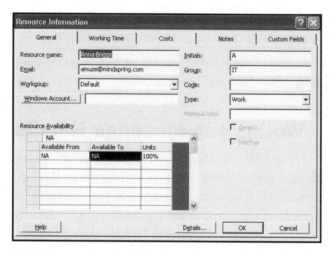

FIGURE 22.22 *Enter the resource's e-mail address in the Resource Information dialog box.*

 NOTE

The messaging options are disabled for material resources. So if you need to send messages regarding material resource assignments, you'll need to enter the recipient as a resource with a 0% Max. Units setting and specify the resource's e-mail address. Then assign that resource to tasks along with the needed material resource—but make sure you assign another work resource or remove effort-driven scheduling from the task. Otherwise, assigning the resource with 0% units will reduce the calculated task duration.

5. By default, the Workgroup drop-down list is set to Default. You don't have to change this option if you've already set up the current project file for e-mail messaging, as described earlier. However, if you set up the file for Web messaging (as described in later chapters), but the resource you selected in Step 2 only communicates via e-mail, open the Workgroup drop-down list and click on E-mail Only to ensure that you can send workgroup messages to the selected resource via e-mail.

 TIP

To disable e-mail workgroup messaging for a resource, choose None from the Workgroup drop-down list on the General tab of the Resource Information dialog box.

6. Click on OK to finish creating the address and setting the messaging method to use.

7. Repeat Steps 2–6 if you want to specify an e-mail address and messaging method for additional resources.

Installing the Workgroup Message Handler

The Workgroup Message Handler enables Project to format messages and communicate with your e-mail program. It also enables e-mail programs to receive and work with collaboration messages. If the recipients of your workgroup messages don't have Project 2002 installed, at the very least each recipient must install the Workgroup Message Handler. You also must install the Workgroup Message Handler on your system. There are three different ways to install it:

◆ You or your resources (message recipients) can insert the Project 2002 CD-ROM in the CD-ROM drive, use Windows to navigate to the WGSETUP.EXE file in the \WGSETUP\ folder (typically found within the \FILES\SUPPORT folder on the Project 2002 Setup CD), and then double-click on the WGSETUP.EXE file.

◆ If the resources are connected to your company's network, you can copy the \WGSETUP\ folder and all of its contents from the CD-ROM to a shared network drive. Then users can run the WGSETUP.EXE file from the shared folder to install the Workgroup Message Handler.

◆ If the resources are at another location and can't access your network or a Project 2002 CD-ROM, you can create Workgroup Message Handler installation disks and ship them to those resources as needed. This process requires two floppy disks. Copy EXTRACT.EXE, PRJ2K_1.CAB, SETUP.INI, WGSETUP.EXE, WGSETUP.INF, WGSETUP.LST, and WGSETUP.TDF from the \WGSETUP\ folder on the Project CD-ROM and transfer them to Disk 1. Copy only PRJ2K_2.CAB and transfer it to Disk 2. Then a resource can run WGSETUP.EXE from Disk 1 to start the setup process, which will prompt the resource to insert Disk 2 when needed. Alternately, you can zip (compress) and e-mail the contents of the folder to a recipient, who can then uncompress the files to a single folder and run WGSETUP.EXE.

Sharing Information with the Workgroup

After you've set up your project file and your resources to use collaborative messaging, in most cases you can use the commands on the Publish submenu of the Collaborate menu to send different types of messages to the workgroup members. This section covers how to use those features, as well as how to send and route files.

E-Mailing or Routing a Project File

Sometimes you might want to send your entire project file as an attachment to an e-mail message, such as when the project schedule is finalized or you receive a request from a superior to review the schedule. Of course, doing so assumes that the recipient of the message also has Microsoft Project installed and will be able to open and review the file. It also assumes that the file is a reasonable size (some e-mail servers limit the size of file attachments for security and capacity reasons), and that the recipient's system can access a shared resource pool if required.

When you send a file, it's sent to your e-mail program's outbox. You then have to launch your e-mail program and send the message from there, as described later in this chapter in the section "Finishing the Send."

To send a project file as an attachment to an e-mail message, follow these steps:

1. Open the file you want to send, make any last-minute changes you want, and then save the file.

2. Choose File, Send To, Mail Recipient (As Attachment). If Exchange or Windows Messaging prompts you to specify a profile, select one from the Profile Name drop-down list and click on OK to continue. The e-mail message window opens with the project file already inserted as a file attachment, as shown in Figure 22.3.

3. If the resource's e-mail address isn't in your Address Book, you can type the address in the text box beside the To button. Otherwise, click on the To button to display either the Select Names or Address Book dialog box, depending on the e-mail system you're using. Click on a name in the list at the left, and then click on To. This adds the name to the list of Message recipients. Add other names as needed, and then click on OK.

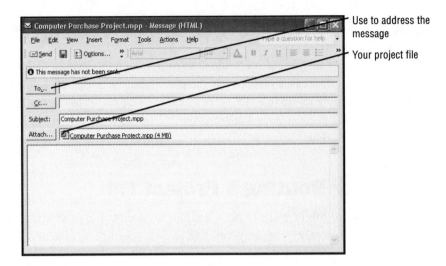

FIGURE 22.3 *Your e-mail program automatically helps you create the message in which to send your file. This message window is from Outlook 2002.*

4. If you want to include text—perhaps to describe what the file contains or to ask the recipient a specific question—click in the message body area and then type in your message (see Figure 22.4).

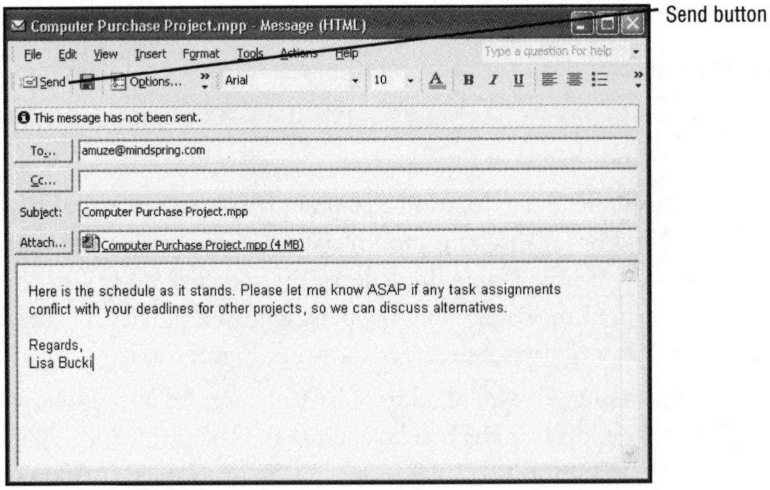

FIGURE 22.4 *The message is ready to go.*

5. Choose File, Send. Alternately, click on the Send button at the left end of the message window toolbar. The message with the file attachment is sent to your e-mail outbox. Later, when you open your e-mail program and send and receive messages, the message will be mailed to the recipient.

You can route a message with an attached file to a number of users and have a copy automatically come back to you when the last recipient closes the file after working with it. You can send the message to all recipients at once, or set it up so that it goes to the first recipient, who then must forward it to the next recipient, and so on.

To route a file, choose File, Send To, Routing Recipient. A security message may appear, asking if you want to allow Project to access e-mail addresses stored in Outlook. Click Yes to continue. The Routing Slip dialog box appears. Click on the Address button to open the Address Book dialog box. Click on a name from the list at the left, and then add this name to the list of recipients at the right by clicking on To. Add all the names you want, and then click on OK to close the dialog box and return to the Routing Slip dialog box.

The Routing Slip dialog box shows the routing order (see Figure 22.5). If needed, click on a name in the To list and click on one of the Move arrows to change the selected name's position in the list. Click in the Message Text area and enter whatever message you want to appear. In the Route to Recipients area, tell your e-mail system and Project messaging whether you want the message to be routed to the listed recipients one after another or all at once. If you want to automatically receive a copy of the routed file after the last recipient in the list has worked with it and closed it, make sure there's a check mark beside the Return When Done option. When the Track Status feature is checked (and when you're routing the file from one recipient to the next), it notifies you when each recipient on the list forwards the file to the next recipient. Click on Route after you specify all the settings you want. This sends the routed file to your e-mail outbox. You can then launch your e-mail program and send and receive messages to forward the routed message.

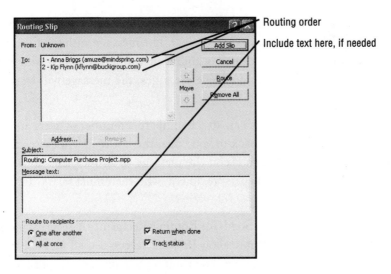

Routing order

Include text here, if needed

FIGURE 22.5   *The Routing Slip dialog box lets you add a cover message to the files you send out.*

Sending Assignments, Updates, and Status Requests

A number of commands on the Collaborate menu and its Publish submenu work in concert with your e-mail program, allowing you to share task information with the resources assigned to particular tasks. These commands take advantage of Project's Workgroup Message Handler. Selecting any of the applicable commands generates a special message in the workgroup messaging format, which is then sent to your e-mail outbox as an attachment to a regular e-mail message.

The workgroup (collaboration) message lists the resources who are receiving the message, and key data about each of the tasks you've selected to send or request information about. It includes suggested message text, so you don't even have to type instructions if you don't want to. It lists information such as the task name, start and finish dates, number of work hours, and percentage of work complete. It also offers a comments column for each task. The recipients of each workgroup message can make changes to the task information and then automatically return the message to you via their e-mail outbox.

TIP

The Collaborate toolbar offers buttons for sending workgroup messages. To display this toolbar, point to any toolbar, right-click, and then click on Collaborate.

There are two commands in particular that you'll use:

◆ **Publish New and Changed Assignments.** Use this command to send e-mail messages about new assignments, or assignments that have changed (such as revised start or finish dates or a new duration). This type of message asks a resource to verify acceptance of an assignment, as well as the schedule you've set for it, as shown in Figure 22.6.

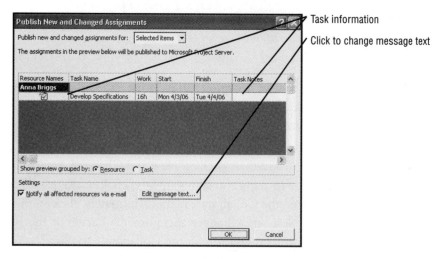

FIGURE 22.6 *This workgroup message asks a resource to verify an assignment.*

◆ **Request Progress Information.** This type of message queries the recipient to tell you how work is progressing on a task (see Figure 22.7).

The steps for sending each type of workgroup message are similar:

1. Update information in the schedule in Gantt Chart view, and then save your file. (Messaging features don't work in other views, such as the Resource Sheet.) If you don't save now, you'll be prompted to save later.

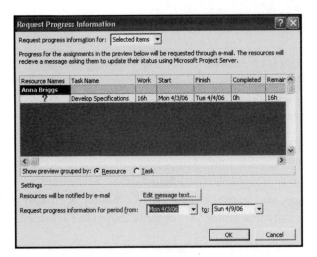

FIGURE 22.7 *You can ask resources to report to you about progress on tasks.*

2. If you want to send a workgroup message about a particular task or group of tasks, select a task and then hold down Ctrl while clicking on any additional tasks.

3. Open the Collaborate menu. To publish assignments, point to the Publish option and then click on New and Changed Assignments in the submenu. To request a status update, click on Request Progress Information on the Collaborate menu. Alternately, click on the either the Publish New and Changed Assignments button or the Request Progress Information button on the Collaborate toolbar.

4. The appropriate message dialog box appears. Open the top drop-down list (which is called either Publish New and Changed Assignments For or Request Progress Information For, depending on the type of message that you're sending). Then specify whether to send a message regarding the entire project or selected items (tasks), as shown in Figure 22.8.

5. Edit any of the information you want, such as adding additional information to the Task Notes cell for the task. To edit the text accompanying the message, click on the Edit Message Text button. The Edit Message Text dialog box appears, as shown in Figure 22.9. Make the changes you want in the dialog box, and then click on OK to return to the main message dialog box.

6. Click on the OK button at the bottom of the message window.

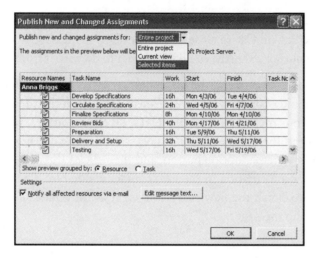

FIGURE 22.8 *Specify whether you want to send a message for all tasks*

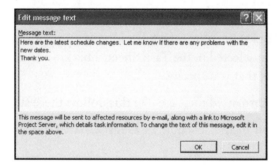

FIGURE 22.9 *You can personalize the text in a workgroup message here.*

 NOTE

Depending on which e-mail system you're using, or whether or not you're presently logged on to your e-mail program, you might be prompted to specify a profile when you send messages of any type. Make the appropriate selection, if prompted, and then click on OK to continue. If you see a security warning that Project is accessing the e-mail addresses in Outlook, and another message that Project is trying to send e-mail for you automatically, click on Yes in each message to continue.

7. A message box may confirm that your project information has been published. Click on OK to close it. The workgroup message is sent to your e-mail outbox. Shortly, you'll learn what to do with it from there.

When you send a file or send one of the team message types (described later), the Check Names dialog box may appear if Project needs to verify the e-mail address for any of your message recipients. Click on the resource's name in the list of matches and then click on OK. If necessary, use the Create a New Address for "Resource Name" option button, and then click OK twice. Enter the resource's contact information in the new contact dialog box. Then click on Save and Close to finish the new entry and use it as the contact's e-mail address for workgroup messages.

Sending Notes to the Team

Project can set up an e-mail message for you automatically, building the recipient list based on options you specify and enabling you to select whether the attached file should hold your entire schedule file or just a graphic picture (BMP file) of any tasks you selected in the Task Sheet. This kind of note can be sent to e-mail addresses that you specify.

To send an automatically formatted message like this, follow these steps:

1. Update information in the schedule in Gantt Chart view and save your file.

2. If you want to send a message about a particular task or group of tasks, you need to select the task or tasks. Select a single task, and then hold down Ctrl while clicking any additional tasks you want to select (you may be limited to 10 or so).

3. Choose File, Send To, Mail Recipient (As Schedule Note). The Send Schedule Note dialog box appears, as shown in Figure 22.10.

4. In the Address Message To area, specify the recipients for the message and whether the list should include the resources and contacts from the entire project or selected tasks.

5. In the Attach area of the dialog box, specify whether the attachment message should be the entire file or just a picture of selected tasks.

6. Click on OK. If any of the selected recipients lacks an e-mail address on file, you're prompted to specify the needed address as described

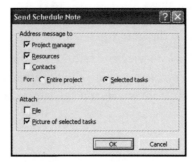

FIGURE 22.10 *Specify who will receive a schedule note and what attachment it will contain.*

earlier in this chapter. (You may be prompted to choose a profile or confirm access to e-mail addresses and messaging in Outlook. Do so, and then continue.) Then the message appears onscreen, as shown in Figure 22.11.

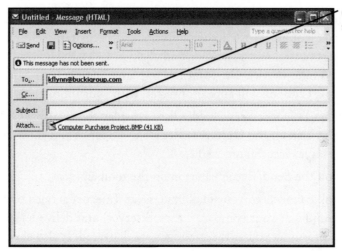

Contains a picture of selected tasks

FIGURE 22.11 *The e-mail message appears so that you can type the note. The correct recipients have already been entered.*

 TIP

You can delete the attached file from the message if you want. All your addressing information remains intact. To delete the attachment, click on its icon and then press the Delete key.

7. Type in a subject for the message. Then click in the message area above the attached file and type in the note you want to send.

8. Choose File, Send. Alternately, click on the Send button at the left end of the message window toolbar. The message with the file attachment will be sent to your e-mail Outbox, from which you can later send it.

Finishing the Send

All the workgroup messages you've learned to create so far in this chapter were sent from Project to your Outbox folder within your e-mail program. This makes sense, because Project and the Workgroup Message Handler aren't e-mail programs. They simply prepare your information to be sent via e-mail.

Now you need to send your messages from the Outbox to the intended recipients. To send workgroup messages from an e-mail program, you use whatever method you normally would use to send messages from the Outbox. For example, to send messages from Outlook 2002, follow these steps:

1. Go to your Windows desktop and double-click on the Microsoft Outlook icon to start Microsoft Outlook 2002. Alternately, click on the Start button on the taskbar, and click on E-Mail Microsoft Outlook (Windows XP). Or, point to Programs, and click on Microsoft Outlook. Outlook will appear onscreen with your Inbox folder open.

2. (Optional) Choose View, Folder list to display the available Outlook folders. Click on the Outbox folder icon to open it and show outgoing messages (see Figure 22.12).

3. Click on the Send/Receive button on the toolbar.

4. Outlook connects to your mail system (an Internet service provider, for example, or your company's e-mail server) and delivers the messages, informing you as the messages are delivered. It also checks for incoming e-mail messages and places them in your Inbox.

If you need to take any particular steps to retrieve regular messages from your e-mail system, you'll need to take the same steps for workgroup messages. For example, if you need to click on a Connect button to dial your Internet connection, you'll be prompted to do so.

Outbox folder | | Your workgroup messages

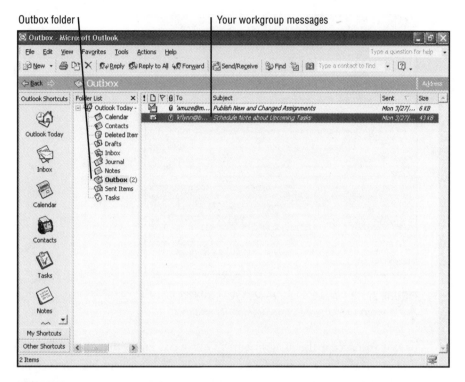

FIGURE 22.12   *The messages you prepared are lined up in the outbox, waiting to be mailed.*

Responding to Assignments and Updates

When you're on the receiving end of workgroup messages, they appear in your e-mail Inbox folder along with the rest of your incoming e-mail messages. To read a workgroup message, double-click on it. If you have received a project file as a message attachment, a routed file, or information sent as a schedule note, the message simply opens like a normal e-mail message. If you're opening a Publish New and Changed Assignments message or a Request Progress Information For message, Project's messaging features launch and open the message. It appears in a special message dialog box (see Figure 22.13).

Click on the Reply button to prepare your response to the message. The window automatically adjusts to enable you to reply, and RE: appears beside the window title and in the beginning of the subject. An insertion point appears in the Message area. Type in your overall reply there. If you're responding to a Publish New and Changed Assignments message, you can double-click on the Accept? cell entry to toggle between Yes and No, which informs the project manager whether

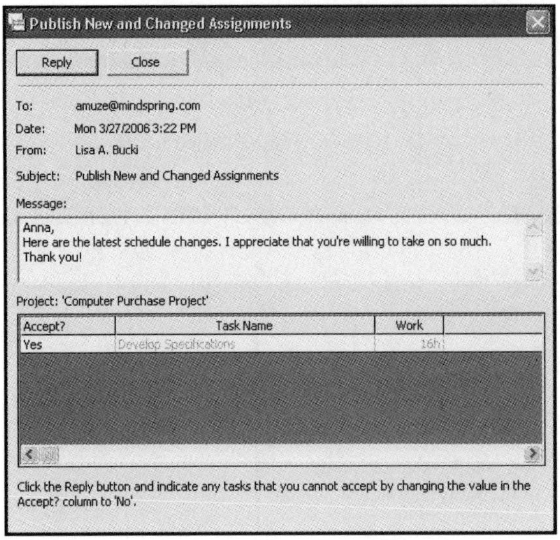

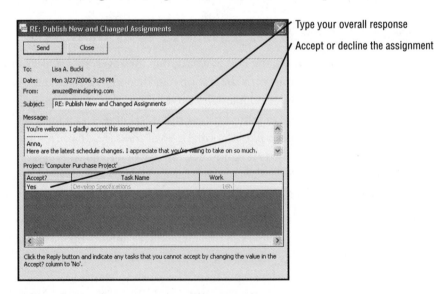

FIGURE 22.13 *Here's how a Publish New and Changed Assignments workgroup message looks to its recipient.*

or not you accept the assignment. (This is crucial so that the project manager doesn't accept your assignment accidentally. If you select No, Project does not finalize the assignment.) Figure 22.14 shows some example entries.

FIGURE 22.14 *Here's a response to the assignment message from Figure 22.13.*

If you're responding to a Request Progress Information message, enter any work completed on a particular day for the report period being shown in one of the blank cells. To make an entry, scroll to the right, click in the cell, type in your entry, and press Enter. Figure 22.15 shows a response to this type of message.

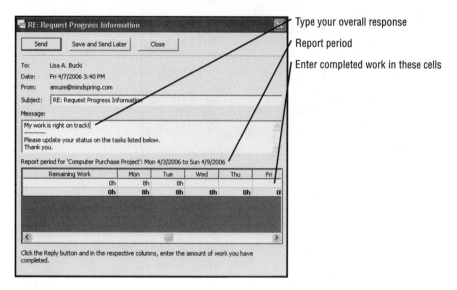

FIGURE 22.15   *Here's a response to a request for progress information.*

Click on the Send button to send the reply to your e-mail Outbox. From the Outbox, send the reply to the project manager using the steps outlined in the preceding section.

If you're a project manager, your resources will send replies to your assignment and status requests. Such responses appear in your e-mail Inbox, and you can double-click on each one to open it. For example, the response shown in Figure 22.15 resembles Figure 22.16 when the project manager opens it.

If the resource's response isn't satisfactory, click on the Reply button to send a follow-up message. If the resource has simply confirmed the existing schedule in response to a Request Progress Information message, you can click on the Close button to close the message, and click on No if you're asked whether to update the Project file. If the response accepts an assignment, suggests some schedule changes, or reports completed work, and you want to enter these changes into your project file, click on the Update Project button. If Project isn't open, it starts up and the file opens for updating. The schedule

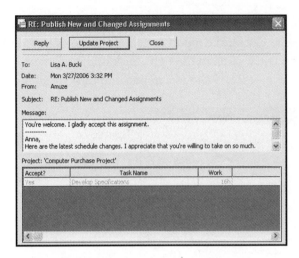

FIGURE 22.16 *This assignment response has been received from a resource.*

changes are made to the appropriate task in the schedule, and the status update message closes. Save your project file to keep these changes.

How Messaging Interacts with Outlook

When you accept an assignment or assignment change via a TeamAssign or TeamUpdate message in Outlook, Outlook automatically adds that assignment into your Outlook Tasks list. When you click on the Tasks icon in the Outlook Bar at the left (which is analogous to the View Bar in Project) or the Folder List, the Tasks list appears and includes any new assignments that you accepted via a team message (see Figure 22.17). Even better, if you respond to a Request Progress Information message and indicate that you've completed a task, workgroup messaging marks that task as completed for you, as in the third task shown in Figure 22.17.

So, if you're the project manager, you'll need to send Published New and Changed Assignments messages and Request Progress Information messages to yourself for your assignments in the project. You need to reply to each message to accept the assignment. Then open the response message and click on the Update Project button to accept the assignment response and add it into the Project file. (Open the response message in your outbox if it isn't sent back to you automatically. You don't have to *send* the message; you just have

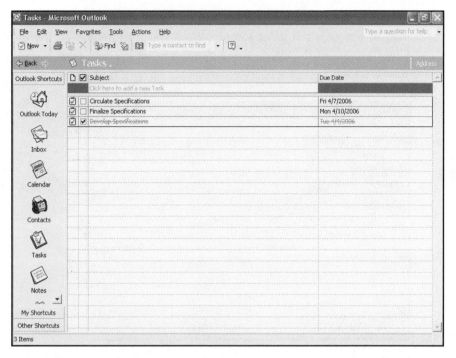

FIGURE 22.17   *Assignments you accept via team messages appear in your Outlook Tasks list.*

to complete the process steps.) You can then delete the message from your Outbox (or Inbox, if the message was sent automatically.)

 CAUTION

> At present, what I've just described is the only way to add your own assignments into your Outlook Tasks list. Although you can copy-and-paste or drag-and-drop a task from Project to the Tasks list, the task information isn't filled in completely in Outlook.

Outlook 2002 can remind you of your tasks that were created via workgroup messages. By default, Outlook reminds you of any task that includes a due date. Because due dates are assigned to tasks created via workgroup messages by default, Outlook will display a reminder on the task's due date.

To set a more specific reminder on your own (specifically, one that precedes the start date for the task), double-click on the task in your Outlook tasks list. The task window opens. To turn on the reminder, check the Reminder check box (see Figure 22.18). You can then use the accompanying drop-down lists to specify the reminder date and time, and use the button with the speaker icon to choose a reminder sound. When you finish, click on the Save and Close button on the task window toolbar to set the reminder and return to your Outlook Tasks list.

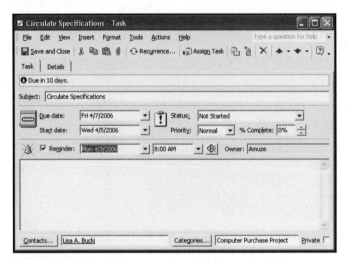

FIGURE 22.18 *Check the Reminder check box to have Outlook display a reminder about a task that's been added to your Tasks list.*

 NOTE

If you're the project manager and you use the Outlook Journal feature to track your work on various types of Office files, you can turn on the tracking for Project files, too. First, choose Tools, Options in Outlook. On the Preferences tab of the Options dialog box, click on the Journal Options button. In the Also Record Files From list, check Microsoft Project. Then click on OK twice to accept your choice and close the two dialog boxes.

Chapter 23

**Using Project
with the Web**

In This Chapter

◆ Browsing the Web

◆ Adding hyperlinks into a Project file

◆ Saving Project information in Web format

◆ Formatting your Web information

With tens of millions of users worldwide, the Internet has become one of the most important communication tools in the business world. The thousands and thousands of sites on the Internet contain information on almost any subject you could imagine. This chapter explains how to use Project 2002's basic features for working with the Web. (Chapters 24 through 27 explain how to use Web workgroup features to manage project progress.)

The Web coverage in this chapter assumes that your system is set up to connect to the Internet, and that you have a Web browser installed and configured to launch when needed.

Embedding a Hyperlink

In Project, hyperlinks not only point to Web pages, but also to files stored elsewhere on your computer or in a shared folder on a network server. You can embed a hyperlink along with a task row or resource row in the Task Sheet or Resource Sheet of any view. Then you can click on the hyperlink indicator in the Indicators column to launch your browser and display the Web page the link points to. Selecting a hyperlink that points to a file opens that file—and its application, if needed.

For example, if an external resource has a Web site where you want to find updated product pricing information, you could add a hyperlink for that Web site to the resource's entry on the Resource Sheet. Or if you want to consult the file for another project that's on your company network before you update a particular task, you could create a hyperlink to that file.

Even better, if a file in another application holds extensive notes you need to keep in association with a project, a contract, a price list, or any other vital information, you can hyperlink to it from Project. This way you don't need to make lengthy note entries (which would inflate the size of your project file), and you can use the right application for each type of information you want to track, while keeping that information close at hand.

To create a hyperlink to a path on your hard disk, use the full path and file name to identify the file, as in C:\My Documents\NewProduct.mpp. You can use the same format if a file is stored on a *mapped network drive*, which is a particular storage area on the network that has a particular drive letter assigned to it (usually H). For other networks, instead you may need to enter the UNC (Universal Naming Convention) address to point to the file on the network server. Enter the UNC address in the format **\\Server\Share\Path\FileName.ext**, where Server is the name of the network server computer and Share is the name of a shared area or partition that network users can access. If you've worked with files on your company's network, you probably know which method you need to use to name and access network files. Use the same method for creating hyperlinks.

To insert a hyperlink, follow these steps:

1. Display the view with the Task Sheet or Resource Sheet holding the task or resource for which you want to add a hyperlink, and then click on the desired task or resource to select it.

2. Choose Insert, Hyperlink, press Ctrl+K, or click on the Insert Hyperlink button on the Standard toolbar. The Insert Hyperlink dialog box will appear.

3. In the Text To Display text box, enter a short name for the hyperlink. (For example, if you're creating a hyperlink to http://www.msn.com, you might enter **MSN** in the Text to Display text box.) This entry will appear onscreen instead of the full path or URL when you point to the hyperlink indicator.

4. In the Address text box, enter the Web page or file address. If you're creating a link to a file on your hard disk, you can click on the one of the buttons to the left of the Look In list, and then select or browse for the desired file or Web page. Figure 23.1 shows a network link address entered in the Address text box.

Insert Hyperlink button

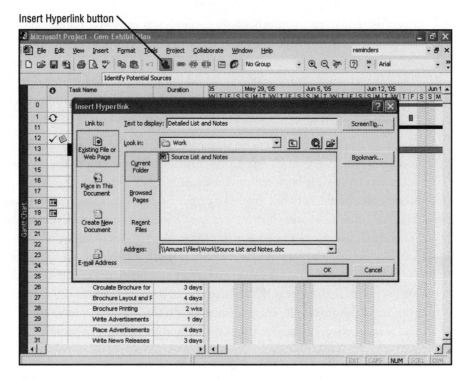

FIGURE 23.1 *Use this dialog box to create a hyperlink.*

 TIP

You can also use the ScreenTip button to increase the amount of information that appears when you point to the hyperlink indicator. After you click on the button, enter text in the ScreenTip Text box and then click on OK.

5. If the file you're opening uses easily referenced labels like cell addresses (spreadsheets), bookmarks (word processors), or a task ID number (Project file), click on the Bookmark button to open the Select Place In Document dialog box. The options will change depending on the type of file or page to which you've linked. When you're done, click on OK.

6. Click on OK to finish creating the hyperlink. An indicator for the hyperlink will appear in the Indicators column.

Your hyperlink is now complete. To see the short text or URL and the ScreenTip (if any) for the hyperlink, move the mouse pointer over the hyperlink indicator, as shown in Figure 23.2.

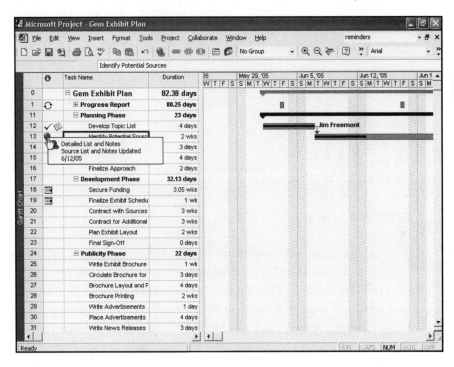

FIGURE 23.2 *Point to a hyperlink indicator to see information about the hyperlink.*

To display the Web page or document that the link points to, click on the hyperlink indicator. Project launches the source application for the specified file and connects to the Internet, if needed, and then it displays the specified file or page. If you open another Project file, the Web toolbar also appears in Project. See the next section to learn how to use that toolbar.

If you need to change the location for the hyperlinked page or file, or you want to remove the hyperlink, you can display the Edit Hyperlink dialog box. Its options are nearly identical to those in the Insert Hyperlink dialog box shown in Figure 23.1. To change or remove a hyperlink, click on a cell in the row for the task or resource that holds the hyperlink. Click on the Insert Hyperlink button on the Standard toolbar. In the Edit Hyperlink dialog box, change the text box entries as needed. Or, to remove the link, click on the Remove Link button. Click on OK to close the dialog box.

Using the Web Toolbar to Surf

When you click on a hyperlink to open a linked Project or Office document, the Web toolbar appears near the top of the screen, just under the Formatting toolbar. You can also display the Web toolbar at any time by right-clicking on another toolbar and then clicking on Web. Figure 23.3 shows the Web toolbar.

FIGURE 23.3   _You can also use the Web toolbar to display files and Web pages._

The Web toolbar offers buttons for displaying particular Web pages or hyperlinked files. Many of the buttons on this toolbar work just like buttons in your Web browser. For example, the Back and Forward buttons move back and forward through pages and files you've displayed during the current project's work session. Click on the Stop Current Jump button to stop loading a hyperlinked file, or click on the Refresh Current Page button to update the Project files that are currently open.

The Start Page button launches your Web browser and displays the start page or home page (the first Web page your browser has been set up to display). The Search The Web button also displays your browser and a page with tools and links for searching the Web for a particular topic. Clicking on the Favorites button opens a drop-down list naming the pages you've added to the Favorites list in your Web browser. Click on a page name to launch your browser and jump to the page. The Go menu offers commands that correspond to some of the buttons already described, as well as Set Start Page and Set Search Page for changing the Web page that either of those Web toolbar buttons display. Click on the Show Only Web Toolbar button to hide or display other on-screen toolbars.

Finally, you can enter a Web address or file path and name in the Address text box, and then press Enter to display the linked page (or the linked file) in your Web browser. To jump back to a previously displayed page, click on the drop-down list arrow beside the Address text box, and then click on the name of the link to follow.

Saving Project Information as a Web Page

The section called "Exporting Project Files" in Chapter 21 noted that one of the formats you can select for exporting data is the Web Page (HTML) format. You can use the File, Save As command and choose Web Page from the Save As Type drop-down list in the File Save dialog box, and then continue exporting the file as described in Chapter 21.

 NOTE

You also can export your project data as an XML (Extensible Markup Language) file. XML files present the project data with special tags that identify the file's contents. The XML data can then be used in a variety of custom applications—such as a Web application for presenting data.

In addition, the File menu includes the Save As Web Page command. This displays the Save As dialog box with the Web Page option already selected, as shown in Figure 23.4. Project suggests the name of the original schedule file as the file name. You can edit that name or the location to which the file will be saved.

Click on Save to continue the export process. The first Export Wizard dialog box appears. Click Next to continue. From there, you can follow the wizard, choosing whether to use an existing data map or create your own map. (Refer to the "Understanding Data Maps" section of Chapter 21 to refresh your memory about the map creation process.) After choosing or selecting a map, follow the rest of the wizard to save the document as the HTML Web page, with the HTML file name extension.

After you create the Web page, you can use it in two ways. First, you can copy it to the Web (http://) server folder (on your company's Internet or intranet Web site), where other users can access it. If your Web site is on an ISP or configured in certain ways, you may need to use a program such as CuteFTP to transfer the file. You can then build hyperlinks in other documents (Web, Project, and other Office applications) to display the Web page from the

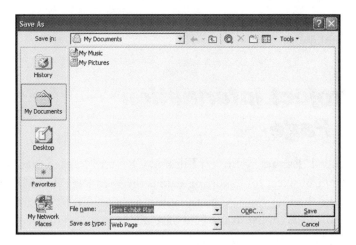

FIGURE 23.4 *Choose the Web Page file type to save the current Project file as a Web page.*

folder where you posted it. If you have trouble with this, consult your company's network administrator or webmaster to learn how to post your pages.

Alternately, you can e-mail the Web page (HTML file) or provide it on disk to anyone who uses it. Any recipient with a relatively recent version of their Web browser will be able to open the file from an e-mail message or from disk. After saving or copying the page file to a folder on the hard disk, the recipient can navigate to the folder using My Computer or Windows Explorer, and then double-click on the file to launch the Web browser and display the file. (You can use this technique to view the file from your hard disk as well.) Figure 23.5 shows information from a project schedule file exported as a Web document and displayed in the Internet Explorer 6.0 Web browser.

 NOTE

If you have a program that lets you open HTML documents, you can use it to edit the exported Project Web page, adding graphics or changing fonts. For example, you can open any HTML (or HTM) file in Microsoft Word 2002 and use Word to improve its look and layout.

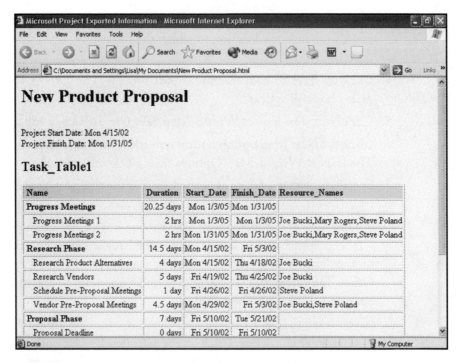

FIGURE 23.5   *Project data saved as a Web page includes title information and a table of fields.*

Specifying a Web Template for a Web Page

The Web page shown in Figure 23.5 looks pretty generic. Happily, Project does offer a few options for improving the page's appearance.

To create a Web page with a custom look, you create a custom map that includes a Web page template to give your data a colorful appearance. You can also add a graphic like a logo. Follow these steps to spice up a Web page generated from your schedule file:

1. Open the schedule file in Project, make any last-minute changes, and then save it.

2. Choose File, Save As Web Page. Project will display the File Save dialog box with Web Page already selected (refer to Figure 23.4).

3. Edit the suggested name in the File Name text box, if needed. You can also change the location to which the file will be saved using the Save In list.

4. Click on Save to continue the export process. The Export Wizard dialog box will appear.

5. Click Next. The Export Wizard-Map Selection dialog box will appear.

6. Click the New Map option button if needed, and then click on Next. The Export Wizard-Map Options dialog box will appear.

7. Specify basic map options as needed, such as the type of data to export.

8. Check the Base Export On HTML Template check box in the HTML options area of the dialog box. The Browse button beside the check box becomes active. Click on it to open the Browse dialog box. Browse to the templates folder for Project (\Program Files\Microsoft Office\Templates\1033), select the template you want to use, and then click on OK to apply the template.

9. If you want to add an image file, check the Include Image File In HTML Page check box. Click on the activated Browse button beside it, use the Browse dialog box to select an image file (it must be a .GIF, JPG, or PNG image), and then click on OK. At this point, your choices might look like Figure 23.6.

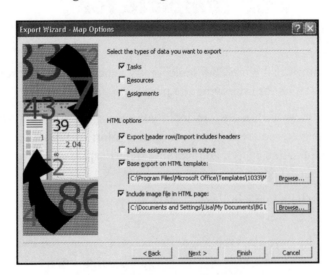

FIGURE 23.6 *In this instance, I'm including both an HTML template and a graphic with the data map.*

10. Click on Next, and then define the fields for your new map in the Export Wizard - Task Mapping dialog box, as described in "Understanding Data Maps" in Chapter 21. Click Next.

11. If you want to use the map again, click on the Save Map button in the Export Wizard - End of Map Definition dialog box. Type an entry in the Map Name text box of the Save Map dialog box that appears, and then click Save.

12. Click on Finish to save the document as the HTML Web page using the map you just created, with the HTML file name extension.

13. Open the new Web page in your browser. It will look something like Figure 23.7.

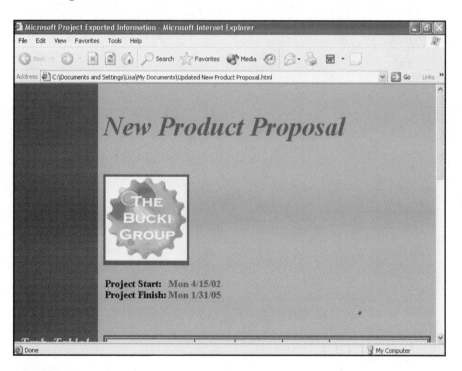

FIGURE 23.7 *Here's the fancy version of my Web page.*

Chapter 24

Project Server
(Administration)

In This Chapter

◆ What is Project Server?

◆ Installing Project Server

◆ Infrastructure Requirements

◆ Administration Basics

The email workgroup functionality covered in Chapter 22, "Communicating with the Team," is merely the tip of the collaborative project iceberg. Used with Project 2000 or Project 2002 Standard Edition, Project Server is a platform for collaborative project and team management. Using Project 2002 Professional Edition as your project manager's interface opens the door to a new world of project level/program level enterprise features. These new features make a compelling argument for moving up to Project Server.

Project Server deployment has intricacies and nuances the surface of which will only be scratched in the next four chapters. This chapter and the next three are an ankle-deep exploration of Project Server and its features, with a strong focus on enterprise features. This is the heart of what's new about the Project 10 family of products. You will likely decide whether to deploy Project Server based on whether the enterprise features are right for you and your company; I will attempt to spotlight what you need to know to make that decision. Topics in this chapter are presented in an order that lends itself to stepping through with the software as you read.

What is Project Server?

Project Server is the second-generation server product that adds a client-server framework to Microsoft Project. Until the introduction of Project Central in 2000, adding centralized management software around Microsoft Project was left to independent software vendors and Microsoft Partners. A host of these, as well as other full-fledged client/server products, are available.

The core of Project Central remains in Project Server, consisting of an assignment and time tracking system realized through Web-based messaging between resources and the project manager, and ultimately the project plan. Time tracking, visibility, and a small set of enhanced collaboration features, such as status reporting, are brought forward and enhanced in Project Server.

Project Server 2002 adds an enterprise-level data layer that enables complex structuring of Project Portfolios supporting highly structured program management requirements. A locked-down project management environment suitable for managing standards-compliance is supported, and Microsoft Sharepoint Team Services is leveraged to provide a full document-and-issues management system integral to the project plan. SQL Server Analysis Services add online analytical processing to project views. All of these features are customizable, and many of them are easily managed through Project Web Access and Project Professional.

Installation

Project Server is not the typical pop-in-the-CD-and-click-Setup Microsoft application we're all used to, despite any impressions you may have gotten from reading its marketing materials. Even in its simplest configuration, which uses MSDE as the database, Project Server can make for an extremely daunting first-time installation, even for a Microsoft Certified Systems Engineer. Project Server is a server product, not a desktop application. At the very least, Project Server relies on IIS (Internet Information Services) and MSDE (Microsoft Data Engine) to function. If you intend to implement enterprise features you'll also be working with Share Point Team Services, SQL Server, and SQL analysis services for OLAP (online analysis processing), as well as substantial server hardware with advanced configurations. Large enterprise installations may require load balancing and clustering schemes. Project Server requires significant manual security configuration and manipulation. You'll need to invest time in reading and planning, and you'll need the patience to survive a false start or two.

If, after reading these warnings, you still find yourself plunging the installation disk into your server's CD drive, heed this last caution: Getting Project Server ready for your organization may be a piece of cake compared to getting your organization ready for Project Server. This is particularly true when time reporting is introduced to the workforce for the first time. Begin your organizational change management well in advance of your rollout. To achieve an effective configuration, you will need to know what your user and business requirements are.

 NOTE

A pilot program is a must for enterprise implementations. The larger and more complex your installation, the more important this becomes. Putting your users through the pain of a poorly thought-out implementation may sour your chances of success.

Explore your installation CD, and make sure that you read every document Microsoft provides. Some of the important Project Server documents you should study include the following:

- The installation guide
- White Papers on the CD
- SVRDB.HTM, which describes the Project Server database
- Deployment and Resource Kits on the Web

Project Server is designed to take advantage of domain security. If you do not have a domain, don't use Windows Authentication for your project managers; instead use Project Server authentication.

You may, however, use Windows authentication for your Project Web Access users who are not managing projects, by creating accounts for them on the Project Server and granting them permission to log on locally.

Project Server Infrastructure

Like its predecessor, Project Central, Project Server can be economically deployed in a work group environment. A single server running IIS, Project Server, and SQL Server will support up to 10 project managers working with up to 100 project resources. Your mileage will vary according to your usage patterns. The demands on your server resources depend on how much your business uses views and reports. A default installation using MSDE as your data engine and Project Standard as your planning tool is supported, but is suitable only for very small workgroups. Your best use of an MSDE configuration is for training and evaluation. Moreover, because it lacks the powerful management tools and convenient interfaces provided with SQL Server, MSDE is much more difficult to manage. Yes, MSDE is free, but you get what you pay for.

 NOTE

Enterprise features are supported only when Project Professional is used with Project Server and SQL Server is used for project storage. Oracle is not supported for Project Server as it was for Project Central. Oracle and other ODBC-compliant databases continue to be supported for project storage without Project Server.

Suitable for large organizations, Project Server supports load balancing for Web farms and SQL Server clustering. Installations supporting hundreds of project managers and thousands of team members are within your reach. The capacity of your hardware, the number of users, and the volume of project activity substantially contribute to performance. For example, a single 1 GHZ processor machine with 1 GB of RAM and a 50 GB hard drive makes a dandy test box and is the least you should have to support a "small shop" installation. Always choose hardware that has been tested and certified to be compatible with the Microsoft operating system and server products you intend to implement. Visit the Microsoft Hardware Compatibility List home page at http://www.microsoft.com/hcl/ to learn more about compatible hardware.

First Post-Installation Steps

Assuming that the installation went well, you're no doubt eager to harvest the fruits of your effort. Wipe the sweat from your brow, type the URL for your server into your browser (http:servername/projectserver/ or the custom URL you chose) and take a look.

The first time Project Server is launched, as shown in Figure 24.1, you must log on using the administrator account automatically created during the installation process. The password is blank; leave it that way until you've verified that Windows authentication is working. You'll likely be logging in and out quite a lot until you've stabilized your installation; leaving the password blank makes this less of a chore. Don't forget to set a password before going into production! Project Central supports both Windows authentication as well as Project Server logons. Typical installations will primarily use Windows authentication—it's easiest to administer and most secure. Project Central accounts are useful for granting access to guests and for remote log on via the Internet.

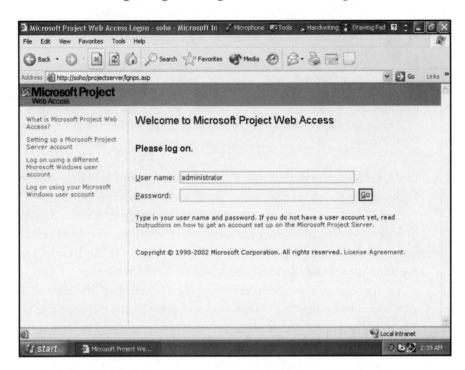

FIGURE 24.1 *Use the administrator account to log on to Project Server for the first time.*

The new style of Project Web access is instantly familiar (see Figure 24.2) if you've worked with Microsoft Share Point. If you're migrating from Project Central you'll also be instantly comfortable navigating the interface. Whether you're a first-timer or a Project Central émigré, you'll probably want to explore a little. Go ahead and click around. There's not much to see or do until you set up some resources and publish a few projects; and you've got some configuration work to do, so go ahead and do so, then hurry back!

With your curiosity about the Web interface satiated, it's time to get this application configured and ready for use. As an administrator, you have access to every feature in Project Server. Functional access is largely defined by Project Server roles and can be managed granularly by user, project, and resource. The interface is logon-sensitive and displays menus and options appropriate to the user.

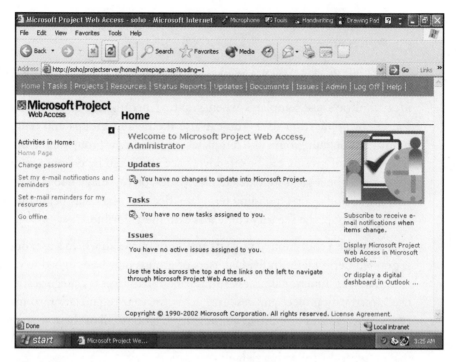

FIGURE 24.2 *The Project Server interface sports a style similar to Share Point and retains the navigational elements familiar to Project Central users.*

Project Server Administration

To effectively manage a Project Server implementation, you must first understand its security matrix. You can manage permissions for individual users or for user groups. A group is simply a collection of users who are assigned the same permissions. Permissions are set for functional access to application components, and for access to data types. Managing by group is the easiest and most effective way to control access to both program functions and data. Project Server Web Access is installed with the following default groups:

- ◆ Administrator
- ◆ Executive
- ◆ Portfolio Manager
- ◆ Project Manager
- ◆ Resource Manager

◆ Team Lead

◆ Resource

Each group installs with a default security template. You can use a template to apply permissions to a group or define permissions individually. It's a good idea to always use templates when granting permission to application resources or application data. You can use the default groups and templates, modify the default groups and templates, or create new groups and templates. Sub-typing of groups can be effectively accomplished by creating templates that reflect the logical subtype characteristics, or you may choose to create a new group and a corresponding template. Because users may belong to more than one group, the security context is extremely flexible.

Categories are a collection of projects and/or resources to which a user or group is granted permission. Individual users or groups may be assigned to categories marrying functional access to informational access. Categories may be used to stratify project and resource access in your organization to meet all types of access and visibility requirements. Combine all of these security features to fine-tune access within your organization. Project Server Web Access installs with the following default categories:

◆ My Organization

◆ My Projects

◆ My Resources

◆ My Tasks

An *organization* refers to all of the projects, users, and data in an installation instance of Project Server. Permissions set at the organization level determine whether features will be available to all users. Any permission set here will override any permission set at all other levels of the organization. Like groups and templates, you may modify the default categories or create custom categories. Data access to categories may also be set by customizable templates, and both users and groups may be assigned to one or more categories.

You can layer security permissions by defining groups and assigning users to multiple groups. Similarly, you can layer access to data by defining categories and assigning users or groups to multiple categories. Combining the two constructs supports complex security requirements. Again, the key to success is a clear understanding of your organizational requirements and as simple an application as possible.

Managing Users and Groups

Project Server's interface contains a main navigation bar across the top of the screen. The options available here reflect a user's security permissions and role. As an administrator, you identify these and Project Server displays the appropriate choices. The left-hand side of the screen is a collapsible activities panel reflecting the subtasks associated with each functional area. You choose a functional area by clicking on the main navigation bar. Clicking on the arrow in the activities panel collapses it, freeing up screen space for the primary work area. Unless you're working on a high-resolution display, you'll likely want to collapse the activities panel while working within a functional area. Expanding it is as easy as clicking on the arrow again.

Choose Admin from the main navigation bar to display the administration interface shown in Figure 24.3. For the most part, the main page of each functional area contains the same navigational choices available on the activities panel; however, there are some exceptions wherein the first choice on the activities list is immediately displayed.

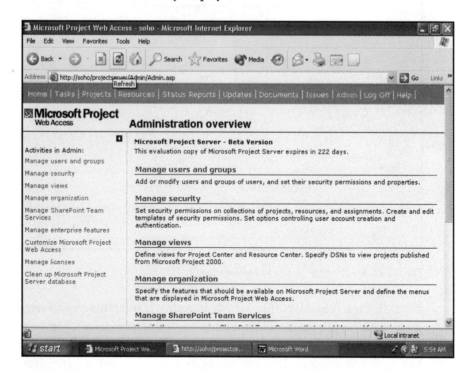

FIGURE 24.3 *A left-hand activities panel displays subtasks associated with the top-level navigational choice. The body of the display contains the work area.*

Choose Add User from the menu. When the Add User screen is displayed, select the Windows Authentication radio button, as shown in Figure 24.4. Type your user name in the format **domainname\username**. If your server is not part of a domain, then substitute the Project Server server name for the domain name. These instructions assume that you already have a domain account or an account on the server with local logon rights.

If you instead select the Microsoft Project Server Authentication radio button, the display changes to display password and password confirmation fields. Create a Windows account for yourself now, in order to verify that Project Server is properly configured to use Windows authentication. You'll use your new account to work with Project Professional in the next chapter.

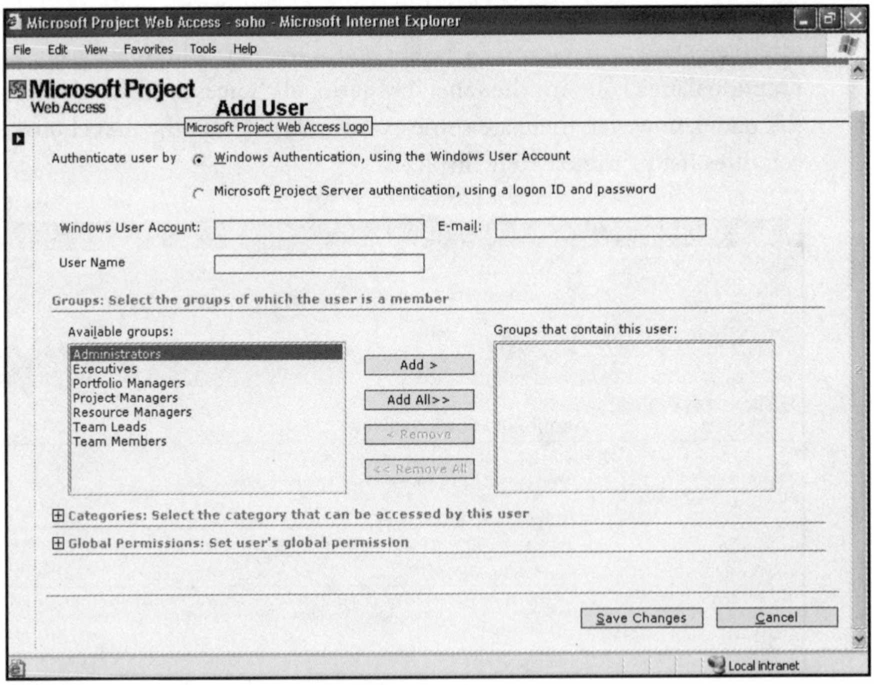

FIGURE 24.4 *Enter the new user information.*

Next click the Add All button (which, in reality, is something you'll rarely ever need to use, as few users will require such broad access rights). Scroll down, if necessary, then define your category permissions and global permissions by selecting Set Permissions by Template using the Administrator template. Take note that permissions can be allowed, denied, or left blank. Click the Save Changes button to complete your user creation. If you've made an error in typing the name, left out the name of the domain or server, or another error was encountered, the system will display the error message shown in Figure 24.5; otherwise, the application will report success, as shown in Figure 24.6.

FIGURE 24.5   *An error occurred during new user creation.*

FIGURE 24.6   *The Add User operation was successful.*

You've now successfully created an account for yourself, but the critical topic of permissions requires additional discussion. More specifically, it is very important that you understand the impact of *allowed* versus *denied* and *not allowed*. Allowed and denied are explicit selections, whereas not allowed is implicit. Once a user is explicitly denied access to a function or data area, either directly or by virtue of group membership, that denial trumps any other permission to that function or data anywhere else in the security schema.

Use the denied value very judiciously. Browsing through the default values in the various templates deployed in Project Server reveals this ethic very clearly. Rarely do you see denied being used. This is because once a user is denied a specific permission in any one group, that user will be denied that permission in all groups. In a simplistic deployment, where each user is a member of only one group, this will not cause much management grief, but the moment you start to take advantage of layering permissions through groups and categories, unintended consequences may result. Don't deny permission unless you're sure that doing so is necessary to meet your requirements.

NOTE

Similarly, if a user is allowed permission in one group, that permission is granted for the user in all groups.

Instead, use this behavior to your advantage. Suppose you had a select group of resources within the Team Members group to whom you want to expose a higher level of visibility. For instance, you may want to give some team members access to assignment views because they're playing a pseudo-role as junior team leads. As long as you haven't explicitly denied access to the Team Members group, you could create a second group called Junior Team Leads, allow access there, and add those users to the new group. Their existing permissions would remain intact while their new permissions were layered on. You may ask, "Why not simply create a new group with all the permissions of Team Members and the added permissions?" That would be a perfectly acceptable approach, but if the permissions are transient, as they might be for a trial period or a special situation, it's easier to remove a group from the system than it is to shuffle resources between them. You must choose which approach is right for your organization.

To manage groups and group permissions, select Manage Users and Groups from the Admin menu, then choose Groups from the Activities menu. From here, follow the screens to create new groups and modify existing groups. You'll see the same groups you worked with while creating your user account, but here you'll be able to modify the existing ones and create new groups for your organization.

 NOTE

Now that you've navigated through a few screens you may have noticed that Project Server remembers the state of your display choices after you leave a screen. If you leave a display element collapsed or expanded, it will return to that state upon your next visit. Project Server uses cookies to accomplish this. If you're not seeing this behavior, cookies may be turned off in your browser.

Manage Security

Choosing Manage Security from the Admin menu brings you to a submenu of activities that include Category maintenance, Security Template maintenance and an interface to maintain global authentication options for your Project Server installation. You've learned how to use categories and security templates to manage security in Project Server; here you have the opportunity to tailor these to your organizational requirements.

Category maintenance (shown in Figure 24.7) is the default display when you choose Manage Security from the Admin menu. Note that the current system categories are enumerated in a table at the top of the page. Project Central users might have noticed that the grid control responsible for creating this table, which touched most displays in Project Central, has been downplayed in Project Server. Microsoft explains this as part of the performance improvements in the new release. Click on a category in the grid to display its detail on the page.

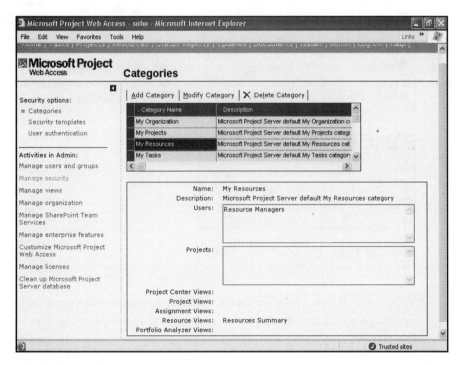

FIGURE 24.7   *The users, projects, and views included in a category are displayed when you click on the category name in the grid.*

Choosing to add or modify a category loads a new page, which allows you to point and click at available category members in each subsection of the category, easily moving them in and out of play. Scroll through the choices and you'll find that the process is very intuitive and self-explanatory, once you understand the underlying concepts. Security templates may be used to create and modify the default permissions for categories in much the same way they're used to define permissions for individual users. The interface is identical.

Maintaining security templates is the second available option under Manage Security. If you're planning on creating a number of categories, you might want to first define the templates you wish to use in the process. The first screen in Security Template maintenance is nearly identical to Category Maintenance. Available security templates are enumerated in a grid, and clicking on a template name displays its detail on the page (See Figure 24.8).

 TIP

The easiest way to create a new security template is to clone an existing template and then make changes to it. When you choose Add Template, the Add a New Template Web Dialog is displayed. Here you enter a template name and description, and you have the option to copy an existing template on which to base your new one. A drop-down selection box allows you to select an existing template that most nearly matches your requirement; alter it to suit your needs.

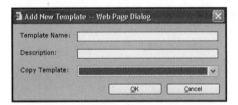

FIGURE 24.8 *Clicking on a template name allows you to see details about it.*

When you choose Add a Template, the dialog box that displays allows you to provide a name and description for your new template, as well as select a template to clone. When modifying a template, the dialog box does not display; from that point on the process is identical. The display shown in Figure 24.9 renders adding and modifying templates a matter of selecting or deselecting check boxes.

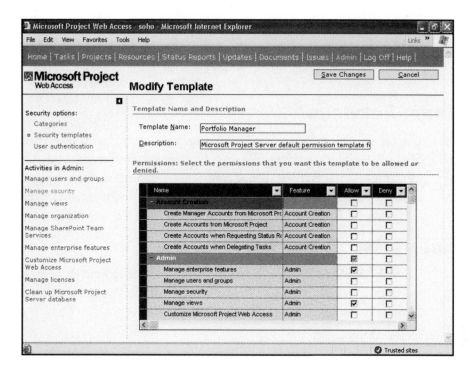

FIGURE 24.9 *Select and deselect as your requirements dictate.*

User authentication options are configurable in the third option in the Manage Security activities pane. Project Server may be set to accept Windows authentication only, Project Server authentication only, or mixed. Mixed authentication is strongly recommended. Unless only one or the other is feasible, it's difficult to imagine an implementation that wouldn't benefit from supporting both Windows and Project Server authentication. Windows authentication demands the least overhead and is the easiest to manage, but installations exposed to extranets and the Internet will likely require Project Central authentication. Use Windows authentication wherever possible and allow for the possibility that you won't be able to use it in every situation.

Manage Organization

New in Project Server is the ability for the administrator to turn core features on and off. The administrator may also set the default intranet and extranet server addresses for the server, which are used in email notifications and reminders. To access these features, click Features in the activity pane under Manage Features.

Click on Menus in the side pane to explore the exciting new menu management facility. The interface allows you to change the name and the order of menus. You can also create custom menus here.

Team Services

Use the features in this section to manage connections with servers running Share Point Team Services. Through the various interfaces provided the administrator can specify or change connections, determine the settings for sub Web provisioning, and choose between automatic and manual functionality.

Enterprise Features

Click the Manage Enterprise features link from the Admin Activities menu to control many of the new features in Project Server. Activities available through this submenu include

- ◆ Features
- ◆ Update resource tables and OLAP cube
- ◆ Check in enterprise projects
- ◆ Check in enterprise resources, and
- ◆ Versions.

Selecting Features allows you to enable or disable the new enterprise features in Project Server. The options found here, combined with the options that are set in the next section, Project Server Customization, give you extensive control over fundamental behaviors in the system. In the Features main pane you can

- ◆ Enable enterprise features
- ◆ Allow master projects in Microsoft Project Server
- ◆ Allow projects to use local base calendars
- ◆ Enforce single currency as specified in the enterprise global template, and
- ◆ Allow only Microsoft Project Professional to publish to this server.

In essence, these options determine whether enterprise features are supported or not. If the Enable Enterprise Features check box is not checked, the other selections in the Manage Enterprise Features Activities menu are disabled. Enterprise projects and resources, OLAP services, and versions are disabled.

Master projects are not recommended for Project 2002 Professional. They are an obsolete construct in the context of enterprise management. You should think in terms of programs and projects, not master projects.

Project Server Customization

Customization options allow you to set a default tracking method or lock down the time tracking method system-wide, requiring users to conform to one enterprise standard. Gantt chart formats used in timesheets and views may be customized, including which elements are displayed, as well as their colors and styles. You may specify grouping formats for timesheets and views as well as for custom groupings. Users may report non-project work hours through their timesheets in Project Server. This is called *non-working time* in the interface. You can create categories for reporting and tracking non-project work; these are specified through this interface. You can add links and simple content items to the home page by clicking the Home Page Format link. An automated reminder service has been introduced with Project Server, and you can customize the standard message by selecting the Notifications and Reminders link in the activities pane.

 NOTE

The term *non-working time* can put off your users when they see it for the first time. Explain to them that non-working means work other than work on this project, not time spent slacking or goofing off. Because Project Server does not provide a full-fledged time reporting system, it should not be used as such. Further, time posted to non-working categories is accessible only through direct query of the database rendering it less useful than it might appear.

Project Server Licensing

This area of administration allows the administrator to specify the number of licenses purchased. Project Server includes five client access licenses along with the server license, and each copy of Project 2002 includes a client access license for project Web access. Users who are not licensed to use Project 2002 must be licensed separately for Project Server Web Access. Bulk licensing is available through Microsoft resellers.

Project Server Database

Although it's no substitute for a good DBA, Project Server administration provides an easy-to-use interface for managing more mundane aspects of database cleanup. Here you can delete tasks, resource task changes, and status reports selectively for one user or all users. Projects and Share Point Team Services subwebs can be deleted as well. Look for a file named svrdb.htm on your installation CD. It contains a detailed data dictionary for the database, as well as code and query samples that will help you get started on your integration and customization projects using the Project Server database.

Chapter 25

**Enterprise
Project
Management
with Project
Professional
and Project
Server**

In This Chapter

◆ Working with the enterprise global file

◆ Importing resources into the enterprise

◆ Understanding generic resources

◆ Learning how to customize enterprise fields

◆ Bringing your customizations to life in views

Chapter 24 explored server administration, which is only half of the administrative picture—and the easier half at that. This chapter looks at administration for the enterprise, a much more complex set of tasks. Used as a suite, Project 2002 Professional and Project Server with enterprise features enabled provides a platform for tightly integrated program management. The features described here apply only to those two programs used in concert.

What Makes It "Enterprise"?

Project Server deploys with a single database. This is a substantial departure from Project Central's architecture and supports much tighter data integration. Project behaves differently when operating in a Project Server enterprise environment—it adheres to an enterprise global file, where customization is managed in a single repository at the organizational level.

Resource pools are gone. In their place are enterprise resources with check-in and check-out capability. A new centralized project data store also supports check-in and check-out, as well as version control, thus enabling shared plan management in the application. This construct was not supported by the last version. A resource substitution engine now provides skill-based, availability-sensitive suggestions for selecting enterprise resources to replace generic resources, a new type of supported resource used for planning.

Finally, we now have project-level custom fields. They're introduced as part of a new layer of enterprise custom fields, which distinguish themselves by their centralized control. They provide a means to build a rich metadata layer to complement your organizational structure. They're also the basis for applying a custom-tailored structure to your project portfolio.

Rounding out the complement of new enterprise features is OLAP portfolio modeling provided by SQL Server analysis services, as well as a document and issues repository provided by Sharepoint Team Services (STS). STS ships with Project Server, but SQL Server analysis services is a component of SQL Server and is licensed separately.

Next Steps

Most of your enterprise management is handled through the Project 2002 Professional interface. First you need to create a server account profile for Project to use to connect to Project Server. Choose Tools, Enterprise Options, Microsoft Project Server Accounts (see Figure 25.1).

FIGURE 25.1   *Create a server account profile to connect to Project Server.*

When the Microsoft Project Server Accounts dialog box appears, click on the Add button to open the Account Properties dialog box shown in Figure 25.2. The same dialog box opens when you click Properties for editing an existing account. Enter the appropriate information and click the Test Connection button to verify the configuration. You'll probably want to make this your default account. Creating additional accounts is optional. This capability supports connections to multiple Project Server instances. By clicking the appropriate option button, you can control the connection state manually or set it to automatic. If you choose manual, you will be required to select your connection state each time you start Project 2002 Professional. However, the default account will be highlighted and you'll never be more than one click away from loading. Choosing Automatic causes the application to immediately attempt to connect using the default account.

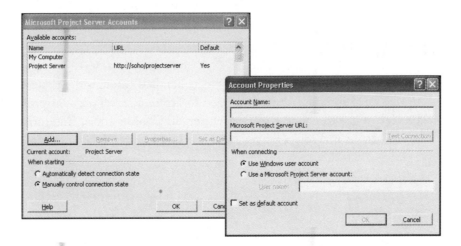

FIGURE 25.2 *Enter your account name and the Microsoft Project Server URL. Test the connection.*

There's one more setup step left. You can either click Tools, Options, and then click on the Collaborate tab, or you can click on the Collaborate menu and select Collaboration Options, which will take you directly to the Collaborate tab shown in Figure 25.3.

Use the options here to determine how your installation of Project 2002 Professional interacts with Project Server. Your project plan is the primary data store, but assignment data lives only in Project Server. The language here is very confusing. If you haven't had experience with Project Central, you must understand the difference between an assignment in Project and an assignment in Project Server. Assigning a resource to a task in Project doesn't immediately push that information to a resource in Project Web Access (the

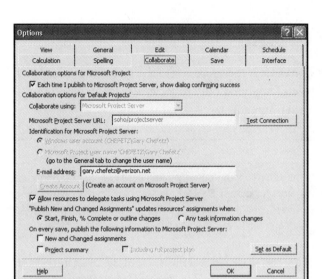

FIGURE 25.3 *The Collaborate tab of the Options dialog box allows you to choose how Project interacts with Project Server.*

name of the Project Server Interface). As a project manager, you control when and how that happens.

When you assign a resource to a task in Project, you are booking that resource's time. The fact that the resource is assigned to a particular task will be visible in your plan in Project, as well as in Project Server views, but it will not appear on a resource's timesheet until you explicitly publish the assignment. The reason for this is manifold. Project Server views draw data directly from the project tables. These simply duplicate, on the Web, what a manager is able to see in a project plan. Although resources may be granted privileges to views, they do not have them by default. A separate set of tables contain assignment information that make up the resource timesheets and resource personal Gantt charts. These provide a staging area for a bidirectional flow between you and your resources, and ultimately the project plan. You choose when data is published to these tables for resource use, and you choose when data is accepted back from these tables to update the plan. In this respect, Project Server acts as a messenger service. Resources never interact directly with plan data, which is a good thing. You'll see how this works in the next two chapters, but it's important for you to understand it now.

Enterprise Global

The Enterprise Global file is the successor to the global.mpt file, which takes on a diminished role of applying only to local files when working offline in the Project Server environment.

> **NOTE**
>
> In the past, the global.mpt file could be controlled centrally by creating a custom network installation, which pointed Project installations to a single copy of the global file on the network. Besides being complex to administer, it suffered from availability issues and was far from an elegant way to centralize project artifacts.

The introduction of a server-based global file is one of the most important (if not *the* most important) new features introduced with Project Server. Certainly, it is the foundation of the Enterprise features and behaviors supported in this release. The global file stores all of the standardized data for projects, including views, tables, filters, macros, and the like, in the same way the global.mpt behaves in prior versions. The most significant difference is the addition of Enterprise Fields and the ability to lock down behavior into a client/server environment.

To work with the Enterprise Global file, a user must be logged on to Project Server as an administrator. Select Tools, Enterprise Options (see Figure 25.4), and then click Open Enterprise Global. The title bar at the top of the screen (see Figure 25.5) will read Checked-out Enterprise Global.

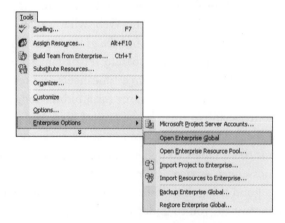

FIGURE 25.4 *Select Enterprise Options from the Tools menu, and then select Open Enterprise Global from the submenu.*

FIGURE 25.5 *The title bar changes to display Checked-out Enterprise Global.*

 CAUTION

Changes you make to the Enterprise Global file will not be active in your project files until you save and close the Enterprise Global file, close Project and restart it, and reconnect to Project Server. This is because the Global file, which is stored in the database, gets cached when you first log on through Project Professional. Even when you check out the Global file, all changes are visible in your personal session, but not active in your personal session, until you have saved and checked in the file and exited fully from Project Professional. This means that you must be very structured in your approach to modifying enterprise fields. For instance, you shouldn't define a custom enterprise field and then try to reference it in a formula for yet another custom enterprise field until you first save the original change and exit fully out of Project Professional and then restart it.

When you set out to make a bunch of changes to the Global file, consider whether the changes have dependencies among them. Also, make the changes in small, controlled steps, verifying each round as you make them. It's a good idea to back up your Global file through the administration feature provided in Project Server before making each round of changes. Be careful: this is probably the biggest "gotcha" in Project Server.

When you are working in a connected environment, all changes made to the Global File override changes made in local files. This includes changes to project views and toolbars outside the realm of those designated as enterprise. Carefully consider the impact to your existing projects when you migrate to a Project Server environment. It may be more palatable to your managers if you introduce new views rather than changing existing ones, as changing views may interfere with changes your managers have made to their local files. Consider focusing your enterprise customization efforts on the new class of enterprise fields, which allow you to introduce new attributes without interfering with existing customizations. Be aware of the innovative changes your managers have made to their plans as part of your implementation planning, and leverage the best of these changes into your enterprise customizations.

Enterprise Custom Fields

Program managers with large-scale deployments will applaud the addition of tightly controlled enterprise custom fields, and will likely be ecstatic when they discover project-level fields. Not only do you have another complete set of customizable fields for tasks and resources, you now have an entire new class of fields available at the project level.

Project-level fields have been sorely missing. They support the addition of meaningful metadata to a project. Use them to store information such as the names of key personnel or stakeholders, departmental information, key target dates, allocated burden costs, or initiation process checkpoints. These fields are very flexible, limited only by your organizational requirements and imagination. Enterprise custom fields may be designated as required, forcing a user to establish a value for them as a requisite to publishing in Project Server. Declaring a field as required will affect all enterprise custom fields at the task, resource, and project level.

Customizing enterprise fields follows the same workflow covered in the discussion of customizing fields in Chapter 13. Names given to enterprise fields take precedence over local items. If a manager creates a local field with an identical name and then connects to Project Server, the system will let him rename the duplicates. Otherwise, it will suppress them in the view.

When you launch Project Professional with a connection to Project Server, the Enterprise Global file loads into memory and caches calendar information from projects opened during your session. Caching is a new feature that boosts performance. Enterprise items are copied from the server on demand, and are not saved in the project file itself. However, when you choose to work offline, these items are copied into your plan until you republish it to the server.

With the Enterprise Global file open, click on the Tools menu and select Customize Enterprise Fields. The Customize Enterprise Fields dialog box will appear, as shown in Figure 25.6. This dialog box is essentially the same as the one for customizing standard custom fields. It contains two tabs, one for enterprise fields and one for a special type of enterprise custom field called

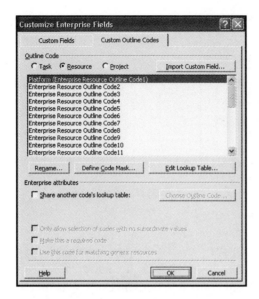

FIGURE 25.6 *The Customize Enterprise Fields dialog box contains two tabs, one for fields and the other for outline codes.*

enterprise outline codes. These codes play a special role in enterprise resource functionality. They're used exclusively by the new resource substitution engine for skill-based resource matching (covered in the next chapter), and are used to filter resources when browsing. Therefore, it's very important to carefully think through how you use these codes to enable the best use of enterprise resource features in Project Server.

The important distinction between enterprise outline codes and standard outline codes is that enterprise outline codes may be used for skill matching and resource substitution. Like other enterprise custom fields, you can declare them to be required.

Click the Rename button to give your new outline code a name, and then click the Define Code Mask button to apply a mask or format to your outline code. Figure 25.7 defines a code for a programming language skill. There are three definable attributes for each outline code level: character type, length, and the separator to be used. Here we're setting up a simple code using one segment as a character with any length. Segments may be defined as numbers, uppercase letters, lowercase letters, and characters. The character type accepts a combination of upper- and lowercase letters, as well as numbers and other characters. The other three adhere strictly to their types.

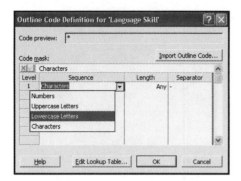

FIGURE 25.7 *When you define an outline code, you must first define the code mask.*

Next, define the lookup table for the code. Lookup table values must adhere to the mask definition. In this example, shown in Figure 25.8, I've used a mask that allows a fairly freeform approach, but you can use as much structure and complexity as you like.

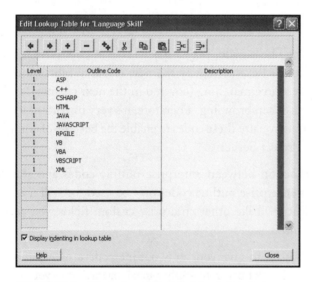

FIGURE 25.8 *The lookup table definition is handled through the Edit Lookup Table dialog box. The system displays the name of the custom outline code in the title bar.*

Lookup tables may be shared with other codes. Suppose that your company classifies resources by the department that they work for, and also classifies projects by the department they originate from or are sponsored by. These elements can share a lookup table, allowing you to maintain your department list in one place. Lookup tables may be maintained only through the outline code for which they were first set up. When a code shares a lookup table, the outline code will be tagged with "shared" in the Enterprise Outline Code dialog box. Likewise, when a code shares a lookup table from another code, it will be tagged with "linked," and the field from which it shares will be displayed in the dialog box shown in Figure 25.9 when it is highlighted by a mouse click.

 TIP

When you define lookup tables for required resource outline codes, consider your skill-matching needs for generic resources. Make certain you have provided a value that is applicable to generic resources. For example, if you define a required code to identify a resource by business location, make sure you provide a value to represent something like "any" or "all." That's easier than creating a distinct generic resource for each location.

One other consideration is that once you add a required field at the resource level, you obligate yourself to assign a value for all of your resources. Otherwise, the system will start nagging your managers for values when they open and attempt to resave their project plans. Project Server provides support for default values in custom fields only, not custom outline codes. (I smell a much-requested feature for the next release!)

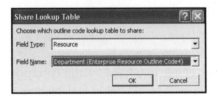

FIGURE 25.9   *When you share a lookup table with another code, the system displays the Share Lookup Table dialog box, which allows you to choose from a list of existing codes.*

You may use formulas that reference enterprise fields and Project's standard fields when you're creating custom enterprise fields. However, formulas can't reference Project local custom fields because they are not tightly controlled by Project Server. You may, however, reference enterprise custom fields in formulas that are embedded in local custom fields.

There are two methods of removing an enterprise custom field. The first is to clear the lookup table, mask, and custom name value. The other, faster, method is to delete it from the Fields tab in the Organizer. You must open the enterprise global file to delete enterprise fields through the organizer, and you must be connected to Project Server as an administrator.

Enterprise Resources

Project Server provides a central repository for resources available to the enterprise. As previously mentioned, the repository replaces the function of resource pools in the Project Standard version and the previous releases of the product. Resource pools are notoriously problematic for large organizations, so Project Server opens new vistas for Microsoft Project. You don't need to be working for a large organization to benefit from using enterprise resources, though.

Resources must be checked out on a resource-by-resource basis to be edited or assigned to tasks. This ensures that two or more project managers don't work with a resource at the same time. The ability to address resources individually in the checkout process is a major advance, and it promises to drastically reduce the occurrence of resource contention, even in very large resource pools. You may want to give some thought to enterprise resource pool etiquette for your organization.

Only the resources stored in the central repository use the calendars and fields defined in the enterprise global file. Resources may be created locally within your project and used there without being imported to the enterprise, but none of the enterprise global goodies will be available for these resources. Enterprise resources are automatically opened when an enterprise project that they are contained in is opened. Additionally, you may check out a resource directly from the enterprise resource pool or through the team builder, which is covered in the next chapter.

Opening the enterprise resource pool is similar to opening the Enterprise Global file. From the Tools menu, select Enterprise Options, Open Enterprise Resource Pool. Project Server will verify your right to access the pool and display the Open Enterprise Resources dialog box shown in Figure 25.10.

The Open Enterprise Resources dialog box displays the check-out status of resources, as well as when and by whom they were checked out. Resources that are checked out may be viewed. You can select all resources for checkout using

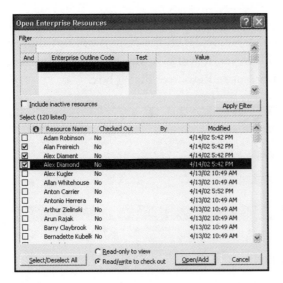

FIGURE 25.10   *The Open Enterprise Resources dialog box allows you to select any or all resources with which to work.*

the Select All button, or you can choose them individually. To make your search easier, use the values of your enterprise outline codes to filter the view in the dialog box. To simply add resources, don't select anything and click the Open/Add button, making sure that the Read/Write to Check Out option button is selected. The enterprise resource pool will open to a blank Resource Sheet view.

Generic Resources

Attributed properly with custom resource outline codes, *generic resources* facilitate a powerful new team-building functionality. To use this power, you must define generic resources around the skill codes and other outline codes you create. With the Enterprise Resource Pool open, display the new Generic field in the Resource Sheet View by adding the Generic column. Now you're ready to define generic resources.

Set the Generic field value to Yes to designate a resource as generic. Give your new generic resource a descriptive name, and double-click on it to open the Resource Information dialog box. Navigate to the Custom Fields tab and enter the required information, as well as your skill attributes. In this example, you'll use the programming language skill code you set up earlier in the chapter. If you don't complete the required fields in the Resource Information dialog box, shown in Figure 25.11, the system will not allow you to save the new resources. However, it will give you a chance to correct your blunder in the Validate Enterprise Resources dialog box.

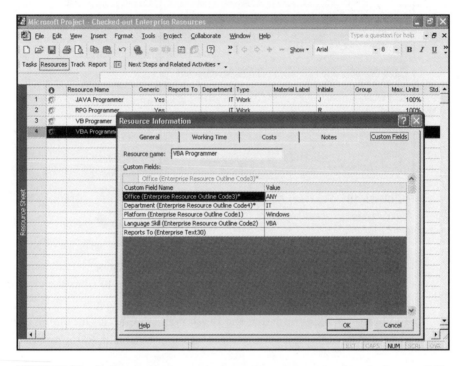

FIGURE 25.11 *Before you can save new resources, you must enter any required custom field information in the Resource Information dialog box.*

After completing the required fields, you will be able to save the resource. But you may have forgotten to enter all your skill code values if they're not required fields. If this is the case, click the Cancel button in the Validate Enterprise Resources dialog box (shown in Figure 25.12), go back to the suspect resource, and complete the entries.

Import Resources

Microsoft has made it very easy to import resources into Project Server's Enterprise Resource Center. A wizard is provided that streamlines the process, including mapping custom field information and automatically creating

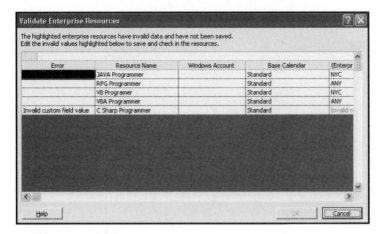

FIGURE 25.12 *The system validates your input and displays the Validate Enterprise Resources dialog box before saving changes. This is your last opportunity to make corrections, because resources with errors will not be saved.*

user accounts in Project Server. From the Tools menu, select Enterprise Options, Import Resources to Enterprise (see Figure 25.13).

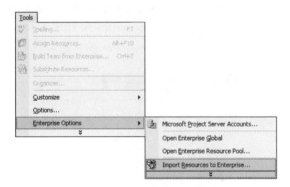

FIGURE 25.13 *Opening the Import wizard*

The Import wizard announces itself with a splash screen. Click Next, and the program presents the Open From Microsoft Project Server dialog box shown in Figure 25.14. Most likely, you don't have anything stored on the server and will want to import your resources from a resource pool. You may also import resources from regular project files. Click the Open from File button to invoke a typical file-browse dialog box, and then locate the file or click the ODBC button to open a series of dialog boxes that step you through DSN selection to open a file stored in a database. Once you have located the file, click the Import button.

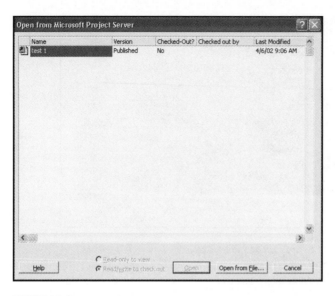

FIGURE 25.14   *The Open From Microsoft Project Server dialog box.*

Next, you must map any custom field data that you want to conserve in the new system. The friendly Import Resources wizard presents you with a dialog box, shown in Figure 25.15, with which to accomplish this. If you don't have any custom information to map, you can skip this step.

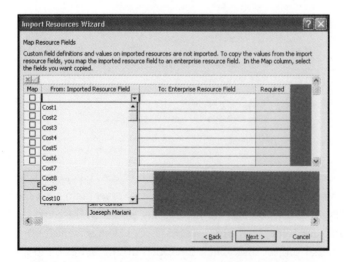

FIGURE 25.15   *The Import Resources Wizard allows you to map custom field values from your existing resource pools or project files and load them to enterprise fields.*

TIP

If you've defined the required custom resource fields, you should add similar custom fields and values to the project or resource pool from which you are importing your resources. Remember that Project Server will not allow you save enterprise resources without valid values in the required fields. If you have many project files from which you want to import resources, build a resource pool from those files first, then add the fields and values there. This makes it an easier task.

Alternately, you may import your resources prior to creating your required custom fields, or mark the fields as required after you import your resources. Keep in mind that the system will insist that you fill in these blanks before it will allow you to save any changes to resources in the enterprise.

Each row of the dialog box has two sides. The left side is the resource field from which the information will be imported, and the right side is the destination enterprise resource field. Creating your custom enterprise fields prior to mapping makes identifying the destination fields a reasonably easy task. Keep in mind that this information is imported into enterprise resource fields, not standard resource fields. Click Next to continue.

Now you're presented with a dialog box that summarizes your import selections. Notice the errors in Figure 25.16. The Import wizard will not import

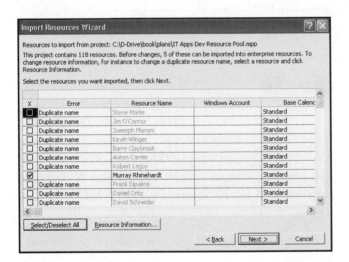

FIGURE 25.16 *The system validates your input selections and displays any errors. Resources with exceptions will not be imported.*

duplicate resources—this is particularly useful for gathering resources from disparate project plans.

However, a word of caution is necessary. The wizard will not be able to distinguish the difference between Mary Jones and Mary J. Jones, and will see the two as distinct resources. It's a good idea to go through your source plans and ensure consistency before importing your resources. Make certain that the Windows account information is entered for your resources if you are going to use Windows authentication for Project Server.

Click Next to complete your import. A completion dialog box will appear, giving you the option to import more resources. When you're done, click Finish.

Enterprise Projects

An *enterprise project* is defined as a project created in Project Professional and published to a Project Server with enterprise features enabled. Once a project is created in or imported to the enterprise it is governed by the Enterprise Global file. Under this umbrella, the project acquires custom enterprise fields. These fields, and the information that they contain, reside on the server and are copied down to the plan when required. Any local customizations that do not adhere to the Enterprise Global file, such as modifications to views and filters, will be suppressed when the plan is opened and manipulated in the enterprise environment.

Import Projects

There are two primary ways to move your projects into the Project Server environment, besides the database migration scripts provided by Microsoft on your installation CD. When you open a Project 2000-created project in Project Professional, the plan becomes eligible to save and publish to the enterprise. Alternately, you can choose Tools, Enterprise Options, and click Import Project to Enterprise, invoking the Import Project wizard, shown in Figure 25.17.

Clicking Next brings up a standard file browse dialog box, allowing you to locate the plan you wish to import. When you locate the plan, the system displays a dialog box allowing you to assign values to your enterprise custom fields. You must provide values for required fields (see Figure 25.18) to continue. You

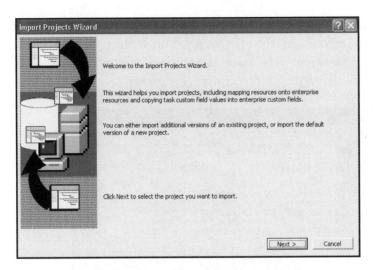

FIGURE 25.17 *Microsoft has provided an Import Projects wizard to quickly move your existing projects into the enterprise.*

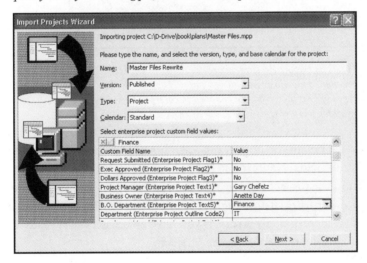

FIGURE 25.18 *The Import Projects wizard lets you add new custom enterprise data to your project during the import process. Required fields must be completed or the Project will fail the import process.*

may choose to enter values for non-required fields at this time, or you can do it later. Required fields are marked with an asterisk (*).

Once you've completed the required entries, click Next. The system brings up a dialog box, shown in Figure 25.19, that allows you to select how the resources contained in the plan will be imported. You have three choices: map the resource to an enterprise resource, import the resource to the enterprise, or keep the resource in the plan locally. This is the perfect opportunity to account for variations in resource names as you import the plans. The mapping feature allows you to import with consistency.

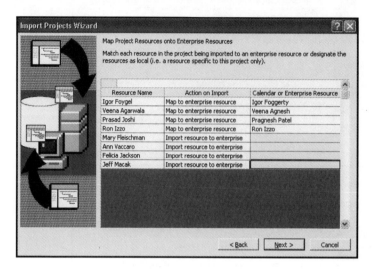

FIGURE 25.19 *The Import Projects wizard will also import the resources in the plan. This dialog box allows you to choose their disposition. Resources may be retained locally, mapped to enterprise resources to deal with duplicates, or imported.*

The last dialog box in the import process, shown in Figure 25.20, allows you to map custom fields to enterprise fields. Custom fields that are not mapped will remain in the project locally. Map any information that you plan on importing to enterprise custom fields. Click Next to display a task import summary that identifies any errors. If you have no errors, you're ready to click the Import button and complete the process.

It is very important that the resource information is correct in your projects before you import them. You are best served by importing all of your resources into the enterprise resource pool first. If you don't already have a resource pool, clean up all inconsistencies by building one from your existing project files. In the pool, make sure that all of your resource information is accurate before you use the Import wizards.

If you end up with multiple versions of the same resource, or if you have a Project Server account when you intended to have a Windows authenticated account,

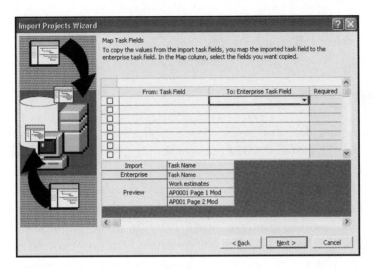

FIGURE 25.20 *Custom task information may be mapped through the Import Projects wizard.*

you may use the Manage Users functions in Project Server administration to create the correct account. Then merge the incorrect account into the new one.

The final dialog box, shown in Figure 25.21, summarizes your import selections and reports any errors. Scroll through the list to find specific errors.

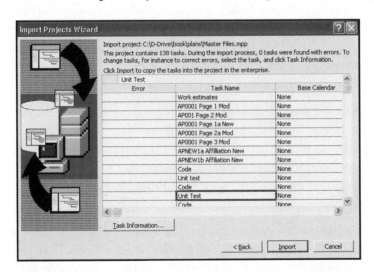

FIGURE 25.21 *The system summarizes and validates your work. This final dialog box allows you make last-minute corrections before processing. Tasks with errors will not be imported.*

If there aren't any, click Import to process your selections. The system imports the project and reports success.

Managing Views

So far, everything described in this chapter applies only to the combination of Project Server and Project 2002 Professional with enterprise features enabled. Views, on the other hand, have been at the core of this application for a while. To top it off, view management is an odd duck in this chapter. The application interface flow dictates that it should go in Chapter 24. Your appreciation of this software feature will be greatly enhanced, however, when you work with your enterprise custom fields. Therefore, it's presented here, now that you've had a chance to see how enterprise custom fields are leveraged.

Project Server views are based on SQL Server views. If you have some SQL knowledge and a burning desire to go table-surfing, there are all sorts of ways to build custom add-on features leveraging the database. If not, you'll be pleased to know that the application data layer is soundly designed.

To get started customizing your views, log on to Project Server through your browser, using an administrative account. From the Admin menu, select Manage Views (see Figure 25.22). The system displays a summary of views by type. The system offers Project, Project Center, Assignment, Portfolio Analyzer, and Resource Center views. In Project Central, views are presented largely through a single menu selection. In Project Server, they have been disbursed into the application where they're most likely to be used.

You may create views outside of the Project Server interface and import them into Project Server by using the Get Additional Views feature from this interface. These can be data access pages, HTML, or ASP pages that you place in the Views folder. See the product documentation to learn which requirements these views must meet to work with Project Server.

Choose Add View to build a new view using some of the enterprise custom fields we created earlier in the chapter. The new view will be added to the Project Center. You may choose any of the five types of views. Give your new view a name and a description, and then choose the fields you would like to include. The field selections automatically change according to the type of view you have selected, so there's no need to worry about whether the field you're choosing applies. If it's there, it does.

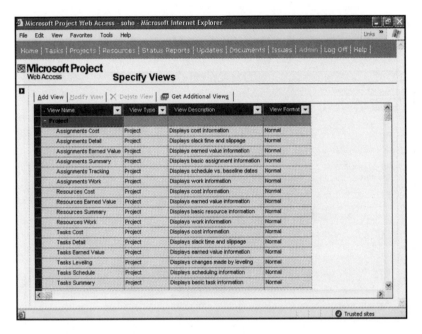

FIGURE 25.22 *The Specify Views screen is displayed when you select Manage Views from the Project Web Access Admin interface.*

Although all of your customized fields are available for your use, the field names in this part of the interface are not displayed with the custom names you gave them. Therefore, it is very important that you have a list to work with. Alternately, you might open Project as well as your browser, and then switch windows while you work.

Next, select the Gantt chart format and the grouping format for the view, and assign the view to categories. This determines who will have access to the view. Click Save; your view will be written to the system. Figure 25.23 shows the screen with your new view included.

The proof is in the viewing, of course, so click Project on the menu to go to the Project Center. Your new view is now listed in the View dropdown menu. Select it to display the view with the projects to which you have access. This example, shown in Figure 25.24, contains enterprise project custom fields, but all fields are candidates, including your custom formula fields and fields containing graphical indicators.

Note that the custom descriptions are displayed in the view, even though they aren't available in the Manage Views interface. Notice that within the view frame, you can drag column widths and slide the divider between the field display and the Gantt display to get a better look at one or the other. You can also scroll vertically and horizontally within the view frame.

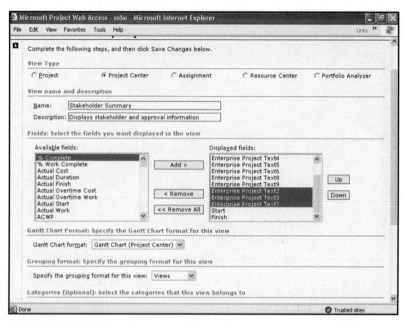

FIGURE 25.23   *The interface accepts information for your new or modified view.*

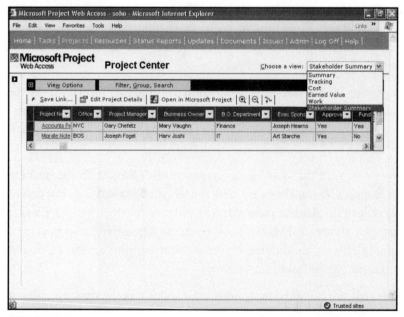

FIGURE 25.24   *Experience your new view in action in the Project Center.*

Chapter 26

Project Server and Project (Managers)

In This Chapter

◆ Team building with enterprise resources

◆ Publishing projects and assignments

◆ Publishing in a multi-manager environment

◆ Working in the Resource Center

◆ Managing to-do lists

◆ Sharepoint Team Services

The two previous chapters have given you a foundational overview of the enterprise architecture supported in Project Server, approaching it from a program manger/administrator perspective. Now it's time to look at a day in the life of a project manager who's using Project Server in an enterprise environment.

Whether you connect automatically upon start-up of Project or you connect manually, you'll notice differences in the way Project behaves when connected to the enterprise. Right away, you'll get a strong sense of the control that Project Server has over Project Professional when enterprise features are enabled. Project's behavior fundamentally changes when you enter this client/server environment.

Until now, as a project manager, you've been completely in the driver's seat when using Project. You were the supreme user. Suddenly you find yourself under an umbrella, where someone else is determining what your views look like, which fields are visible, and which organizational fields you're compelled to enter!

Team Building with Enterprise Resources

Life is a tradeoff. Along with opening the door for new metadata demands that management will suddenly realize it can't live without, Project Server delivers many new features to help make a project manager more effective. Enterprise resource features are a natural place to begin.

Microsoft has made strong advances in resource handling. The enterprise resource pool is the backbone of new features, including the team builder, the skills-based Resource Substitution Wizard, and customizability that enables intelligent, needle-in-a-haystack searches through a very large resource base.

Resources can be added to a plan from an Active Directory, Outlook or Exchange Address book, or Microsoft Server. In an enterprise configuration, Project acts as a conduit to Project Server when you're adding resources from an Active Directory or central address book. It is a conduit in the sense that the resource must be imported through a project plan Save operation, or by using the Enterprise Resource Import wizard (described in the previous chapter), before it can become part of the enterprise. Some companies may demand that only enterprise resources can be used in every aspect of planning and execution, keeping a tight rein on data to support enterprise models.

Click the new Add Resources button in the Assign Resources dialog box (see Figure 26.1) and select Active Directory, Address Book, or Project Server. The Project Server administrator may not have chosen to permit project managers to create Project Server accounts, so these choices may be useless to you. Select Project Server to explore a routine use of the enterprise resource pool.

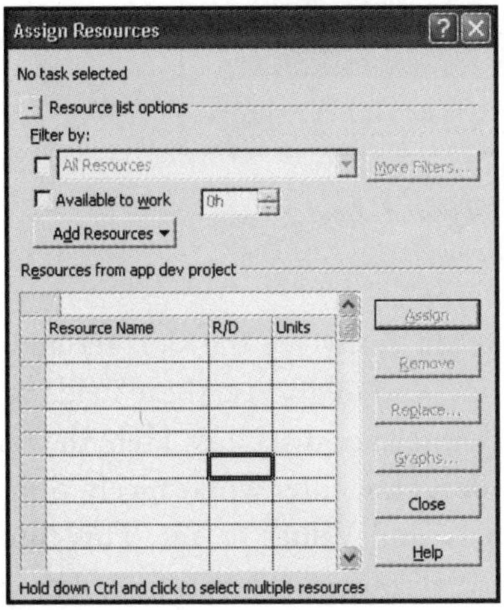

FIGURE 26.1 *The Assign Resources dialog box has a new Add Resources button.*

Click Add Resource, and the system will launch the Build Team dialog box. As shown in Figure 26.2, the ad hoc filter area is expanded to show the possibilities. It also reveals that the interface at times lacks support for an 800x600 resolution display. Try to have your resolution set at 1024x768 or higher, because both Project Professional and Project Web Access are best suited for higher resolutions. If you don't prefer higher resolutions, occasionally you'll be annoyed by the interface.

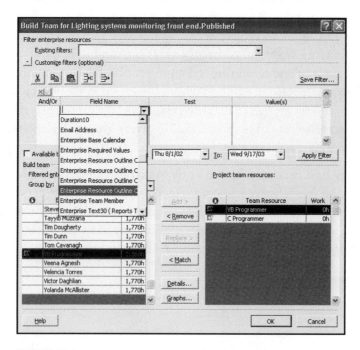

FIGURE 26.2 *Team building, skill set matching, and resource substitution are handled in the Build Team dialog box.*

On a higher-resolution screen, you could easily see the skill set and office location fields, but you can imagine how you might use these fields to make your life easier despite Project Server's interface disability. Here the target is enterprise generic resources, so a simple ad hoc filter works nicely. Simply set Field Name to Generic, Test to Equals, and Values to Yes. This filters the display to show only enterprise generic resources. The ad hoc filter created here would make much more sense if it were added as a stock selection. In this basic example, office location, platform, and primary language skill would be things that everyone assigning development resources would want to use.

Once you select your first resource, you'll notice that the Match button becomes active. This is an important way to use generic resources. Ultimately, you'll use generic resources for skills matching in your typical team building activities—that is, if your organization is large enough to make use of it.

TIP

In the previous chapter, you learned how to open the enterprise global and check-out resources. Once you've added enterprise resources to your plan, it's easy to forget to check them out. Before you begin making any kinds of changes to your plan that affect resources (and how many don't?), make certain you check them out.

Make your selections and assign your generic resources. Now you're ready to use the skills Match function (see Figure 26.3).

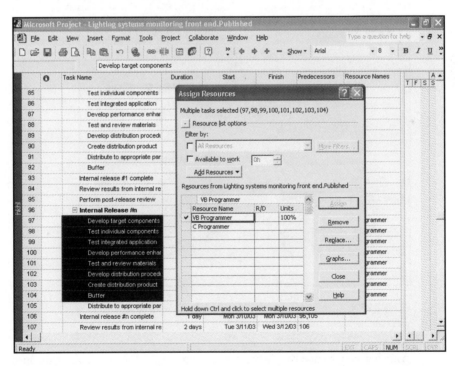

FIGURE 26.3 *Select the tasks for which you want to use skill set matching, and first assign a generic resource with the skill attributes you're looking for.*

Retrace your steps back through Add Resources to the Build Team dialog box, and this time choose the Match function. At the top of the screen, expand the Customize filters and use the skill codes you created in the last chapter. In the example, a code is used to select an office location, and NYC is specified. A combination of platform and language codes is set to narrow the selection. Select the generic resource you want to replace and click Match. The system selects all resources with availability for the time period.

As you can see, a brand new team is available for the example project in Figure 26.4. Select a resource or multiple resources on the left and a corresponding generic resource on the right, and then click Replace. The system will substitute the selected resource(s) for the selected tasks in the plan.

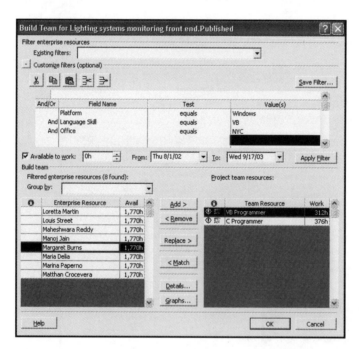

FIGURE 26.4 *Select the generic resource on the right, click Match, and view the system-matched resources on the left.*

Another way to use this feature is through the Resource Substitution wizard. Start the wizard from the Tools menu by choosing Substitute Resources. The Resource Substitution wizard's welcome screen, shown in Figure 26.5, cautions you that enterprise resource outline codes must have already been set up in order for you to use this feature. As you've already done that, click Next.

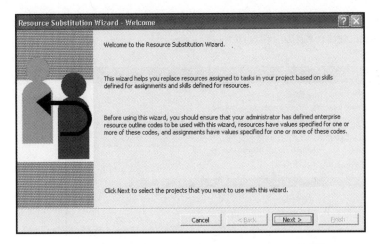

FIGURE 26.5 *The Resource Substitution wizard's welcome screen.*

In Step 1, you're asked to select a project or project(s) to work with. Select your project in the dialog box shown in Figure 26.6 and click Next.

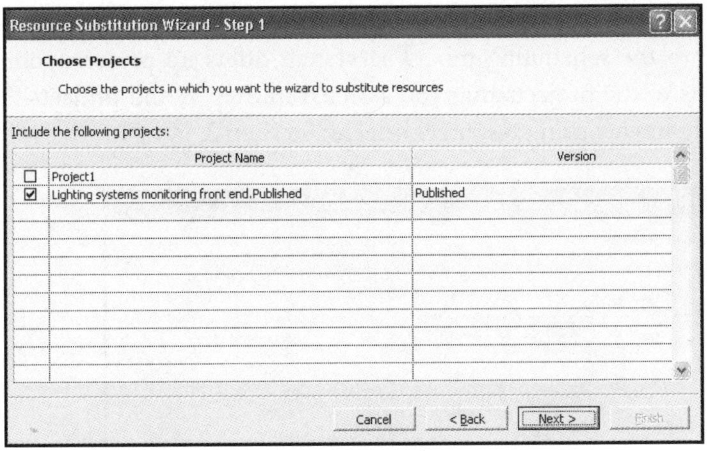

FIGURE 26.6 *Select the projects to work with in Step 2.*

Step 2, shown in Figure 26.7, allows you to select resources. If you've already checked out resources and added them to your plan, selecting the In the Selected Projects option button is an option. Otherwise, you can specify by resource breakdown structure level, or choose Specify Below and click Add. This displays a screen almost identical to Figure 26.4, except the title bar now reads Build Pool for Resource Substitution. Setting the Resource

Freeze Horizon limits how far the wizard will reschedule the resources that you've selected for it to consider.

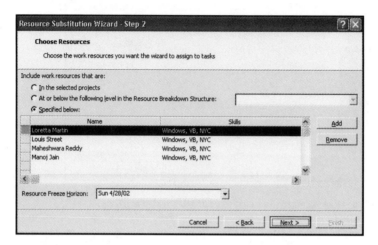

FIGURE 26.7   *Step 3 allows you to select resources to work with.*

The third step, shown in Figure 26.8, lets you select additional related projects to toss into the scheduling mix. The system offers up projects containing cross-links to the projects that you selected in Step 1, and projects that include assignments using resources selected in Step 2.

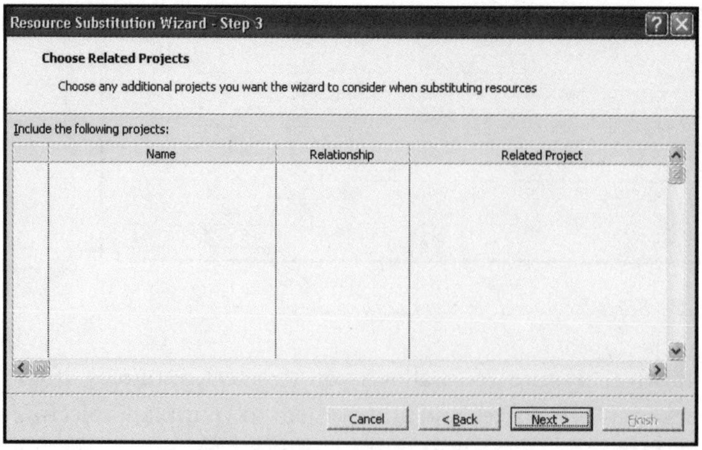

FIGURE 26.8   *If any of the primary projects are linked, you can include them in Step 3.*

Fourth, you define priorities for the selected projects and their related projects. The wizard schedules available resources to projects from highest to lowest priority. Specifying Use Resources in the Project limits the wizard to using resources already contained in the project. Shown in Figure 26.9, selecting Use Resources in Pool allows the wizard to consider the resources you selected from the pool in Step 2, as well as the resources already in the plan.

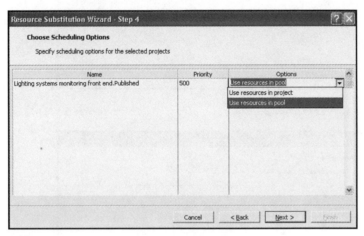

FIGURE 26.9   *Specify scheduling options in Step 4.*

The wizard gives you one last opportunity to bail out in Step 5, (see Figure 26.10) while presenting you with a summary of your selections. Click Run to activate the wizard, and then click Next to review the results. Not to worry—the results aren't applied to the plan until you choose to apply them.

As shown in Figure 26.11, in Step 7 it's your choice to update the plan. The results can also be written to a file, and you can select both options. If you choose to write the results to a file, the Browse button will be activated.

Upon completion, the wizard advises you to level your plan and determine whether you're happy with the results. You have one last opportunity to discard the changes that the wizard proposes. Close the project without saving it to discard the changes, or save the project to the database to commit the changes.

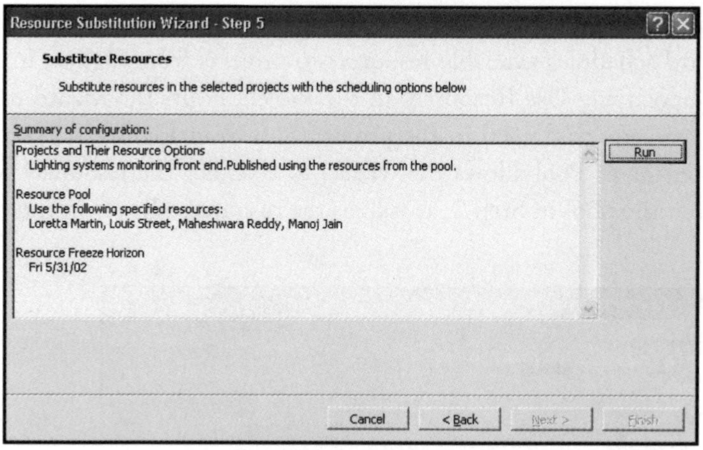

FIGURE 26.10 *The wizard displays a summary of your choices in Step 5.*

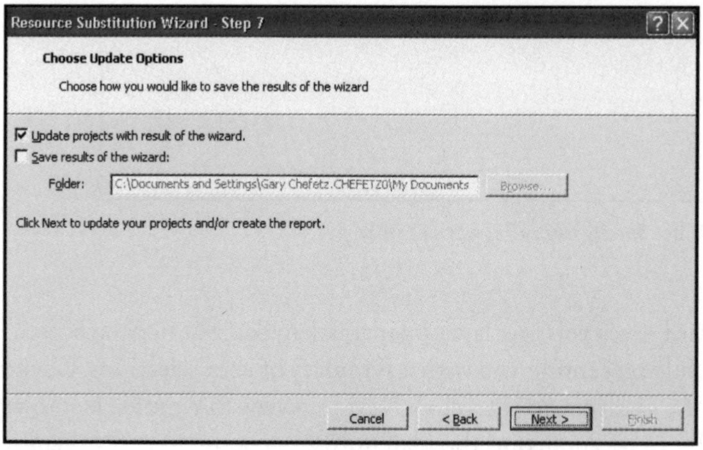

FIGURE 26.11 *The final step is to select how you would like to save the results.*

Publishing Projects and Assignments

You're now ready to explore the wonderful world of Project Server collaboration, which starts with the concept of publishing.

Sometimes the terminology Microsoft chooses is a tad confusing. Such is the case with the use of the word *published*. A plan becomes published by being saved to Project Server in an enterprise environment. However, assignments aren't *published to resources* until you execute a separate process. In other words, assignments don't show up on a resource time sheet until the Project Manager has deliberately caused that to happen.

Once a plan is published to resources, it's visible through views in the Project Center. The impact on resource availability is also visible through views in the Resource Center once a plan is published. Both of these areas derive project data directly from the project plans. With the proper permissions, you can browse through Project Web Access views of the project. However, a resource will be unaware of an assignment until you publish it, because assignments are contained in a different set of tables in the database. These are populated only when you cause them to be.

Publishing assignments can be transacted in a number of ways. Selecting Publish from the top of the Collaborate menu reveals a number of choices:

◆ All Information
◆ New and Changed Assignments
◆ Project Plan
◆ Republish Assignments

If you select All Information, the plan summary information and all assignments that are new and changed are updated. Selecting New and Changed Assignments publishes only assignment information for task assignments, or assignments that have changed in some way and require updating as you specify in the dialog boxes. The Project Plan selection applies more to non-enterprise implementations. Republish Assignments allows the project manager to resend assignment data to a resource. This is particularly useful when a resource inadvertently deletes a task from the timesheet.

Select New and Changed Assignments. The system warns you that the project will be saved after you have made your assignments. Click OK to continue. The Publish New and Changed Assignments dialog box will be displayed, summarizing your selections. Notice that you can choose the entire project, the current view, or what's currently selected in your plan before invoking the menu option. As in the example in Figure 26.12, select Selected Items. Selecting the Notify All Affected Resources Via E-Mail check box will cause Project Server to send a notice of the assignment to each affected resource via e-mail. You can customize that message for this instance by clicking the Edit Message Text button.

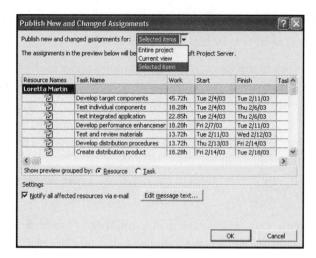

FIGURE 26.12 *When you're publishing assignments, eligible tasks are automatically selected by the system. You have the final say.*

You can modify the default e-mail before sending, or delete it and completely change it. The Edit Message Text dialog box, shown in Figure 26.13, is displayed when you click the Edit Message Text button. The e-mail notifications the resources receive will contain a hyperlink back to Project Server.

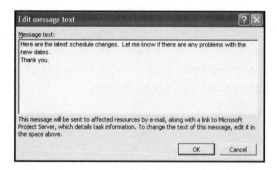

FIGURE 26.13 *Accept the default message, add comments, or author your own.*

Selecting OK sends the assignments to the user's Inbox in Project Server, sends the e-mail notification if you've chosen that option, and saves the plan to the server. Next you'll see a confirmation alert box that allows you to choose not to see it again in the future.

Publishing in a Multi-Manager Environment

Project Server now supports collaborative project management. Project Central uses the project manager ID as part of the unique key for a project in the database. This makes it impossible for anyone but the holder of the original user account to maintain the plan without either sharing a logon or unintentionally creating a duplicate copy of the plan. As it is, many organizations employ project administrators or share responsibility for time approval and acceptance between different project managers and resource managers. The Project product team removed this restriction, along with the infamous proclivity to create dupes.

The rules of the road for multiple managers controlling assignments within the same plan are simple. The logon who publishes the assignment becomes the de facto owner. A task assignment will belong to the manager who published it until someone else takes it over. To take over an assignment, use the Republish feature. In the dialog box, check the option Become the Manager on These Assignments.

Processing Updates

Everyone's home page in Project Web Access summarizes important pending business within the system (see Figure 26.14). Each person only sees the navigational selections he or she has permission to access. Log on to Project Server Web Access using Windows Authentication or your Project Server account.

You can plainly see in Figure 26.14 that this project manager has updates from resources. Clicking the Update link takes you to the View Task Changes Submitted by Resources page, shown in Figure 26.15. A number of options present themselves. In the update submitted, one task had time reported against it and one task assignment was declined. In the example, the time update is accepted but the task rejection was countermanded and marked for rejection. Clicking Update opens the project plan targeted for update. The system then applies the updates and asks if you'd like to save the plan (see Figure 25.16).

Click OK to save the project plan and commit the changes. Your updates will be applied and finalized (see Figure 26.17).

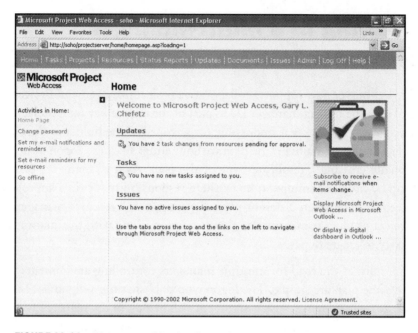

FIGURE 26.14 *Your personal Project Server home page*

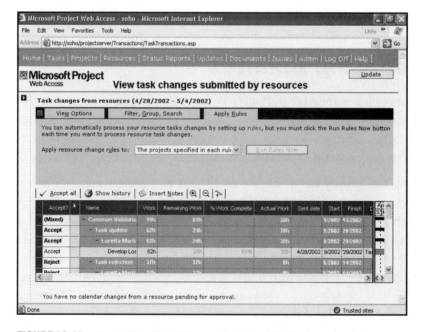

FIGURE 26.15 *In the View Task Changes Submitted By Resources interface, you can choose to accept or reject updates from resources.*

FIGURE 26.16   *Project Server acknowledges your update.*

FIGURE 26.17   *Server displays one final confirmation alert.*

Create Rules to Manage Updates

Processing updates looks rather easy when there's only one resource reporting against one task. When dozens of resources are reporting to you over numerous projects, your work can be made easier using the Update Rules feature in Project Server. Access Update Rules from the Updates activities menu in Project Web Access. Selecting New Rule from the Rules home page opens the Set Rules for Automatically Accepting Changes page shown in Figure 26.18.

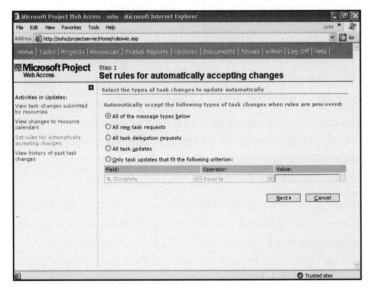

FIGURE 26.18   *Setting rules for automatically accepting changes can save time. First choose what you'd like to automatically update.*

Rules can be set to automatically accept task changes based on

◆ All of the message types below

◆ All new task requests

◆ All task delegation requests

◆ All task updates, and

◆ Only task updates that fit the following criterion.

The first four choices are shotgun approaches to building automatic acceptance. They paint in broad strokes. On the other hand, the last choice allows for a great deal of granularity and flexibility, providing laser-like accuracy. For example, if you set up a custom enterprise resource code or field that identifies whether a resource is trusted for auto-accepting, you can use the value set in that field to base your automatic acceptance decision by finding the field in the drop-down list and specifying the operator and the value. This simple approach gives you control of automatic acceptance at the individual resource level by simply flagging them as trusted, yes or no. Click Next to advance through the interface.

Step 2 of 3, shown in Figure 26.19, provides a number of options. Here you can set rules to define the perpetuity of your rules, or how they'll be handled over time. Rules can apply to all current and future projects, or one or more existing projects by individual selection. All of the projects in your personal portfolio are displayed in the Available Projects window.

Click Next to continue. The options available at the resource selection level mirror those at the project level. Make the appropriate selections, as shown in Figure 26.20, and then click Next.

Once you've completed the third and final step, you're ready to save your rule. Clicking Finish returns you to the Set Rules main page, where your new rule will now appear in the grid. Your new rule will also be available to you during update activities in Project Server.

Project Server provides a new view that allows you to view the history of the updates you've made. Select View History of Past Task Changes from the Updates activities menu to access this view. Like all Project Server views, rich filtering can be applied to reduce the selection set to a workable size, and a number of options are provided to tailor the presentation.

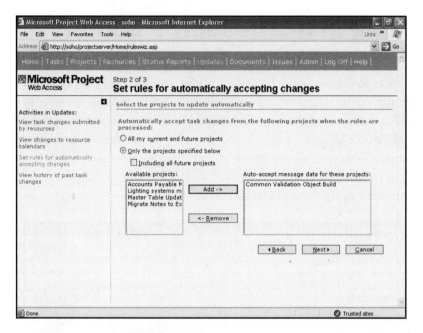

FIGURE 26.19   *Next, choose the projects to which you'd like to apply automatic updates.*

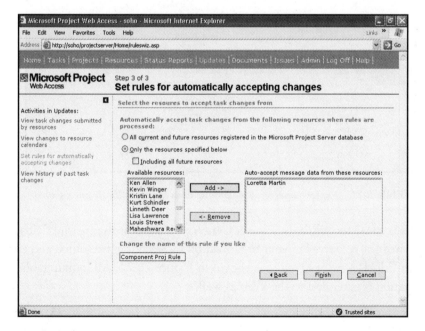

FIGURE 26.20   *Select the resources to whom automatic updates apply.*

Working in the Resource Center

The Resource Center can be opened and displayed from within Project. Choose Resource Center from the Collaborate menu in Project, or click Project on the main navigation bar in Project Web Access. You can see, in Figure 26.21, that some of the same filtering capabilities available through the Project and Project Wizard interfaces are extended to the Web. Like other areas of Project Web Access, you can add and modify views and filters for the resource center. This saves your users lots of time in getting the information they want in the format that suits them best.

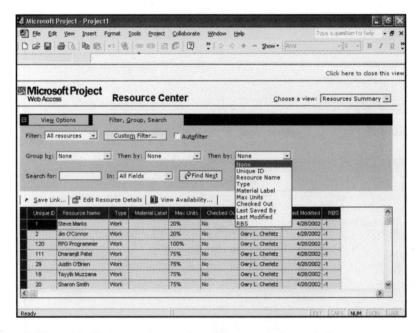

FIGURE 26.21   *Project managers and administrators can access the Resource Center.*

As is consistent with the Project Center, you can edit the custom fields established for resources in your organization by selecting a resource and clicking on Edit Resource Details, as shown in Figure 26.22. All lookup table information is extended to the Web as well.

Resource availability graphs, like the one shown in Figure 26.23, are created with the assistance of Office XP Web parts, which must be installed on a client computer for the graphs to work. You can view the assignment work of one or more resources, the availability, or the assignment work grouped by

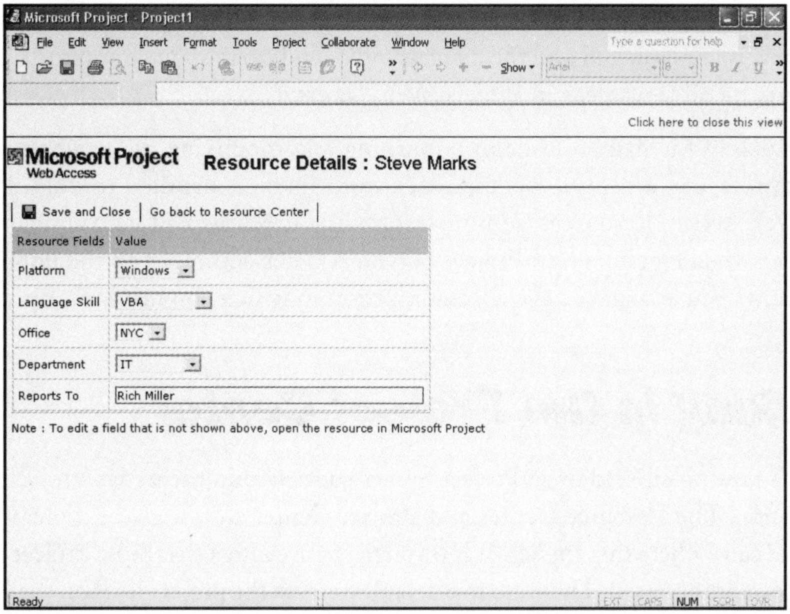

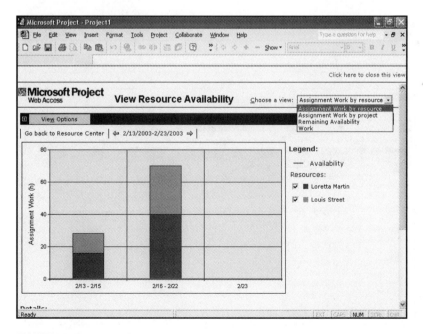

FIGURE 26.22 *Custom field information is editable through the Resource Center.*

FIGURE 26.23 *View Resource Availability displays a bar graph of one or more selected resources.*

project. When you navigate away from any view in Project Server, your last view is remembered and the display will default to it upon your return. This is true for all view areas in Project Web Access.

Much of the daily routine of publishing and modifying assignments for resources, and accepting updates back from them, is handled through Project Web Access. Resources, administrators, and executives all see a similar interface when logging on to Project Server. A quick summary on the home page shows you at a glance the communication to which you need to respond.

Working in the Project Center

It's now possible to open Project Server pages within the native Project application. The Resource Center and Project Center are the two new features of the suite where this applies. It is through these centers that most Project Server views are accessed. There are five default views at the project level on the Project Center home page, plus any additional views you may have created. The Stakeholder Summary view created under Manage Views is shown in Figure 26.24.

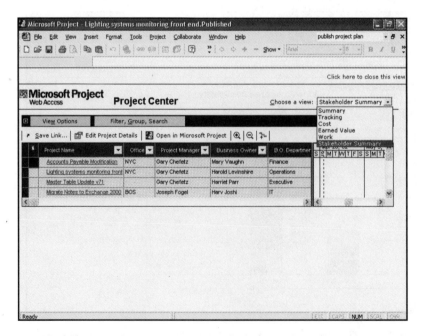

FIGURE 26.24 *The Project Center displays all projects to which you have security access.*

Selecting a project to drill down on brings you to the View a Project page shown in Figure 26.25. From here, many Project Sever standard views are available, as are any custom views you have chosen to create at the task, assignment, or resource level. Selecting a view from the drop-down list on either page causes the display to change accordingly.

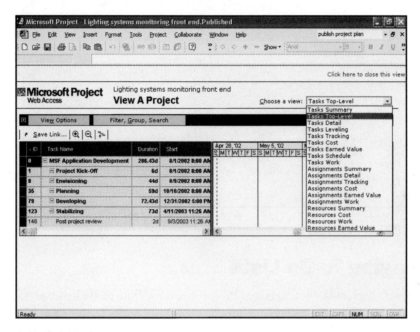

FIGURE 26.25 *Numerous detailed project views are available when you drill down into a project.*

A couple of more features worth mentioning in the Resource Center are accessed from the Project Center home page. You can open a selected project by selecting the Open in Microsoft Project icon or link. Clicking Edit Details displays a new page that allows editing of custom information, as shown in Figure 26.26. The Project Center can be accessed from either Project Professional or a browser. Some of these features seem to duplicate one another; this replication is often driven by the need to provide access through both avenues. Interestingly enough, these details can only be edited through the Project Center when the plan isn't open in another session, including the one you're in if you open the Resource Center while the plan you wish to modify is open.

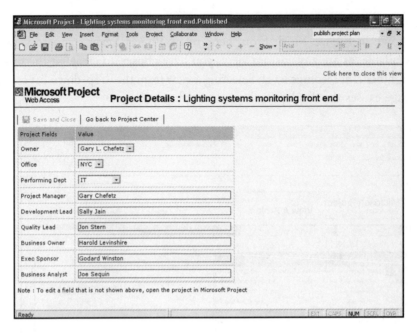

FIGURE 26.26 *Enterprise custom fields can be edited in the Project Center interface.*

Managing To-Do Lists

To-do lists make their debut in Project Server. While to-do lists provide more than scratch-pad project functionality, there are limits to their use. Tasks can be created and assigned, priorities set, start and finish dates determined, work completed, and notes stored and tracked. To-do lists are essentially a loosely structured collection of tasks. Typical project features such as dependencies, tracking, and scheduling are not operative in to-do lists.

Most interesting is that to-do lists are managed completely within the Project Server environment and can be promoted into projects. You can leverage to-do lists to manage small, informal mini-projects that don't require a full-blown project management application.

The first step in creating a new to-do list, shown in Figure 26.27, is to give it a name and select who will have access to it. To-do lists can be available to everyone, to only the resources who are assigned tasks in the to-do list, or completely private—for personal management purposes only. After making your choices, click Next to continue.

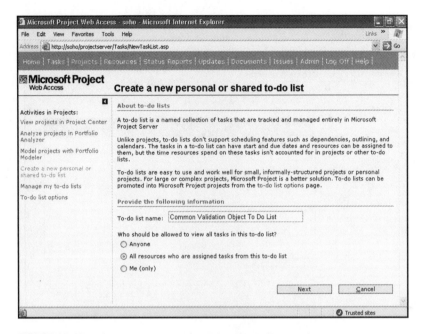

FIGURE 26.27 *To-do lists are managed through the Project Center.*

The system displays a task entry grid, shown in Figure 26.28, where tasks are defined and assigned. Resources are selected from a pick list in the Assigned To column of the grid. Date pickers are operative for applying start and finish dates. You can enter notes at this point, but this particular interface makes it very difficult. Adding them in the to-do list maintenance interface is facilitated by a much more user-friendly approach.

The Manage My To-Do Lists interface, shown in Figure 26.29, is accessed from the Projects activity menu in Project Web Access. This particular feature is an oddity because of its rudimentary appearance and isolated functionality. Microsoft suggests that to-do lists can be used to manage informal projects, but the simple functionality will relegate it to the level of a project bulletin board. You can create and manage multiple to-do lists, and the system allows you to manipulate the display to suit your tastes.

The Manage My To-Do Lists facility provides much better text entry than the Create a New To-Do List interface does; it is shown in Figure 26.30. Selecting a task and clicking Insert Notes opens a text entry form labeled

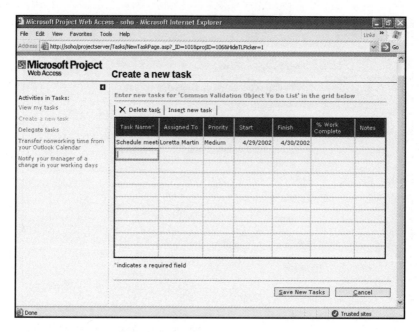

FIGURE 26.28 *The to-do list task interface is structured in a simple grid.*

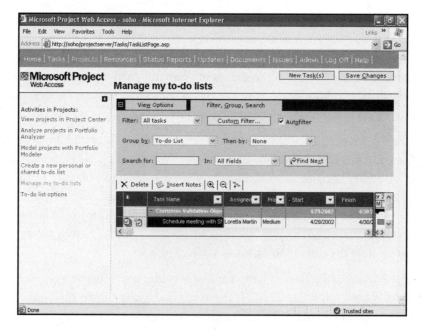

FIGURE 26.29 *Once you have created a to-do list, you manage it through the Manage My To-Do Lists page.*

Project Web Access Assignment Notes. Word wrapping is supported and automatically applied within the entry area. Click OK when you're done entering your note.

FIGURE 26.30 *Text entry for to-do list notes is best handled from the Manage My To-Do List page.*

Choosing Manage My To-Do Lists from the Project Center activities menu allows you to maintain the list-level data you entered when creating a to-do list (see Figure 26.31). The most notable options in this interface are Transfer Ownership of This To-Do List To and Promote to Project. The ownership transfer is a handy feature. Promote to Project is handy as well, but a mixed bag of surprises awaits you there.

The system warns you, as shown in Figure 26.32, that when you click the Promote To Project button from the Promote a To-do List Into A Project page, the action is irrevocable. Click the button to create a new project in memory.

In the beta version used to author this book, it's possible to abandon the conversion after clicking the button, by choosing not to save the project. A lot can change in the early life of a product release, so verify this for yourself before you count on it.

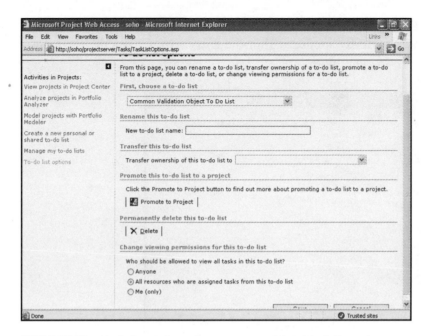

FIGURE 26.31 *To-do list configurations are managed from To-do list options.*

The new project has you listed as the project manager and your to-do list items imported as tasks. When the process is completed, the project is opened and ready to go in Project Professional. To save the project, you'll be obligated to provide the enterprise's required data. The plan is ready to take on a project life of its own once it's saved to the enterprise. Any resources defined in the to-do list are brought into the new plan as local plan resources. The promotion process offers no direct mapping capabilities, unlike the import process, which allows you to map field values. Therefore, you will need to use resource substitution or the team builder to map these manually.

Status Reports

Status reports can be either requested or responded to. As a project manager, you'll find yourself on the requesting side more often than not, unless your company has a C-level manage-by-project mentality. Select Status Reports from the main navigation bar in Project Web Access, and choose between responding to a status report or requesting one. When you select Request a Status Report, the Request a Status Report screen, shown in Figure 26.33,

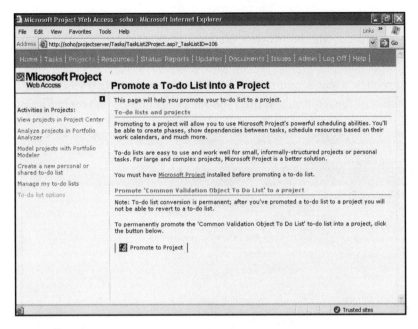

FIGURE 26.32   *To-do lists can be promoted to projects.*

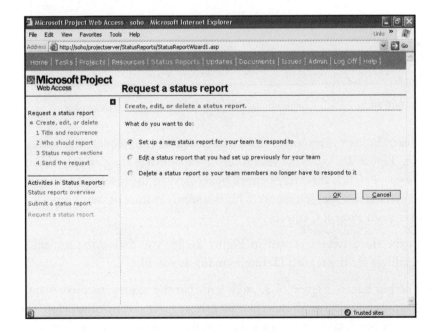

FIGURE 26.33   *Status reports are typically requested by the project manager, but users may choose to send unrequested status reports as well.*

appears. Status reports are defined by a number of user options. Your initial selections are whether to view, create, update, or delete a status report. Click OK to set up a new status report.

To request a status report, first you provide a name, then you define the frequency of the request, and then you set a start date, as shown in Figure 26.34.

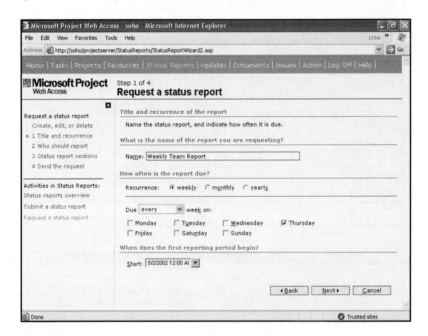

FIGURE 26.34 *Give your status report a name and determine its recurrence.*

Next, choose the resources from whom you wish to request this status report (see Figure 26.35). Note that filtering capabilities are glaringly absent from this page. Click the Merge check boxes next to the resources you would like to include in a merged report. This is a handy feature of status reports carried over from Project Central.

In the third screen, shown in Figure 26.36, you define the topical section headings for the report. Define as many as you like.

The last screen, Figure 26.37, tells you that the request succeeded and offers you the choices to send, cancel, or save the request. At any time before you click Save or Send, you can go back through the screens and make changes. When you save or send the status report, it's created in the database and activated.

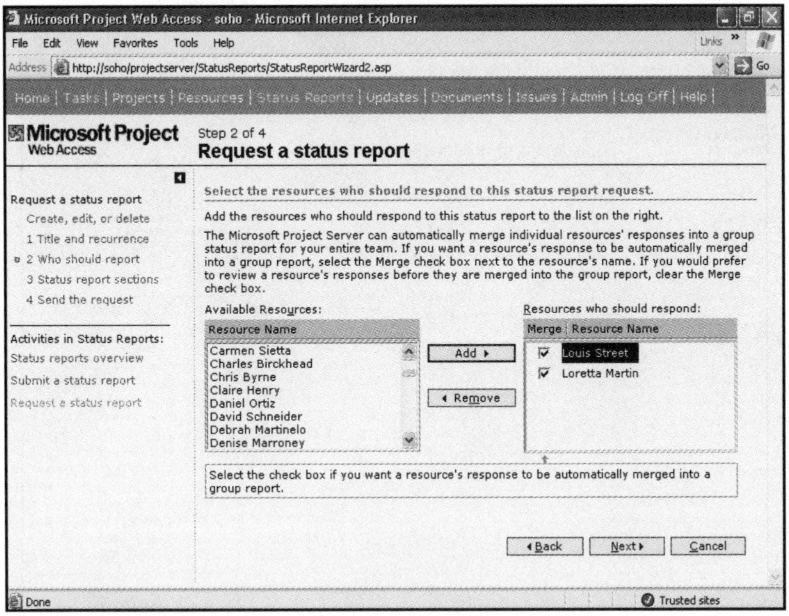

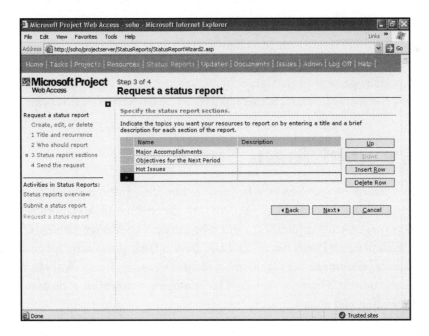

FIGURE 26.35 *Choose the resources for your request.*

FIGURE 26.36 *Specify the section headings for your status report request.*

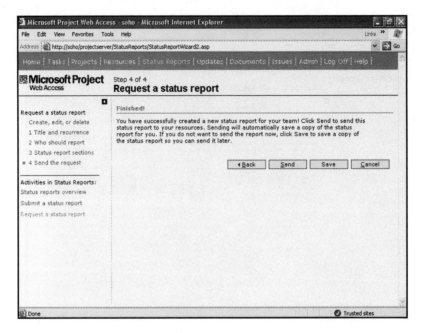

FIGURE 26.37   *Save and send a status report when you're finished requesting it.*

To view status reports from your resources, select View Status Report Responses from Your Team Members in the Status Reports activities menu. In the View Status Report Responses from Your Team Members in the Status Reports page, shown in Figure 26.38, you can select reports individually or view the merged report. Status reports can be deleted from this page.

Sharepoint Team Services

To sweeten Project Server, Microsoft is bundling in Sharepoint Team Services (STS). Project Server's interface is modeled after this collaborative active server page (ASP) application, right down to the basic design elements. Throw in a Sharepoint Portal Server and you have a fairly good suite for managing projects, document management, and issues management. Although these are the newest Microsoft Internet technologies, a powerful code base awaits the willing and able.

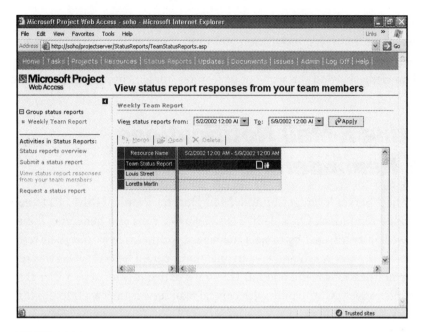

FIGURE 26.38 *View status reports submitted by resources.*

 NOTE

Sharepoint Portal Services and Sharepoint Team Services are two distinct Microsoft Server products. SPS is Microsoft's offering in the enterprise portal market. Its focus is knowledge management/document management. Microsoft Office integrates with SPS, with open-from and save-to integration to its libraries, featuring version control, document check-in, and rich search functionality. STS features include discussion lists, issues management, document libraries, and subscription-based notification.

STS is database-dependent. It has a flexible document-and-issues-management system with lots of linking capability, made meaningful to enterprise projects by allowing you to extend linking to Project tasks. Project Server can be linked with other document management systems, but for users that don't have these or SPS, the document library feature that comes with STS is a nice addition.

While it is a tempting notion to throw this onto the same box as Project Server, Microsoft's scalability and stability model favors dedicated boxes for server products. STS is an active server application that, applied as a serious conduit for business information, deserves its own server. On a related note, the Project

Web Access interface is intuitive enough to use without needing a software reference. However, installation and integration with your corporate network requires some skill. To get the most from STS, you should plan on acquiring knowledge beyond the scope of its features implementation in Project Server.

Setting E-Mail Notifications and Reminders

Project Server leverages Simple Mail Transfer Protocol (SMTP) to generate e-mail reminders. On a daily basis, a service runs and generates the notices based on criteria set by project managers, for themselves and their resources. Resources may set their own personal reminders. The SMTP service required for notifications is included in IIS so it's native to your server if enabled administratively. Companies with central mail servers may want to point Project Server at these instead.

E-mail notifications are a new feature in Project Server. The criteria selection is broad enough to cross the border between informative and annoying very quickly. Be sensible and ask your team what they find helpful. Figure 26.39 shows the My E-Mail Notifications and Reminders interface for project managers. In addition, you can set automated notifications to be delivered to your resources for the following:

◆ Upcoming tasks

◆ Overdue tasks

◆ Tasks that require status updates

◆ Upcoming status reports

◆ Overdue status reports

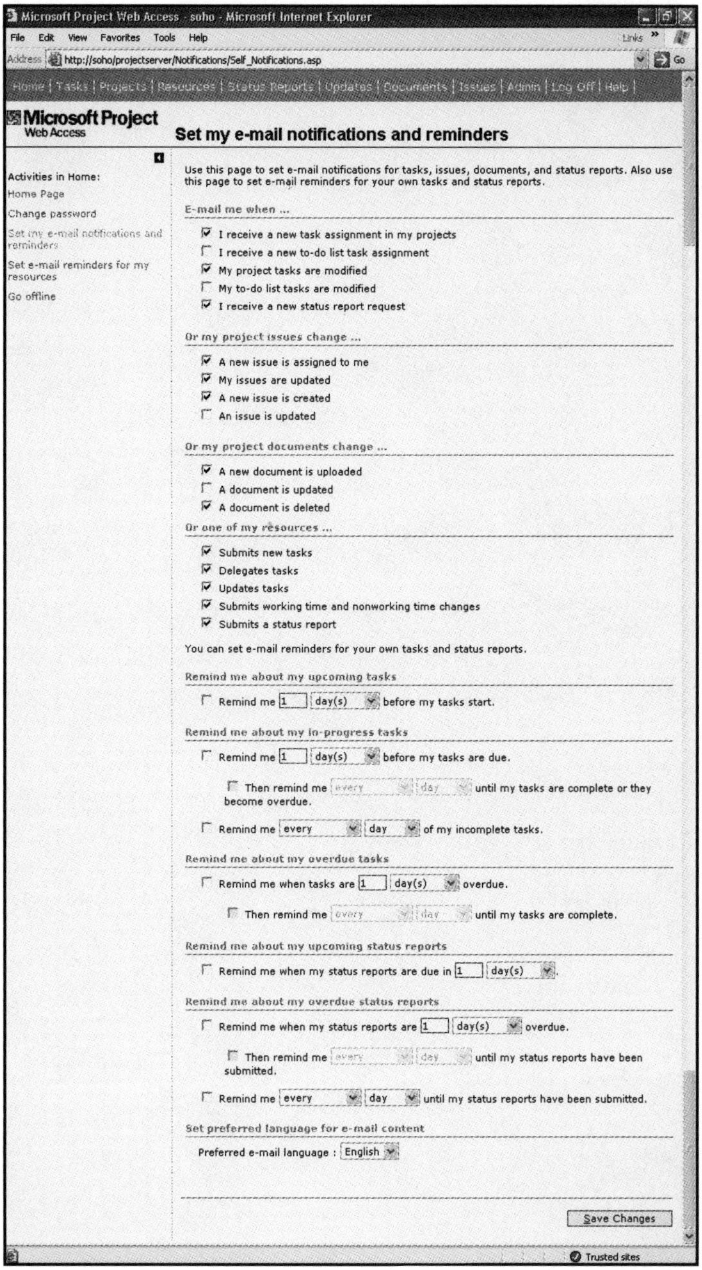

FIGURE 26.39 *Automated e-mail notifications and reminders keep you in touch with your resources while you sleep.*

Chapter 27

Project Server for Executives and Resources

In This Chapter

◆ Project Web Access and resources

◆ An executive view of Project Server

◆ Building an OLAP cube

◆ Working with Portfolio Analyzer

◆ Working with Portfolio Modeler

Now that you have a feel for how to set up, administer, and publish with Project Server, it's time to take a look at how your team and the extended enterprise interact with it as well. This chapter closes the loop on time reporting and status reports through a resource view. It also explores information delivery to stakeholders and management.

Information sharing is not universally accepted as a good thing in all organizations, but companies that want to implement Project Server will likely spend a lot of time tailoring the program's views and using new analysis features. Generally, the hungrier the enterprise is for information, the more customization it will demand.

In a Resource World

If time tracking is new to your organization, make certain you've done your homework on organizational change management. This is not an easy transition for some groups to make, and your organization must be mentally prepared for it.

By default, resources have limited access in Project Web Access. Besides a personalized home page, resource functionality consists primarily of access to tasks and status reports. Most of a resource's work in Project Web Access is conducted in the time sheet view of tasks.

The Resource Home Page

A resource who accesses Project Server Web Access is greeted with a personalized home page, the same way all users are. However, the navigational choices are much more limited than those of the administrator account. Figure 27.1 shows the home page for a resource, with a status report coming due. By default, a resource has access to tasks, issues, and documents according to the specific privileges of the categories to which he or she is assigned.

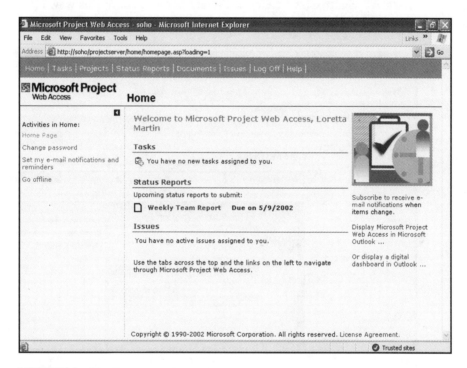

FIGURE 27.1 *Not all sections of the Project Server pages are displayed at all times. For instance, the Status Reports section would not appear if no status reports were overdue or near due.*

Tasks Are the Center of My World

If Microsoft were more consistent about interfaces and nomenclature, they might have called it the Assignment Center or Work Center instead of the Tasks Area. A resource sees a highly personalized presentation of task work. Not even the fact that other resources are assigned to the same task is visible to the resource. But it could be visible, if you wanted it to be. In fact, you may want to open this type of information to some resources and not others. Perhaps you would like a new category of leaders?

Resources have two primary ways of looking at tasks: a Timesheet view and a personal Gantt Chart view. Figure 27.2 shows the personal Gantt Chart view. When you hover the mouse pointer over the center bar in the grid, the pointer changes to a pair of reverse brackets. Click and hold on the center bar and drag it in either direction to display more or less of the fields or the Gantt chart. All Gantt Chart views in Project Server behave this way. Filters and date range selections are available.

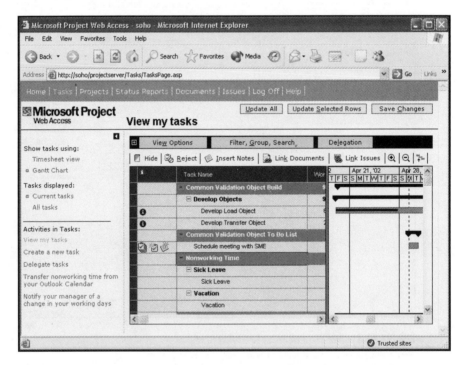

FIGURE 27.2 *Your personal Gantt Chart view displays all of your tasks and to-do list items.*

The core of Project Server resource functionality is extended through the Timesheet view. Greatly improved over the previous version, the Timesheet interface has a number of handy features that allow users to reject tasks, add notes, link issues and documents to tasks, delegate tasks, and of course, report time against tasks and update the project manager.

Resources may use the task delegation and rejection feature if the project manager enables it. Figure 27.3 shows the Timesheet with the center divider dragged far to the right at a resolution of 800x600. As a result, columns with recent weekly history totals are hidden from view. The tracking method has been set to require resources to report actual and remaining work. To-do list items, as well as task work, are shown in the Timesheet. Notice also the Nonworking Time category.

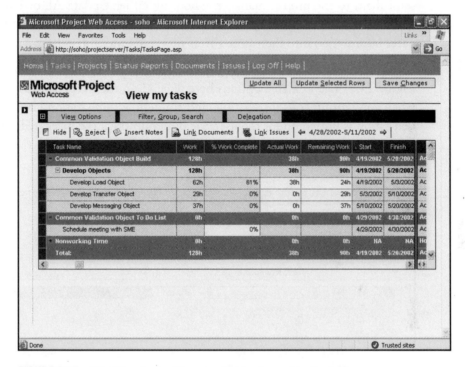

FIGURE 27.3 *The Timesheet with center divider dragged to the right.*

To reject a task, a user highlights the task in the grid to select it and then clicks the Reject button. The system displays a warning, as shown in Figure 27.4. Clicking Yes will process the request.

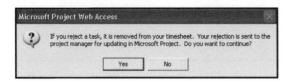

FIGURE 27.4 *The system warns the user before completing a task rejection.*

Selecting Insert Notes invokes the same text interface you've seen used in to-do list management. Clicking on Documents or Issues invokes the Sharepoint issues and documents management interface linked to the project. Notice that when sending an update, a user may choose to send selected rows or all information. Choosing Save keeps the changes in the database, but it doesn't send them to the project manager. Choosing either Update All or Update Selected Rows actually sends the updates. In other words, users may build or enter information into their time sheets now and send it days later.

Click the Delegation tab to bring up the delegation view options shown in Figure 27.5. The available options here depend on the selections you made when configuring your installation, and through administration later on. If delegation is turned on for the user, the option to track the delegated task is available as well. Selecting this option means the task will remain visible in the Timesheet, as will its progress.

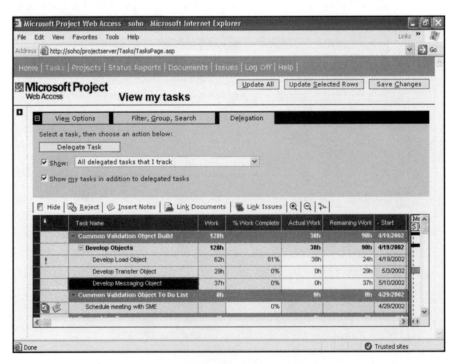

FIGURE 27.5 *To delegate a task, first highlight it in the Timesheet.*

Highlight a task and click Delegate. The first page of Delegate Tasks will be displayed, as shown in Figure 27.6. The drop-down list in the first section allows you to choose from all resources. Section 2 accepts a yes or no answer to assume the lead role for the task. Selecting this option negates the third selection, which determines whether the task will remain visible in your Timesheet if you do not select the lead role.

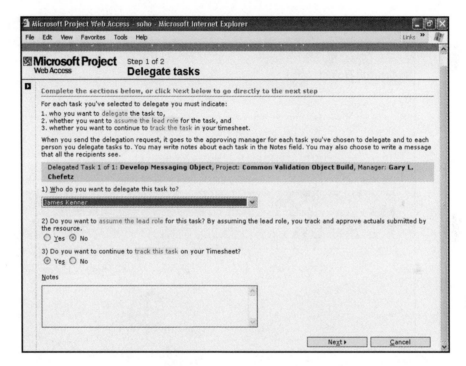

FIGURE 27.6 *Step one of task delegation allows you to select the recipient of the delegated task, as well as whether or not to assume the lead role or simply continue to track its progress on your Timesheet.*

 TIP

The lead role takes on new significance in Project Server. When the person delegating the task assumes this role, he or she can approve actual work data submitted by the delegated resource. This feature now supports the behavior of an intermediary role, whereby a team leader or resource manager can participate in the team structure with the same resource control functionality as the project manager. Use this feature to model your reporting structure in Project Server.

Click Next to go to Page 2, shown in Figure 27.7. The system summarizes the delegation choices prior to committing them. Click Send to complete the delegation and notify both the project manager and the resource to whom the task has been delegated. The delegation remains subject to the project manager's approval. The system displays a completion alert box to let you know your actions have been successful.

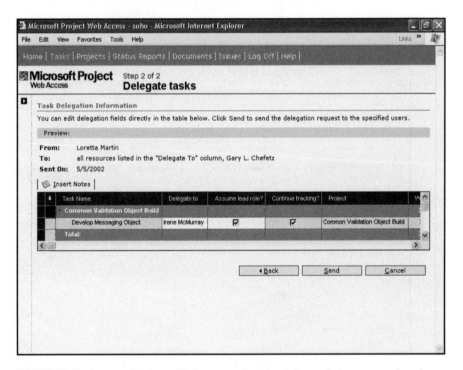

FIGURE 27.7 *Page 2 of Delegate Tasks summarizes the choices and gives you one last chance to make changes.*

As a resource, you can create or request a new task from your project manager. Selecting Create a New Task from the Tasks Activity menu displays the Create a New Task page, shown in Figure 27.8. This page reveals what some will consider one of Project Server's shortcomings. The pull-down project selector contains all projects in the system, exposing this information to all resources, unmindful of access rights in the application. If a resource chooses to create a new task in a project to which he or she is already assigned, the new task requested will appear in the timesheet immediately after the change is saved.

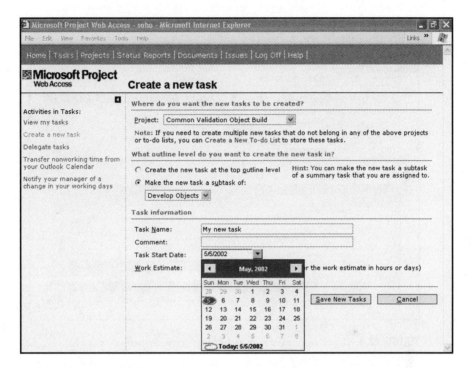

FIGURE 27.8   *Creating a new task takes the form of a request that must be approved by the project manager.*

The reporting fields for your new task will not accept data until the task is approved by the project manager. The new task is highlighted in yellow on the timesheet, as shown in Figure 27.9. To actually send your updates to the project manager for approval, you must click either Update All or Update Selected Rows. Alternately, clicking Save Changes writes your pending activity to the database for later retrieval and updating.

Resources report working time changes to their project manager(s) by selecting the Report Working Time Changes from the task center activities menu. The first page is shown in Figure 27.10. Resources can submit these changes to either make working time, nonworking time, or vice versa. Choose the period that the change applies to and click Next.

In Step 2, choose the managers to notify of the change, as shown in Figure 27.11.

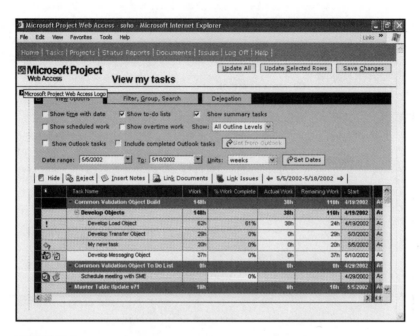

FIGURE 27.9 *Until the project manager approves the delegation, the task is highlighted on the timesheet.*

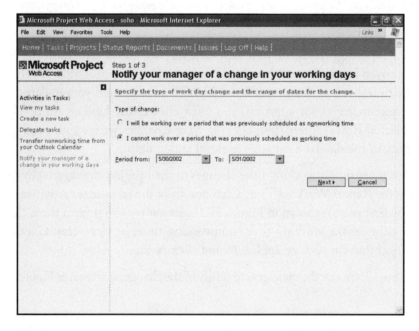

FIGURE 27.10 *In Project Web Access, notifying your manager of a change in working time is easy.*

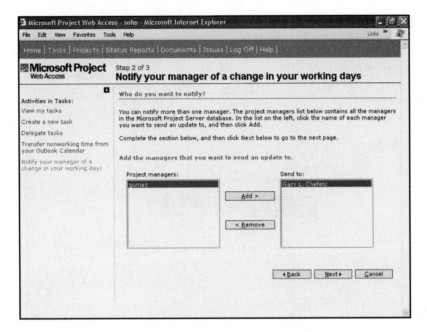

FIGURE 27.11   *Choose the managers to notify by moving them to the Send To category.*

The system displays a summary of the changes you are about to submit, as shown in Figure 27.12. Click the Send button to commit the changes and notify the selected managers.

You've now seen nonworking time mentioned in more than one context. In the context of work day changes, nonworking time represents time away from work. In the context of the timesheet, it's entirely different. For working days on the calendar, hours are reportable against nonworking time.

Hours reported against nonworking time, which might be better termed *non-project time*, are stored in the database, but Project Server provides no native access to this data through any of its interfaces. To access or display this information, you must use direct queries against the database.

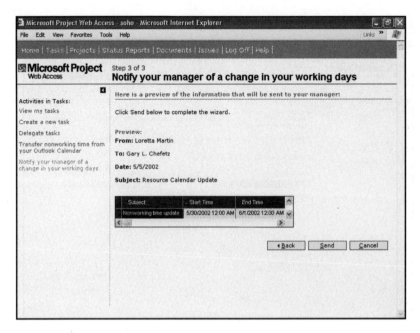

FIGURE 27.12 *Approve the summary of changes, or go back to make more changes.*

 TIP

Many businesses want to get more granular in their reporting of non-task time spent working. They want to know how much time is spent on meetings, telephone support, or maintenance tasks. To capture work effort more specifically, it's best to set up a project for this purpose using fixed-unit type tasks. This makes it possible to preserve and represent availability more accurately.

Status Reports

Resources can submit non-requested status reports by clicking the Activities link in the Status Reports overview page, shown in Figure 27.13. The overview display is the Status Reports default page. Click on a report name to respond to a status report request.

Figure 27.14 shows that the sections you specified as a project manager in Chapter 26 are represented as text entry boxes with titles. When you click in a text box, an editing and formatting toolbar appears that offers the option to insert tasks from the timesheet.

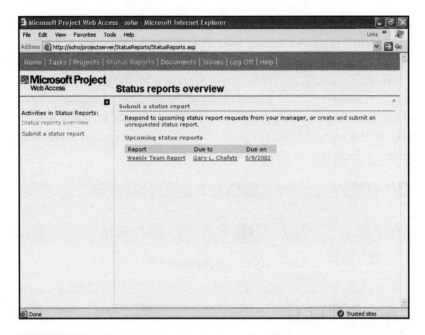

FIGURE 27.13 *All of your status report requests are displayed on your personalized Status Reports Overview page.*

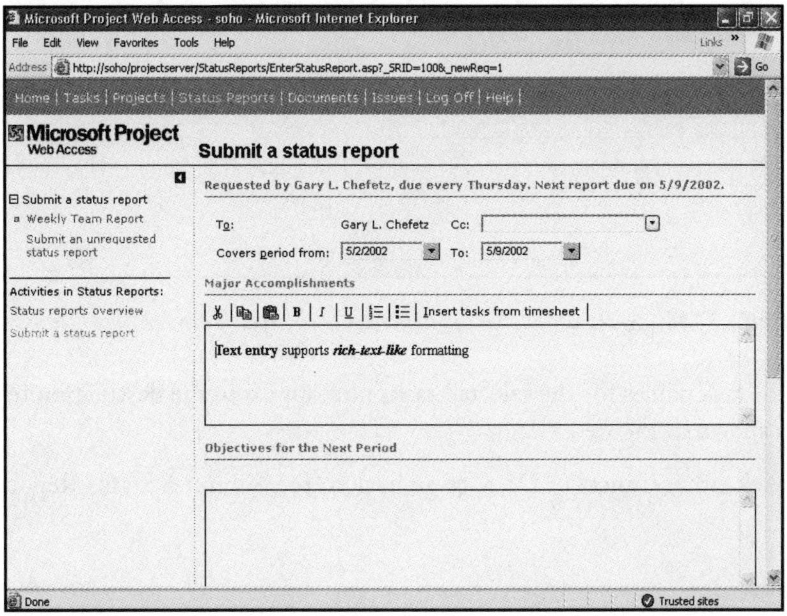

FIGURE 27.14 *To submit a status report, fill in the blanks.*

Select a section by clicking in the text box to activate the toolbar. Click Insert Tasks from Timesheet to load your available task selections. Click the check boxes to indicate the task(s) you want to insert into your status report, as shown in Figure 27.15. Notice that Section 1 is displayed beneath the task grid. You must scroll the page past all of the sections to expose your choices: Insert Task, Done, or Cancel. Choosing Insert Tasks adds the names of the tasks to the section from which you initiated the insertion. Click Cancel to abandon these changes or Done to save them.

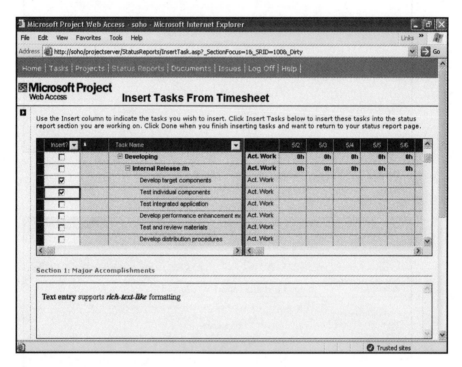

FIGURE 27.15 *Automatically move task names to any text box in the timesheet.*

The task names for the selected tasks now appear in the destination text box, as shown in Figure 27.16.

Click either Cancel or Done to go back to the Submit a Status Report page.

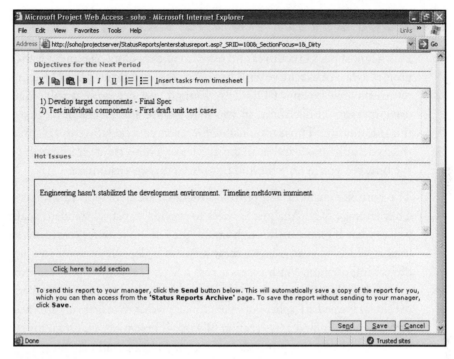

FIGURE 27.16 *Click Send to file this report with your manager.*

The Project Center

Resources have no access to Project Center views until you change the default categories or begin customizing categories and assigning users. Oddly enough, that's an advantage, because none of the standard installed views are particularly useful for resources. Given that custom fields are plentiful, you may see publishing opportunities in this area that Microsoft hasn't already provided for.

 TIP

Remember to approach the changes to the Enterprise Global, as discussed in Chapter 25, and then perform the following steps (Steps 1 and 2 are interchangeable):

1. Create views.

2. Create categories if necessary.

3. Assign users and views to categories.

Project Server for the Executive

For the most part, executives and other members of management want timely project data. An executive with financial responsibilities might be focused on return-on-investment (ROI) data. Earned and net present value data help drive investment decisions, so you may expose and create views that render this information. Those responsible for resource scheduling and planning will welcome utilization and availability views. These views are plentiful out of the box, but you're only limited by your ability to customize.

The portfolio analyzer and portfolio modeler are new tools in Project Server. They leverage SQL Analysis Services to provide statistical standard analyses, as well as what-if modeling through various project and resource cost scenarios. The level at which you can exercise these analyses is dependent upon your access to project information. With access across a large portfolio of projects, executives can plan at the enterprise level. With access limited to projects and resources within an immediate sphere of operation, a project manager can use these tools across a more limited cross-section of work. These tools are useful for studying the feasibility of a new project, as well as for strategic staff planning.

Project managers do not have access to modeling functionality out-of-the-box in Project Server. The default group can be modified to change that, of course. Executives *do* have access to the analyzer and modeler by default, so it would seem that Microsoft considers this to be an executive-level feature. Either that or it limits access by default because it knows that this service could render a box useless if more users than the box was sized for started using it at one time. Project Server's documentation explains how to install it with the analysis service run on its own box. For scalability, the message is clear: *Give it its own box.*

As an executive or administrator, you can choose Analyze Projects in Portfolio Analyzer, or choose Model Projects in Portfolio Modeler in the Project Center. In order for these features to function, an administrator must enable them. An OLAP cube must be built to enable the analyzer, which is also an administrator's task. Now that you have some projects and resources recorded on your server, going back to administration to build the cube is the last preparatory step. If you've been following this text using the software on a small test computer with everything installed on one box, generating your first cube will give you a sense of how resource-hungry the analysis service is. It takes a very long time to process.

Setting Up an OLAP Cube

Project Server provides a simple interface for exercising OLAP capabilities. Generating the cube is almost ridiculously simple. The power of it, though, lies in your ability to craft meaningful enterprise fields with which to drive your queries.

1. Log on as an administrator and select Manage Enterprise Features from the Admin Activities menu.

2. From the side-menu, choose Update Resource Tables and OLAP Cube. The Update Resource Tables and OLAP Cube page, shown in Figure 27.17, will appear.

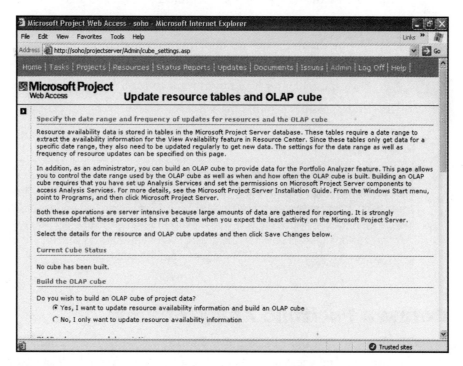

FIGURE 27.17   *The OLAP cube must be built before Portfolio features can be used.*

As you can see, you control more than just portfolio tools from this administrative interface. Use Resource Availability to feed the Resource Center availability views and graphs. This interface also exercises the OLAP cube, causing it to be built and setting its data and refresh parameters.

3. First, decide whether to update resource availability information and build an OLAP cube, or only update resource availability information.

4. Click Yes.

5. Give your cube a name. Referring to the time period covered is one useful naming convention.

6. Choose the date range for the project's finish and start dates.

7. Select the date range for updating resource availability.

8. Define the frequency for updating this model, and schedule the first update run.

9. Save your changes (you might want to read the tip below first).

10. Wait, possibly a good long while.

 TIP

Saving your changes doesn't build the cube, but it does schedule it to be built on its first refresh date. You probably want to build one now. Either save the changes and reopen this screen, or click Update Only When Specified and then choose Save Changes to kick off the cube-building process immediately. You want to schedule your cube-build when there won't be other traffic on your server, so do it now only if you're certain it won't cause contention for resources.

Define a Portfolio Analyzer View

The last step that must be completed before your executives will have access to Portfolio Analyzer views is to create a Portfolio Analyzer View. Remember when you defined a new Project Center view in the Manage Views administrative interface in Chapter 26 Project-level views are but one of two new view types introduced with Project Server. The Analyzer Views category is the other type. From the first page of Manage Views, click the Analyzer Option button. The result is shown in Figure 27.18.

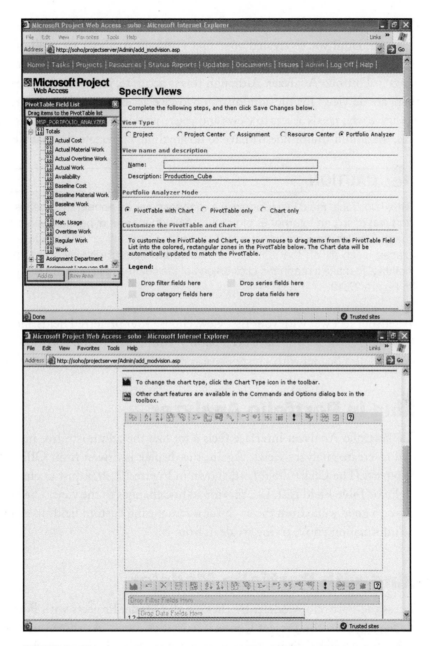

FIGURE 27.18 *Specifying a view for the Portfolio Analyzer is a prerequisite to using it.*

Office XP Web parts are used to render charts and pivot tables for the Portfolio Analyzer. Until you've created your first Portfolio Analyzer view, all of your users will be told that the administrator hasn't given them permission to any views in Portfolio Analyzer. Although this is accurate, it's misleading because there are no views for the administrator to give access to. In fact, if you're an executive who needs access to views and you're working with a default installation, the administrator doesn't have to do anything but create the first view.

CAUTION

The Pivot Table Field List window is a slippery devil. Its appearance belies the fact that it isn't an Internet Explorer window but rather a dynamic display element. Clicking the screen causes it to disappear. Hunting for it in the usual places, such as on the task bar or behind the current display, will turn up nothing. To make it reappear, click on one of the colored field drop areas shown in Figure 27.19.

To get your feet wet with your first view, choose your preferred fields and save your changes. Users who have been defined with access to the Portfolio Analyzer will now be met with a responsive system when they make that selection.

Working in Portfolio Analyzer

The Portfolio Analyzer interface feels a lot like the administrative interface used to create analyzer views. Again, the display is driven from Office XP Web parts. The Chart Field List, shown in Figure 27.20, is just as elusive as the Pivot Table Field List. Use this for ad hoc changes to the view. The key to getting a good value from the analyzer is structuring custom fields to support the information you're trying to glean from it.

Working with Portfolio Modeler

Access the Portfolio Modeler by clicking the Model Projects with Portfolio Modeler link on the Project Center's Activities menu. As shown in Figure 27.21, the Modeler displays your existing models. Whether you choose to create a new model or modify an existing one, the interface flow is the same.

Before you can analyze a model, you must create it. Create a new model by clicking the New button above the model display grid. The interface flow is the same for adding new models and modifying existing ones. Click on New to

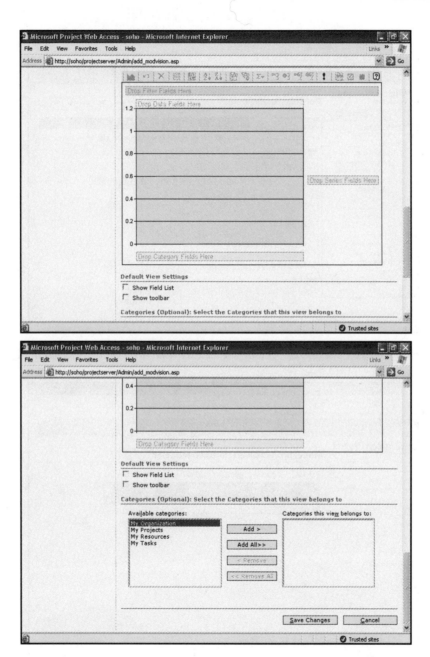

FIGURE 27.19 *Fields can be dragged and dropped onto the report areas.*

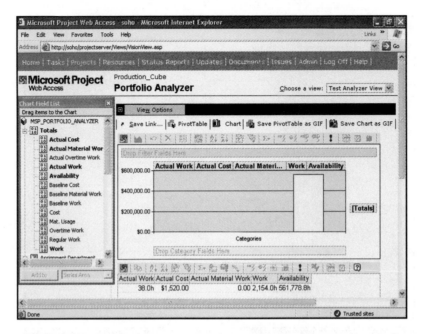

FIGURE 27.20 *The interface for using the view is similar to the one used to create it.*

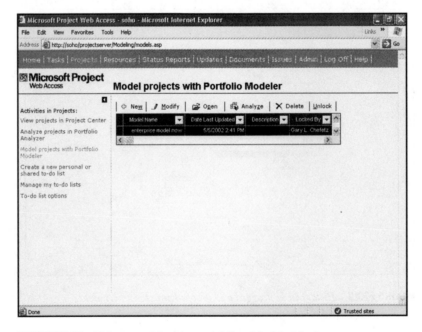

FIGURE 27.21 *You can model projects with Portfolio Modeler home page.*

display the first step in new model definition, shown in Figure 27.22. Give your new model a name and a description (optional). Select the project scope of the model. All projects are displayed, and you can use as few or as many as you like. When you're scoping resources to include in the model, you have three primary modes: Use only resources in the model projects, use only resources at or below

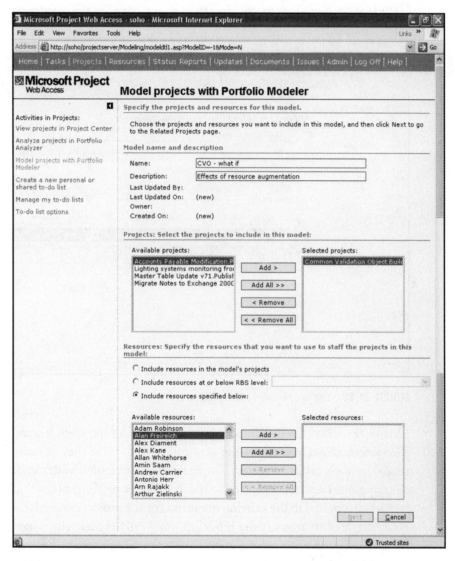

FIGURE 27.22 *Specify the projects and resources to use in the new model.*

a specified RBS level, or use resources that are specified in the interface. Clicking the latter activates the resource selection windows. When you're satisfied with your selections, click Next.

Related projects are displayed in the grid on the Include Related Projects page, shown in Figure 27.23. Note that the relationship is defined. You can include related projects by clicking their check boxes in the display grid.

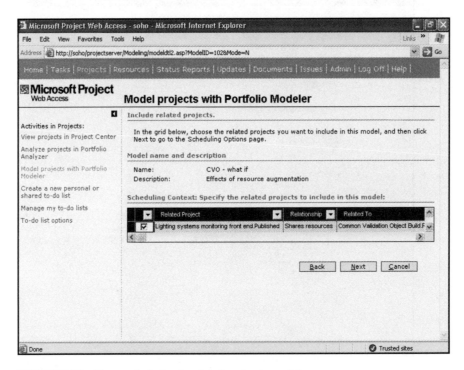

FIGURE 27.23 *You can include related projects in the model.*

Finally, the scheduling options page is displayed. As shown in Figure 27.24, the system allows you to set the scheduling options as they pertain to the model for each project selected. The options are presented in descending order, from most restrictive to least restrictive. Choosing Keep Start/End Dates restricts the model to the existing durations for the project selected. Use Current Assignments restricts the model to using only the current assignments, rather than proposing reassignments. Reassign Resources in Project allows the model to make reassignments only in the project for which it's selected.

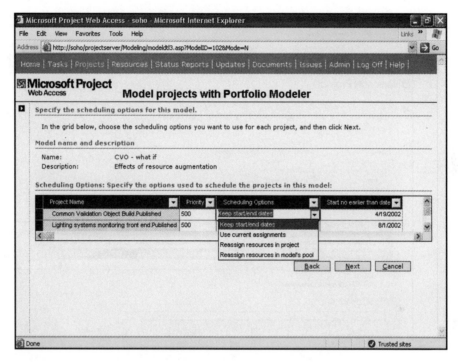

FIGURE 27.24 *Specify the scheduling options to use in the model.*

Reassign Resources in Model's Pool will take full liberty with regards to reassigning tasks within the entire model. Click Next to go back to the Model Projects with Portfolio Modeler main view.

Select a project in the main view and click Open to display the model you've created, as shown in Figure 27.25. The display contains a grid display of information, with a Gantt chart that functions like all Project Server Grids. In the figure, the divider has been dragged to the right to expose more of the field display. The chart at the bottom of the display shows resources across the selected projects, and the degree to which they're overallocated is indicated by a color-coded display. This figure shows a single model view. Click Compare to select another model to compare in the view.

This model shows the result of a what-if scenario: "What if these two projects were executed with two additional resources?" To see what the system suggests, click Analyze from the Task menu above the grid. Analyzed results are

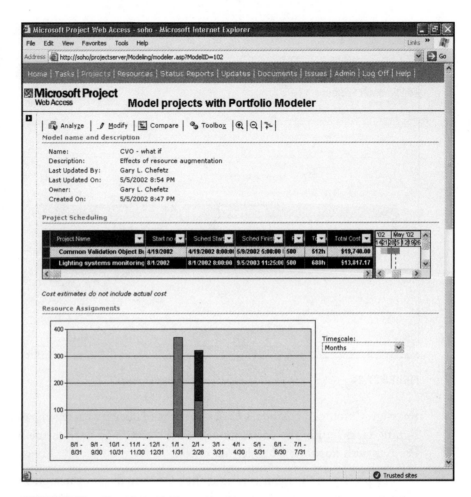

FIGURE 27.25 *View the model by opening it.*

displayed, as shown in Figure 27.26. The system suggests the shortest hypothetical schedule based on the parameters it was given. Of course, this doesn't account for the nuances of scheduling and assignments, but it does provide an ad hoc analysis "sand pit," as Microsoft calls it. Goal-seeking activities are a natural for this type of analysis.

The Portfolio Model Property toolbox can be invoked from an open model. The toolbox, shown in Figure 27.27, allows you to make changes to a model's properties at the same time you're changing the parameter selections. The toolbox can remain open while you're making your other changes.

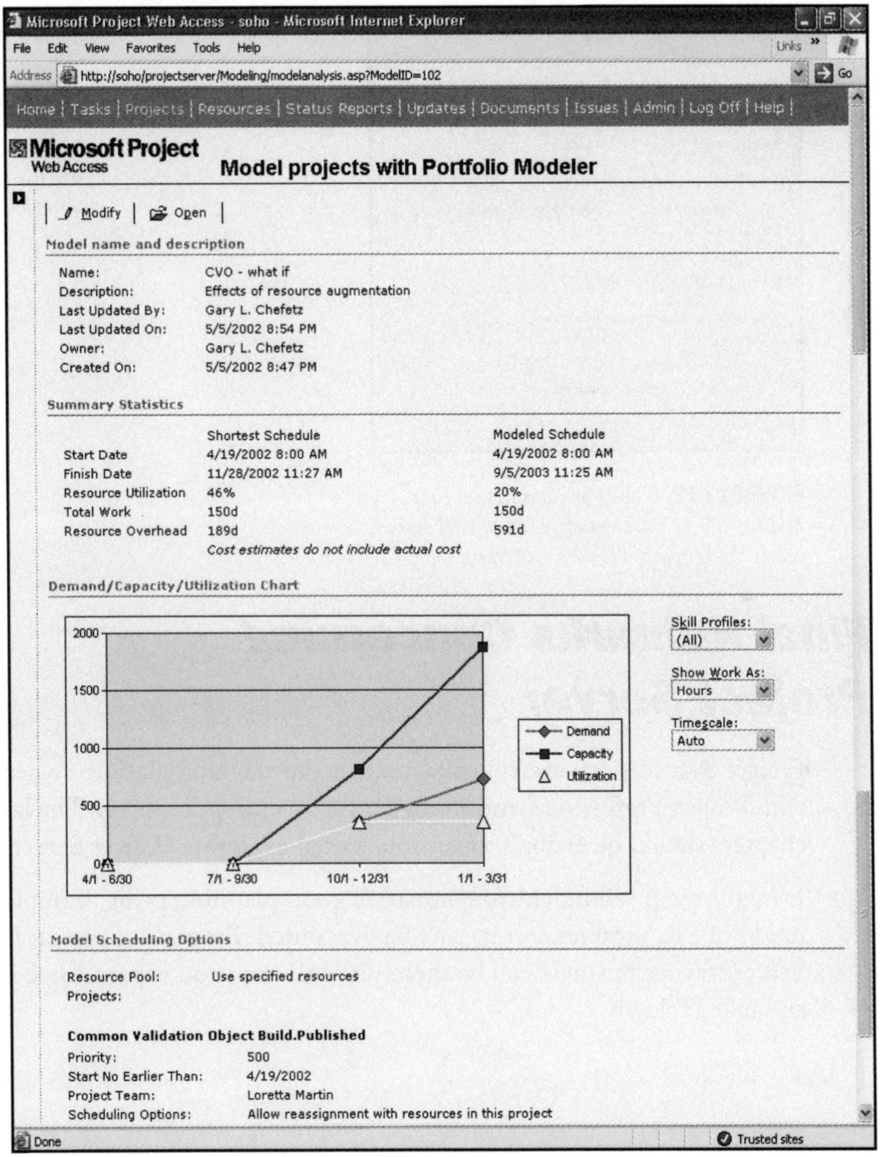

FIGURE 27.26 *Click Analyze to get system recommendations and the graphing of demand, availability, and utilization.*

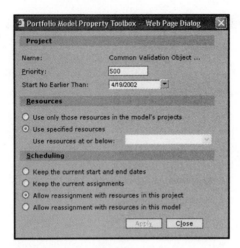

FIGURE 27.27   *The Portfolio Model Property toolbox allows you to manipulate model options while changing model data selections.*

Final Remarks Concerning Project Server

Project Server is a powerful collaborative and tracking platform when used with Project Professional and configured as an enterprise server. The last four chapters should be enough to get you started exploring Project Server.

It might seem redundant to emphasize good planning prior to implementation of this product, but it can't be overstated. Properly mapping Project Server to your business can be more difficult than you expect. Give it time and take it slowly.

PART VII

Working with Advanced Features

Chapter 28

**Customizing
Microsoft
Project**

In This Chapter

◆ Making adjustments to menus

◆ Hiding and displaying toolbars, and working with toolbar tools

◆ Adding Add-Ins

◆ Working with the Options dialog box

Throughout the book, I've noted numerous situations where you need to tweak how Project 2002 reacts to your commands, or even how you communicate with Project to give it commands. This chapter provides an overview of all the customization options available to you in Project. It explains how to make Project look and work the way you want it to.

Creating a Custom Menu

Early on, many computer programs deserved their reputation for being difficult to learn. Each program used its own terms for particular operations. For example, opening a file was called "getting," "retrieving," and so on, depending on the program. Moreover, each program had different menus that grouped commands differently. From one program to the next, you never knew exactly how to navigate. Software publishers have come a long way toward standardizing terms and menus so that the things you learn in one program apply in another, and they've also been kind enough to leave in plenty of flexibility for controlling the way menus look and work.

In fact, in Project and many other applications, you can create custom drop-down menus and custom menu commands to suit your needs and working style. The menus you create or modify can execute standard program commands, macros that come with the programs, or macros you create.

To work with menus in Project, choose Tools, Customize, Toolbars. Or, right-click on the menu bar and then click on Customize. The Customize dialog box (see Figure 28.1) displays the list of menu bars and toolbars available in Project. (In Project 2002, you use similar steps to create menu bars and toolbars.) Each menu bar offers a list of menus, which in turn list commands. To display a different toolbar onscreen, click the Toolbars tab, check the toolbar's check box, and then close the dialog box. If you no longer want a particular menu to appear onscreen, clear the check box next to its name before closing the dialog box.

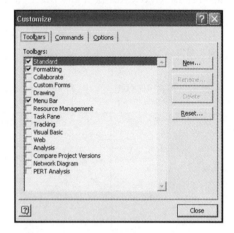

FIGURE 28.1 *Work with menus and toolbars using this dialog box. On the Toolbars tab, place a check next to any menu bar or toolbar to display it.*

 TIP

To display a menu bar you've created, right-click on any onscreen menu bar or toolbar to open a shortcut menu, and then click on the name of the menu.

You can also use the Customize dialog box to add a new command to a menu, add a new menu to a menu bar, or create an entirely new menu bar. For example, to create a new menu bar, click on the New button on the Toolbars tab. The New Toolbar dialog box appears. Type a name for the menu in the Toolbar Name text box, preferably a name that distinguishes the new bar as a menu bar rather than a toolbar. Click on OK, and the new menu bar appears onscreen as a small, blank floating toolbar.

Next, you want to create the first menu on the menu bar. Click on the Commands tab in the Customize dialog box. Scroll down the Categories list and click on New Menu. A New Menu option appears in the Commands list at the right side of the dialog box. Drag New Menu from the dialog box onto the new menu bar. A New Menu placeholder appears on the menu bar. Right-click on the placeholder, or click on it and then click on the Modify Selection button in the Customize dialog box. Then, type a menu name in the Name text box, such as **Favo&rites** (see Figure 28.2). Press Enter. Project knows that you intend the entry to be a menu name and automatically places a drop-down arrow next to it. The ampersand (&) before the "r" is how you tell Project to format that letter as a selection letter. Your custom menu will be called Favorites, and pressing Alt+R will open it when you're finished.

Drag this placeholder onto the menu bar   Right-click on the new menu   Enter the menu name

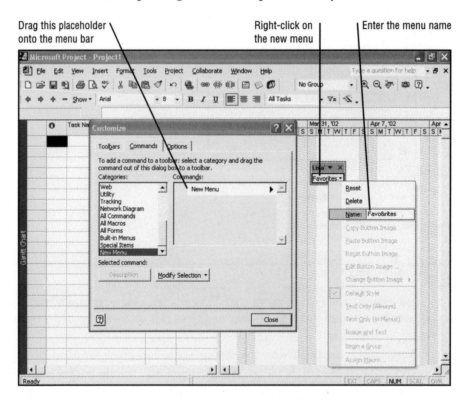

FIGURE 28.2 *You can create a completely new menu on a menu bar.*

For obvious reasons, you can't use the same selection letter for two menu names on the same menu bar, or for two commands on the same menu. Also, you should be careful not to duplicate selection letters in menu names if you plan to display more than one menu at a time.

TIP

You can also add a menu to any toolbar that's displayed onscreen by dragging the New Menu placeholder onto the toolbar rather than onto a menu bar.

On the Commands tab of the Customize dialog box, scroll through the Categories list and click on the category that holds the first command or macro you want to add to the menu. If you're not sure what category to choose, click on the All Commands or All Macros option. Then scroll down the Commands list until you see the command you want to add to the menu. Drag the command from the Commands list to the new menu name on the menu bar. When the blank menu opens below the menu name, drag the command onto the menu and release the mouse button. The command appears on the menu, which remains open. If you want to rename the command or change its selection letter, right-click on the command, or click on it and click on the Modify Selection button in the Customize dialog box. Edit the Name text box entry, and then press Enter. To add each additional command to the menu, simply click on the Categories option you want and drag a command from the Commands list to the position on the menu where you want it to appear. Then drop it into place, as shown in Figure 28.3.

NOTE

You have to leave the Customize dialog box open to make all your menu changes. Otherwise, the techniques described in this section won't work. If you need to reopen the Customize dialog box, choose Tools, Customize, Toolbars.

If you want to create a command to display a submenu, select New Menu in the Categories list on the Commands tab, and then drag the New Menu option onto a menu. Name the submenu just as you would name a menu. Then select command categories from the Categories list and drag commands from the Commands list onto the submenu you added to the menu.

You might want to be able to group commands on your menu, for easier access. You can do so by inserting a separator line. Open the new menu, and then click on the command above which you want the separator line to appear. Click on the Modify Selection button in the Customize dialog box, or right-click on the selected command. To insert the separator line, choose the Begin a Group option in the menu that appears. To remove the separator,

Indicates where the new command will appear

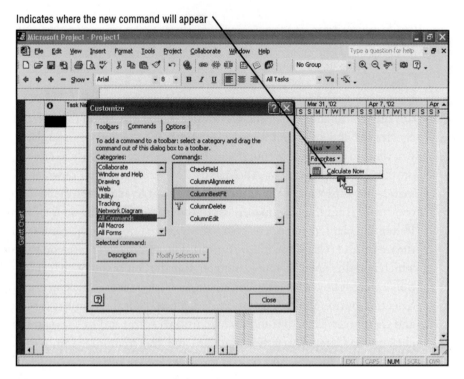

FIGURE 28.3 *Drag additional commands from the Customize dialog box to the new menu.*

reopen the shortcut menu for the selected command and click on the Begin a Group option to toggle it off.

Continue using these techniques to add additional commands to your menu. Anytime you want to start a new menu on the menu bar, click on the New Menu option in the Categories list, and then drag the New Menu placeholder from the Commands list to the desired position on the menu bar. If you make a mistake and add an unwanted menu bar or command, simply drag the menu or command off the menu bar where it resides and onto the Project work area, and then release the mouse button. Alternately, you can drag a menu name to change its position on a menu bar, or drag a command to move it up or down in a menu. For example, if you're right-handed, you may want to move the File menu on the default menu bar to the right.

When you finish making your menu bar changes, close the Customize dialog box. Then you can drag the new menu bar to where you want it onscreen. If you drag it to the top of the screen, you can drop it above an existing toolbar or menu bar to "dock" it in a horizontal position.

Although it's fine to start from scratch when you're creating a menu, you may be better off adding a copy of an existing menu to your menu bar and modifying it to suit your needs. Click on the Built-In Menus option in the Categories list on the Commands tab. Then drag the name of the menu that most approximates your needs from the Commands list to the appropriate position on a menu bar or menu. Finally, make changes to the menu and commands as needed.

TIP

If you make changes to the Standard menu bar and later you want to undo the changes, display the Customize dialog box, click on Menu Bar in the Toolbars list on the Toolbars tab, and click on the Reset button.

NOTE

By default, your custom menu bars and toolbars are stored with the GLOBAL.MPT file, where Project settings are stored. If you want to e-mail a schedule file with the custom menu bar or toolbar, you need to copy that custom menu bar or toolbar—as well as any macro modules holding macros for commands or toolbar buttons—to that particular file. Use the Organizer command on the Tools menu to display the Organizer, which enables you to copy the custom feature. See Chapter 13, "Working with the Different Project Views," to learn more about the Organizer.

Working with Toolbars

Toolbars are as easy to customize as menu bars, and most users find toolbars easier to use. Throughout this book, you've seen that displaying different toolbars or working with particular toolbar buttons can help you get the most out of certain Project features. This section shows you how to work with Project's toolbars.

Displaying and Hiding Toolbars

Every toolbar is accessible via the other toolbars. You can right-click on any toolbar to display a shortcut menu. Then click on the name of another toolbar you want to display, or click on the name of a toolbar that's already onscreen that you want to hide. Similarly, you can open the View menu and point to the Toolbars option to display a submenu of toolbars and menu bars. In this submenu, you just click on the toolbar you want to hide or display.

An alternate method of choosing which toolbars appear onscreen and which don't, as well as accessing other commands for working with toolbars, is to choose Tools, Customize, Toolbars. The Customize dialog box appears (refer to Figure 28.1). To open the Customize dialog box using the mouse, right-click on any toolbar and then choose Customize.

In the Toolbars list on the Toolbars tab, click on the check box next to any toolbar you want to display. If you want to hide a toolbar that's onscreen, simply click on its check box in the Toolbars list to remove the check mark. Click on the Close button to close the Customize dialog box and finish making your choices.

Customizing the Buttons on a Toolbar

You can make any changes that you want to the contents of a toolbar. It's very similar to creating and editing a menu, which you learned about earlier in the chapter. You can remove buttons, add buttons, or edit the function of any button. To add and remove buttons on a toolbar, following these steps:

1. Open the toolbar that you want to edit onscreen.
2. Choose Tools, Customize, Toolbars. Alternately, you can right-click on any toolbar and then choose Customize. The Customize dialog box will appear.
3. To add a button to one of the displayed toolbars, click on the Commands tab to display it. Click on one of the Categories list choices to display the available buttons and commands in that category. Then drag a button or command from the Commands list over to its desired position on the toolbar, as shown in Figure 28.4. Release the mouse button to drop the new toolbar button into position.

 NOTE

To add a toolbar button or menu command for a macro you've created, select All Macros from the Categories list box on the Commands tab. Then drag the macro from the Commands list to a menu bar or toolbar.

Button being dragged   Click to display a description   A choice with an icon appears
                            of the command or button   as a button on the toolbar

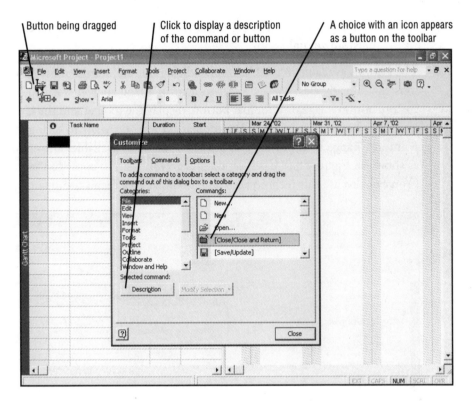

FIGURE 28.4 *You add a button to a toolbar by dragging the button from the Customize dialog box.*

 TIP

The Commands list on the Commands tab tells you whether a command you add to a toolbar will appear as a picture button only or as a text command only. A choice that has an icon will appear as a picture button when you drag it onto a toolbar. If a choice lacks an icon, the command name itself will appear on the button.

4. To move an existing toolbar button to a new position on the same toolbar, which you must do while the Customize dialog box is open, just drag and drop it into the new location.

5. To remove a button from a toolbar while the Customize dialog box is open, drag the button off the toolbar and release the mouse button. (Make sure that you don't accidentally drop it onto another toolbar.)

6. When you finish moving buttons around on your toolbars, close the Customize dialog box.

The buttons available in the Customize dialog box are, for the most part, buttons that already exist on a Project toolbar or menu. If you want to place a custom button image on a toolbar button, display the toolbar and the Customize dialog box. Right-click on the toolbar button you want to change. Then point to Change Button Image to display a palette of available button images, as shown in Figure 28.5. Click on the image you want to apply to the button. (You can also use this technique to add an image to a menu command.)

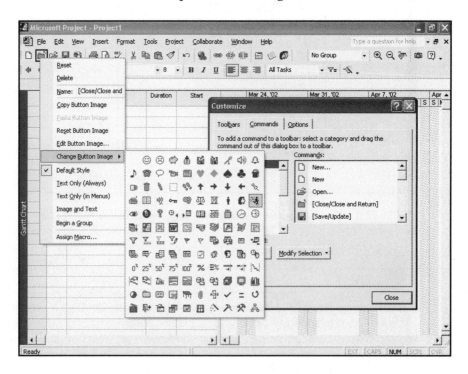

FIGURE 28.5 *Click on a new image in this palette of choices to apply it to the current toolbar button.*

If you can't find a button that's exactly what you need, click on a button that's close in appearance. Then right-click on the toolbar button with the image you want to edit and click on Edit Button Image in the shortcut menu that appears. The Button Editor appears, as shown in Figure 28.6. Click on a color or in the Erase box in the Colors area. Then click on a square (called a pixel) on the picture to change that pixel to the selected color. Click on OK when you finish making changes. The edited image appears on the toolbar button only (it's not available on the palette for other buttons).

Click on a color or the Erase choice here . . .   . . . then click on a pixel here

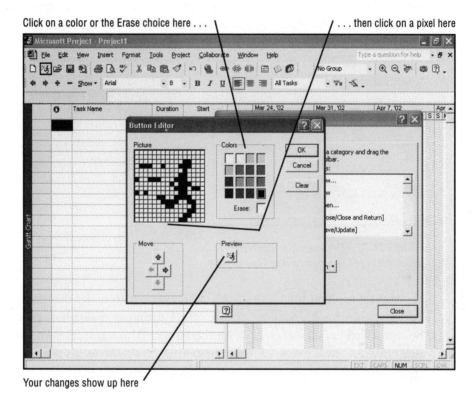

Your changes show up here

FIGURE 28.6 *If you can't find an existing design that's exactly what you want, edit the button art.*

You can change the command or macro assigned to a button or its status bar description by using the Customize Tool dialog box. (This technique applies to menu commands, too.) With the Customize dialog box open, click on the toolbar button (or menu command). Then click on Modify Selection on the Commands tab, or right-click on the toolbar button. In the menu that appears, click on Assign Macro. The Customize Tool dialog box appears. To change the existing command, macro, or custom form assigned to the button (or menu command), open the drop-down list for the Command text box. Scroll through the list and click on the selection you want to assign to the button. (Forms and macros are listed under "f" and "m," respectively. For example, a custom form might be listed as *Form "Summary"* and a macro as *Macro "Adjust_Dates."*)

Click on the Name text box and type or edit the button name, which will pop up as a ScreenTip to describe the button whenever you point to it with the mouse. Then click on the Description text box and type a description for the button, which will be used to explain the button in the status bar whenever you point to it. Figure 28.7 shows some sample entries. Click on OK to finish editing the toolbar button, and then adjust other buttons or close the Customize dialog box.

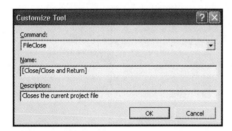

FIGURE 28.7   *Here are example entries for a button in the Customize dialog box.*

If you want to open the Customize Tool dialog box to make changes to any button on any toolbar without opening the Customize dialog box, press and hold the Ctrl key, and then click on the button. Make any adjustments you want in the Customize Tool dialog box, using the same techniques just described for creating a custom button. Then click on OK.

Creating a Custom Toolbar

You can create a brand new toolbar, or one that's based on an existing toolbar. To do so, right-click on a toolbar and then choose Customize. Alternately, choose Tools, Customize, Toolbars. The Customize dialog box appears. On the Toolbars tab in the dialog box, click on the New button, type a toolbar name in the New Toolbar dialog box, and click on OK. This displays a blank toolbar.

After the new toolbar appears, click on the Commands tab in the Customize dialog box to add or remove toolbar buttons, as described earlier. You can also right-click on any individual button on the toolbar to display a menu of commands for modifying that button.

Deleting a Custom Toolbar or Menu Bar

Project does not let you delete any menu bar or toolbar that comes with the program. You can delete the custom menu bars or toolbars you create, however.

To delete a custom menu bar or toolbar, right-click on any menu bar or toolbar onscreen, and then open the Customize dialog box. In the Toolbars list of the Toolbars tab, select the name of the custom menu bar or toolbar you want to delete. Click on the Delete button. Project asks you to confirm that you want to delete the menu bar or toolbar. (You're warned because you can't undo the deletion.) Click on OK to do so. Then close the Customize dialog box.

Using Add-Ins

In the section called "Comparing Two Project Versions" in Chapter 11, you learned that you can add the COM Add-Ins option to the Tools menu or any toolbar. A COM (Component Object Model) Add-In is a specially designed program that extends the features of Project. When you load a COM Add-In, the new features become available in Project. When you unload the COM Add-In, those features are no longer available. As saved programs, Add-In files typically have the EXE or DLL file name extension.

Although you may not have the programming skills to write your own COM Add-Ins, you may obtain additional Add-Ins from the Microsoft Web site or another source. To use them, you must once again ensure that the COM Add-Ins option is available on a menu bar or toolbar.

To add the COM Add-Ins option to a menu or toolbar, right-click a toolbar and click Customize. Click the Commands tab, choose the Tools category, drag the COM Add-Ins option to the desired menu or toolbar, and then click OK.

When you choose COM Add-Ins from the menu or toolbar where you placed it, the COM Add-Ins dialog box appears, as shown in Figure 28.8.

This dialog box enables you to manage, install, and uninstall Add-Ins, as follows:

◆ To unload an Add-In, uncheck its check box in the Add-Ins Available list.

◆ To load an Add-In, check its check box in the Add-Ins Available list.

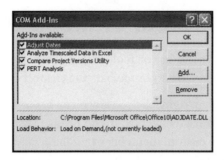

FIGURE 28.8 *Use this dialog box to load, unload, add, and remove Add-Ins.*

◆ To remove an add-in, click on its name in the Add-Ins Available list, and then click on the Remove button. Project removes the Add-In immediately, without displaying a warning message.

◆ To install an Add-In, click on the Add button. In the Add Add-In dialog box that appears, use the Look In list to navigate to the folder that holds the Add-In you want to install. Double-click on the Add-In file to finish loading it, and return to the COM Add-Ins dialog box.

When you finish working with Add-Ins, you can click on OK to close the COM Add-Ins dialog box.

Customizing Workgroup Message Fields

Chapter 22, "Communicating with the Team," explains how to send specialized messages called *workgroup messages* to make resource assignments, send task updates, and request status reports from resources. In each of these messages, Project lists certain fields for each task you're communicating about, such as Task Name or Remaining Work Hours. You can add more fields for tasks listed in these messages by following these steps:

1. Choose Tools, Customize, Published Fields. The Customize Published Fields dialog box will appear, as shown in Figure 28.9.

2. To add a new field, scroll through the Available Fields list at the bottom-left corner and click on the name of the field you'd like to insert. Click on the Add (>) button. The field moves to the Fields In The Tasks View list at the bottom-right corner (see Figure 28.10).

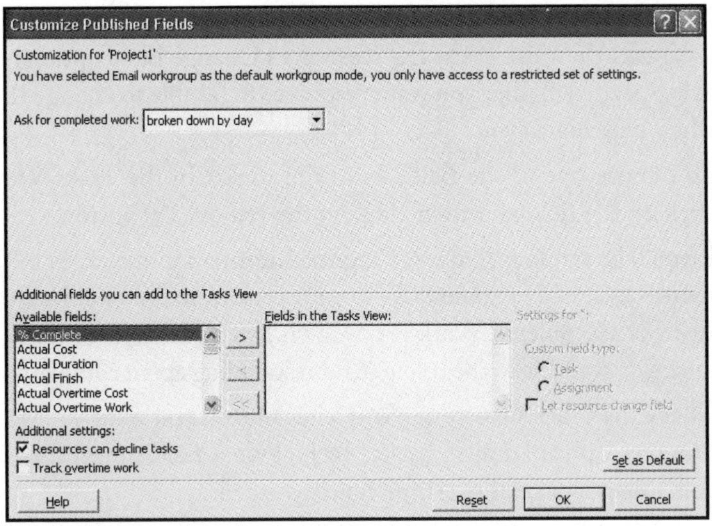

FIGURE 28.9 *You can add additional fields for the task information in workgroup messages.*

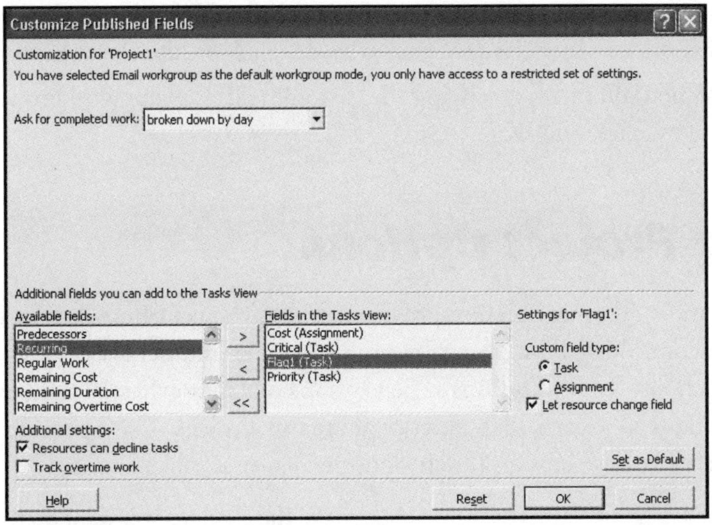

FIGURE 28.10 *The Fields in the Tasks View list shows the fields added to workgroup messages.*

3. To change the settings for a particular field, click it in the Fields In the Tasks View list. If the Let Resources Change Field option is available, specify whether you want resources to be able to change the field when replying to you.

4. To remove one of the fields from the Fields In the Tasks View list, click on the field and then click on the remove (<) button.

5. If you'll be sending Request Progress Information messages to the resources assigned to some tasks in your project, make a choice from the Ask For Completed Work drop-down list. Your choice here controls the fields available to the resource for responding about completed work.

6. Check the Track Overtime Work check box if you want your Request Progress Information messages to include a field prompting recipients to report actual overtime hours worked.

7. If you want to include a field enabling recipients to decline tasks (via e-mail) you assign through Publish New and Changed Assignments messages, check the Resources Can Decline Tasks check box.

8. If at any point you're not satisfied with the Fields in the Tasks View list or the other changes you've made, click on the Reset button.

9. When you finish specifying the custom fields for your workgroup messages, click on OK.

Setting Project Options

As with most other application programs today, Project offers dozens of options for controlling how the entire program looks and behaves. To set these options, choose Tools, Options. The Options dialog box has 10 tabs, each of which relates to a particular functional area of Project. The upcoming sections describe these tabs and their options.

Click on a tab to display its options. Then make the changes you want on that tab. When you finish specifying your options for all the tabs in the Options dialog box, click on OK to close the dialog box and put your changes into effect.

View Options

The first tab in the Options dialog box, the View tab (see Figure 28.11), specifies how Project looks onscreen when you run it.

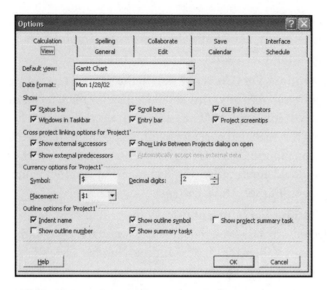

FIGURE 28.11   *Project offers options for controlling its onscreen appearance.*

Here are your choices:

◆ **Default View.** This is the view Project uses for the current schedule when you start the program.

◆ **Date Format.** This specifies how dates appear in the Task Sheet for any column with date information.

◆ **Show.** In the Show area, you specify which of the following should appear—Status Bar, Scroll Bars, OLE Links Indicator, Windows In Taskbar, Entry Bar, and Project ScreenTips. Place a check mark next to each feature that you want to appear.

◆ **Cross Project Linking Options For (Current File).** If you've linked tasks between files or consolidated projects (see Chapters 18 and 20), use these options to control whether and how the links appear. If you want tasks that are linked to other projects to appear in the current project file, check the Show External Successors or Show External Predecessors check box (or both). Clear these check boxes to hide the linked tasks. Check the Show Links Between Projects Dialog On Open check box if you want Project to prompt you about updating links when you open a file that contains linked tasks. When that check box is cleared, you can check the Automatically Accept New External Data check box to make Project update the tasks without displaying a dialog box. Alternately, clear both check boxes to simply open the file without updating the linked tasks.

◆ **Currency Options For (Current File).** In the Symbol text box, specify the currency symbol (if any) that should appear to the left of columns containing cost information. The Placement drop-down list lets you control how the specified currency symbol appears in relation to the currency value. In the Decimal Digits text box, enter how many decimal places should appear after whole numbers in currency values. For example, enter **0** to see whole currency values only.

◆ **Outline Options For (Current File).** When the Indent Name check box is selected, any tasks you indent will move to the right in the Task Name column. When the Show Outline Number check box is selected, Project displays an outline number, which you can't edit, next to each task in the Task Name column of the Task Sheet. You can use the Show Outline Symbol check box to turn on or off the display of the outlining + (summary task) and – (subtask) symbols. If you clear the check mark beside the Show Summary Tasks option, summary tasks won't appear in the Task Sheet, so you won't be able to use outlining features. The Project Summary Task option inserts a summary task for the whole project file, as described in Chapter 4.

General Options

Click on the General tab to display the options shown in Figure 28.12.

Here's what you can do with each of these options:

◆ **Show Startup Task Pane.** Leave this option checked if you want to see the task pane at the left side of the application window when you start Project.

◆ **Open Last File on Startup.** Check this option to tell Project to automatically reopen the last schedule file you worked in when you restart Project.

◆ **Prompt for Project Info for New Projects.** Check this option to make Project ask you for Project schedule information when you create a new project.

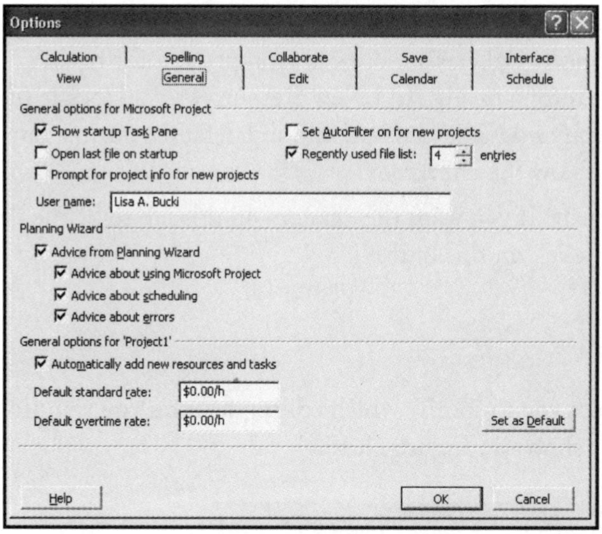

FIGURE 28.12   *Control the most common Project options in this tab of the Options dialog box.*

◆ **Set AutoFilter on for New Projects.** When checked, this option automatically turns on the AutoFilter feature in all new project files. As you learned in Chapter 13, the AutoFilter arrows on Task Sheet and Resource Sheet column headings are a speedy way to display only entries with similar information in a particular field.

◆ **Recently Used File List.** Check this if you want the names of files you've worked with recently to appear at the bottom of Project's File menu. Use the spinner buttons next to the Entries text box to tell Project how many file names should appear on the File menu. Clicking one of those file names on the menu quickly opens the file.

◆ **User Name.** Type your name in this text box.

◆ **Planning Wizard.** When no check mark appears next to the Advice from Planning Wizard option, no Planning Wizard options are available. You can determine whether you want Project to display advice about using Microsoft Project, advice about scheduling (asks whether you want to create links where they're possible, and so on), or advice about errors (informs you when your changes will create a scheduling conflict or some other problem).

◆ **General Options for (Current File).** A check mark next to the Automatically Add New Resources and Tasks option means that any name you type when making assignments becomes a row entry in the Resource Sheet. Otherwise, Project prompts you for resource information. If Automatically Add New Resources and Tasks is selected, you can specify a default standard rate and default overtime rate in the text boxes below the check box.

◆ **Set as Default.** If you want the changes on this tab to be the defaults for Project, click on this button.

Edit Options

The Edit tab enables you to specify which editing features you want to use in Project. This tab is shown in Figure 28.13.

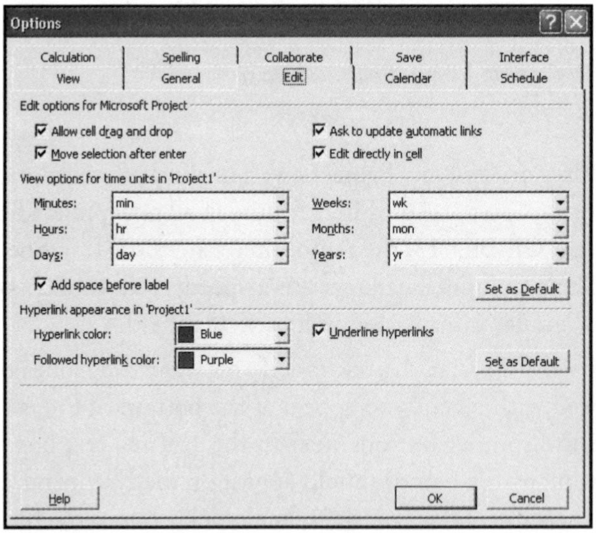

FIGURE 28.13 *Project offers numerous editing features, and here's where you choose whether to use them.*

The first option, Allow Cell Drag and Drop, controls whether you can drag information into the Task Sheet or Resource Sheet. Move Selection After Enter means that when you press Enter after making an entry in the Task Sheet or Resource Sheet, the cell selector moves down to the next row. Ask to Update Automatic Links means that Project prompts you about links if you update a file that's linked to task or resource information in another file. Edit Directly in Cell lets you make changes in a Task Sheet or Resource Sheet cell, rather than having to click on a cell and then click in the Entry bar to make needed changes.

The options under View Options for Time Units In (Current File) allow you to choose how time measurements are displayed in the Task Sheet and Resource Sheet. You can use the six drop-down lists to control the labels (abbreviations) for minutes, hours, days, weeks, months, and years. In addition, check the Add Space Before Label check box to insert a space between the number and label for any time value in the Task Sheet or Resource Sheet. Click on the Set as Default button to make your time label setting change the defaults for Project.

If you use hyperlink fields in your project plan, use the options under Hyperlink Appearance In (Current File) to control the link colors. Choose colors from the Hyperlink Color and Followed Hyperlink Color palettes. Leave Underline Hyperlinks checked if you want Project to format hyperlinks with underlining, as well. Click on the Set as Default button to make your hyperlink settings the default for all Project files.

Calendar Options

The Calendar tab of the Options dialog box (see Figure 28.14) enables you to specify the default base calendar for the current schedule file. Use the top two drop-down lists to specify the start of each work week and fiscal year in your calendar for the current schedule file. Depending on which month you select from the Fiscal Year Starts In drop-down list, the Use Starting Year for FY Numbering check box may be enabled. Use that check box to tell Project which year to use for your company's fiscal years. Click on the check box to label the fiscal year according to the starting year (for example, call it fiscal '03 if the fiscal year spans 2003 and 2004). Clear the check box to label the fiscal year according to the ending year (call it fiscal '04 if the fiscal year spans 2003 and 2004).

The remaining choices affect only the current file:

◆ **Default Start Time.** The time you enter here is the time of day Project uses for new tasks you add to the Task Sheet, unless you specify otherwise.

◆ **Default End Time.** Sets the time of day when Project cuts off work on tasks for the day, unless you specify otherwise for a particular task or its assigned resource.

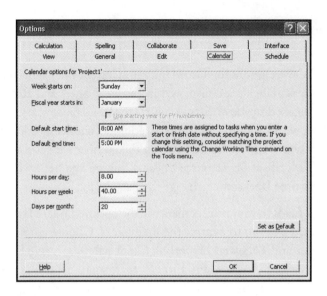

FIGURE 28.14 *Use the Calendar tab to establish the default calendar for the current schedule file.*

◆ **Hours Per Day.** When you enter durations in terms of days, this entry determines how many working hours each day contains.

◆ **Hours Per Week.** As with the preceding option, the number of hours you enter here is reflected in the schedule. If you enter **35**, each work week contains 35 hours by default.

◆ **Days Per Month.** Use this setting to control the number of workdays per month that Project assumes when you assign durations in terms of months. For example, if you change this setting to **22,** each one-month task you create will be scheduled for 22 days of work.

◆ **Set as Default.** Click on this button and your changes in this tab become the default settings used by Project.

Schedule Options

The default scheduling options, displayed by clicking on the Schedule tab of the Options dialog box (see Figure 28.15), control how Project responds when you enter information in the Task Sheet. The first option is Show Scheduling Messages. When this option is checked, Project warns you if you make a mistake that will cause a scheduling error.

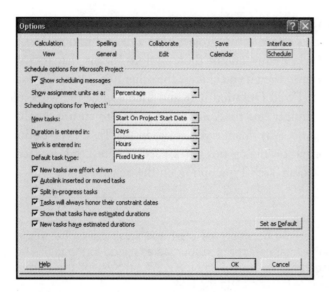

FIGURE 28.15 *This tab enables you to specify how Project handles scheduling choices.*

This tab offers numerous key settings for the current file, as well:

- ◆ **Show Scheduling Messages.** Project can't prevent you from making certain errors when you enter date information in the Task Sheet, but when you check this box, it can warn you when an entry will create an error.

- ◆ **Show Assignment Units as a.** Choose an option from this drop-down list to specify whether assignment units appear as a percentage or decimal value. To display assignment units for individual assignments, you must display the Task Usage view and then add the Assignment Units field to the Task Sheet. (See Chapter 13 to learn more about displaying different views, and Chapter 4 to learn how to add a column or field to the Task Sheet in a view.)

- ◆ **New Tasks Start On.** Choose whether the default start date that Project enters for new tasks is the project start date or the current date.

- ◆ **Duration Is Entered In.** Your choice here specifies the time units (minutes, hours, days, weeks) that Project assigns to Duration column entries if you don't specify a unit.

- ◆ **Work Is Entered In.** Your choice here specifies the time units (minutes, hours, days, weeks) that Project assigns to Work column entries if you don't specify a unit.

◆ **Default Task Type.** Your choice from this drop-down list specifies whether tasks in the active project have a fixed duration, fixed units, or fixed work. Fixing one of these options means that its value remains constant, even if you change the other two values. For example, if you select Fixed Duration here and then double the work allowed for a task, Project cuts the Units value in half to ensure the duration stays the same. Any change you make in the Task Type option the Task Information dialog box for a particular task takes precedence over the Default Task Type option on the Schedule tab.

 NOTE

The *duration* is the time between the start and finish dates that you enter. *Units* represent the total number of resources assigned to the task—two resources working full-time, for example. *Work* stands for the number of person-hours required to complete the task.

◆ **New Tasks Are Effort Driven.** This check box controls whether or not adding resources to a task or removing them affects the task duration by default. Check this option if you want task durations to be adjusted when you add or remove resources.

◆ **Autolink Inserted or Moved Tasks.** If you insert or move tasks within a series of tasks linked by Finish-to-Start (FS) relationships, and this option is checked, Project links the inserted tasks within the group of linked tasks. If you reschedule tasks, Project automatically asks whether you want to create links where they're possible.

◆ **Split In-Progress Tasks.** When this option is checked and you automatically reschedule uncompleted work, uncompleted work on in-progress tasks is rescheduled, in addition to work scheduled for tasks that haven't yet begun.

◆ **Tasks Will Always Honor Their Constraint Dates.** This check box controls the behavior of tasks with negative total slack (that is, tasks that cannot slip or move out without delaying the entire project's finish date). When this option is checked, tasks will honor their constraints and won't move to correct the negative slack situation. If you prefer that tasks move according to their links, to help compensate for negative slack, clear this check box.

◆ **Show That Tasks Have Estimated Durations.** Leave this option checked if you want Project to display a question mark in the Duration field for tasks where you've specified an estimated duration only. This visual cue allows you to judge where you may need to check with resources to verify the duration you've plugged in, for example.

◆ **New Tasks Have Estimated Durations.** Leave this option checked if you want Project to assume that all new tasks you add have an estimated duration. Again, this reminds you that you may need to revisit the duration and adjust it later.

◆ **Set as Default.** Click on this button if you want your choices on the Schedule tab to apply to all new project files you create.

Calculation Options

Calculation options (see Figure 28.16) indicate whether Project automatically updates all calculated values (such as actual cost figures that equal actual hours worked, multiplied by hourly rates). In the Calculation Options area of this tab, specify whether calculation should be automatic or manual. Calculate All Open Projects tells Project to recalculate all open files each time it recalculates. If you do so and you have large consolidated or linked files open, recalculation may be slow. In such a case, you may want to choose Calculate Active Project instead, to recalculate only the current file. If calculation is set to Manual, you can display this tab and click on the Calculate Now button to recalculate all values in all open projects.

The following settings in the Calculation Options for (Current File) area of the dialog box apply to the currently open schedule file:

◆ **Updating Task Status Updates Resource Status.** Select this check box if you want information you enter into task views to be reflected in the calculated fields in resource views. For example, if you enter an actual task completion amount, it's reflected in terms of actual hours worked and costs for a particular resource.

◆ **Move End of Completed Parts After Status Date Back to Status Date.** Check this check box to make the Gantt bars for partially completed tasks sync up with the status date you've entered in the Project Information dialog box. If a task is scheduled to begin after the status date,

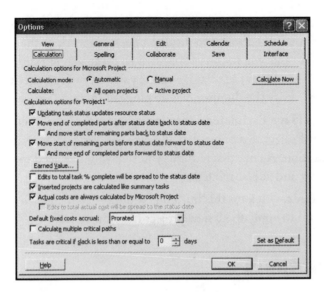

FIGURE 28.16 *Set calculation options here to control when and how Project calculates certain fields based on your entries elsewhere.*

but you then mark work as complete on the task, the portion of the Gantt bar representing the completed work moves to the left, before the status date. You can check the accompanying check box, And Move Start of Remaining Parts Back to Status Date, to move the uncompleted portion of the task to start from the status date as well.

◆ **Move Start of Remaining Parts Before Status Date Forward to Status Date.** This option also moves the Gantt bars for partially completed tasks to sync up with the status date you've entered in the Project Information dialog box, but it applies to tasks that are running late. If a task was scheduled to finish before the status date, but you mark only partial work (or no work) as complete on the task, the portion of the Gantt bar representing the uncompleted work moves to the right, after the status date. You can check the accompanying check box, And Move End of Completed Parts Forward to Status Date, to move the completed portion of the task to finish at the status date, perhaps reflecting that the work started late on the task.

◆ **Edits to Total Task % Complete Will Be Spread to the Status Date.** Check this option if you want your % Complete entries to spread to the next status date set for the schedule or the finish date for the task.

For example, if you enable this check box, and your project has a status date of 4/18/03 and the finish date for a task is 4/28/03, marking the task as 100% complete marks it complete only through 4/18/03.

◆ **Inserted Projects Are Calculated Like Summary Tasks.** When you consolidate project files, this option tells Project to recalculate schedules when you insert and link subproject files.

◆ **Actual Costs Are Always Calculated by Microsoft Project.** Check this option to make Project calculate actual costs for each task until it's marked as 100% complete, at which point you can then enter a differing actual cost value. This ensures that you won't enter an actual cost value prematurely. However, if you've already entered an actual cost, don't turn on this check box unless you want to reenter that information.

◆ **Edits to Total Actual Cost Will Be Spread to the Status Date.** When the preceding check box is cleared, this check box becomes active. Clicking on it then specifies that the actual cost information you enter for a task applies only through the status date of the file, not through the task finish date.

◆ **Default Fixed Costs Accrual.** Your choice from this drop-down list tells Project when and how to add cost information for new tasks with fixed costs into the actual costs calculated for the task and project. For example, if you want to assume that the task's fixed cost is spent as soon as the task begins, as with a nonrefundable retainer fee you pay in advance, click on Start. If you won't pay a resource at all until a task is finished and you've inspected and accepted the work, click on End. If you've agreed to pay the resource a partial fee even if the resource doesn't complete its work, or you're paying a monthly fixed fee for the resource's work, you can choose Prorated.

◆ **Calculate Multiple Critical Paths.** If you have a few different groups of linked tasks that span your project duration, rather than a single string of linked tasks, you can enable this check box to make Project calculate multiple critical paths. More tasks will be marked as critical, so you'll be able to identify all the tasks that could delay the project finish date if they slipped out.

◆ **Tasks Are Critical If Slack Is Less Than or Equal to.** Enter a value here to control how many tasks are part of the critical path. Higher values mean that fewer tasks are marked as critical.

◆ **Set as Default.** Click on this button if you want your choices on the Calculation tab to apply to all new project files you create.

Spelling Options

By default, the spell-checker in Project reviews most task and resource text information. Using the options on the Spelling tab (see Figure 28.17), you can speed up the spell-checker by selecting which information it checks. You can also specify other options related to the spell-checker.

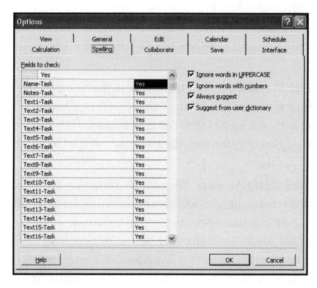

FIGURE 28.17 *If you don't want the spell-checker to review particular fields, specify them here.*

To tell the spell-checker not to review information in a particular task or resource field, select the field in the Fields to Check list. Then click on the drop-down list arrow in the right column and click on No.

The next options on the Spelling tab are the Ignore Words In UPPERCASE check box and the Ignore Words with Numbers check box. When these options are checked, the spell-checker does not check the spelling for words typed entirely in uppercase (such as **IN**) or words including numbers (such as **Qtr1**), respectively. Always Suggest means that the spell-checker displays a list of suggested corrections for any unrecognized word it finds. Suggest from

User Dictionary means that the spell-checker includes corrections from your user dictionary with the suggestion list.

Collaborate Options

Click on the Collaborate tab to display options for controlling how some online features work by default (see Figure 28.18). Chapters 22 through 27 discuss how to work with online features in more depth.

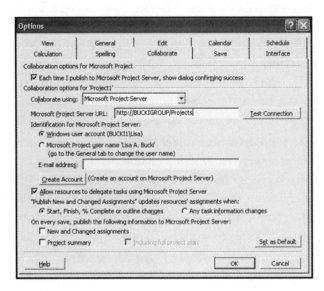

FIGURE 28.18 *Use these options to control how some online features work and look.*

The top check box, Each Time I Publish to Microsoft Project Server, Show Dialog Confirming Success, displays a message box confirming when you've successfully sent a workgroup message via e-mail or Project Server.

The options in the Collaboration Options for (Current Project) area of the tab enable you to specify defaults for workgroup messages you send and project information you publish to Project Server. You can set the following options for those activities:

◆ **Collaborate Using.** Your choice from this drop-down list controls how Project attempts to publish project information. The E-mail Only option sends messages to the outbox of your e-mail program, so you can then launch the e-mail program and send the messages. The Microsoft Project Server option sends the messages to a Web server on the Internet or your internal company intranet. You can also choose to send each message in both ways.

◆ **Microsoft Project Server URL (Current File).** If you're using a Project Server Web server to communicate with team members, and you chose Microsoft Project Server for the preceding option, enter the URL for the Web server in this text box. For example, if you've set up a Project Server site on your computer and connected it to your company's network, your URL might be something like this: http:// BUCKIGROUP/Projects. Note that you have to choose Microsoft Project Server from the Collaborate Using drop-down list and then enter the URL here to enable the remaining options on this tab. You also can use the Test Connection button to test Project's ability to communicate with the server you've specified.

◆ **Identification for Microsoft Project Server.** Choose whether to log on to the Project server as a generic Windows user or under a specific user name. If you choose the Microsoft Project User Name (Current User) option, click on the Create Account button to tell Project to create a new account for your user name. (You must be connected to the Project server for this to work.)

◆ **Allow Resources to Delegate Tasks Using Microsoft Project Server.** Leave this option button checked to allow resources to use automated features in the Project Server to reassign work to other resources.

◆ **"Publish New and Changed Assignments" Updates Resources Assignments When.** These options control how often assignment changes will be published to the Project server (and the resource thus will be notified of the change). The Start, Finish, % Complete or Outline Changes option button limits resource updates to when information changes in one of the fields identified in the option name. In contrast, the Any Task Information Changes option publishes changes to the server when any field of task information has been changed.

◆ **On Every Save, Publish the Following Information to Microsoft Project Server.** Use these options to control which changes are published to the Project server every time you save the project file. New and Changed Assignments republishes only changes to individual assignments. Project Summary republishes project summary statistics.

When it's checked, you can check Including Full Project Plan to re-publish every field of information to the server.

Finally, if you're comfortable with your choices on the Workgroup tab and want those choices to apply no matter which file is open, click on the Set as Default button.

Save Options

The Save options (see Figure 28.19) give you more control over how, when, and where project file information is saved.

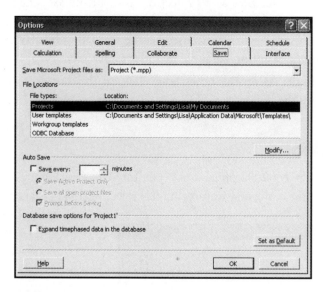

FIGURE 28.19   *The Save options in Project 2002.*

Here's the lowdown on how these options work:

◆ **Save Microsoft Project Files as.** Use this drop-down list to specify that you want Project to save files in an alternate file format by default, such as Microsoft Access Databases (*.mdb).

◆ **File Locations.** Click on a choice under File Types, and then click on the Modify button to change the default drive and folder in which Project stores the specified type of file. After you navigate to the proper location using the Look In list in the Modify Location dialog box, click on OK.

◆ **Auto Save.** Like its Microsoft Office siblings, Project can now save your files automatically as you work. This ensures that you don't lose all your work if your system crashes or restarts unexpectedly. To enable Auto Save, check the Save Every check box, and then adjust the setting in the Minutes text box to control how often the saves occur. If you want to auto-save all open files, click on Save All Open Project Files rather than Save Active Project Only. I also recommend that you clear the check mark next to Prompt Before Saving, just to avoid having to verify every save.

◆ **Expand Timephased Data in the Database.** If you use the very first option to save your files as a Project or Access database, check this option to ensure that the database contains all the time-based details—how work occurs and costs accrue on a day-by-day basis. Otherwise, the resulting database includes totals only.

◆ **Set as Default.** As on the other tabs, click on this button to make your settings the default for all files.

Interface Options

Finally, Microsoft Project 2002 offers a new tab, Interface (see Figure 28.20), that controls how some of the new features in this Project version look and work.

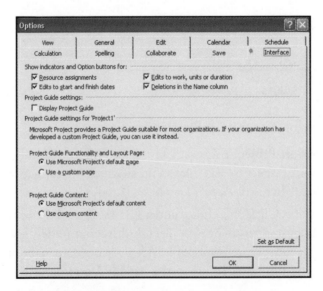

FIGURE 28.20 *The Interface options control some of the new features in Project 2002.*

Here's an overview of the available settings:

◆ **Show Indicators and Option Buttons For.** Check and uncheck check boxes here to specify when feedback indicators appear onscreen when you change resource assignments, for edits to start and finish dates, for edits to work, units, or duration, or for deletions in the Name column.

◆ **Display Project Guide.** Check this check box to display the Project Guide in the Task Pane.

◆ **Project Guide Settings for (Current File).** If you're using the Project Guide, the settings in this section help you control its functionality and layout. If you click the Use a Custom Page option (which disables the Use Microsoft Project's Default Page option), a URL text box and Browse button appear so that you can enter or select the URL for the .HTM file with the custom Project Guide functionality and page layout that your organization has developed. Similarly, if you click the Use Custom Content option (which disables the Use Microsoft Project's Default Content option button), an XML File for Custom Content and Browse button appear so that you can select the XML file that holds the custom content your organization has developed.

Chapter 29

**Creating and
Using Macros**

In This Chapter

◆ Adjusting macro security levels

◆ Recording and playing back macros

◆ Changing macro information, such as the shortcut key

◆ Making changes in or removing macros

◆ Finding more help about VBA

◆ Creating your own command or button for a macro

◆ Looking at a few last ideas about macros

Every company's needs and projects are unique. Even seasoned temporary workers need a bit of on-site training to conform to the specific processes of a new client company.

While company A might want temps to organize files and information by project name, company B might want the information to be ordered by job number. Although such differences seem trivial, misunderstanding the requirement or making filing mistakes can create hours of work down the line for someone else who is searching for particular files.

Like a temporary worker, Project can conform to your unique needs in building schedules. Project does this by enabling you to create *macros*, which are mini-programs that you create to perform certain tasks.

Setting the Macro Security Level

Even if you don't create your own macros, you may be using Project files from other sources that contain custom macros. If you've heard about Word macro viruses, you know that macro viruses can cause you to lose data or can completely corrupt a file. While I haven't yet read about or encountered any macro viruses that affect Project, the possibility certainly exists.

As a result, both Project 2000 and 2002 include macro virus protection. To benefit from it, the VBA project developer must acquire a *digital certificate* and sign the VBA project with the certificate. (Organizations such as VeriSign and Microsoft issue certificates as a means of tracking macro, Web, and programmed content. These organizations can help track down the source of particular content based on the information stored in the certificate.) When you open a Project file that includes a digitally signed VBA project or macros, or when you try to run macros from other sources, Project asks whether you want to add the macro developer to your list of *trusted sources*. If you do so, Project copies the digital certificate for that source to your system.

 TIP

A *VBA project* or *VB project* stores extensive macro code in a Microsoft Project file. You have to create a VB project programmatically. In other words, you don't create a VB project when you simply record a macro. However, the security settings do apply to individually recorded macros, too.

Once the digital certificates for trusted sources are on your system, you can choose Tools, Macro, Security to open Project's Security dialog box (Figure 29.1). Use the options on the Security Level tab to control whether macros run and whether you're given warnings.

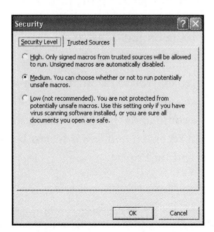

FIGURE 29.1 *These options enable you to choose how to handle Project files that contain macros.*

The Low option enables all macro projects and macros, and it displays no warnings. If you select Medium, Project displays a warning when you open a file with a project that's not signed or isn't on your list of trusted sources, or when you try to run a macro that's unsigned or from an unknown source. You can choose whether to enable the macros and whether to add the source to your list of trusted sources. If you select High, Project doesn't open unsigned macros at all, and it doesn't give you the option of using them. If the macro or macro project comes from a trusted source, it's enabled automatically. If macros are signed with an unrecognized certificate, you can choose whether to enable the macros and whether to add the source to the list of trusted sources.

To remove a source from your list of trusted sources, click on the Trusted Sources tab in the Security dialog box, click on the source you want to remove, and then click on the Remove button.

Click on OK to close the Security dialog box after you finish making your security choices. Then save and close all your files, exit Project, and restart Project for the new settings to take effect.

Creating Macros

Macros store a series of commands or steps as a single entity, so that you can execute the entire series via the single step of selecting the macro. In earlier computer applications, macros had to be created manually via *scripting*, which was a "user-friendly" euphemism for programming. Thus, most people didn't use macros because they were too difficult to create.

Today's applications, including Project, enable you to record macros. You don't have to be a whiz to create one. All you need to know is how to start the macro recorder and how to execute the commands that you want to save as a macro. Unless you specify otherwise, a recorded and saved macro becomes available to all the files that you work with in Project.

 NOTE

The macros you record in Project are built behind the scenes with Visual Basic for Applications (VBA), a macro programming language used in all Microsoft Office applications. Each macro is stored in a VBA Macro module, which is like a single sheet that can hold multiple macros. By default, the modules and macros are saved with the GLOBAL.MPT file, which saves your default information for Project. You can use VBA programming to develop more powerful macros. However, programming with VBA is beyond the scope of this book.

These are the two basic situations in which you should record macros to automate a task:

◆ **When the task is lengthy and requires many steps.** Creating a macro to store such a process helps other users work with the file, particularly if the file is stored on a network. If several users need to create and print a particular report, for example, you can create a macro for that purpose rather than try to teach each person all the steps that are involved.

◆ **When the task is repetitive.** Even though it takes only a few steps to format the text in a cell as red, you might regularly need to format cells that way. If so, you'll save time with a macro that does the job for you.

Project enables you to record and work with macros by means of commands in the Tools menu or tools in the Visual Basic toolbar (see Figure 29.2). To display that toolbar, right-click on any toolbar and then click on Visual Basic.

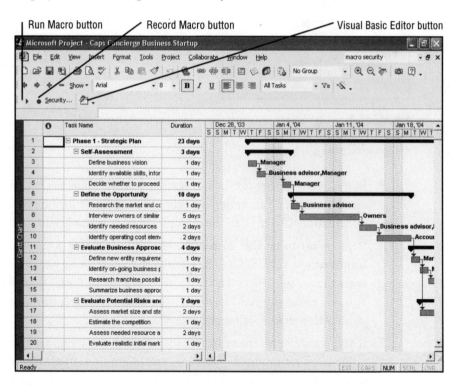

FIGURE 29.2 *The Visual Basic toolbar offers you tools for recording, editing, and running macros.*

To record a macro, follow these steps:

1. Take any preparatory steps that are necessary before you begin recording the macro. If you want to record a macro that formats a selected task's Gantt bar to make it green and use new end symbols, for example, go ahead and select a cell in that task in the Task Sheet.

2. Choose Tools, Macro, Record New Macro, or click on the Record Macro button on the Visual Basic toolbar. The Record Macro dialog box will appear, as shown in Figure 29.3.

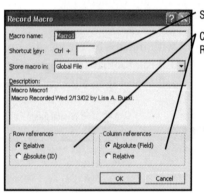

Specifies where the macro will be saved

Controls how the macro will behave with Task or Resource Sheet rows or columns

FIGURE 29.3 *Assign a name and settings for your macro after you start the recording process.*

3. In the Macro Name text box, enter a unique name for the macro. The name can include an underscore character but can't include spaces or punctuation. Green_Bar, for example, is an acceptable name.

4. If you want to be able to run the macro by pressing a shortcut key combinations such as Ctrl+K, click in the Shortcut Key text box and enter the second keystroke for the combination in the Ctrl+ text box. You can enter any A–Z keyboard character. You can't use numbers, punctuation marks, or function keys.

5. If you want the macro to be stored only with the currently open file (which isn't recommended, because you might need to use that macro in future files), open the Store Macro In drop-down list, then click on This Project. If you leave Global File selected instead, Project stores the macro in GLOBAL.MPT, the file that stores macros, forms, settings, and other default and custom information you specify for Project.

NOTE

You need to select This Project if you'll be saving the open project file as a template file and you want the macro to be part of that file.

6. If you want, edit or add more detail to the macro's description.

7. The options in the Row References area control the way the macro interprets row selections in the Task and Resource Sheets, and the way it handles those selections during playback. Select one of the following options:

   ◆ **Relative** means that during playback, the macro selects rows based on the location of the selected cell. Suppose that you selected three rows or cells in three rows (such as rows 1–3) when you recorded the macro, and that before you play back the macro, you select a cell in row 4. The macro selects rows 4–6, or the specified cells in those rows, during playback.

   ◆ **Absolute (ID)** means that during playback, the macro always selects the same rows (by row number) that were selected when the macro was recorded.

8. The options in the Column References area control the way the macro interprets column selections in a Task Sheet or Resource Sheet, and the way it handles those selections during playback. Select one of the following options:

   ◆ **Absolute (Field)** means that during playback, the macro always selects the same field (by field or column name) that was selected when the macro was recorded.

   ◆ **Relative** means that the macro selects columns based on the location of the selected cell. Suppose that you select two columns or cells in two columns (such as the Start and Finish columns of the Task Sheet) when you recorded the macro. Before you play back the macro, you select a cell in the Predecessors column. The macro selects the Predecessors and Resources columns of the Task Sheet (or the specified cells in those columns) during playback.

9. After you make all your selections, click on OK to begin recording the macro.

If you specified a shortcut key that's already assigned (back in Step 4), at this point Project displays a warning (see Figure 29.4). Click on OK, specify another shortcut key, and click on OK in the Record Macro dialog box to continue.

FIGURE 29.4 *Project warns you when the shortcut key you specified isn't available.*

10. Perform the steps that you want to record in your macro.

11. When you finish performing all the steps, stop the macro recording by clicking on the Stop Recorder button on the Visual Basic toolbar, or by choosing Tools, Macro, Stop Recorder.

 TIP

If you're creating a macro and you want to select only the range of cells in the Task Sheet or Resource Sheet that currently contain entries, select the cell in the upper-left corner of the range. Then press Ctrl+Shift+End. This method is better than selecting the entire sheet. It's also the method to use when you might end up running the macro on different sheets or filtered lists of differing lengths. That's because it ensures that the macro highlights all the rows that contain entries, not just the number of rows that was correct during macro recording.

Running a Macro

After you create a macro, it's immediately available for use. Running a macro is sometimes referred to as *playing back* the macro. To play back any macro, follow these steps:

1. Perform any preparatory tasks you need to complete before running the macro. If your macro applies green formatting to a Gantt bar, for example, select the tasks whose bars you want to reformat.

2. Use one of the following methods to execute the macro, depending on how you set up the macro when you created it:

   ◆ Press the shortcut key combination that you created for the macro.

   ◆ Click on the Run Macro button on the Visual Basic toolbar, or choose Tools, Macro, Macros. The Macros dialog box appears. If you want the Macro Name list to display only macros contained in a particular file (which narrows down the display and may make the macro you want easier to find), open the Macros In drop-down list. Then click on the name of the file you want, select the name of the macro in the Macro Name list (see Figure 29.5), and click on the Run button.

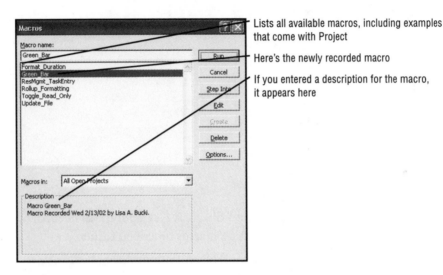

Lists all available macros, including examples that come with Project

Here's the newly recorded macro

If you entered a description for the macro, it appears here

FIGURE 29.5   *This dialog box enables you to run and manage macros.*

Changing Macro Options

The information and options that you specify when you create and store a macro aren't carved in stone. If you initially don't assign a shortcut key to the macro, for example, you can go back and add one. If you want to change the description for a macro, you can do that too.

To adjust the options for a macro, follow these steps:

1. Choose Tools, Macro, Macros. Or click on the Run Macro button on the Visual Basic toolbar. The Macros dialog box will appear.

2. In the Macro Name list, select the name of the macro for which you want to change the options. If you don't see the macro you want, open the Macros In drop-down list, click on the name of the file that holds the macro, and then select the macro when it appears on the Macro Name list.

3. Click on the Options button. The Macro Options dialog box will appear, as shown in Figure 29.6.

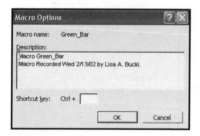

FIGURE 29.6 *Use this dialog box to adjust the macro description or shortcut key.*

4. Edit the Description and Shortcut Key options, as needed, by using the techniques for creating macros described earlier.

5. Click on OK to close the Macro Options dialog box.

6. Click on Close in the Macros dialog box, which activates your new macro options.

Editing Macros

Unless you have time to learn VBA programming, you probably don't want to bother with editing macros, especially if the macros are fairly simple. In such cases, the fastest way to make changes in a macro is to delete it (as described in the following section) and rerecord it. In other cases, however, making a change or two in a macro is much speedier than creating it again from scratch.

This section explains the basics of macro editing so that you can experiment with it if you're so inclined. (Chapter 30 will help you get started with programming your own macros.) Macros and their VBA coding are stored in modules, which are like pages in the Project GLOBAL.MPT file. Each module can store numerous VBA macros. You use the Visual Basic Editor to open a macro and display it (within its module) for editing. In the module, you edit the commands just as you would edit text. When you save your changes and exit the Visual Basic Editor, Project returns you to Gantt Chart view (or whichever view you prefer to work in) and your changes to the macro take effect.

 NOTE

Even if you are experienced in editing VBA code, there's always the chance of introducing an error that really fouls up the macro. As a precaution, print the original macro code before you make any changes. That way you have a record of what the macro's contents were when the macro still worked. To print Project macros, simply click on the Print icon on the Standard toolbar when the macro is displayed in the Code (Module) window of the Visual Basic Editor.

Project and the Visual Basic Editor can provide help about using specific VBA commands in Project, but this help doesn't install by default. Therefore, before you begin editing macros, install Visual Basic Help:

1. Click on the Visual Basic Editor button on the Visual Basic toolbar to display the Visual Basic Editor.

2. Choose Help, Microsoft Visual Basic Help. The Office Assistant will appear.

3. In the Office Assistant's yellow thought bubble, click on the Install Missing Help Files option button to install Visual Basic Help.

4. Insert your Project 2002 CD into your CD-ROM drive if prompted, and then click on OK. After the update finishes, you can start using the Office Assistant in the Visual Basic Editor and in Project to get Visual Basic Help.

After Visual Basic Help is installed, you can use Project's online help to learn more about the overall process of VBA programming with Project. Also, you can use online help within the Visual Basic Editor to learn more about specific VBA commands, syntax, and more.

After you make Help available and review key topics, you'll definitely be ready to try some basic macro editing. Suppose you've created a macro that enters a new task—named "Staff Meeting"—in the Task Sheet, and you've assigned the task a duration of **2h** (two hours). You can use the macro to plug in the

Staff Meeting task at any point in any project. Later, you may decide that you no longer want to have staff meetings, and you just want to prepare and distribute staff reports. Accordingly, you want the macro to specify the task name as "Staff Report." To make this change, follow these steps:

1. Choose Tools, Macro, Macros. Or click on the Run Macro button on the Visual Basic toolbar. The Macros dialog box will appear.

2. In the Macro Name list, select the macro that you want to edit—Staff_Meeting, for this example. If you don't see the macro you want to edit, open the Macros In drop-down list, click on the name of the file that holds the macro, and then select the macro when it appears on the Macro Name list.

3. Click on the Edit button to display the Visual Basic Editor, with the module for the macro displayed in its Code window. The Code window for the Staff_Meeting macro appears in Figure 29.7.

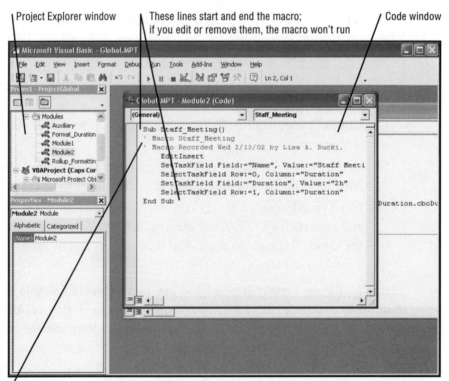

Project Explorer window   These lines start and end the macro;   Code window
if you edit or remove them, the macro won't run

To create a note or remark, use a single prime (single quote) at the beginning of the statement

FIGURE 29.7 *The macro looks like specially aligned text in the module.*

4. Make your changes in the macro's contents, using the same editing techniques that you would use in a typical word processing program such as WordPad or Word 2002.

For this example, because you want to change the task name, first look for the line that defines the Name column (TaskField) and then look for the value assigned there, which is what you want to change. You can double-click on the word *Meeting* to select it, as shown in Figure 29.8. Be careful not to select the quotation marks. Then simply type **Report** to replace the selection.

When text is highlighted, simply begin typing to replace it

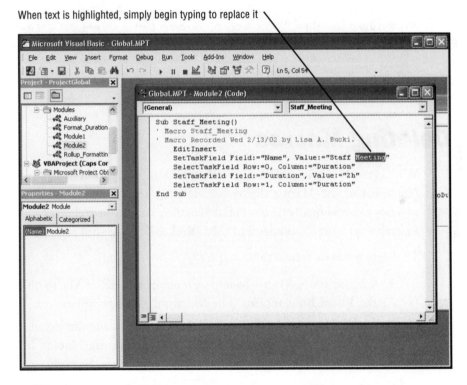

FIGURE 29.8 *To modify a macro's contents, edit it just as you would in a word processing program.*

5. When you finish making your changes, open the Visual Basic Editor File menu and click on Save (File Name) to ensure your changes are saved. To close the Visual Basic Editor and return to Project, open the File menu again, and then click on Close And Return To Microsoft Project.

6. Test the macro to make sure that your changes work correctly.

TIP

Project comes with several macros, which provide a good illustration of how to structure VBA code. These macros are excellent learning tools for would-be macro gurus. If you want to see how one of these macros is written, select it in the Macro Name list in the Macros dialog box, and then click on Edit. Alternately, if the Microsoft Visual Basic window is already open, double-click on a macro in the Project Explorer window to display the macro's contents in a Code window.

 TIP

When the Visual Basic Editor is open, you can open Code windows for multiple modules (holding macros), by double-clicking each module to open in a file's Modules folder in the Project Explorer. Then you can cut, copy, and paste code between macros, switching between Code windows with the Window menu.

Deleting Macros

When you no longer need a macro, you can simply delete it from the Macro Name list in the Macros dialog box. If you use many macros, it's a good practice to occasionally review and delete the macros you no longer need, just to keep your macro modules and GLOBAL.MPT file slim and trim.

To delete a macro, follow these steps:

1. Choose Tools, Macro, Macros. Or click on the Run Macro button on the Visual Basic toolbar. The Macros dialog box will appear.

2. In the Macro Name list, select the macro you want to delete. If you don't see the macro you want to delete, open the Macros In drop-down list, click on the name of the file that holds the macro, and then select the macro when it appears on the Macro Name list.

3. Click on the Delete button. Project asks you to verify that you want to remove the macro (see Figure 29.9).

4. Click on Yes to delete the macro.

5. Close the Macros dialog box.

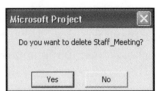

FIGURE 29.9 *Verify that you want to delete the selected macro.*

Creating a Menu Command or Toolbar Button for a Macro

Although you can create shortcut keys for the macros you create, remembering shortcut keys can be as difficult as remembering the exact names of macros.

In Chapter 28, "Customizing Microsoft Project," you learned the general steps for editing Project's menus and toolbars. You can use that knowledge to edit any Project menu bar, adding a menu that lists all your macros. This procedure not only provides quick access to your macros, but also provides more room for listing macros than the Tools menu does. In addition, you can add a command for an individual macro to any menu, or add a button for any macro to a toolbar.

Adding a Menu Listing All Macros

If you want to be able to run any macro simply by selecting its name from a menu, you can add a special menu that lists all the macros available in the GLOBAL.MPT file in Project. You can add this menu to Project's default menu bar, or to any toolbar. To create a menu for your macros, follow these steps:

1. To add the macro menu to a toolbar, display that toolbar.
2. Choose Tools, Customize, Toolbars. Alternately, right-click on any onscreen menu bar or toolbar and click on Customize. The Customize dialog box will appear.
3. Click on the Commands tab to display its options.
4. Add a brand new menu for the macros to the menu bar or toolbar where you want the macros menu to appear, as described in Chapter 28, "Customizing Microsoft Project." Briefly, scroll down the Categories

list and click on the New Menu option. Drag the New Menu place-holder from the Commands list to the menu bar or toolbar that will hold the menu, and then drop the placeholder into the appropriate location, as shown in Figure 29.10.

Drag the New Menu placeholder from here... \   \ ...and drop it into place on a menu or toolbar

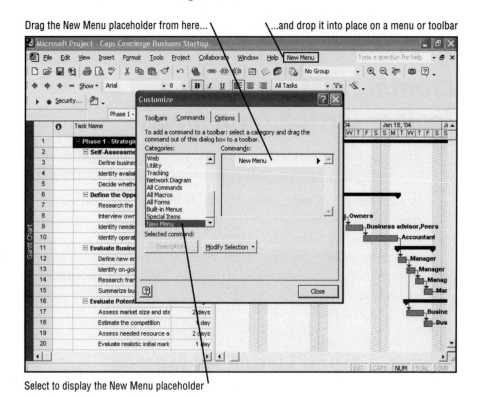

Select to display the New Menu placeholder

FIGURE 29.10   *You can create a new menu that lists all available macros.*

5. To rename the placeholder for the new menu, right-click on it, edit the contents of the Name text box in the menu that appears, and then press Enter. Remember, if you want the menu name to have an underlined selection letter, insert an ampersand (&) before that letter in the menu name.

6. In the Categories list on the Commands tab of the Customize dialog box, click on the Special Items option.

7. In the Commands list, scroll down to display the [Macros] option, and then drag it onto the new menu, as shown in Figure 29.11. Release the mouse button to drop it onto the menu.

Drag from here...   ...over the menu name, and down onto the menu

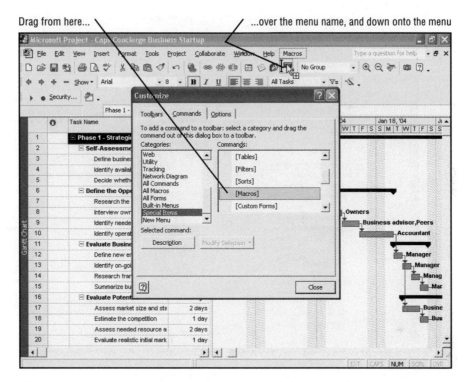

FIGURE 29.11   *Drag the [Macros] option onto the new menu to place a list of macros on that menu.*

8. Close the Customize dialog box.

When you open the new menu later, it lists available macros, as shown in Figure 29.12.

Adding a Macro Command or Button

Although adding a menu for macros gives you easy access to all of them, it can be cumbersome if you've created dozens of macros. Such a menu is slow to appear onscreen, and you still have to take the time to scan through the menu to find the macro you need. For the ultimate in easy access to the macros that you create, add a custom menu command or toolbar button for the macro to any menu or toolbar. Then you can execute your macro simply by selecting its name from a more streamlined menu, or by clicking its toolbar button.

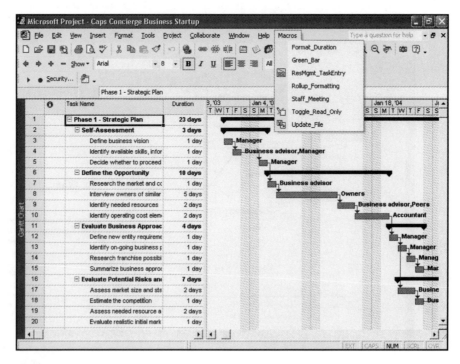

FIGURE 29.12 *You now have a menu listing all the macros.*

 CAUTION

Although you can assign a macro to an existing toolbar button, replacing the command that was originally assigned to that button, this procedure is not recommended. It might be difficult to recall what the button's original command was if you ever want to reinstate it.

To create a menu command or toolbar button for a macro, follow these steps:

1. As you learned in Chapter 28, start by displaying the menu bar or toolbar that will hold the command or button.

2. Display the Customize dialog box by choosing Tools, Customize, Toolbars. Alternately, right-click on any toolbar or menu bar and click on Customize.

3. Click on the Commands tab to display its options.

4. Scroll down the Categories list and click on the All Macros option. The Commands list then lists all the macros available in Project.

5. Scroll down the Commands list until you see the macro for which you want to create a menu command or toolbar button.

6. Drag the macro from the Commands list to the menu or toolbar that you want to work with. Then drop the macro into the appropriate location. Note that if you drag the macro over a menu and drop it into place, it becomes a menu command. If you drop the macro directly onto a toolbar, it becomes a toolbar button. See Figure 29.13 for an example of each.

Choose this option to list   I've added this macro as a   ...and a button
macros in the Commands list   command on this menu...   on the toolbar

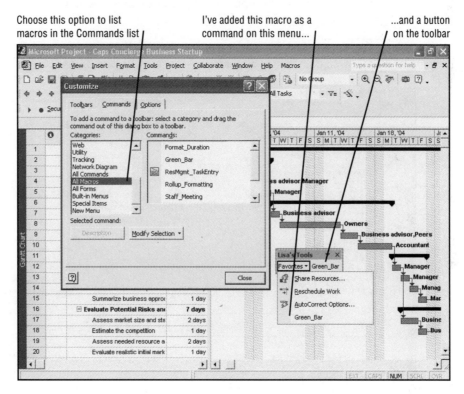

FIGURE 29.13 *Drag the macro from the Customize dialog box onto a menu or toolbar.*

7. Click on the Close button to close the Customize dialog box and finish your menu and toolbar edits.

Adjusting the Macro Command or Button

After you add your menu command or toolbar button for a macro, you might want to fine-tune it a bit. For example, you might want to display an icon rather than the macro name on a toolbar button, or change the wording of the macro command on the menu.

Chapter 28 covered how to make changes to a command or button in more detail, but here's a refresher:

1. Display the menu bar or toolbar that holds the command or button you want to edit.

2. Choose Tools, Customize, Toolbars. Alternately, right-click on any toolbar or menu bar and click on Customize. The Customize dialog box will appear.

3. Right-click on the menu command or toolbar button to edit. A shortcut menu of commands appears, as shown in Figure 29.14.

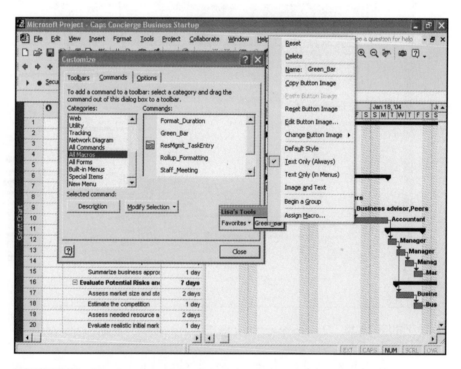

FIGURE 29.14 *Use the commands here to edit a custom menu command or toolbar button.*

4. To make changes to a menu command (or text that you want to appear on the toolbar button), edit the Name text box contents and press Enter.

5. If you're working with a toolbar button and you want it to display an icon only, right-click on the button and then click on the Default

Style option in the shortcut menu to toggle that option on. (The default for buttons is to show only an icon.) Then right-click on the blank button to return to the shortcut menu, point to the Change Button Image option, and click on an icon in the pop-up palette that appears. Figure 29.15 shows the toolbar button for the Green_Bar macro, which has been changed to display only an icon.

Green_Bar macro toolbar button

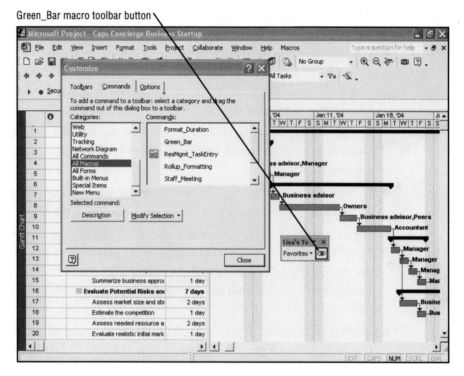

FIGURE 29.15   *You can display a custom button with an icon instead of a text label.*

6. If you're working with a menu command or toolbar button and you want it to display text and an icon, right-click on the command or button. Then click on the Image And Text option in the shortcut menu to toggle that option on. Then right-click on the menu command or toolbar button to return to the shortcut menu. Edit the contents of the Name text box. (Do not press Enter.) Point to the Change Button Image option and click on an icon in the pop-up palette that appears.

7. Close the Customize dialog box.

A Few More Macro Ideas

This chapter has shown you how to create macros to make your work in Project faster and more efficient. Here are a few other ideas about how to use macros to get the most out of Microsoft Project:

◆ Create a macro that inserts a new task—with a particular name and duration—that you want to use more than once. Assign a shortcut key to run the macro and add the task.

◆ Create a macro to format summary tasks in a way that calls even more attention to them. The macro can apply a particular font, color, or emphasis (such as italic), or it can adjust the summary task Gantt bars. Add a button for the macro to the Formatting toolbar.

◆ Create a macro that inserts your company logo where you specify (such as in a Gantt chart), so that the logo appears on printouts you send to clients.

◆ Record macros that change the active view or display a particular Task Sheet table. Create a shortcut key or button for each macro.

◆ If you supervise a team of people and use Project to manage multiple tasks, create a macro that assigns each person (as a resource) to the currently selected task. Then you can assign a task to a particular worker with a single shortcut key, reducing the time that you spend making assignments.

◆ If you regularly need to print a particular form or report, create a macro that automates the process and assign that macro to a toolbar button.

Chapter 30

**Starting to
Write VBA
Macros for
Project**

In This Chapter

◆ Working with digital certificates

◆ Learning about the Visual Basic Editor

◆ Creating a macro using some basic VBA techniques

◆ Checking for macro problems with debugging tools

Getting Started

In the first section of Chapter 29, you learned that Microsoft Project and Office XP applications include a macro security feature. It works by checking whether a macro is signed with a digital certificate. If you choose the highest security level, Project only runs macros that have been signed with certificates from trusted sources.

This chapter will get you started with macro programming, but your organization may require every macro to be signed with a digital certificate in order to run. If that's the case, you can obtain your certificate in one of three ways:

◆ If your organization has its own internal certification authority (usually based on Microsoft Certificate Server), you can request a certificate from the administrator or group that's handling your company's certifications.

◆ If your organization has no certification authority and/or you intend to create macros for a number of organizations (perhaps clients), obtain a digital certificate from a certification organization such as VeriSign. Go to http://www.verisign.com, click on the Products link, and then click on the Code Signing IDs link. Click on the option button for the Microsoft Office and VBA Signing Digital ID product type, scroll down to the bottom of the page, and click on the button for the certificate package you want. At present, $400 and $695 certification packages are offered.

◆ Finally, if you plan to create a limited number of macros for individual use or use in a small workgroup, there's a utility provided with Office XP that lets you create your own certificate so you can self-sign your macros.

If you need to use the last approach and self-sign your macros, install the Create Digital Certificate utility with Office. Follow these steps to install the utility (under Windows XP) and create your digital certificate:

1. Click on the Start button, and then click on Control Panel in the Start menu.

2. Click on the Add or Remove Programs category in the Control Panel window that opens. The Add or Remove Programs window opens.

3. Click the listing for your version of Microsoft Office XP, and then click on the Change button beside it. The Windows Installer launches the setup, and then it displays a dialog box with Maintenance Mode Options.

4. Make sure that the Add or Remove Features option button is selected, and then click on Next. The next Setup dialog box presents the list of features to install.

5. Click on the plus sign beside the Office Shared Features option to expand it.

6. Click on the icon to the left of the Digital Signature for VBA Projects option, and then click on Run from My Computer, as shown in Figure 30.1.

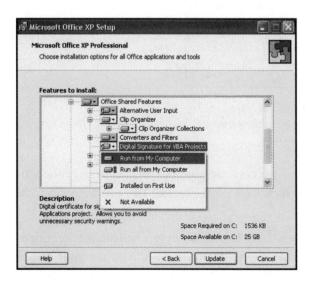

FIGURE 30.1   *If you have the Office software, you can install a utility that enables you to digitally sign your macros.*

7. Click on Update, insert the Office XP CD-ROM when prompted, and click on OK.

8. At the final Setup dialog box that informs you that Office has been updated successfully, click on OK. You can then close the Add or Remove Programs window and the Control Panel.

9. To create your certificate, click on the Start button and click on My Computer in the Start menu.

10. Use the My Computer window to navigate to the \Program Files\ Microsoft Office\Office10 folder. This is where Setup placed the Create Digital Certificate utility.

11. Scroll down the through the files in the folder, if needed, and then double-click on the SELFCERT.EXE file. The Create Digital Certificate dialog box appears.

12. Type your name into the Your Name text box (Figure 30.2), and then click on OK.

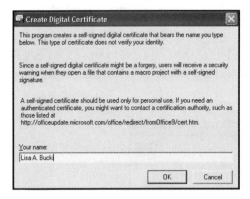

FIGURE 30.2 *The certificate you create identifies you as the macro creator any time you sign a macro with that certificate.*

13. In the SelfCert Success message box that appears, click on OK to finish the certificate creation process. You can then close the open folder window.

You don't have to do anything further for now. The later section titled "Signing and Saving the Macro" will demonstrate how to use your certificate to sign a macro that you've created.

NOTE

When you self-sign your macro with the certificate that you've created, any user who has macro security set to medium will be asked whether or not to enable the macros and can view your digital certificate in the Visual Basic Editor.

TIP

You can use the Microsoft Management Console application to manage your certificates in Windows XP. To start the console, click on Start and then click on Run. Type **mmc** and press Enter or click OK. The Windows XP help system and the Microsoft Management Console help system provide further details about managing your certificates.

Starting the Visual Basic Editor

Because macros in Project use Visual Basic for Applications (VBA), you use the Visual Basic Editor (VBE) to write and edit macros. To start the Visual Basic Editor, choose Tools, Macro, Visual Basic Editor. Or, if you've displayed the Visual Basic toolbar, click on the Visual Basic Editor button.

TIP

Writing your own macros can be quite a trial-and-error process, especially if you're new at it. It's a good practice to use a "dummy" file—a copy of one of your other project files with some data in it that you can use to test the macro and iron out errors. If you're working in a dummy file, you won't make any unwanted changes to your data. Also, it's useful to change to the view or table where you can best test your macro (unless the macro itself changes views, that is).

Understanding the Windows in the Visual Basic Editor

When the Visual Basic Editor initially appears, it won't show you any macro information. You need to enter the code window to be able to enter the macro code. Choose View, Code in the Visual Basic Editor window. Then, you'll see all the windows you need to get started (Figure 30.3).

Project Explorer   Properties Window   Code window

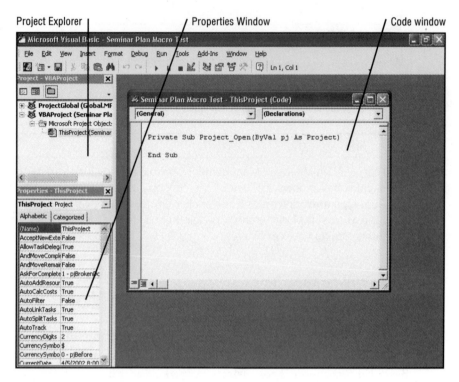

FIGURE 30.3   *Build your macros in the Visual Basic Editor.*

The code window is where you enter the programming information. You use the Project Explorer to specify where a macro should be placed—in the current file or the global file (GLOBAL.MPT). For certain types of items, you use the Properties window to change properties.

Using Help to Learn More About Project's Object Model

VBA streamlines programming because it is an object-oriented language. This means that in each application, VBA can refer to elements of the application using standard names. For example, VBA refers to the current project file as the ActiveProject object. You can refer to all the resources (the collection of resources) in the current project by using ActiveProject.Resources. VBA refers to the available objects in Project as its Object Model.

You can learn more about the objects in Project and how to manipulate them by examining the VBE's help on the subject. To start, choose Help, Microsoft

Visual Basic Help in the VBE, which you learned how to install in Chapter 29. The Office Assistant appears. Type **objects** into the Office Assistant's search text box, and then click on Search. Click on any of the topics the Office Assistant presents, and then click on the Contents tab in the Microsoft Visual Basic Help window that opens. (You can hide the Office Assistant at this point.) Expand the Microsoft Project Visual Basic Reference Topic in the left pane of the Help window, and then click on Microsoft Project Objects. A diagram of the objects appears, as in Figure 30.4. You can click on any object to learn more about it.

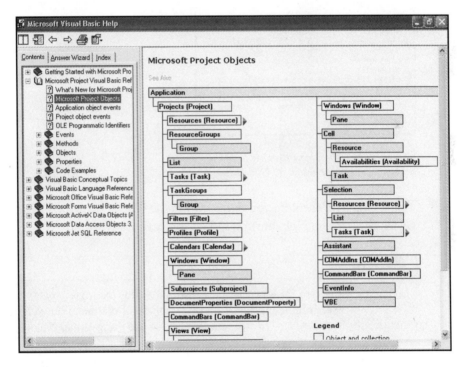

FIGURE 30.4   *Get help about Project's objects.*

 TIP

Another great section of Help you should review is the Visual Basic Conceptual Topics. This section presents valuable definitions and fundamental programming topics to help you get started.

In addition to Microsoft Visual Basic Help, the VBE Object Browser can help you learn more about objects (and other items such as functions) on the fly. To display the Object Browser window, choose View, Object Browser. To learn more about an object or item, select a class from the Classes list at the left, if needed, and then click on the desired item in the list at the right. The bottom of the Object Browser window then displays a brief description of the selected item and its syntax (the proper way to enter its code). Figure 30.5 shows an example, the `FilePageSetup` function.

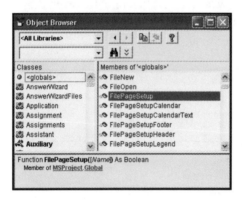

FIGURE 30.5 _The Object Browser helps you find and learn about objects and functions._

To get help with the item you've selected in the Object Browser, press the F1 key or click on the Help button in the Object Browser window.

 TIP

Functions represent Project's menu commands. For example, you can use the `FilePageSetup` function (on a line by itself or in combination with other instructions in the macro) to have a macro open the Page Setup dialog box.

Creating an Example Macro

You don't need to be a programming ace to start writing your own VBA macros. A lot of books that include information about VBA programming (such as this book) assume the reader has a lot of programming knowledge. That's not the approach here. (Primarily because I'm no ace programmer myself.) The macro example here presents the most basic aspects of macro programming. After you work through this example, you can build on your knowledge by getting a book that provides more in-depth coverage of VBA programming (such as *VBA Professional Projects* from Premier Press), or you can take a class on the subject.

The example macro here provides an alternate way to make a new entry in the `Complete` field for tasks in the project. You would create a macro like this if, for example, you have a number of tasks to update with various completion percentages and want a method that's faster than using the Update Tasks dialog box. The macro will perform these steps:

1. Tests whether or not a task is a summary task, skipping any summary task and moving on to the next task.

2. Presents an input dialog box presenting the task name and the current entry in the `Complete` field, along with a text box for making a new entry.

3. Evaluates your entry and proceeds as follows:

   ◆ If you leave the entry text box Empty and click OK or Cancel, a new message box will ask if you want to skip the task. Click Yes to do so, or click No to exit. (If you skip the task, another message box appears to verify whether you want to quit the application.)

   ◆ If you make a value entry in the Entry text box—even 0—and click on OK, the macro enters the value in the `Complete` field and moves on to the next task in your project.

Although an advanced program might create special dialog boxes (forms) and other elements to accomplish these steps, you can build a macro procedure to achieve similar results with some straightforward statements and functions. (Statements and functions refer to particular types of coding syntax. *Statements* generally declare or define something in the code, or indicate a particular action. *Functions* typically perform a task, and sometimes return a value.)

Naming the Macro

When you create a macro in the VBE, you must start out by identifying where you want to place the macro and then creating and naming the basic procedure. In most cases, you'll want to add the ProjectGlobal (GLOBAL.MPT) project to make the macro available to all of your project files. To do this, you use the Project Explorer to add a new module:

1. In the Project Explorer, click on the plus icon beside the ProjectGlobal (GLOBAL.MPT) option to expand its folders.

2. Right-click on the Modules folder that appears, point to the Insert option in the submenu, and click on Module. A module (Module1 if it's the first module you've added) appears in the Project Explorer tree, and a code window opens for the new module.

3. The insertion point automatically appears in the Code window for the new module, so you can immediately begin typing code. To establish the procedure and macro name, type the following and press Enter:

```
Sub UpdateTaskCompletePercent()
```

In this statement, UpdateTaskCompletePercent specifies the macro name. Pressing Enter automatically adds the End Sub line, which specifies the end of the procedure. (See Figure 30.6.) You must add all subsequent code between the Sub () and End Sub statements, which is why VBE places the insertion point there for you.

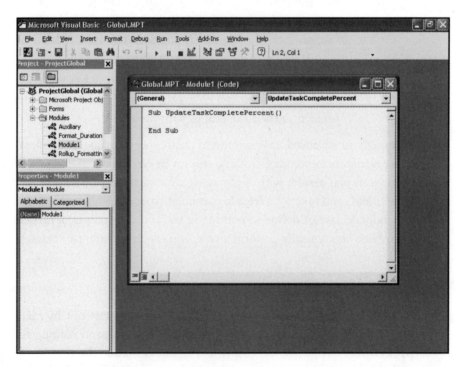

FIGURE 30.6 *The new macro module holds your first code, which defines the beginning and end of the procedure, as well as the macro name.*

Specifying Variables

For most macros, you will next need to define the *variables* that the macro will use. You can think of a variable as a container for values generated by the macro or entered by the user. As the macro executes, it can replace the contents of each variable, which also can help direct the execution of the macro. To *dimension* (that is, to reserve a memory space for) or declare a variable, you use the Dim statement.

In this example, you'll use a variable to identify the current task. Each time your macro runs through its instructions, it will increase the task number held in the task variable. When it loops back to the start, its instructions will work on the next task in the list. To declare this variable (which represents the Task object), enter the following line into the Code window for the macro and then press Enter:

```
Dim T As Task
```

TIP

VBE automatically corrects minor errors, like capitalization errors.

Next, you need to define another variable to hold the user's input for each task—the value that will be inserted into the Complete field. In this case, the variable you create will be a *string variable*. String variables hold a string of sequential characters, which can include numbers. So, to declare your second variable, type the following line into the Code window and press Enter:

```
Dim PC As String
```

Finally, you want to declare another last variable that will hold the user's response to the message box that asks whether the user wants to quit the application. Enter the following line into the Code window, and then press Enter twice:

```
Dim NextTask As String
```

At this point, your code should look like Figure 30.7.

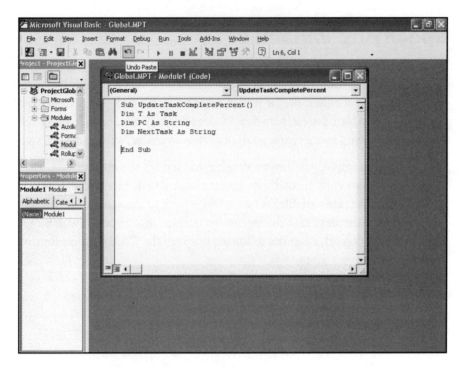

FIGURE 30.7 *Declare variables with the* Dim *statement.*

Documenting Your Macro

You may have seen macro examples that include lines (or parts of lines) that start with a single quote or single prime. The single prime indicates comment (or remark) text. This text does not affect the macro's operation. It simply helps you and others who examine your macro code to understand what a particular line or section does. You also can use include a remark at the top of the macro to describe the macro itself. For your macro, type the following remark and press Enter twice:

```
'The looping begins here
```

Setting Up a Looping Structure

When you set up a macro to *loop*, you're controlling the order in which it executes. In this case, you're making it repeat a selected set of instructions. VBA offers several different statements you can use to create loops and other types of control structures, including Do...Loop statements and For...Next statements.

For your macro, you'll use a third type of looping statement, the `Fore Each...Next` statement. It's designed to go through each item in a collection (in this case, each task in the collection of tasks), perform steps designated by additional code, and then stop running automatically when the macro has finished with the last item in the collection.

To establish the looping for the example macro, type the following lines into the Code window:

```
For Each T In ActiveProject.Tasks

Next
```

This statement tells the macro to look at the first `T` (the variable you set up earlier, representing the current task in the collection) in the collection of tasks in the active project (represented by the `object.collection ActiveProject.Tasks`), and then execute the subsequent code. When the macro reaches the `Next` statement, it moves on to the next task in the list and continues the macro. The looping continues until the macro finishes operating on the last task of the collection, and then the macro ends. Figure 30.8 illustrates the macro at this point.

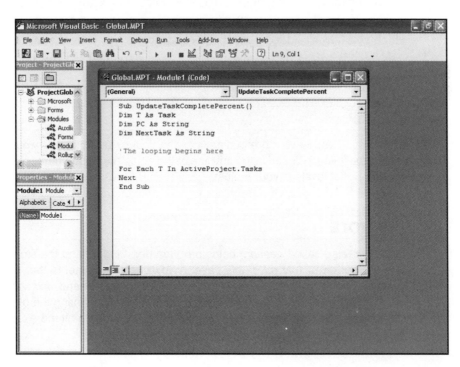

FIGURE 30.8 *Control the macro execution with a looping statement like* `For Each...Next`.

Using an If...Then Statement

Next, you need to build the code that the macro will perform on each loop. You also can use logical statements to control macro execution. The most basic logic statement is an If...Then statement, in which you specify a condition (or test) and tell the macro what action to take if the condition is true in a given instance (for the current task on which the macro is operating, for example).

For your macro, you need to test each task and make sure that it's not a summary task, because you don't want to enter Complete values for summary tasks. (That would override the calculated values for those tasks.) So, click at the beginning of the Next statement line and press Enter. Press the Up Arrow key and then the Tab key, and then type the following lines:

```
If T.OutlineLevel > 1 Then

End If
```

The first line specifies the condition. It tells the macro to look at the contents of the OutlineLevel field (property) for the current T (task). If the outline level is greater than 1 (meaning that the task is not a top-level task like a summary task), the macro will execute on the next line following the Then (which you haven't added yet). If the condition is not true, the macro proceeds directly to End If, exiting the If...Then statement. At this point, the macro appears as in Figure 30.9.

 TIP

Of course, if you have more outline levels in your project file, you would increase the value included in the first line of the If...Then statement to reflect the number of levels in your project.

 NOTE

Indention (also called *nesting*) helps programmers understand the structure of the program or macro. In this case, many of the statements that you're using require an ending line: Sub () and End Sub, For Each and Next, and so on. Placing each pair on the same indention level, and indenting the pairs of statements within each pair, illustrates the macro structure a bit more clearly.

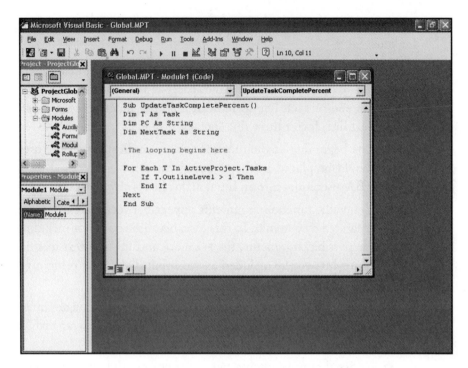

FIGURE 30.9 *Use logical statements like* If...Then *statements to test conditions and control execution in a macro.*

Prompting for User Input

For each task, you want the macro to prompt the user to enter a new value for the Complete field. In this case, you will use the InputBox function, which automatically displays an Input dialog box. You'll use a number of *arguments* (values or other pieces of information that tell a function how to operate) to specify the exact contents of the Input dialog box. Click at the beginning of the End If line you just added, press Enter, press Tab, and then enter the following function:

```
PC = InputBox(Prompt:="Enter task completion percentage for" _
& Chr(13) & Chr(13) & T.Name & Chr(13) & T.PercentComplete _
& Chr(13) & Chr(13) & "(Leave box blank and click OK to skip)", _
Title:="Completion Percentage")
```

That's quite a mouthful for a single function, so I'll clarify the various pieces for you:

- First, if you have a function like this that will consume more than one line of code, you can press the spacebar and type an underscore (_) at the end of each line to indicate that the function continues on the next line. Insert these line "breaks" at logical locations.

- The beginning of the function (`PC = `) indicates that the user input should be placed in the `PC` string variable you declared earlier. (In VBA, user input into an Input dialog box is always treated as a string.)

- Generally, function arguments appear between parentheses and are separated by commas. In this case, because you're not including all of the possible arguments, the `Prompt:=` and `Title:=` text identifies the arguments you've included as the Input dialog box prompt text and Title bar text.

- To concatenate (string together) different items for an argument, type a space, an ampersand, and another space (`&`). To wrap text (create a line break) in argument text, use `Chr(13)`.

- Notice that the contents' particular objects and object properties can be used as arguments. In this example, `T.Name` will display the name property of the current task (`T`) in the input box, and `T.PercentComplete` will display the current contents of the `Complete` field for the current task in the Input dialog box.

Figure 30.10 illustrates the macro at this point.

Rounding Out the Macro

The example macro next needs information about what to do with the user input from the Input dialog box, based on the nature of the input. To cover all the possibilities, you can use an `If...Then...Else` statement. This statement defines a condition and tells the macro what to do based on whether the condition is true or false. You also can include `ElseIf` statements to specify what the macro should do if an additional condition is true. To continue building the macro, click at the end of the function you just added if needed, press Enter and Tab, and then enter the following code:

```
If PC = Empty Then

NextTask = MsgBox("Do you want to skip this task?", vbYesNo)
```

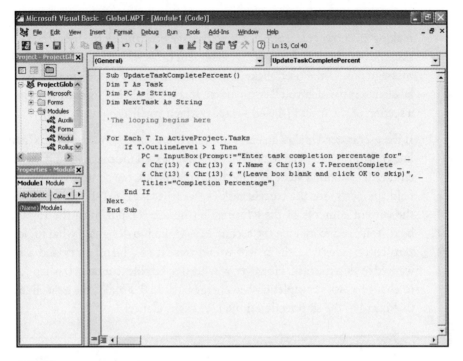

FIGURE 30.10   *This function displays an Input dialog box and defines its contents. Maximize the code window if you need more room to work.*

```
If NextTask = vbYes Then

GoTo Skip

Else

GoTo BailOut

End If

ElseIf PC <> "0" Then

T.PercentComplete = PC

ElseIf PC = "0" Then

T.PercentComplete = PC

Else

GoTo Skip

End If
```

This code covers a lot of ground in telling the macro how to handle the user's Input dialog box entry, which was placed into the PC variable declared at the top of the macro. First the macro says that if the user clicks on OK or Cancel without making an entry (PC = Empty), a new message box will ask the user if she wants to skip the current task. A nested If statement deals with the user's response to this message box. If the user clicks Yes, the macro jumps to a section of the macro labeled Skip (which you'll create next). If the user clicks No, the macro jumps to a section of the macro labeled BailOut, which you'll also create next.

If the user instead makes an entry into the Input dialog box, the ElseIf and Else lines tell the macro what to do. The ElseIf lines tell the macro that if the user has entered **0** or another value into the Input dialog box, the contents of the Complete field (property) for the current task (T.PercentComplete) should be set to equal the current contents of the PC variable (the user's input from the Input dialog box). You need to include the second ElseIf line to designate what to do with a zero entry; otherwise the macro would treat it as a blank entry and ask if you wanted to skip the task. However, you need to be able to enter a 0 when you want to change a task's completion percentage back to 0. Finally, the Else line directs the macro to the skip section if the user clicks Cancel.

 TIP

While you're typing the macro, you can press Shift+Tab to jump back out to a higher indention level.

Click at the End If line of the code you just added and press Enter. Now you can create the new Skip section. Whenever the user's earlier choices divert the macro execution to the Skip section, it will display another message box asking if the user wants to quit the macro. To create a section like this, you include a label that appears on a line by itself and is followed by a colon. Enter the following code to create the Skip section:

```
Skip:
If MsgBox("Do you want to exit the macro?", vbYesNo) = vbYes Then
GoTo Bailout
End If
```

Finally, you need to designate the end of the procedure as the BailOut section. To do so, click at the end of the Next statement line, press Enter, and type

```
BailOut:
```

Code Listing 30.1 illustrates the final code for this macro.

Code Listing 30.1

```
Sub UpdateTaskCompletePercent()

Dim T As Task

Dim PC As String

Dim NextTask As String


'The looping begins here


For Each T In ActiveProject.Tasks

    If T.OutlineLevel > 1 Then

        PC = InputBox(Prompt:="Enter task completion percentage for" _

        & Chr(13) & Chr(13) & T.Name & Chr(13) & T.PercentComplete _

        & Chr(13) & Chr(13) & "(Leave box blank and click OK to skip)", _

        Title:="Completion Percentage")

            If PC = Empty Then

              NextTask = MsgBox("Do you want to skip this task?", vbYesNo)

                If NextTask = vbYes Then

                    GoTo Skip

                Else

                    GoTo BailOut

                End If

            ElseIf PC <> "0" Then

                T.PercentComplete = PC

            ElseIf PC = "0" Then

                T.PercentComplete = PC

            Else

                GoTo Skip

            End If

Skip:

        If MsgBox("Do you want to exit the macro?", vbYesNo) = vbYes Then

            GoTo BailOut
```

```
        End If

    End If

Next

BailOut:

End Sub
```

 WEB

You can download the finished `UpdateTaskCompletePercent Chapter 30.txt`
file, which contains the final macro code, from the Premier Press download
page at www.premierpressbooks.com/downloads.asp.

Signing and Saving the Macro

You conclude the process by applying your digital signature to the macro and
then saving the macro. To add the digital certificate you created earlier, follow these steps:

1. In the VBE, choose Tools, Digital Signature. The Digital Signature
   dialog box opens.

2. Click on Choose. The Select Certificate dialog box will appear.

3. Click on the certificate to use in the list, if needed, and then click on
   OK. The Select Certificate dialog box closes and the Certificate Name
   appears in the Digital Signature dialog box, as shown in Figure 30.11.

4. Click on OK to finish signing the macro.

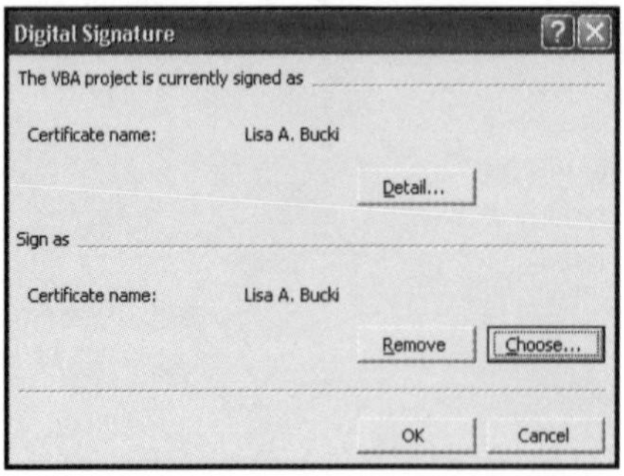

FIGURE 30.11 *You can sign macro work with a digital certificate.*

To save the macro (which in this case also saves the GLOBAL.MPT button), click on the Save button on the VBE toolbar. You can then choose File, Close and Return to Microsoft Project to finish your work in the Visual Basic Editor.

Debugging Your Code with Available Tools

Whether or not you know how to write elegant, programmer-caliber VBA code, the real test is whether the macro runs correctly and does what you wanted it to do. If you try to run the macro from Project and it contains an error, an error message will appear as in Figure 30.12.

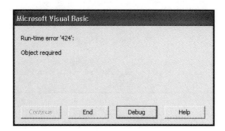

FIGURE 30.12 *If you don't catch the bugs in your macro, Project and Visual Basic will force you to fix them.*

Click on the Debug button to start the Visual Basic Editor. Your macro will load and the VBE will highlight the line with an error, as shown in Figure 30.13.

If you hover the mouse pointer over the highlighted code, a pop-up tip will tell you which value has been assigned to a variable, object, or property. Press the F1 key to open the Microsoft Visual Basic Help window and get help about the statement, function, or other contents of the line with the error.

After you diagnose the code and save the macro again, click on the Reset button on the VBE toolbar to exit Break mode. Then click in the Code window within your code and press F5 to rerun the macro.

To run the macro one step at a time, you can use the Step Into option on the Debug menu in the VBE, or press F8. This moves you through each step in the macro until you pinpoint any problems. When you finish, click on the Reset button before running the macro.

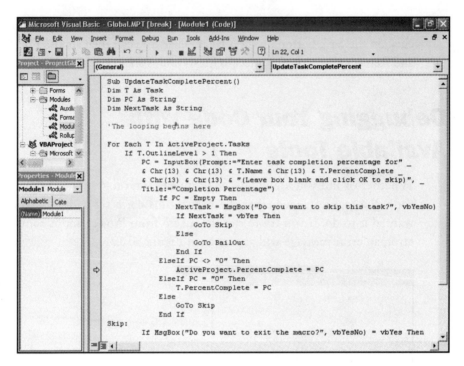

FIGURE 30.13 *The Visual Basic Editor helps you diagnose macro bugs.*

Appendix A

**Additional
Online
Resources**

Online resources for Microsoft Project help aren't quite as plentiful as the resources for other major Microsoft applications, particularly those in the Office Suite. And the resources about project management are likewise limited. However, this appendix points out a few key resources you can consult when you need further help working with Microsoft Project 2002.

Downloading Practice Files and Other Support Items for This Book

Premier Press, Inc. works hard to expand your opportunities to master a particular application. The Premier Press Web site offers a Web page with downloads for each book. This book's downloads page offers a number of files that you can use to practice key skills in this book, as well as a glossary of key terms. To access the available downloads for this book, go to http://www.premierpressbooks.com/downloads and click on the link for *Managing with Microsoft Project 2002*.

Other Online Resources

There are online resources you can consult when you need an answer to a technical question (and don't want to be on hold with a technical support line), want to find a Microsoft Project or project management consultant, or would like to check into add-on products available for Microsoft products.

Here are the key online resources that I've consulted in using Microsoft Project:

 CAUTION

These links were all correct as of the date when I wrote this appendix. As the Web continues to evolve rapidly, you may find changes that apply in this list. If you do, please be sure to make a note of it here in the book.

◆ **http://www.pmi.org**. The Web site for the Project Management Institute (PMI) includes links to copious educational and certification materials, books about project management, and some links to Project consulting companies.

◆ **http://www.microsoft.com/office/project**. This is the main Microsoft Web page for the Microsoft Project product. Consult it from time to time to get news, order product updates and patches, and get hints about using Project. (Note that this page is different from the page you see when you choose Help, Office On The Web in Project.)

◆ **http://www.microsoft.com/office/project/resources** . This page includes links to Project and project management consulting companies, as well as links to user groups and training resources. If your organization needs a custom Project solution, visit this page. The page also includes a link that you can click on to subscribe to an e-mail newsletter about Project called the Microsoft Project Report, so Microsoft will deliver the latest news and updates directly to your e-mail address. In addition, the newsletter provides information about downloadable files to enhance your use of Project, as well as news of local seminars and tips for using the product.

◆ **microsoft.public.project.2002 newsgroup**. You can visit this public Internet newsgroup to post your questions about using Microsoft Project and to view questions posed by other users. This group is staffed by a number of Microsoft Most Valuable Professionals (MVPs), many of whom work with top Project software and consulting companies, and boasts a very active group of key users who respond quickly to questions. When I've posted questions here, I've typically been able to return in a couple of hours to see multiple responses to my question.

◆ **http://www.mvps.org/project**. The Microsoft Project MVPs maintain this most valuable Web site, which covers Frequently Asked Questions, companion products that you can purchase and use with Project, sample VBA code, and links to valuable downloads like Project training materials. You can find a lot of great answers at this site!

◆ **http://www.mpug.org**. This is the Web site for the Microsoft Project User's Group (MPUG). If you join MPUG (for a modest individual, corporate, or student rate), you'll receive newsletters, invitations to members-only regional and national professional meetings and breakout discussions, and access to both a private Web site and a private newsgroup for MPUG members.

◆ **http://www.zdnet.com/downloads**. Go to this site, enter Microsoft Project in the Search For text box, and then click on the Go button to find downloadable Project add-ins. If you go to http://www.zdnet.com and just search for "Microsoft Project," the results will include a much more expansive list of downloads, articles, and reviews.

Index